Applied Social Psychology

To my Scottie and Christopher, Kimberly, Kinsman, Holly, and Kelly

—FWS

To Michi

—JAG

To Jacinthe, Sarah, and Juliane

—LMC

Applied Social Psychology

Understanding and Addressing Social and Practical Problems

Edited by

Frank W. Schneider
University of Windsor, Canada

Jamie A. Gruman
University of Toronto at Scarborough

Larry M. Coutts
University of Windsor, Canada

SAGE Publications
Thousand Oaks ▪ London ▪ New Delhi

For information:

Sage Publications, Inc.
2455 Teller Road
Thousand Oaks, California 91320
E-mail: order@sagepub.com

Sage Publications Ltd.
1 Oliver's Yard
55 City Road
London EC1Y 1SP
United Kingdom

Sage Publications India Pvt. Ltd.
B-42, Panchsheel Enclave
Post Box 4109
New Delhi 110 017 India

Printed in the United States of America

Library of Congress Cataloging-in-Publication data

Schneider, Frank W.
Applied social psychology : understanding and addressing social and practical problems / Frank W. Schneider, Jamie A. Gruman, Larry M. Coutts.
    p. cm.
Includes bibliographical references and index.
ISBN 1-4129-1539-2 (pbk.)
    1. Social psychology. I. Gruman, Jamie A. II. Coutts, Larry M. III. Title.
HM1033.S36 2005
302—dc22

                                                          2004023043

This book is printed on acid-free paper.

05   06   07   08   09   10   9   8   7   6   5   4   3   2   1

Acquiring Editor:	Jim Brace-Thompson
Editorial Assistant:	Karen Ehrmann
Production Editor:	Sanford Robinson
Typesetter:	C&M Digitals (P) Ltd.
Copy Editor:	D. J. Peck
Indexer:	Karen McKenzie
Cover Designer:	Michelle Kenny

CONTENTS

PREFACE

Applied social psychology began to emerge as a clearly identifiable field during the early 1970s with benchmark events such as the publication of the first issue of the *Journal of Applied Social Psychology* in 1971 and the inauguration at Loyola University of Chicago of the first graduate program in applied social psychology in 1974. In the more than 30 years since then, many developments that have occurred in this young field have entrenched applied social psychology more firmly, including the opening of a number of graduate programs (we counted 19 in the United States and Canada). Kurt Lewin's legacy—promotion of the integration of theory, research, and practice—continues to be realized as social psychology is being increasingly applied in the amelioration of social and practical problems in many arenas of life.

The three editors of this book followed very different paths into the field of applied social psychology. Frank Schneider, having come to the University of Windsor as an experimental social psychologist, eventually cofounded the graduate program in applied social psychology in 1980. Larry Coutts, after being trained at the University of Windsor as an experimental social psychologist, worked in the public sector for 23 years before joining the University of Windsor's applied social psychology program in 2000. Jamie Gruman was educated as an applied social psychologist, receiving his Ph.D. from the University of Windsor in 2002. A big reason why we have put this book together is our desire to share with others, especially students, the promise of the field of applied social psychology and our mutual excitement about it.

One of our major objectives has been to produce a book that is compatible with the abilities and interests of students at the undergraduate level. In our view, most other texts in the field are too advanced for many undergraduate students and/or lack sufficient coverage of the field. While emphasizing the importance of maintaining the academic integrity of the book, we encouraged the contributing authors to write in a reader-friendly way, for example, drawing connections between academic material and students' real-world experiences. The book is most appropriate for students with some course work in psychology. However, students with little or no formal background in psychology, including those in allied fields (e.g., sociology, communication studies), should feel comfortable in reading the book because of the instructional approach it takes. The instructional features come, in particular, in the first four chapters, which provide readers with the necessary foundation for understanding the processes by which applied social psychologists develop theories, acquire knowledge, and design interventions. Chapter 1 defines applied social psychology as a branch of the science of social psychology and places the field in a historical and intellectual context. The chapter identifies social psychologically based interventions as occupying a central position in the field. Chapter 2 defines and illustrates the nature of theory and the process of theory development. Chapter 3 reviews basic research designs and data collection methods used by applied social psychologists. Chapter 4 defines and illustrates the steps involved in the design, implementation, and evaluation of interventions, including how they draw on theory, research evidence, and research methods.

In light of the potential applicability of social psychology to virtually any domain involving human interaction, this book addresses a broad range of topic areas. Chapter 5 introduces the idea of personal uses of social psychology by illustrating how individuals can benefit from applying social psychology in their daily lives. This chapter is followed by "content" chapters that focus on social and/or practical problems in a number of major topic areas: clinical practice (Chapter 6), sports teams (Chapter 7), media (Chapter 8), health (Chapter 9), education (Chapter 10), organizations (Chapter 11), criminal justice (Chapter 12), community (Chapter 13), environment (Chapter 14), and diversity (Chapter 15). Chapter 16, the final chapter, stretches students' thinking about research methods by considering action, participatory, and activist research.

To foster students' understanding of the material, we avoided an "encyclopedic" approach (i.e., reviewing many topics) within content chapters but ensured adequate breadth by having the authors of each chapter explore from two to four major topic areas. Content chapters also include at least one "Focus on Research" and one "Focus on Intervention." These features provide readers with a more detailed, in-depth appreciation of the processes of designing, executing, and evaluating research studies and interventions. Also, because the overriding focus of the book is on the contributions of applied social psychology with respect to social and practical problems in North America, content chapters include a "Culture Capsule." These brief considerations of possible cultural differences are intended to help readers to recognize that generalization from one cultural context to another cannot be assumed. The one exception where a content chapter does not have a Culture Capsule is Chapter 15, which has cultural influences as a major focus.

Although the book has been written by a number of authors, we have worked very hard to ensure that it is organized and reads like a textbook written by a single individual. To this end, authors of content chapters followed specific guidelines regarding organization and format. In many places, to achieve increased coherence and continuity, we inserted chapter-to-chapter connections such as recognizing that a theory had been considered in an earlier chapter.

In Appreciation

We truly appreciate the contributions of the many individuals who helped with this project. We certainly express our gratitude to those colleagues who contributed chapters for doing their best to follow our guidelines and for their "patience" when asked to make revisions. The final product was significantly improved by the incorporation of suggestions from the reviewers selected by Sage; our appreciation goes to them as well. Also, we are very grateful to two individuals at Sage who, throughout this long process, were always there with a friendly greeting and a readiness to help with our questions: Jim Brace-Thompson, our editor, and Karen Ehrmann, his assistant. We add that without Jim's initial enthusiasm for the idea of this book and his continued support, this could still be a work in progress or possibly a work in the basket. We likewise greatly appreciate the contribution of our copy editor, D. J. Peck, whose careful rewording made the writing of all of us seem much more like that of one.

We express our appreciation to our secretaries, Katherine Hamel and Angela Papas, who over and over again—always with smiles on their faces, we think—helped with a variety of clerical tasks. Thanks also go to Natalia Camargo Santos and Sarah-Jane Renaud for volunteering to assist by typing editorial changes. Way beyond the call of duty, Fatima Kazoun volunteered endless hours working to ensure proper formatting of references in all chapters. Many thanks go to Fatima and also to her helper, Christa Ryan.

Finally, we cannot fail to mention our families and friends for their encouragement and patience. Yes, it's finally done!

Frank W. Schneider

Jamie A. Gruman

Larry M. Coutts

1

DEFINING THE FIELD OF APPLIED SOCIAL PSYCHOLOGY

FRANK W. SCHNEIDER

JAMIE A. GRUMAN

LARRY M. COUTTS

CHAPTER OUTLINE

The purpose of this book is to introduce you to the field of applied social psychology. Before reviewing some of the contributions of the field in various domains of life (e.g., education, health, sports), it is important to define the field of applied social psychology, including placing it in the context of its parent field, social psychology. We begin by describing an event involving the three of us that occurred early in April 2003—a meeting to review a draft of one of the chapters in this book. Although it was simply a task-focused get-together involving the three of us, the interaction reflected (as most any social interaction does) a great variety of social psychological phenomena. These phenomena enable us to illustrate for you first the focus of the science of social psychology and then the focus of applied social psychology, which we define as a branch of social psychology.

We had agreed to meet at 10 o'clock in the morning at a coffee shop. Two of us (F. S. and L. C.) were careful to be on time because we had recently been chastised (by J. G.) for being late for meetings. After being waited on by a friendly waitress, we were soon deeply involved in a discussion of the strengths and weaknesses of the draft chapter. Much discussion revolved around what changes we should recommend to the chapter authors. Periodically, frustrations were expressed over how painstakingly long it was taking for us to work through each section of the draft. Also, although we agreed for the most part on revisions we would recommend, one of us (F. S.) had to work hard before he finally convinced the other two to advise a major change in the chapter's organization. Then, given this decision, we spent considerable time discussing how best to sell the proposed change to the authors.

During a break, the conversation drifted to the war in Iraq that had begun barely 2 weeks earlier. The conversation intensified as many thoughts and feelings poured out of us. Like the divided world around us, we too did not agree. All three of us expressed grave concerns about the impact of the war on international relations. For weeks, we had witnessed worldwide massive protests against the war and mounting anti-Americanism. Now that the war was in progress, we were bombarded with an incredible array of powerful media images, ranging from the very worst horrors (e.g., the devastation in Baghdad, maimed and dead soldiers and civilians) to uplifting acts of compassion and heroism (e.g., American soldiers caring for child victims, the Iraqi man who risked his life to help in the rescue of American prisoner of war Jessica Lynch). We wondered what impact this "living room" war would have on people's attitudes—toward this particular war, toward war in general, toward U.S. policies, toward Americans, toward Iraqis, and so on. Although we felt confident that the coalition forces would win the war on the battlefields, we were much less confident that they would win the "hearts and minds" of the Iraqi people. The attitudes of the Iraqi population toward their "liberators" would greatly determine the success of postwar

efforts to rebuild their society. And even if the coalition nations did gain general support, would Iraq's major ethno-religious groups be able to set aside their long-standing differences to cooperate in effective nation building? (You, of course, are aware of the events in Iraq that transpired since our coffee shop meeting.)

SOCIAL PSYCHOLOGY

Defining Social Psychology

So, what about the preceding coffee shop interaction helps us to define the field of social psychology? For one thing, the meeting was rich in social psychological phenomena. Drawing on the definitions in several social psychology textbooks (e.g., Feldman, 1998; Myers, 2002), **social psychology** may be defined as the science that seeks to understand how people think about, feel about, relate to, and influence one another. Given this definition, you should be able to identify many examples of social psychological subject matter in our coffee shop interaction by looking for instances of thinking about others, feeling about others, relating to others, and influencing others. J. G. *thought* that F. S. and L. C. had been inconsiderate in their tardiness and was frustrated and annoyed (*feelings*) by their behavior (how they had *related* to him). He *related* to F. S. and L. C. by vocalizing his annoyance and insisting that they begin to show up for meetings on time. His admonition did *influence* F. S. and L. C.; they arrived at the coffee shop on time. Secure in our respect for (*thoughts about*) each other's abilities and liking (*feelings*) for each other, we *related* to each other in reviewing the chapter by freely asserting our views and sometimes challenging each other's views. F. S. was able to persuade (*influence*) J. G. and L. C. about the merits of revamping the organization of the chapter and so on. We want you to recognize that one can do a similar analysis with virtually any kind of social situation.

Social Psychology as a Science

So, those are the kinds of phenomena that social psychology—as a science—seeks to understand. Do not pass lightly over the phrase "as a science" because the fact that social psychology is a science is fundamental to its meaning. The *essence of science* involves (a) a set of research methods that in combination make up what is known as the scientific method and (b) a foundation of core values.

Scientific method and core values. The research methods (e.g., correlational, experimental) that fall under the scientific method are those that depend on **empirical tests,** that is, the use of systematic observation to evaluate propositions and ideas. An empirical test of an idea (e.g., people are happier in sunny weather) entails a research study that is (a) set up in such a way as to allow for the idea to be either refuted or supported and (b) conducted so that what is done can be readily evaluated and replicated by other researchers (Cozby, 2004).

Undergirding and guiding research methods is a set of *core values* (Baron & Byrne, 2000; Heiman, 2002). The following are some of the most important values that are absolutely essential for scientists to adhere to in their work:

- *Accuracy:* precise, error-free measurement and collection of information (i.e., data)
- *Objectivity:* minimization of bias in data collection and proposition testing
- *Skepticism:* refusing to believe findings and conclusions without rigorous verification
- *Open-mindedness:* readiness to accept as valid evidence that which may be inconsistent with one's initial, and perhaps strongly held, beliefs or theories
- *Ethics:* acceptance of the absolute importance of ethical behavior in conducting research

Adherence to the first four values is necessary to ensure that findings of research validly reflect the phenomenon under study. The fifth value, ethics, also pertains to the validity of findings (e.g., researchers should not wittingly alter or misrepresent their results) but also encompasses the need to safeguard the dignity and well-being of research participants.

Scientific understanding. Thus, to seek an understanding of social psychological phenomena, social psychologists, as scientists, are guided by certain core values and rely on research strategies that fall under the scientific method. But what is meant by "understanding"? In science, including social psychology, *understanding* involves the accomplishment of four goals: description, prediction, determining causality, and explanation (Cozby, 2004). We define these goals and illustrate them by considering the possible influence that having a pet has on the adjustment of the elderly.

The goal of **description** entails identifying and reporting the details and nature of a phenomenon, often distinguishing between the classes or types of the phenomenon and recording its frequency of occurrence. In the case of the adjustment of the elderly, a researcher might distinguish between emotional adjustment and social adjustment and then measure and record the incidence of older persons in the community who fit this classification. The researcher could also find out whether or not each elderly person has a pet, perhaps listing information about the kind and number of pets. Achieving accurate descriptions of phenomena is one aspect of understanding. Understanding also entails prediction.

The **prediction** form of understanding requires knowing what factors are systematically related (i.e., correlated) to the phenomenon of interest. In our example, if research showed that there is a relationship between adjustment and having a pet—those who have a pet tend to be better adjusted—we would understand that adjustment in the elderly can be predicted in general by the presence or absence of a pet. This relationship would represent an important insight and lead us to consider the third form of understanding: ascertaining whether or not there is a causal relationship between having a pet and adjustment.

Determining causality between two factors means determining that changes in one factor produce (i.e., cause) changes in the other factor. Just because two factors are related does not necessarily mean that they are causally related. For instance, having a pet might have no effect whatsoever on the adjustment of the elderly even though a relationship may exist. A third factor could be responsible for the existence of the relationship. For instance, physical health could influence both how well-adjusted people feel and whether they have a pet (because it is easier to care for a pet if one is healthy). So, it is important not to be misled by a common tendency among people to assume that if two things are correlated, a causal relationship necessarily exists.

Identifying the cause(s) of phenomena is a very important component of understanding. If research were to establish that having a pet does indeed lead to improvements in adjustment (i.e., causes better adjustment), there could be clear-cut practical implications in terms of providing help to the elderly. But pursuit of understanding does not end with the establishment of causation. Understanding also involves explanation, the fourth goal. **Explanation** pertains to establishing *why* a phenomenon or relationship occurs. We may understand that one factor causes another factor without knowing exactly why the effect occurs. If having a pet does lead to improvements in the adjustment of the elderly (and this does seem to be the case [Beck & Katcher, 1996]), what is the explanation? Is it because having a pet reduces loneliness, because it increases feelings of security, because it gives the elderly person a chance to feel needed by nurturing a living thing, or because of some other factor?

Social psychological understanding: The formation of intergroup attitudes. Let us return to the coffee shop and use another example to illustrate social psychology's approach to understanding social psychological phenomena. During our discussion of the war in Iraq, much of our concern was with its possible impact on intergroup attitudes and with the importance of intergroup attitudes and relations for Iraq's future. Thousands of social psychological investigations have been carried out on an array of important basic questions about attitudes in general, including what the internal structure of attitudes is, what the relationship between attitudes and behavior is, and what the factors that influence attitude change are (Eagly & Chaiken, 1993). Another major area of research focuses on understanding how attitudes are formed (i.e., how people come to possess their attitudes). Let us focus specifically on intergroup attitudes and consider a small portion of the research that sheds some light on how negative intergroup attitudes develop in people. Note that this is essentially a question of causality.

First, an **attitude** may be defined as "a person's overall evaluation of persons (including oneself), objects, and issues" (Petty & Wegener, 1998, p. 323). Thus, *intergroup attitude* refers to a person's overall evaluation of members of a group to which the person does not belong. One approach that social psychologists have taken in the study of intergroup attitudes is to examine the role of various agents of socialization in the formation of attitudes. This research indicates that children tend to take on the racial attitudes of important people around them (e.g., parents, teachers, peers) and that at least part of the explanation is that these individuals influence the development of such attitudes through the basic principles of learning such as instrumental conditioning, classical conditioning, and imitation (e.g., Oskamp, 1991).

So, intergroup attitudes are learned partly from others. But as is the case with many social psychological phenomena, multiple factors must be recognized when exploring the determinants of intergroup attitudes. Social psychologists also have found that people's attitudes toward other groups may be influenced by the simple fact that they see themselves as members of a particular group. When people see themselves as belonging to one group (e.g., Americans), that group is referred to as the in-group; nonmembers of the in-group (e.g., non-Americans) are called the out-group. Many investigations confirm the existence of a very robust phenomenon called **in-group/out-group bias,** which means that in-group members tend to evaluate and relate to the in-group favorably and tend to evaluate and relate to the out-group less favorably (or unfavorably). This might not seem especially surprising. What is remarkable, however, is that in-group/out-group bias is such a basic social psychological phenomenon that it can show up even in a situation where there is just the slightest differentiation between the in-group and the out-group. In many laboratory experiments, Tajfel and his colleagues (e.g., Tajfel & Billig, 1974) and others (e.g., Allen & Wilder, 1975) divided participants— all strangers—into two groups on the basis of trivial criteria (e.g., those who underestimate and those who overestimate the number of dots on slides). Consistently across experiments, participants have assigned more favorable rewards and traits to in-group members than to out-group members. So, we know that simply being a member of a group contributes to the development of negative attitudes toward other groups.

What other factors lead to the development of negative intergroup attitudes? Around 1950, Muzafer Sherif and his research team took the investigation of intergroup relations into the field, where they studied the role of competition between groups (Sherif, 1966b; Sherif & Sherif, 1953, 1969). The researchers conducted an ingenious series of 3-week experiments with 11- and 12-year-old boys at isolated camp settings. The investigations were conducted in phases. During phase 1—group formation—the boys were divided into two groups of approximately 10 each. Each group's members lived together in a separate cabin from the other group and, as arranged by the experimenters, engaged in a series of appealing activities that required cooperative interdependence (e.g., camping, building a rope bridge). Members of each group soon developed a sense of "we-feeling" as their group developed a definite role structure (e.g., leaders, followers) and set of norms (e.g., expectations about how things should be done). During phase 2—group conflict—the researchers investigated conditions that result in negative intergroup attitudes and behavior. They drew on theory and research evidence suggesting that intergroup antagonism often results from intergroup competition, including the frustration that a group experiences because the other group interferes with its ability to achieve its goals. During this phase, the experimenters implemented a series of competitions (e.g., tug-of-war, skits) between the two groups in which only the victorious group won a prize. By the end of the week, the relations between the two groups had deteriorated to a very antagonistic situation involving strongly negative stereotypes (e.g., "sneaky," "stinkers") and behavior (e.g., name calling, food fights, damage to property).

In all of the preceding examples of research on intergroup attitudes, we can see that the social psychologists focused on furthering the understanding of one or more of the following: how people think about, feel about, relate to, and influence each other. All of the research

reviewed fits under social psychology's umbrella. Now let us look under applied social psychology's umbrella.

APPLIED SOCIAL PSYCHOLOGY

Sherif's (1966b) field research on intergroup relations involved a third phase. During this phase—reduction of conflict—the researchers developed and evaluated an intervention strategy to improve the relations between the groups of boys. The strategy was designed on the basis of the Sherifs' understanding of the existing research literature on the determinants of positive attitudes and relations among groups that are divided along racial, political, and industrial lines (Sherif & Sherif, 1953). The strategy was based on the idea that groups in conflict would experience improved relations if they cooperate in the attainment of **superordinate goals** (i.e., goals that are highly appealing to both groups but that can be attained only through their cooperative effort). During this phase, the groups of boys were introduced to a series of superordinate goals that could not be achieved without their joint effort (e.g., pulling together on a rope to start a broken-down truck that had been on its way to get food). Over the course of several days, hostile interaction between the groups declined considerably and friendships began to cross group boundaries.

In Sherif's research on breaking down the barriers between the groups of boys, we have an example of the use of social psychology to effect positive social change. Notice how his emphasis shifted from trying to understand the causes of a social problem—intergroup antagonism—to trying to come up with a strategy for doing something about the problem. This concern with contributing to positive change brings us more fully into the area of social psychology that focuses on application—applied social psychology.

Applied social psychology refers to the branch of social psychology that draws on social psychological theories, principles, methods, and research evidence to contribute to (a) the understanding of social and practical problems and (b) the development of intervention strategies for improving the functioning of individuals, groups, organizations, communities, and societies with respect to social and practical problems. In this definition, *functioning* is broadly viewed as encompassing how well people perform or operate with respect to any one of many criteria, including emotional and social adjustment, physical health, and performance in school, work, or athletics.

In our view, it is *the concern with the development of intervention strategies* that is unique to applied social psychology and sets it off as a branch of social psychology. The remainder of this chapter elaborates on the meaning and focus of applied social psychology and, in so doing, defines its position in the context of its parent field, social psychology.

Applied Social Psychology as a Science

As a branch of social psychology, applied social psychology is by definition a science and, accordingly, relies on the scientific method and is guided by the core values of science. Moreover, applied social psychologists likewise are motivated by the aforementioned goals of science: description, prediction, determining causality, and explanation. However, they are distinguished from other social psychologists by also having a strong interest in what may be regarded as the fifth goal of science: control (Christensen, 2004; Goodwin, 2003). In science, **control** means being able to manipulate conditions that will cause changes in a phenomenon. Thus, once scientific research has identified the causes of a phenomenon, the potential for scientific control will have been established. Returning to the pets–adjustment example, once researchers determine that having a pet frequently improves adjustment in older people, a "pets visit nursing home" program might be implemented as an intervention strategy. Another example is that once the basic principles of attribution theory were formulated, clinical psychologists began to use them to develop interventions designed to alleviate depression (see Chapter 6).

Although their ultimate goal is to effect positive change—to improve the functioning of people—applied social psychologists themselves may conduct research that helps them to understand the nature and causes of phenomena

that concern them. This is seen in Sherif's (1966b) research on how competition can negatively affect intergroup relations. As another example, applied social psychologists who are interested in reducing bullying among school children may investigate the correlates or causes of such antisocial behavior with a view toward using the results of their research to develop effective intervention strategies. However, it is often the case that they will draw on knowledge accumulated by other researchers who may or may not be interested in the direct application of research findings. For example, many social psychologists are very interested in conducting research that will enhance our understanding of social problems but in their own work do not address how that understanding can be applied. Regardless of the origin of the research evidence, interventions that applied social psychologists are involved in developing, such as bullying reduction strategies (see Chapter 10), will have solid scientific bases to them.

Thus, just as research studies designed to enhance the understanding of a phenomenon are guided by the researchers' best understanding of the existing theory and research evidence, so too are intervention strategies designed by applied social psychologists based on existing theory and knowledge. Furthermore, applied social psychologists' responsibility does not stop with careful, science-based design of intervention strategies but rather extends, for both scientific and ethical reasons, to the evaluation of the consequences of the interventions. The scientific obligation stems from our responsibility to test the theoretical rationales and hypotheses underlying intervention strategies. The ethical obligation stems essentially from the need to ensure not only that the intended beneficiaries of interventions gain from them but also that they (or others) do not experience unintended negative consequences. We return to the design and evaluation of intervention strategies in Chapter 4.

The Role of Personal Values

As we have noted, in conducting research, scientists are guided by a universally agreed-on set of core values. We must also recognize the role of personal values in the conduct and application of science. Although one of the core values of science is objectivity, it is widely recognized that the individual's personal values influence many decisions that he or she makes as a scientist. For example, a social psychologist's concerns about racial injustice in society may lead him or her to choose as an area of research one that focuses on the causes of prejudice and discrimination and also to search for evidence that implicates certain political groups or institutions in the perpetuation of prejudice in society.

As social psychologists become involved in implementing control—developing strategies to change people's lives—personal values take on added importance (Mayo & La France, 1980; Sapsford & Dallos, 1998). In contributing to the development of an intervention, the applied social psychologist has determined that a problem exists. However, the determination of what constitutes a problem is not always objective. When someone breaks a leg while skiing, a physical problem unequivocally exists and the services of a medical professional are clearly required. Unlike the medical professional, the social psychologist's choice of whether or not to intervene in a situation is often based on personal values. Consider the example of affirmative action programs attempting to overcome the historical disadvantages experienced by certain minorities by requiring employers to hire members of these groups. The basic value underlying affirmative action is equality. However, some people argue that affirmative action is unfair because giving preferential treatment to selected groups may exclude more qualified people from consideration. The value underlying this second line of reasoning is merit. Whether or not an employer decides to voluntarily implement an affirmative action program is based partly on his or her values. Similarly, the applied social psychologist who contributes to the development of affirmative action initiatives also is promoting a specific set of values.

So, interventions developed by applied social psychologists are value laden in that the psychologists' values play a role in determining what social and practical problems to address, including which people should be targeted for change and what should constitute change. As Mayo and La France (1980) noted, "Improving quality of life may entail social changes [that are] not always to everyone's liking" (p. 85). For example, not all organizational interventions, such as redesigning people's jobs, may meet the needs or wishes of all employees. Thus, the goal of control through intervention is sometimes controversial.

Historical Context of Applied Social Psychology

The scientific foundation of applied social psychology can be traced at least as far back as the 1930s to the thinking and work of social psychologist Kurt Lewin (Lewin, 1936). Lewin conducted research on a variety of practical issues and social problems such as how to get people to eat healthier diets and how interpersonal relations and productivity are affected by different supervisory styles. For instance, in the latter case, Lewin and his colleagues (Lewin, Lippitt, & White, 1939) conducted an experiment in which they had groups of school boys work on hobbies under the direction of a male adult who varied his leadership in one of three ways: autocratic (controlling, gave orders, made the decisions), democratic (asked for input, allowed boys to make choices), or laissez-faire (interacted little with boys, mainly observed). The results for interpersonal relations and productivity generally favored the democratic style. For example, compared with boys under the laissez-faire leadership style, boys under autocratic and democratic leaders spent more time working; however, when the leader left the room, the amount of work done by the autocratic groups dropped sharply, whereas this did not happen in the democratic groups.

It is important to recognize that Lewin's goal was not only to further the scientific understanding of these topics but also to contribute to their solutions. Very important to him was linking psychological theory to application, and the following words of Lewin (1944/1951a) represent probably the most commonly cited quotation in social psychology:

> Many psychologists working in an applied field are keenly aware of the need for close cooperation between theoretical and applied psychology. This can be accomplished in psychology, as it has been

accomplished in physics, if the theorist does not look toward applied problems with highbrow aversion or with a fear of social problems and if the applied psychologist realizes that there is nothing so practical as a good theory. (p. 169)

Lewin left a solid scientific legacy for applied social psychology in his emphasis on the integration of theory, research, and practice.

The 1930s and 1940s witnessed, among social psychologists such as Lewin, a flurry of concern with applied issues and practical problems, much of which stemmed from the rise of Nazism and World War II (Jones, 1998). In fact, Brehm, Kassin, and Fein (1999) went so far as to suggest that Adolph Hitler had more influence on the field of social psychology than did any other person, including leading social psychologists: "Hitler's rise to power and the ensuing turmoil caused people around the world to become desperate for answers to social psychological questions about what causes violence, prejudice and genocide, conformity and obedience, and a host of other social problems and behaviors" (pp. 12–13). Reich (1981) observed that the foundation of applied social psychology was set by 1950 because the potential of using scientific methods to address social problems had been demonstrated successfully by, for instance, Lewin and colleagues' (1939) work on the effects of autocratic leadership and Sherif's (1966b) work on conflict resolution. It seemed as though an applied psychology centered in the field of social psychology was poised to take off. Yet the "takeoff" did not occur for another 20 years or so.

In fact, in social psychology, there occurred a backlash to applied developments. The negative reaction emanated largely from a widespread concern that "applied" was synonymous with low quality and, thus, threatened the scientific integrity of the discipline (Reich, 1981; Streufert & Suedfeld, 1982). During the late 1940s and the 1950s, social psychology experienced a concerted movement away from applied concerns to a "pure science" emphasis on theory and laboratory experiments focused on basic social processes (e.g., processes of attitude formation and change, group structure, impression formation). In fact, the relationship between research on basic processes and applied research was described with terms such as "estrangement" and "schism."

Just as the events around World War II sparked interest in applied social psychology, so too did the events of the 1960s. A host of powerful social and political occurrences (e.g., assassinations of John F. Kennedy and Martin Luther King, Jr., war in Vietnam, race riots, campus protests, civil rights movement, women's liberation movement) forced increased attention on a variety of pressing social issues endemic to American society. Many of the problems were the same as those that had come to a focus during the 1930s and 1940s (e.g., violence, prejudice), and some were new (e.g., social injustice). There were increased cries—both within psychology (including from students) and in the broader society—for psychology to become more socially relevant (Jones, 1998; Reich, 1981). At the same time, many social psychologists had begun to criticize the overreliance on laboratory experiments, pointing out that the field would benefit from methodological approaches that also included field research and a variety of nonexperimental research methods. Very instrumental in setting the stage for the emergence of a clearly defined field of applied social psychology was a 1969 series of articles in *American Psychologist* that focused on the interface between science and social issues. Some of the titles of the articles reflected the emerging applied emphasis of the field: "Psychology as a Means of Promoting Human Welfare" (Miller, 1969); "Social Psychology in an Era of Social Change" (Weick, 1969); "Socially Relevant Science: Reflections on Some Studies of Interpersonal Conflict" (Deutsch, 1969); "Experimental Psychology and Social Responsibility" (Walker, 1969); and "Reforms as Experiments" (Campbell, 1969).

In response to such developments, applied social psychology surfaced during the 1970s as a clearly identifiable field (Reich, 1981; Streufert & Suedfeld, 1982). There were several notable benchmarks, including the establishment of a journal devoted specifically to applied issues and research, the *Journal of Applied Social Psychology* in 1970–1971 and the founding of the first doctoral program in applied social psychology at Loyola University of Chicago in 1974 (Bickman, 1981). These soon were followed by other developments that reinforced the identity of applied social psychology, including another journal (*Journal of Basic and Applied Social Psychology*) in 1980, the first textbook in applied social psychology (Fisher's *Social Psychology: An Applied Approach*) in 1982, and more doctoral programs, not the least of which was the one founded in 1980 at the University of Windsor (our institution). So, after some delay, the field of applied social psychology finally took off—"an actualization of long-term fundamental trends in the science" (Reich, 1981, p. 65). Here we are today, some 30 or so years later. In our view, a lot has happened in the meantime that has reinforced the initial promise of Lewin's legacy of integrating theory, research, and practice. Applied social psychology is firmly entrenched as a branch of social psychology.

A Problem Focus

Social problems. At the very heart of applied social psychology is a regard for addressing social problems. Morawski (2000) observed that since its very early days around the turn of the 20th century, social psychology has had "an appreciation of its immediate connectedness with pulsing social conditions—crises, dysfunctions, or tensions" (p. 427). Recently, social psychologist Philip Zimbardo, as president of the American Psychological Association, affirmed the central role of psychology in the solution of many of the most serious problems facing the United States. Zimbardo (2002a) listed problems such as AIDS, substance abuse, prejudice and discrimination, minority student dropout rates, crime and juvenile delinquency, and "lethal hostility" (e.g., gang fighting, war). According to Zimbardo, the "solutions and prevention require changes in attitudes, values, behavior, and lifestyles" (p. 5). Although Zimbardo was extolling the potential contributions of psychology in general, the centrality of the field of social psychology is readily apparent: To ameliorate many of the most serious problems facing us today, changes must occur in the very phenomena that constitute the core subject matter of the field of social psychology—people's attitudes, values, and lifestyles.

For instance, for health-related problems, a very big part of the solution often comes down to behavior (i.e., lifestyle) change. For example, stop smoking if you do not want to be one of the half billion people living today who will die from cigarette smoking (Myers, 2002), engage in regular exercise if you want to do the one thing that will most benefit your physical and psychological well-being (DeAngelis, 2002), or choose not to get in a car with a drunk driver (Branswell, 2003). Let us consider in more detail one of the problems mentioned by Zimbardo (2002a)—AIDS. Without a doubt, the AIDS epidemic is one of the most serious crises facing humanity. The statistics are terrifying. More than 40 million people in the world live with HIV/AIDS (UNAIDS/World Health Organization, 2002). In 2002 alone, 3 million people died from AIDS and 5 million became HIV positive. AIDS has become the fourth leading cause of death in the world, with the epidemic still in the early stages (Kiragu, 2001). In North America in 2002, approximately 980,000 people were living with HIV/AIDS. The massive death rates in some countries already have torn apart their social, educational, and economic systems.

There have been successful AIDS prevention programs in a number of countries. However, without global intervention strategies of epic proportions, the amount of death, suffering, and social, political, and economic turmoil will continue to escalate. The most successful prevention efforts focus on young people and on changing behavior, for example, delay of sexual experimentation, abstinence, and use of condoms. For now, let us bring the issue of AIDS prevention closer to the personal lives of many readers—to applied research on the college campus. Hodges, Klaaren, and Wheatley (2000) investigated ways in which to increase the likelihood of females engaging in "safe sex" discussions, a critical aspect of AIDS prevention behavior. They noted that college students know the risks of unprotected sex and know that they are supposed to discuss condom use with their partners but too often fail to carry out such discussions. The researchers observed that students "generally find it easier to have unsafe sex than to discuss safe sex" (p. 332) and noted the paucity of safe sex role models in the media, where most "couples collapse onto the nearest horizontal surface in the heat of passion without broaching issues of safe sex" (p. 332). In brief, the research of Hodges and her colleagues suggested that the willingness of females to have safe sex conversations with males would increase if they were provided with a positive experience in actually discussing safe sex practices with a male and if they were informed that such discussions become easier with repeated occurrences. The implications of the findings for the development of AIDS prevention campaigns are fairly straightforward.

A point that we wish to underscore with regard to the AIDS issue is that although, at the most basic level, HIV/AIDS is a biological and medical problem, it is also very much a social problem. The virus is spread by people relating to people; therefore, prevention efforts necessarily must have a very strong social psychological component, as the work of Hodges and colleagues (2000) suggests. This, of course, applies to many other health-based problems (e.g., smoking is very much a socially precipitated and sustained behavior). There are other critical problems that at one level clearly are the domain of the nonsocial sciences (e.g., biology, geology, physics, engineering) yet are strongly rooted in social behavior and, thus, are amenable to social science-based solutions. As Bjork (2000) affirmed, the answers to many of the most complex problems rest with the behavioral sciences: "Overcoming the problems that beset our schools, for example, does not lie with making computers and associated devices better, faster, and more available. . . . Overcoming the violence in our society does not lie in more and better metal detectors or surveillance cameras" (p. 27). A prime example is what many people regard as the most serious crisis facing humanity—the continuing devastation of the earth's environment by factors such as acid rain, global warming, ozone layer destruction, and the depletion of forests, fisheries, agricultural land, and water supplies. Many scientists believe that on our current course, our planet will be "irretrievably mutilated" (Union of Concerned Scientists, 1993, p. 1) and the earth "will be nearly uninhabitable for future generations" (Oskamp, 2000, p. 496). These environmental threats can be addressed in part by physical science initiatives (e.g.,

increasing agricultural productivity, decreasing toxic emissions). Nonetheless, a strong case can be made for the idea that escape from ecological disaster requires social science-based solutions because the causes of the most critical environmental problems are directly traceable to human choice and behavior, particularly to two categories of behavior: overpopulation and overconsumption (Howard, 2000; Oskamp, 2000).

Practical problems. Beyond any doubt, applied social psychology has enormous potential in the prevention and reduction of social problems. However, a singular focus on social problems misrepresents the past and current accomplishments and potential contributions of the field. As you will discover as you read this book, the field's applicability extends well beyond social problems. Applied social psychology addresses other undesirable or unsatisfactory circumstances that do not qualify as social problems in the conventional sense. For example, in Chapter 7, improvements to sports team cohesiveness and communication are considered as means of dealing with the problem of poor team performance, and in Chapter 11, decision making is addressed in the context of improving both individual work performance and organizational functioning. Although poor team performance and ineffective decision making are not typically defined as social problems, they are certainly social in that they occur in the context of groups, organizations, and people interacting with other people. We refer to such unsatisfactory circumstances that people (e.g., groups, organizations) face as *practical problems* to distinguish them from conventional social problems and to acknowledge their centrality to the field of applied social psychology.

Without wanting to confuse you, we should also put a positive spin on the focus of applied social psychology in that application can be extended to the improvement of an already acceptable or even very favorable situation. For instance, in sports, strategies may be implemented to improve the goal-focused communications of a team that already has an outstanding record of wins versus losses.

Personal uses. Also, with respect to issues in everyday life, individuals can look to social psychology for assistance. Murphy (1998) referred to personal uses of social psychology, meaning how each of us can use social psychological knowledge to improve his or her own life. In our coffee shop scenario, to improve the size of the tip, the female server might draw on the research literature on the role of server behavior that shows the importance of facilitating positive mood in customers, for example, by giving them an amusing task or by briefly touching or smiling at them (Rind & Strohmetz, 2001). A customer interested in receiving attentive service might be sure to use the server's name given the evidence that when others use their names, people regard this as a rewarding stimulus—as complimentary—and tend to respond with positive acts in kind (Howard, Gengler, & Jain, 1997). These would be personal uses/applications of social psychology. Chapter 5 considers the personal relevance of social psychology to two areas of life: the classroom and close relationships.

Social Influences on Behavior: The Power of the Situation

A core assumption of the field of social psychology is that *the behavior of individuals is strongly influenced by the social situation or context.* Both social psychological theory and research focus on understanding how and why people are influenced by social factors. Examples of the powerful role of situational determinants abound in social psychological research, including the results of some of the classic and best-known studies. We saw the power of social influence in the work of Sherif (1966b), where competition between groups of campers led to a marked deterioration in relations. Asch (1955), in his research on independence and conformity, demonstrated that on a very simple judgment task (e.g., distinguishing between the lengths of lines) in which the correct judgment was perfectly obvious, many participants chose to go along with the erroneous judgments of others rather than to publicly disagree with them. Depending on the particular study, 50% to 80% of participants conformed at least once over a series of trials. Dozens of bystander intervention studies—laboratory and field—that contrast the behavior of individual bystanders when alone and when with other bystanders have demonstrated that an individual's tendency to intervene in an emergency is sharply inhibited by the presence of others (Latané & Nida, 1981).

Stanley Milgram's obedience research is perhaps the most widely recognized illustration of the power of the situation. In Milgram's (1974) research, each participant was told by the experimenter that the study was about the role of punishment in learning. The participant had to administer apparently painful shocks to a learner (an experimental accomplice who only pretended to receive the shocks) every time the learner made a mistake on a learning task. The learner (accomplice) made a total of 30 mistakes in 40 opportunities. In a series of studies, Milgram examined the effects of different situational variables on people's compliance with the experimenter's insistent directives to increase the shock intensity with each successive error made by the learner up to the maximum shock level of 450 volts. The 30 shock levels ranged from a low of 15 volts, labeled "slight shock," to a high of 450 volts, which was beyond the label of "danger, severe shock." Table 1.1 shows, for seven of the situations that Milgram manipulated, the percentages of participants who obeyed completely by shocking the learner all the way up to the 450-volt maximum. The numbers showing maximum obedience ranged, depending on the situation, from nobody (0%) to a strong majority (65%). This clearly is a striking demonstration of what may be called situational control. Although all of the participants in the situations in the table were adult male volunteers from the community (in Connecticut), a replication of the first situation with females showed exactly the same level of maximum obedience (65%). Further attesting to the power of the situation was a control condition in which participants were not directed by the experimenter to increase the severity of shocks and were free to choose any shock level. In this situation—with pressure from the experimenter removed—only 1 participant of 40 (2.5%) chose the maximum shock intensity, and the mean (average) level selected by participants across all 30 learner errors was level 4 of 30 levels (in the slight shock range). You should be careful not to dismiss Milgram's findings as reflecting a bygone era given that research during the intervening 30 years has indicated similar levels of obedience (Feldman, 1998). Social psychologists have drawn parallels between the obedient behavior of Milgram's participants and actual examples of "destructive obedience," including military personnel following "orders" in Nazi Germany, in Bosnia, and (more recently) at Abu Ghraib prison in Iraq. Everyday life abounds with examples of the strong influence of the power of the situation on people's behavior, for example, when we turn on our best behavior when we enter a place of worship or begin a job interview and then may turn the good behavior sharply off when we are horsing around with friends or imbibing at a local drinking establishment. You may be thinking something like, "Sure, people are influenced by the situations they are in, but not everybody is influenced the same way." If you are, you have a good point. After all, the amount of conformity in Asch's (1955) experiments varied greatly, with some participants showing no conformity at all. Likewise, in each of the other classic studies described earlier, people differed in how they reacted to the situation. For instance, we can see in Table 1.1 that in every condition in the obedience research, there were some participants who resisted the authority of the experimenter. What is being suggested here is the relevance of individual differences. **Individual differences** refer to characteristics or qualities of an individual (as opposed to characteristics of a situation) and include things such as personality variables, attitudes, values, and abilities as well as demographic variables such as gender, ethnicity, religion, and age.

Although social psychology is primarily concerned with social determinants and explanations of behavior, the field recognizes the important role of individual difference variables in understanding the behavior of people. The idea that behavior is a function of both the person and the situation was advanced by Lewin (1936): "Every psychological event depends upon the state of the person and at the same time on the environment, although their relative importance is different in different cases"

Table 1.1 The Milgram Experiments: How Variations in the Experimental Situation Influenced Levels of Obedience to Authority

Experimental Situation	Percentage of Participants Who Showed Maximum Obedience
1. Learner is in adjacent room; participant cannot see learner but can hear his protests about the shocks and complaints about having a heart condition	65.0
2. Similar to No. 1 except that there is no mention of the learner having a heart condition	62.5
3. Participant is a few feet away from learner and can readily see and hear his protests; no mention of a heart condition	40.0
4. Participant is beside learner and must hold (force) learner's hand onto shock plate; no mention of a heart condition	30.0
5. Same as No. 1 except that, after giving initial instructions, experimenter departs and directs participant by telephone	20.5
6. Same as No. 1 except that participant and two other participants (actually accomplices) jointly teach learner; the others begin to defy the experimenter	10.0
7. Same as No. 1 but involves two experimenters; one begins to direct participant to stop shocking the learner, whereas the other one encourages him to continue	0.0

SOURCE: Based on Milgram (1974).

(p. 12). That is, at any given moment, what we are doing usually is a reflection of our personalities and the surrounding social and physical contexts. This position also was recently expressed aptly by Myers (2002): "The great truth about the power of social influence is but half the truth if separated from its complementary truth: the power of the person" (p. 200). Social influences on behavior and personal influences on behavior should not be viewed as incompatible. Instead, social psychologists commonly view them as demonstrating an *interactive relationship* (Snyder & Ickes, 1985). One way in which personal and social influences interact with each other is that social situations may have different effects on different people. For example, people with different personalities may react to a situation differently because they do not construe it in the same way (Ross & Nisbett, 1991; Shoda, 2004), as would have been the case if some of Milgram's (1974) participants had viewed the experimenter as a powerful authority figure, whereas others had not.

Underestimating the role of situational influences. When we observe people's behavior, we explain it by making internal attributions, external attributions, or a combination of the two. **External** (situational) attributions explain behavior by focusing on factors in the observed person's social environment. **Internal** (dispositional) attributions explain behavior by focusing on factors within the person who has been observed. Despite the fact that behavior results from both personal and social influences, we have a tendency to underestimate the role of situational factors in influencing other people's behavior. For example, imagine showing up for the first day of class and meeting your new psychology professor. Imagine further that your new professor is dressed in a dirty suit, speaks in a monotone voice, does not seem to care about the lecture material, and is short with you when you ask a simple question about the format of the exams. In this situation, you are likely to infer that the professor is a bitter curmudgeon, and because of that you might even consider dropping the course. Notice that in this situation, you would have made an internal attribution for the professor's behavior; you explained his behavior by inferring something about his

personality. However, it is entirely possible that the professor is in fact a pleasant, caring, and helpful individual who had a flat tire and ruined his favorite suit on the way to class. Had you known this, you would have been more likely to make an external attribution of the professor's behavior. You would have chalked up his poor mood to unfortunate circumstances.

This tendency for us to underestimate the influence of situational factors and focus on individual factors in explaining other people's behavior is called the **fundamental attribution error** (Ross, 1977). Because people themselves are more salient to us than their situations when we are observing them, we tend to focus on people rather than situations when explaining their conduct. You can see from the data provided earlier the great extent to which situational factors influenced the behavior of participants in Milgram's (1974) studies. However, if you had been an observer in one of Milgram's sessions, you probably would have made an internal attribution for the participants' behavior (e.g., that the participants who administer high-voltage shocks are aggressive individuals or perhaps even sadists) (Myers, 2002). However, such a conclusion would have been inaccurate. As we mentioned earlier, in one version of his experiment, Milgram gave participants the opportunity to administer whatever voltage shock they desired. Under this experimental condition, the vast majority of participants chose to administer very low-voltage shocks. Clearly, situational factors (e.g., the demanding experimenter) played the primary role in prompting participants to administer high-voltage painful shocks. However, if you did not know about the results of Milgram's "free choice" condition and, thus, had not been made aware of the power of the situation, you would likely explain participants' cruel behavior in terms of the participants' character rather than the situation. Applied social psychology, by focusing on effecting change in people's social environments as a means of bringing about changes in their behavior, helps us to counteract a person's propensity to fall victim to the fundamental attribution error and, instead, to be attentive to the importance of social influences on behavior. More will be said about the fundamental attribution error in subsequent chapters.

Intervention strategies as social influence.
Consider the intervention strategies that we have mentioned so far, for example, Sherif (1966b) using superordinate goals to reduce intergroup conflict and Hodges and colleagues (2000) providing positive safe sex discussion experiences to increase college females' tendencies to engage in such discussions prior to having sex. Notice how each strategy involves introducing the target individuals to a social situation devised for the purpose of effecting changes in their attitudes and/or behavior. Thus, each strategy entails a social influence attempt, that is, an attempt on the part of some social agent (e.g., person, group, organization) to induce changes in behavior that will contribute to more effective functioning (e.g., more harmonious intergroup interaction, safer sex). The focus of this book is on how social psychological understanding of social influence processes can be applied to improving the lives of people. In essence, we are saying that the field of applied social psychology rests on the power of the situation. That is, fundamental to the field is the assumption that the systematic exercise of situational control (i.e., intervention strategies) can be employed to improve the functioning of people.

Levels of Analysis

We have underscored that the social psychological perspective emphasizes the importance of social influences on people—that how we think, feel, and behave is greatly affected by aspects of the social situation or context. To explore further what may be viewed as constituting one's social situation, let us consider your current activity, that is, reading this chapter. As you review this section of the chapter, what is the social situation that is possibly causing you to read the material with more or less motivation and diligence? Is it a social stimulus in the immediate situation? For instance, are you being encouraged by a motivated friend with whom you are—at this very moment—reading and studying the material or perhaps by other students earnestly studying around you in the library? Also, it might be helpful to look beyond your immediate situation to the broader social context to understand your current level of

motivation on this task. Are you reading intently because you are concerned that the instructor may call on you during the upcoming class? Or, are the perceived expectations of significant others, in addition to your instructor, having an influence on you? For instance, are you applying yourself because your family or close friends expect this of you, or (conversely) is your heart not really in this task because of the pull of friends who really want you to be out having fun with them? Beyond the influence of significant others, are you working hard (or not so hard) because the academic standards at your school are quite high (or not so high) and you feel a lot of pressure (or little pressure) to do your best?

From this personal example, you can see that the social situation can be conceived broadly, ranging from the direct influence of specific others to the influence of more general factors. The social situational determinants of an individual's behavior may be viewed as falling into the following categories: interpersonal, group, organizational, community, and societal/cultural. Based on categorizations similar to this one, in social psychology we refer to *levels of analysis* (or explanation) that correspond with the various categories of determinants. For example, we seek to explain a person's behavior (e.g., studying) by investigating the effect of individuals on him or her (explanation at the interpersonal level) or by investigating the effect of groups on him or her (explanation at the group level). Of course, what is missing is the possible role of individual difference variables. In the example of studying, a dispositional explanation would suggest that your current level of diligence stems from your personality; for instance, you have (or do not have) a high drive to achieve (of course, social psychology would also investigate the influence of the social environment on your achievement drive). It is customary to combine personal determinants with situational determinants to come up with a more complete list of explanatory variables. It is also important to understand that the term "level" does not imply superior in any way; all levels may be important in establishing a thorough understanding of a phenomenon, although the relative importance of explanatory levels may vary from phenomenon to phenomenon.

A study by Riksheim and Chermak (1993) allows us to consider further the meaning of the social situation as a determinant of behavior and illustrates the notion of levels of analysis. Riksheim and Chermak were interested in examining factors that lead police officers to engage in various behaviors such as providing service (e.g., assisting motorists), making arrests, and employing force on suspects. They distinguished among four categories of determinants of police behavior: (a) immediate situational variables such as characteristics of the incident (e.g., seriousness of crime) and of the parties involved (e.g., demeanor of the suspect), (b) organizational variables such as differences among police units in policing style and enforcement strategy, (c) community variables such as the crime rate and ethnic makeup of the neighborhood, and (d) officer individual difference variables such as gender and racial attitudes. Riksheim and Chermak's classification of variables divides the determinants of police behavior into three situational categories and one individual difference category.

Table 1.2 summarizes what Riksheim and Chermak (1993) found in their review of 40 studies that examined factors that predict police officer use of force (use fists, firearms, stun guns, pepper spray, etc.). The researchers pointed out the importance of understanding the determinants of officer use of force because of its potential alienating and inflammatory effects on communities. Table 1.2 shows, for each category of variable (level of explanation), those variables reported by Riksheim and Chermak that showed a relationship to use of force. For instance, under the immediate situation, use of force was related to the number of officers present (occurring more often with more officers present) and the suspect's conduct (occurring more often with antagonistic suspects).

Further inspection of Table 1.2 clearly shows that to gain a more complete understanding, it is also necessary to investigate police use of force from the perspective of the other levels of analysis—individual difference, organizational, and community—because variables at these levels are shown to be related to use of force. The distinction among levels of analysis is an especially important one for applied social psychology because it begs the question of toward

Table 1.2   Variables Found to Predict Police Use of Force

Individual differences (officer characteristics)
  Gender (male)
  Racial attitudes (prejudicial)
  Skilled in handling overt conflict (most skilled)

Immediate interpersonal situation
  Number of officers (more officers)
  Suspect's conduct (e.g., antagonistic, consumed alcohol)
  Bystanders (not present)
  Weapon (used by citizen)

Organizational
  Department policy (less restrictive about use of force)
  Assignment/Nonassignment to specialized unit (e.g., narcotics)
  Supervisory review process (in place)

Community
  Ethnic composition of community (more non-white)
  Racial heterogeneity (more heterogeneous)
  Transience of population (less transient)

NOTE: Factors in parentheses are associated with more use of force.

SOURCE: Based on Riksheim and Chermak (1993). Reprinted with permission from Elsevier.

what level(s) and toward what variable(s) intervention strategies should be directed. Given the results in Table 1.2, what do you think? One possibility is to intervene at the organizational level by ensuring the consistent application of supervisory review of questionable incidents involving force, thereby ensuring greater accountability of officers for their actions. We imagine that you can see some other intervention possibilities, perhaps especially at the organizational and individual difference levels.

The Need for a Broad Approach

As we noted earlier, applied social psychology can be relevant to addressing social and practical problems in virtually *all areas of life*. Although the field certainly does not have all of the answers, applied social psychology has provided us with useful information, important insights, and fresh approaches to many different areas of social life (Sadava, 1997). There are at least three other important ways in which applied social psychology represents a broad approach: the use of multiple research methods, the adoption of an interdisciplinary orientation, and the application of evolutionary, personality, and cultural perspectives.

To truly understand and address social and practical problems in diverse organizations and communities, research undertaken in applied social psychology requires that social psychologists must be first and foremost social scientists. That is, we must be knowledgeable of the *research methods* of other allied disciplines such as cognitive science, communication studies, sociology, political science, program evaluation, marketing, organizational studies, and public health (Crano & Brewer, 2002). You will see examples of a variety of research methods throughout this book.

Advancements in finding solutions to social and practical problems also require that applied social psychologists adopt an *interdisciplinary approach.* Not only must we be knowledgeable of the research contributions and knowledge bases of many of the disciplines just listed, we also must increasingly pursue cross-disciplinary research and collaboration to take advantage of the perspectives and knowledge of social scientists within these disciplines.

There is a third way in which the breadth of applied social psychology has expanded during recent years. Although social psychologists devote primary attention to the role of the social context in understanding and explaining the complexities of human social behavior, we now appreciate more fully that a richer and more thorough understanding of many aspects of social behavior must also take account of *evolutionary (or biological), personality, and cultural perspectives.* The evolutionary perspective, which focuses on inherited tendencies to respond to the social environment in ways that enabled our ancestors to survive and reproduce, has been used to explain a diverse array of social behaviors and attitudes, including genetic influences on interpersonal attraction and job satisfaction. As we noted earlier, individual difference factors, including personality characteristics, also have a substantial influence on how people behave, think, and feel in a social context.

Moreover, to understand behavior in a social context, we must consider the influence of culture—the attitudes, values, beliefs, and behaviors shared by a group of people. Culture plays a subtle but powerful influence in our lives. As Triandis (1994) pointed out, people are often not aware of their own cultures until they come into contact with other cultures. In this book, issues are discussed from a North American vantage point. We recognize, however, that this perspective might not always be relevant to the consideration of problems in other cultures. Therefore, to maintain awareness of the importance of considering the role of culture in understanding and addressing social and practical problems, many of the chapters include a "Culture Capsule" that helps us to keep in mind the importance of cultural differences in understanding and addressing social and practical problems.

Various Roles of Applied Social Psychologists

Whereas the goal of social psychology in general is to develop and empirically test theories of social behavior, applied social psychology is concerned more specifically with understanding and finding solutions to social and practical problems by drawing on the knowledge base of existing theory and research, conducting research, and developing intervention strategies. Within these broad objectives, applied social psychologists may assume many different roles. For example, Sadava (1997) listed several roles, including planner, organizer, evaluator, consultant, advocate, and activist. Fisher (1982) grouped many of these roles into two major categories: applied scientist and professional practitioner. Drawing on the thinking of both Sadava and Fisher, we see at least six major roles for applied social psychologists: researcher, program developer, evaluation researcher, consultant, action researcher, and advocate.

Researcher. The applied social psychologist conducts research on social and practical problems. That is, the applied social psychologist seeks to understand social and practical problems through the application of both the core values and research strategies embodied in the scientific method. Thus, in the role of researcher, the applied social psychologist functions in a manner similar to other social scientists.

Program developer. Using existing theory and research evidence, the applied social psychologist may be involved in developing or improving interventions designed to resolve or ameliorate social and practical problems. As noted by Fisher (1982), this role combines theory, research, and practice; therefore, in the tradition of Lewin, it embraces a true scientist/practitioner model. The role of program developer is a central focus of Chapter 4.

Evaluation researcher. As an evaluation researcher (or a program evaluator), the applied social psychologist applies social science research methods to evaluate the process and outcomes of interventions (e.g., social programs and policies). The role of program evaluator also is addressed more fully in Chapter 4.

Consultant. During their careers, many (if not most) applied social psychologists will serve in some capacity as consultants to various groups, organizations, or communities. In the role of consultant, the applied social psychologist provides his or her expertise in social process and social theory to help clients resolve particular difficulties they are experiencing.

Action researcher. In the capacity of action researcher, the applied social psychologist works closely with an organization or a community group to resolve a particular issue or problem. This is accomplished through a collaborative cycle of data collection and interpretation leading to the development of appropriate action strategies. Action research is discussed in particular in Chapter 16.

Advocate. In the role of advocate, the applied social psychologist functions within the political arena. As stated by Fisher (1982), "The advocate uses his or her expertise to press for social change, usually in collaboration with a specific group, lobby, or institution that is working to change some aspect of the sociopolitical

system" (p. 19). Examples of the advocate role are provided in Chapter 16.

OVERVIEW OF BOOK

The first four chapters set the context of the field of applied social psychology. They provide a conceptual, theoretical, and methodological background to help you more fully appreciate the subsequent 11 chapters that focus on content areas of the field (e.g., sports, organizations). Each content chapter introduces you to research that seeks to develop understanding of relevant social and practical problems as well as to the application of social psychological knowledge to the design of intervention strategies for the amelioration of the problems. Each content chapter covers a selection of important topics; however, the chapters are not meant to be comprehensive in their coverage of these topic areas. Chapter 16, the final one, deals primarily with action and participatory research that describes both a way of approaching research (i.e., epistemology, values, assumptions about research) and a particular research process in which participants become active collaborators with the researcher.

SUMMARY

Applied social psychology is the branch of the science of social psychology that focuses on (a) developing social psychological understanding of social and practical problems and (b) drawing on that understanding to design intervention strategies for the amelioration of social and practical problems. As scientists, applied social psychologists are guided by a core set of values (e.g., accuracy, objectivity, skepticism, open-mindedness, ethics) and by the scientific method that includes specific research methods used to provide empirical tests of hypotheses. Scientific understanding of phenomena, including social and practical problems, entails the accomplishment of five goals: description, prediction, determining causality, explanation, and control.

The embracement of the goal of control (manipulation of conditions to cause changes in phenomena) particularly distinguishes applied social psychology as a separate branch of social psychology. That is, at the heart of applied social psychology is a concern with developing social influence strategies (i.e., interventions) to improve people's functioning with respect to social and practical problems. Although the field of applied social psychology is particularly concerned with addressing social and practical problems on a general level (e.g., education, environment), individuals also can use social psychology to improve their own lives.

The core assumption of the field of social psychology, and of applied social psychology, is that people's attitudes and behavior are greatly influenced by situational factors. In fact, intervention strategies may be viewed as involving the use of knowledge about social situational influence to effect improvements in people's functioning. However, applied social psychology also recognizes that to understand and address problems, individual difference variables (e.g., personality) must be considered. Moreover, the social situation can be viewed as reflecting different levels of analysis (e.g., interpersonal, group, community); accordingly, interventions may be directed at different levels.

Applied social psychology requires a broad approach to social and practical problems, including the use of multiple research methods, an interdisciplinary orientation, and recognition of the value of evolutionary, personality, and cultural perspectives. In his or her work, the applied social psychologist can assume several roles, some of which include researcher, program developer, evaluation researcher, consultant, action researcher, and advocate.

2

SOCIAL PSYCHOLOGICAL THEORY

SHELAGH M. J. TOWSON

CHAPTER OUTLINE

How can we understand the role of theory in applied social psychology? A good place to start is with the realization that we all are applied social psychologists. Although most of us would probably not think of ourselves in this way, all of us are constantly engaged in a process of making observations, constructing theories based on these observations, testing hypotheses derived from our theories, and applying these theories in our lives.

Let us imagine that you are 16 years old again and that you will be taking your driver's test in just a few months. Now, as you see it, the purpose of getting your driver's license is so that you can drive a car, and your reasons for wanting to drive a car are to have increased access to places you cannot get to with public transportation, more opportunities to spend quality time with friends, and greater freedom from parental supervision. Once you have your license, there will be only one obstacle standing in the way of your goal, and that is the fact that you do not have a car and are unlikely to be able to afford one in the foreseeable future.

You realize that your dream of independence will be fulfilled only if you start now on what you anticipate will be a long and hard campaign to get permission to use the family car on a regular basis. Your first step in this campaign is careful observation of the tactics your friends use with their own families, tactics that include "borrowing" their family cars without actually asking; prolonged begging, whining, and pleading; and, when all else fails, completing homework and assigned responsibilities around the house without having to be nagged to do so and even volunteering to do some helpful things.

On the basis of your observations, you conclude that some of these tactics work better than others. But what distinguishes the tactics that work well from those that do not? The "borrowing" first and asking later approach seems to result in severe negative consequences, and begging, whining, and pleading seem to succeed only occasionally. However, more often than not, acting responsibly and being helpful seem to increase your friends' chances of using their family cars. So, putting all your observations together, you construct an "adolescent car acquisition theory" that goes something like this:

1. Parents believe that their primary role as parents is to raise their children to be responsible adults.

2. Because of this belief, parents are always looking for indications that their efforts have been successful, and when they see evidence of positive adult behavior, they reward it.

3. Therefore, parents are more likely to accede to a request allowing the enactment of adult behavior (e.g., borrowing the family car) if the request is preceded by the demonstration of different but positive adult behavior.

While you are waiting to apply for your license, you design a research study to test your theory. You develop specific hypotheses such as the following: Volunteering to babysit younger siblings instead of going out with friends on Friday night results in a higher probability of car acquisition on Saturday night. You then recruit your friends to test these hypotheses with their families. Your hypotheses are supported; when your friends demonstrate responsible adult behavior, their rates of car acquisition increase markedly. Therefore, after you get your driver's license, you apply your theory by becoming a model (at least for a teenager) of adult maturity

and responsibility. You take out the garbage without being asked, you leave the bathroom sparkling clean after you use it, and so on. Sure enough, when you pop the question, "May I borrow the car Saturday night?," the answer is usually yes.

But wait, there is more. Based on your observations of its successful application, you revisit your theory and realize that it may apply to more behaviors than just car acquisition. You generate and test additional hypotheses such as the following: "If I finish my homework, my chances of having a later curfew will increase" and "If I mow the lawn, my band might be able to practice in the basement." Once more, your hypotheses are supported, and your confidence in your theory grows. You apply the knowledge you have gained, consistently demonstrate adult behavior, and become the envy of your friends for all of the privileges you get. Your parents are happy because they believe that your new maturity is the result of their excellent child-rearing techniques, and you are happy not only because of all the privileges you have gained but also because you have constructed, tested, and applied your first social psychological theory. (In fact, you might be beginning to contemplate social psychology as a career.)

Would you have gotten to use the family car if there had been no adolescent car acquisition theory? Probably, but without the theory, your opportunities to drive would have occurred less often and would have been chance occurrences rather than planned ones. Your theory helped you to accomplish the five goals of science described in Chapter 1 by providing you with a better *understanding* of what was going on in your parents' heads, thereby enabling you to exert more *control* over the car acquisition process.

This chapter discusses theory in the context of applied social psychology. First, it examines the role of theory in the scientific process. Then, it describes three functions fulfilled by social psychological theories and some of the characteristics of these theories. Finally, the chapter explores two influential theories—cognitive dissonance theory and groupthink theory—in terms of their functions, characteristics, and contributions to applied social psychology.

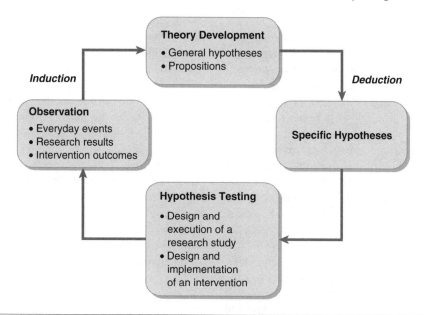

Figure 2.1   The Scientific Process

The Scientific Process

The five goals of science are description, prediction, determining causality, explanation, and control. Fulfilling these goals involves carrying out the steps in the scientific process outlined in Figure 2.1—from the observation of phenomena, to the development of theory, to the deduction of specific hypotheses derived from the theory, to testing these hypotheses through research and interventions. You might be interested in knowing that this was the path you followed, albeit unwittingly, in getting the keys to the family car and other privileges.

The first step in the process is *observation.* For social psychologists, the observation stage might consist of a single vivid incident from everyday life, a systematic program of descriptive data gathering (such as you used to construct your adolescent car acquisition theory), a review of existing research evidence, or the analysis of intervention outcomes. The helping behavior theory of social psychologists John Darley and Bibb Latané, for instance, was triggered by their perception of the events surrounding a murder in New York City that took place in front of many bystanders who did not intervene to help the victim (Darley & Latané, 1968). One

of the theories discussed in this chapter (see also Chapter 11), Irving Janis's groupthink theory, was based on Janis's (1972) observations of many situations involving group decision making. Leon Festinger's cognitive dissonance theory, also discussed in this chapter, grew out of a review of research on rumors (Festinger, 1957).

The next step in the scientific process is *theory development,* with **theory** defined as "a set of interrelated hypotheses or propositions concerning a phenomenon or set of phenomena" (Shaw & Costanzo, 1982, p. 4). In your case, the phenomenon in question was the adolescent pursuit of the family car. You thought about (i.e., analyzed) all of your observations of your friends' behaviors in attempting to get their family cars and their parents' reactions, looked for a common thread, and you found it: Parents reward evidence that they have succeeded in their mission to raise responsible adults. On the basis of your observation of many examples of a variety of behaviors and resulting consequences, you constructed a theory that explained all of the examples. This process of moving from the specific to the general is known as **induction** (i.e., inferring general principles from observing specific instances), and it is the way in which the vast majority of social psychological theories are constructed.

The third step in the scientific process outlined in Figure 2.1 is the development of *specific hypotheses* through a process of **deduction** (i.e., deriving specific hypotheses from the general hypotheses and propositions of the theory). A **hypothesis** may be defined as a prediction that specifies the relationship between variables. The relationship that is specified may be causal in nature (i.e., one variable causes change in another variable) or may simply suggest that the variables are correlated but not in a causal manner (see Chapter 3). Your adolescent car acquisition theory includes the general causal hypothesis that the voluntary enactment of particular adult behaviors by an adolescent will result in parents' granting permission for other adult behaviors (e.g., driving the family car). Based on this general hypothesis, you developed a series of specific hypotheses that attempted to specify the relationship between particular adult behaviors enacted by your friends (e.g., baby-sitting, washing dishes) and the particular adult behavior for which they would request permission (i.e., borrowing their family cars).

The fourth step in the scientific process is *hypothesis testing*. To test hypotheses, social psychologists use a variety of strategies, including conducting research and carrying out interventions. As indicated in Chapter 1, many social psychologists focus primarily on the goals of science that center on understanding social psychological phenomena. For these psychologists, the goal of control through the application of social psychological knowledge is not a central concern, and hypothesis testing is carried out through the design and execution of systematic research studies. The results (observations) of such research may provide support for the hypothesis and, thus, for the theory from which it was derived. Observations that do not support the hypothesis may lead to modifications of the original theory or to the development of a new one.

However, many social psychologists, particularly those who define themselves as applied social psychologists, are interested in pursuing the fifth goal of science—control. Thus, these social psychologists are interested in the *application* of the knowledge gained through theory development in the design and implementation of interventions. As a teenager who is eager to drive, your careful analysis of the adolescent request/parental resistance phenomenon enabled you to influence your parents so that they would give you the car keys nearly every time you asked. Applied social psychologists use theories in a similar way, that is, as the source of intervention strategies designed to improve the functioning of individuals, groups, or organizations. And as Figure 2.1 shows, the process does not end there. Intervention strategies derived from theory and research results lead to further observations, to the modification of existing theories or the construction of new ones, to the testing of hypotheses derived from these theories, and to new possibilities for application (through a continuing process of induction and deduction).

THEORY IN SOCIAL PSYCHOLOGY

Functions of Social Psychological Theories

We noted in Chapter 1 that Kurt Lewin, one of the founders of social psychology, believed that there was "nothing so practical as a good theory" (Lewin, 1944/1951a, p. 169). Why is a good theory practical? Or, to put it another way, what functions does theory perform? One way in which to think about the functions of a theory is to see theory as the one component of the scientific process outlined in Figure 2.1 that ties the other three components together by providing organization, direction, and guidance for the development of interventions.

The first function of a theory, which is related to observation, is to provide *organization*. Just as an architect needs a blueprint to turn a heap of stones into a house, the social psychologist needs a theory to discern the pattern that underlies and connects observations of relevant phenomena. The move from observation to theory is a critical one because the most careful compilations of fact—the most detailed descriptions—do not tell us possible ways in which the observed phenomena are interrelated. Referring once more to your adolescent car acquisition theory, some of your friends found that their chances of using their family cars increased if they mowed the lawn, whereas others observed the same result if they volunteered to babysit. However, it was only when you organized these two observations (and others) within the framework of your theory that you were able to identify a common theme that connected them. It was not solely lawn mowing or babysitting that earned your friends' use of their family cars; it was the meaning of these behaviors to your friends' parents.

The second function of theory, which is related to hypothesis testing, is to provide *direction.* When you are traveling to a new destination, you use a road map to chart your course, perhaps noting alternate routes that you may try on future trips if your initial choice is not satisfactory. In the same way, social psychological theories may suggest possible heretofore unconsidered relationships between observed phenomena and may provide stimulation and guidance for further hypothesis testing and the possible alteration of the theory or even the generation of new theories. For example, your adolescent car acquisition theory led you to demonstrate previously untried mature behaviors to your parents in pursuit of permission for other adult behaviors besides driving the car.

The third function of a theory, which is related most directly to application, is to guide *intervention.* The goal of medical science is to identify the causes of disease, not out of idle curiosity but rather to prescribe actions that will prevent its occurrence. In the same way, theories in social psychology provide prescriptions for the solutions to social and practical problems. So, for example, you used your adolescent car acquisition theory as the basis for an intervention strategy that solved your practical problem of getting access to the family car as frequently as possible.

Characteristics of Social Psychological Theories

Social psychological theories differ in terms of a number of characteristics, including scope, range, testability, and parsimony. The **scope** of a theory refers to the number of different human behaviors that the theory attempts to explain. Social psychology, like other branches of psychology, has been influenced by several broad perspectives that explain most human behaviors

by reference to a single central concept. For example, according to psychologist John Watson's (1913) *behaviorist perspective,* all human behaviors are learned responses to external rewards and punishments. Sigmund Freud's (1935) *psychoanalytic orientation* suggests that humans behave as they do because of unconscious motivations, and Lewin's (1944/1951a) *phenomenological perspective* advances the notion that human behavior is the result of the way in which we subjectively interpret our environment. Many social psychological theories incorporate some aspects of these perspectives, recognizing the importance of learning (behaviorist), motivation (psychoanalytic), and internal cognitive processes (phenomenological). However, social psychological theories do not claim to be able to explain all kinds of human behavior and, thus, are more limited in scope than the perspectives they reflect.

Many social psychological theories, such as cognitive dissonance theory (discussed in more detail later in this chapter), are *mid-level theories* that attempt to explain one way of thinking or behaving that is relevant in a number of different situations. Other theories are *mini-theories* that attempt to explain a particular human behavior when faced with a particular set of circumstances. Groupthink, the second theory reviewed in this chapter, could be described as a mini-theory because it focuses on the decision-making behavior of people in a cohesive group when faced with an urgent need to make a decision during a crisis.

Range refers to whether a theory predicts the behaviors of only a specific group of people or all humans. Until relatively recently, the assumption shared by many social psychologists was that it is possible to identify certain universal principles that shape the behavior of all humans; therefore, the theories they developed were thought to apply to people in general. Social psychologists have come to realize, however, that people's behavior may be influenced by individual differences, such as intelligence and temperament, as well as by group differences, such as gender and cultural background. Therefore, to determine possible limits to a theory's range, increased attention has been paid, for instance, to testing hypotheses with men and women separately and with people who differ on individual- and group-level attributes.

Another characteristic of a theory, and perhaps the most important one, is its **testability**. Testability refers to the idea that a good theory is capable of being refuted or disproved. In our individualistic culture, the idea that you can accomplish anything you want so long as you try hard enough is a very powerful theory. Unfortunately, it is not a good theory because it is impossible to disprove. Did you accomplish your goal? If so, it must be because you tried very hard. If not, it must be because you did not try hard enough. How does one know that you did not try hard enough? One knows because if you had tried hard enough, you would have succeeded. The theory that anything is possible with enough effort is not testable because it does not specify what "enough" effort means. Many of the variables in which social psychologists are interested, such as values, attitudes, and beliefs, are internal states that are not directly observable, and so for some time theories about these variables were thought to be untestable. Thus, social psychologists were hampered in their theorizing until methods to measure these internal variables were developed (Jones, 1998), and much current social psychological research is devoted to developing new and better measurement methods so that promising theories can be tested.

A theory should also demonstrate **parsimony,** meaning that it should use the fewest possible number of propositions to explain the phenomenon in question. Perhaps in part because social psychologists have focused on mid-level theories and mini-theories rather than attempting to construct and test grand theories (i.e., those that are broad in scope) of human behavior, their theories tend not to include an overabundance of propositions. However, given the complexity of social behavior, social psychologists sometimes have to sacrifice some parsimony to provide adequate theoretical explanations.

Probably the best way in which to understand theories' functions and characteristics, as well as the interplay of observation, theory construction, hypothesis testing, and application, is to look at actual theories. We now consider two influential theories in social psychology—cognitive dissonance and groupthink theory—and examine their function in terms of organization, direction, and possibilities for intervention.

COGNITIVE DISSONANCE THEORY

Description

How would you react if you felt the tremors of an earthquake but, fortunately, did not suffer any direct injury or property damage? Prasad (1950) observed that, curiously, people in India who were in exactly this situation after a severe earthquake started spreading rumors of even worse disasters to come. When Festinger and his colleagues read Prasad's descriptive study, they wondered whether perhaps the people spread these rumors not to provoke more anxiety but rather to justify the anxiety they still felt, even though the earthquake was over and they had suffered no injuries or damage. Festinger wrote, "From that germ of an idea, I developed my theory of dissonance reduction—making your view of the world fit with how you feel or what you've done" (cited in Myers & Spencer, 2004, p. 132).

As indicated in Figure 2.2, the core of cognitive dissonance theory is the idea that humans are motivated to maintain consistency among their cognitions (e.g., opinions, attitudes, knowledge, values) because cognitive dissonance, the situation that exists when two cognitions are psychologically inconsistent with one another, is psychologically uncomfortable. Festinger's cognitive dissonance theory would suggest, in the case of Prasad's (1950) rumor spreaders, that their cognition that "the earthquake didn't hurt me in any way" was inconsistent with the cognition that "I'm still feeling very frightened." For them, apparently the easiest way in which to reduce their dissonance-caused discomfort was to justify their fear by adding new cognitions (Figure 2.2), that is, by generating rumors of impending disasters. They might have taken a seemingly more logical approach (e.g., moving away from the earthquake zone), but an additional key element of cognitive dissonance theory is the proposition that people will reduce dissonance in the easiest way possible. For example, the cognition that "exercising is good for my health" is dissonant

Cognitive Dissonance Theory

Central Hypotheses

- Cognitions can be irrelevant to, consonant with, or dissonant with each other.
- Humans are motivated to maintain cognitive consonance.
- The presence of cognitive dissonance is psychologically uncomfortable and creates pressures to reduce dissonance.

Some Dissonance Producing Situations

- *Post decisional dissonance.* Dissonance almost always exists after a decision has been made between two or more alternatives.
- *Effort justification.* Dissonance almost always exists when a person engages in an unpleasant activity to obtain some desirable outcome.
- *Insufficient justification.* Dissonance almost always exists after a successful attempt has been made to elicit overt behavior that is at variance with private opinion by offering a reward that is just sufficient to elicit the overt behavior.

Some Ways to Reduce Dissonance

- Change one or more of the dissonant cognitions.
- Add new cognitions to make existing cognitions consistent.
- Downplay importance of dissonant cognitions.

Figure 2.2   Cognitive Dissonance Theory

SOURCE: Adapted from Festinger (1957) and Aronson and Mills (1959).

with the cognition that "my only exercise is the trip between my couch and refrigerator." The most logical action for me to take would be to start exercising. However, because breaking old habits and acquiring new ones is very difficult, I probably will reduce my dissonance in one of several other ways. I might change my cognition that exercise is good for my health ("Joggers drop dead from heart attacks every day"), add new cognitions that rationalize my "couch potato" existence ("Relaxing is also good for my health") (Festinger, 1957), or trivialize the importance of my inconsistent cognitions ("What's the big deal? Nobody lives forever") (Simon, Greenberg, & Brehm, 1995).

captured in a few sentences. But think about what is implied by this seemingly simple theory. Human inconsistency is not a new phenomenon. We all can think of examples when we knew we were behaving in ways that contradicted our attitudes or beliefs and managed to find ways in which to rationalize the contradictions. But what cognitive dissonance theory does, in fulfilling the first function of a theory, is to organize what we know about human inconsistency in such a way that we are led to some nonobvious conclusions about the relationship between attitudes and behavior, particularly the idea that we may change our attitudes to match our behavior rather than the other way around.

Organization

Although Festinger (1957) wrote an entire book detailing the definitions, assumptions, and hypotheses of his theory, its essence can be

Direction

The second function of a theory is to provide direction for research, and by this criterion, cognitive dissonance theory is one of the best.

Festinger derived a number of intriguing hypotheses from cognitive dissonance theory that have been tested in hundreds of experiments. Figure 2.2 illustrates the three dissonance situations that have received the most attention. They involve postdecisional dissonance, effort justification, and insufficient justification.

Postdecisional dissonance. Let us start with postdecisional dissonance. Have you ever had to choose between two attractive alternatives? You go back and forth considering the pros and cons of each alternative, but eventually you have to make up your mind. Dissonance theory predicts that, whichever alternative you choose (e.g., when purchasing a car), you will feel dissonance because of the two conflicting cognitions: "I bought the BMW" and "Maybe I should have bought the Audi because there are some great things about it." But it is too late to change your mind; you have already signed the papers and driven the car home. Your decision has been made, so you cannot reverse your behavior. What will you do? The dissonance theory prediction, supported by extensive research (e.g., Brehm, 1956; Heine & Lehman, 1997; Knox & Inkster, 1968; Shultz, Léveillé, & Lepper, 1999), is that you will reevaluate the chosen and unchosen alternatives so that the chosen alternative appears to be clearly superior to the unchosen alternative. In other words, two cars that were judged to be very close together before you made your decision are now perceived to be much further apart. Note what has happened here and how in some ways it contradicts common sense. We like to think that our attitudes guide our behaviors: "I like BMWs better, so I bought a BMW." But in this instance, your behavior actually contributed to a change in attitude: "I bought a BMW, so I guess I must like BMWs better."

Automobile salespeople are very aware of the practical implications of postdecisional dissonance. They use what is called a *low-ball* technique by offering such a good deal on a car that the customer commits to buying it. In some cases, the customer is even allowed to take the car home overnight to reinforce the commitment made. When the customer returns the next morning to pay for the car, just before money

changes hands, the salesperson explains that some costs in the total price had accidentally been omitted by the sales manager, so that the car will actually cost more than the amount to which the customer had originally agreed. The logical decision at this point is to refuse the deal (because it is no longer such a great deal). But by now the customer has had many hours to justify choosing this car instead of any others that had been considered. The chosen alternative now looks so much better than the unchosen ones that the customer does not mind shelling out a little extra cash. After all, it is clearly a superior car (Cialdini, Cacioppo, Bassett, & Miller, 1978).

Effort justification. Cognitive dissonance theorists have also tested the effects of effort justification on attitude change. Have you ever worked very hard to achieve a goal—say, admission to the college you are now attending—only to have a sinking feeling, after you attained the goal, that all that effort might not have been worth it? In this case, your two dissonant cognitions are "I worked very hard to get accepted by this college" and "So far, my college experience doesn't seem to be as good as I expected it to be." Cognitive dissonance theory predicts, again with research support (e.g., Aronson & Mills, 1959; Gerard & Mathewson, 1966), that in this situation, where (once again) you cannot change your behavior (changing schools during mid-semester is difficult), you will instead reevaluate the goal you have attained and convince yourself that it was in fact a very worthy goal (e.g., "I doubt that I would have a better experience at any of the other colleges I considered").

The idea of effort justification may be applied to practical problems. For example, Axsom and Cooper (1985) recruited overweight female college students to participate in a weight loss experiment in which participants were told that they would be completing a series of cognitive tasks (e.g., reciting nursery rhymes with delayed auditory feedback) designed to increase neurophysiological arousal that supposedly would enhance emotional sensitivity and, in turn, lead to increased weight loss. (In actuality, there was no evidence that the cognitive tasks helped with weight reduction.) For some participants, the cognitive tasks were relatively difficult; for others, the tasks were relatively easy. A control group of participants completed no cognitive tasks and were simply weighed. After four sessions over 3 weeks, the high-effort women had lost more weight than had the low-effort and control group women. The dissonance theory interpretation for the high-effort women goes like this: "After I have expended all this effort to lose weight, I am more convinced than ever that weight loss is a good goal, and so I will try even harder to lose weight." Furthermore, despite the fact that there were no more sessions and the participants were not aware that they would be contacted again, the beneficial effects of the high-effort condition were still apparent a year later. When they weighed in at that time, the high-effort women had lost an average of 6.7 pounds, compared with less than 1 pound for the low-effort women and a gain of nearly 2 pounds for the control group women. Further research by Axsom and his colleagues (Axsom, 1989; Cooper & Axsom, 1982) suggested that psychotherapy patients who had to work hard at their own treatment are more likely to report feeling better when the treatment is over than are those patients who did not have to work as hard.

Insufficient justification. Insufficient justification is the most difficult dissonance theory hypothesis to understand and is also the most intriguing. Suppose that your friend has just gotten a haircut that makes him look like a badly plucked chicken. When he asks you for your opinion, you can either tell him what you really think and hurt his feelings or lie and tell him that the new haircut looks great. Normally, your knowledge that you lied would be dissonant with your belief that you are an honest person and you would feel uncomfortable. In this case, however, your concern for your friend's feelings provides you with considerable external justification for your lie, so you do not feel dissonance and you do not change your real opinion (i.e., you still believe that the haircut was a big mistake). But what happens if you lie about something and there is very little external justification for doing so? When this happens, cognitive dissonance theory predicts that because you cannot take back the lie (it has already been told), you will provide yourself with internal justification for your behavior. You will convince yourself that you were not really lying by changing your attitude regarding whatever it is you lied about.

In the original test of the insufficient justification hypothesis (one of the classic experimental studies of social psychology), Festinger and Carlsmith (1959) had college students participate in a very boring study and then induced them, for either $1 or $20, to tell another student that the study was very interesting. The participants were then asked to indicate how they really felt about the experiment. Consistent with cognitive dissonance theory predictions, students who had lied to a fellow student for only $1 evaluated the experiment as more interesting than did students who had lied for $20. Why? According to Festinger and Carlsmith, both the $1 students and the $20 students had two dissonant cognitions: "I thought that the experiment was boring" and "I just told a fellow student that it was interesting; I just told a lie." For the students who had lied for $20, the inconsistency was resolved with the addition of the cognition, "I'm a poor student, and I got paid a lot of money for telling a harmless lie." But for the students who had lied for $1, the knowledge that they had lied to a fellow student could not be externally justified (who lies for a paltry $1?), so they had to provide internal justification for their behavior by convincing themselves that the study had actually been kind of interesting.

The cognitive dissonance aroused by insufficient justification has been demonstrated in many experiments (e.g., Brehm & Cohen, 1962; Hobden & Olson, 1994; Riess & Schlenker, 1977) and also has been used to change people's attitudes about important issues. Leippe and Eisenstadt (1994) either told (high external justification) or asked (low external justification) white college students at a U.S. university to write an essay in support of doubling the scholarship funds available to African American students, even though this would mean halving the funds available to other students. Consistent with cognitive dissonance theory predictions, only the students who had written the essay voluntarily subsequently expressed more favorable and supportive attitudes toward African Americans than they had before engaging in the attitude-discrepant behavior.

As illustrated, good theories provide direction for research by generating testable hypotheses. The results of hypothesis testing research also can lead to theory modification. This has happened with respect to cognitive dissonance theory. One modification of cognitive dissonance theory with significant implications for application is Aronson's (1968, 1992) reinterpretation of cognitive dissonance as always involving some form of *self*-justification. Think about the following cognitions: "I'm driving at night on a lonely country road and just got a flat tire" and "I don't have my tire jack with me." In his book, Festinger (1957) argued that a person in this situation, although frustrated, would not feel dissonance because the two cognitions are not psychologically inconsistent; that is, the two cognitions do not contradict each other in the way that the following cognitions do: "I smoke" and "I know that smoking is bad for me" (pp. 277–278).

Aronson (1999) disagreed, stating that the dissonance would come from the fact that the driver, like most of us, likes to think that he is a reasonably intelligent individual, but his two cognitions lead him to conclude that he must be a total idiot to drive down a country road in the middle of the night without a jack. This observation led to Aronson's *self-consistency dissonance theory,* which posits that situations evoke dissonance because of an inconsistency between self-concept and awareness of one's behavior. In other words, people experience dissonance when they behave in ways that they view as reflecting negatively on themselves (that they are incompetent, immoral, irrational, etc.). Research supports this idea, and as Aronson (1968, 1992) pointed out, the results of many cognitive dissonance experiments can be interpreted in accordance with his modification of cognitive dissonance theory. Furthermore, Aronson's reworking of dissonance theory provides a good illustration of how cognitive dissonance theory has fulfilled the third function of theory: helping in the design of interventions.

Intervention

Do you believe that we need to do more to conserve our natural resources? Now, do you behave in a way that is consistent with your beliefs? It is quite possible that your behavior is not necessarily consistent with your beliefs. Let us take recycling as an example. How many of us look for the recycling box every time we have something to throw out, and how many of us "cheat" quite often, or at least occasionally, because it is just easier to toss that bottle into the nearest garbage can?

But what would happen to your behavior if you were asked to write and deliver a speech on the importance of recycling, a speech that would be videotaped and shown to various audiences as part of a community campaign to increase participation in recycling programs? Now, suppose that you do not recycle very much, if at all, even though you think that it is a good idea. You still would probably be able to give the speech, coming up with some pretty good arguments in support of recycling. However, it is unlikely that your own recycling behavior would change much at all. But suppose that, just before you write the speech, you are questioned about your own recycling behavior. Now that you must focus on your behavior, you have two dissonant cognitions: "I will be preaching recycling to my community" and "I don't practice what I preach." In other words, you are now very aware of your hypocrisy.

This is exactly the manipulation that Fried and Aronson (1995) used in their experiment. College students were asked to write and deliver a pro-recycling speech, but prior to writing the speech, half of the participants (the hypocrisy condition) were asked to list examples of recent times when they had failed to recycle. After they had written their speeches, all participants were asked whether they would volunteer to make phone calls for a local recycling organization. Just as predicted, the participants in the hypocrisy condition (who had been reminded that their actual behavior was not consistent with their expressed attitudes) volunteered significantly more often, and for longer periods of time, than did those students who had only written the speeches. Aronson and his colleagues have reported similar results in experimental studies involving the induction of hypocrisy to increase condom use (Aronson, Fried, & Stone, 1991; Stone, Aronson, Crain, Winslow, & Fried, 1994) and to encourage water conservation (Dickerson, Thibodeau, Aronson, & Miller, 1992).

Summing Up Cognitive Dissonance Theory

How can we sum up cognitive dissonance theory? Based on the "germ of an idea" triggered by his reading a study on rumors, Festinger developed a theory that, given its applicability to a number of different situations, could be described in terms of scope as a midlevel theory. As originally proposed, cognitive dissonance theory had a broad range because it was presumed to apply to people in general rather than to particular individuals or groups. Further research on individual and cultural differences has modified this presumption somewhat. The central premise of cognitive dissonance theory is that psychological inconsistency makes people uncomfortable. However, Cialdini, Trost, and Newsom (1995) developed a Preference for Consistency scale and discovered that some people have a low preference for consistency, whereas others have a high preference for consistency. Consistent with cognitive dissonance theory predictions, both high- and low-consistency preference individuals changed their attitudes when they were induced to behave in attitude-inconsistent ways and had low external justification for doing so. However, contrary to cognitive dissonance theory predictions, people with a low preference for consistency changed their attitudes to match their behaviors even when they had high external justification for behaving as they did and could have avoided attitude change by attributing their behavior to the external pressure.

As discussed elsewhere in this book, cross-cultural psychologists have identified a reliable cultural difference known as individualism–collectivism (Hofstede, 1991). In individualistic cultures, the integrity of the individual is most important, whereas people in collectivistic cultures are expected to behave in ways that preserve the integrity of the group, regardless of their own attitudes. Therefore, Kashima, Siegal, Tanaka, and Kashima (1992) hypothesized that the preference for internal psychological consistency would be stronger in individualistic cultures than in collectivistic cultures. Consistent with their hypothesis, they found that Australians, whose culture is relatively individualistic, had stronger beliefs about the importance of attitude–behavior

consistency than did Japanese, whose culture is relatively collectivistic. Future research will determine whether these cultural differences in attitudes about consistency translate into different reactions to supposedly dissonance-arousing situations.

Without a doubt, cognitive dissonance theory fulfills the criterion of testability. Since its inception, it has inspired many hundreds of studies and continues to influence research (e.g., Abelson et al., 1968; Harmon-Jones & Mills, 1999; Wicklund & Brehm, 1976). Cognitive dissonance theory also provides a good example of parsimony given that the essence of the theory can be captured in a few propositions.

In short, cognitive dissonance theory provides an excellent example of how theory serves three main functions: (a) organizing the existing literature, (b) providing direction for the testing of hypotheses derived from the original theory and for the generation of new hypotheses and new theories, and (c) suggesting many possibilities for intervention. Recapitulating the scientific process (see Figure 2.1) and emphasizing the relationship that should exist between experimentation and application, Festinger (1999) said it very well:

> I think we need to find out about how dissonance processes and dissonance reducing processes interact in the presence of other things that are powerful influences of human behavior and human cognition, and the only way to do that is to do studies in the real world. They're messy and difficult. . . . But out of them will emerge more ideas which we can then bring into the laboratory to clarify and help to broaden and enrich the work. (p. 385)

GROUPTHINK THEORY

Description

In 1961, President John F. Kennedy authorized covert military support for an invasion of Cuba by a brigade of Cuban exiles who had been armed and trained in the United States. The purpose of this secret mission was to engineer the overthrow of the Cuban government in such a way that it would be perceived as an

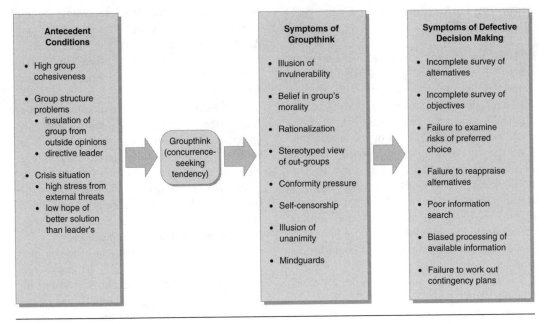

Figure 2.3   Groupthink Theory

SOURCE: Adapted from Janis and Mann (1977). Reprinted with permission.

internal uprising with no U.S. involvement. The invasion was an unmitigated disaster, from the brigade's landing at the Bay of Pigs to its capture and imprisonment by the Cuban army 2 days later. U.S. involvement in the debacle was painfully obvious and resulted in widespread condemnation.

In retrospect, Kennedy sometimes referred "incredulously to the Bay of Pigs, wondering how a rational and responsible government could ever have become involved in so ill-starred an adventure" (Schlesinger, 1965, p. 292). Janis (1983) found himself asking the same question and wondering whether "the poor decision-making performance of the men at those White House meetings might be akin to the lapses in judgment of ordinary citizens who become more concerned with retaining the approval of the fellow members of their work group than with coming up with good solutions to the tasks at hand" (p. vii).

Using an inductive case study approach, Janis analyzed poor policy decisions made by five American presidents: the lack of preparation for Pearl Harbor (Franklin D. Roosevelt), the invasion of North Korea (Harry S. Truman), the Bay of Pigs invasion (Kennedy), the escalation of the war in Vietnam (Lyndon B. Johnson), and the Watergate cover-up (Richard M. Nixon). On the basis of these analyses, Janis developed the theory of groupthink.

Janis (1983) defined **groupthink** as the "deterioration of mental efficiency, reality testing, and moral judgment that results from in-group pressures" (p. 9). Examination of the groupthink theory in Figure 2.3 indicates that three antecedent conditions must exist for groupthink to occur: high group cohesiveness, structural problems in the group, and a situational context that exerts great pressure on the group to make a decision. These conditions lead to groupthink (concurrence seeking) among group members that is reflected in eight symptoms, including the illusion of the group's invulnerability, stereotyped views of outsiders, and strong pressures toward conformity. These symptoms of groupthink lead to a process of defective decision making, including the group's failure to consider possible alternative courses of action. The defective decision-making process results in an increased probability of arriving at an unsuccessful outcome, that is, of the group arriving at a poor/bad decision or solution.

Organization

Janis was able to take the same observations available to many other observers of group decision making and to frame and organize these observations in the construction of an interdisciplinary theory that is discussed and analyzed in many different fields—social psychology, political science, communications, organizational theory, management, computer science, information technology, engineering management, health care, marketing, and others (Turner & Pratkanis, 1998).

Direction

Analysis of the available research also indicates that groupthink theory, like cognitive dissonance theory, has fulfilled the second function of a theory—providing research direction by suggesting new relationships among existing phenomena, thereby stimulating hypothesis testing. Groupthink is a complex theory because it concerns many possible relationships among many variables and it requires an analysis of all members of a group rather than just individual members. Because of this complexity, groupthink theory has stimulated less hypothesis testing than have other theories that are simpler to research such as cognitive dissonance theory. Despite these difficulties, however, groupthink research has proceeded through the same phases of hypothesis testing as has cognitive dissonance theory—direct tests, extensions, and reformulations (Turner & Pratkanis, 1998).

Direct tests of groupthink, including laboratory experiments (e.g., Flowers, 1977) and archival and case studies (e.g., Herek, Janis, & Huth, 1987; Tetlock, 1979), confirm the existence of at least some of the variables included in the original groupthink model but suggest that they might not influence group decision making in exactly the way that Janis predicted. The role of group cohesiveness has come under particular scrutiny (see antecedent conditions in Figure 2.3). Janis believed that although group cohesiveness was not always sufficient for groupthink to occur, it was a necessary condition for its occurrence. However, various studies have suggested that this might not be the case. For example, in their analysis of 10 decision-making

episodes, Tetlock, Peterson, McGuire, Chong, and Field (1992) found that neither group cohesiveness nor situational stress was as important an antecedent of groupthink as were structural problems. The effect of cohesiveness seems to depend on its interaction with other antecedent conditions. In their review of research on groupthink, Mullen, Anthony, Salas, and Driskell (1994) found that high cohesiveness impairs a group's decisions (as suggested by groupthink theory) when other conditions leading to groupthink are present, for example, a controlling leader and a stressful situation. They found, however, that high cohesiveness does not negatively influence decision making when these conditions are absent.

Partly because of the preceding evidence, other research has extended groupthink by exploring antecedent conditions not included in the original version of the theory. One of these studies, an experiment by Kameda and Sugimori (1993), provides a good example of how social psychologists can combine elements of two theories, in this case groupthink theory and cognitive dissonance theory. Imagine that you are a member of one of Kameda and Sugimori's experimental groups. Your group must decide which one of two job applicants to recommend for a position. Opinion in the group is split, and to make matters worse, a simple majority vote is not sufficient; you have been told that the group's decision must be unanimous (in the other experimental conditions, groups merely have to reach a majority decision). It takes a lot of effort to convince everyone in your group which applicant should be hired, but finally all group members agree, and by the time they agree they are a very cohesive group. Now, imagine that you find out that the applicant your group recommended for the job not worked out very well. Her probationary period is nearly over, and your group now has to decide whether to fire her or to stick with its original decision and hire her permanently.

How likely is it that your group will reverse its original decision? Kameda and Sugimori reasoned that it was very unlikely for several reasons. First, research on postdecisional cognitive dissonance suggests (as you know) that as soon as your group had chosen one applicant over the other, the group members would have begun to convince themselves that she was clearly superior to the rejected applicant. A decision to fire her now would be inconsistent with that judgment. Second, in light of the fact that the members of your group initially disagreed, reaching the initial decision required a lot of effort, and cognitive dissonance theory and research on effort justification suggest that the way in which each group member justified that effort was to evaluate the outcome of that effort (the recommendation to hire) very highly. Finally, consistent with groupthink theory predictions, the initial pressure on your group to reach a unanimous decision rather than merely a majority decision would have created a highly cohesive group that is vulnerable to groupthink symptoms, including the inability to believe that the group's initial decision could possibly have been wrong (i.e., the illusion of invulnerability). Sure enough, Kameda and Sugimori found that the members of unanimous decision groups were much more likely to recommend permanent hiring than were the members of groups that merely had to reach a majority decision on whom to hire.

In addition, Moorhead, Ference, and Neck (1991) applied groupthink to a real-life situation and, on the basis of their analysis, reformulated groupthink theory just as Aronson had reformulated cognitive dissonance theory. The morning of January 28, 1986, was a very exciting one for the National Aeronautics and Space Administration (NASA) as well as for members of the general public. The space shuttle *Challenger* was scheduled to be launched with a crew of seven, including the first civilian to win the chance to go into space, a New Hampshire schoolteacher named Christa McAuliffe. It was also a very cold morning at the Kennedy Space Center in Florida with temperatures below freezing, and some engineers had expressed concern that the O-ring seals on the rocket might disintegrate at these temperatures. But the launch had already been cancelled once, and the way in which to ensure continued funding for the space program was to demonstrate its usefulness. So, NASA authorized the launch, and 73 seconds after liftoff, the *Challenger* exploded, killing all seven people on-board. On analyzing the *Challenger* disaster, Moorhead and colleagues concluded that it illustrated the groupthink

characteristics included in the original theory. However, they also argued that time pressures and a directive leadership style were much more important than Janis had indicated in the original groupthink theory; in fact, they believe that groupthink occurred only when these two factors were present.

The presidential commission that investigated the *Challenger* disaster identified "a flawed decision-making process as a primary contributing cause" (Moorhead et al., 1991, p. 540), and so the legacy of the *Challenger* tragedy should have been the assurance that the space program would no longer be susceptible to groupthink. But on February 1, 2003, people watched in horror as the space shuttle *Columbia* disintegrated during reentry, killing all seven astronauts on-board. The immediate cause of the disaster was the piece of *Columbia*'s foam insulation that fell off during the shuttle's launch and ripped a hole in the shuttle's left wing. However, according to the Columbia Accident Investigation Board, NASA's organizational culture was as much to blame for this accident as the damage caused by the foam (Cabbage & Harwood, 2004). So, it would seem that the headline of the *New York Times* article comparing the *Challenger* and *Columbia* disasters might well be correct: "Groupthink Is 30 Years Old, and Still Going Strong" (Schwartz & Wald, 2003).

Intervention

As suggested by the *Challenger* analysis, one of groupthink's strengths is its fulfillment of the third function of a theory, that is, its application in interventions to improve group functioning. Janis (1972) encouraged the application of groupthink as part of his initial presentation of the theory and later provided prescriptions for its prevention (Janis, 1983). As shown in Figure 2.4, virtually all of the prescriptions are directed at ensuring that there is free and comprehensive consideration of all relevant information and alternatives so that concurrence-seeking tendencies (pressures) do not lead to premature and bad decisions or solutions.

The combination of a complex but clearly constructed model and these prevention guidelines has made groupthink theory so "user-friendly" that it is used as a management training tool by

> **Recommendations for Preventing Groupthink**
>
> - Group leader should assign role of *critical evaluator* to each member.
>
> - Leader should be *impartial* and not state preferences and expectations.
>
> - Organization should set up *independent* groups to work on same problem.
>
> - Group should from time to time divide into separate *subgroups* to work on problem.
>
> - Each group member should discuss group decisions with a *trusted associate*.
>
> - *Outside experts* should be invited to group meetings to challenge group views.
>
> - At least one member should be assigned the role of *devil's advocate*.
>
> - Survey rival group's (e.g., competition's) *warning signals*.
>
> - After preliminary consensus, group should hold *second chance* meeting.

Figure 2.4   Preventing Groupthink

SOURCE: Adapted from Janis (1983).

private and public organizations. Moorhead and colleagues (1991) referred to a best-selling video illustrating groupthink that is used in classroom presentations, leadership seminars, and executive decision-making workshops. They also noted that the executive branch of the U.S. federal government adopted decision-making procedures based on groupthink.

Social psychologists have generated additional strategies to prevent groupthink. For instance, Kroon, Hart, and van Kreveld (1991) found that individual group members who believe they will be held accountable for their decisions are more likely to express their disagreement with the group, and Miranda (1994) recommended using specialized interactive computer programs as part of group meetings as a way of preventing groupthink. Among other advantages, these programs enable group members to raise their concerns anonymously, reduce the directive role of the leader, and provide all group members with an equal opportunity to express their opinions.

What is groupthink's potential for application in the 21st century? During the early 1990s, Manz and Sims (1993) and Verespej (1990) estimated that by the year 2000, more than 40% of employees in the United States would be working in self-managing teams. Furthermore, far from guarding against the dangers of groupthink, Locke and colleagues (2001) described this as "the age of groupomania. Teams have become endowed with almost mystical qualities [and] will cure almost any organizational disease, solve any problem, achieve any goal" (p. 502). Thus, as the enchantment with groups in the workplace increases, the potential for negative outcomes associated with groupthink phenomena likewise increases. Moorhead, Neck, and West (1998) identified five distinguishing characteristics of self-managing teams and showed the similarity between each of these characteristics and the groupthink conditions included in the original groupthink theory. They then proposed a number of prescriptions for avoiding groupthink in self-managing teams, for example, providing leadership training to team leaders so as to discourage directive leadership patterns. It is hoped that the hypothesis testing and application of the prescriptions to these teams will provide an antidote to the uncritical glorification of group processes.

Summing Up Groupthink Theory

Janis's groupthink theory focuses on the way in which the interactions among the members of a group can affect the quality of group decisions. In scope, groupthink can be described as a mini-theory, designed to explain a category of behavior in one specific kind of situation (i.e., decision making in groups).

As with cognitive dissonance theory, research suggests that groupthink theory may be limited in range by individual differences. Hodson and Sorrentino (1997) found, as predicted by groupthink, that groups with directive leaders made more biased decisions than did groups with more nondirective leaders. However, the effect was especially pronounced when the groups led by directive leaders consisted of individuals with a certainty-oriented personality, that is, a tendency to avoid new information so as not to reduce one's certainty in what one already knows.

Culture may also moderate the tendencies of groups to be vulnerable to groupthink. In a study of flight attendants and pilots from the United States and from several Asian countries, Merritt and Helmreich (1996) found that the Asian attendants and pilots preferred pilots to have an autocratic leadership style, whereas the American flight attendants and pilots preferred consultative or participative leadership. Further research may determine the implications of these differences in cultural preferences for group functioning and the operation of groupthink.

What about testability? Although the original theory has not been fully supported by data collected as part of the hypothesis testing process, these inconsistencies have led to constructive extension and reformulation of the theory rather than to its dismantling. As indicated previously, groupthink deals with a complex phenomenon and, therefore, has not been as easy to test as have other theories. However, researchers have solved that problem to a certain extent by testing subsets of the variables included in groupthink.

Groupthink is not particularly parsimonious, positing a large number of variables that could interact in many different ways. However, it would seem that, overall, groupthink theory has admirably fulfilled the three key functions of theory: organization, direction, and intervention. In Paulus's (1998) words,

> The original model represents a brilliant construction founded in part on the existing group dynamics literature. What we need to do now is continue to build on the current literature and insights in group and intergroup behavior ... for developing an adequate model of group decision making. ... The field could use a few more Janises who develop compelling, coherent ... perspectives of real-world groups and organizations. (p. 371)

SUMMARY

The scientific process involves a continuing cycle of observation, theory development, deduction of hypotheses, and hypothesis testing (in research and applications). Theory development is central to this process—organizing our observations, directing our hypothesis testing, and guiding our efforts to intervene in solving real-world problems. The two theories discussed in this chapter—cognitive dissonance and groupthink—illustrate the way in which the process works, with the original theory leading to hypothesis testing, observation of results, and theory revision (if needed). As you read through this book, you will discover the many different contexts in which social psychology has been applied and the importance of theory to the development and implementation of intervention strategies designed to improve the functioning of individuals, groups, organizations, communities, and societies.

3

RESEARCH METHODS IN APPLIED SOCIAL PSYCHOLOGY

KENNETH M. CRAMER

LOUISE R. ALEXITCH

CHAPTER OUTLINE

We often look at the work of social psychologists and wonder, "Why would anyone study love and communication? Everyone knows they go together!" The truth is that although much of what social psychologists study might seem to be common sense, it is clear that we cannot always come up with reliable scientific principles based *solely* on common sense (Babbie & Benaquisto, 2002). Consider the following example.

Years ago, the State of California was suffering severely under an extreme drought. In an effort to conserve water, the state urged large institutions, such as businesses and universities, to come up with strategies to use less water (Dickerson, Thibodeau, Aronson, & Miller, 1992). For instance, officials at the University of California, Santa Cruz, noticed that a good deal of water was consumed in the campus athletic facilities and reasoned that if they could reduce the duration of student showers, significant water savings would result. But how could that be accomplished? At first, they simply mounted signs on the change room walls urging students to shower in less time. This commonsense strategy had no effect. What if the signs were made more noticeable? To explore this possibility, each sign was mounted on a stand and positioned right in the doorway to the showers so that students would have to notice it. This decision would prove to be folly. Not only did the strategy fail to curb shower duration, it actually had the opposite effect. The signs were thrown around, and students took especially long showers in defiance. Despite these noble intentions, the university's efforts were ineffective and costly. What could be done?

The University of California, Santa Cruz, eventually did find a solution (which we share at the end of this chapter) based on research methods and tools often employed by social psychologists to tackle relevant social and practical problems. Problems encountered in areas such as education, health, the environment, and the criminal justice system all are addressed using these same research methods and techniques. Specifically, decisions about how to set up and conduct research in applied social psychology are made on the basis of three research dimensions: method of data collection, research design, and research setting. This chapter introduces you to the three research dimensions. Let us begin by considering how we gather information (i.e., data) from the world around us.

METHODS OF DATA COLLECTION

Before reviewing the basic methods of data collection, we should recognize that all research data reflect the researcher's attempt to study and measure specific variables. Accordingly, we first briefly consider the meaning and measurement of variables.

Variables and Their Measurement

All research begins with a research question. For example, Chapter 1 considered research stemming from questions such as whether children learn intergroup attitudes from their parents and whether competition between groups leads to negative intergroup attitudes. Moreover, Chapter 2 considered what groups can do to reduce groupthink, and the beginning of this chapter considered how a severe drought led to the question of how to get college students to reduce the use of water while taking showers. Researchers often translate their research questions into hypotheses such as the following: If "use less water" signs are placed in highly visible locations, water use will decline.

Each research question (and hypothesis) specifies the variables of interest. A **variable** refers to a property of a person, an object, or an event that can vary in quantity (e.g., amount, degree) or in quality (e.g., kind). Some of the variables indicated in the preceding research questions were intergroup attitudes, learning, competition, water use, and groupthink. When researchers investigate research questions, they must measure the variables of interest; thus, an important decision they must make is how exactly they will measure each variable. As an example, a researcher might measure water use by having students themselves time and record the duration of their showers or by using a mechanical meter that automatically records volume of water used.

The specific way in which a researcher measures a variable is referred to as the **operational definition** of the variable. The choice of an operational definition is very important because some operational definitions will reflect what the researcher means by a variable more closely than will other definitions. A measurement procedure that reflects the meaning of the variable accurately is said to have a form of validity called **construct validity.** For instance, a measure of water use that entails having students monitor and record their shower times may have questionable construct validity because it does not accurately reflect the amount of water consumed and there is a definite possibility that some students might alter the data they provide to the researcher so as to make a good impression. On the other hand, the mechanical meter accurately calculates water volume and is much less susceptible to distortion; thus, it would have higher construct validity as a measure of water use.

Measurement of variables provides researchers with the data (information) they analyze in trying to answer their research questions. In the water use study, possible data included the students' written reports of how long they showered on each occasion and the mechanical meter's numerical output of the volume of water consumed.

To address their research questions, applied social psychologists use a variety of data collection tools. For instance, data may be gathered through mail surveys, face-to-face or telephone interviews, focus groups, and observations of behavior in natural settings. We distinguish between two basic and broad categories of data collection: those that rely on self-report procedures (e.g., surveys, personality scales, aptitude tests, single-item ratings) and those that rely on observational procedures (e.g., visual, auditory, and physiological observations). We begin with an examination of self-report procedures and follow with considerations of observational techniques and qualitative methods.

Self-Report Methods: The Special Case of Surveys

Self-report data collection procedures are those that require participants to report (either orally or in writing) on themselves with respect to the variable(s) of interest. Examples of self-report measures include surveys, personality scales, vocational interest inventories, and single-item rating scales. This chapter focuses on surveys because of their versatility and widespread use in applied social psychology.

Surveys involve a series of questions about one's attitudes toward, views on, and behaviors regarding a variable or set of variables. Like face-to-face interviews, surveys have had a long history in psychological measurement and continue to be a popular option for social researchers. Of the 129 studies cited in the 2001 volume of the *Journal of Applied Social Psychology,* 60 had used a survey. Given that the survey is one of the key tools of the applied social psychologist, it is important to understand how a survey is constructed. How should survey questions be worded? Does question order matter? Should people answer questions in a free-flowing, open-ended manner, or should they be presented with structured, close-ended response categories? The following subsections deal with the issues of question type, wording, sequence, and response formats typically considered in survey development.

Question type. Regardless of how you plan to administer a survey, you must first decide on the question type. There are three basic question types used in surveys: factual, attitude, and behavioral. Each has its strengths and weaknesses. Do you want to find out about a person's current situation or about what has happened to him or her in the past? These are called **factual questions** and are used to collect demographic data (e.g., age, gender, level of education) and information regarding events or circumstances about which a person is knowledgeable. Although these questions aim at tapping objective information, they are susceptible to lapses in memory or even conscious withholding of information. Alternatively, **attitude questions** measure a person's feelings, beliefs, or views that cannot be easily ascertained from his or her behavior or other sources of information (Azjen, 1991). Because attitudes are complex, responses to attitude questions are often difficult to interpret. For example, a person might not have an opinion about a topic but may feel obligated to provide a response, or two people might have the same attitude toward an event (e.g., they are positive about it) but differ in how strongly they feel about it. Attitude questions must be as specific as possible. For example, a study of attitudes toward recycling household products should be tackled using a series of questions about the recycling of newspapers, cans, bottles, and so on. Finally, **behavior questions** tap into specific aspects of current or past behavior such as its frequency, intensity, and timing. Because they are subject to memory gaps and distortions, behavior questions are best asked about recent behaviors (Kraus, 1997).

Question wording. Research shows that even minor differences in question wording can have a significant impact on responses. Questions have to be worded carefully to avoid bias or misinterpretation. Listed below are some general guidelines for developing survey questions. These guidelines are not exhaustive and are only meant to give you an idea of the complexity of question construction in surveys.

1. *Wording should be exact* so that it reflects precisely what you want to measure. For example, it is very common to see the words "frequently," "usually," and "sometimes" in surveys. What if you want to determine the

potential demand for public transportation in a city? It might not be enough to know that a person will "sometimes" use the bus because it is uncertain what exactly this means. You would obtain more precise and useful information if you asked respondents to estimate the number of times they would take the bus during a certain period (e.g., a month).

2. *Wording and terminology should be simple* so that even people with poor literacy skills, with little education, or from different backgrounds can understand them. Avoid jargon, abbreviations, acronyms, and terms that may be unfamiliar to respondents.

3. *Loaded questions should be avoided.* These are questions that are phrased so that respondents are led to choose one response over another (often reflecting the bias of the researcher). Consider the following "yes/no" question: "Should the city council fix the dangerous playground equipment in the public parks?" The word "dangerous" would suggest to respondents that you are looking for a "yes" answer.

4. *Questions should be kept short and relatively simple.* Do not use complex lengthy sentences that may be hard to understand. It may be prudent to split such questions into multiple questions. In this regard, avoid **double-barreled questions** that involve having more than one question embedded within a sentence. Consider the following "yes/no" question: "Do you think that the city council should allow skateboarding and roller-blading on public sidewalks?" If an individual responds "yes," does he or she support both skateboarding *and* roller-blading on sidewalks or only one of them?

5. *Questions should not make assumptions* about respondents such as about their experiences or demographic status. Consider the following example: "How long have you owned a cellular phone?" How could a person respond if he or she does not own a cell phone?

Question sequence. The sequence of survey questions is important for three reasons. First, you want to capture respondents' interest from the beginning and maintain it throughout. One

way in which to do this is to start with a general, easy-to-answer question that is both nonthreatening and important to respondents and also is clearly relevant to the topic of study. Unless you are screening for particular respondents (e.g., a specific age group), *never* start your survey or interview with demographic questions. These are boring to respondents and are highly personal. Put demographic questions at the end. Second, one question can affect responses to subsequent questions, a process called a **context effect** (Dillman, 2000; Fowler, 1998; McFarland, 1981). Consider the following example:

Question 1: Indicate how often in an average month you recycle each of the following materials: Newspapers _____ Cardboard _____ Aluminum cans _____ Plastic containers _____

Question 2: In your opinion, what is the most important environment-friendly behavior that an individual can engage in? _____

Do not be surprised if the majority of responses to Question 2 feature recycling. Other possible responses (e.g., using public transportation) will be less likely to be mentioned because Question 1 will *prime* the respondents to think about recycling. It is prudent to present general questions first, followed by more specific questions (i.e., reverse the order of Questions 1 and 2).

Third, questions about sensitive and controversial topics (e.g., mental illness, drug use, abortion) should be presented near the end of the survey. By this time, you have established better rapport with the respondents, and they may feel more comfortable answering such questions. If such questions are presented too early, respondents may choose not to answer them or may provide inaccurate or socially desirable responses. Do not end the survey with sensitive or controversial questions because respondents may complete the survey feeling uncomfortable or embarrassed.

Response format. You need to select the format of your responses. There are two basic response formats: close-ended (fixed-alternatives) response and open-ended (free) response. Each of these formats serves a different purpose and carries unique advantages and disadvantages.

Close-ended questions provide respondents with a specified predetermined set of possible responses. Examples include checklists, multiple-choice items, rankings, and rating scales. Here is an example of a multiple-choice question:

Recycling is a worthwhile endeavor.

 a. Strongly disagree
 b. Disagree
 c. Agree
 d. Strongly agree

Close-ended questions can be easily and quickly answered by respondents and easily coded and analyzed by the researcher. However, these questions are relatively time-consuming to design and require (in advance) some knowledge of the possible responses. That is, you need to make sure that all conceivable response categories are presented, often including a nondefined alternative such as "no opinion," "don't know," or "not applicable." Close-ended questions invite other issues. Consider the same question using a rating scale:

To what extent do you think recycling is a worthwhile endeavor?

Not at all 1 2 3 4 5 6 7 To a great extent

If you use rating questions, should they involve a 7-point scale (as in this example) or a 5- or 9-point scale? How should you label the endpoints? Should you include a middle neutral point? Should you include a "don't know" option? These are the kinds of decisions one has to make in designing rating questions.

One solution to the constraints of close-ended questioning is to "open up" the questions by using an open-ended format, akin to writing an essay question on a test. **Open-ended questions** allow individuals to respond freely in their own words to survey or interview questions. An example might be the following: "In the space below, please describe your views about recycling." The researcher codes responses to open-ended questions in terms of key words, categories, or themes. This format is ideal when you are not familiar with the range of possible responses on a topic or an issue or when you want to explore fine distinctions in attitudes, opinions, or beliefs among your respondents. But this approach is not without disadvantages. A major one is that the process of interpreting and coding data from these questions can be time-consuming and difficult.

Observational Methods

Self-report approaches, such as surveys and interviews, are common means of data collection but are not the only ones. Instead of asking participants to report about themselves, the researcher may observe participants and record his or her observations. For instance, the researcher may measure physiological processes (e.g., using a polygraph during job interviews for high-ranking security positions). The researcher may audiotape phone conversations to track how employees deal with customer complaints. Also, the researcher may record actual behavior as it happens (e.g., counting the number of cars that run a red light at an intersection) or has happened (e.g., measuring floor tile erosion in front of various museum exhibits as an index of exhibit popularity).

Indeed, the latter two examples invite discussion of an important measurement problem in both the social and natural sciences—the possibility that measurement of a variable (e.g., a person's attitude) changes that variable. In other words, measuring floor tile erosion in a museum has no bearing on the people who once stood there. However, if you instead measure exhibit popularity by standing with a clipboard and stopwatch at each exhibit, you might well scare off some museum patrons and possibly obtain a biased set of responses about the exhibits. Fortunately, observational techniques that permit the researcher to get close to respondents without unduly influencing their behavior are available.

In the method of **participant observation,** the researcher is an active participant in the social situation that he or she has chosen to observe. In some cases, the researcher may pose as another member of the situation (e.g., joining a street gang to observe how gang members interact). Alternatively, participants may be made aware that the researcher not only is participating in the event but also is studying their behavior (e.g., attending meetings of an organization's advisory board to study how the group makes decisions). By using participant observation, the researcher still risks changing the behavior under study (especially if people know that they are being observed) or losing objectivity if he or she adopts a role in the setting. For many social situations, however, there is no way in which to remain unobtrusive, and valuable insights may be gained by actively participating in the events of interest.

With a different approach, **nonparticipant observation,** the researcher remains separate from the event being observed so as not to influence (i.e., contaminate) the natural behavior and dynamics of the situation. The researcher can engage in nonparticipant observation either by observing the behavior of interest directly or by gathering observations through indirect means. **Direct (systematic) observation** involves selecting a naturally occurring set of behaviors, making observations of the behaviors using checklists or a coding system (developed ahead of time), and categorizing these observations for analysis. This method has been widely used to study a variety of behaviors, including people's facial expressions when lying, people's reactions to receiving religious pamphlets, and latent prejudice in selecting a checkout line at a cafeteria (Page, 1997). The observer may be hidden or in the open, but he or she usually makes an effort to avoid interfering in any way with the relevant behavior. That way, participants either are entirely unaware of being observed or quickly get used to the presence of an observer.

So, how is systematic or direct observation different from the everyday "people watching" that we do? Direct observations (a) serve a specific research purpose (i.e., address specific questions or hypotheses), (b) are carefully planned ahead of time, and (c) are recorded systematically. Efforts are made to focus on behaviors that are relevant to the variables under study. Suppose that you wished to study playground aggression in children. Many decisions must be made. For instance, you would have to determine exactly what you mean by aggression and define it operationally. Is it the number of times that a child strikes another child? Does it include swiping possessions or name-calling? (All of these observable behaviors are consistent with at least some theoretical definitions of aggression.) In addition, you would have to decide when, where, and how often you would make observations. Would you go to different playgrounds or observe behavior in just one playground? What time of day would you record observations? Would you record behavior continually, every hour, or every 5 minutes? Finally, would you record the behavior using paper and pencil, camcorder, or microphone?

Another type of nonparticipant observation, **indirect observation,** involves recording physical traces of the target behavior (e.g., floor tile erosion to measure exhibit popularity, empty alcohol containers in recycling boxes to track drinking patterns). In addition, one can review previously collected (**archival**) data to examine behaviors that are difficult to observe or occur infrequently or to determine patterns of behavior over long periods of time (e.g., comparing crime and weather statistics to determine whether tempers rise with temperature).

Qualitative Methods

Before we leave the topic of data collection, let us briefly mention one technique based on the information obtained largely through open-ended interviews that has received increasing attention during recent years. The challenge is determining what to do with the overwhelming amount of data that the researcher has obtained through the interview process, including descriptions of feelings, detailed accounts of experiences or events, and explanations of behaviors. How does one organize or reduce the amount of information acquired so that response patterns among participants may be identified? One way is to classify the responses based on identified themes or categories. This technique falls under the heading of *qualitative methods* because the emphasis is on discerning themes or categories of ideas rather than on assigning numerical values.

In one major qualitative method, **grounded theory** (Glaser & Strauss, 1967), the researcher (as in other data collection techniques) enters the setting with a theory, some research questions, knowledge of how he or she will collect and analyse the data, and an acknowledgment of his or her own biases and preconceived notions (Fetterman, 1998). Data collection and analysis go on throughout the study and involve organizing field notes and transcribing hours of recorded interviews with research participants. The researcher identifies concepts and themes that emerge from the data, begins to form connections among the emergent themes, and uses the relationships among the themes or categories to build theoretical models. Finding links among themes is called **memoing,** that is, a process of writing down one's thoughts and hypotheses about the data; indeed, these thoughts become the basis for the researcher's theory or conceptual model. During this time, the researcher may continue to collect data, constantly checking emerging connections among variables and concepts and adjusting for new or inconsistent information and for inconsistent cases. Once the researcher has decided how everything fits together in the model, he or she presents the model along with **exemplar (direct) quotes** from respondents that help the reader to understand the nature of the themes and the basis on which they were derived. This **content analysis** codes and transforms data into a standardized form so that responses are usually classified on the basis of some preexisting conceptual framework (Babbie & Benaquisto, 2002). Specifically, the researcher may look for the occurrence of certain phrases or words or for how many positive or negative references are made to particular events. The frequencies of certain responses can then be examined in relation to other variables in the study.

For example, the grounded theory approach would be appropriate if you interview first-year undergraduate students about their reasons for coming to the university. Their responses could reflect a variety of reasons such as a desire to acquire knowledge, an interest in gaining marketable skills, a need for social interaction, and a desire to get away from home. You might then categorize your participants' responses on the basis of either previous research conducted with university students or theoretical assumptions related to intrinsic motivation (attending the university for the goal of learning) versus extrinsic motivation (attending the university for goals unrelated to learning). This might mean that you have specific categories established a priori, or you may have only some general ideas about the range of responses that you would expect.

Social psychologists investigate their research questions and test their hypotheses based on the data they obtain from either self-report or observational methods of data collection. The next section reviews the four basic research designs used to investigate research questions and test hypotheses. Both self-report and observational methods can be employed with any of the four research designs (Hendricks, Marvel, & Barrington, 1990).

RESEARCH DESIGNS

The four basic research designs are true experimental, quasi-experimental, correlational, and descriptive. Each of these designs has unique advantages and disadvantages. The researcher's choice of design depends chiefly on the type of research question being asked, and this depends on what the researcher currently knows about the phenomenon. No matter which research design is chosen to investigate a topic, the design will have limitations. Ideally, a research program (i.e., a series of studies) on a topic, including a social or practical problem, should employ different designs. In this way, one design's limitations will be addressed by another design's strengths. Table 3.1 provides an overview of the four designs. You should refer to Table 3.1 as a guide to the designs as they are reviewed in the following subsections.

True Experiments

What leads people to litter? Is lack of awareness the chief reason why people fail to recycle? If governments invest more money in health promotion campaigns, will people choose healthier lifestyles? Note that these questions seek to uncover the reason(s) behind a phenomenon, that is, the *cause* of the behavior. An experimental design enables the researcher to answer causal questions. Specifically, a **true experiment** allows the researcher to assess whether, and the degree to which, a variable (the possible cause) manipulated by the experimenter leads to a change in another variable (the effect). There are three kinds of variables relevant to experiments: independent, dependent, and extraneous.

Table 3.1   Comparison of Research Designs

Design Type	Features	Questions Addressed
Experimental	• Manipulation of independent variable(s) • Random assignment of participants to conditions • Comparison of groups on measured dependent variable(s)	• Does one variable affect another variable? • Can causality be demonstrated?
Quasi-experimental	• Manipulation of independent variable(s) or use of preexisting groups • No random assignment • Comparison of groups on measured dependent variable(s)	• Do nonequivalent groups differ on a variable? • Can possible causality be suggested, especially when manipulation is used?
Correlational	• Measurement of variables without manipulation • Examination of relationship between variables	• Is one variable correlated with another variable? • Is a (noncausal) relationship demonstrated?
Descriptive	• Measurement of variables without manipulation • Summarization of measurements of variables	• How is something described with respect to a certain variable(s)?

Independent variables are those that are actively *changed or manipulated* by the experimenter. A thermostat dial in a house is like an independent variable in that it can be manipulated to regulate how much heat the furnace generates. Experiments involve at least two *levels* (i.e., variations) of the independent variable (e.g., setting thermostat at either a warm setting or a cool setting). Participants who are introduced (i.e., exposed) to a level of an independent variable are said to be in a particular experimental condition (e.g., warm setting condition). Experiments often involve more than one independent variable. For example, you might be interested in the effect of warm and cool temperatures on male and female participants. This study would be referred to as a "two by two" design. If you were reading about it in a journal article, it would be represented as a 2 (cool vs. warm) × 2 (male vs. female) design.

Dependent variables are those that are *measured* by the experimenter and are expected to change in response to the manipulation of the independent variable. Thus, house temperature (dependent variable) depends on adjustments of the thermostat dial (independent variable).

Extraneous variables are those that the experimenter wishes to hold constant across levels of the independent variable so as to rule them out as possible reasons why the dependent variable changes in accordance with the manipulation of the independent variable. In the home heating example, extraneous variables might include other heat sources (e.g., open windows, lit fireplace) that could affect house temperature and make it difficult to determine the exact influence of the thermostat setting.

Experimenters rule out the possible biasing effects of extraneous variables by using *two basic types of* control. One form of control is **random assignment of participants** to experimental conditions (i.e., levels of the independent variable). This involves using a procedure (e.g., coin toss, table of random numbers) that ensures that all participants have the *same* probability of being assigned to each of the conditions. Random assignment minimizes the likelihood that the participants in one condition differ from those in another condition on extraneous variables (e.g., intelligence) that might influence how they respond to the measurement of the dependent variable. The second form of

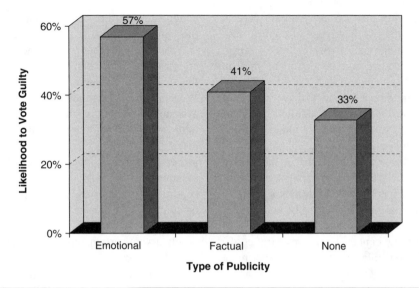

Figure 3.1 Likelihood That Jurors Would Vote Guilty as a Function of Exposure to Pretrial Publicity

SOURCE: Kramer, Kerr, and Carroll (1990).

control is **experimental control**, which involves ensuring that participants in the different experimental conditions are exposed to the *same* environmental stimuli (e.g., room, experimenter, instructions) with the exception of the independent variable. Thus, with good experimental control, there will be no uncontrolled environmental stimuli (e.g., an experimenter who is warm and friendly vs. one who is gruff and distant) that might account for differences in behavior across the experimental conditions.

Consider the following experiment conducted in the area of social psychology and the law. Kramer, Kerr, and Carroll (1990) asked whether pretrial publicity (in the form of newspaper and television news reports) would negatively bias juror verdicts. In other words, if investigators varied the details revealed to jurors (independent variable) prior to jury duty, would they be more likely to judge a suspect as guilty (dependent variable). Undergraduates (mock jurors) watched a videotaped trial of a man accused of robbing a supermarket. Before the jurors viewed the trial, they were randomly assigned to one of three conditions of pretrial publicity. Some jurors received *emotional publicity,* seeing reports that the car matching the description of the one used in the robbery also was seen to have fatally struck down a 7-year-old girl. Other jurors

received *factual publicity,* seeing reports that the suspect had an extensive criminal record. Still other jurors received *no pretrial publicity* (i.e., a control condition).

After watching the trial and deliberating in six-member juries, participants rated whether they would vote to convict. All jurors were instructed that their decisions were not to be influenced by the pretrial information (an extraneous variable); if they indicated otherwise, their data were not included in the analysis. The results showed a substantial influence of pretrial publicity on voting decisions. As the researchers had expected, jurors who heard emotionally charged pretrial publicity were significantly more likely to judge the suspect as guilty. As shown in Figure 3.1, the manipulation of pretrial publicity led to differential conviction rates, suggesting that the likelihood of voting guilty in a trial is at least in part *caused by* information available to jurors prior to the trial. We are confident in reaching that conclusion because we cannot identify any other variable as differing among the conditions.

Although true experiments may allow us to draw causal conclusions, steps must be taken in conducting an experiment so that our confidence that a cause-and-effect relationship has been demonstrated remains high. The steps involve ensuring that we use extreme care in carrying out the two key types of control: random assignment and experimental control. Actually, when we can be confident that an experiment has demonstrated a causal relationship, the experiment is said to have a type of validity known as internal validity. **Internal validity** refers to the extent to which one can infer that an independent variable has influenced the dependent variable, that is, has caused the difference in behaviors among the participants in the experimental conditions. Failure to achieve internal validity seriously undermines the value of an experiment because conclusions about causality cannot be made with confidence, and the whole objective of an experiment is to investigate questions (or hypotheses) about cause and effect. Internal validity is directly related to how well the experimenter has nullified the influence of possible extraneous variables through experimental control and random assignment.

A **threat to internal validity** refers to a failure to adequately control for an extraneous variable. We saw in Kramer and colleagues' (1990) pretrial publicity study how the researchers attempted to minimize threats to internal validity by, for example, using random assignment to conditions and holding constant exposure to news reports of the original trial. Let us briefly consider a few hypothetical breakdowns in *experimental control* in the pretrial publicity experiment as examples of possible threats to internal validity. First, imagine that the three conditions had been conducted at different times of the day. The exposure to different events or experiences, such as meal times, could result in speedier, less reasoned decision making by some groups (e.g., the hungrier ones). Second, imagine that Kramer and colleagues had conducted only one publicity condition each day of the week but that on the first day there was a problem with the heating in the building (someone was likely fiddling with that thermostat again), resulting in participants from that one condition being especially cold and making speedier decisions so that they could leave early. As a result, we could not be sure whether their guilty convictions were due to the type of pretrial publicity or just to impatience. Therefore, two aspects of experimental control would involve

conducting the three experimental conditions on the same days and at roughly the same times.

Also, we know that people tend to grow more conservative with their advancing years, and this could lead to sterner handling of criminals. What if the researchers had unintentionally assigned more mature students, or even seniors, to the emotional publicity condition because, for instance, they were more likely to be available at certain times of the day? Could we then assume that the mean harsher penalty in that condition was due solely to the type of publicity, or could age also have affected the outcome? Again, we can see why it is important to randomly assign participants to conditions because with this form of control the likelihood of getting a disproportionately high number of prosecution-favoring jurors in one condition is remote and, thus, helps to eliminate an alternative explanation (threat to internal validity) based on possible differences among participants. That way, you can say that the groups were roughly equivalent *before* manipulation of the independent variable so that you are more confident that the independent variable was the reason for any observed differences in the dependent variable.

It is worth mentioning that although random assignment works reasonably well (especially with large samples) at ensuring that experimental groups are roughly equivalent on participant characteristics relevant to the dependent variable, an experimenter might not be fully satisfied. Suppose that in the publicity study the researcher wanted to be absolutely certain that the groups were equivalent on age. To the rescue is a procedure called **randomized matching,** which involves identifying one or more dimensions of the participants and assigning them evenly to the various conditions. If there were 30 participants between 21 and 25 years of age, the researcher could randomly assign each of them to one of the three publicity conditions, do the same for participants between 26 and 30 years of age, and so forth. That way, the conditions are matched for age, and one can definitively rule out age differences as a threat to internal validity (i.e., why the verdicts varied among groups). There are, however, several key things to remember before matching across conditions. First, we cannot always readily identify a dimension that is relevant to the dependent variable on which we should match participants. If age were not used in the publicity study, what else could have been used? Could some personality trait have been used? If so, which one? Second, matching procedures can be expensive and time-consuming. Finally, the previous two problems are compounded if one wishes to match along several dimensions.

Quasi-Experiments

As we have seen, true experiments permit causal conclusions because they entail randomly assigning participants to the conditions and exerting experimental control, thereby eliminating a host of alternative explanations. However, many events worthy of study are outside of the researcher's control (e.g., people's exposure to a natural disaster). In addition, people are already members of particular groups or categories (e.g., gender, religion, socioeconomic level, right- or left-handedness), and so random assignment to those groups is either unethical or impossible. Finally, in many cases where the researcher may implement a treatment (i.e., independent variable), he or she might not be able to assign participants randomly to the different levels of that treatment because participant assignment is not under the researcher's control (e.g., using humorous examples in teaching one section of a course but not a second section where students themselves choose their sections when registering). So, how do we address questions involving differential effects on the basis of *preassigned groups*? The researcher may employ any one of a collection of research designs known as quasi-experiments. **Quasi-experiments** allow comparisons to be made in observations across time and among groups with the assumption that these groups may not be equivalent to each other (for a thorough review of these designs, see Cook & Campbell, 1979).

Pretest–posttest designs. Drunk drivers are a major concern in many communities. Drunk driving has been linked to serious accidents and traffic fatalities. As a response to this problem, police monitoring programs have been launched in many places in the United States and Canada, and penalties for drunk driving have become more severe. Do these strategies have any effect on the number of people who engage in this behavior? To address this question, we could employ a **pretest–posttest design** (Reichardt & Mark, 1998). Briefly, initial observations are taken (the pretest), the treatment (e.g., an intervention) is implemented, and observations are taken again (the posttest) so that a comparison can be made between what happened before the treatment and what happened after the treatment. This design is depicted as follows:

Observations Before → Treatment → Observations After

Does implementing more severe penalties for drunk driving actually reduce the number of drunk driving incidents? Suppose that a researcher used a pretest–posttest design to evaluate the effect of legislative reforms on alcohol-related fatal and injury accident rates. By determining that rates before the reforms were higher than those after the reforms, the researcher concluded that the reforms had been effective.

Now the question is, based on the research design used in the preceding hypothetical study, can we conclude with confidence that harsher penalties reduced alcohol-related injuries and deaths? Not necessarily. There are a number of other extraneous factors that may have led to the reduction, posing serious threats to the internal validity of the study. For instance, an event in the community may have coincided with the introduction of the new penalties. Perhaps there was a particularly serious traffic accident attributed to drunk driving, and in the aftermath many people may have become more reluctant to drive while intoxicated. In addition, a natural process of time could yield such an effect among drivers. That is, even before the introduction of severe penalties, the people in the community may have already started curbing their drinking and driving behavior. We would then see a decline in the number of drunk driving cases from the pretest to the posttest that had very little, if anything, to do with the new penalties (the treatment).

Interrupted time series design. To address the limitations of pretest–posttest designs, we may want to use a different quasi-experimental design, the **interrupted time series design,** which involves an *expanded* version of a pretest–posttest design. In this case, numerous observations are taken over time before a treatment (i.e., the interruption) is administered, and then numerous observations are taken afterward. This design is represented as follows:

$$O_1 \ O_2 \ O_3 \ O_4 \ \text{Treatment} \ O_5 \ O_6 \ O_7 \ O_8,$$

where O = observation. In this way, we can detect any patterns of behavior occurring before the treatment and whether the treatment affected this pattern. So, if drunk driving rates were already declining in the community months (or years) before the new penalties were introduced, we would still be able to determine whether the penalties had any impact on this pattern of decline. For instance, the penalties might speed up the rate of decline in drunk driving. As an added advantage, by including numerous posttest observations, we also can determine whether the treatment has a long-term effect on drinking and driving behavior. In fact, Rogers and Schoenig (1994) employed an interrupted time series design to study the impact of legislative reforms (including stiffer penalties) in California by tracking alcohol-related injury and death rates over several years. They concluded that the reforms did lead to lower rates, and their conclusion could be made with more confidence than would have been the case with a simple pretest–posttest design.

Nonequivalent control group designs. But what if we simply do not have the time or opportunity to conduct an interrupted time series study? How can we increase the internal validity of a study? An improvement on the pretest–posttest design would be to use a control group. The addition of a control group would be an improvement because we would have a comparison group that was not exposed to the treatment. However, unlike with a true experiment, random assignment is not used; the control group usually is a preexisting group and is not assumed to be equivalent to the treatment group. This approach involves a **nonequivalent control group design** in which the treatment group is compared with a nonequivalent control group. In the drinking

intervention study, the researcher could try to match the treatment community with another comparison community on things such as economic level, population size, and number of drunk driving cases during the pretest period. Whereas both the treatment and control groups receive initial and follow-up observations, only the treatment group receives the unique element (e.g., intervention) that is thought to yield the desired effect. The nonequivalent control group design is shown as follows:

Treatment Group: Pretest →
Intervention → Posttest

Control Group: Pretest →
No Intervention → Posttest

If the treatment group, but not the control group, displays a decline from pretest to posttest (e.g., in drunk driving incidents), our confidence in internal validity (i.e., that the treatment worked) would be greater than it would with the simpler pretest–posttest design because with this design we have evidence that change did not occur without the treatment.

As you may have guessed, a nonequivalent control group also can be added as an improvement to an interrupted time series design (called a **control time series design**). This involves a series of the same observations for the control as for the treatment group but without exposure to the treatment.

It is important to remember that although quasi-experiments resemble true experiments, they are more vulnerable to threats to internal validity than are true experiments. Consequently, the baggage of quasi-experimental studies is that they are much more limited than true experiments with respect to being able to make inferences about cause-and-effect relationships.

Correlational Studies

Our research questions often address the relationships among variables. Are home repair stresses more severe if the homeowners are older? What if they have less money? To address these questions, we can use a correlational study. A **correlational study** involves measuring variables and determining the correlation between them. A **correlation coefficient** is a measure of the degree of association between different variables, so that knowing one thing about a person may tell you something else (e.g., knowing a person's height may let you predict his or her shoe size).

Mathematically, correlation coefficients (denoted by r) range from -1 to $+1$. This boundary allows us to compare coefficients and understand both the strength and direction of the relation between two variables. When two variables are positively correlated ($r > 0$), high values of one variable typically are found among high values of the other variable (and, of course, low values of one variable typically are found among low values of the other variable), so that the values of the variables move together in the same direction. Figure 3.2 shows a positive correlation in a scatterplot graph comparing years of university education and earned income. Each diamond signifies one person and shows both that person's years of university and his or her earned income. Alternatively, two variables can be negatively correlated ($r < 0$), where high values of one variable typically are found among low values of the other variable (and vice versa), so that the values of the variables move in opposite directions. Figure 3.2 shows a negative correlation between number of annual dental problems and income. Note that whereas the sign in front of the correlation coefficient reveals only the direction of the relation, the absolute magnitude of the coefficient reveals its strength. That is, larger correlation values signify a greater connection between the variables. For example, a correlation of $+.80$ is a stronger relationship between two variables than is a correlation of $+.60$, but it reflects the same magnitude of relationship as does a correlation of $-.80$.

We can also observe correlations in nature that, although either positive or negative in value, are so small in magnitude that we can say there is no observable relation between the variables. That is, high values of one variable may be observed with low values, high values, or moderate values of another variable. In short, we cannot really predict the value of one variable just by knowing the value of the other variable. Figure 3.2 shows little correlation between the number of churches in a neighborhood and earned income; that is, there may be few, some, or many churches in an affluent neighborhood.

To better understand the nature of correlations, let us consider a study of marital satisfaction. A growing area of research has explored the extent to which we can predict whether a marriage will survive or falter based on a variety of characteristics. Holman, Larson, and Harmer (1994) administered a survey to husbands and wives concerning not only their current marital relationships but also their perceptions of the marital relationships of their parents. The researchers hypothesized that a marriage might be in trouble if one or both partners witnessed marital discord in their parents' marriage(s). The results showed a positive correlation between husbands' premarital perceptions and couples' marital satisfaction ($r = +.43$). That is, in general, when men perceived that their parents' relationships were positive while they were growing up, they were more satisfied with their current marriages.

Correlations are quite useful at uncovering relationships among variables and prove to be effective during the initial stages of a research program. However, no matter how tempted we might be, we cannot derive causal explanations from a correlation because there could be any number of alternative explanations. Suppose that we found a positive correlation between crime and poverty so that the incidence of violent crime (e.g., armed robbery, murder) was higher in more impoverished neighborhoods. Based on this relationship, can we say that poverty causes violent crime? Not necessarily. It is possible that the reverse holds true. Can you think of a reason why the incidence of crime might promote poverty in a neighborhood? And perhaps we are being overly simplistic to look at only two variables when, in fact, many social problems are far more complex. For instance, the variable of crowding might help to account for the crime–poverty relationship. With a possible adverse influence on interpersonal relationships and cognitive development, crowding could contribute to both crime and poverty. In other words, by considering a *third variable,* crowding, we have one possible explanation for why crime and poverty might be related but not necessarily in a causal way. There could, of course, be many other variables not yet

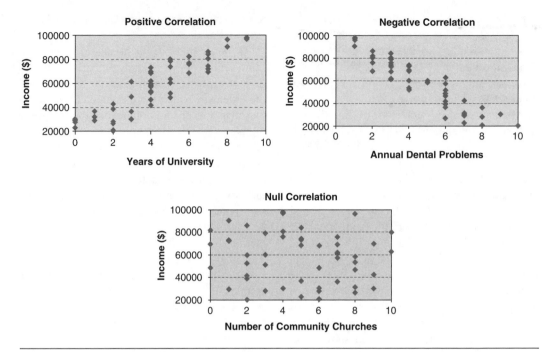

Figure 3.2   Scatterplot of Positive, Negative, and Null Correlations

considered such as sanitation, health problems, and drug use. Also, beware of words/terms such as "influence," "leads to," "results from," and "affects" in reference to correlational evidence. This is causal language and misleadingly suggests that one variable causes another. We should more accurately refer to a correlation as a "relationship," a "linkage," or an "association" between variables.

Descriptive Studies

Let us suppose that you want to study home repair stress but do not quite know where to begin. In fact, yours may be the very first study on the subject. You may not know enough about stress experienced in home repair to suggest what factors either promote or reduce that stress. In that case, an experiment might be premature, and so would a correlational study if you cannot even hypothesize what variables might be related to home repair stress. Therefore, your research aims might be more exploratory in that you wish simply to describe the phenomenon in an effort to identify important variables. In that case, you would conduct a descriptive study. In **descriptive**

research, no attempt is made to manipulate the situation or behavior of interest. The objective is to observe variables and summarize the observations by using descriptive statistics such as means, frequencies, and percentages. In your home repair study, you would merely record relevant behaviors, for example, by asking people (using interviews or a survey) about their home repair experiences, observing home repair activity, and measuring stress levels. Of course, with a purely descriptive approach, you would lack the ability to determine *why* the behavior occurs. Nevertheless, the scope of questions that descriptive designs can address is quite vast.

Consider the following descriptive field study by Page (1997) on racial preferences in a cafeteria checkout line. The purpose was to study whether students preferred to give their money to a white checkout clerk or a black checkout clerk. Page unobtrusively situated himself in front of two checkout counters in a university cafeteria: one stationed by a white clerk and the other stationed by a black clerk. After taking into account the length of each line, Page tested the assumption that there should be an equal likelihood of line queuing across race. His results suggested otherwise; students were less inclined to go to the black checkout clerk even if that line was shorter. To use one more example of descriptive research, let us return to the issue of drunk driving. Monto, Newcomb, Rabow, and Hernandez (1992) surveyed university students with items tapping whether their friends had ever driven drunk and, if so, whether the students had intervened. The results showed that among those who reported having been in cars with friends who were too drunk to drive, only 65% reported having confiscated their friends' keys, driving them home, or calling a taxi.

RESEARCH SETTINGS

One of the first decisions that a researcher makes is whether to conduct the study in a laboratory or out in the "real world" (i.e., the field). Research conducted in a laboratory typically offers more definitive support for theories than does research conducted in the field. This is achieved by getting rid of "noisy," unwanted extraneous influences on the phenomenon. That is why biologists sterilize instruments before adding germs to a Petrie dish in case unwanted biotoxins get in the dish by mistake.

So, why do we not conduct all research in the laboratory? One answer is simply because laboratories are not typical environments for people, and so people might behave differently in laboratories than they normally do. The alternative, then, is to conduct studies in the real world to enhance their ecological validity. **Ecological validity** signifies the extent to which the experiences and behaviors we observe in research are genuine in the sense of being similar to those that occur in everyday life. That is, we have more confidence that participants' behavior is not merely an artifact of being in a laboratory or participants' knowing that they are being observed.

Studies conducted in the natural environment are called **field studies.** In field studies, we typically do not have as much control over unwanted influences as we have in laboratory studies. Let us consider some research on helping behavior. In an experiment in a laboratory setting, Darley and Latané (1968) found that roughly 85% of solitary participants helped a seizure victim,

compared with only roughly 30% of participants who helped when four other people who also could have helped were present. But how often do people find themselves in a laboratory with a seizure victim? What if an incident occurred in the real world? Would more people still help when they are alone than when they are with others? This is a question of another kind of validity, external validity, which is closely tied to ecological validity. **External validity** refers to the extent to which research findings can be generalized beyond a particular study to other people, times, settings, and so forth.

Latané and Darley (1970) investigated the external validity of their laboratory finding on helping by conducting a field experiment in a liquor store. Two men (sufficiently muscle-bound so that one would not tangle with them) waited until there were either one or two customers remaining (independent variable) in the store (this was determined randomly). When the clerk went into the back room to check on price and inventory, the two men picked up a case of beer close to the exit. One loudly announced that "they won't miss this" as they fled the store with the beer. Supportive of the external validity of the laboratory evidence, the likelihood that a customer reported the theft to the store clerk (dependent variable) was higher when the customer was the only witness to the crime.

As this discussion implies, there is a trade-off between laboratory studies and field studies. As noted previously, laboratories allow us to identify and eliminate the influence of extraneous variables. In experimental research, for instance, this means we can be more confident that the manipulation of the independent variable led to the observed differences in behavior, that is, to be more confident about internal validity. But increasing control, and hence internal validity, may invite problems associated with low ecological validity and low external validity. Therefore, increasing confidence in these two kinds of validity often requires leaving the laboratory setting in favor of a field setting. This move, of course, usually means giving up some control over extraneous variables and, thus, impairs internal validity.

In short, any good researcher will appreciate that both laboratory studies and field studies have their strengths and weaknesses; thus, both are needed to get a complete picture of a social psychological phenomenon. As Crano and Brewer (2002) wrote,

> The interplay between laboratory and field research is critical to the development of effective applications in social sciences. Basic experimental research may isolate important causal processes, but convincing demonstrations that those processes operate in applied settings are essential before theory can be converted into practice. (p. 120)

Before concluding this section on research settings, the third major dimension of research, we emphasize that both laboratory research and field research can involve either kind of data collection strategy—self-report or observational—and also can be used with any of the four basic research designs: true experimental, quasi-experimental, correlational, or descriptive. Thus, the three research dimensions are what may be called completely balanced, such that research entailing any combination of the three dimensions is, under the appropriate circumstances, not only feasible but also potentially very informative (Hendricks et al., 1990).

RESEARCH ETHICS

As psychologists, we want our studies to resemble the real world as much as possible and to be as sound and well controlled as we can make them. Alternatively, we want to avoid causing our participants to endure unnecessary stress. But these two goals often conflict. We are concerned about the health and welfare of individual participants. However, we also wish to make important discoveries surrounding human social behavior and believe that it would often be immoral *not* to carry out research. Indeed, some studies have caused widespread controversy because people have regarded them as unethical and claim that they should not have been conducted in the first place. Milgram's (1963) experiments on obedience, where "teachers" believed that they were giving increasingly dangerous levels of shock to a "learner," are widely cited in this context. But more important, does the pursuit of knowledge condone the means by which it is achieved? At what point do we say that someone is suffering unjustifiable personal harm or mental distress from taking part in a research study?

Suppose that you want to study how people look at each other during conversations. How do you set up your study to measure looking behavior? One possibility is that you could place two people in a laboratory equipped with concealed, closed-circuit television. When two participants turn up, you escort them to the laboratory and have them converse for 15 minutes. But suppose that one participant asks, "What's this all about?" Do you conceal the truth and merely satisfy their curiosity (e.g., "I'm studying how two people get acquainted"), or do you tell the full truth and face the consequences (e.g., "It's an investigation about looking behavior between two people in a conversation; see that video camera hidden behind the wall?"). If the participants know what the study is about, imagine how their behavior might change as a result. Two people engaged in a conversation will likely be more conscious of how they look at each other, making it difficult for them to act as they normally do. Because they feel self-conscious, they might avoid looking at each other or might look at each other in atypical ways. This example illustrates why it may be necessary to *deceive* participants so that they are not sensitized to the behaviors being observed. That is why Milgram's participants were led to believe they were giving lethal shocks to a helpless learner and why Darley and Latané's (1968) participants "believed" a fellow participant was suffering an epileptic seizure and needed help. Nevertheless, there are major concerns about using deception in research. These concerns include the fact that deception is morally wrong and violates individuals' right to autonomous behavior and that participants suffer personal harm, for example, to their self-concepts (they can be so easily duped) and to their trust and respect for research and the discipline of psychology. In turn, the discipline suffers because of the damage to its reputation. Notwithstanding such concerns, participants deceived in research typically regard deception as both acceptable and of value (Christensen, 2004).

So, what solutions exist to the problem of deception? Fortunately, the American

Psychological Association (APA, 2002) has a set of guidelines for researchers to follow with respect to deception and other ethical issues: *Ethical Principles of Psychologists and Code of Conduct.* Following are some of the main principles:

1. *Respect for the dignity of persons.* As the central ethical principle, psychologists' respect for human dignity underlies all of the others. Note, for instance, that we refer to those persons who take part in a study as "participants" rather than as "subjects" (which had been the term used for most of the history of psychology) because it reflects the dignity and respect afforded to the people we study.

2. *Minimization of harm and reduction of risk.* Psychologists must take steps to avoid harming participants.

3. *Informed consent.* Researchers should describe the procedures to participants before they take part in a study and should document their agreements to take part in the study as it was described.

4. *Freedom to withdraw.* Participants must be informed that they are free to withdraw from a study at any point with no negative consequences for doing so.

5. *Privacy and confidentiality.* All information obtained from individual participants must be held in strict confidence. Confidentiality is not to be confused with anonymity. Confidentiality refers to restricting access to the data and to releasing results in such a way that each individual's privacy is not violated. Anonymity refers to collecting and storing data in such a way that individual identities cannot be ascertained.

6. *Minimal use of deception.* Deception may be used only if the research has potential value (scientific, educational, or applied) and if there are no other viable means of investigating the research questions or hypotheses. Also, it can be used only if it does not put participants at undue risk and if, on completion of the study, participants are provided with a full description (i.e., debriefing) of the study's true purpose and an explanation of all procedures, including the need for deception.

All researchers are responsible for abiding by the ethical guidelines. Furthermore, many institutions require approval of research projects by an institutional review board (e.g., department or university ethics committee). Moreover, at the chapter authors' institutions (University of Windsor and University of Saskatchewan), we follow the APA guidelines as well as the Canadian Code of Ethics for Psychologists (Canadian Psychological Association, 2000), which articulates four principles that both scientists and practitioners are expected to apply in their decision making and conduct. In generally decreasing order of weight in decision making, the principles are (a) respect for the dignity of persons, (b) responsible caring, (c) integrity in relationships, and (d) responsibility to society.

EPILOGUE

Having learned more about the tools that applied social psychologists use to address their research questions, we return to our initial question of how officials at the University of California, Santa Cruz, handled their water shortage problem. The researchers hypothesized that students (in this case females) would take shorter showers if they were (a) made more aware of their conservation attitudes or (b) asked to commit to the conservation effort. The researchers' reasoning stemmed from the theory of cognitive dissonance (reviewed in Chapter 2), which posits that we are motivated to reduce the discomfort we feel when our attitudes and behavior are inconsistent (e.g., "I favor conservation of resources, yet I use up a lot of water when I shower").

In this field experiment, before students entered the change room, they were approached by a female researcher who identified herself as a representative of a campus water conservation office (deception). She invited them to participate (following informed consent) in a study on water conservation. The students were randomly assigned to one of four conditions that were manipulated by the experimenter. Students in the first condition completed a brief survey about their water use, making them more *mindful* of their water conservation attitudes. Students in the second condition signed a petition as a

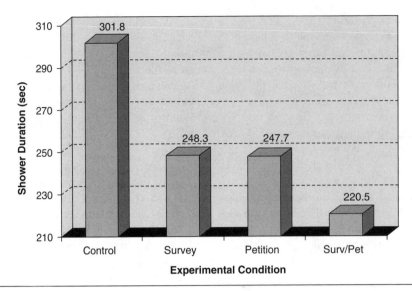

Figure 3.3   Shower Duration (in seconds) as a Function of the Experimental Manipulation

NOTE: sec = seconds; Surv/Pet = Survey and Petition.
SOURCE: Dickerson, Thibodeau, Aronson, and Miller (1992).

public commitment to the water conservation effort. Students in a joint condition completed the survey and also signed the petition. Students in a fourth condition, the control condition, received no manipulation. A second female experimenter waited in the change room and measured each participant's shower time. Note that after the manipulation of the independent variable, the researcher did *not* tell the students that the study had not yet ended (another element of deception) because doing so might have cued them to monitor their shower durations. However, this procedure and the rest of the deception were explained to each participant in a debriefing after the participant emerged from the change room.

The results showed that the duration of shower time was lowest among students in the group whose members completed the survey and also signed the petition (so that they were both committed to and mindful of water conservation issues), averaging approximately 3.5 minutes of water use. Employment of either the survey or petition alone was less effective (averaging less than 4 minutes of water use), but all three manipulations were more effective than the control group (averaging just over 5 minutes of water use). Overall, this study suggests that it is possible to change people's behavior with respect to conserving on water (and possibly to change other conservation behaviors) based on sound theory, well-established research tools, and an explicit ethical code of conduct.

SUMMARY

Decisions concerning how to conduct research in applied social psychology are made on the basis of three research dimensions: method of data collection, research design, and research setting. Self-report methods (e.g., surveys, interviews, attitude scales) are often used to evaluate hypotheses. Surveys are used to illustrate self-report methods of data collection. Survey construction requires careful consideration of question wording, question format (open-ended vs. close-ended questions), and question sequence. Observational techniques include physiological measures, audio and visual measures, and behavioral measures. Also, researchers can engage in either participant observation (i.e., the researcher is an active participant in the situation) or nonparticipant observation (i.e., the researcher remains separate from the people, situation, or event). Qualitative methods provide an in-depth, nonnumerical analysis of the themes underlying many social issues.

True experiments involve the manipulation of one or more variables in the environment (independent variables) so as to observe possible changes in the responses of participants (dependent variable). Through random assignment to groups and experimental control of extraneous variables, researchers can assess cause–effect relationships between variables. When researchers are unable to randomly assign individuals to groups or to manipulate certain variables, they may use a quasi-experimental design. Depending on the specific type of quasi-experimental design, data may be collected at different points in time (pretest–posttest and time series designs) and may involve one or more nonequivalent groups. Correlational studies test for relationships between variables. Correlation coefficients can vary both in direction (positive or negative) and in magnitude (values of correlations get stronger as they deviate from zero up to a maximum of 1). Researchers must be cautious not to draw causal conclusions from correlational evidence because variables can be related yet not in a causal manner. Finally, descriptive studies measure the incidence and magnitude at which specified variables occur.

Researchers must decide where to conduct a study—in a controlled laboratory environment (which typically controls extraneous variables and increases internal validity) or in the field (which typically provides less control but often with more external validity). Whereas internal validity represents the confidence researchers have that the observed effect resulted from the factor in question, external validity represents the generalizability of findings to other settings and participants.

Applied researchers need to respect and protect the dignity of their research participants. Although understanding and addressing research issues is important, the safety of research participants is paramount. Researchers in psychology guide their research on the basis of the ethical guidelines articulated in the APA code of ethics. Some of the major guidelines include protection of the respect and dignity of participants, use of informed consent, freedom to withdraw without penalty, minimization of harm to participants, assurance of confidentiality, and conclusion with full debriefing.

4

INTERVENTION AND EVALUATION

ADAM LODZINSKI

MICHIKO S. MOTOMURA

FRANK W. SCHNEIDER

CHAPTER OUTLINE

Contributing to the development of inter-vention strategies that lead to improve-ments in the lives of people is the defining feature of the field of applied social psychology and, in our view, is the most exciting thing about being an applied social psychologist. Imagine the great sense of accomplishment and

gratification that Sherif (1966b) and his col-leagues must have experienced when they, in fact, did reduce conflict between rival groups of boys by using a strategy that involved having the groups work together toward common goals. Imagine how rewarding it is for those who are involved in designing community-based interventions that influence people to adopt healthier lifestyles (e.g., engaging in regular exercise, employing safe sex practices), thereby reducing the incidence of serious health problems (e.g., heart disease, sexually transmitted diseases). Throughout the remainder of this book, you will be provided with many examples of successful interventions that are grounded in social psychological theory and research. Likewise in this chapter, several social psychologically based interventions are reviewed. In particular, the chapter focuses on an intervention strategy that has been implemented on many college campuses to deal with the high rates of alcohol abuse.

Given that interventions are so central to the field of applied social psychology, it is important for you, as a student of the field, to have a good understanding of their nature. The major goal of this chapter is to consider how applied social psychologists draw on their understanding of theory, methods, and research evidence in the design and evaluation of interventions. The chapter takes you through the steps involved in developing and evaluating interventions, using examples of actual interventions to illustrate the steps. It also recognizes social psychology's role in influencing social policy, which is another very important way of applying social psychology and is closely related to the application of the field through the implementation of interventions. Near the end, the chapter considers some of the practical and ethical issues that are confronted by people who practice applied social psychology.

Design of Interventions

Nature of Interventions

An **intervention** may be defined as a strategy (or procedure) that is intended to influence the behavior of people for the purpose of improving their functioning with respect to some social or practical problem. Some interventions might not target people's behavior directly, for example, those that are designed to increase knowledge or awareness (e.g., of the environmental benefits of recycling) or are designed to change attitudes (e.g., becoming more supportive of recycling). However, the ultimate goal of most interventions is behavior change (e.g., increased recycling). As pointed out in Chapter 1, interventions can be conducted at different levels of analysis (e.g., individual, group, organization, community). Although interventions can be directed at different levels, it can be argued that ultimately they are directed toward individuals in that for changes to occur, such as in a group or in an organization, the individual members must change in some way.

Moreover, to understand the focus of this chapter, it is helpful to distinguish between two broad types of intervention: personal and programmatic. **Personal interventions** are those that people carry out in the course of their daily lives, that is, when they use their knowledge of social psychology to improve their own circumstances or those of people around them. Examples of personal interventions were provided in Chapter 1 where "personal uses" of social psychology were considered (e.g., the waitress using her social psychological toolbox to improve her tips). Clearly, all of us can benefit from applying social psychology in our lives. However, personal interventions are not the focus of this chapter or the major focus of this book, although they are the subject of Chapter 5, which illustrates the relevance of social psychology to everyday life.

In the current chapter, our primary concern is with **programmatic interventions,** which commonly are referred to simply as programs. In this chapter (and in the book as a whole), the terms "intervention" and "program" are used interchangeably. Royse, Thyer, Padgett, and Logan (2001) defined a **program** as "an organized collection of activities designed to reach certain objectives" (p. 5). In the context of applied social psychology, the activities that comprise a program are directed toward addressing a social or practical problem with the objective of preventing, reducing, or eliminating its negative consequences. In some instances, interventions may be directed at reinforcing and strengthening a positive situation (e.g., improving the productivity of an already effective work group). Except for the personal interventions that have been mentioned, all of the interventions discussed so far in this book fall under the category of programmatic interventions. For example, one program involved the procedures and activities that Hodges, Klaaren, and Wheatley (2000) employed in getting female college students to engage in comfortable safe sex discussions, and another example entailed the set of procedures and activities that Sherif (1966b) used to get groups of boys to work cooperatively toward superordinate goals.

We also can identify some interventions as trial interventions. **Trial interventions** are those that are implemented to determine whether the interventions, as designed, in fact have the intended positive consequences. These are also known as program efficacy studies (Crano & Brewer, 2002). Trial interventions typically are associated with programmatic interventions, although theoretically personal interventions can be "tried out" as well. There are two basic kinds of trial intervention. One is when researchers design a study to test out a possible intervention strategy. The interventions of Sherif (1966b) and Hodges and colleagues (2000) represent this type of trial intervention. The second kind of trial intervention is when an organization conducts a pilot program to determine its effectiveness before implementing it on a more permanent basis or before implementing it on a wider scale. For example, as police departments in North America transition to community policing, which is a new model of policing, they frequently test its efficacy by trying out a community policing unit in one or two neighborhoods. Many interventions considered in this book are trial interventions, particularly the kind that involves a research test of an intervention design. We now turn to a consideration of the main tasks in intervention design and delivery.

Key Tasks in Intervention Design and Delivery

The process of intervention design and implementation follows four overarching steps that reflect the general problem-solving approach adopted by many areas of applied psychology and are applicable whether the recipient of the intervention is one individual or many individuals. These steps are (a) identifying a problem, (b) arriving at a solution, (c) setting goals and designing the intervention, and (d) implementing the intervention. (Oskamp & Schultz, 1997).

Step 1: Identifying a problem. Programs are initiated to address social problems or practical problems. The first step in program design is to identify the existence and severity of a problem. A problem usually is identified and defined by stakeholders. **Stakeholders** are individuals or groups who have a vested interest in the possible development of a program in that they may be affected by it in some way. Stakeholders include not only the potential recipients of the program but also individuals such as program funders, administrators of the organizations responsible for delivering the program, program managers, and frontline staff members (i.e., the employees who actually carry out the program activities). As you might imagine, difficulties arise when different stakeholders disagree about whether a problem exists, how serious a problem is, or which problems should be given highest priority.

A **needs assessment** is the term that is commonly used to refer to the process of establishing whether or not there is a need or problem (these words are used interchangeably) to sufficiently warrant the development of a program. A needs assessment may be *informal* in nature, for example, when a coach determines that a team-building exercise is necessary based on her own experience with her team or when a manager decides that his department needs a workshop on sexual harassment after overhearing some of his staff members making sexually inappropriate remarks. In general, we have more confidence in the conclusions of a *formal* needs assessment that relies on systematic research procedures for collecting data that are relevant to problem severity and prevalence. Problems may be investigated using a variety of procedures, for instance, by means of interviewing representatives of various stakeholder groups or administering questionnaires to them. Also, a formal needs assessment gauges the availability of existing programs or services as well as possible barriers to or gaps in service.

Step 2: Arriving at a solution. Ascertaining the existence of a problem or need is one thing; determining how best to address it is quite another. To arrive at a solution, it is important to identify the factors responsible for causing the problem. When identifying causal factors, one should distinguish between **precipitating factors** (i.e., those that triggered the problem) and **perpetuating factors** (i.e., those that sustain the problem and keep it from being solved). Making the distinction between precipitating factors and perpetuating factors is critical to the design of an intervention because the factors or events that lead to a problem are not always directly involved in its continuation. For instance, factory employees may be laid off for one reason (the precipitating factor may be a slowdown in the economy) but unable to secure new employment for another reason (the perpetuating factor may be a lack of skills that are demanded by alternative jobs). In this case, one must identify the perpetuating cause—lack of important skills—as the factor to be targeted so as to solve the problem (inability to find new employment).

Once causal factors have been identified, the next step is to find out (often through a literature review) whether interventions that have effectively addressed the same needs already exist. Such interventions can be used to guide the development of a solution to the current problem. If previous interventions cannot be located, then a solution must be developed independently. When possible, solutions should be based on relevant social psychological theory and research evidence as well as theory and evidence from any other field that may contribute to a solution. Ross and Nisbett (1991) cautioned against the development of interventions based on conventional lay understanding and intuition because "lay predictions are often both wrong and too confidently made" (p. 18). They added, "The hard won lessons of social psychology . . . constitute a repertoire of strategies with which to supplement the guidance of common sense in constructing interventions" (p. 245).

Consider the following example of an effective smoking prevention intervention that was based on McGuire's (1964) research on the "inoculation effect." McGuire discovered that just as it is possible to be immunized against a disease, such as polio, by being inoculated with a vaccine containing a weak strain of the virus, so too is it possible for people to be immunized against attacks on their beliefs. In a series of laboratory experiments, he demonstrated that if participants are immunized by first receiving a small challenge to their beliefs and have an opportunity to prepare a rebuttal to this weak attack, they are better able to resist a subsequent more powerful attack. In a creative leap from research to application, McAlister, Perry, and Maccoby (1980) wondered whether it is possible to apply the inoculation effect to an actual social problem, namely, helping seventh-grade students resist inducements to smoke. Drawing on McGuire's (1964) inoculation theory and his innovative methodology, McAlister and colleagues (1980) developed a program involving role-playing that was successful in getting children to resist peer pressure to smoke.

For clarity of conceptualization and communication, solutions to problems should be expressed as intervention hypotheses (Lodzinski, 2003). **Intervention hypotheses** are "if–then" statements that summarize the intervention and the expected outcomes. In the case of McAlister and colleagues' (1980) smoking prevention program, the intervention hypothesis could be stated as follows: "If seventh-grade students are provided the opportunity to rehearse rebuttals to inducements to smoke in realistic role-playing, peer pressure scenarios, then in their daily lives they will be more likely to resist pressures to smoke and less likely to begin smoking."

Step 3: Setting goals and designing the intervention. Once the need and the proposed solution have been determined, it is necessary to develop the **program activities,** which refer to the specific components and procedures of the program. The best place to begin this process is to set the goals and objectives of the intervention. Knowledge of goals and objectives serves to guide the selection of program activities. **Goals** refer to the ultimate or long-term results that one hopes to accomplish through an intervention. For example, a goal for a substance abuse program might be to have the clients abstain from alcohol and other drugs. Once goals have been established, it is important to define the program objectives. **Objectives** refer to short-term changes (e.g., during or immediately after an intervention) and intermediate-term changes (e.g., 1 or 2 months later) that occur as a result of the intervention and are required for (i.e., support) the attainment of the program goals. In other words, goals refer to the

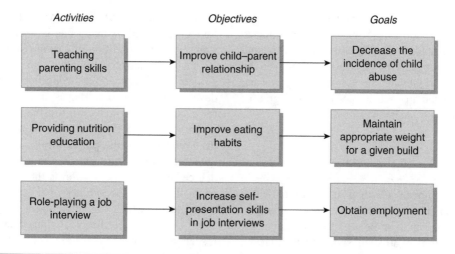

Figure 4.1   Examples of Activities, Objectives, and Goals for Three Programs

ends, whereas objectives refer to the means or steps by which the ends are achieved. For instance, if the goal is for clients with substance abuse problems to remain abstinent, one objective might be for them to understand why they use drugs in the first place.

Once the goals and objectives have been set, the next step in intervention design is to determine the program activities. When choosing activities, one of the most important questions is the following: What objective (and ultimate goal) will the proposed activity help to meet? For example, for clients to learn the reasons for their drug use (objective), they might need to have individual counseling sessions with a certified counselor (activity). Figure 4.1 illustrates additional examples of intervention activities, objectives, and goals.

The process of specifying the various components of a program—goals, objectives, and activities—requires a sound rationale, often referred to as a program logic model. A **program logic model** is an explanation or a blueprint of how the program activities lead to the attainment of the program objectives and, in turn, how the objectives logically and operationally contribute to the eventual achievement of the program goal(s) (Wholey, 1983). Logic models vary in complexity and detail, but all of them stress a "cause and effect" flow as expressed in the intervention hypothesis. Program logic is the glue that holds the activities, objectives, and goals together.

Fundamental to a program logic model is its theoretical basis (Unrau, Gabor, & Grinnell, 2001). That is, a logic model should be based on a theoretical rationale that explains the causal connections among its various components, for example, why rehearsing rebuttals will induce resistance to peer pressure to smoke. From the point of view of intervention design, this means that one should be able to point to any component of the intervention and indicate not only what its contribution is but also why the effect should occur. The use of a program logic model ensures a careful theoretically and empirically based articulation of the program and increases the likelihood of its success. This, of course, helps to ensure that program resources are used as effectively as possible. Unfortunately, in applied settings, too often it is the case that programs are designed without formal articulation of logic models.

Step 4: Implementing the intervention. As the term implies, **implementation** refers to the actual process of enacting the intervention activities, that is, of delivering them to the recipients of the intervention. A point worth noting is that there are many practical details that might need to be in place to implement programs properly. Depending on the complexity of an intervention, determined by factors such as its size and structure, practical details might include securing an appropriate facility, hiring staff members, ensuring adequate training, and developing things such as operating budgets, management structures, job descriptions, performance appraisal methods, promotional strategies, and cross-agency referral protocols. Moreover, an intervention always should be designed and implemented in such a way that its degree of effectiveness can be evaluated.

EVALUATION OF INTERVENTIONS

Donald Campbell, a leading authority on research design in the social sciences, spoke often and strongly on behalf of the need for program evaluation. More than 30 years ago, Campbell (1969) called for a culture of evaluation:

> The United States and other modern nations should be ready for an experimental approach to social reform, an approach in which we try out new programs designed to cure specific social problems, in which we learn whether or not these programs are effective, and in which we retain, imitate, modify, or discard them on the basis of apparent effectiveness. (p. 409)

Campbell's proposal was driven by the recognition that no matter how carefully conceived and convincing a program hypothesis is, it is only a proposition until the program is actually designed, implemented, and *evaluated*. Although this chapter considers evaluation in a separate section, be assured that evaluation is an integral part of the process of intervention design and implementation and may be considered a fifth step in the process. In fact, a good intervention design includes a plan for program evaluation (Lodzinski, 1995). Testimony to the importance of evaluating interventions is the existence of a separate field in the social sciences called evaluation research (or program evaluation).

Reasons for Evaluating Interventions

The effectiveness of *all* programmatic interventions should be subjected to evaluation. (Actually, this also applies to personal interventions in the case of individuals who want to avoid repeating the same mistakes in their lives.) There are several reasons why programmatic interventions should be evaluated (e.g., Lodzinski, 1995). A major one is *scientific* and stems from the tradition of Lewin (Cartwright, 1951), who viewed all applied work as being guided by theory and as contributing to the development of theory. That is, a major reason for evaluation research is to test the theoretical assumptions underlying the intervention (i.e., the foundation of the program logic model). If the intervention is implemented as designed, its degree of effectiveness informs those involved in its design of the validity of the theoretical rationale on which the intervention is based. This evaluative feedback is important with respect to attempts to develop theories that have utility in the world of application.

Another important reason for evaluating interventions is an *ethical* one. Royse and colleagues (2001) listed 14 major social problems (e.g., substance abuse, poverty, unemployment, domestic violence, adolescent pregnancy, illiteracy) and suggested that for each problem in the United States, there are hundreds—often thousands—of programs. The existence of that many programs translates into millions of program recipients whose lives are affected by program activities in various ways (e.g., physically, socially, educationally, economically) and to varying degrees. Whereas the goals of such programs are to improve the functioning of their recipients in various ways, the only appropriate means of ensuring that they do so is through evaluation. Those responsible for the implementation of programs have an ethical responsibility to determine whether their recipients are receiving the intended benefits *and* whether they are experiencing any unintended undesirable consequences. The ethical responsibility also extends to a readiness to modify or even discontinue ineffective programs and to improve on programs that have been evaluated as effective. Later in this chapter, further ethical issues in the design and evaluation interventions are considered.

The need for *financial accountability* is another reason for program evaluation. Imagine the billions of dollars needed to fund the many thousands of social programs that exist. Most of us likely would say that the money is worth it— if the programs in fact do improve people's lives as intended. On the other hand, most of us would be pretty put off if all those tax dollars (our money) were being wasted on ineffective programs. Royse and colleagues (2001) pointed to a government-sponsored $2 billion anti-drug media campaign that was initiated when there were "no well-controlled studies showing that media campaigns are effective in changing behavior" (p. 15). This astonishing example of fiscal irresponsibility very clearly highlights the need for rigorous research on the effectiveness of programmatic interventions. For the sake of the funders of programs, there should be accountability in the sense of convincing demonstrations of program effectiveness. Moreover, even if a program is found to be effective in accomplishing its goals, the program might be too costly. That is, an effective program might cost too much given the available resources that might instead be used for other purposes, including the implementation of other beneficial, yet less expensive, programs.

Finally, *program development* may be viewed as the overriding reason for evaluation research. Programs are evaluated as part of the process of developing the most effective programs possible. In fact, the three reasons for evaluation mentioned previously dovetail into program development by seeking to ensure that programs (a) are based on sound empirically tested theoretical assumptions, (b) are conducted with appropriate ethical safeguards, and (c) have a satisfactory ratio of benefits to costs.

Ineffective Interventions

As suggested, programs must be subjected to evaluation research because their success—even that of the most carefully rationalized and designed ones—cannot be assumed. If we can generalize from the literature on program evaluation, the intervention world is replete with ineffective programs. An early dramatic example of a failed intervention was the Cambridge–Somerville project (described in Ross & Nisbett, 1991). What is especially noteworthy about the intervention, as observed by Ross and Nisbett (1991), is the fact that although the program was the "kind of multifaceted intervention that many social scientists would love to see implemented today" (p. 214), it turned out to be a dismal failure. A major goal of the intervention

was prevention, that is, to reduce the likelihood of young boys from lower class backgrounds in a Boston suburb—some of whom were identified as delinquency prone—from going down a criminal path. The program was a model of intervention design, with approximately 250 boys randomly assigned to the program and another 250 or so randomly assigned to a control group. The boys were involved in the program for 5 years and received a wide variety of supports (i.e., program activities). For instance, all boys received twice-monthly visits to their homes from caseworkers, and substantial percentages received academic tutoring, psychiatric attention, medical attention, and opportunities for involvement with the Boy Scouts and summer camps.

The long-term effects of the program were evaluated in series of studies for (remarkably) 40 years following the intervention. Two kinds of evaluative data sharply contradicted each other. On the one hand, the subjective impressions of caseworkers and many program participants presented a positive picture of the benefits of the program. On the other hand, the more reliable statistical evidence indicated that the program participants, as compared with the control group, had no fewer juvenile and adult offenses and did not fare better on a number of other indicators such as health, mortality, and life satisfaction.

Ross and Nisbett (1991) offered several plausible explanations for the failure of the Cambridge–Somerville project, including the fact that the situational factors (i.e., program activities) that were manipulated as the intervention, although impressive in terms of expenditure of time and human resources, were "trivial" compared with the environmental forces that the boys faced on an ongoing basis. They also mentioned the possibility that being identified with the program might have had a stigmatizing effect on the boys, such that they and others would have viewed them as troubled and delinquent prone, with such a view becoming a self-fulfilling prophecy (see Chapter 10). This explanation raises the unfortunate possibility that the intervention actually may have had a harmful effect on the boys. In fact, on several indicators (e.g., multiple offenses, alcoholism, achievement of professional status), the program participants were less well off than the control participants during adulthood. Another possible reason why the program may have worked to the detriment of the participants is that because the boys could be seen as already receiving help from the program, the usual community sources of help (e.g., clergy, teachers, social service agencies) might have been less likely to provide their assistance. The possibility of unanticipated negative consequences must always be recognized and assessed in the evaluation of a program.

Our main purpose here is not so much to account for the failure of the Cambridge–Somerville project as to underscore that an apparently well-designed and intuitively compelling intervention can fail. If the program evaluation had not been properly designed (i.e., if it had relied solely on the subjective testimonies of key stakeholders), its failure would not have been detected; in fact, it may very likely have been deemed a success and regarded as an exemplary model of prevention. As suggested by the possible explanations for the failure of the Cambridge–Somerville project, there is a wide variety of factors that can contribute to the failure of an intervention to achieve its goal(s).

Here are four more possible reasons for program failure. One is that the theoretical rationale—the program logic model—may be inadequate and require revision. A second is that the program might not be implemented as designed (see next section on process evaluation) despite a sound theoretical and research basis. A third cause of program failure can be the operation of reactance in program recipients (Rothman, Haddock, & Schwarz, 2001). **Reactance** refers to the idea that when a source of influence threatens people's sense of freedom to think or behave as they see fit, people will act against the influence to protect their freedom (much like Romeo and Juliet did when their families opposed their love for each other) (Brehm & Brehm, 1981a). Thus, even though an intervention is intended to help people, if people feel pressure to change, they might resist the social influence attempt that the program represents. Thus, designers of interventions often must take steps to minimize the undermining effects of reactance, for instance, by avoiding the use of overly strong (i.e., reactance-triggering)

persuasive communications and by helping (as much as possible) to sustain in individuals a sense of choice or control about being exposed to program activities.

A fourth program failure may stem from an incompatibility between program design and cultural context. An example of major magnitude occurred during the 1990s when the United Nations came to recognize, after a number of failure experiences, that HIV/AIDS prevention programs that are effective in some countries or regions are less effective or completely ineffective in other countries or regions. For example, school-based HIV/AIDS prevention programs are regarded as perhaps the most effective way in which to reduce rates of HIV/AIDS (Gallant & Maticka-Tyndale, 2004). However, their potential in some developing countries is curbed enormously by the fact that the majority of children do not attend school and are illiterate and, thus, would be unable to benefit from information-based program activities in the first place. Also, the goal of condom use, which is a fundamental component of HIV/AIDS prevention programs, is opposed by very powerful cultural forces in many countries where having children is an important symbol of sexual and economic potency as well as a tremendous source of pride and status. The paramount importance of addressing culture in the design of intervention efforts was formalized in UN policy during the late 1990s (e.g., Kondowe & Mulera, 1999).

Types of Evaluation

In assessing the effectiveness of an intervention, there are two main types of program evaluation: process and outcome (Posavac & Carey, 1997). **Process evaluation** is undertaken to determine whether the program has reached its target audience (as identified in the intervention hypothesis) and whether the program *activities* (as outlined in the program's logic model) have been implemented in the prescribed manner. Basically, one wants to answer the following question: Is the program being implemented in the way in which it was planned? For instance, if an alcohol addiction program's activities include giving addicted people five individual counseling sessions and five group counseling sessions, a process evaluation would ensure that the clients were in fact addicted to alcohol and did indeed receive the prescribed number and types of counseling sessions.

Outcome evaluations typically are conducted after process evaluations. An **outcome evaluation** assesses how well a program meets its objectives (as described in the program logic model), and in a more comprehensive evaluation, it also assesses how well the program is achieving its goals. Essentially, the overriding purpose of an outcome evaluation is to determine whether the hypothesized improvement in functioning occurs among the recipients of the program. For example, an outcome evaluation of an alcohol treatment program might assess whether participants publicly (e.g., among all other participants) express strong commitment to long-term abstinence by the end of the program. Evaluation of the goal of actual long-term abstinence would occur after a specified period of time (e.g., 1 year) following completion of the program.

As suggested previously, program evaluation is an integral part of program development. The results of a program evaluation often will lead one to revisit and revise the program logic model and, accordingly, to make changes in the goals, objectives, and activities. For instance, the logic model for an alcohol addiction program might have to be amended to include the important role of family support, thereby necessitating the inclusion of new program activities (e.g., family counseling) and objectives that emphasize family involvement.

Importance of Research Design in Evaluating Interventions

Chapter 3 stressed the advantages of experimental designs in the study of causal relationships. Heightened confidence in *internal validity* (i.e., the independent variable did in fact cause changes in the dependent variable) comes with sound experimentation. Similarly, as Campbell (1969) and others (e.g., Crano & Brewer, 2002) have argued, if we want to know whether an intervention does indeed result in its intended consequences, evaluators are in a much stronger position to reach a confident conclusion with an intervention that is conducted as an

experiment. In such a case, potential program participants are randomly assigned to either the intervention group or a "no intervention" control group. Assuming that all other environmental factors are similar for the two groups (this assumption becomes less tenable with interventions in the field than with those in the laboratory), differences between the groups (e.g., gains in students' self-esteem) can be attributed to the intervention with some confidence.

Confidence about program effects will be lower in the case of interventions conducted as quasi-experiments, for example, when random assignment is not used and the outcomes for the intervention group are compared with those for a group of individuals whom the researchers deemed to be similar to the intervention group (e.g., the groups may be matched on a few characteristics such as income level and intelligence quotient [IQ]). This is not to say that evaluations of interventions conducted as quasi-experiments are not of value. In fact, when it comes to interventions in the "real world," experimentation frequently is not feasible for a variety of practical reasons (e.g., an agency cannot afford to run a program as an experiment, random assignment cannot occur because the evaluator is faced with an intervention group that is preselected). When experimental procedures are not possible, quasi-experimental procedures should be employed. However, with such procedures, conclusions about program effectiveness must be more guarded (Campbell, 1969).

Recently, Biglan and his colleagues proposed standards that scientific organizations should apply before recommending programs and policies (see later section on policy development) directed toward the prevention of behavior problems in youth (Biglan, Mrazek, Carnine, & Flay, 2003). Such organizations include the Center for the Study and Prevention of Violence, the Center for Substance Abuse Prevention, and the Collaborative for Academic, Social, and Emotional Learning. Biglan and colleagues proposed that before an organization recommends adoption of a given prevention program or policy, its positive outcomes for the target group should be demonstrated by at least two well-designed experimental trials or three well-designed interrupted time series experiments (one of the more rigorous quasi-experimental designs, as described in Chapter 3). According to Biglan and colleagues, the use of this "standard would mean that scientific organizations would put their resources into disseminating the programs and policies that . . . would concentrate the limited resources of scientific, government, and nonprofit organizations on the policies and programs that are most likely to have an impact" (p. 436).

The following section further clarifies intervention design and evaluation by taking you through each step of design and evaluation of an actual program.

AN INTERVENTION EXAMPLE: REDUCING ALCOHOL PROBLEMS ON CAMPUS

As noted previously, when designing an intervention, it is important to draw on relevant theory and research to develop the most effective intervention possible. This section describes an intervention that involves the direct application of social psychological theory and research evidence. The goals of the intervention, which was developed and implemented at Northern Illinois University (NIU), were to reduce high-risk drinking among students and to reduce the incidence of injuries due to alcohol consumption. The intervention was conducted by the Health Enhancement Services Office of the University Health Service at NIU and was initially funded by a grant from the U.S. Department of Education's Fund for the Improvement of Postsecondary Education (Haines, 1996).

Identifying the Problem

Alcohol consumption is a very big problem on many college campuses. The level of alcohol consumption among college students has long been a concern of school administrators, parents, and other community members. The Harvard School of Public Health surveyed students at 119 colleges and universities in the United States (Wechsler, Davenport, Dowdall, Moeykens, & Castillo, 1994; Wechsler et al., 2002). The results showed that, overall, 44% of students had engaged in "binge drinking" (defined as having five or more drinks in a row)

during the 2 weeks prior to the survey. The survey also showed that a higher percentage of binge drinkers had experienced alcohol-related problems since the beginning of the school year than had non-binge drinkers. Frequent binge drinkers were 7 to 16 times more likely than non-binge drinkers to have reported the following: missed class, fallen behind in schoolwork, engaged in unplanned sexual activity, had sex without protection, found themselves in trouble with campus police, damaged property, and been physically hurt or injured. A survey of NIU students (details reported later) confirmed that NIU was not an exception with respect to having a serious campuswide alcohol problem.

To deal with problem drinking on campus, many colleges, including NIU, have tried "traditional" methods of intervention such as alcohol education and awareness campaigns, which are based on the idea that increased knowledge of the negative consequences of alcohol consumption will reduce drinking levels. However, there is little research evidence that education-oriented programs reduce alcohol consumption among college students (Moskowitz, 1989). Consistent with the research, NIU found that these traditional methods did not reduce drinking rates or alcohol-related injury rates among its students. It was clear that there was a need for a new kind of intervention to deal with problem drinking among NIU students.

Developing a Solution: Forming the Intervention Hypothesis

To reduce alcohol consumption among NIU students, an intervention that represented an application of **social norm theory** was designed (Berkowitz, 2003; Perkins, 2003). Fundamental to social norm theory is the central role that norms play in people's lives. **Norms** refer to shared beliefs about which behaviors are acceptable and which behaviors are not acceptable for members of a given group to engage in. Essentially, norms are prescriptions for how people should act in particular situations. There is ample research evidence that people do tend to guide their behavior in accordance with what they perceive to be the situation-relevant norms (Secord & Backman, 1974). Social psychologists have long recognized the influence of social norms on people. However, what is distinctive about social norm theory is its emphasis on the idea that people often perceive norms incorrectly and use such erroneous perceptions to guide their actions. In fact, social norm theory is based on the following three principles. First, individuals tend to conform to what they perceive to be the norm for a particular behavior. Second, in some instances, individuals may behaviorally conform to misperceived norms. Third, if misperceptions of norms are corrected, individuals will change their behavior to agree with the corrected perceptions.

Research on social cognition has identified some thinking errors that can lead people to misperceive norms. Two are particularly relevant to the problem of drinking on college campuses. One cognitive error is **false consensus,** which is the tendency for people to believe that others are like them when in fact they are not (Ross, Green, & House, 1977). For instance, heavy drinkers may believe that most of their peers (e.g., students at their school) are also heavy drinkers when in fact they are not. We can see how this kind of thinking would allow heavy drinkers to rationalize their own levels of alcohol consumption as normative—socially acceptable—and, thus, help to sustain their excessive drinking. Another way in which norm misperception can occur is through **pluralistic ignorance,** which is when the majority of individuals incorrectly assume that others behave or think more differently from themselves than they actually do (Toch & Klofas, 1984). For instance, students may believe that others drink more than they do when in fact they do not. In fact, survey studies on a variety of college campuses have shown that these two types of misperception, especially pluralistic ignorance, are very common. That is, most students think that other students on their campuses drink more than is actually the case (Graham, Marks & Hansen, 1991; Perkins & Berkowitz, 1986). At NIU, similar results were found. A 1988 survey indicated that less than half (43%) of students reported that they drink more than five drinks when they "party," whereas 70% of students reported that they believed most NIU students drink more than five drinks when they party. Thus, at NIU, the norm was that most students did not drink more than five drinks

when partying, yet a solid majority misperceived the norm (suggesting the operation of pluralistic ignorance).

As the second principle of social norm theory suggests, not only do college students misperceive the norm for drinking behavior to be higher than it really is (e.g., "everyone is doing it"), but they also behave in ways that conform to this misperception. As evidence of this, studies have determined that if students believe that their peers are drinking more than they themselves are drinking, drinking rates tend to rise (Graham et al., 1991; Prentice & Miller, 1993).

The third principle of social norm theory—that people will conform to corrected perceptions of norms—leads directly to the hypothesis that if misperceptions of the drinking norm are corrected, levels of high-risk drinking will decline. Social norm theory and related research, therefore, led NIU to use the following intervention hypothesis for the design of its program: If NIU students are led to perceive the campus norm for drinking levels more accurately (i.e., the levels are lower than believed), drinking levels among students should decrease.

Goal Setting and Designing the Intervention

The main goals of the intervention were to reduce high-risk drinking and alcohol-related injuries among students at NIU. The objective of the intervention was to reduce the misperception of the amount of drinking on campus. It was reasoned that reaching this objective would lead to the achievement of the main goals of the intervention. The campaign plan was to target all students who drank alcohol. Because nearly all students (90%) at NIU drank alcohol, a campuswide intervention was planned. Four rules used to guide the development of the campaign message to the student body were to (a) keep it simple, (b) tell the truth, (c) be consistent, and (d) highlight the norm of moderate drinking. Reflecting these rules, the message was that most NIU students (55%) drink five or fewer drinks when they party.

Because of the limited resources available (one full-time staff person) for this project and the large number of students at NIU (23,000), it was decided that the main program activity

Figure 4.2   One Poster Used for Social Norm Media Campaign at Northern Illinois University.

would be to use a mass media campaign. Given that most students at NIU reported that the campus newspaper was their primary source of information about campus activities, it was decided that a print media campaign would reach the largest number of students at the lowest cost. The print media campaign included campus newspaper advertisements, a campus newspaper column, press releases, flyers, and posters (Figure 4.2). It was also important that students perceived the source of the message as credible. A survey determined that NIU students rated health professionals as more believable than educators and friends. As a result, a print media campaign that was endorsed by health professionals on campus was deemed to be the most effective method of communicating the intervention message to NIU students.

An additional program activity involved a means of increasing the likelihood that students would read and remember the campaign message. This entailed rewarding students who remembered the message and spread the message to others. For example, groups of students were approached at random and asked, "Who knows how many drinks most NIU students drink when they party?" The student with the correct answer received $1. Students also received $5 for putting campaign posters on their dorm room walls.

Implementing the Intervention

The media campaign was first implemented at the beginning of the fall semester in 1989. The long-term intervention strategy was to initiate the media campaign at the beginning of each fall semester and to keep it highly visible until spring break. The messages would taper off after spring break and begin again at the start of the following academic year. Because new students arrive every year bringing their own misperceptions about drinking levels, it was important to conduct the intervention at the start of each school year. This social norm-based intervention has been ongoing at NIU since its inception during the early 1990s.

Evaluating the Intervention

An outcome evaluation of the social norm media campaign at NIU was conducted to determine whether the intervention was able to reach both its main objective and its two key goals. The evaluation sought to answer three questions. First, did the perceived rate of high-risk drinking (defined as having more than five drinks when partying) among peers decrease to a more accurate perception? Second, did the rate of actual high-risk drinking decrease? Third, did the rate of alcohol-related injuries decrease? To answer these three questions, baseline information was collected from the students in 1988, that is, before the intervention was implemented. **Baseline information** refers to data that are collected on the target population prior to an intervention (i.e., the pretest) and that are compared with data collected after the intervention has been implemented (i.e., the posttest). A student survey was used in 1988 to collect three pieces of information about NIU students: the perceived rate of high-risk drinking among other students, the actual rate of high-risk drinking, and the rate of alcohol-related injuries. This pretest information was used both to justify the need for the intervention and to compare with data collected after the intervention was implemented (posttest). To rule out other possible explanations of the evaluation results (i.e., high-risk drinking is reduced because of reasons beyond the intervention), data on national drinking levels among U.S. college students during this same time period were also recorded. This evaluation study demonstrates a quasi-experimental design because a nonequivalent comparison group of U.S. college students was used.

Data were collected at the end of each academic year from 1988 to 1998 (Figure 4.3). From 1989 to 1990, after the first year of implementation, researchers found that there was a 12% reduction in *perceived* high-risk drinking, an 8% reduction in *actual* high-risk drinking, but no significant reduction in alcohol-related injuries to self or others. Over a span of 10 years using the social norm media campaign, NIU experienced a 37% reduction in perceived high-risk drinking, a 30% reduction in actual high-risk drinking, and a 20% reduction in alcohol-related injuries to self or others (Haines, 2003). In addition, the overall rate of binge drinking among U.S. college students (i.e., the nonequivalent comparison group) remained virtually the same over the same time period (Johnston, O'Malley, & Bachman, 1999). These data suggest that the NIU social norm intervention has been very successful in reaching its goals.

The social norm approach has also been used to reduce high-risk drinking among students at many other colleges and universities across the United States, including Hobart and William Smith Colleges, the University of Arizona,

Rutgers University, and the University of North Florida (Berkowitz, 2003). The social norm theory also has been applied to other social issues where individuals tend to misperceive the norm. For example, an intervention to reduce tobacco use has been implemented at the University of Wisconsin–Oshkosh and in DeKalb County, Illinois; an intervention to prevent sexual assault has been implemented at Mary Washington College and the James Madison University; a pilot project to improve the participation and retention of women in mathematics has been implemented at NIU; and a program to increase seatbelt use has been implemented in Montana (Berkowitz, 2003).

Application of Social Norm Theory to Different Levels of Analysis

As noted earlier in this chapter, interventions vary in terms of levels of analysis. The intervention work based on social norm theory represents an excellent illustration of how a basic intervention model can be applied at different levels of analysis. Berkowitz (2003) distinguished among three levels of intervention using the social norm approach: universal, selected, and indicated. Berkowitz defined **universal interventions** as those that target an entire population without selecting out special members of that population. For instance, the social norm intervention at NIU was directed at the entire student population. **Selected interventions** aim toward improvement of a select group of individuals within a population, for example, individuals who may be in particular need of receiving assistance. The social norm intervention has been used to target groups that are at especially high risk for abusing alcohol such as members of a fraternity or sorority. **Indicated interventions** target single individuals who may already exhibit signs of the unwanted behavior. It is at this level where some form of counseling often takes place. The social norm approach has been delivered on a one-on-one basis with individuals who are known to engage in high-risk drinking.

The application of social norm theory in programmatic interventions that successfully reduce a variety of high-risk behaviors aptly demonstrates the potential for the development

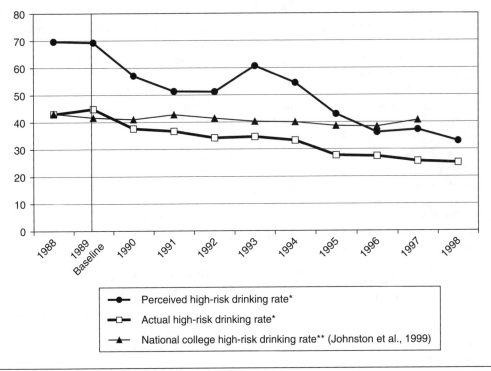

Figure 4.3 Effects of the Social Norm Media Campaign at NIU on Students' Perceptions of and Actual High-Risk Drinking Behavior

*High-risk drinking defined as having more than five alcoholic drinks when "partying."
**High-risk drinking defined as having five or more alcoholic drinks at a sitting within the past 2 weeks.

of beneficial interventions based on social psychological theory and research. The following section briefly describes two other examples of applying social psychological theory to intervention design.

Examples of Other Interventions

Among the many examples of how social psychological theory can be applied successfully to interventions is the work of Stone, Aronson, Crain, Winslow, and Fried (1994). These social psychologists drew on *cognitive dissonance theory* (reviewed in Chapter 2) to design an intervention to encourage young adults to use condoms. Recall that cognitive dissonance theory (Festinger, 1957) suggests that dissonance—a form of psychological discomfort—may occur in individuals when they are made aware of the fact that they are being hypocritical (i.e., they do not "practice what they preach"). In this

intervention, college students were asked to develop a persuasive message about AIDS and practicing safer sex and to deliver it in front of a video camera as part of an AIDS prevention program for high school students. Then participants were asked to recall the circumstances surrounding their past failures to use condoms. The intervention hypothesis was that the inconsistency between their public commitment to promote safer sex and the awareness of their own risky sexual behavior would cause cognitive dissonance. Furthermore, to reduce dissonance, the students were expected to begin to practice what they preach by having safer sex through the use of condoms. Stone and colleagues found support for the hypothesis that students who both made a videotape and recalled unsafe sexual behavior (hypocritical condition) were more likely to buy condoms and bought more condoms than did students who only made a videotape or who only recalled unsafe sexual behavior.

There are also interventions that incorporate more than one theory into their designs. For instance, Hansen, Meissler, and Ovens (2000) used aspects of social learning theory and the fundamental attribution error to create group play–therapy programs for children with attention deficit hyperactivity disorder (ADHD). The major tenet of **social learning theory** is that we learn new behaviors by observing and imitating others (e.g., role models) as well as by observing consequences of behaviors (Bandura & Walters, 1963). The group play–therapy program allows children to learn from others through the process of modeling and the enforcement of positive or negative consequences for actions. As reported in Chapter 1, the **fundamental attribution error** refers to the notion that people tend to underestimate the role of situational determinants of people's behavior and tend to overestimate the role of dispositional determinants (e.g., personality) (Ross, 1977). For children with ADHD, this means that the behaviors that they display (e.g., excitement) tend to be attributed (e.g., by significant others) to their condition, whereas situational influences (e.g., fun event) are ignored. The group play–therapy intervention attempts to reduce this bias in judgment by conducting the therapy groups in a community-based setting away from stigmatizing mental health facilities and by increasing awareness of the attribution error and its potential consequence for children with ADHD.

INFLUENCING SOCIAL POLICY

This chapter would be remiss if it did not recognize another avenue of application—influencing the development of social policy. The potential of psychology and other social sciences to contribute to public policy has long been recognized. Also long recognized is the existence of a considerable gap between the actual amount of social scientific knowledge about social issues and the impact of this knowledge on social policies (Hennigan, Flay, & Cook, 1980; Miller, 1969). Two recent American Psychological Association (APA) presidents, DeLeon (2002) and Zimbardo (2002b), challenged psychologists to become more involved in public policy development. Zimbardo noted that many of the most serious problems facing the United States (e.g., animosity of the Arab world against the United States, education failures, addictions) have psychological causes and/or consequences and that "psychologists need to be heard and to be at the table of influential leaders and policy makers because psychologists have more to say about these issues than do members of any other discipline" (p. 432). Among the strategies for enhancing psychology's voice in social policy development, Zimbardo proposed a "psychological advisory council to the president of the United States, akin to that of economists" (p. 432).

Probably the best-known example of social psychological research having a role in policy formation occurred in 1954 when the U.S. Supreme Court, in its *Brown v. Board of Education* ruling, struck down the 1892 *Plessy v. Ferguson* separate but equal doctrine, thereby making racial segregation in public schools unconstitutional (Benjamin & Crouse, 2002). In making its ruling, the court cited seven social science publications as having a role in its decision. The main thrust of the social science argument was that segregation negatively affected the self-esteem of African American children and also fostered interracial prejudice. This event is particularly noteworthy because it marked the first time that the Supreme Court had recognized psychological research in a decision, and the ruling was perhaps the most socially significant one made during the 20th century. Recently, in recognizing the 50th anniversary of *Brown v. Board of Education* and the important influence of Kenneth B. Clark on the court's decision, Tomes (2004) appropriately titled his article "The Case—and the Research—That Forever Connected Psychology and Policy."

A more recent example of social science research contributing to policy development comes from the criminal justice field in North America, which during the past 20 years has witnessed a shift in philosophy and operational strategy. The change has been from less emphasis on the traditional law enforcement model of policing (a reactive, response-driven approach) to more emphasis on the community-oriented model of policing (a proactive, police–community partnership approach). In embracing this transition, leaders in policing and relevant government agencies drew considerably on the research evidence that pointed to the limited effectiveness of the core operational procedures used in traditional policing and to the need for more attention to quality of life issues and improving police–community relations (Schneider, Pilon, Horrobin, & Sideris, 2000).

Thus, social psychology can contribute to both the development of policy and the development of interventions. The difference between policy and intervention is that **policy** refers to a general course of action endorsed by an organization, whereas an *intervention* refers to the specific concrete action(s) (i.e., program activities) that the organization chooses to take to implement the policy. For instance, on the one hand, the leadership of a police agency may decide on the policy of implementing community policing on an organization-wide basis. On the other hand, interventions pertain to exactly how the agency chooses to implement the policy, that is, the actual steps taken to carry out the policy of community policing (e.g., involving officers in courses on community policing principles, setting up a neighborhood ministation, conducting foot patrols).

Without a doubt, influencing social policy is a very important applied function of the social science disciplines, including social psychology. However, instead of focusing on social policy influence, this chapter (and this book overall) concentrates on the role of social psychology in the design of interventions that are viewed as the sine qua non of applied social psychology. The path from social psychological knowledge to influencing social policy is seldom straightforward. Many factors that preclude the direct use of knowledge in policy decision making have been identified (e.g., Hennigan et al., 1980), including the failure of researchers to adequately communicate research findings to policymakers, time pressures on decision makers that undercut thorough assimilation of research evidence, resistance to change stemming from comfort with the status quo, pressures from stakeholders whose positions do not accord with the scientific evidence, and so forth. In the case of the development of interventions, the route from knowledge to practice is more direct in that there are likely to be fewer obstacles to application than is the case for social policy.

Intervention Issues

Process Issues

The focus of this chapter has been on programmatic intervention. We have described the basic steps in the design of interventions, and although these steps are fundamental to the development of effective programs, it is important to recognize that they are not carried out in a vacuum. All interventions—and by extension, intervention designs—have to operate within constraints, and it is sometime very challenging to both work within these constraints and maintain the integrity and effectiveness of the interventions. The most prevalent constraint is budgetary. Other constraints are subtler. Following are three general constraints.

First, interventions must be paid for, and funding typically is rooted in policy directions that, in turn, are embedded in the funder's broader political philosophy or ideology (whether conservative or liberal). Thus, the view that interventions are driven exclusively by the emergence of empirically validated methodologies is naive (Mark & Bryant, 1984). To be sure, empirical validation is critical to the successful application of social psychological theory and knowledge, but interventions based on such insight must, to varying degrees, conform to funders' needs and wants. Ideas for interventions, no matter how well validated, will always have to be vetted for approval by those who have been approached to fund them.

Second, intervention design is a collaborative process in which the responsibility always is shared among stakeholders. For example, intervention design often involves professionals from different disciplines (sometimes together with program participants) working as a team. Hence, designing an intervention to assist in relapse prevention in a substance abuse clinic is likely to involve—in addition to the applied social psychologist—medical professionals and clinical psychologists as well as social workers and counselors. Each professional group will contribute a unique experience and perspective on the design of the intervention. To be effective, therefore, an intervention's designer(s) must be able to take into account a wide range of stakeholder ideas while at the same time ensuring that the key elements of the design remain linked with one another both logically and operationally to form a cohesive and integrated whole. Also note that the challenge is not only intellectual but also interpersonal given that listening, relationship building, and negotiating become part of the toolbox of every applied social psychologist involved with intervention design. (You likely will find that your grounding in basic social psychology is extremely helpful in this regard. For an excellent chapter on the practice skills of the applied psychologist, see Fisher [1982].)

Third, constraints that are specified by the law, and by various organizational policies and established procedures, also exist. Organizational constraints that must be accommodated include restrictions to access, availability of facilities, hours of operation, staffing availability, and scheduling restrictions.

None of these constraints can be ignored, so all must be addressed in the process of intervention design and eventual implementation. Sometimes it is possible to work around them, and sometimes it is not; for example, some constraints are nonnegotiable (e.g., maintaining confidentiality of client records, being required to accept nonvoluntary participants), whereas others may be negotiable to varying degrees. Typically, designers have to advocate for certain parameters, for example, getting more flexible intake or referral criteria to give access to more people and getting agreement from management to change the program delivery model in response to participant feedback.

Ethical Issues

As this chapter has illustrated, applied social psychologists contribute to improving the quality of life and the betterment of society as a whole through the application of social psychological theory and research. Recall from Chapter 3 that social psychological research undertaken to develop an understanding of social phenomena is guided by codes of ethics (American Psychological Association, 2002; Canadian Psychological Association, 2000). Just as ethical issues exist in the conduct of basic research, concerns also can arise around the ethical use of both research methodology and research findings in applied

settings. In fact, the focus on effecting change in the functioning of individuals, groups, and organizations raises a host of ethical issues beyond those that typically emerge in understanding-focused research. Ethical issues can arise in both the design and evaluation of interventions, and they can challenge a practitioner's professionalism and integrity.

Although psychologists are guided by their national associations' codes of ethics, and often by specialty-specific codes of ethics such as those for clinical and educational psychologists, some have pointed out (e.g., O'Neill, 1989, 1998) that ethical standards for much of applied psychology focus on issues that typically arise between a psychologist and an individual. These writers point out that these ethical guidelines have been designed specifically to protect the *individual rights of clients* (e.g., maintenance of confidentiality, prohibition of sexual contact). As such, they are not wholly adequate for dealing with issues that arise with regard to programmatic interventions, which by definition involve multiple stakeholders (e.g., program participants, program personnel, funders, members of the community at large). Two key questions that arise from this observation were voiced by O'Neill (1989). The first question is to whom (i.e., which stakeholder group) the applied psychologist is responsible. The second question is for what (i.e., which end product) the applied psychologist is ultimately responsible.

As a practical matter, the *contract* that is drawn up between a practitioner (e.g., applied social psychologist) and his or her employing organization can be very helpful by providing some clarity with respect to both of these questions. For example, contracts specify the individual or committee to whom the practitioner will report, the scope of the work expected, the end product of the work (e.g., a program evaluation report outlining conclusions and recommendations), timelines for the completion of the work, agreement on who owns the data collected or copyright to any materials produced, whether publication of the findings is permissible, and so forth. Typically, contracts do not spell out generally accepted norms of professional conduct (e.g., confidentiality of information, objectivity, prohibitions on profiting from privileged information), but adherence to these is assumed.

Contracts cannot anticipate every dilemma that may occur. Ethical issues in program intervention typically arise when the applied social psychologist is aware of, or discovers, information that, if divulged, will further the interests of one stakeholder group at the expense of another. As an example, consider an applied social psychologist who is hired to head the design of an intervention and finds that the employing organization (a government agency) only supports a politically popular intervention that, it turns out, has questionable support in evaluation research. The dilemma is that if the applied social psychologist does not reveal the lack of evidence for the program's hypothesis, it is likely that considerable resources will be wasted on an intervention that is ineffective, and so the intended program recipients will not be well served. On the other hand, if the lack of evidence is revealed, not only may the psychologist's job be at stake, but also the program may well be implemented anyway.

To take a parallel example from intervention evaluation, consider the case of an applied social psychologist who has been hired to conduct an outcome evaluation of a major program offered by a social service agency. The evaluation determines that although the program benefits the community in incidental ways, it is largely ineffective. Such results may lead to the closure of the agency because this program represents the bulk of the funding that the agency receives. The practitioner is asked by the agency's management to focus more on the positive than on the negative in the evaluation report, and this in effect would distort the overall findings of the evaluation. If the psychologist refuses to misrepresent the findings, his or her relationship with the agency (and possibly future contracts) may be jeopardized along with the survival of the agency. On the other hand, if the psychologist does comply with the request, the people who need the services will not be served as well as they could be, and financial and other resources provided by the government will not be invested optimally.

It is important to note that these are just two examples and that dilemmas can stem from many factors such as cross-cultural differences (e.g., among client groups, funders, and policymakers) and competing value systems. Some argue (e.g., Riger, 1989) that such ethical dilemmas are essentially political conflicts arising from the presence of many needs and scarce resources and the resulting necessity to compete for these resources. Kimmel (2004) suggested that applied social psychologists have frank and open discussions with the organization prior to embarking on any program design or evaluation project. The purpose of the initial discussion is to clarify the psychologist's role as well as to articulate the professional and ethical standards and any limits they may place on the extent to which the organization can be assisted.

Kimmel (2004) pointed out that occasionally it is necessary for the applied social psychologist to refuse to participate in projects that have the potential to conflict with the ethical standards of the profession. For the applied social psychologist, there is rarely an "easy" way out of ethical dilemmas. It must be remembered that one's expertise carries with it the responsibility to always act in ways that place the interests of those who are in the greatest need of help above the self-interests of the professional. This is the essence of acting ethically.

SUMMARY

This chapter has outlined some of the key components involved in the development of intervention strategies designed to address social and practical problems. It noted that although we can design personal interventions, the focus of this chapter was on programmatic interventions or programs—a collection of activities designed to prevent, reduce, or eliminate negative consequences as well as to promote positive outcomes.

The chapter noted that there are a number of steps involved in the development of programs: (a) identifying the problem, (b) developing a solution, (c) goal setting and designing the intervention, and (d) implementing the intervention. It also discussed the evaluation of interventions and noted that evaluation can be considered as a fifth step in the process of program development.

There are two main types of program evaluations. Process evaluations focus on whether programs have been implemented as planned, and outcome evaluations focus on whether programs meet their objectives. It is important to evaluate programs because they are not always effective and can sometimes produce unintended consequences.

The chapter also presented a detailed example of an intervention aimed at reducing problem drinking at NIU. This intervention demonstrated the value of using theory in the design of programs.

The chapter then explored how the results of interventions can be used to inform public policy and, finally, noted a number of intervention issues, including program constraints and ethics.

For the Applied Social Psychologist, It Is Not Enough to Know Only That an Intervention Has Worked

Although this chapter has emphasized the importance of developing a program logic model to explain *why* an intervention will result in a particular outcome or set of outcomes, the applied social psychologist involved in designing and evaluating interventions may be the only stakeholder who is particularly concerned about understanding the intervening processes that link intervention to outcome. Generally speaking, other stakeholders care little, if at all, regarding how intervention outcomes come about as a result of program activities (cf. Mark & Bryant, 1984). For them, the bottom line is whether the intervention works. An overriding emphasis on results makes sense for most stakeholders because their investment in the intervention is predominantly practical. Program funders want visible, cost-effective returns on their dollars, program managers and staff members want to demonstrate their value to the organization through program accountability, and the only important thing for program recipients is that they experience the purported benefits of the intervention. Needless to say, it is of great importance to the applied social psychologist that the intervention proves to have its intended beneficial consequences. However, unlike other stakeholders, focusing on the practical aspects is not enough. As a scientist, it is necessary for the applied social psychologist to avoid giving insufficient attention to understanding why an intervention works and why it does not work. It is vital that the applied social psychologist does not compromise the scientific integrity of the intervention–evaluation process by dwelling only on the practical "does it work" question (i.e., the question of cause and effect) and giving insufficient attention to the "why it works" question (i.e., the question of explanation). Answers to both questions are required for applied social psychology to move toward fulfilling its potential as a social science to contribute to a better world.

5

APPLYING SOCIAL PSYCHOLOGY IN EVERYDAY LIFE

RANDOLPH A. SMITH

ANN L. WEBER

Chris dreads the end of the semester. As a transfer student, Chris had struggled to adapt to a new campus and to keep up with a more demanding curriculum. Some things were the same, of course; reading assignments were excessive, all tests were scheduled at the same time, and professors still seemed to be in a different world, that is, to think so differently from students. It took constant effort to figure out how to "play the game" at the new campus.

But other challenges were new and daunting; Chris had felt lonely and even shy, a rare and unwelcome experience. At Chris's hometown campus, there had been familiar faces and old friends to ease the adjustment to college life. But now, far away from the familiar environment, this "better school" was surprisingly isolated. Chris had felt excluded and a little lost, going through the motions of classes and studying but with no direction or optimism.

Until Lee, that is. From the first time they sat beside each other in psych class, Chris and Lee had struck up conversations easily. Lee actively participated in class and chatted easily with other students—a social ease and self-confidence that Chris envied and admired. Lee had a year's more experience on campus than did Chris and offered good advice about getting around and fitting in. Where Chris frequently felt self-conscious, Lee seemed relaxed and spontaneous. Chris was more scholarly and helped Lee to study better.

They found much in common. They liked the same courses, shared the same jokes about some professors' idiosyncrasies, and enjoyed the same sports and movies. They both loved hiking and outdoor activities. As they shared talk, time, and pastimes, they quickly became close friends. They used their differences to help each other. Chris discovered that Lee was not invariably at ease but rather had seemed so because so many classmates were familiar acquaintances. Lee had participated actively in psych class because a high school course had made the subject matter more familiar. When they both took modern poetry, however, Lee was quieter and it was Chris who participated more and drew Lee into the discussion. Helping each other, they grew even closer. As months passed, they also felt personally attracted to each other, and friendship soon included romantic closeness.

Lee and Chris became inseparable partners. Chris began to feel confident and socially comfortable. Lee enjoyed academic success and worried less about grades. Superficial differences made their relationship interesting but could be surprising to others. Lee is the talker, telling the stories and getting the laughs. Chris is the quiet one, chiming in less often but paying close attention to the goings-on. Friends still call them "the odd couple" and point out that "opposites attract." Professors react to the two of them in different ways for some reason. But despite some contrasting habits and traits— or maybe because of them—Chris and Lee now feel content and well matched. They seem better together than either one seems when apart.

But now, as summer break approaches, Chris realizes that so much remains unsaid. Soon Chris and Lee will part ways and travel in different directions to their distant homes and summer jobs. In one sense, it is only a few months apart, but in another sense, that is equal to nearly half the time they have already been together. Visits would cost too much, so they will have to rely on e-mail and telephone calls. Chris pictures living back at home, working hard to keep busy, missing Lee, and losing some of that self-confidence so recently gained.

Feeling depressed at the thought, Chris frowns, only to be interrupted by Lee's familiar voice: "Hey, didn't you see me? I've said your name twice. You're lost in thought. So, what's the matter? You look like you've lost your best friend." Startled by Lee's apparent mind-reading, Chris laughs and shakes off the concern for now. They walk off in search of coffee. Chris thinks, "Now might be the right time to talk about it—but I feel too good to have a heavy conversation. So, why spoil the moment?"

- What leads people like Chris and Lee to get together in the first place?
- What factors account for the strengthening of relationships such as Chris and Lee's?

- Nothing was said about how physically attracted the two students were to each other. How important is physical attractiveness in the development of personal relationships?

- What do the worries about the effect of the summer separation on their relationship tell us about Chris's attachment needs?
- Do you agree with Chris that professors and students seem to think differently and be in a different world? If so, is it possible that you might benefit academically if you gained insight into the differences between faculty and student perspectives?

"Chris" and "Lee" are common names for both men and women. This vignette deliberately provides no clues as to whether Chris and Lee are a heterosexual couple, two men, or two women. Do you think this matters in terms of the outcome? Why or why not?

Social psychology can be applied usefully in every imaginable social and personal sphere of life. In Chapter 4, a distinction was made between personal interventions and programmatic interventions (i.e., programs). Whereas the remaining chapters of this book focus on programmatic interventions in different areas of life (e.g., clinical practice, health, organizations), the focus of this chapter is on the immediate personal relevance of the field of social psychology to individuals. Thus, the focus is on **personal interventions**, that is, how individuals can use social psychological knowledge to improve their day-to-day lives. The goal is for the material in this chapter to help you appreciate the immediate relevance of the field to people's lives.

In bringing the application of social psychology closer to you, this chapter focuses on two everyday concerns of most college students: their personal relationships and their academic lives. You have plenty of experience with both relationships and school; after all, you have been dealing with these two areas of life since you were a child. However, aspects of relationships and school may have been confusing or mysterious to you. This chapter may provide you with answers to some of those mysteries and, perhaps, make dealing with your social life and academic life a bit easier in the future.

PERSONAL RELATIONSHIPS

The story of Chris and Lee, as even Chris realizes, is not the kind of grand romance that makes a good movie plot. Their love began with friendship, not the heavy looks and passionate clutches portrayed by gorgeous actors on screen. Their good times are not scripted; their laughter involves neither great wit nor wacky comedy. And the challenge they face, in parting for summer break, is hardly the stuff of Shakespearean tragedy.

Most of us do not lead the magical lives of fictional characters. Our romantic experiences might not seem as thrilling—or as traumatic—as those of characters in movies and books. But love and friendship are necessarily important to us, and that partly explains why romantic tragedies and comedies are so appealing to wide audiences. Like Chris and Lee, and like Romeo and Juliet, you also need closeness and passion in your life. You also risk challenge, conflict, and disappointment (Figure 5.1).

To apply social psychology to your relationship experiences, begin by recognizing two practical realities. First, humans are social creatures who cannot live without closeness to others. Second, the skills we need to succeed in relationships do not "come naturally." Like other social skills, relationship behaviors must be learned. This means effort, mistakes, and trial and error—as well as a certain amount of luck.

This section begins where relationships themselves usually begin—with the very human need to affiliate with and become close to others. It then examines what it means to feel attracted only to specific others. During infancy, the process of attachment might become our blueprint for developing later adult intimacy. What are the qualities and experiences that draw us to others? What makes others seem attractive, and how then do we become closer?

Circumstances sometimes throw people together. Simple coincidences, such as enrolling in the same class as someone else and just happening to sit beside him or her, can prompt interaction and liking, eventually friendship, and possibly even love. Social psychology offers several principles to account for such transformations. The most consistent lesson of social psychology is the *power of situational influences*. You live your life in a social context, considering and reacting to the events and conditions surrounding you. In human experience, thoughts, feelings, and actions are shaped, at least in

Figure 5.1   Love and Friendship

part, by the social and physical environment. Personal relationships are not determined exclusively by personality and intention.

Chris and Lee were *pushed* together by common circumstances (e.g., a small campus, the same class) and *pulled* together by mutual interests (e.g., perceiving common preferences in pastimes, developing shared friendships). What circumstances have brought you into contact with others? How have your social perceptions, and even wishful thinking, shaped your social life as it is today?

The Need to Be Close

How much do you value relationships? How important is it for you to get close to others? Look at Table 5.1, a listing of several pairs of personal qualities. If you could possess only one of the traits in each pair; which would you choose? Make your choices before continuing.

This "forced-choice" task requires you to make a series of decisions that may be difficult in some cases. All of these traits are desirable qualities, but one quality in each pair reflects more of a *social orientation,* that is, a greater interest in *relating to others* (e.g., kindness) than

Table 5.1   Personal Qualities Menu

Instructions: If you could have only one personal quality from each pair, circle the one you would choose. (An explanation of scoring is provided in the text.)

1. Strong or kind?

2. Intelligent or generous?

3. Friendly or brave?

4. Helpful or artistic?

5. Popular or sympathetic?

in *developing a personal ability or talent* (e.g., strength). (In real life, of course, there is no reason why you should not cultivate both qualities in each pair, and there are many good reasons to do just that.)

To score yourself on this simple assessment of social interest, give yourself 1 point for choosing each of the following: *kind, generous, friendly, helpful,* and *sympathetic.* Each of these qualities requires a partner or recipient—someone to whom you can be kind or generous. These qualities can be expressed only in social situations. If you circled all or most of these traits, this (very crude) assessment suggests a stronger social orientation than if you had circled none or very few of them.

Some people are more skilled at social interaction than are others. But all humans are social creatures (Aronson, 1999b). Humans did not evolve to survive alone. Our earliest human ancestors lived in groups, cooperating in their efforts to obtain food and shelter and to raise their offspring. Without a clan or community, we would be vulnerable, homeless, and hungry. For this reason, the ancient practice of punishing an offender by exile was often a death sentence.

As social animals, humans need social relationships. In his classic theory of a hierarchy of needs and motives, humanistic psychologist Abraham Maslow listed "belongingness" as the third most important motive, after physiological needs and safety needs (Maslow, 1970). Thus, not far from food, water, and safety, one's closeness to others is vital to one's survival and well-being.

Long before people form particular friendships or romances, they seek out the company of others, whether strangers or acquaintances. The presence of "any warm bodies" can seem reassuring and soothing. You are not alone; you face your fate with others of your own kind. Affiliating also provides unique rewards, including information about what is going on, strategies for how to behave and what to do, companionship, and humor. Imagine the casual conversation and joking that can erupt among the people seated in a dentist's waiting room. Ominous sounds that make a lone patient fearful can prompt laughter and social support in a group, even though the individuals do not know each other.

Stanley Schachter investigated whether fear increases the desire to affiliate. Schachter (1959) recruited women attending the University of Minnesota as participants. Students in one of two randomly assigned groups met with an "experimenter" (clad in a lab coat along with a stethoscope) who explained the procedure to come. The experimenter explained that this was a study of the effects of electric shock. Each volunteer would receive a series of electric shocks, and the physical effects would be measured. Women in the low-fear condition heard reassurance that the shocks would be mild, resembling a tickle or tingle. But women in the high-fear condition were specifically warned that the shocks would be severe; that is, the shocks would be painful and would hurt.

As the women pondered what was to come, they were asked to wait elsewhere while the scary-looking equipment was set up. Each woman was then asked to indicate in writing one of three preferences: (a) prefer to wait alone, individually, in their own comfortable rooms; (b) prefer to wait with some of the other women in a larger waiting room; or (c) no preference. In fact, here the experiment ended. No shocks were administered. As noted, Schachter's (1959) experiment did not examine the effects of shock; rather, it examined the effects of fear on preferring to affiliate. The results indicated that, indeed, fear did affect affiliative behavior. Some 63% of the women in the high-fear condition preferred to wait with others, whereas only 33% of those in the low-fear condition preferred to wait with others. The effect is summed up in a familiar aphorism—"misery loves company."

Schachter (1959) concluded that fear motivates individuals to affiliate with others. His results certainly accord with the idea that we gain from affiliating with others. Affiliation reduces the feeling of being alone, provides comfort, and even demonstrates how others are coping with a common threat. All of us have moments of anxiety and fear, and these are times when many of us would feel better with others around—even mere strangers. If you expected a painful procedure at the dentist's office, would you rather be alone or share the waiting room with other patients? To meet our social needs, we affiliate with others, endeavoring to become close with some of them.

Attraction

Affiliation is a search for "any warm body"; in contrast, attraction is a pickier process. **Feeling attracted to someone** means knowing that not just anyone will do; you want especially to be with that particular person.

What attracts you to someone else? The very term "attraction" suggests almost a force of physics, powerfully drawing you to another person regardless of your conscious wishes or circumstances. In fact, some factors in interpersonal attraction are not a matter of taste or choice; they may seem like "outside" influences, almost like magnetism or gravity. Factors such as *proximity* and *familiarity* demonstrate social psychology's lesson on the power of situations. Let us briefly examine these factors in attraction and apply their lessons in everyday life.

Proximity and Familiarity

Most relationships begin with **physical proximity,** that is, being near or accessible to each other. In the vignette that opened this chapter, Chris reflects on first meeting Lee when they sat next to each other in class. Being near someone makes eye contact easy and makes conversation natural. Two people sit near enough to learn about each other—their clothing preferences, their voices and accents, when and how they laugh, other classes they might be taking, and so forth. The beginning of Chris and Lee's relationship laid in their *proximity,* that is, their nearness and frequent interaction—and, therefore, what they could learn about each other.

Proximity. With proximity comes interaction and the possibility of a relationship. Like many students, you might uncover the effects of proximity in relationship formation by considering your friendships. Think of your friends, especially childhood friends. Jot down the initials of their (original) last names. Are many of them from the same region of the alphabet as the initial of your own (original) last name? If so, proximity has determined some of your friendships. In grade school and later, pupils are often assigned classroom seats on an alphabetical basis. You get to know best those you sit near; Ts meet Rs, Ss, Us, and Vs but not so many As, Bs, or Cs. Thus, proximity might affect early, even lifelong, relationships.

The **proximity effect**—the tendency for physical nearness to increase interpersonal liking—was identified in a classic study by Festinger and his colleagues (Festinger, Schachter, & Back, 1950). In a large university housing complex, the researchers asked students who their closest friends were. Although the students had been assigned living spaces randomly, they overwhelmingly identified as their friends students who lived nearby and with whom they had the most frequent contact rather than others with the same hometowns, majors, or pastimes. Some locations make people more approachable or likable than others. For example, if you live near an exit or elevator, more people will pass your door than if you live at the far end of a hall. Even such accidental interactions increase people's liking for each other. It is not people's nearness to the exit that makes them appealing; rather, it is the fact that using the exit brings these people and others into regular contact with each other.

Applying the proximity effect. This research suggests one obvious application of the proximity effect: If you want to meet people and form friendships, try to secure a living space, work space, and/or even parking space that brings you into contact with as many people as possible. At least some people may be regular passers-by, and more frequent interactions with them could be the beginning of friendships. In effect, you can use the power of the situation by deliberately manipulating the locations you frequent and then enjoying the social benefits of situational influence.

Familiarity: Breeding contentment. Why should proximity and contact make someone likable in the first place? It does not always work that way. The more contact you have with an unpleasant person, the more you will dislike him or her—an effect known as **environmental spoiling** (Ebbeson, Kjos, & Konecni, 1976). Ebbeson and colleagues (1976) surveyed residents of a condominium complex, asking how much they either liked or disliked fellow residents. Each respondent's list of those he or she either liked or disliked identified neighbors living in the same section of the complex as the respondent was living.

Increased exposure to someone generally enhances preexisting feelings toward that person, whether positive or negative (Zajonc, 1968). In the absence of any prejudgment, however, frequent contact usually increases positive affect. This may be because mere exposure increases another person's *familiarity*—a quality that most people find reassuring and pleasant. Familiar faces are comforting; familiar people seem predictable, even after only superficial contact. And predictability offers a sense of order and control—an experience of competence during an age of uncertainty and anxiety.

Frequent contact also increases *perceived similarity* (Moreland & Zajonc, 1982). Suppose that you visit the library to search for a journal article and find another student searching the same part of the stacks. You make eye contact, nod, and smile but do not speak. Another day, you visit your favorite coffee shop and notice that same student sitting at a table reading. Still another day, you go to a movie and see that same person standing in line for the same show. By this time, you are making assumptions that you and the stranger have several things in common—similar course work, restaurant preferences, and taste in movies. The stranger seems less strange; each time you notice him or her, you feel more comfortable, warmer in your greeting, and closer to making conversation.

Applying the familiarity effect. How can you apply the familiarity effect in your own life? If you want an appealing stranger to like you, make yourself *familiar* somehow. Do not "stalk" him or her, but when you have the chance, do make eye contact. Hang around before or after class and make sure that person notices you. When the other person returns eye contact, smile—but do not push it. If you interact, keep it pleasant. You want to become associated with all that is good about familiar others—predictability, safety, reliability, and so forth. As Zajonc (1968) and Ebbeson and colleagues (1976) noted, exposure can increase existing negative attitudes as well as positive attitudes; familiarity can indeed breed contempt. But do not forget that the more common outcome of familiarity is liking (Zajonc, 2000). Familiarity is not enough for true closeness, but it is a vital first step in intimacy. It usually does not breed contempt; rather, it usually breeds a sort of contentment and paves the way for real interaction and communication.

Physical Attractiveness

Once you have made contact with someone, how do you know whether this is a relationship you want to pursue? In addition to words and action, most people judge each other to some extent by physical attractiveness. This reliance on looks may be a form of the **primacy effect,** referring to the tendency to be especially influenced by information that is presented first. Physical appearance is usually the earliest information you get about another person who you have seen but not yet met. Even if you hear someone before you see him or her, such as by making phone contact before meeting, it is irresistible to imagine what the other person looks like.

But what if, instead of forming impressions based on scanty data, you had an early opportunity to get to know the person? Could genuine interaction overcome the primacy of looks alone? To study this question, researchers had to "rearrange" reality somewhat so that prospective dates would meet to interact on the basis of something other than evaluating each other's physical attractiveness.

The computer date study. Nearly 40 years ago, researchers at the University of Minnesota explored reasons for dating choices by inviting new students to a Welcome Week dance (Walster, Aronson, & Abrahams, 1966). Several hundred first-year students signed up to attend. They were told (deceptively) that a computer would use each student's personal data to effect his or her best match for the evening. On arriving at the dance, the students were paired up. In exchange for free entertainment and soft drinks, the participants were asked to check in a couple of times during the dance to complete a few forms. These questionnaires asked students to provide self-ratings (e.g., about their self-esteem) and ratings of their partners (e.g., about their physical attractiveness, about how similar they were to themselves). At the end of the evening, participants privately reported whether they would like to see their "matched" dates again.

When all of the data were analyzed, only one variable predicted whether a given person wanted to see his or her date again: not the date's conversational skills, not the respondent's own self-esteem, and not the individuals' similarity to each other but rather the date's physical attractiveness. This surprising finding (at the time), confirming a human preference for looks over other qualities, has been reported countless times in psychology texts and classrooms.

During the decades since the computer date study, the power of looks in selecting dates and mates has been supported (Hatfield & Sprecher, 1986; Sprecher, 1989), although with some qualifications. For example, men seem to value looks more than do women (Feingold, 1990; Sprecher, 1986). What, then, does physical attractiveness "mean" to us? Why is it important?

The importance of looks. Good-looking people are assumed to possess other appealing qualities such as being kind, strong, and exciting (Langlois et al., 2000). And if nothing else, attractive people are at least pleasing to look at. It might even increase your social capital to be seen with a good-looking person. For example, an employer who is offered similar résumés from two people, one good-looking and the other not, generally will prefer the attractive job applicant, inferring that he or she will be a better employee (e.g., Hamermesh & Biddle, 1994).

There is a definite bias for beauty. Attractive people are expected, purely on the basis of their looks, to be better people—sensitive, sexually responsive, interesting, sociable, and so forth (Dion, Berscheid, & Walster, 1972). Such common assumptions make up the **physical attractiveness stereotype,** that is, the general expectation that a physically attractive person has positive qualities, whereas an unattractive person has negative qualities. The physical attractiveness stereotype has powerful consequences. Those people who are considered to be unattractive may be passed over for dates and/or job advancement and even may be assumed to be more capable of criminal behavior (e.g., Efran, 1974; Esses & Webster, 1988; Hatfield & Sprecher, 1986).

But a bias is not a rule, and in the case of the physical attractiveness stereotype, it is not even accurate. Ample research shows that despite expectations, for virtually every quality and virtue measured (e.g., intelligence, friendliness, honesty), good-looking people are no better or worse than people of average looks (Brehm, Miller, Perlman, & Campbell, 2002). Still, the attractiveness stereotype is a strong bias, as demonstrated by the computer date dance study. Must only the best-looking people win the competition for closeness? Apparently not. Looks

matter, but in the long run, the typical person is looking not so much for a prize as for a match.

The matching effect. Think of some local and international celebrities—movie stars, politicians, athletes, writers, and so forth—and list several whom you consider to be extremely physically attractive. On a scale from 1 (very unattractive) to 10 (very attractive), assign each celebrity a rating. Now, what rating would you give yourself? If you rated the celebrities as higher than average but rated yourself low (compared with them), how does this make you feel? What are your chances of being attractive to the sort of person you consider to be most physically attractive?

It can be sobering for many of us to realize that our looks sometimes do not match the looks of the people we find desirable. If you rate yourself a 5—or maybe a 6 on a good day—how can you capture the heart of a 9 or 10, even a 10 whom you know and have things in common with, for example, an extremely good-looking classmate? Fortunately, despite any evolutionary preferences for beauty, most people seek long-term partners who do not exceed but rather *match* their own perceived levels of attractiveness. If a 5 asks a 10 for a date, what are the chances the 10 will accept? You are more likely to be rejected if you aim too high, but you will be disappointed and dissatisfied with your partner if you keep thinking you aimed too low and could do better. The **matching effect,** or when a person prefers a long-term partner who is similar himself or herself in looks, reduces the chances of either rejection or dissatisfaction (Carli, Ganley, & Pierce-Otay, 1991; Folkes, 1982).

Test the matching effect by taking a good look at the long-term couples you know. Do they seem to "belong" together looks-wise? Now look at couples who have not been together that long. Could you predict, on the basis of whether their attractiveness levels match, whether they are likely to stay together for long?

Applying the lessons of looks. So much research and writing has been done on the power of physical appearance that it is impossible to choose any single application. Knowing that looks matter, you should take your appearance seriously any time others will be evaluating you—as a potential date, friend, partner, or employee. If you think of yourself as less than a 10 in physical appearance, identify your other fine qualities and emphasize them. Make them visible, mention them, and act on them, for example, by demonstrating your kindness, wit, generosity, helpfulness, loyalty, courage, and humor.

Keep the importance of looks *in perspective*. Evolution may have shaped a few general preferences for "good looks" of a certain kind, but human behavior is complex, being influenced by biology but not driven by instinct. The looks and qualities that people find attractive differ across cultures around the world. See the Culture Capsule for a perspective on how interpersonal attraction varies from one culture to another.

CULTURE CAPSULE: CULTURE AND INTERPERSONAL ATTRACTION

To whom are you attracted? Your list of preferences might seem personal and unique to your history, needs, and taste. But much of what you find appealing about someone else is determined by your culture—what you have *learned* to value and seek. Mate preference is more strongly associated with one's culture than with one's sex (male or female) or gender (masculine or feminine) (Goodwin, 1999).

Ours is an **individualistic culture,** where personal successes and accomplishments are valued. We like winners, people who stand out, and people whom others will prize, admire, and even desire. But a different set of values emerges in cultures that value group success over individual achievement. In **collectivistic cultures** such as China and India, community cooperation is valued more than individual distinction and a potential mate is especially prized for practical virtues such as possessing money and household management skills (Goodwin & Tang, 1991; Sprecher & Chandak, 1992).

A culture's economic and family values affect relationship values. In urban and mobile cultures such as those in the United States and Canada, a given individual seeking a friend or partner has available a much larger "pool" and might have the luxury of choice. In contrast, individuals in rural and isolated regions have far less choice. In such areas, close relationships depend greatly on proximity and availability and, therefore, are hard to replace. For someone in a poor, farm-based economy, an arranged marriage is greeted not with scorn but rather with gratitude; if not for the arrangement, how else would this individual even find a mate (Moghaddam, Taylor, & Wright, 1993)? In this sense, culture is a very large-scale version of "situational influence" on relationship choices. How would you react if an arranged marriage were advised for you? Your likely reaction gives apt testimony to the extent to which we truly are products of our cultures.

Attachment

Have you ever had your heart broken? The loss of a close relationship is universally painful. How did you feel and behave? Common reactions are distraction, anger, sadness, and despair. You may have lost sleep or the ability to concentrate. Perhaps you argued or wept. Compare these reactions to those of a baby whose mother leaves, even if only briefly. The child is placed in a crib or in the arms of the babysitter and watches as the mother walks away. (If you have ever cared for younger siblings or other children, you may have been the "villain" in a similar scenario.) The baby cries out, wailing in apparent sadness or screaming in what certainly seems like rage.

What is happening in these interactions? The child is reacting to *separation*, that is, the loss of the most important person in his or her life. In the process of *attachment*, the human infant associates satisfaction and need gratification with only one or two specific others (Bowlby, 1969/1982). Many years later, the human adult similarly sees an intimate partner as essential to well-being and happiness and becomes attached to that individual. And if that relationship ends, the adult expresses grown-up versions of the symptoms of infantile *separation distress,* that is, attention focused on the lost other and extreme discomfort at that person's inaccessibility (Weiss, 1975).

Many psychologists argue that the blueprint for later life relationships is drawn when you are still a baby by your first experience of being cared for by your parents, particularly your mother or primary caregiver. To be fed, cuddled, and protected, you must be sure that your caregiver is near or signal your need for that person. Missing or losing your *attachment figure* triggers a series of attachment behaviors—looking for the person, pleading for contact, moving toward the person, clinging to prevent abandonment, and so forth (Shaver & Hazan, 1994). This action pattern evolved as a very effective way in which to bring back a too distant caregiver.

Attachment Styles

Individuals differ in how they express separation distress. For all their variety, however, individuals' attachment behaviors have been found to fall into a few basic patterns. Understanding these patterns—your own as well as those of other people—can help you to achieve more satisfactory relationships.

Infant attachment. Research by developmental psychologist Mary Ainsworth and her colleagues revealed that, among infants, three patterns of attachment behavior could be identified (Ainsworth, Blehar, Waters, & Wall, 1978). Infants were separated from their mothers by barriers or were introduced to a strange person or environment—all situations that triggered separation distress. Although the trigger situation was the same for all of the babies, reactions reflected one style of secure attachment and two styles of insecure attachment.

1. *Secure attachment style.* Most infants were unhappy while the attachment figure was away but quickly soothed when she returned

2. *Insecure attachment style, anxious/ambivalent:* Infants acted unhappy about being separated but were still fretful and clingy when the mother returned

3. *Insecure attachment style, avoidant:* Insecure Infants behaved as though they were unconcerned about the presence or absence of the mother (they did not cry when she left, and they avoided contact when she returned)

Why the differences? Children's attachment patterns most likely develop from a combination of biological influences (e.g., inherited traits, temperament) and social learning (e.g., the attachment figure's responsiveness to the child's actions such as insufficient attention). A nervous or unwell child with a stressed or overworked parent is likely not to receive "enough" attention, contributing to an insecure style (Shaver & Hazan, 1994). Set in place early in life, the attachment categories of infancy appear to endure as attachment styles in adult relationships. Secure babies grow to be secure adults, with measurably different relationship choices and experiences, as we now consider.

Adult attachment. Your infantile attachment was not a matter of choice for you; you were born into a particular family arrangement. But as an adult, you are not assigned friends and partners; you must choose them. As an adult making such choices, you know that every relationship entails risks. To get close to someone else, you must open up, self-disclose, and become vulnerable. In developing closeness with someone, you run *two great risks:* rejection and betrayal. Another person may *reject you,* that is, refuse to get close to you. Or, once another person is close, he or she might *betray* you, that is, deceive or harm you with more painful consequences than if you had never become close in the first place. Is intimacy worth such risks? Based on experience, do you believe that you can count on people, or do you mistrust them? Are you optimistic about love, or do you expect others to abandon you sooner or later?

Infants' distinctive patterns of attachment appear to continue into childhood and later. These patterns characterize adults' reactions to love, threat, and loss in their romantic experiences. Shaver, Hazan, and their colleagues invited

Table 5.2   Views of Self and Others

Instructions: From the following four statements, choose the one that best reflects your attitude toward close relationships. (See the text for an interpretation and explanation.)

1. I am comfortable being emotionally close to another person. I enjoy depending on others and having them depend on me. I enjoy socializing with others. I feel optimistic about my close relationships.

2. I need a close relationship to feel good about myself. I often find that others do not want to get as close as I want to get. I worry about losing my partner. I feel jealous if our relationship seems to be threatened.

3. I generally feel shy in social situations. I have difficulty in trusting others or in depending on them. I fear being hurt or rejected by others if I attempt to become close to them.

4. I do not need close relationships and prefer to rely on myself. I would rather have independence than intimacy. Getting close to someone just is not worth the trouble involved.

SOURCES: Adapted from Bartholomew (1990) and Brehm, Miller, Perlman, and Campbell (2002).

adults to provide descriptions of attachment behaviors in response to newspaper question-naires about life, love, and work. Their partici-pants' attachment patterns fell into patterns similar to those of secure and insecure infants (Hazan & Shaver, 1987; Shaver & Hazan, 1994; Shaver, Hazan, & Bradshaw, 1988).

At about the same time, Main, Kaplan, and Cassidy (1985) used interviews to assess the attachment styles of parents and to relate these to their infants' response styles. Combining such techniques, attachment researchers have confirmed that in our adult relationships, we replay early-life patterns of dealing with close-ness, separation, and loss. Bartholomew (1990) developed more complex assessment tech-niques, identifying not just three but rather four styles of adult attachment.

Before reading further, pause for a minute to consider your own adult relationship experi-ences. Now, based on your reflections, examine Table 5.2 and read over the different patterns that have been found in people's attitudes toward closeness. Choose the one pattern that best sums up your particular approach to being close. Then we will examine how to interpret your choice.

The four patterns listed in Table 5.2 refer to four patterns of adult attachment style identified by Bartholomew (1990; see also Brehm et al., 2002):

1. *Secure:* Trusting, comfortable with closeness and interdependence

2. *Preoccupied:* Needful of closeness, worried about abandonment

3. *Fearful:* Afraid of rejection, mistrustful, shy

4. *Dismissing:* Self-reliant, independent, uninter-ested in intimacy

Each of these adult *attachment styles* balances people's view of themselves with their view of others. Secure individuals have positive views of both themselves and the trustworthiness of close others. Preoccupied individuals have poor views of themselves but want to be close to others. Fearful persons are unhappy with themselves and do not trust closeness. And dismissing individu-als see themselves as all right, especially if they are untroubled by closeness with others.

Applying attachment lessons. You can apply research on attachment by considering the dynamics of different combinations of attach-ment styles. Suppose that, in one couple, a woman has developed a preoccupied attachment style, whereas her male partner is more dismiss-ing. She seeks his presence, reaching for him and making plans for their time together. But he feels uncomfortable with that much closeness and pulls away so as to feel more independent. As he does so, canceling plans or behaving coolly, the woman feels threatened and needy. She becomes more clingy, hoping for warmth and contact—but he only pulls away that much more. Both are unhappy but perhaps are unable to explain why or what to do about it.

In your life, you can be more practical in identifying what you need and how best to inter-act with others. Identify your feelings about yourself and others and be realistic about how to meet both your own needs and others' complex needs. Begin by being honest in your early interactions and communicating your needs and goals as best you can. If you need reassurance in relationships, say so to your friend or partner; do not expect anyone to read your mind. Listen carefully to what your partner seems to be saying and seeking. How well will you be able to respond to someone who needs reassurance that things are okay between the two of you? The combination or confrontation of your two styles is also important. If one of you needs reassurance and the other does not even feel like making eye contact, both of you will suffer.

Suppose that you started life with an insecure attachment style but that you want to feel and act secure. Is change possible? Learning and unlearning are possible over time, but to alter your patterns you must first know where you stand with regard to relationships, where you want to go, and how to close the gap. This journey begins with self-awareness, so keep in mind that you and everyone else need attachments and that your life experience has taught you a distinctive style in forming them.

The Selection Process

Physical attractiveness is studied extensively because it figures importantly in how people initially *select* each other as friends, dates, and mates. Besides physical attraction, other factors have been studied and found to be equally or more important in determining what people find attractive in each other: *reciprocity,* or liking those who like you (Curtis & Miller, 1986; Muehlenhard & Miller, 1988); *similarity* in attitudes, values, and social and personal characteristics (Botwin, Buss, & Schackelford, 1997; Newcomb, 1961; Tesser et al., 1998); and even *barriers* to closeness such as parental disapproval and obstacles to overcome to be together—experiences that, for some couples, can provoke mutual desire all the more, at least for a while (Brehm & Brehm, 1981b; Driscoll, Davis, & Lipetz, 1972; Pennebaker et al., 1979).

Whatever the mix of factors, most people do find at least some others attractive and then face the next hurdle—establishing real closeness, that is, an interaction or relationship that is

real for both parties and not just a fantasy in the mind of the one who feels attracted to the other. Keeping your attraction to yourself gets you nowhere. Similarly, finding another person appealing to look at, without knowing whether the two of you have important values in common, leaves much yet to be done. You must meet, interact, and assess the desirability of getting closer. This process risks rejection or the possibility of discovering no further attraction because "there is nothing there." How do you begin?

The T-shirt study. Even before the Internet made it possible to "meet" and learn about others in cyberspace by way of anonymous matchmaking websites, people have always relied on other strategies—blind dates, friends' recommendations, personal ads, and so forth. Alan Gross and his colleague, India Fleming, created an ingenious study of the first meeting between prospective dates, combining strategies of two popular sources of information: parties and personal ads (Gross, 1983). Participants were college men and women who first provided personal information about several topics such as their college majors, religions, sports and music preferences, drinking and smoking habits, and personalities. The 200 participants attended a mixer, with each one donning a T-shirt (yellow for women and blue for men) custom-printed with his or her "ad" and an assigned number. For example, a T-shirt might read,

(19)

Alex

Psychology

Squash, Jazz

Sense of Humor

No Smoking, Chardonnay

The goal was for the participants to talk to as many others as possible and to identify possible dates. Each person was to interact with a member of the opposite sex for no more than 5 minutes and then move on. After 1 hour of excited number seeking, participants made final rankings of those others they would most like to date. (They were not prevented from exchanging contact information if they hit it off during their 5-minute meetings.)

Among other findings, Gross (1983) discovered that once these face-to-face interactions had taken place, the selection power of physical appearance waned. Looks had not been used to select prospects; conversations were made easier by the introductions printed on the T-shirts. It was not necessary to notice or track down people who *looked* promising because each shirt's "ad" offered information needed to decide whether to interact. Instead of using looks (which usually represents the first kind of information a person gets about another) as a *filter* for choosing others and forming impressions, participants could consult "labels" as a guide to the "contents" of other persons attending—eerily similar to deciding on preferred brands before visiting a store.

Drawing on these findings, Gross (1983) "envisioned rooms throughout the social world filled with singles sporting descriptive T-shirts or at least lengthy nametags." Two decades later, the Internet now offers widely broadcast matchmaking sites, chat rooms, and other shortcuts to making friends and dates. Most such "meetings," just like face-to-face interactions, occur because similar interests and circumstances bring people together. The protagonists in the 1998 movie *You've Got Mail* first meet in a chat room discussing books without realizing that they both are in the book-selling business—and are archrivals for the same customer base.

General lessons and applications. Selection of dating or mating partners is a process. Conversations do not happen to you; you have to start or join them. However much you long for attachment and however attractive another person may be, you and/or the other person must *do or say* something to establish a connection. After all, the T-shirt study suggested that once you learn to enjoy each other's company, you can overlook the fact that the other person's looks rate somewhat less than a perfect 10.

But even when you feel well matched to the person in whom you are interested—another 6 to your own 6, for example—you may still hesitate to express your interest. Fear of rejection can overwhelm desire. The longer it takes for either person to express interest, the less likely anything will happen at all—an opportunity lost, a road not taken. The "first move" is difficult for both men and women to make, yet each wishes the other would make it (Regan, 2003). For example, Vorauer and Ratner (1996) asked men and women in their study to imagine meeting an attractive person and having a good conversation, after which neither person expresses interest in seeing the other again. How did respondents explain this failure to follow up? Participants generally blamed their own inaction on fear of rejection (an aspect of the situation) but blamed the other person's inaction on lack of interest (an internal influence)—a classic case of attribution bias.

Unfortunately, when you assume that the other person is simply not interested in you (when in fact the other person may be just as afraid of rejection as you are), your silence guarantees the relationship will end before it ever gets started. The lesson? Avoid making assumptions except to infer that the other person's concerns and motivations are a lot like yours. Learn to express interest while still saving face. The next time both you and another person fear rejection, take responsibility yourself and say something.

Conclusion: The Science of Closeness

This section began with the assertion that relationships are so important and useful that most people will endure disappointment and difficulty in their search for intimacy. The social psychological study of relationships is likewise important and useful. We have reviewed the power of social situations in developing personal relationships. It is true that people are different, and these individual differences may lead us to prefer different others and to express ourselves differently.

However, no one is immune to situational influence. As you understand the situational forces that affect your closeness to others, you can act more effectively in beginning and developing your social and personal relationships. Circumstances can throw people together and offer (or deny) opportunities to pursue friendship and passion. Anticipate these influences and work with situations, and you will lead your life instead of being led by it. Will your personal relationships be shaped more by chance or by choice? That may be up to you. If you opt for choice rather than chance, then happy choices are those that are *informed* ones.

Begin by appreciating the value of applied social psychology in your everyday personal life. You will find that the more you understand and apply the evidence on personal relationships, the better and more fulfilling they become. As explored in the next section, the benefits of understanding social psychology extend to your experiences as a student as well.

The Classroom as a Social Psychology Laboratory

Although many social psychology texts examine the application of social psychological knowledge to various arenas of life, such as education, law, health, and the environment, no leading texts come down to a more personal level by systematically addressing two of the arenas that most affect (and perhaps most interest) you: personal relationships and the classroom. The first section of this chapter considered the application of social psychology to personal relationships. This section turns to the classroom, particularly to how students and instructors think about and relate to each other. The neglect of the classroom as a "social psychology laboratory" in social psychology texts seems unusual because the classroom dynamics between student and teacher involve many important social psychology phenomena.

This section delineates several classic social psychological findings and demonstrates how they apply to your classroom experiences and interactions. One thing this section requires of you is to recognize that to understand the dynamics of the classroom, you must take into account two main perspectives: that of the student and that of the instructor (Figure 5.2).

Furthermore, be advised that several of the phenomena that we review can interfere with how effectively you deal with your academic life (as well as your life beyond academia). If being forewarned is being forearmed, the material considered may help you to anticipate these social psychological patterns and, perhaps, to take steps to minimize their negative impact on you. For example, Beaman, Barnes, Klentz, and McQuirk

(1978) found that undergraduate students' rates of helping could be increased by alerting students to the bystander effect, that, as noted in Chapter 1, refers to the finding that a person is less likely to help in an emergency with other bystanders present. Other research evidence likewise has shown that alerting an audience to social psychological phenomena may help them to avoid mistaken judgments. In examining social psychology concepts at work in the classroom, you will find two major categories of phenomena: cognitive errors and self-perceptions.

Cognitive Errors

Cognitive errors are errors that people make in their thought processes. Because of these errors, people make predictable mistakes where interacting with and judging others. This section discusses three common cognitive errors. It is quite likely that you will recognize yourself in some of the descriptions of these errors. If so, do not worry; they are quite common. However, do pay attention to these errors so that you may be in a position to try to minimize them in the future.

Fundamental Attribution Error

Have you ever found yourself wondering why a teacher holds a belief that you think is outlandish? For example, you may have listened to a professor talk about Sigmund Freud and wondered to yourself, "How can an educated person believe that stuff?" If so, you may have been guilty of making the fundamental attribution error, which was first introduced in Chapter 1 and, as a concept of widespread relevance, appears in several other chapters in this book.

Classic study of the fundamental attribution error. Much social psychology research has focused on the **fundamental attribution error,** that is, the tendency people have to focus on personal causes of other people's behavior (i.e., to make internal attributions) and to downplay the influence of situational causes (i.e., to not make external attributions). Thus, to put a different spin on the example provided in Chapter 1, if you walk into class late because you had a flat tire on the way to school, and if your teacher concluded that your tardy behavior was due to

Figure 5.2   Different Perspectives in the Classroom

SOURCE: Photos courtesy of the University of Windsor

the fact that you were a lazy student who had overslept, then your teacher would be guilty of making a fundamental attribution error.

Jones and Harris (1967) conducted a classic study on the fundamental attribution error. They had college students read either pro-Castro or anti-Castro essays dealing with Fidel Castro's rule of Cuba and told the students that the writer either had chosen the position or had been assigned the position (as in a debate). Then the researchers asked the students to infer the attitudes of the writers. The results showed that students made pro- or anti-Castro attributions based solely on the content of the essays. If an essay was pro-Castro, the students assumed that the writer held pro-Castro attitudes *regardless* of whether the writer had chosen the position or the position had been determined by an external situational factor (i.e., being assigned to the writer). Assuming that someone assigned to write an attitudinal essay actually holds that attitude illustrates making a fundamental attribution error.

Attributions based on lectures. Coren (1993) had college students read hypothetical lectures and make attributions about the professors' attitudes and motivations for lecturing on the specific topics. Coren found that students made negative attributions about professors who lectured that genetic factors could explain some racial differences in intelligence quotient (IQ) scores (e.g., that the professor was racist) and that sex differences in cognitive skills could be due to genetic factors (e.g., that the professor was sexist). This evidence supports the notion that students think that faculty members necessarily believe everything they teach. However, consider this situation logically. Teachers have to cover a good deal of material that may very well include some ideas or theories that might be controversial or seem foolish or inappropriate to you. To do an effective job of teaching, faculty members must be evenhanded in their coverage, seeming to give equal weight and emphasis to a diversity of topics and viewpoints. Also, to challange students' thinking, instructors may purposely express controversial ideas that they may not personally agree with (i.e., play the devil's advocate). Thus, to assume that faculty members are proponents of virtually everything they say is to make the fundamental attribution error.

The vignette that opened this chapter noted that Chris committed the fundamental attribution error after first meeting Lee. Chris observed Lee's active class participation and social interactions and attributed them to a self-confident personality. It turns out that Lee's social comfort and academic comfort were not so much direct reflections of personality variables as they were *a function* of the social context. Chris mostly saw Lee greeting old friends, and it is easy to act friendly with longtime friends. Also, the class they took together was on a subject that Lee had studied before and about which Lee felt confident. Chris's early selective observations led to an impression of Lee as someone with great social and academic self-confidence, but this was not an entirely accurate impression.

Overcoming the fundamental attribution error. Is there a "cure" for the fundamental attribution error? Certainly, if people could somehow learn how to guard against a biased mode of viewing others that involves insufficiently recognizing possible situational determinants of their actions, their interpersonal understanding and relations would improve. For help we look to a study by Gilbert, Pelham, and Krull (1988), who had college students watch a silent video of a woman talking with a stranger. The woman exhibited several anxious behaviors such as twirling her hair and biting her fingernails. The experimenter told half of the participants that the woman was discussing an "anxious topic" (e.g., sexual fantasies, secrets) and told the other half that the woman was discussing a "relaxing topic" (e.g., vacations, hobbies).

The participants who believed that the woman was discussing an anxious topic rated her lower on the trait of anxiety than did those who thought that she was discussing a relaxing topic. Thus, participants made the attribution of "anxious person" when they thought that the woman should not be anxious. Those participants who believed that the woman was discussing a sensitive topic apparently attributed her anxiety to the topic (situation) rather than to her personality. Gilbert and colleagues (1988) hypothesized that the fundamental attribution error occurs automatically and that people have to devote cognitive effort to overcome it, for example, by getting additional information or being thoughtful about the situation. That is, the participants had to make extra effort to look past the woman's behavior and take the topic into account. Thus, if you wish to avoid making the fundamental attribution error about people, try to find out more about their situations or try to think of reasons why they might behave the way they do. Teachers should attempt to find out why their students enter class late, fall asleep in class, and do not turn in assignments so as to avoid unfairly drawing negative conclusions about them. Perhaps the undesirable behavior was due to situational factors that were largely or entirely beyond the students' control, for example, the tardiness due to a flat tire, the sleepiness due to holding a night job, and the late assignment due to caring for a sick child. Likewise, students should attempt to discover teachers' motivations for covering class material that seems to indicate a certain set of attitudes. Although a teacher may lecture on Freud or race differences in aptitude test performance, such a lecture does not make the teacher a Freudian or a racist.

Belief Perseverance

Belief perseverance means that people tend to maintain their initial ideas or beliefs despite exposure to disconfirming evidence. They may discredit, ignore, misinterpret, or give the disconfirming information little weight, but the effect is the same in that their ideas or beliefs persist.

Classic study of belief perseverance. Wegner, Coulton, and Wenzlaff (1985) had college students (referred to as "actors") read 25 pairs of suicide notes and guess which one of each pair was genuine. Half of the actors received success feedback (24/25 correct) and half received failure feedback (10/25 correct). While each actor was working, another student observed. Afterward, the actor and observer were informed that the feedback was not genuine; that is, it had been predetermined and did not reflect the actor's actual performance. Then both the actor and the observer were asked to predict how well the actor would perform on an additional 25 trials. Curiously, their predictions were not affected by learning that the feedback was false. Instead, both actors and observers predicted that "successful" actors would perform better than "failure" actors. Their initial beliefs about the actors' ability had persevered and led them to predict future behavior despite the evidence that their initial beliefs had been based on erroneous information. The participants' failure to factor into their predictions the fact that the initial feedback had been predetermined is similar to what happens with the fundamental attribution error in which the role of the situation is downplayed.

Wegner and colleagues (1985) devised an interesting twist to their experiment that produced even more striking evidence of belief perseverance. Using a nearly identical procedure, they informed the actors and observers *beforehand* that the feedback they would receive would be false and not based on the actors' performance. Then the experiment took place as before. When asked to predict the actors' future performance, the observers' predictions still were influenced by the success and failure feedback. Believing that actors had been successful (or unsuccessful) was apparently very difficult to ignore in predicting future performance.

Belief perseverance in the classroom. Unfortunately, belief perseverance also takes place in the classroom. If you have used a word for many years to mean one thing, it may be difficult to learn a different or more specific meaning for it in a class. For example, psychology students often confuse "negative reinforcement" and "punishment" despite having encountered the terms since their first psychology course. Teachers also may be prone to belief perseverance if they expect you to perform or behave in the same fashion that your older brother or sister performed or behaved for those teachers in the past. In an academic example, Prohaska (1994) found that students with medium or low grade point averages (GPAs) were very prone to overestimate their future grades. Thus, despite their poor performance in the past, low-achieving students continued to believe that they would get good grades in the future.

There is substantial literature dealing with popular misconceptions about psychology. Much of the work shows that taking a psychology course does not remove those misconceptions (e.g., Vaughan, 1977). When students have completed a course but still hold the misconceptions with which they entered the course, this problem illustrates belief perseverance. Gardner and Dalsing (1986) administered a 60-item "test of common beliefs" (which were actually incorrect) to more than 500 students taking psychology courses (e.g., "To change people's behavior toward members of ethnic minority groups, we must first change their attitudes"; "In love and friendship, more often than not, opposites attract"). On average, students agreed with more than 20% of the misconceptions. The only significant drop in misconceptions occurred for students who had taken at least six psychology courses. Thus, it appears to take repeated exposure to disconfirming information for students to overcome belief perseverance. As an interesting aside, faculty members from other disciplines are also likely to hold misconceptions about psychology (Gardner & Hund, 1983).

Reducing belief perseverance. By now, you may have recognized that belief perseverance is not necessarily a good thing. In fact, more often than not, it is maladaptive for the individual who steadfastly clings to beliefs in the face of information suggesting that the beliefs may be, or in fact are, wrong. Is it possible to overcome belief perseverance? An experiment by Hirt and Markman (1995) shed some light on how it can be done. Hirt and Markman gave introductory psychology students one of several hypothetical relations (e.g., risky firefighters are more successful than less risky firefighters or the exact opposite) and asked them to generate an explanation for the relationship. Afterward, the experimenters told the participants that the relationship they gave them was bogus; that is, there was no truth to it. Then they asked the participants to decide what the true relation was between risk-taking behavior and firefighting ability. As you would probably predict from the concept of belief perseverance, the participants tended to presume that the true relation was the one they had previously heard and explained. However, with a second group of participants, Hirt and Markman presented one of the same hypothetical relations (e.g., risky firefighters are better) and asked the participants to generate an explanation for it *and* an explanation for any alternative relation (e.g., risky firefighters are *not* better). After these participants learned that the original relation was not true and chose what they believed to be the true relation, they were not as likely to stick with their first impressions. Thus, they showed much lower levels of belief perseverance.

You might wish to guard against belief perseverance when you encounter new ideas or theories in class, both because an open mind better facilitates learning and to prepare for upcoming tests. If so, the results of the research by Hirt and Markman (1995) suggest that you should listen carefully to the professor's account of the new information even though it may conflict with your viewpoint. Then try to think of an explanation as to why that new information is correct and why the old information you believed is incorrect. Hirt and Markman referred to this as adopting a **consider an alternative strategy.** Considering an alternative should reduce the tendency to cling to your former belief. For example, you may cover interpersonal attraction in your social psychology class. Suppose that all your life, you have believed that "opposites attract" because you have heard that phrase so often. However, extensive social psychology research has not supported this notion; David Buss wrote that this tendency for opposites to marry or mate "has never been reliably demonstrated" (Buss, 1985, p. 47). To get rid of this belief and to avoid belief perseverance, you should read the available evidence *and* think about why "opposites attract" could be wrong.

We would not be surprised if your belief still is struggling to persevere, that is, if you still have difficulty in believing that opposites do *not* attract. It is true that someone who is *different* from you in some ways can be especially attractive, but "different" is hardly the same as "opposite." If opposites truly attracted, then rich people would be attracted to poor people and smart people would want dumb partners, but this seldom happens in real life. In the vignette that opened this chapter, it is clear that although Chris and Lee are different in some important ways, they are not opposites. One may be talkative, whereas the other may be a good listener. One may be confident, whereas the other may be a bit shy. But they agree about matters of taste, life values, and goals. Their similarities outweigh their differences. Chris and Lee are not opposites; rather, they are complements.

Social Categorization

Do you ever find yourself in a gripe session with other students complaining about "those professors"? Does it sometimes seem like school turns into mini-battles between students and teachers? Unfortunately, what should be a mutual adventure of learning between two groups interacting in a positive manner sometimes can seem like an adversarial experience.

Classic study of social categorization. According to the principle of **social categorization,** we tend to classify other people into groups on the basis of certain social characteristics (e.g., race, gender, status, occupation). Because of social categorization, as soon as the sorting process begins, we form in-groups and out-groups (discussed in Chapter 1 in the context of how intergroup attitudes form). These groupings, in turn, create an "us versus them" mentality. In a school setting, one logical set of categories is students and teachers. Which group is the in-group and which is the out-group depends on the group to which you belong. From this perspective, if you were at one of the chapter authors' universities, for you we would be the out-group and for us you would be the out-group.

One vivid example of social categorization occurred in a study by Rabbie and Horwitz (1969) in which the researchers simply flipped a coin to divide junior high school participants into two groups. Then they had the participants rate both the groups and the individuals in the groups on eight characteristics (e.g., responsibility, consideration, fearfulness, openness). Rabbie and Horwitz found evidence of **in-group/ out-group bias;** that is, students rated their own group more favorably on the characteristics than they did the other group, and they rated individuals in their group more favorably than they did individuals in the other group. These ratings occurred despite the fact that the participants had been divided into groups by the mere flip of a coin. There is considerable laboratory research and anecdotal evidence of the divisive role of in-group/out-group biases in intergroup relations (e.g., Brewer & Brown, 1998). It is certainly likely that social categorization is pertinent to the relations between faculty members and students.

Another outcome of social categorization is the **out-group homogeneity bias,** which is the tendency to perceive less variability among members of an out-group than among members of the in-group. Thus, when we look at out-groups, we tend to think that all of their members are similar; they act alike and possibly even "look alike." Linville, Fischer, and Salovey (1989) asked undergraduates and people living in a retirement community to rate 100 hypothetical elderly people and 100 hypothetical college students on eight attributes (e.g., friendliness, motivation, interesting, irritability, attractiveness). Each group gave less variable ratings to the other age group than to their own age group, meaning that they saw the out-group members as more similar than the in-group members. Thus, the out-group homogeneity effect could

lead to the similar refrain, "They're all alike." For example, teachers may tend to see fewer differences among students, and students may tend to see fewer differences among faculty members.

Reducing in-group/out-group biases. There is an extensive research literature that addresses how to ameliorate the negative effects of in-group/ out-group biases and other factors relevant to intergroup attitudes and relations (see Chapters 10 and 15). Here we briefly consider the implications of an experiment by Gaertner and colleagues (1999) and the evidence on cooperative learning.

Gaertner and colleagues (1999) had groups of three college students who shared similar political preferences (i.e., Republican or Democrat) work together on a problem-solving task dealing with survival after a plane crash. After a group had completed the task, the experimenters had the group work on a new problem with another group whose members had the opposite political preference. Each of the groups was able to win money for good solutions. Gaertner and colleagues varied the amount of interaction—full interaction or no interaction—the two groups could have as they worked on the new problem. Also, with regard to the monetary reward, some groups had a common fate (both groups won the same amount of money) and some did not have a common fate (each group could win differing amounts of money). After all of the various pairings of groups completed the experiment, Gaertner and colleagues found that interaction was a more important variable than was common fate given that the groups having full interaction performed the best. Thus, for groups composed of different types of people, it is to their benefit to overcome those differences and communicate with each other fully so as to achieve the best outcomes.

In terms of the interaction between students and teachers, the preceding results imply that the parties should focus on interaction and communication in an attempt to overcome their differences in perspective and find common ground to have the best possible class. Cooperative learning between students and faculty members should best achieve this goal. Both parties should understand that they have common goals (e.g., having students do well in the course) and must work toward the same ends (i.e., student learning and achievement). On the other hand, if teachers and students find themselves in an antagonistic "us versus them" situation, the atmosphere of the class will suffer and learning (and satisfaction) will be lower.

Self-Perceptions

In addition to cognitive errors that we make in dealing with other people, social psychological research has shown that we also make certain predictable *errors in thinking* about ourselves. Most of these errors show that we tend to misjudge our motivations or ourselves. Not surprisingly, in many cases we judge ourselves more favorably than we should.

Self-Handicapping

Have you ever found yourself walking into an exam knowing that you studied less than you should have or that you went out with friends instead of studying the night before the exam? Similarly, have you ever begun a competition (athletic or otherwise) for which you know you did not prepare enough? If any of these situations describe you at some point in your life, you may have been guilty of self-handicapping. According to the social psychological concept of **self-handicapping,** people act in ways that may undermine their subsequent performances, thereby having anticipatory excuses for potential failures. In other words, if you studied less than you know you should have, you have a handy excuse in case your grade is lower than you would prefer. Table 5.3 includes items from a self-handicapping scale. A person who tends to engage in self-handicapping would endorse these kinds of items.

Classic study of self-handicapping. Berglas and Jones (1978) conducted the classic study of self-handicapping. The experimenters gave college students analogies to solve, after which all participants were told that they had performed well—although some of the analogies were unsolvable. Before working on a second set of analogies, the students had the choice of taking a performance-enhancing drug or a performance-impairing drug. Men (but not women) who had done well in the unsolvable analogies condition

Table 5.3   Items Indicating Self-Handicapping

1. When I do something wrong, my first impulse is to blame circumstances.

2. I tend to put things off until the last moment.

3. I suppose I feel "under the weather" more often than most people do.

4. I am easily distracted by noises or my own creative thoughts when I try to read.

5. I would do a lot better if I tried harder.

6. I sometimes enjoy being mildly ill for a day or two because it takes off the pressure.

7. Sometimes I get so depressed that even easy tasks become difficult.

SOURCE: Rhodewalt (1990).

chose the drug that would hinder their performance, presumably because they had no confidence that they would continue to perform well (Figure 5.3). According to Hirt, McCrea, and Kimble (2000), subsequent research has shown that men (but not women) tend to self-handicap through strategies that will actually hamper their performance (e.g., by failing to practice or study). On the other hand, the research shows that both men and women tend to claim excuses ahead of time; for instance, prior to the time of performance, they may point to potentially debilitating stress or physical illness. Relatedly, Mello-Goldner and Jackson (1999) discovered that female college students who reported premenstrual syndrome (PMS) symptoms scored higher on a self-handicapping measure than did those who did not report such symptoms.

Self-handicapping and academics. There is ample research evidence that self-handicapping takes place in academic settings. Beck, Koons, and Milgrim (2000) administered self-report measures of self-handicapping (as illustrated in Table 5.3) and procrastination to more than 400 college students and found that self-handicapping and procrastination were positively correlated. They also found that self-handicappers (i.e., those who scored high on the self-handicapping measure) not only began studying for tests later than non-self-handicappers but also earned lower grades. Similarly, Zuckerman, Kieffer, and Knee (1998) found that, among college students, higher self-handicapping scores correlated with lower GPAs, less time spent on academic work, and less efficient exam preparation. Sikorski and colleagues (2002) found that roughly 20% of students at two universities admitted to not buying a textbook for an introductory college course, whereas nearly 80% reported either not reading or reading only sparingly a text they had bought for an introductory course. Clearly, self-handicapping can be a problem for college students.

Why might students self-handicap regarding classes and exams? To answer this question, consider the consequences of *not* self-handicapping. Suppose that a student prepares as well as he or she can for an exam and then fails the exam (or earns a grade that is below expectations). How can this student explain this outcome? Having studied hard, a logical and disturbing answer goes something like "I'm stupid" or "I'm not smart enough to handle that kind of exam." On the other hand, if the student waits until the night before the exam to begin studying or goes out for pizza instead of studying, he or she has a ready-made excuse for not doing well on the exam. In other words, self-handicapping prevents a blow to the student's self-image. In some cases, faculty members might also try to protect their self-images. You might be surprised to know that many faculty members would admit that they have waited until the last minute to begin working on an important paper or grant application. Perhaps some are motivated by the ego-protective function of self-handicapping.

Reducing self-handicapping. Clearly, not everyone is a self-handicapper, although we imagine that most people can recall at least one or two times when what they did (actually, what they did not do) might fit the meaning of the term. The problem, of course, is that whereas self-handicapping might protect one's self-image on a particular occasion, it clearly undermines the possibility of performing at an optimal level on that occasion. Moreover, people should recognize that self-handicapping is self-defeating in the long run. Also, other people might not respond to self-handicapping in a positive manner. For

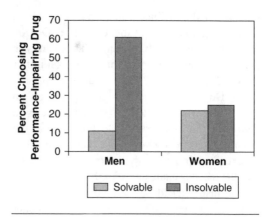

Figure 5.3   Results Indicating That Men (but not women) Self-Handicapped (chose a performance-impairing drug) on Very Hard Tasks

SOURCE: Results from Berglas and Jones (1978).

example, Rhodewalt, Sanbonmatsu, Tschanz, Feick, and Waller (1995) asked college students to evaluate a hypothetical coworker who gave one of three excuses for performing poorly on a task. The students consistently evaluated persons making self-handicapping excuses lower on ability, on actual performance, and on 20 different personality traits (e.g., friendly, pleasant, egotistic). Thus, if you do tend to self-handicap and give excuses for your poor performance in hopes of getting other people to "cut you some slack" in their evaluations of you, that type of behavior may boomerang on you. Instead of creating more positive evaluations of you, you may actually be creating more negative evaluations.

Is there anything that might lessen self-handicapping? It is important to recognize the short- and long-term self-defeating aspects of self-handicapping. Even the short-term protection of one's self-image is soundly offset by the long-term havoc brought on by repeated underperformance experiences. Therefore, people with self-handicapping tendencies would be better off devoting their energies to preparing for major events than to making excuses ahead of time for potential poor performances.

Self-Serving Bias

It may be expected that, from time to time, you will receive an exam grade that is lower than you had anticipated. In such a case, whom do you tend to blame for the low grade? Do you own up to not studying enough, or do you perhaps blame the teacher for making an unfair or too difficult exam? Here is a different scenario. Do you ever get a higher grade on an exam than you expected? If so, whom do you credit for the high grade? Do you decide that you must have really known the material and did an excellent job of studying, or do you decide that the teacher made an exam that was too easy or you just "lucked out"? If you are like most people, you are more likely to blame the teacher for the low grade but take personal credit for the high grade. This pattern of explanation for good and bad performances exemplifies the self-serving bias.

Classic study of the self-serving bias. According to the principle of the **self-serving bias,** we have a tendency to attribute our positive outcomes to internal causes (e.g., our traits or characteristics) but to attribute our negative outcomes to external causes (e.g., chance, difficulty of a task). Thus, we are likely to take credit for our successes but blame others or circumstances for our shortcomings. For example, in an experiment by Streufert and Streufert (1969), pairs of undergraduate students played a tactical economics game against what they thought was another team. The other team was actually a computer that was used to provide standardized success or failure feedback regarding game performance. After playing the game, participants rated how much of their performance was due to their team or to the other team. Streufert and Streufert found that participants who had been informed that they succeeded at the game gave the lion's share of the credit to their team. Participants who had been informed that they failed, however, tended to say that the other team was responsible for the outcome, thereby deflecting the blame for poor play (Figure 5.4).

Self-serving attributions in academics. In two studies, McAllister (1996) looked for evidence of the self-serving bias in the academic arena. First, in a laboratory experiment, he paired introductory psychology students and had them engage in a teacher–learner interaction about

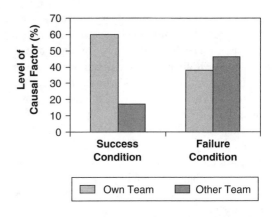

Figure 5.4   Results Indicating That Participants Tend to See Their Own Team as Responsible for Its Success But Tend to See the Other Team as Responsible for Its Failure

SOURCE: Results from Streufert and Streufert (1969).

reading an article in a psychology journal. In each student pair, one student was assigned the role of the teacher and the other was assigned the role of the learner. The learners received false feedback of either failure (50% correct) or success (90% correct). In their attributions for their performance, learners took credit for their performance in the success condition and blamed the teachers in the failure condition. In the follow-up study, McAllister asked students to think about the most recent courses in which they had received an A and an F (or their best and worst grades) and to make attributions for their performance. The results were virtually identical to those of the laboratory experiment in that students believed they had deserved (earned) the high grade but believed that the instructor was the cause of the low grade.

In the same two studies, McAllister (1996) also examined the teachers' perceptions. In the laboratory study, the students who served as the teacher in the success conditions believed that they had played a large role in the student learners' success. However, those who were in the failure condition believed that the student learners were more responsible for their poor performance. In the second study, McAllister asked actual college faculty members to think of the most recent courses in which they had graded students as receiving an A or an F and to make attributions for those grades. Again, the reversal was present such that instructors believed that they played a large role in students' successes but that the students were to blame for their failures.

Adaptive nature of the self-serving bias. Just as with self-handicapping, the self-serving bias can be an adaptive mechanism in terms of guarding one's self-image. If we take credit for our successes but explain away our failures, our self-esteem is left intact. In fact, our self-esteem probably becomes somewhat inflated. Research on the **depressive realism** phenomenon has shown that depressed people are actually more accurate than nondepressed people at assessing their abilities and self-images (Taylor, 1989). This research implies that most of us are viewing our lives through rose-colored glasses—believing that we are better than we actually are. Thus, it is a simple matter for faculty members to believe that they are excellent teachers but that their students should work harder. By the same token, students tend to think that they are smart and hard-working but that faculty members could teach better or be more fair in their grading.

Overjustification Effect

Have you ever wondered why your teachers seem so excited about classroom material that you *have* to absorb for the course but find boring? Have you ever read a textbook and thought, "This might be a good book if I didn't *have* to read it"? Or, have you ever been aware that people were raving about a certain book or movie, but when you read or watched it as a course requirement, you thought it was a drag? If you have ever had these kinds of experience, you have experienced the overjustification effect.

According to the **overjustification effect,** if people see an external reason (e.g., reward or punishment) for their behavior, they may view the behavior as controlled by the external reason (i.e., the reward or punishment) rather than see it as intrinsically appealing (i.e., something they just like to do). Thus, it is possible that students, by virtue of *having* to learn about psychology for a course, might find the content of psychology

less enjoyable than if they learned about it on their own.

Classic studies of the overjustification effect. Lepper, Greene, and Nisbett (1973) conducted an often-cited experiment of the overjustification effect. They matched preschool children on their interest in drawing and divided them into three groups. All children had the opportunity to draw pictures with markers. One third of the children were shown an award they could win by drawing good pictures, one third were given an unanticipated award after drawing a picture, and the other third got no award. Judges, who were unaware of the three conditions, rated the children's pictures for quality. Lepper and colleagues found that the children drawing to win an award somewhat counterintuitively drew lower quality pictures. In a follow-up session 1 to 2 weeks later, the experimenters observed the children during free-play time (drawing with markers was one of the free-play choices). Children who had originally drawn pictures to win awards spent less time drawing during this subsequent period. Thus, rewarding the children for something they already enjoyed doing produced lower quality output and undermined subsequent motivation to perform the task.

Deci (1971) found similar results in an experiment where undergraduates first solved puzzles. Then some, but not all, of the students were paid to solve puzzles. Finally, all students returned to the baseline condition. In this condition, the students worked longer on the puzzles if they had not been paid to solve puzzles. Are faculty members any different? Perhaps not. A few years ago, faculty members at the former college of one of the chapter authors formed a voluntary reading group. The group met once a month to discuss a book of mutual interest. Each month, the leader of the group would bring the next month's book to pass around, presumably to pique the members' interest and curiosity. Within a matter of a few months, the group members acted just like the examples at the beginning of this section, where *having* to engage in an activity required for a course seemed to sabotage student interest in the activity. They quickly examined each book to see how large or small the print was and to find out how many pages it had, complaining if the print was too small or the book was too long. *Having to read made it less fun.*

Unfortunately, parents appear to be unaware of the overjustification effect. Boggiano, Barrett, Weiher, McClelland, and Lusk (1987) had parents read scenarios in which elementary school children showed either high interest or low interest in academic activities. Then the parents rated several social control techniques as to how good they would be to maintain the children's enjoyment or interest in an activity. The parents did not differentiate between high- and low-interest scenarios; in either case, they opted for the use of reward as the control technique of choice. The research on overjustification clearly indicates that reward would be a bad choice for children who already have high interest in academics.

Immunization against overjustification. There is hope, however, for mitigating the overjustification effect. Hennessey and Zbikowski (1993) attempted to immunize fourth-grade children against the effect by showing them videotapes of target children discussing their work at school. The target children said that getting rewards was nice but that the real reason they did their schoolwork was because of how much they enjoyed it. A day later, the children and a control group, whose members had not seen the videotapes, took part in an apparently unrelated study. A researcher asked the children to make up a story to accompany a picture book with no words (a measure of creativity). Half of the children from the treatment group and the control group were offered a reward and half were not. The children who had watched the videotapes of the target children showed higher creativity scores than did those in the control group. The control group children who had been offered a reward produced the least creative stories, demonstrating the overjustification effect. Therefore, it appears that focusing on intrinsic motivation may reduce or eliminate the overjustification effect.

What should people do to avoid the overjustification effect? As an example, let us consider individuals who may have suffered a decline in enthusiasm for the content of the courses they are taking. First, they should remind themselves why they have chosen to go to college. Presumably, they are in college because they are interested in learning new information. If they behave like they did when they were children—full of curiosity about the world—they should be able to avoid the negative effects of overjustification. On the other hand, *if they find themselves working for grades rather than knowledge, overjustification becomes more likely.* Along the same lines, if you are studying psychology because it interests you, remind yourself of that intrinsic interest when the going gets tough. Focusing on your internal reasons for studying and learning will help you to avoid focusing on the external factors that could lead to the overjustification effect.

Conclusion: Social Psychology in the Classroom

The interaction patterns that take place in the classroom show predictable social psychology phenomena. This section has spotlighted several of those phenomena, and no doubt there are others. As a psychology student, you are well qualified to notice the occurrence of these phenomena and understand them. Coping more successfully with one's classroom experiences may be easier as a result of knowing the social psychological processes at work in the classroom.

EPILOGUE

We hope that spotlighting the role of social psychology in close relationships and in the classroom has been instructive. Actually, this chapter has barely scratched the surface regarding the relevance of social psychology to your life. We challenge you to be on the lookout for other aspects of your life that social psychology touches. We predict that you should find many such applications (i.e., personal interventions) and that seeing them may make many aspects of your life more understandable and subject to your control. Enjoy your search for social psychology all around you.

Summary

This chapter has dealt with two important topics to most college students: personal relationships and the classroom environment. Although the topics are complex, we believe that social psychology provides some valuable insights into them.

Personal relationships are affected by several major factors. The desire or need to be close to others varies between people; you may express this need differently from other people you know or with whom you interact. Being attracted to another person is a function of several factors, including proximity (we are more attracted to people who are near us), familiarity (we are more attracted to familiar people), and physical attractiveness (we tend to be attracted to physically attractive people, although we are more likely to look for a long-term partner who is equal to us in physical attractiveness). Some researchers have found evidence that personal relationships are affected by events during childhood. The type of attachment patterns we have as children with our caregivers seems to affect the relationships we form as adults. In light of these many factors that affect relationships, people must still act on their attractions. That is, to select a partner, a person must meet, interact, and assess the likelihood of establishing a relationship with the person.

Social psychology plays important roles in the classroom in terms of cognitive errors and self-perceptions. The chapter considers three basic cognitive errors: fundamental attribution, belief perseverance, and social categorization. When making the fundamental attribution error, students may assume that faculty members are proponents for all of the positions they present in the classroom. The error of belief perseverance may lead students to continue to hold beliefs that have been shown to be incorrect in a class. Social categorization makes it likely that students and faculty members will see each other as opposing groups (us vs. them) rather than as cooperating teammates in the educational venture. There are also three problematic self-perceptions: self-handicapping, self-serving bias, and the overjustification effect. Students may self-handicap by giving less effort in a class so as to have an excuse for a less than stellar performance. Self-serving bias can occur when students take credit for good performance but blame faculty members for poor performance. The overjustification effect predicts that because students *have* to read or study class material, they will tend to like it less than if they simply chose to learn about it.

6

Applying Social Psychology to Clinical and Counseling Psychology

Kenneth E. Hart

David M. Ledgerwood

A few years ago, one of the chapter authors (K. H.) had a troubled student in a class he taught on personality and adjustment. Halfway through the semester, Deena (not her real name) began to pay visits to K. H. during his office hours. Deena was a single, attractive, 20-year-old woman who had moved out of her parents' home to attend college in another city 2 years earlier. She was anxious, lonely, and depressed, and her schoolwork was suffering because she had difficulty in motivating herself to study. When she did sit down to study, she could not keep her mind focused enough to concentrate. As a result, her schoolwork had been piling up and she said that she felt "snowed under" by a mountain of backlogged homework.

Deena disclosed to K. H. that in high school she was an average student who had difficulty in making and keeping close friends. She also was sad because she had never had a long-term romantic relationship. During her 2 years at college, she had not made any new friends, and during her first 1½ years away from home, she had been on a total of only three dates with two different men. She said her "boring personality" was the reason why these men never called her back. Because no one had asked her out for more than half a year, she felt rejected, blue, and despondent. She was very pessimistic about her future chances at romance. She described her mother as domineering and perfectionistic. Deena said that she could never please her mom.

In terms of personality, Deena described herself as a loner. Her only hobby was playing online video games on her computer, and she said that she was losing interest in this. When she went to see the latest movies, she often went alone, and when she ate lunch at the school cafeteria, she usually sat in the corner at the table by herself while reading a newspaper. She commented with envy and sadness in her voice on the public use of cell phones by others, saying, "A cell phone for me would be a waste because I don't have anything to say and I don't have anyone to talk to." She added, "Who would want to talk to me anyway?" Her self-esteem was obviously very low. Deena also paid very close attention when she saw people who seemed to be enjoying life and having fun. Once she commented on how much other people smiled and showed their teeth. She said, "I could have rotten teeth and no one would know because I never smile. There's nothing to smile about."

Deena was extremely concerned about how she appeared to other people. She worried obsessively that others might not like her. She dressed herself impeccably in the latest fashions and wore a lot of accessories. She also liked to wear perfume and makeup. Most of the money from her part-time job as a checkout clerk at the local supermarket went to pay for things that could help to make her look good in the eyes of others. Examples included her fitness club membership, clothing, and hair care and personal grooming.

During the spring semester of her sophomore year, Deena struck up an acquaintanceship with a man she had met in the library. Eventually, he asked her out for dinner and a movie. Before they went on their date, K. H. had the occasion to speak with Deena. She was an emotional wreck and was seriously considering canceling the date. In anticipating the dinner and movie, she exclaimed with muted enthusiasm, "He's so perfect. I've never liked anyone this much before!" But then a minute later, with a worried frown on her face, she also said, "I don't think I'll have much to say that's worthwhile. He'll think I'm boring." It was quite clear to K. H. that Deena was feeling overwrought with anxious anticipation. At the same time, she was also feeling pessimistic and discouraged enough to consider calling the fellow to cancel their date. She thought that she should be happy, and it bothered her that she was so anxious and sad.

As you read through this chapter, keep Deena's case in mind and try to answer the following questions:

- How might social psychological theory be useful in understanding Deena's emotional difficulties?

- Can social psychological theory and research be useful in helping Deena's anxiety and depression?
- In trying to diagnose Deena's problems, what potential biases should one (e.g., K. H.) guard against?

Of what relevance is behavioral science to a distressed person such as Deena? It is hoped that after reading this chapter, you will be able to apply social psychological theory and research findings to understanding why people such as Deena suffer from emotional distress. If you were a practicing psychotherapist who had Deena as a client, you could potentially use your understanding of social psychological theory and research to guide your choice of intervention strategies and avoid making mistakes during the process of diagnostic assessment.

So, why was Deena in so much emotional pain, and what could be done to help her? Biomedical scientists have identified a number of factors as important in the cause and cure of emotional and behavioral problems. Genetic factors and factors related to abnormal brain chemistry obviously play important roles, but these factors alone do not give the whole picture. Behavioral researchers have provided a more comprehensive view of human suffering by identifying psychosocial causes and psychosocial treatments. Social psychologists are among the mental health professionals who have taken a lead role in uncovering factors that may influence the onset and resolution of emotional and behavioral disorders.

The goal of this chapter is to demonstrate the relevance of social psychology to understanding, diagnosing, and helping people such as Deena. In particular, the chapter describes some of the theoretical and practical breakthroughs that have elevated social psychology to a place of prominence in behavioral science efforts to improve our ability to understand psychological disorders. The chapter focuses in particular on two of these disorders: depression and anxiety. Because improved understanding of how and why people become depressed and anxious has implications for intervention and therapy, this chapter also demonstrates how social psychology has contributed to advances within the fields of clinical and counseling psychology.

Metaphorically, social psychologists who study the onset and resolution of depression and anxiety have helped to build an intellectual bridge between social psychology and the subdisciplines of abnormal psychology and clinical psychology. The abbreviated term given to this three-pronged bridge is the **social–clinical interface** (Leary & Miller, 1986). Although this chapter focuses mainly on depression and anxiety, it should be noted that the social–clinical interface involves efforts to understand, diagnose, and modify a broad spectrum of other types of psychological problems, including those that involve jealousy, anger, shame, guilt, embarrassment, regret, and remorse. Moreover, a large number of social psychological principles have been applied to these problems. These include many of the better known theories of self (e.g., self-efficacy, self-esteem, self-presentation, self-awareness, self-concept, self-handicapping) as well as social psychological models based on attribution theory, expectancy theory, social comparison theory, cognitive dissonance theory, learned helplessness theory, and social support theory.

This comprehensive body of work is described in a book titled *The Social Psychology of Emotional and Behavioral Problems: Interfaces of Social and Clinical Psychology* (Kowalski & Leary, 1999). Kowalski and Leary defined the interface as consisting of issues of mutual concern to the discipline and profession of psychology that have caused social and clinical/ abnormal psychology to converge and commingle. These issues of common concern have been categorized as falling into one of three *subdomains* known as (a) the social–dysgenic domain, (b) the social–diagnostic domain, and (c) the social–therapeutic domain.

The **social–dysgenic subdomain** addresses the social and psychological factors that contribute to the onset or maintenance of emotional and behavioral problems. For example, in Deena's case, she appears to have had a perfectionistic and overcontrolling mother who may have caused her to become insecure, shy, and lacking in assertiveness and social skills. Within the social–dysgenic subdomain (*dysgenic* means origins of abnormality), several social psychological models have been developed to understand why psychological disorders arise. Indeed, a wide variety of disorders have been studied, with depression and anxiety being perhaps the best understood. In this chapter, each of these two disorders is examined from the point of view of a particular social psychological perspective.

The **social–therapeutic subdomain** involves social and psychological processes that influence the treatment (and prevention) of psychological problems. Interface researchers who study within this domain attempt to answer questions about how and why people change as a result of counseling and psychotherapy. In addition to studying the processes of therapeutic change, work in the social–therapeutic domain involves testing new interventions, many of which are grounded in social psychological principles. This chapter examines the relevance of two different social psychological models in the treatment of anxiety and depression.

Finally, the **social–diagnostic subdomain** involves studying the social and psychological processes that might cause therapists to be less than 100% objective in how they assess and diagnose their clients' emotional and behavioral disorders. Social psychologists who work in this area study factors that might bias the process of identifying the nature of a client's difficulty. They also study the impact of giving a diagnostic label to a client on the client's welfare. This chapter presents examples of theory and research that have identified the stigmatizing impact of giving a client a psychiatric diagnosis. It also describes research that seeks to understand and prevent potential errors that mental health professionals sometimes make based on faulty ways of thinking and of questioning clients.

After reading this chapter, you should be able to answer the following four questions:

- Why do people become so anxious and depressed?
- Of what value are social psychological theories in helping to better understand, diagnose, and treat people with problems such as depression and social anxiety?
- What can we do to help alleviate or prevent this suffering?
- What errors and biases should clinical and counseling psychologists guard against when diagnosing clients as having a disorder worthy of treatment, and how are such errors and biases prevented?

THE SOCIAL–DYSGENIC SUBDOMAIN

"I probably sound stupid." "What do they think of me?" "I feel so inadequate around these people." Have these or similar thoughts ever popped into your head in social situations with new acquaintances? If you are like most people, these types of thought will enter your mind from time to time. For people such as Deena, they occur with a very high frequency and tend to be quite bothersome, causing extreme upset and intense feelings of distress. Technically, we call this type of distress **social anxiety.** Well-known signs of social anxiety include feeling tense and uptight or prone to embarrassment when interacting with acquaintances, blushing during conversations with strangers, feeling dread about having to speak to others whom one does not know well, feeling apprehensive about meeting new people, and avoiding social gatherings (Figure 6.1).

Anxiety associated with interpersonal interaction can be so overwhelming as to cause some people to act in an unnaturally awkward, inhibited, and "stiff" fashion. This apparent aloofness stimulates others to draw pejorative inferences about friendliness, self-confidence, and poise. For some people (e.g., Deena), anticipatory dread can also be so debilitating as to cause them to shy away from entering social situations in the first place. If socially avoidant behavior becomes habitual, it can gradually cause a person to become more and more detached and isolated from others. The resulting alienation, in turn, is experienced as loneliness and depressive-type symptoms.

Loneliness is defined as the sad yearning for intimacy that results from deficiencies in the number and quality of friendships. There are two types of loneliness: social and emotional. The intensity of **social loneliness** is related to the degree of discrepancy between one's desired number of friends and one's actual number of friends. How much **emotional loneliness** one feels is determined by the discrepancy between one's desired level of intimacy and one's actual level of intimacy. Loneliness can sometimes be a stepping-stone to depression, which is a more serious emotional disorder. Well-known signs of depression include feeling tired and worn out, feeling overwhelmed by struggling with daily life, feeling unable to cope, experiencing thoughts about worthlessness and not playing a useful role in life, having a lack of interest in otherwise pleasurable activities (e.g., eating, sex), feeling sad and blue, and having so little

Figure 6.1   Speaking in Front of a Group of People, a Situation That Is Debilitating for Someone With High Social Anxiety

SOURCE: Photo courtesy of the University of Windsor

energy that even the easiest task seems too difficult.

Think back to Deena in the opening vignette. Try to identify how many of the telltale signs of depression she has. Also, try to assess whether or not she has most of the signs of social anxiety. Although Deena is certainly distressed and has several symptoms indicating possible depression and social anxiety, there is insufficient information to give a formal diagnosis of *clinical depression* or *social anxiety disorder* (you would have to be a trained psychotherapist and perform a formal diagnostic interview to give her these psychiatric labels). Despite an absence of an official diagnostic label, we think that it is safe to assume Deena is so distressed that she could benefit from counseling.

But how did Deena come to feel so distressed? We encourage you to try to unravel the causal chain of determinants. As you read along, this section describes social psychological theories of symptom onset. You are invited to consider how they might apply to Deena's case. These theories seek to provide conceptual frameworks for understanding the role that psychological and social processes play in rendering

people vulnerable to becoming depressed and anxious. In particular, this section discusses *cognitive–social risk factors*.

The Social Psychological Roots of Social Anxiety

Generally speaking, symptoms of social anxiety fall along a graded continuum of unpleasant emotions that are experienced by susceptible people when interacting with others. As such, social anxiety is a type of emotional distress that can vary in intensity. Feelings of nervousness tend to be especially pronounced in social settings where others are not well known. People at the highest end of the distress continuum are sometimes diagnosed as suffering from a debilitating impairment known as either social phobia or social anxiety disorder. The most extreme form of the condition is serious enough to merit professional intervention. People with full-blown social phobia have a pervasive, self-defeating, and debilitating fear of interpersonal situations. They feel an exaggerated sense of social inadequacy and dread severe embarrassment. According to the fourth edition of the

American Psychiatric Association's (1994) *Diagnostic and Statistical Manual of Mental Disorders* (DSM-IV), **social phobia** (i.e., **social anxiety disorder**) is defined as "a marked and persistent fear of one or more social or performance situations in which the person is exposed to unfamiliar people or possible scrutiny by others. The individual fears that he or she will act in a way (or show anxiety symptoms) that will be humiliating or embarrassing" (p. 416).

If you were a social psychologist and you were asked to offer an explanation to account for why some people are more prone to debilitating levels of social anxiety than are others, what would you say? Take a moment now to anticipate what social psychologists have suggested. Identifying specific cognitive–social culprits involved in the onset and perpetuation of symptoms of social anxiety is important because their identification improves our theoretical understanding of how symptoms develop. Furthermore, a good theoretical understanding has practical value because it provides practitioners with a blueprint for developing treatments that work to reduce anxiety in people who are already suffering. Having a blueprint can also lead to preventive interventions aimed at inoculating nonanxious people against developing the disorder.

Self-presentation theory. Leary and Kowalski (1995) developed a broad social psychological blueprint for social anxiety that sheds light on its origin, maintenance, and treatment. In other words, the theory is useful because it not only explains the psychological chain of events leading up to anxiety but also describes how symptoms of social anxiety might be reduced (and prevented). Leary and Kowalski's **self-presentation theory** (SPT) emerged from a cognitive–social framework that was applied to understanding clinical samples of socially anxious people. This framework assumes that individuals attempt to manage or control the impressions that others form of them. According to SPT, other people's impressions of us are important because their impressions influence whether they behave in ways that reward us or punish us. Moreover, how we behave toward others influences, to a certain extent, how they behave toward us. SPT maintains that people

can get others to treat them as they wish by paying close attention to the impressions they communicate to others and by intentionally altering these impressions for strategic impact.

Furthermore, according to Leary and Kowalski (1995), a person becomes prone to experience a fearful response in social circumstances when two conditions are present: high self-presentational motivation and low self-efficacy. **Self-presentational motivation** refers to the degree to which people are concerned with how others perceive them. Obviously, some people are more concerned than others. When self-presentational motivation is high, people are very concerned with ensuring that others have a particular image of them. In contrast, people who have low self-presentational motivation do not care as much. But why should people care what others think of them? In the opening vignette, why did Deena care? According to SPT, a person becomes motivated to communicate a particular impression to others in proportion to how much the person has at stake. If you are an employee, for example, you might be anxiously concerned about your supervisor's opinion of you because you know that your chances of promotion or for a pay raise depend, in part, on whether you are seen as competent and reliable. In Deena's case, she may have felt that the man she met in the library could turn out to be the "Mr. Right" she was yearning to find. Desperation often creates motivation.

Self-presentational theory maintains that people who are most vulnerable to developing social anxiety are those who are most strongly motivated to convey a particular impression to others. However, this is a "double-barreled" theory. For high self-presentational motivation to create high anxiety, a second process must also be in operation. Specifically, a person must also doubt his or her ability to successfully make the desired impression. Emotionally speaking, then, the "lethal combination" is wanting to impress others, on the one hand, but feeling unable to do so, on the other.

Social self-efficacy is defined as a person's level of *confidence* in his or her ability to convey a particular image to another person. Someone with low social self-efficacy has little confidence in his or her ability to influence the perceptions of others. A person with high social self-efficacy will possess a sense of certainty and confidence. If a person strongly doubts his or her ability to communicate a particular image (e.g., interesting, sexy, trustworthy, talented, reliable, loyal, competent), this person's social self-efficacy is said to be low. In this situation, if the doubting person's self-presentational motivation also happens to be high, SPT predicts that the combination will produce high levels of social anxiety.

To summarize, according to SPT, a person experiences social anxiety only if two cognitive–social conditions are present simultaneously, namely, that the person must (a) really want to make a particular impression and (b) doubt his or her ability to succeed. These two conditions, however, do not produce social anxiety directly; they produce it only indirectly. What this means is that the first two conditions produce a third condition in the chain of causal antecedent. According to SPT, it is this third condition that directly causes symptoms of social anxiety. This third condition is called negative outcome expectancies. Negative outcome expectancies are said to mediate the association of motivation and self-efficacy to anxiety. In other words, expectancies explain how and why motivation and self-efficacy work to produce fear. People with high self-presentational motivation who also have low social self-efficacy are assumed to respond with fear because they have pessimistic (negative) expectancies about their future well-being. According to SPT, the fearful person's gut feeling of dread is directly caused by expectations that bad things are likely to happen because the person has failed to convey a certain impression. Thus, **negative outcome expectancies** are defined as anticipated aversive repercussions that are contingent on creating an undesirable impression. These repercussions or consequences can involve either not receiving a consequence that is desirable or receiving a consequence that is undesirable. People can fear the future for both reasons.

In the case of social anxiety disorder, the content (or focus) of the negative outcome expectancy often involves being convinced that one will be humiliated or embarrassed in public and that this will result in irrevocable social rejection or other types of horrific aversive consequences. **Anticipatory embarrassment** is the name of the emotion resulting from expecting short-term harm to one's social reputation. Social psychologist June Tangney and her colleagues found that anticipatory embarrassment is common among people who are socially anxious (Tangney, Miller, Flicker & Barlow, 1996). Because embarrassment is defined contextually as an emotional reaction to a particular interpersonal situation, it is more of a *state* variable, meaning that it is a temporary condition caused by the situation.

Think back to Deena again. If you were a professional counselor who subscribed to SPT, how would you judge Deena's level of social self-efficacy? What about the strength of her self-presentational motivation? Try to determine whether the cognitive–social conditions would be conducive to the development of negative outcome expectancies and social anxiety. Do you think that knowing why Deena feels anxious might be useful in helping her to relax? As you continue to read on, see whether you can apply the cognitive–social concepts therapeutically to help ease Deena's emotional suffering.

 ## CULTURE CAPSULE: PUBLIC SHAME IN JAPAN

Cross-cultural differences in the prevalence of social anxiety disorders may be systematically related to variation along the sociocultural dimension known as **individualism–collectivism** (emphasized in several other chapters in this book, e.g., chapters 5 and 11), that is, the degree to which a culture encourages its members to define their personal identities as independent of others (individualism) or as interdependent and connected to others (collectivism) (Kleinknecht, Dinnel, Kleinknecht, Hiruma, & Harada, 1997). Relative to countries in the West such as the United States, Canada, and the United Kingdom, people's identities (i.e., how they define the self) in areas of the world such as East Asia, Africa, Central America, and South America tend to be interlinked with and dependent on relationships with others. For example, a typical Japanese woman might see her "self" as more connected and interwoven into the social fabric of her family and community than would a typical American woman, who might see herself as more self-sufficient and autonomous.

The East–West differentiation in the foundational underpinnings of the self-concept has implications for understanding social anxiety in a cross-cultural context. In the West, embarrassment and humiliation tend to occur in response to threats to a person's individual self. Also, negative outcome expectancies in the West tend to occur in response to threats to one's own self-interests. In more collectivistic cultures, however, a person may be more likely to feel embarrassed and humiliated for other people. Similarly, as a result of sharing a common identity with others, a person in a collectivistic society may experience more negative outcome expectancies when the welfare of others is in jeopardy. For these reasons, social anxiety may be experienced more often and more intensely in collectivistic countries such as those in the Far East.

Taijin kyofusho is a form of social anxiety that is especially prevalent in Japan and other collectivistic cultures. Some authors have gone so far as to suggest that this type of social anxiety does not even exist in Western cultures. **Taijin kyofusho** has been described as a pathological obsession involving a fear of being embarrassed and shamed in public. It has also been described as an intense morbid fear of offending others by a number of means. These means include blushing in public, displaying improper facial expressions, displaying a visible blemish or physical deformity, and even emitting offensive odors or making improper eye contact (Dinnel, Kleinknecht, & Tanaka-Matsumi, 2002).

As you read the following subsection, compare and contrast the definition of taijin kyofusho with the definition of social anxiety disorder provided by the American Psychiatric Association (1994). Although the Eastern and Western forms of social anxiety are different in certain regards, you will also notice that they share much in common. Continue reading to discover the relevance of social psychological theory to understanding the causes of taijin kyofusho. As described in what follows, self-presentation theory would suggest that high levels of interdependence are likely to cause people to acquire a strong need for social approval. This, in turn, could contribute to symptoms of social anxiety through the influence of high levels of self-presentational motivation.

Tying the research to self-presentation theory. Research results support Leary and Kowalski's (1995) two-factor explanation for how symptoms of social anxiety develop. For example, the scientific literature has reported significant inverse relationships linking social self-efficacy to social anxiety. As expected, this research has found evidence that low self-efficacy is associated with high anxiety, whereas high self-efficacy is associated with low anxiety. This association seems to have *external validity* (i.e., generalizability) because it has been found in "normal" adults (Leary & Atherton, 1986), clinically distressed treatment-seeking adults (Gaudiano & Herbert, 2003; Rosser, Issakidis, & Peters, 2003), and normal adolescents (Muris, 2002).

Other studies have also provided support for the *motivational* aspect of SPT. For example, research has found overreliance on others to be positively associated with social anxiety symptoms (Davila & Beck, 2002). Other support comes from negative expectancy research with clinical samples of persons classified as suffering from social anxiety disorder who overestimate the cost ("harmfulness") of negative interpersonal interactions (Foa, Franklin, Perry, & Herbert, 1996). These results, together with a host of similar findings reported by other authors, suggest that anxious-prone individuals tend to (unrealistically) anticipate that catastrophe will follow from minor social blunders. In the context of clinical models of psychotherapy such as the Beck (1976) and Ellis (1962) approaches, this maladaptive style of thinking is termed *negative automatic thoughts* and *irrational beliefs,* respectively. From the perspective of Leary and Kowalski's (1995) two-factor model, overestimating negative repercussions simply connotes greater self-presentational motivation. Similarly, it is easy to reinterpret research linking social anxiety to greater need for social approval (e.g., Mallet & Rodriguez-Tome, 1999) as supporting

SPT because desire for approval reflects the principle of self-presentational motivation. Thus, in addition to being a theory of causation and a model for guiding clinical intervention (by identifying targets for therapeutic change), SPT serves as a useful heuristic device for organizing and giving order to a wide range of seemingly unrelated research.

Despite the fact that SPT provides an elegant organizing theoretical framework, surprisingly few studies linking cognitive–social processes to social anxiety explicitly couch themselves within the framework offered by SPT. It is hoped that future empirical work in this area will give greater attention to systematically testing ideas based on SPT.

FOCUS ON RESEARCH

Self-presentation theory (SPT) has proved to be useful in helping shed light on factors that might cause or contribute to social anxiety in young people. In particular, research has provided evidence to support the idea that symptoms of social anxiety in children and adolescents may have their roots in overinflated levels of self-presentational motivation coupled with underinflated levels of social self-efficacy.

Chansky and Kendall (1997) studied 9- to 15-year-olds. The research participants consisted of two subgroups known to differ on social anxiety. The *socially anxious group* consisted of a clinical sample of 47 participants enrolled in the Child and Adolescent Anxiety Disorders Clinic at Temple University. The *comparison group* consisted of a same-age sample of 31 nonanxious counterparts.

In a laboratory setting, research participants were exposed to a situation in which they anticipated social interaction with an unknown peer of the same age. Participants in both groups were shown a videotape of another child playing a game and were told that the child was in an adjoining room. In anticipation of joining the other child to play, participants filled out a number of self-report assessments of their thoughts and emotions in response to the (anticipated) social situation. SPT would predict that the socially anxious children, as compared with the comparison group children, would report more negative outcome expectancies, lower social self-efficacy, and higher social anxiety when anticipating joining their playmate in the adjoining room.

Self-presentational motivation was assessed using a scale called the Social Expectancies Questionnaire, which taps the strength of both positive and negative outcome expectancies (i.e., anticipating acceptance or rejection). Anxiety and self-efficacy were assessed using the Social Anxiety Scale–Revised (La Greca & Stone, 1993) and the Perceived Competence Scale from the Self-Perception Profile (Harter, 1985), respectively.

The results showed that the two groups of participants did respond differently to the situation involving anticipated social interaction. In accordance with SPT, the socially anxious group reacted with more social anxiety. When the two groups were compared in terms of self-presentational motivation, the results showed that the socially anxious group responded with greater anticipation of rejection. There was a positive correlation between social anxiety and fear of rejection (i.e., negative outcome expectancies), suggesting (in line with SPT) that fear of rejection contributed to levels of social anxiety. Other results showed that the clinical group reported lower levels of social self-efficacy (i.e., confidence) than did the nonclinical group. As would be expected based on SPT, the treatment sample participants felt less confident in their social skills than did those in the nontreatment sample.

To summarize, Chansky and Kendall's (1997) study showed that young people receiving treatment for social anxiety disorder responded to an anticipated social situation just as SPT would predict. They felt less socially competent relative to control children and were presumably more concerned with the type of image they might portray. Thus, their self-efficacy was low and their motivation was high. Furthermore, this combination of influences was uniquely related to heightened symptoms of social anxiety.

A Social Psychological Model of Depression

Have you ever received a lower than expected grade in a course, experienced a romantic breakup, or lost a job? Most students have experienced undesirable events or situations. This is because the human condition is inherently stressful. Social psychological theory and research looks at how the way in which people think about stressful events makes a difference to their mental health. It is not so much what happens to you that is important; rather, it is how you perceive it. This section discusses how one's explanations for past events can affect vulnerability to symptoms of depression.

Let us start off with a brief exercise. Write down the numbers 1 to 3 in a notebook. Think back over the past 24 months and try and remember the three worst things that have happened to you. Also think about why these situations occurred. Try to explain them briefly. Beside each number, write a sentence to indicate what happened and why. Do it now before reading further.

You likely offered a number of different explanations for your difficulties. These explanations are called *causal attributions,* as noted in earlier chapters. Sometimes people will respond to the difficulties in their lives with explanations that are rather pessimistic. For example, in accounting for your own situations, you may have written something like this: "What made this happen is something that will never change and something that is undermining my whole life." Specific examples of pessimistic attributions for a job loss might include chronic illness, lack of intelligence, and discrimination.

This section reviews theory and research suggesting that people who habitually offer pessimistic explanations like this may be at risk for developing depressive symptoms. As you read on, you will come to understand the process by which a pessimistic attribution style works to make people vulnerable to symptoms of depression. You will see that this type of thinking is related to depression through feelings of helplessness and hopelessness. Later, the chapter, discusses what counselors can do to help people resolve their bouts with depression and what can be done to prevent depression from happening in young people who are developmentally vulnerable.

Martin Seligman, a respected social psychologist, has spearheaded pioneering efforts to build bridges between social psychology and clinical psychology. Early in his career, in a series of experiments in which he exposed dogs to stressful events, Seligman (1975) administered painful electric shocks that could not be avoided or escaped. The dogs learned that the painful situations (the shocks) were uncontrollable. Later, these same dogs were placed in a similar "stressful situation," but this time the circumstances were slightly changed so that the dogs were given greater ability to cope. Specifically, during their second exposure to the stressful situation, the dogs could escape the electric shock.

The results of these experiments showed that dogs that had previously been exposed to uncontrollable shocks learned to passively accept new shocks. Even though the dogs could have escaped the new shocks if they wished, they did not even try. They seemed to have given up on the idea of coping by escaping. Instead of trying to do something to change their situation, they suffered passively when receiving the new series of painful jolts of shock.

Why would these dogs not try to do something to improve their situation? Seligman (1975) proposed that prior experience had taught the dogs that there was nothing they could do to change the situation. He suggested that the dogs, like humans who are depressed, had become psychologically helpless. Seligman's model became known as the **learned helplessness model of depression.** When applied to humans, the basic idea is that life experiences can sometimes teach people to give up in their attempts to cope.

In extending the animal model to humans, Seligman and his colleagues (Abramson, Seligman, & Teasdale, 1978) developed a cognitive–social model of human depression. This new model added some of the thinking components that were missing in the animal model. The 1978 human model was called the **attributional reformulation of the learned helplessness theory of depression.** The attributional model proposed that people were depressed because of the attributions they make for why unfortunate things happen. According to the model, people who are prone to depression make pessimistic attributions that cause them to believe that there is nothing they can ever say or do that would change their unfortunate circumstances. Technically, such a state of mind is called a *negative outcome expectancy* (discussed earlier) or simply *helplessness.* According to the 1978 model developed by Seligman and his colleagues, helpless thoughts about the future prompt symptoms of depression.

Recall the opening vignette about Deena, the student who came to K. H. for counseling. Although Deena appeared to be generally depressed in life, she was particularly depressed and dejected in anticipation of going out on a date with the fellow she met in the library. She even wanted to give up on the date before it happened. From the perspective of the attributional reformulation model, Deena had very strong negative outcome expectancies. She was convinced that the man would reject her, and she was probably also convinced that there was nothing she could do to change this eventuality. But why was she so sure the situation would turn out poorly? Why did she have such a strong negative outcome expectancy? According to Seligman and colleagues' (1978) attributional model, Deena was probably making dysfunctional causal attributions for the imagined outcome. She was probably attributing her anticipated rejection to (a) something about herself (an *internal,* as opposed to *external,* causal attribution), (b) something that would not change (a *stable,* as opposed to *unstable,* causal attribution), and (c) something that would undermine her whole life (a *global,* as opposed to *specific,* causal attribution). In fact, she did tell K. H. that she had a boring personality and that she was unlovable. This would certainly classify as an internal, stable, and global attribution. If indeed Deena believed that this was the reason for her (anticipated) rejection, you can see how she might become depressed. After all, not being an interesting or lovable person is a hard thing to accept about oneself and is virtually impossible to change. These qualities would likely contribute to additional romantic failures in the future and lead to bleak expectancies.

The hopelessness theory of depression. Seligman and his colleagues reformulated the 1978 model of depression, calling their updated model the hopelessness theory of depression (HTD) (Peterson, Maier, & Seligman, 1993). The **hopelessness theory of depression** represents a clinically relevant theory of depression that features social psychological principles and processes. It suggests that depressive symptoms are most likely to occur when two factors are present at the same time: (a) a vulnerable person and (b) negative environmental circumstances. Although either factor by itself may be only loosely connected to risk of depression, the co-occurrence of the factors is thought to be especially likely to make people susceptible to becoming depressed.

According to HTD, a *vulnerable person* is someone who has a characteristically negative style of interpreting the causes of aversive life events. This interpretative bias is sometimes called the **depressogenic attribution style** or **pessimistic explanatory style.** The term *style* connotes consistency of perceptual response across diverse types of stressful life events. A person who believes that "the root cause that made this bad thing happen is something that will never change and something that is undermining my whole life" is displaying the depressogenic attribution style. Such an explanation involves making stable and global causal attribution. **Stable attributions** represent a broad class of diverse causes that share one thing in common: The person thinks that the cause will endure over time and that it will be present in the future. A stable cause is one that is not likely to change over time (e.g., physical attractiveness). **Global attributions** also come in all shapes and sizes. However, each member of this class of causes has one thing in common: The person thinks that the cause has widespread influence on many aspects of his or her life; for example, physical attractiveness can serve as a global attribution because a person may think that being unattractive will affect many aspects of his or her life.

Let us look at some concrete examples of stable and global attributions. Imagine for a moment a situation in which you told someone that your lack of intelligence is what caused you to experience a stressful academic event (e.g., getting a poor grade on a psychology exam). Your lack of intelligence explanation is an example of an attribution that is both stable and global in nature. It is global because low intelligence could also give rise to many different stressful life events beyond just a poor psychology grade. In contrast, thinking that a low mark on an exam is due to insufficient effort spent studying is an example of a causal attribution that is *unstable* and *specific*. It is unstable because it can change in the future because you have control over it. You can always expend more effort studying in the future and thereby avoid suffering a similar fate again. It is also specific in that it is unlikely that lack of effort in studying for a psychology exam will have widespread adverse repercussions in other spheres of your life. There is likely a unique cause-and-effect relationship between the occurrence of this type of academic stressor (i.e., poor grade) and not studying enough. Thus, specific (vs. global) attributions for unpleasant events allow a person to have positive expectancies for the future. People who think this way feel more hopeful about their future chances of success, and their hope protects them against lapsing into depression. Conversely, attributing a poor grade on a psychology exam to lack of intelligence (a stable and global cause) has the opposite effect. It increases thoughts involving hopelessness, and this in turn causes emotions such as depressed feelings to occur.

One chief advantage of HTD is that it offers useful and testable predictions that enable researchers to account for both the duration of depressive episodes over time and the severity of depression. Some depressed people have short-lasting episodes of depression, whereas others have longer episodes. Why is this? A useful theory should be able to account for differences among clients. According to HTD, the duration of an episode of depressive symptoms is influenced by the level of perceived stability of the root cause of the precipitating bad events. Take, for example, a person who is depressed and believes that his or her past academic failure is due to a lack of intelligence. By definition, a stable cause is unlikely to change in the future. According to HTD, a depressed student who accounts for academic failure in this manner

will be depressed longer than will a student who believes that his or her academic failure is due to insufficient studying (an unstable/changeable cause).

Also, in terms of clinical observations, psychotherapists have noted that some clients suffer from a type of depression that is pervasive and all encompassing. These clients experience symptoms of depression that are very widespread. They not only feel hopeless about their schoolwork but also anticipate a bleak future in all of their life domains (e.g., romance, health, finances). Other depressed people, in contrast, have circumscribed "pockets" of depression. For instance, they might be hopeless with regard to their academic future, whereas their athletic futures and romantic futures seem bright. Why is this? According to HTD, the pervasiveness of symptoms of depression is related to whether a person offers specific or global explanations for past negative events. Accounts that are global lead to much more pessimism about the future than do accounts that are more specific in nature. Having more negative expectancies about the future, in turn, tends to breed a more all-encompassing type of depression.

As noted by Seligman and colleagues (1993) in their landmark book titled *Learned Helplessness: A Theory for the Age of Personal Control,* there is plenty of research to support the idea that explanatory style is a risk factor for the onset and maintenance of depressive symptoms. In terms of research evidence, these authors described several studies showing a link between the magnitude and presence of depressive symptoms and the tendency to make stable and global (and sometimes internal) explanations to account for why bad events happen. Although relatively fewer studies have examined the hypothesized role of negative outcome expectancies as a mediator between depressogenic attribution style and depressive symptoms, those that have tested this link have provided supportive evidence (e.g., Buchanan & Seligman, 1995; Peterson & Vaidya, 2001).

It is important to emphasize that the attributions identified by HTD are thought to work in concert to generate depression through the mediating influence of generalized negative outcome expectancies. The theory itself calls these types of anticipatory cognitions *hopelessness expectancies.* Sometimes *hopelessness* is used as a shorter term. **Hopelessness** has been defined as "the expectation that highly desirable outcomes will not occur and that one is powerless to change the situation" (Needles & Abramson, 1990, p. 156). The flip side of this definition is that hopelessness also includes the expectation that highly undesirable outcomes will occur and that one is powerless to change the future outcomes. In either case, the heart of the cognitive problem for the person suffering from hopelessness is the belief that he or she is disempowered. This explains why depressed people seem to have given up on life. They "throw in the towel" because they believe that nothing they say or do will make a difference. Social psychologists would say that people who have given up or thrown in the towel do so because they believe (rightly or wrongly) that their future rewards and punishments in life are beyond their control.

The particular type of depression generated by generalized hopelessness expectancies is thought to be unique. This unique type of depression has a special name: **hopelessness depression.** Although many of the symptoms overlap with "regular" clinical depression as defined by the DSM-IV (American Psychiatric Association, 1994), other symptoms are specific, including increased interpersonal dependency and decreased self-esteem (Abela & D'Alessandro, 2001) in addition to apathy and lethargy. In contrast, people who suffer from "regular" depression experience marked irritability, appetite disturbances, physical/medical complaints, and anhedonia (i.e., inability to enjoy or experience pleasure). There is considerable evidence from research to support the hypothesis that hopelessness depression exists in nature and is distinguishable from traditional forms of (non-hopelessness) depression (e.g., Alloy & Clements, 1998; Joiner, Steer, Abramson, Metalsky, & Schmidt, 2001). Additional research shows that depressogenic attribution style predicts increases in hopelessness symptoms of depression (Abela & Payne, 2003).

Knowing why people develop emotional problems such as depression and social anxiety can be very useful. For example, if attributions and expectancies explain how people get depressed or anxious, it should also be the case that therapies might help clients to reduce their suffering by modifying attributions and expectancies. Thus, mental health professionals who work with clients can use this information to help them be more effective in their therapeutic interventions. The next section describes how social psychological knowledge has been applied in clinical settings.

THE SOCIAL–THERAPEUTIC SUBDOMAIN

To this point, you have learned how social psychology has contributed to an improved understanding of how people become vulnerable to experiencing depressive symptoms. The chapter has also discussed social–cognitive determinants of symptoms of social anxiety. As you have seen, both SPT and HTD suggest that social psychological processes that are cognitive in nature play a role in the onset and maintenance of these disorders. Thus, social psychology has helped to improve our understanding of the origins and maintenance of emotional problems.

In addition, social psychology has been instrumental in improving our understanding of the underlying processes by which therapeutic interventions help to ameliorate various psychological problems (Figure 6.2). This section discusses the social–therapeutic subdomain of the social–clinical interface. This facet of the interface seeks to identify social psychological processes that may play a role in explaining how and why clients change as a function of therapy. The social–therapeutic subdomain is also concerned with using social psychological insights to design new interventions and improve techniques for treating people with mental illness. Although social psychology has been applied to understanding a wide range of therapeutic interventions (for a review, see Kowalski & Leary, 1999), for the purpose of consistency, this section focuses on treatments for anxiety and depression.

As you read further, consider each of the therapy approaches in terms of Deena's case presented in the opening vignette. She experienced significant feelings of hopelessness, depression, and social anxiety. How might social psychologically derived treatment models

Figure 6.2   Using Social Psychologically Based Approaches to Therapy to Treat a Person With
Psychological Problems

SOURCE: Photo courtesy of Rebecca Purc-Stephenson

for anxiety and depression help Deena to become happier and more socially outgoing?

Self-Presentational Approach to Treating Social Anxiety

Previously, we discussed SPT as a social psychological model of how social anxiety develops and persists. This model has several implications for the treatment of social anxiety disorder. First, by identifying the nature of cognitive–social targets for change, it helps to guide therapeutic interventions. (Do you remember Lewin's idea, from Chapter 1, concerning the practical usefulness of good theories?) The model suggests, for example, that interventions should seek to modify social self-efficacy and self-presentational motivation. Specifically, interventions should seek to increase the former and decrease the latter. Second, the model provides a useful theoretical blueprint for understanding how and why improvement occurs (or does not occur). For instance, if an existing treatment for social anxiety has been used and it does not reduce the client's anxiety, one might use SPT to infer the

reason why it was ineffective. Specifically, this model could lead to the hypothesis that the treatment was ineffective because it failed to bolster a client's sense of confidence in communicating with others. In addition, the model suggests that an absence of therapeutic improvement might be attributable to a failure of therapy to diminish the client's motivation to project a desired image. Thus, SPT guides the change process by suggesting targets for therapeutic intervention. As you may recall, the theory hypothesizes that social anxiety is most likely to occur in people who lack social self-efficacy and who have high self-presentational motivation to impress others. Sometimes by design and sometimes by coincidence, existing cognitive–behavioral treatments for social anxiety disorder intervene in such a way as to reduce the excessive need for social approval. From the perspective of SPT, interventions that reduce the need for social approval benefit clients by decreasing their self-presentational motivation. In this regard, it is likely that reduced motivation to impress others is one of the chief benefits of *rational–emotive therapy* (RET) (Ellis, 1962) for socially anxious people. RET is designed to help clients by reducing or eliminating their irrational and unrealistic concerns, in this case with respect to what others will think of them. The application of RET to social anxiety is a good example of how SPT helps to explain the change process in existing therapies.

Other interventions, such as *social skill therapies,* may reduce symptoms of social anxiety by bolstering the client's sense of social self-efficacy (Leary & Miller, 1986). This is precisely what Bandura's (1977a) *theory of self-efficacy* would predict. Specifically, Bandura would suggest that the most effective way in which to increase self-efficacy among socially anxious clients is to provide them with "mastery" situations in which they can practice their interpersonal skills successfully. This probably explains why role-play enactments work to help socially anxious clients. The more people practice engaging in social situations with others, the less difficult and anxiety provoking they will be.

Gaudiano and Herbert (2003) conducted one of the first intervention studies to rigorously apply the concept of self-efficacy to clients suffering from social anxiety disorder. Consistent with SPT, self-efficacy was defined as the client's confidence in being able to convey a favorable impression to others. Research participants were a large sample of employed adults, most of whom suffered from avoidant personality disorder, a psychological problem that is characterized by debilitating levels of social anxiety. During the therapeutic intervention, the clients were engaged in a type of cognitive–behavior therapy that sought to reduce anxiety by teaching social skills. A key feature of the treatment included role-play enactments of social situations in which difficult social interactions were practiced and mastered. It was reasoned that learning social skills would naturally bolster clients' levels of social self-efficacy.

The research clients were assessed for levels of self-efficacy and anxiety prior to beginning the treatment program and after it was finished. You may recall from Chapter 3 that this quasi-experimental method of investigation is called a pretest–posttest design.

The results provided support for the relevance of SPT in understanding how therapy produces change. From pretest to posttest, mean levels of social self-efficacy increased and social anxiety decreased. Moreover, the magnitude of increases in self-efficacy ratings from pretreatment to posttreatment was associated with the magnitude of decreases in social anxiety. That is, the amount of reduction in anxiety paralleled the amount of increase in self-efficacy. This pattern is significant because it is precisely what one would expect to see if SPT offered a valid explanation for how and why therapy works to produce symptom reduction in clients.

Impressively, changes in self-efficacy associated with therapeutic involvement remained a significant predictor of reductions in social anxiety independent of other potential biasing extraneous influences. This latter finding suggests that the connection between self-efficacy and social anxiety is genuine and cannot be explained away as trivial or as secondary to other factors. A liberal interpretation of this study's main finding (remember that it was a quasi-experiment) is that changes in social self-efficacy mediated the effects of the treatment involvement on client improvement. In other words, there is evidence to suggest that the main reason why therapy worked as well as it did was because it bolstered levels of social self-efficacy.

As discussed in Chapter 2, when results from intervention studies are consistent with expectations based on a theoretical model, the results strengthen our confidence in the validity of the model. In this connection, the therapy study by Gaudiano and Herbert (2003) is significant because it provides empirical support for the validity of the SPT model of social anxiety. If we apply these findings to Deena's case, helping her to improve her own sense of social self-efficacy might give her the skills she needs to develop the close relationships for which she has been longing. In this treatment model, this skill building is done through role-playing and practice. Deena may be less worried about what others are going to think about her if she knows how to relate to them.

The findings reported by Gaudiano and Herbert (2003) also suggest that clinical psychologists may find this model of social anxiety as a practical blueprint for treating clients. In particular, the study is relevant to mental health professionals because it points to social skills training and role-play enactments as techniques for helping clients to decrease their interpersonal anxiety by increasing their social self-efficacy. It is hoped that future studies will further validate these techniques. Given that a multitude of social–cognitive factors (e.g., values, beliefs, expectancies, attributions) seem to be involved in the maintenance of symptoms of social anxiety, it is likely that future clinical research will show additional therapeutic techniques to be effective in remediation.

Hopelessness Theory Approach to Treating Depression

HTD also has implications for therapeutic intervention. With respect to the treatment of depression, hopelessness has always been a concept that is implicitly relevant to cognitive approaches such as those developed by Beck (1976; see also Peterson et al., 1993). Technically speaking, HTD was a model developed to account for why people become depressed in the first place. Later, when the model started to be applied to understanding remediation of depression, the therapeutic goal shifted away from hopelessness and toward *hopefulness*.

Hopefulness is defined as expecting good things to happen in the future. This principle of hopefulness was articulated by Needles and Abramson (1990), who extended the principles of HTD by suggesting that people recover from depression by becoming more hopeful. This section describes how knowledge of HTD has the potential to help clients overcome depression.

Theoretically, how can a psychological intervention help clients to develop increased levels of hopefulness? The hopefulness approach developed by Needles and Abramson (1990) suggests that counselors should attempt to do two things. First, they should engineer their clients' social environments in such a way as to increase the frequency of occurrence of positive life events. Recreational therapy might be considered. Role-play enactments might also help. Setting modest goals and achieving them on a daily basis may also result in pleasurable experiences. Second, counselors should encourage clients to think differently and to use an **enhancing attributional style.** This style is the opposite of the depressogenic attributional style. Thus, clients are encouraged to make global and stable attributions for positive events.

● FOCUS ON INTERVENTION

The Penn Optimism Program (Gillham, Reivich, & Shatte, 2001) is an excellent example of a psychotherapeutic intervention that was carefully crafted to target change in cognitive–social processes identified by the hopelessness model as being important mediators of depressive symptomatology.

The Penn Optimism Program was tested with 69 fifth- and sixth-grade students who were considered to be at risk for developing depression. The main goal was to demonstrate that this theory-based intervention could prevent the onset of depression. Given that depressive symptoms have been shown to increase slightly over the middle school years and then rise with entry into high school, the researchers reasoned that they might be able to intervene during this developmental period. The means of preventing depression involved modifying explanatory style. In fact, the intervention consisted of two parts: cognitive restructuring and skills acquisition.

Cognitive restructuring. The program sought to teach children about the nature and impact of depressogenic (pessimistic) versus nondepressogenic (optimistic) interpretations of life events. Because children in the fifth and sixth grades are less able to engage in high-level mental abstraction normally associated with cognitive–behavioral therapy in adults, a number of creative techniques were employed to make cognitive restructuring procedures more accessible and engaging to the young "clients." Important cognitive–behavioral therapy concepts were introduced and elaborated on using novel delivery modalities such as skits, stories, role-plays, and cartoons. Consistent with cognitive therapy models developed by Beck (1976) and Ellis (1962), these modalities were used to teach students attending the program to link how they feel and how they behave with the contents of their thoughts. For example, in one set of worksheets involving cartoons (story boards), students were asked to generate beliefs that would lead to a behavioral or an emotional consequence shown in the final frame of a cartoon story. Sometimes the children had to generate an explanation for an emotional outcome depicting a happy face with an upturned smile, and sometimes they had to do so for an outcome portraying a sad face with a down-turned frown.

The consequences of optimistic and pessimistic explanatory styles were also communicated by skits involving two characters: Gloomy Greg and Hopeful Holly. In one particular set of skits, both Greg and Holly were described as attending a school dance. At the dance, when the music started to play, both Greg and Holly asked peers to dance with them, only to be met with rejection. However, the skits diverged at this point, with Hopeful Holly responding much differently from Gloomy Greg. Greg was depicted as attributing the rejection (negative social interaction) to stable and global causes (e.g., "I'm a loser and no one likes me"). Greg also made pessimistic predictions representing negative outcome expectancies (e.g., "No one will dance with me—ever," "I'll never have fun at dances"). He gave up on dancing and sat down dejected on a wooden bench alongside the bleachers for the rest of the evening. Feeling hopeless about his future chances of dancing, he had a miserable and depressing time.

Hopeful Holly, in contrast, was depicted as attributing the negative interpersonal interaction to more unstable and specific causes (e.g., "Maybe I didn't smile enough," "Maybe he was too nervous to dance"). The skit also depicted Holly's predictions as more hopeful.

Skill acquisition. A vital second component of the Penn Optimism Program is skill acquisition. It is true that shifting one's attributional style can provide hope that problems will dissipate and that some change is possible. However, modifying explanatory biases does not provide the behavioral skills required to enact or realize that hope of change. The second half of the program teaches problem-solving skills. These include emotion control techniques as well as strategies for relaxing, being assertive, negotiating with others, and avoiding procrastination. As with the cognitive component, skills were taught (illustrated) using skits, stories, and cartoon characters (e.g., Say-It-Straight-Sally). These skills were enacted through participation in role-play scenarios.

The at-risk children who received the program were compared with a group of matched children who were also at risk but did not receive the intervention. Results of this experimental intervention revealed that children involved in the program, as compared with control children, showed both improved explanatory style *and* reduced depressive symptoms. Importantly, these therapeutic benefits were maintained a full 2 years after the program ended. Major benefits occurred with respect to moderate to severe levels of depressive symptoms. The 2-year follow-up showed that 44% of children in the control group reported moderate to severe levels of symptoms, compared with only 22% of children in the sample who received the program. Thus, the Penn Optimism Program was successful in reducing the expected upward trajectory of depression for an appreciable number of these young adolescents.

Positive life events and self-enhancing attributions (i.e., global and stable for positive events) are believed to combine to promote the growth of hopefulness. Hopefulness, in turn, is thought to offset depression, causing a person's mood to lift. Thus, to reduce symptoms of depression, one may alter how clients explain the good things that happen to them in life. Missing in the Needles and Abramson (1990) model is any mention of the importance of altering how clients explain the bad things that occur. This omission is a limitation, as we will see.

In addition to the research conducted under the Penn Optimism Program (Gillham et al., 2001), a number of other studies provide evidence supporting the validity of the hopefulness approach to alleviating depression (Needles & Abramson, 1990; Johnson, Han, Douglas, Johannet, & Russell, 1998). One study, for example, monitored changes in depression before and after treatment in a clinical sample of psychiatric patients (Johnson et al., 1998). These patients received cognitive–behavioral treatment for depression. Consistent with expectations based on the hopefulness approach to treatment, attributions for positive life events predicted decreases in depressive symptoms over time. These decreases in depression were directly linked to increases in hopefulness expectancies. Patients who made stable, global, and internal attributions for positive events had more hopefulness and less depression after treatment than did patients who did not attribute positive events in a manner consistent with this self-enhancing style.

Clinical research testing the Needles and Abramson (1990) model is contributing to its further empirical refinement. For example, we have seen that a *depressogenic attributional style for negative events* can lead to depression and that an *enhancing attributional style for positive events* can promote hopefulness. Is it reasonable to wonder whether these two styles interact in some way? Consider a recent study that examined the combined effect of both enhancing *and* depressogenic attribution styles (Voelz, Haeffel, Joiner, & Wagner, 2003). In this study, depressed inpatients were assessed at intake to a psychiatric hospital and again at discharge approximately 9 days later. Patients received standard cognitive–behavioral treatment. Treatment efficacy was assessed by monitoring changes in hopelessness and depression from pretreatment to posttreatment. Note that by virtue of being hospitalized, these patients experienced a stable and supportive environment over the course of the study. Negative life events were unlikely to occur during this period (this fact itself serves as a positive life event), thereby permitting an enhancing attributional style to interact with positive life events to possibly produce hopefulness.

The results extended the Needles and Abramson (1990) model by suggesting that a depressogenic attribution style for negative events interacts with an enhancing attributional pattern for positive events to predict changes in hopelessness. Specifically, Voelz and colleagues' (2003) study showed that patients exhibiting a high degree of enhancing attributional style for positive events reported only moderate levels of hopelessness at the time of

discharge regardless of whether they displayed a depressogenic attributional style for negative events. In comparison, patients showing a low degree of enhancing attributional style and a high degree of depressogenic style displayed high levels of hopelessness at the time of discharge.

Clearly, these data provide evidence that the Needles and Abramson (1990) hopefulness model is in need of modification. Specifically, a thorough model of the causes of hopefulness appears to require the integration of both an enhancing attributional style for positive events and a depressogenic attributional style for negative events. If the results of Voelz and colleagues' (2003) study can be replicated, they suggest that mental health professionals working with depressed clients may wish to broaden the range of cognitive–social targets they attempt to modify. In particular, practitioners may wish to encourage clients to make stable and global attributions for positive life events and to make unstable and specific attributions for negative events. Thus, when good things happen, it might help to alleviate depression if clients can be made to believe that these things are due to (their own) personalities, attitudes, or intelligence. Conversely, when bad things happen, depression might be decreased in proportion to the extent to which clients can be persuaded to blame these things on fleeting extenuating circumstances.

By now, you should have a fairly good understanding of how social psychological theory can help us to explain why people develop certain emotional problems. You also should have an improved understanding of how social psychological theory and research can be applied in designing clinical interventions. Specifically, you have seen how social psychologically based therapeutic interventions are useful in helping clients to resolve symptoms of anxiety and depression.

THE SOCIAL–DIAGNOSTIC SUBDOMAIN

The first two sections of this chapter considered why people become depressed and socially anxious and what can be done to overcome such problems. Those sections emphasized the social psychology of therapeutic clients. The focus of this section shifts from clients to mental health clinicians—the therapists. The study of mental health practitioners is the purview of the social–diagnostic subdomain of the social–clinical interface. Research within this subdomain focuses on understanding the processes by which clinicians assess and diagnose their clients.

Imagine for a moment that you are employed in a psychiatric setting as a clinical psychologist. Your job is to diagnose and treat people suffering from a wide range of disorders. Some of the clients are depressed, whereas others have social anxiety disorder. Still others have drug or alcohol problems, schizophrenia, or other difficulties. Imagine that you have a new client coming for a first appointment with you. You have never met him, and you are not sure what his difficulties are. For all you know, he could have schizophrenia or be depressed or alcoholic. The client knocks on your office door, and you invite him in. How would you go about deciding which disorder (if any) this particular client has? Making such a decision is what *clinical diagnosis* is all about. Given that your goal is to be as accurate as possible, you should avoid pitfalls that might bias your judgment. Just as people who become depressed or anxious may be predisposed to think in certain ways, so too are clinicians (and people in general) predisposed to fall victim to certain patterns of thought. After reading this section, you will come to appreciate how important it is to remain as objective and unbiased as possible in judging others. You will also learn that this is not always an easy thing to do.

Clinicians, whether they are psychologists, psychiatrists, social workers, or others, are generally highly skilled professionals whose goal is to identify and alleviate people's emotional and behavioral problems. Research in clinical psychology has demonstrated that mental health practitioners are effective at treating mental illness. However, clinicians are also humans. As a result, they sometimes make the kinds of errors in judgment and thinking that afflict all people from time to time (Kowalski & Leary, 1999, Leary & Miller, 1986; Lichtenberg, 1997). In what follows, you will find a brief review of certain biases and errors in thinking that social psychologists believe practitioners should guard against when making clinical decisions. By **clinical decision making,** we mean the process of judging what is wrong with clients (assessment/diagnosis) and choosing among alternative approaches to treatment.

Imagine two scenarios. In the first, a person suffering from a serious anxiety disorder goes to a mental health professional for help, but the therapist fails to diagnose the problem accurately. In the second scenario, a client is inappropriately diagnosed with an anxiety disorder that he or she does not in fact have. With the first scenario, if a clinician mistakenly diagnoses a client's symptoms and fails to provide proper treatment, the client will continue to suffer from anxiety and the client's level of emotional disability might even get worse over time. The first scenario describes a case where a **false-negative** judgment is made. This error involves not recognizing a bona fide problem that exists. In this case, an anxiety disorder diagnosis should have been made but was not. Obviously, steps should be taken to avoid this type of mistake, and there is a need for more research on how to reduce false negatives.

Research within the social–diagnostic subdomain, has given somewhat more attention to **false-positive** judgments. A false positive exists when a diagnostic label is inappropriately given to the client as in the second scenario above. An example of a false-positive judgment is when a mental health professional incorrectly diagnoses a client with depression when in fact the client is mourning the death of a loved one and is actually suffering from a normal grief reaction. False positives and false negatives are further described in Table 6.1.

One of the most famous research demonstrations of the existence of a false positive came from an investigation by Rosenhan (1973). Rosenhan showed how context or setting can cause clinicians to distort their judgments of a client's problems. The lesson learned is that being in a therapeutic setting can influence clinicians to see apparent problems where none exists (i.e., to make false-positive judgments). As you read about Rosenhan's famous study, try to answer the following question: Why did the staff members make these errors in judgment? Following this research example is a discussion of how different types of influences can sometimes contribute to distorted perceptions among highly trained mental health professionals.

Table 6.1   Correct and Incorrect Diagnostic Decision Making and Outcomes

	Actual Condition of Client	
Clinician Conclusion	*Client Has Depression*	*Client Does Not Have Depression*
	True Positive	*False Positive*
Client is diagnosed with depression	• Client appropriately receives treatment for a condition that he or she actually has; potential to benefit from treatment exists	• Client receives treatment for a condition that he or she does not have; receives unnecessary treatment or fails to be treated for a condition that he or she actually has
	False Negative	*True Negative*
Client is not diagnosed with depression	• Client does not receive treatment for a condition that he or she actually has; condition might not improve and might actually get worse	• Client is appropriately not treated for a condition that he or she does not have; opportunity to consider other diagnoses exists

FOCUS ON RESEARCH

During the early 1970s, D. L. Rosenhan carried out a controversial study that raised many questions about the accuracy of psychiatric diagnoses. Rosenhan's research sparked a heated debate in clinical and social psychology that still goes on today. In his article, titled "On Being Sane in Insane Places," Rosenhan (1973) described an experiment in which eight "normal" (mentally healthy) research confederates gained admission to 12 different inpatient psychiatric hospitals. These "pseudo-patients" came from a variety of backgrounds. Importantly, none was known to be suffering from psychiatric problems. The pseudo-patients approached different psychiatric hospitals faking psychiatric complaints. They told the staff members that they had been hearing voices. In each case, the pseudo-patient reported that the voices said "empty," "hollow," and "thud." All of them were admitted to hospitals. Once the pseudo-patients were hospitalized, they told the staff members that the auditory hallucinations had stopped. From the point of admission onward, the pseudo-patients acted normally.

The results of the study were astonishing. In all cases, false-positive judgments were made. Of the pseudo-patients, 11 were incorrectly diagnosed as having schizophrenia. The remaining pseudo-patient was given the diagnostic label of "manic depression." None of the pseudo-patients had his or her diagnosis reconsidered over the course of the hospital stay. On average, the pseudo-patients were hospitalized for 19 days, although 1 pseudo-patient was kept for 52 days before being discharged. This occurred in spite of the pseudo-patient acting normally during the stay. When the pseudo-patients took notes on what they were observing on the ward, the nursing staff members pathologized this behavior, seeing it as an expression of assumed underlying psychopathology. When the pseudo-patients were discharged from the hospitals, they were released with essentially the same diagnoses they received when they entered the hospitals. The only difference was that their mental illness diagnosis was qualified with the term "in remission."

Rosenhan's research provides evidence showing how false-positive errors are sometimes made in clinical decision making and how the consequences of such errors can harm the very people whom professionals are trying to help. The study also illustrates the biasing effects that labels derived from first impressions can have on subsequent assessments. Although "in remission" at their times of discharge, the pseudo-patients would continue to carry a stigmatizing label (e.g., "schizophrenic," "mental patient") with them after they left the hospitals. As you will see in the subsequent discussion, and in Chapter 13 on applying psychology to the community, other people often react in a negative manner to stigmatizing labels.

Keep Rosenhan's (1973) research example in mind while reading the next subsection on biases and errors in clinical decision making.

Biases in Clinical Decision Making

The effect of labeling on judgments of mental illness. Social psychologists have found that preexisting information (i.e., labels) may sometimes bias clinicians, resulting in false-positive or false-negative judgments. The **labeling effect** refers to a tendency to perceive clients in ways that are erroneous owing to the reactive effects of an existing psychiatric label. In the clinic, labeling refers to the possibility that a clinician may perceive a client's symptoms differently after the client has been given a diagnosis compared with before the client has been diagnosed.

For example, past medical records on new patients can result in labeling. Providing practitioners with clients' files is common practice when new clients have been referred. Although this practice seems innocent enough, information in client records may inadvertently "contaminate" a clinician's thinking, causing him or her to lose objectivity due to labeling bias. When a mental health professional gives a client a diagnostic label indicating the presence of a psychiatric disorder, the label quite often takes on a life of its own and has an influence beyond the therapeutic context. Members of society often react to the label, and sometimes a person labeled with a psychiatric diagnosis can be seen as "deviant" rather than in need of help. This *stigma* can even result in a loss of supportive services (Rosenfield, 1997). It can also cause the stigmatized person to experience a reduction in life satisfaction (Rosenfield, 1997).

The negative effects of psychiatric labels have been illustrated in research by Link, Phelan, Bresnahan, Stueve, and Pescosolido (1999) that surveyed people's perceptions of clients with mental illness. One third (33%) of the people surveyed fell prey to the myth that a depressed person was "somewhat likely" to "very likely" to commit violence against someone else. Of course, this is an erroneous perception because it is not consistent with what mental health practitioners know about depression. In reality, depressed people tend not to be any more dangerous than nondepressed people. The myth of being dangerous was particularly prevalent for clients labeled as schizophrenia (66%), alcohol dependent (71%), or cocaine dependent (87%).

This same study (Link et al., 1999) also examined stereotypes of distressed people who have not been stigmatized by a diagnostic label. In particular, the researchers asked their research participants to rate a target person who was described as being distressed due to having had "a rough time" in life. Participants were not told that the target person had a diagnosis of a mental illness. The effect of the absence of a psychiatric label was dramatic. Only 17% of the people surveyed believed that the distressed person was prone to violence. This is convincing evidence of the biasing effects of labels because the person being judged differed only on the basis of the existence of a psychiatric diagnosis.

Unlike members of the general public, mental health practitioners are much less likely to experience such biases toward people who have been labeled as having a psychiatric disorder. Although professionals who work with clients are less prone to obvious forms of prejudice, there is nevertheless some evidence that clinicians occasionally exhibit negative stereotypes. The existence of clinical prejudice is very subtle, but it is worth knowing about because it potentially can have an adverse impact on clinical diagnosis and treatment. If social psychologists can help their clinical counterparts to eradicate even subtle biases, client welfare should improve.

In a study that examined judgments of mental health service providers, Burk and Sher (1990) found that children of alcoholics were perceived by clinicians as having equally poor emotional health regardless of whether they were described as "class leaders" or as having "behavior problems." Normally, one would expect decisions about mental health to vary with these two descriptions. In fact, Burk and Sher did find that clinical ratings of emotional well-being of the children of nonalcoholics fluctuated (as one would expect) from being positive when the children were described as class leaders to being negative when the children were considered to have behavior problems. What can be concluded from the fact that the two sets of findings were so different? Although clinicians make every effort to remain impartial and generally succeed in so doing, they can sometimes fall prey to biased clinical decision making. As we will see, clinicians have begun to use this kind of research to improve the ways in which they make clinical decisions.

The effects of group stereotypes on clinical judgments. Perhaps you have noticed that clinical bias resulting from labeling can be induced by culturally provided labels and culturally acquired stereotypes. Mental health practitioners cannot help but notice the ethnicity or gender of their clients. Social psychologists have demonstrated that culturally perpetuated labels and stereotypes can sometimes bias judgments made by mental health professionals (Solomon, 1992). Social–clinical research has focused on several categories of stereotypes, including those based on gender, race, ethnicity, religion, and sexual identity. Clinicians work hard to be objective and try not to let individual stereotypes and biases get in the way of providing clients with the best care. However, all people are susceptible to stereotyping other groups, and it is unfortunate that stereotypes may lead mental health professionals to misattribute or misdiagnose their clients' symptoms. As we will see, the sometimes unconscious nature of culture- and gender-based stereotypes can make it difficult for clinicians to take preventive or corrective steps aimed at guarding against racism or sexism (or other forms of bias).

What is the evidence to show that judgments of mental health professionals may sometimes be distorted by their clients' *social, racial,* and/or *economic* standing? Jenkins-Hall and Sacco (1991) conducted an experiment in which white male and female therapists were shown a videotape of a therapy client. The videotapes were made to differ based on the race of the client (black or white), the presence of a disorder (depressed or nondepressed), and the gender of the client (male or female). Therapists were asked to rate each of the videotaped clients on a number of dimensions.

Some interesting biases were revealed. For example, white therapists were more likely to make false-positive diagnoses for black clients. In particular, white therapists incorrectly rated nondepressed black clients as having more depression than nondepressed white clients. Depressed black clients were also rated more negatively than depressed white clients on an interpersonal rating scale that assesses assertiveness, attractiveness, social skills, and other factors. Thus, this research suggests that mental health professionals can sometimes hold culturally derived biases that result in false-positive diagnoses. Also, a therapist's race may have a subtle and mostly unconscious influence on his or her clinical decision making when it comes to treating and diagnosing people from other cultures. This type of bias in perceiving symptoms in clients of other races may help to account for the results of research showing that the diagnosis of mental illness in ethnic minorities is unusually high (Solomon, 1992).

The idea that mental health practitioners may sometimes display a type of "psychiatric racial bias" is also illustrated in other research showing that African Americans are more likely to be diagnosed with schizophrenia than are Caucasians (Loring & Powell, 1988; Pavkov, Lewis, & Lyons, 1989). Evidence showing differential rates of clinical diagnosis is especially interesting given that there is little objective evidence for actual differential prevalence of schizophrenia in the two groups. It is quite possible that the tendency to attribute schizophrenia to African Americans more often than to Caucasians is related to culturally based stereotypes. In terms of explaining this bias, it could be that race-related stereotypes bias the attentional focus of Caucasian clinicians in a way that causes them to pay excessive attention to client symptoms that are consistent with their own beliefs about the client's cultural reference group (Garb, 1996). Conversely, biased clinicians may ignore or discount client symptoms that are inconsistent with their (erroneous) stereotypes of people who are members of the client's race.

There has been considerable research within the social–diagnostic subdomain to suggest that clinicians' judgments are sometimes vulnerable to being influenced by *gender bias* as well. In a classic study conducted more than 30 years ago, Broverman, Broverman, Clarkson, Rosenkrantz, and Vogel (1970) found that clinician beliefs about mentally healthy adults were frequently closer to their concept of a psychologically healthy man than to that of a psychologically healthy woman. Despite the fact that our society has witnessed increased equality between the sexes, contemporary research is still finding gender biases among clinicians. Unfortunately, these biases provide conditions that discriminate against women. Take, for instance, a study by Danzinger and Welfel (2000) that showed that clinicians, on average, rated female clients as less competent (and hence more needful of therapy) than male clients.

What can we conclude from the research on gender bias? First, just as there is a type of "psychiatric racial bias," there is also a type of "psychiatric gender bias." It is likely that mental health professionals are being influenced by this gender bias in a way that causes them to "over-diagnose" psychiatric disorders in women relative to those in men (Mosher, 2002).

Even a client's *age* can have a biasing effect on clinicians' judgments (Danzinger & Welfel, 2000; Meeks, 1990). This idea has been borne out by research conducted by Suzanne Meeks, who examined clinicians' perceptions of client suitability for psychotherapy (Meeks, 1990). In this study, a sample of clinical psychologists (and trainees) read case histories of potential clients. Then they proceeded to rate the potential clients in terms of how responsive each client would be to a course of treatment. The cases differed in terms of how old the client was. There were three age groups: young, middle-aged, and seniors. Can you anticipate which group received the worst prognoses?

If you guessed seniors, you are correct. Overall, clinicians assumed that elderly clients would be less likely to get well in therapy. This age bias was largely an unconscious one. When asked, clinicians could not give logical reasons to explain their prognostic decisions. What can we conclude from this study? First, subtle factors such as a client's age can distort practitioners' judgments about treatment efficacy. If older clients are systematically being given poorer prognoses, it could be that treatment services are being erroneously withheld. Also, the study by Meeks (1990) suggests clinicians are sometimes vulnerable to making diagnostic and prognostic mistakes without realizing they are doing so. If this is true, it is difficult to imagine how we could design educational programs designed to eradicate this type of bias.

Information about a client's *sexual orientation* can also distort clinicians' judgments and cause them to make decisions that are less appropriate than they otherwise could be. Wisch and Mahalik (1999), for example, examined pairs of male clients and male therapists. These researchers wanted to know whether male therapists who held more sexist views of gender roles were less comfortable with (and more likely to "pathologize") male clients who did not fit traditional gender role stereotypes. In this experiment, therapists were presented with a number of case vignettes of clients in which sexual orientation (heterosexual or homosexual) and emotional state (e.g., angry, sad) were manipulated. The results of this study showed that therapists with more rigid views of sexual identity experienced less comfort with and less willingness to work with a client who was gay and experiencing anger than did therapists who held less rigid views of sexual identity. Thus, gender role traits of therapists and clients can interact to cause bias and distortion in diagnostic decisions.

The effect of anchoring and confirmatory bias. Labels and culturally based group stereotypes can act like psychological "anchors." Like anchors on ships, labels and stereotypes can have a constraining effect. Anchoring effects influence people's judgments and decisions in every sphere of life. In the context of clinical judgment, psychological anchors can make practitioners reluctant to deviate from their first impressions when they receive new information that might conflict with earlier information. In a clinical context, the **anchoring effect** is defined as a bias that occurs when a therapist's first impression about the nature of a client's problem artificially constricts the therapist's subsequent assessments (Leary & Miller, 1986; Meehl, 1960; Tversky & Kahneman, 1974).

Social psychological research examining clinical decision making shows that information presented early in the process of assessment and therapy can have a disproportionately strong impact on how subsequent information is attended to and interpreted (Friedlander & Stockman, 1983; Rosenhan, 1973; Temerlin, 1968). For example, mental health professionals who initially diagnose their clients as being clinically depressed may get stuck in their first impressions. Later, when new and perhaps different information becomes available, clinicians might find it tough to change their initial diagnoses. This is what happened in the case of the pseudo-patients in Rosenhan's (1973) study discussed earlier. As the therapeutic relationship with a client unfolds over time, new information that is inconsistent with old information will sometimes be uncovered. Ideally, when this occurs, the clinician should pause and consider revising the earlier assessment. Unfortunately, the anchoring effect suggests that revisions likely occur less often than they should. Instead, when the clinician is faced with new information that is discrepant with old information, the new information tends to be either ignored or misinterpreted.

The very existence of the anchoring effect is due mainly to a process called confirmatory bias. Without confirmatory bias, anchoring would not pose a problem because it would not exist. As you will see from the discussion that follows, **confirmatory bias** is a process in which people (e.g., clinicians) tend to seek out information that confirms their initial hunches (e.g., diagnoses) and to ignore relevant information that disconfirms their initial hunches. So, it is a lopsided method of gathering evidence that is rife with problems.

Have you ever seen a television courtroom drama in which a lawyer asks "leading questions" of the witness in front of a jury? The lawyer's questioning strategy is obviously biased because it is directed in a way that increases the likelihood that the answers provided will confirm an initial premise. There is a problem with this method for gathering information. Even if the initial premise is wrong, asking leading questions might still produce apparent evidence to make the jury members think that the premise is correct.

Something similar may occasionally happen when a mental health professional becomes involved in the process of making a psychiatric diagnosis. The clinician starts off with an initial impression or hunch. Given the existence of a tentative hunch about the nature of a client's problem, confirmatory bias is the tendency to be more likely to try to confirm the hunch rather than try to disconfirm it. Like blinders on a racehorse, this bias channels the clinician's attention and perception, causing the clinician to selectively focus on evidence that is likely to confirm the initial diagnosis. Confirmatory bias not only points a clinician's attention in a certain direction but also colors the interpretation of information that does not fit the first impression. In this way, irrelevant information and neutral information are perceptually distorted in a way that makes it conform to the preexisting premise (Snyder & Swann, 1978).

The process of confirmatory hypothesis testing accounts, in part, for why initial impressions (e.g., diagnostic labels provided by client records or others) are so difficult to disconfirm later in time. Imagine a mental health professional who has interviewed a client for the first time and has a feeling that the client suffers from social anxiety disorder because the client does not look her in the eye. Like the lawyer in our example, the clinician may be more likely to ask questions that "pull" from the client information that supports the diagnosis of social anxiety (Haverkamp, 1993; Klayman & Ha, 1987; Pfeiffer, Whelan, & Martin, 2000). The bias makes it more likely that the clinician would ask questions such as "Have you ever felt shy and awkward when speaking with people?" Conversely, confirmatory bias makes it unlikely that the clinician in this example will ask a question that seeks information that disconfirms the initial impression or diagnosis, that is, a question such as "What would be an example of a time when you felt self-assured and confident when interacting with others?" At the same time, a clinician who is seeking to confirm that a client's problem is social anxiety will be unlikely to probe for information relevant to other possible problems such as drug/alcohol abuse and depression.

The implication for improving clinical assessment and making it more accurate is that counselors should be taught to be more even-handed in their questioning; in fact, there is research evidence to suggest that therapists do pursue disconfirmatory strategies more than do laypeople (Tutin, 1993).

Although anecdotal evidence seems to support the process of confirmatory bias, there is also evidence of this phenomenon from experimental research. In a classic experiment, Temerlin (1968) demonstrated that confirmatory bias can compromise the accuracy of clinical diagnoses. In this study, mental health practitioners were asked to evaluate a case interview with a patient. Specifically, they were asked to analyze the evidence in the case and make a professional judgment concerning the nature and severity of the patient's problem. Using random assignment, half of the practitioners were initially told that the patient might be psychotic. This label (or anchor) was not given to the other professionals, who were not given an initial hunch at the start. In fact, the client being interviewed was actually in good emotional health; however, this information was withheld from both groups. The professionals' responses in the two groups were significantly different. Professionals who were told that the patient might be psychotic were more likely to find evidence to confirm the patient was mentally ill and in need of therapy than were professionals who were not told about the diagnosis of psychosis. Thus, even though all of the professionals were presented with the same client history, the two groups came to interpret this information very differently.

As mentioned previously, clinicians try to remain objective, and they also go through intensive training to avoid the types of pitfalls identified in the this chapter. Furthermore,

Barak and Fisher (1989) argued that methodological problems in bias research make it impossible to draw sweeping conclusions about the prevalence or severity of clinician biases. Thus, we do not really know how widespread or problematic the biases are. About all we know for sure is that mental health practitioners will sometimes make mistakes in how they assess and treat their clients and that some of these mistakes are rooted in biases and constricted thinking that occurs in anchoring. Correcting for these confirmatory biases may be difficult because clinicians (as well as laypeople) fall into this trap *unconsciously*. If you do not know that you are being affected in the first place, it is hard to catch yourself and make corrective changes. However, as we will see in the next subsection, there are some techniques that clinicians can use, and do use, to reduce this source of bias, among others.

Reducing errors and biases among professionals. Clinicians are, at times, susceptible to falling victim to the same decision-making biases as are laypeople. This is because these biases are rooted in cognitive–social processes that represent fundamental aspects of human information processing. However, clinicians are significantly less likely than laypeople to experience these biases in their work.

Just because laypeople fall into these traps more often than do professionals is no reason to be complacent. Improving the ability of practitioners to make accurate and unbiased decisions is important because the welfare of clients could be improved if the incidence of the biases were diminished.

How can these biases and errors be reduced or eliminated? As you have seen, clinical and social psychologists have taken steps to understand the biases, and this understanding has suggested solutions. For example, in terms of reducing racial/ethnic biases in treatment settings, clinical psychologists are paying more attention to cultural competency in both research and treatment (Bernal & Scharron-del-rio, 2001; Sue, 2003). Furthermore, clinical and counseling psychology training programs that are accredited by the American Psychological Association are required to include education on cultural diversity. This includes attention to the influence of a client's age, gender, race, ethnicity, religion, sexual orientation, disability, socioeconomic status, language, and national origin (American Psychological Association Committee on Accreditation, 2000).

Less work has focused specifically on reducing errors involving cognitive distortions that do not involve biases toward particular groups of people. However, some research evidence suggests that education directed at reducing cognitive errors may produce improvements. For example, one experiment involved trainees in a professional program who were studying to be counselors (Chen, Froehle, & Morran, 1997). Trainees were divided into three groups. One group received specialized education on attribution processes. The second group received specialized education on how to be empathetic toward clients; that is, they were taught how to adopt their clients' perspective so as to feel what the clients were feeling. The third group formed a control condition and did not receive any specialized education.

Trainees in the first two groups were less likely than those in the third group to commit the fundamental attribution error and make dispositional (internal) attributions for clients' symptoms. Chen and colleagues' (1997) study suggests that it is possible to counteract biases in thinking so as to help clinicians become more accurate in their judgments of their clients.

This hopeful viewpoint is supported by evidence from other social psychological studies (Garb, 1996; Pfeiffer et al., 2000; Tutin, 1993). For example, with regard to confirmatory hypothesis testing, Pfeiffer and colleagues (2000) gave psychology doctoral candidates cases to analyze and judge. These mental health trainees were more likely to exhibit confirmatory bias if they were initially given highly plausible diagnostic explanations of clients' difficulties rather than less plausible diagnoses. Trainees who were presented with unlikely hypotheses subsequently found evidence that disconfirmed the initial premises. What is remarkable about this study is that it demonstrated the possibility of shifting clinicians from a confirmatory strategy to a disconfirmatory strategy. This provides a reason to be optimistic because it suggests that a clinician's method of gathering information is amenable to being influenced.

Tutin (1993) also studied clinical decision making in students and clinicians. She found that clinicians evidenced less confirmatory bias than did students when discussing the likelihood of a particular event (i.e., a potential patient's suicide). That is, clinicians were less biased than students. However, Tutin also found that when some of the students were asked to give counterexplanations to their original arguments, their confidence ratings in their original arguments were significantly lower, meaning that educating people to scrutinize their own initial beliefs and entertain different possibilities may help to reduce cognitive errors.

Final Thoughts

Obviously, understanding the nature of a problem is necessary to identify solutions to that problem. For this reason, clinical psychologists and other mental health service providers have a vital interest in understanding why their clients are distressed. Ideally, a professional's understanding should be accurate. After all, if it is accurate, it will direct a professional toward the best treatment. To the extent that solutions are properly matched to problems, clients are more likely to benefit and get better. Unfortunately, as this section has shown, a clinician's understanding is not always unbiased and accurate. Clinicians are sometimes prone to biases and cognitive distortions. Although practitioners are certainly accurate more often than not in their assessments, they do sometimes make poor decisions and faulty assessments. Efforts to reduce biases in treatment, research, and training are central in the work of clinical and social psychologists. Future studies at the interface between social psychology and clinical psychology will likely yield continued improvement in techniques to decrease biases and cognitive distortions in treatment settings.

SUMMARY

As noted at the outset of the chapter, scholars who have originated theory, research, and practice at the intersection of social psychology and abnormal/clinical psychology have constructed a special type of applied psychology. This broad interdisciplinary interface is known as the social–clinical interface. It involves the convergence of issues of mutual concern to social, abnormal, and clinical psychology. The interface has three subdomains: the social–dysgenic subdomain, the social–diagnostic subdomain, and the social–therapeutic subdomain.

This chapter provided a brief introduction to research that has been conducted within each of the three subdomains. It is hoped that you are now better able to understand how social psychological theories, concepts, and research can be applied in improving the understanding, diagnosis, and treatment of social anxiety disorder and depression. Although the scope of the interface encompasses far more than just anxiety and depression, and although the chapter discussed only a few of the theories and concepts that have been applied, it is hoped that the chapter provided you with enough of an overview to make the social–clinical interface understandable.

With regard to social anxiety, the chapter attempted to show how debilitating emotional and behavioral symptoms of social anxiety are consequences that result from the operation of negative outcome expectancies rooted in joint influence of (a) a very strong desire to make a favorable impression and (b) doubts over one's ability to make a favorable impression. Literature was also described to show how self-presentation theory helps us to understand the

theoretical processes through which professionally administered therapeutic interventions work to provide clients with relief from the debilitating symptoms of social anxiety.

The chapter reviewed theory and research suggesting that depressed mood may be caused by the expectation that highly undesirable outcomes will occur (and that desirable outcomes will not occur) and that one is powerless to change the situation. It suggested that the heart of the cognitive problem for people suffering from hopelessness is the subjective belief that events and circumstances in their lives are beyond their control. The chapter also reviewed literature showing how the hopelessness theory of depression can help to (a) identify targets for therapeutic change and (b) understand the underlying cognitive–social dynamics that explain how treatments help to reduce depressive symptoms.

The chapter also described the social psychology of mental health professionals. The final section reviewed concepts relevant to understanding pitfalls and shortcomings associated with clinical judgment and decision making. It suggested that improved knowledge of the types of cognitive–social biases that professionals fall prey to should benefit clients. This benefit will occur in proportion to the extent to which mental health professionals become resistant to making errors in how they diagnose and treat clients.

7

APPLYING SOCIAL PSYCHOLOGY TO SPORTS TEAMS

PHILIP SULLIVAN

DEBORAH L. FELTZ

CHAPTER OUTLINE

Team Dynamics
   Team Cohesion
   Team Confidence
   Effective Communication
   Team Goal Setting

Team Building
   Family Psychology Intervention
   Communication Training Intervention
   Performance Profiling Intervention
   Summary

Every year in Britain, the universities of Oxford and Cambridge compete in a boat race. The participants are true student-athletes (with no scholarships), and the coaches are volunteers, but this is a significant sporting event that draws international attention. The race has been called one of "the most brutal, harsh, and uncompromising struggles in all of sport" (Topolski, 1989, p. 9).

After losing the race in 1986, the Oxford boat club faced a long year before meeting Cambridge again. Aside from the wounded pride and standard training, those 12 months included an inordinate amount of drama. One of the 1986 Oxford crew members, an American named Chris Clarke, returned the following year with several experienced American rowers who had enrolled in Oxford. Their plan was, simply, to put out as strong a team as they could, one that could not possibly lose to Cambridge again.

As often happens in sports, things did not go as well as planned. The team had little camaraderie, and members even showed outright hostility toward each other and the leaders of the club. The newer rowers did not agree with the established training routines; they felt that the training routines were not necessary to ensure success. Disagreements over training methods resulted in an attempt to oust the club president (who also rowed on the team). When this revolt failed, half of the team members, led by the American contingent, quit the club with just 6 weeks to go before the boat race.

A poorly trained, substandard crew was left to prepare for the race. The team showed no unity, had little confidence in their leaders, and was largely disinterested in the race. Training runs and exhibition competitions resulted in poor times, further decreasing team confidence. Team members admitted to each other that they had little chance of winning the race and provided a wide variety of reasons for this impending failure.

However, the team did not fail. Instead, it pulled off a historic upset victory against Cambridge. From a social psychological perspective, one key aspect to this triumph was that, during a final team retreat, the team voted on the lineup for the race with Cambridge, inserting the maligned club president into a key position in the boat. From that point onward, although time was running out, the crew's training performances were excellent.

This one story shows two separate examples of the importance of social dynamics within groups in sport. In the first case, a team that on paper easily should have won every race it entered typically underperformed and could not even remain intact for one full season. Later, a team that did not have the skills and abilities to match its opponent nonetheless won the race. In both cases, something more than the individual attributes of the players contributed significantly to team performance. These collective attributes and processes, and their impact on performance and other outcomes, are the focus of this chapter. Consider these questions:

- After the Americans joined, the Oxford rowing team members did not get along well, and members disagreed frequently. What might have been done to avoid such problems?
- Which one factor do you think was most responsible for the team's eventual success during the race? Why?
- Do you think that the team, after winning the race, would have become a more united group? Why or why not?

In a column in *The Sporting News* on February 4, 2003, Matt Hayes discussed the University of Florida's men's basketball team. Instead of commenting in-depth on the talents and skills of the players, Hayes focused on "chemistry." He noted that "college sports live off of emotion and motivation and a strange, subtle, and significant thing called chemistry," adding that this chemistry is "the reason the line between champs and chumps isn't as wide as you would think" (Hayes, 2003). The picture of the head coach accompanying the article included a caption indicating that he had "earned a Ph.D. in team chemistry this season." More recently, when the underdog Detroit Pistons upset the Los Angeles Lakers to win the 2004 National Basketball Association (NBA) championship, Tayshaun Prince of the Pistons told reporters, "Words can't really describe how I feel right now. It's the best feeling in the world. This is a family. The chemistry around this team has been unbelievable."

Chemistry is an often-cited notion within sports. Although fans, athletes, coaches, and sport psychologists all seem to recognize it, chemistry is a vague concept. In Hayes's (2003) column and Prince's comments, as well as in untold other anecdotal commentaries of sports teams, chemistry appears as an all-encompassing component of team functioning and as a panacea for all team ills. The layperson's term "chemistry" is implicitly understood to be the sum total of intangible attributes within a team. It can be perceived to include everything from respect between teammates, compatibility between players and coaches, and a lack of conflict within the team. It is dynamic, mysterious, and very valuable. It appears that at least part of the reason why teams are successful—or unsuccessful—lies in this notion of chemistry. As Hayes intimated, it can mean the difference between winners and losers—"champs" and "chumps." However, it is important to note that team performance is not the only outcome of chemistry. Player and coach satisfaction, motivation, and a variety of other factors are also important consequences.

The comments of Hayes (2003) and Prince may serve as a poignant introduction to the topic of applied social psychology in sport. However, as familiar as teams like the Detroit Pistons and University of Florida's men's basketball team may be, they are still somewhat irrelevant to the typical psychology student. These are the things of sports pages, not personal experiences. However, think for a minute about your own sporting experiences. Have you ever played a team sport at any level, recreationally or competitively? If you have, what lasting impressions has this experience left with you? Have you made some of your strongest friendships through sport? Have you ever dropped out from a sport or team just because of the "bad blood" within a group of athletes? Have you ever played on a team that overachieved or grossly underachieved? If so, then the topics of this chapter, which are the essence of chemistry, will be relevant to you.

Go beyond your personal experiences as an athlete and think about the diversity of activity choices offered by your campus recreation program or the abundance of such programs for the youth and elderly in your community. Consider the place in our society of professional sports, the Olympics and Paralympics, and the X Games. When one stops to consider how significant sports (and particularly team sports) are in our everyday lives, one may find their presence to be overwhelming. Considering the relevance of these activities, it is not surprising that psychology has a specific field designated to the study of human behavior within a sporting context—sport psychology.

This chapter deals with the applied social psychology of sports teams. As a final part of this introduction, two points must be made. First, in accordance with the literature on the topic, the social psychology of sport is limited to the in-group social dynamics of sports teams. The vast majority of social psychological research in sport has focused on these attributes and interactions (i.e., this chemistry); thus, it is what is reviewed in this chapter. Second, the applied nature of social dynamics is seen in how these attributes and interactions have been conceptually and empirically linked to team performance and other valuable outcomes.

Figure 7.1 gives a schematic view of the application of social psychology to sports teams. Within any team situation in sport, there are certain "givens." A team will have a certain amount of ability, players will have certain personality characteristics, and coaches will have certain coaching styles. These may be considered the "input" into the team sport experience. The output would include variables such as the satisfaction that individuals derive from their involvement with the team and team performance. In this model, social psychological factors (i.e., team chemistry) operate between these inputs and outputs. These factors occur at a collective level, are distinct from individual factors such as personality, and have direct effects on outcomes such as team performance. The operation of the social psychological factors that make up chemistry represents the "throughput" of this model. By understanding what team chemistry is and how to influence it (i.e., through intervention strategies), one can maximize the positive outcomes of a team.

TEAM DYNAMICS

Scientists studying social behavior typically have to choose between using groups that exist naturally in the real world and artificially creating groups that possess certain desirable characteristics. Thus, studies can vary from a contrived "team" composed of five or so undergraduate psychology students who are asked to solve a puzzle to a natural team such as doctors and nurses who actually perform open-heart surgery. For the purpose of conducting research, does it seem that one is too artificial and the other is too uncontrollable? One context that allows researchers to combine and balance both the need for reality and the need for controllability is sports.

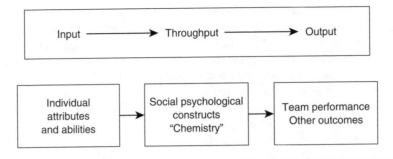

Figure 7.1   Framework for Understanding the Application of Social Psychology to Sports

According to Forsythe (1999), *groups* are best characterized by certain key features. These features include structured patterns of communication, interdependence between members, shared identity, and identifiable roles and structures. Although most of these features can be established in artificial groups, such groups likely lack a certain amount of generalizability to naturally occurring groups and, therefore, offer less insight into the dynamics of sports teams.

As groups, sports teams have been a boon to both basic research and applied research within social psychology. Sports teams at any level typically contain a rich and recognizable structure. They have clear, agreed-on roles that define the behavioral expectations for each member as well as norms that define and reinforce what behaviors are acceptable within the team. For example, the norms and expectations pertaining to coaches are clearly different from those pertaining to players. Individuals must balance their own motives and abilities with those of the team members around them to achieve conjoint, mutually desirable outcomes. These groups operate within a larger social system that includes fans, parents, communities, and leagues. There is a wide variety of clear feedback; teams win and lose, player and team statistics are maintained, players are cut or quit, and so forth.

Given the characteristics of sports teams, it is understandable that most of the social psychological work has focused on their internal social dynamics. The most significant of the topics examined in sports teams are team cohesion, communication patterns, team confidence, and group goal setting. These topics are covered in this chapter. Consistent with the bulk of the research, primary consideration is given to team performance as an outcome of team processes while recognizing the importance of other outcome variables (e.g., satisfaction, morale). Finally, most of the research in this field has focused on interacting team sports (e.g., soccer, basketball) rather than on individual team sports (e.g., golf, wrestling) because performance outcomes in the former depend much more on the dynamics of group interaction.

Team Cohesion

If you have ever played a team sport, one of the issues that may be immediately recognizable is the importance of how much you liked or disliked your teammates. In fact, your attitudes toward teammates may be the main reason why you are or are not a member of that team today. Even professional athletes, such as the NBA's Prince, will comment how their team is "like a family." Obviously, team unity and interpersonal attraction are important issues in sport (Figure 7.2).

The notion of unity (or camaraderie) has been the focus of much of the research in sport psychology. Typically, this has been referred to as **cohesion,** which has been defined as "a dynamic process which is reflected in the tendency for a group to stick together and remain united in the pursuit of its instrumental objectives and/or for the satisfaction of member affective needs" (Carron, Brawley, & Widmeyer, 1997, p. 3). Looking back at the story of the Oxford rowing club in the opening vignette, it is clear that for a large part of that season, the team showed very

Figure 7.2   The Important Dynamic of
Cohesion in Team Sports

little cohesion. Players feuded with one another and rebelled against the coach. It was obvious that they had little regard for instrumental objectives (e.g., how to win the race) or their teammates' affective needs (e.g., accepting them as friends). This lack of cohesion is most noticeable in the fact that the team that started the season together did not stick together; half of the team members quit.

Conceptual nature of team cohesion. The preceding definition of cohesion posed by Carron and colleagues (1997) reflects four key characteristics of the construct, namely, that cohesion is (a) multidimensional, (b) dynamic, (c) affective, and (d) instrumental (Carron et al., 1997).

Being **multidimensional** simply means that cohesion is not one simple factor but rather the sum of several interrelated factors. This reflects one of the earliest notions of the concept of cohesion. Festinger, Schachter, and Black (1950) stated that cohesion is the sum total of all forces that cause members to remain in the group. This sum total can include a wide variety of factors. For instance, players may stay on a team because they like their teammates and/or the

coach, because staying on the team gives them the best opportunity to be successful, because they have no other teams to play for, or even because they are being paid. The notion that cohesion is **dynamic** means that although it is relatively stable, cohesion does tend to fluctuate over time. Team cohesion tends to wax and wane over the course of a season. You may have heard the sentiment that "winning cures everything." One thing that team success may "cure" is a lack of cohesiveness. The relationship between performance and cohesion is discussed more fully later, but for now it is enough to understand that players may (and often do) like each other more when the team is performing well. Thus, team performance is one factor that contributes to the dynamic fluctuating nature of cohesion. For example, despite all of the hostility displayed among members of the Oxford rowing team, it would not be difficult to imagine the team members hugging one another after beating Cambridge.

Finally, it is important to note that cohesion is both affective and instrumental in nature. **Affectivity** refers to the emotional state of the athletes. You cannot understand cohesion unless you recognize that part of what keeps a team united is how the players feel about one another. Likewise, another big part of how cohesive a team is has to do with its goals and objectives. Goals and objectives are the most obvious features about which a team of players will remain united; this is the **instrumental** nature of cohesion. For example, members of a team who do not socialize very much may still be very united over their goal to win a championship. The affective and instrumental aspects of cohesion suggest two main dimensions of cohesion: *social cohesion* and *task cohesion*. There are teams that may be highly united as a social group but are not organized or united with respect to accomplishing team goals. A senior adult softball team may be more concerned with team get-togethers and how members interact socially than with how the team performs on the field (i.e., high on social cohesion and low on task cohesion). Alternatively, there are teams that are highly cohesive with respect to their instrumental purpose but not as social units. For example, Major League Baseball's (MLB) Oakland Athletics team during the early 1970s won back-to-back World Series championships but was notorious for clubhouse fighting and animosity among players. To say that either the senior adult softball team or the Oakland Athletics is not cohesive ignores the notion that there is both social cohesion and task cohesion. It is safe to say that most teams will display at least some amount of each aspect of cohesion.

Measurement of team cohesion. Cohesiveness in sports teams has been measured using a variety of instruments. Most studies have relied on standardized, quantitative self-report scales. The most commonly used measure is the Group Environment Questionnaire (GEQ) (Widmeyer, Brawley, & Carron, 1985).

The GEQ presents team cohesion as a four-factor structure reflecting two separate dimensions of cohesion. First, as we have seen, team cohesion can be social or task in nature; the group can be united as a social-oriented entity, a task-oriented entity, or both. Second, the notion of cohesion can mean different things from an individual perspective compared with looking at the group as a whole. The group may be a very united bunch (either socially or instrumentally), but that does not mean that every player identifies equally with the team. For instance, imagine a university varsity team in which one player is married and the rest are single. The married player might not socialize much with the team because of other commitments, but he or she can still recognize that the team is a tightly knit social group. These two dimensions result in four factors of team cohesion: **group integration–social,** which refers to perceptions of the group as a whole regarding social issues (e.g., "our team would like to spend time together in the off-season"); **group integration–task,** which refers to perceptions of the group as a whole regarding degree of task orientation (e.g., "our team is united in trying to reach its performance goals"); **individual attraction to group–social,** which deals with individual perceptions of the group as a social unit (e.g., "some of my best friends are on this team"); and **individual attraction to group–task,** which refers to individual perceptions of the group's task orientation (e.g., "I'm unhappy with my team's level of desire to win") (Widmeyer et al., 1985). Each factor of the GEQ is measured by the sum of its

items, so that higher scores indicate a greater level of cohesion. The GEQ allows researchers to measure the multidimensional nature of cohesion and to examine the various antecedents and consequences of its multiple dimensions. Given its dynamic and multidimensional nature, there is a variety of antecedents and consequences of cohesion.

Antecedents of cohesion. Consistent with the overall theme of this chapter (Figure 7.1), cohesion is a construct that cannot be understood independent of its inputs and outputs. This also can be seen in Figure 7.3, which shows cohesion as a central mediating process in team dynamics. Both individual antecedents (e.g., personality variables) and social antecedents (e.g., leadership style, role aspects) contribute to social unity and task unity, which in turn lead to individual and team outcomes. For example, individual consequences include member satisfaction and performance, and team consequences include overall team confidence and performance.

This section focuses on the inputs to cohesion, that is, those antecedent factors that shape and influence team unity. Both individual and social factors contribute to the cohesiveness of a group. Individual factors typically involve the personalities and demographic characteristics of teammates. Although conventional wisdom may suggest that people feel closer to those who are similar to them on the most obvious characteristics, simple demographic similarity does not appear to be very important for cohesiveness in sports teams. Widmeyer, Silva, and Hardy (1992) found that team sport athletes rated social and racial similarities as minimally important for both task cohesion and social cohesion. Nondemographic individual attributes, such as personality and attitudes, may have a greater impact on cohesion. For example, the tendency of the individual to self-disclose (Stokes, Fuerher, & Childs, 1984) and the individual's satisfaction with the team as whole (Widmeyer & Williams, 1991) both are positively related to team cohesion. Thus, on one level, how cohesive a team is may depend on the individual attributes and perceptions of its members.

Although it may be important that teammates are alike in certain ways, that does not necessarily

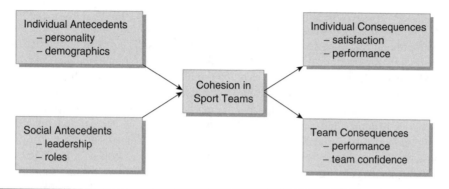

Figure 7.3   Conceptual Model of Team Cohesion

mean that they will work well together. There is also reason to believe that it is important to have teammates that have *complementary attributes* as opposed to similar ones. For example, although leadership is important to team success, having a team full of leaders would most likely not be as functional as having a mix of leaders and nonleaders. Copeland and Straub (1995) discussed the importance of interpersonal compatibility with respect to attributes such as friendliness, dominance, and acceptance of authority. Having individuals who complement each other on these attributes appears to result in greater team cohesion and more effective conflict management within the group.

Examples of social factors that influence cohesion are group size, leadership style, and member roles. With respect to *group size,* it appears that size affects task and social cohesion differently. A series of studies by Widmeyer and his colleagues using the GEQ showed that in laboratory-designed basketball and volleyball teams ranging in size from 3 to 12 members, task cohesion was always greater in groups of 3, whereas social cohesion was greater in larger teams and appeared to be optimal in groups of 6 (e.g., Widmeyer, Brawley, & Carron, 1990). The higher task cohesion in small teams likely is due to the fact that task coordination is easier, whereas larger groups are more likely to suffer from problems of coordination. On the other hand, a wider variety of sources for reliable social support contribute to higher social cohesion in larger groups.

Another group attribute related to team unity, at least task unity, is the coach's *leadership* style.

Correlational studies with samples of high school athletes in baseball, softball, and football have shown that **autocratic leadership** (i.e., the coach as leader makes all decisions and refrains from delegating any power) is associated with lower levels of task cohesion, as measured by the GEQ (Gardner, Light-Shields, Bredemeier, & Bostrom, 1996; Westre & Weiss, 1991). On the other hand, **democratic leadership** (i.e., the coach involves his or her athletes in making decisions that affect the team) is related to higher levels of task cohesion. Thus, with respect to task cohesion, the most appropriate method of leadership would appear to be one that empowers the group and allows team members to have input into decisions and policies.

Although the coach has an obvious role in sports teams, all team members are asked to fill certain roles. **A role** refers to a set of behaviors expected of a person in a particular social position or setting. On a sports team, roles may be formalized (e.g., the coach and team captain) or informal (e.g., the "practical joker"). There are several different aspects to how roles may affect cohesion. **Role clarity** refers to the extent to which one's role has been clearly defined. This is distinct from **role acceptance,** that is, the degree to which the person expected to fill a role agrees to comply with the requirements of the role. Finally, **role performance** refers to how well the individual actually completes the responsibilities of the role. To maximize cohesiveness, each of these aspects of one's role must be satisfied. For example, reconsider the plight of the Oxford rowing crew in the opening vignette. For many months, this elite and previously cohesive team experienced splintering into subgroups, poor performance, and intense personal dissatisfaction. It is likely that many of these negative outcomes would have been avoided if team members had accepted the roles that were best suited to them. It appears that the issues confronting the team originated with a small number of team members who did not like or accept the roles they were expected to fulfill. They spent much energy in trying to take over the duties and responsibilities attached to the roles of other members (e.g., the club captain and coach). Their actions included protesting training methods and altering norms of team decision making. As a result, eventually half of the team members quit. Imagine that, instead of having conflicts over the roles of the crew members, all of the rowers had clearly defined roles (e.g., concerning decision-making authority) and openly accepted their own roles. It seems obvious that the turmoil of the season would have been avoided and that a cohesive, satisfied, and successful team would have existed.

Research on how role clarity, acceptance, and performance affect both social cohesion and task cohesion has yielded two significant conclusions. First, the aspects, although interrelated, are also distinct. For example, just because a coach clarifies a nonstarting role for a player does not mean that the player will accept it. The player may fully believe that he or she should be a starter. The rejection of a clearly defined role could easily detract from both social cohesion and task cohesion in the team. The second major finding with respect to member roles and cohesion is that, of the three aspects of member roles, role acceptance has the most influence on team cohesion (Dawe & Carron, 1990). Thus, although it is important for roles to be clear and to be filled by competent people, with respect to team cohesion, the greatest benefit will accrue when team members accept the roles they are asked to fill.

Cohesion and performance. We now consider the possible consequences of cohesion, concentrating in particular on indexes of performance (Figure 7.3). At the *individual level,* there is ample evidence that members of cohesive teams tend to work harder and experience more success. Bray and Whaley (2001) investigated the relationship between team cohesion (using the GEQ) and the individual efforts of male and female high school basketball players over the course of a season. An individual performance measure consisting of shooting percentage, rebounds, assists, steals, and total points was used. The researchers found that by the end of the season, team cohesion predicted individual performance. These results supported earlier findings on collegiate baseball players (Apple, 1993). Bray and Whaley also found that social cohesion offered the best prediction of individual performance, suggesting that improved individual success may be due to the greater effort invested by individuals in the context of a socially cohesive team. Similarly, Prapavessis and Carron (1997) found a positive relationship between task cohesion and aerobic work rate in athletes from a variety of team sports. Thus, the evidence suggests that cohesion is related to the performance of individual team members, although it cannot be stated with certainty whether social cohesion or task cohesion is more strongly related.

The preceding research links team cohesion with individual performance. We also can consider the connection between cohesion and *team* performance. In this regard, there is considerable anecdotal and research evidence that teams high in cohesion perform better than do teams low in cohesion. For instance, Mullen and Copper (1994) conducted a meta-analysis of the cohesion–performance relationship in many different groups, including sports teams. A **meta-analysis** is a statistical procedure for combining and integrating the results of separate studies to derive an overall assessment of the results, for example, the direction and magnitude of the relationship between variables (causal or otherwise). Mullen and Copper found that task cohesion significantly predicted team performance. Of particular relevance, this relationship was most significant with sports teams. Considering the multidimensional nature of cohesion, it is important to note that the Mullen and Copper analysis suggseted that a team's task cohesion in particular is strongly related to performance. Teams that have clearly defined and mutually agreed-on objectives tend to perform well. This reflects the often-quoted sentiment heard in sports of "everyone rowing in the same direction" or "everyone being on the same page."

The evidence connecting cohesion with team performance may be viewed as suggesting that cohesion leads to better performance (as depicted in Figure 7.3). This is probably why many teams, from high school sports teams to professional sports teams, sometimes go on retreats and take part in team-building exercises. However, keeping in mind the discussion of correlation and causation in Chapter 3, it is also possible that the relationship is reversed, that is, that better performance (individual or team) results in greater cohesion. That certainly is a reasonable possibility. Everyone likes winning, and when you contribute to and share such a positive event with teammates, it makes sense that everyone will like each other more.

The true causal nature of the cohesion–performance relationship has been difficult to ascertain. Just read the following quote from pitcher Damien Moss of MLB's Atlanta Braves: "I think this is the best team we've ever had . . . just the feeling of camaraderie. Everybody is happy to be here. They want to win. They're on the same page" ("Business as Usual," 2002). Undoubtedly, Moss, a professional athlete on an elite team, knows that cohesion and performance go hand in hand. However, it is much harder to determine whether he has any idea of which causes which. Is this the best team the Braves have ever had because everyone is on the same page, or is everyone on the same page because this is the best Braves team ever?

In an early study, Carron and Ball (1977) attempted to clarify the causal nature of the cohesion–performance relationship by assessing cohesion at different points in the season of intercollegiate hockey players. They administered the Sport Cohesiveness Questionnaire (Martens, Landers, & Loy, 1972) at three times during the season: within the first two regular season games, at midseason, and after the regular season had been completed. Team performance was assessed by means of a win/loss ratio at midseason and at the end of the season. Carron and Ball concluded that performance was a much better predictor of cohesion than cohesion was of performance. Causation was inferred because performance accounted for a greater amount of the variation in cohesion than cohesion did in performance.

Recently, Grieve, Whelan, and Meyes (2000) found similar results in an experiment where they created basketball teams with participants who were novice basketball players. Half of the teams were exposed to a cohesion-building intervention, and the remaining teams were subjected to a cohesion-reducing exercise. The cohesion-building intervention was designed to promote task-oriented self-disclosure by facilitating a discussion about role definitions (e.g., perceived roles on the team, communication styles). The cohesion-reducing condition was designed, first, to foster social cohesion by having players disclose information about themselves (e.g., major, year in school, social activities) and, second and immediately prior to competition, to give individual players a change of team assignment so that teams were composed of members who had not communicated with each other previously. Grieve and colleagues found that cohesion (measured by the GEQ) had no effect on performance but that successful teams subsequently reported higher levels of task cohesion.

Finally, Carron, Colman, Wheeler, and Stevens (2002) conducted a more complete examination of the cohesion-performance question: a meta-analysis of studies that related the cohesion of sports teams to performance and that had used the GEQ to measure cohesion. They concluded that there are consistently strong relationships between performance and both social cohesion and task cohesion. More important, in contrast to the findings of Carron and Ball (1977) and Grieve and colleagues (2000), Carron and colleagues found that cohesion was as strong a predictor of performance as performance was of cohesion. Interestingly, the authors also found that the relationships between performance and both social cohesion and task cohesion were stronger for female teams than for male teams. It appears that the relationship between cohesion and performance is robust within sports teams as well as bidirectional. That is, teammates who experience success together probably will perceive more team cohesion, but the likelihood of team success can be increased by facilitating team cohesion, particularly with regard to team goals and objectives. The evidence of bidirectionality suggests that the arrows in Figure 7.3 connecting cohesion to consequences should point in both directions.

Cohesion and other outcomes. Although team performance is the most widely studied variable in relation to team cohesiveness, it is not the only one. In the opening vignette about the Oxford rowing team, low cohesion among team members seemed to be connected not only to poor performance but also to low levels of satisfaction and confidence in the team. Research has shown that cohesion is related to a variety of nonperformance outcomes for both the individual athlete and the team. At the individual level, members of cohesive teams tend to be more satisfied and committed to the team. At the team level, cohesive teams tend to be more confident and interact with each other better (e.g., with respect to communication). These group attributes are further clarified in the following sections. It is worth noting that although cohesion and team confidence do tend to share a reciprocal relationship (as do other group factors), we cannot necessarily assume that the variables are causally related, much less specify the direction of causality.

Team Confidence

Although cohesion was the first group dynamic that attracted a lot of research in sport, it is not the only important one. Level of self-confidence clearly is an important factor in sports teams. Some teams are composed of a collection of talented members who are confident as individuals but lack confidence in their teams as a whole. Other teams might not have very many especially talented members but have a common belief that, as groups, they can integrate their talents to perform successfully. Still other teams may collapse when the self-doubts of a few members become contagious. For example, Longman (2000) related the story of how the U.S. women's soccer team lost the semifinal match against Norway in the 1995 World Cup because the lack of confidence of a few players seemed to infect the entire team. A few years later, however, the 1999 World Cup had a very different ending, with the U.S. women beating China in a shootout for the

championship. The U.S. team members said that they won because they believed in each other. Like cohesion, and consistent with the theme of this chapter, the concept of team confidence is best understood as an intermediate dynamic that both is influenced by certain factors and leads to certain outcomes.

Self-efficacy refers to the belief that one can act to successfully produce a given outcome under a given set of circumstances. It is essentially a situation-specific form of self-confidence. Self-efficacy has long been established as one of the primary psychological factors in human performance. Self-efficacy and self-confidence are used interchangeably in sport psychology and are used accordingly in this chapter (Feltz & Chase, 1998).

Bandura (1986), recognizing that much of human activity takes place in social contexts, proposed the notion of collective efficacy, also known as team confidence. Bandura (1997) defined **collective efficacy** as a group's shared belief in its ability to organize and execute the courses of action required to obtain a certain outcome. Bandura noted that one of the primary areas in which individuals work together to achieve a shared outcome is sports. Therefore, much of the research and theorizing about team confidence has focused on sports teams.

Team confidence and individual attributes. Because teams are composed of individuals, team confidence can be largely affected by the psychological characteristics of the members of the group. Perhaps the most obvious of these is the self-efficacy of each member. If all members of a team feel very confident about their abilities, it would seem to follow that confidence in the team as whole would be quite high. Similarly, one would expect a team to display low team confidence if the members lacked confidence in their own abilities. In reality, however, most teams usually are somewhere between these two extremes. Some players feel quite confident in themselves, whereas other teammates might not.

Although the link between self-efficacy and collective efficacy has been noted several times (e.g., George & Feltz, 1995; Spink, 1990a), to date only two studies have researched the issue. Feltz and Lirgg (1998) examined the self-confidence and team confidence of male college hockey players on six different teams. Feltz and Lirgg measured how confident each player was in performing his role in an upcoming game as well as how confident the player was that the team as a whole would accomplish certain collective goals (e.g., outshoot the opposing team, "kill off" penalties). The measures of perceived self-efficacy and team efficacy were administered within a 24-hour period prior to each of 32 games. The researchers found that the aggregated self-efficacies of the players were significantly related to the collective efficacy of the team. In addition, Magyar, Feltz, and Simpson (2004) examined determinants of collective efficacy with junior rowers at a regional championship regatta. They found that the self-efficacy beliefs of rowers were related to their beliefs in the efficacy of their boat team (i.e., team efficacy). Magyar and colleagues also found that rowers' perceptions of the type of motivational climate that a coach creates were related to their team efficacy beliefs. Specifically, the more a coach emphasized a **mastery-oriented climate** (i.e., an emphasis on learning, improving, and working together), the higher the rowers' efficacy beliefs in the team.

Other individual-level factors that have been researched in conjunction with collective efficacy include precompetitive anxiety and affect. For example, by assessing the levels of individual anxiety and mood of a sample of male rugby players prior to competition, Greenlees, Nunn, Graydon, and Maynard (1999) found a relationship between individuals' perceptions of confidence in their team and how they felt prior to competition. Specifically, team members' concerns that the team would not perform well (i.e., low collective efficacy) were associated with higher levels of anxiety and negative affect.

Another way in which to consider the individual attributes that influence team efficacy judgments is to ask athletes what they think contributes to their confidence. Chase, Feltz, and Lirgg (2003) examined the sources of information that female collegiate basketball players provided in making self-efficacy and collective efficacy judgments prior to 12 basketball games. They found that the athletes rated past performance as a primary contributor to both self-efficacy and collective efficacy. However,

there were some sources that were noted particularly for self-efficacy and not for collective (or team) efficacy. Specifically, the athletes reported that outside sources (e.g., social distractions, school assignments) were influential with regard to their own confidence but not with regard to that of the group.

Team confidence and cohesion. Given the aforementioned wealth of literature on cohesion, it is not surprising that cohesion has been linked to team confidence. Spink (1990b) found that collegiate female volleyball teams that were high in collective efficacy were also high in both social cohesion and task cohesion. Paskevich, Brawley, Dorsch, and Widmeyer (1999) also conducted an extensive study examining the relationship between collective efficacy and cohesion in a sample of collegiate volleyball players. They found that collective efficacy was significantly related to task cohesion, with both factors of task cohesion (group integration and individual attraction to group) significantly discriminating between high- and low-efficacy groups. Using a different sport as a sample, Kozub and McDonnell (2000) found that team cohesion, particularly task cohesion, was highly related to collective efficacy for male rugby players. Thus, cohesion and collective efficacy are highly interrelated. Furthermore, Paskevich and colleagues' (1999) findings suggested that task cohesion might be more closely related to a team's confidence than is social cohesion. This makes sense: How confident a team is in its ability to achieve a specific goal is tied to the unity that the team has around the task of achieving the goal.

Team confidence and performance. According to Bandura (1986, 1997) and a wealth of research in sport psychology (cf. Feltz & Chase, 1998), the most powerful factor affecting confidence is previous experience. Simply put, individuals and teams are confident about doing things that they have done well in the past, and they lack confidence about doing the things that they have not done well in the past. Furthermore, research supports Bandura's contention that confidence beliefs are major determinants of athletic performance (Feltz & Lirgg, 1998, Kane, Marks, Zaccaro, & Blair, 1996; Myers, Feltz, & Short, 2004).

Thus, the relationship between confidence beliefs and performance is believed to be recursive: "Mastery expectations influence performance and are, in turn, altered by the cumulative effect of one's efforts" (Bandura, 1977a, p. 194). This relationship goes a long way toward explaining the phenomena of winning streaks and losing streaks. If a team wins, it is likely to be more confident that it can win again the next time. Conversely, if a team loses, it might lack the confidence needed to perform well in the next game. These two effects result in potential spirals that can be hard to escape. Success leads to confidence, which leads to success; conversely, failure detracts from confidence, which may result in further failures. Needless to say, the players on a team on a winning streak feel as though they can "beat the world," whereas players on a team that has not won lately often lack any faith in their team.

FOCUS ON RESEARCH

Several laboratory experiments have addressed the relationship between team confidence and performance, and their results have consistently pointed to a strong association between these two variables. For example, Hodges and Carron (1992) had three-person groups engage in a competitive task against another group. Unbeknownst to the participants, the group they were competing against was made up of experimental confederates who were familiar with the purpose of the study and enacted a predetermined script. The two groups were told that they would be competing in two tasks: a hand dynamometer task (a measure of hand strength) and a medicine ball task (a muscular endurance exercise). Each participant was told to squeeze the dynamometer as hard as possible. Strength scores for each group member were then summed to produce a total strength score for his or her group. The hand dynamometer task was used to manipulate the collective efficacy of the groups. After the strength scores had been calculated, each experimental group was given bogus feedback about its combined strength relative to the confederate group. In the *high-collective efficacy condition,* the experimental groups were informed that their group strength scores were substantially higher than that of the confederate group. Experimental groups in the *low-collective efficacy condition* were told that their combined strength scores were substantially lower than that of the confederate group. Each experimental group then participated in a series of four performance trials on the medicine ball task in which the group had to hold up the ball for a longer time period than the confederate group. Before doing so, the experimental group was asked to indicate, on scales ranging from 0% to 100%, how likely it was that the group would win and how confident the group was in its assessment of its chances. The product of these two scores served as a measure of collective efficacy. Had they known the truth about the materials used in the experiment, the experimental groups likely would have indicated that their chances were 0% because the medicine ball used by the confederate group was actually filled with foam, even though it looked identical to the one used by the experimental groups. Not surprisingly, the experimental groups lost every time.

The results revealed that the bogus feedback on the dynamometer task was effective in influencing collective efficacy. Groups in the high-collective efficacy condition had higher expectations of success in the subsequent medicine ball task than did those in the low-collective efficacy condition. The results concerning performance were more interesting. Following the inevitable initial loss to the confederate group, groups in the low-collective efficacy condition demonstrated decrements in their performance on the medicine ball task over subsequent trials. However, following their initial failure, groups in the high-collective efficacy condition actually demonstrated improvements in their performance. These results clearly demonstrate the value of positive feedback in producing collective efficacy and affirm the application of Bandura's self-efficacy theory to groups.

Two other studies employed similar designs to assess collective self-efficacy. In one experiment (Lichacz & Partington, 1996), team participants engaged in a tug-of-war against a device that measured the strength of the their collective pull. In another experiment (Greenlees, Graydon, & Maynard, 2000), the amount of time the team spent on a biking machine was measured. In each of these studies, after the group had performed, team members were given misleading feedback about their performance. In both studies, teams that were told they had performed well were more confident than those that were told they had performed poorly. Subsequently, the high-confidence teams performed better during a second performance trial.

To date, only two published studies have examined the relationship between team performance and confidence with actual sporting groups over the course of a season. These studies corroborate the laboratory evidence. Feltz and Lirgg (1998) followed six collegiate male hockey teams over the course of a season and measured individual and collective efficacy before each game as well as subsequent team performance. Team confidence was measured by asking each player how confident he was that his team could accomplish certain goals (e.g., beat the opposing teams, force more turnovers than the opposing teams). Feltz and Lirgg found that team confidence positively predicted team performance. They also found that although collective efficacy increased after wins and decreased after losses, individual self-efficacy was not affected by team performance. This finding supports the notion that collective efficacy is indeed a group attribute rather than an individual attribute. The researchers suggested that a team's accomplishments are more apparent and less ambiguous to a team member than are his or her own accomplishments in the team context. Therefore, the visible team wins and losses may have a greater effect on players' team efficacy judgments than on efficacy judgments about themselves.

In a subsequent study, Myers and colleagues (2004) examined the influence of efficacy beliefs on the offensive performance of American football teams and the reciprocal relationship between collective efficacy and offensive performance over a season of competition. The reciprocal relationship between collective efficacy and performance had not been measured previously in a field setting. The Feltz and Lirgg (1998) study had not examined the week-to-week influence of aggregated collective efficacy on team performance, nor had it examined the week-to-week influence of previous performance on subsequent collective efficacy. Myers and colleagues (2004) surveyed 10 football teams within a 24-hour period prior to each of eight games over eight consecutive weekends. Their results were consistent with those of Feltz and Lirgg (1998): Team performance by the offense (i.e., points scored, total yardage, average yardage gained per play, number of punts, and game outcome) significantly predicted collective efficacy, and collective efficacy significantly predicted the next game's offensive performance. Together, both laboratory and field studies suggest that to affect team performance and alleviate anxiety and negative affect, coaches and athletes should focus on confidence in the collective capabilities of a team rather than emphasizing individual confidence.

It is also possible that teams may become overconfident as a result of past success, and this in turn may lead to complacency, lack of focus, and less willingness to try new strategies (Vancouver, Thompson, Tischner, & Putka, 2002). Such complacency behaviors may lead to future failures. Anyone who watches sports on television has seen teams lose to weaker opponents because the stronger teams did not take their opponents seriously enough. Although this possibility has not been studied empirically in sport, Marks (1999) found with work teams that high-collective efficacy teams performed worse than low-collective efficacy teams in terms of coordination processes in situations that were novel or nonroutine. Thus, it might be that in sport situations that demand flexibility (e.g., a change in offensive or defensive strategy), high-efficacy teams may be reluctant to give up the strategies that have led to their previous successes.

Effective Communication

If a team is a group of people acting together to achieve a shared goal, it goes without saying that team members must communicate with one another to achieve the goal. How could players who cannot talk or signal to one another decide how to play together? If you try to imagine such a situation, you begin to realize just how many interpersonal behaviors communicate meaning and information—not just words and hand signals but also eye contact, body language, and physical touch.

As essential as communication is to groups, team communication still has not been widely studied. Perhaps this is not that surprising. Communication may be difficult to study because it is so ubiquitous. If **communication** can be defined as interpersonal acts that exchange meaning and information, then what is not communication? One player can ignore a teammate, and that would still be considered communication. No wonder so little research has been done.

Nature of team communication. Recently, a relatively precise conceptualization of communication emerged in the work of Sullivan and Feltz (2003), who defined communication in a very specific sense. They used the phrase "effective communication in sports" to refer to those interactions that enhance the operation of the team and its members. For instance, messages between teammates that result in improved team performance or more satisfied players would be considered effective communication because they contribute to a better functioning team. This notion is based on the definition of communication as "a symbolic process by which two people, bound together in a relationship, provide each other with resources or negotiate the exchange of resources" (Roloff, 1981, p. 30) and is couched within the theoretical framework of social exchange theory (e.g., Foa & Foa, 1974). A **resource** is any commodity, whether material or symbolic, that can be exchanged through interpersonal behavior (Foa & Foa, 1974).

Social exchange theory refers to a school of theories of interpersonal interaction that have been used to explain nearly everything from marriage to traffic jams. These theories assume that all interactions are a form of negotiation and an exchange of resources that are valued by the actors. The various social exchange theories tend to offer different classifications of these resources, but they may be said to include both tangible (e.g., money) and intangible (e.g., love) resources. Basically, anything that may be given by one person to another and is valued can be a resource.

There are several key characteristics in a social exchange interaction. First, the people are assumed to be interdependent; that is, their actions and decisions rely in part on the actions and reactions of the other people in the situation. Second, these relationships work best if, in the long run, they are reciprocal and mutually beneficial. Thus, in any one discrete interaction, people may actually give more than they receive so long as they can expect to derive some long-term benefit from that relationship.

Social exchange theories also tend to assume that people are rational actors. People not only evaluate the costs and benefits of their current relationships but also evaluate the ratio of costs and benefits in other possible relationships. For example, a player on a team will have some sense of all the benefits he or she derives from being a member of the team (i.e., in terms of resources such as respect and information). He or she also will have evaluated the costs of this membership (i.e., in terms of resources such as money and time). Based on the balance between these costs and benefits, as well as on the expected costs and benefits ratio of being a member of another team, the player may decide to stay with the current team, switch teams, or quit playing altogether.

The main benefit of social exchange theory is that it offers concrete boundaries for what can be seen as "communication." Any interaction that rewards (or punishes) another through the exchange of resources is an act of communication (Kelly & Thibault, 1978). Thus, the interactions between teammates or partners are characterized by what one individual "provides" to the other (e.g., information, emotional support) and what the other person has to "pay" for these resources (e.g., respect, reciprocated emotional support). Obviously there are many types of this kind of communication within sports teams, for example, coaches giving players tips and athletes patting each other on the back.

Communication resources in sport. Despite the limited research on communication in sport, there is a consistent theme of identifying types of communication that involve valued resources. Typically, researchers have focused on the task-oriented messages between teammates, even though sports teams are also important as social groups. For example, based on an analysis of communication patterns in elite volleyball teams, Hanin (1992) identified four main styles of communication. Messages that dealt with planning strategy or technique were labeled **orientation messages,** whereas those between teammates that served to motivate or energize team members were labeled **stimulation messages.** Discussions that focused on assessments of play, ability, or effort were labeled **evaluation messages.** All other communications were termed **task-irrelevant messages.** Not surprisingly, a distinct, performance-based pattern of communication was observed. Teams tended to display orientation messages before performance, stimulation messages during performance, and evaluation messages after performance. Overall, stimulation messages were the most frequent type of communication, and the amount of task-irrelevant communication was negligible. Although these results are based only on a sample of teams from one sport, it is not unreasonable to suggest that the general communication pattern reflects the functioning of most elite sports teams. Such teams will be extremely task conscious, and interactions within the team will reflect this focus, whether before, during, or after games.

Other task-oriented resources reported in the literature include giving tips to teammates about their play (Williams & Widmeyer, 1991). Other social resources that have been investigated include displaying understanding and acceptance (Sullivan, 1993) and displaying both trust and expressions of warmth (DiBerardinis, Barwind, Flanningam, & Jenkins, 1983).

An important, but little studied, aspect of communication in sports teams is nonverbal communication, particularly given how physical the context of sport is. Kneidinger, Maple, and Tross (2001) investigated the role of gestures and touch among baseball and softball players. Teams were observed for a total of 20 games. The researchers found that females displayed touching behaviors more frequently than did males and that females tended to show different touching behaviors, particularly those that involved multiple actors, for example, team hugs and hand piles (Figure 7.4). In contrast, males were more likely to engage in one-on-one interactions (e.g., high fives). Furthermore, females tended to engage in more touching behaviors (e.g., back slaps, butt pats) after negative game events than did males. The incidence of more touching among the female ball players is consistent with gender role norms that support the display of physical expressiveness in females more than in males.

Communication and performance. Like much of the work applying social psychology to sport, research on communication shows a dual nature involving social and task issues. Actually, with communication, this dichotomy goes beyond sport and dates back to Bales's (1950) distinction between social communication and task communication in groups. For instance, consider the following two quotations from the tale of the Oxford rowing crew's 1987 race against Cambridge described in the opening vignette (Topolski, 1989). Before the race, the coach addressed the team in a motivational speech:

> "This is your weather," I told the crew, "and out there it's your water—no one can cope with those waves like you guys can, least of all Cambridge. You have the weight and technique for rough water—and better still, you have the nerve for it. And, I don't think Cambridge has that nerve. If it stays like this, I really think you could pull it off tomorrow." (pp. 274–275)

> After winning the race, the captain of the team had these words for the coach: "We could have been disqualified out there, Dan . . . because we had ten men in our boat [including you] and they only had nine." (p. 300)

Whether discussions within the team are the type of "fire 'em up" speeches (as the rowing coach made) or a sincere statement of recognition (as the captain of the rowing team subsequently made), there are undoubtedly many important effects of such messages.

The research that has focused on task communications (e.g., motivating, strategizing, teaching technique) has indicated that these

Figure 7.4   Gender Differences in Physical Communication: Females Hugging

messages are positively related to a team's performance (Dale & Wrisberg, 1996; Widmeyer & Williams, 1991). Interestingly, social communication, which is more concerned with expressions of emotion and how members are treated and accepted, also has been shown to be related to performance (DiBerardinis et al., 1983) and team cohesion (Sullivan, 1995; Sullivan & Feltz, 2003).

Team Goal Setting

In the sport psychology literature on individual performance, goal setting is a major topic. Research showing the importance of goal setting with individual athletes suggests the potential value of goal setting with groups.

Nature of goals and goal setting. Athletes can have different types of goal orientation (Burton, 1989). **Outcome goals** focus strictly on the competitive result of an event. These goals are based on social comparison, that is, how one does relative to others. With outcome goals, individuals focus on winning, and if they do win—regardless of how it comes about—their goal has been

achieved. Alternatively, if an athlete plays the best game of his or her life and loses, it would be considered a failure. **Performance goals** focus on achieving success based on self-comparison. The objective is to improve one's own performance; the actual outcome of the competitive event might not be considered important at all. **Process goals** are focused on the skills to be performed during competition such as trying to complete all passes during a hockey game (Kingston & Hardy, 1997).

Regardless of which goals are endorsed, there is little doubt that setting goals improves performance (Kyllo & Landers, 1995). Although there is a variety of conceptual explanations of why goal setting might be so effective, most researchers in sport psychology endorse Locke and Latham's (1985) direct mechanistic view of how goals work. According to Locke and Latham, setting goals can have four direct effects on performance, namely, that (a) goal setting may increase someone's effort toward the requisite behavior, (b) goal setting may prolong persistence once the behavior is initiated, (c) goals may direct the performer's attention to important elements of the performance, and (d) goals may foster development of new learning strategies.

Research has revealed several important aspects of effective goal setting. Goals should be specific, realistic, and challenging. The timeframe should not be ignored when setting goals, and both short-term and long-term goals should be used. Evaluation and feedback based on these goals should be carried out in a consistent and timely fashion in both competitive and training situations (Weinberg & Gould, 1999).

Group goal setting. Brawley, Carron, and Widmeyer (1992) conducted an exploratory investigation of the nature of group goals with team sport athletes. They found that most team goals, as opposed to individual goals, were vague and imprecise. This was true with respect to both the exact nature of the goals (e.g., the goals were not stated in terms of an objective standard such as time of possession) and the timeframes for their accomplishment (e.g., no deadlines would be set). With respect to types of team goals, Brawley and colleagues found that the majority of team goals endorsed during practice were performance goals (e.g., give maximum effort in each drill), whereas goals during a competition comprised a balance among outcome goals (e.g., win the game), process goals (e.g., perform each skill as it should be done), and performance goals.

Widmeyer and Ducharme (1997) proposed a model of the effective use of goal setting for teams as a whole. Their model outlined four principles for team goal setting, namely, to (a) establish long-term goals first and then use short-term goals to establish clear paths to those long-term goals, (b) involve all team members in establishing team goals, (c) monitor progress toward these goals and reward team progress, and (d) take steps to enhance the shared confidence of the group to achieve these goals (i.e., collective efficacy).

If the Oxford rowing club could be used as an example of applying team goal setting, the long-term goal decided on after losing to Cambridge in 1986 would be to win the race the following year. In the short term, goals might include certain training regimens and trial races. If the team as a whole were involved in deciding these steps (in reality, the decisions were made largely by the coaching staff of the club), one could expect that the rowers would have shown greater commitment to the goals and goal achievement and subsequently would have been more united and confident with respect to beating Cambridge. It might even be concluded that if the rowing team had followed Widmeyer and Ducharme's (1997) guidelines, the team might not have experienced the drama and disruption that it did.

TEAM BUILDING

Team building refers to the active planned process of optimizing the abilities of teammates toward maximizing individual performance, team performance, or social outcomes. To a considerable extent, team-building interventions typically are directed toward improving a team's internal social dynamics (i.e., chemistry). In other words, interventions are aimed at one or more of the very social psychological factors that have been reviewed in this chapter: cohesion, confidence, communication, and goal setting. There is some research on the explicit practice of team building within sports.

Family Psychology Intervention

A unique approach to team building is the use of family therapy for sports teams. As Schindler-Zimmerman (1993) observed,

> Athletic teams look like and function much like families.... The coaching staff, especially at the university level, assumes a surrogate parental role.... The more experienced or older players take on older sibling roles teaching the new recruits "the ropes" and generally taking on more team responsibility. (p. 29)

It has been noted that many of the issues dealt with by sport psychologists (e.g., conflict resolution, role clarification, group unity) also are issues for which family psychologists have well-designed group-based interventions (Grau, Möller, & Gunnarsson, 1988; Schindler-Zimmerman, 1993; Schindler-Zimmerman & Protinsky, 1993; Schindler-Zimmerman, Washle, & Protinsky, 1990).

Schindler-Zimmerman and colleagues (1990) developed one such intervention dealing with a college female volleyball team over the course of a season. The consultants focused on developing in team members the perception that the team, like a family, is a social system. As a social system, teammates and coaches have a great impact on each other; therefore, treating any one person individually is not very beneficial. With this goal in mind, one intervention strategy involved having the team members discuss issues such as labeling and rituals, including the meanings they convey (e.g., how meaningful it can be to simply say someone has "bad hands") and how to change the boundaries of the system.

Schindler-Zimmerman and colleagues (1990) designed a program based on repeated short meetings that addressed four specific problems: (a) one player receiving special attention from the coaching staff, (b) the team's propensity to complain during practice, (c) the coaches' polarized roles on the team, and (d) the need for a sense of team confidence. Each of these issues was approached with a specific objective and an individualized consultation plan. Let us consider one example. The issue of one player receiving special attention had to do with one of the team's star players, who was perceived as unmotivated. To

Table 7.1 Seven Stages of Sullivan's (1993) Communication Training Program

Stage	Objective	Activity
1	Effective listening	Teammates generate list of good listening skills and guidelines for implementing them
2	Self-assessment	Teammates share and comment on self-completed personality assessments
3	Identification of problems	Pairs of teammates generate a list of problems facing the team; team consensus is reached on total list of problems
4	Self-disclosure	Each athlete participates in an exercise involving completing a sentence (e.g., "On the team, I need to improve my ability to . . . ") in front of the team
5	Concerns about current season	Team members write down one fear and one hope for the season; these comments are reported (anonymously) to the team
6	Norm of acceptance	Small groups within the team share personal stories about mistakes made and lessons learned
7	Self-evaluation	Each player evaluates the team's progress on team members' being genuine with one another, communicating in an understanding fashion, valuing each other as individuals, and accepting one another

motivate her, the coaches treated her differently from the other players and encouraged her teammates to do the same. This was interpreted as a coalition between different levels of the team (i.e., coaching staff and players) that was resulting in a poorly functioning team. The consultants designed an intervention consisting of the coaches and teammates of the star player first recognizing the harmful consequences of these behaviors (e.g., decline in cohesiveness) and then actively "backing off" when they initiated or witnessed such interactions. This intervention was deemed a success based not just on the subjective evaluations of all the players (including the star) and coaches but also on the subsequent performance of the star player and the team as a whole.

Communication Training Intervention

Sullivan (1993) developed an extensive communication training program for sports teams designed to optimize the interpersonal communication skills of the athletes. Although Sullivan did not present a theoretical rationale for why communication would affect team performance, she did base her intervention on an empirical link between the two concepts. Summarizing the applied literature in the field, she argued that team communication appeared to influence performance indirectly through team cohesion. As a team communicates more openly, the sense of cohesiveness in the team is enhanced. And as we have seen, team cohesion is positively related to performance.

Sullivan's (1993) communication training program was applied to seven teams, including their coaches. In total, more than 80 male and female team sport athletes participated. The intervention lasted for the entire season and consisted of seven stages. Each stage entailed a specific objective with corresponding activities that were designed to enhance different interpersonal communication skills of the teammates.

Table 7.1 summarizes the seven stages of the communication program. Sullivan (1993) concluded that the program successfully enhanced "team members' awareness of their own communication skills and/or competence" (p. 90). This conclusion was supported by numerous comments made by the athletes, including "we have increased awareness of our team communication issues" (p. 88), "we are following through on the court with what we're discussing in these activities" (p. 89), and "I will give my opinion more to people with whom I feel intimidated" (p. 89).

Performance Profiling Intervention

As reflected by Schindler-Zimmerman's family psychology approach and Sullivan's communication training approach, sport psychologists often apply their understanding of social dynamics to enhance team functioning. Another effective intervention strategy involves performance profiling. The work of Dale and Wrisberg (1996) with this technique is detailed in the Focus on Intervention box.

● FOCUS ON INTERVENTION

Although Dale and Wrisberg had worked extensively as consultants for various sports teams, their published account (Dale & Wrisberg, 1996) deals with an intervention designed for a 12-person collegiate (NCAA) women's volleyball team. In the season prior to the intervention, the team had a record of 14 wins and 16 losses. The main objectives stated by the coaching staff members when they contacted the consultants were that they wanted to increase the focus and unity in the team as well as the communication between the coaching staff and the players.

Dale and Wrisberg suggested using *performance profiling* as the basis for this intervention. Performance profiling involves reaching a consensus opinion of the profile of a "successful" situation and then comparing the team's performance to this profile. This process is based on Kelly's (1955) *personal construct theory,* a phenomenological framework that holds that an individual's identity is formed by how he or she views the world. Thus, personal change can be a proactive process rather than a reactive one. By using performance profiling, the participant(s) in an intervention establish their own phenomenological frameworks for functioning. In this intervention, this process was enacted three times: for the team as a whole, for each individual player, and for the coach. Each athlete was asked to think about the characteristics of an elite performer at her position. The team as a whole decided on the characteristics of both a successful team and the ideal coach. In all cases, the participants were reminded to think of performance or process goals rather than outcome goals. Both the players and the coaches then used these characteristics throughout the season.

The criteria identified by the team to be indicative of a successful team were as follows: communicates well on court, has a winning attitude, has sound fundamentals, is mentally tough, is physically strong, is unselfish, is dedicated to giving maximum effort, and is talented. The ideal coach was seen as someone who is dedicated to the job, encourages players, is a good communicator, has confidence in the program, is calm under pressure, is knowledgeable about the game, has realistic expectations, and treats all players equally.

At regular points throughout the season, the coach and team members evaluated themselves against these criteria. Using the identified profiles as a basis for discussion, open and constructive communication was fostered about these criteria, the team's perceived evaluation on each criterion, and steps to improve these evaluations. To illustrate, the team perceived the head coach as often agitated in stressful situations (recall that one criterion of the team's ideal coach was someone who could remain calm under pressure). The coach's initial response was surprise at this rating; he thought he was a calm individual in most game situations. But when presented by the players with examples of situations in which he had lost his composure, the coach agreed to take steps to improve on this characteristic by asking the sports psychologists for articles about stress and anxiety and agreeing to work with the psychologists toward better stress management during competitions.

At season's end, the team as a whole perceived marked improvement on several of its criteria and reported that the performance profiling technique was an extremely valuable experience. Dale and Wrisberg (1996) cautioned that this technique is quite time-consuming but also noted that it need not be limited to teams that are experiencing difficulties.

CULTURE CAPSULE: TEAM DYNAMICS ACROSS CULTURES

Physical activity has been a significant aspect of every recorded culture, and sport has no national or social boundaries. Theoretically, one would expect that teams in different societies and cultures would operate similarly in terms of psychological constructs. Most of the theories and theoretical constructs touched on in this chapter do not recognize cultural boundaries. Conceptually, the importance of role clarity for an Indian cricket player is equivalent to that of a linebacker in the National Football League. Likewise, team confidence, as a social cognition, would be expected to be as influential a construct in a wide variety of sports.

However, much of the published research in the field has been based in North America and Western Europe. Given the importance of social dynamics for group processes such as leadership, cohesion, and communication, one cannot assume that the concepts and research discussed in this chapter are equally applicable to different cultures. It is encouraging to note that the researchers currently working in the field appreciate this issue. For instance, Carron and colleagues (1997), in summarizing the research on team cohesion in sport and the use of the GEQ, noted that the most serious challenge to the measurement is the validity of the GEQ across cultures. Cohesion and its behavioral indicators may have very different meanings in different cultures. Carron and colleagues suggested using great care in applying a particular conceptual model to other cultures. Heuze and Fontayne (2002) followed these suggestions in applying the GEQ to a French sporting sample. Like the English version, their adapted scale measures both social cohesion and task cohesion in four interrelated factors. However, Heuze and Fontayne had to rewrite some items, drop other ones, and add new ones that were culturally relevant.

We can look with excitement to increased research on the meaning of team chemistry—including its antecedents and consequences—in various cultures around the world and to discovering the extent to which the kinds of findings about sports teams in North America reviewed here surface elsewhere. For instance, is cohesion, which appears to be a vital component of successful teams in North America, even more important to teams in collectivistic cultures with their greater valuation of groups over individuals? Furthermore, is the relative importance of social cohesion greater than that of task cohesion in collectivistic cultures?

SUMMARY

This chapter has presented some of the relevant theory and research on the application of social psychology to sports teams. Sports teams provide a valid and realistic venue for conducting applied social psychological research. Sport has been a valuable context within which to increase our understanding of issues such as team cohesion and confidence, styles of communication, and team goal setting. The application of this understanding can be seen in the development of team-building interventions in sport.

Based on the material presented in the chapter, we can now elaborate the initial framework for understanding the application of social psychology to sports that was presented in Figure 7.1. This more extensive framework is shown in Figure 7.5. This is a causal model whereby input influences throughput, which in turn influences output; moreover, output is conceived as in many cases influencing input and/or throughput. The "input" in this framework is still the individual attributes of the team members that include players' abilities and characteristics (e.g., self-confidence, the tendency of individuals to self-disclose, goal orientation). The "throughput" of the model still represents the notion of team chemistry, but now we can be more specific concerning the meaning of this term—dynamic interpersonal factors such as team cohesion, collective efficacy, effective communication, and team goal setting. Given that these group dynamics represent the central

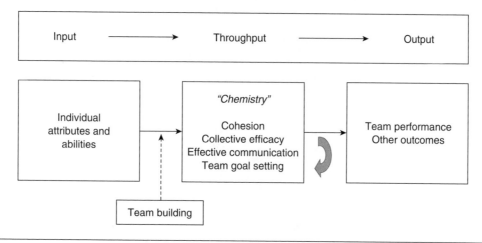

Figure 7.5   Detailed Framework for Understanding the Application of Social Psychology to Sports

part of the model, the framework can now include applied strategies specifically designed to affect team chemistry. This is noted by the inclusion of team-building strategies as a separate part of the model. Note that these are interventions designed to affect team chemistry (e.g., task cohesion) and, thus, have an indirect effect on team performance and other outcomes. Finally, as with the input component of the model, it is possible to be more specific concerning the output component. Although output refers primarily to team performance, other outcomes can include, for example, individual performance and satisfaction.

Thus, it can now be seen that well-studied psychological constructs, such as cohesiveness and collective efficacy, are what social psychologists intuit when they hear the word "chemistry." Such notions are indeed characteristic of how teams function; they have a definite impact on performance and can be influenced to optimize team performance. The team-building process may occur somewhat coincidentally, as with the Oxford rowing crew described in the opening vignette or, more likely, through explicit team-building programs.

8

APPLYING SOCIAL PSYCHOLOGY TO THE MEDIA

DAVID R. ROSKOS-EWOLDSEN

BEVERLY ROSKOS-EWOLDSEN

On October 30, 1938, the Mercury Theatre broadcast Howard Koch's radio adaptation of H. G. Wells's The War of the Worlds. The production was directed by, and starred, Orson Wells. After the opening credits for the Mercury Theatre, the radio play began with the announcement that the audience was listening to the music of Ramon Raquello's orchestra from the Meridian Room of the Park Plaza (a fictional hotel) in New York. During the next 45 minutes, the music was frequently interrupted, and then completely stopped, by news reports. The reports told of flashes of light from Mars and a metallic cylinder landing in a farm in Grover Mills, New Jersey. A later news flash declared that Martians were emerging from the cylinder and using a heat ray to attack spectators. At one point, the radio broadcast was apparently taken over by the military to coordinate efforts against the Martian invaders. Civilians were advised to flee from towns in central and northern New Jersey, and a list of the best escape routes was provided (Koch, 1970). Unfortunately, many people missed the opening announcement that this was a production of the Mercury Theatre. An estimated 6 million people heard the War of the Worlds broadcast. Of those, approximately 28% thought that the news reports were real. People fled from their homes by car, bus, and train. Other people tried desperately to seal their homes against the Martians' poison gas. Still other people called their families and friends to warn them of the attack by the Martians and to talk with their loved ones for perhaps a final time (Cantril, Gaudet, & Herzog, 1940). The Mercury Theatre's production of The War of the Worlds has gone down in history as a prime example of how a powerful media can shape people's social reality.

At the other extreme, Republican Senator William Knowland held a 20-hour telethon on October 31 and November 1, 1958, in an attempt to salvage his campaign for governor of California. By all accounts, the telethon was run professionally and competently. Schramm and Carter (1959) conducted a phone survey of 563 persons living in San Francisco to study the effects of this extraordinary effort by Knowland. The results of the survey are interesting in terms of what they tell us about the limitations of the media. The survey found that the majority of people who watched the telethon were already committed supporters of Knowland—not the audience that Knowland wanted to reach if he hoped to convince more people to vote for him. Did the telethon have any effect on how people voted? Of the 563 people surveyed, 2 reported that it did. Of these 2 people, 1 reported that the telethon convinced him to vote for *Knowland and the other reported that it convinced him to vote* against *Knowland. Knowland's telethon demonstrates one of the limitations of the media: People often watch programs that reflect what they already believe. If that is the case, can the media change people's minds? It might be the case that the media may reinforce what people think but will not change what they think.*

The media have become an integral part of our lives. By 1971, more than 95% of all households in the United States and Canada had televisions (TVs) (Centerwall, 1989). Do you know anyone who does not own at least one TV? Can you think of anyone who does not listen to the radio, read newspapers or magazines, or go to see movies? Indeed, you can now watch TV while pumping gas for your car or while riding an elevator. What are the effects of the media on our lives?

- Do the media create a violent society?
- Can the media increase our level of general fearfulness?
- What happens when people watch pornography?
- Do the media influence what we think are important issues?
- Can the media have an effect on elections?

The *War of the Worlds* broadcast suggests that the media can have profound effects on our lives. Yet Senator Knowland's telethon indicates that the media have little or no impact on what we think. What does the research say? Research on the psychological effects of the media has covered many areas. This chapter explores the effect of media violence, pornography, and political coverage because these three issues have been studied extensively by social psychologists and have important social implications. There are many other areas not covered in this chapter, including the effects of the media on racism, education, body image, and diffusion of information. The overwhelming majority of the research focuses on U.S. media because most of the research has been done in the United States and because the U.S. media are quickly dominating the world's major media systems (McChesney, 1999).

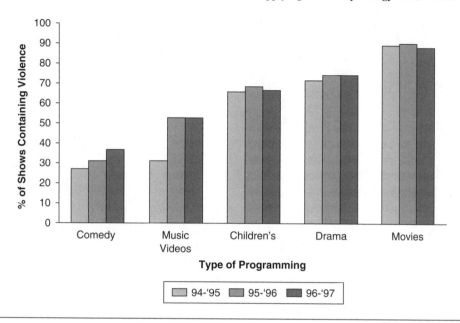

Figure 8.1   Percentages of TV Shows Containing Violence for Different Types of Shows for the
1994–1995, 1995–1996, and 1996–1997 Seasons

SOURCE: Adapted from Wilson and colleagues (1997, 1998) and Smith and colleagues (1998).

HOW DOES MEDIA VIOLENCE AFFECT US?

How difficult is it to turn on a TV for an entire evening and not watch some type of physical violence? Based on studies of media violence on TV programming in the United States, it is extremely difficult. Focusing only on intentional physical violence, 58% of all TV programs during the 1994–1995 season contained some type of physical violence or a credible threat of physical violence (Wilson et al., 1997). This figure rose to 61% during the 1995–1996 and 1996–1997 seasons (Smith et al., 1998; Wilson et al., 1998). If you are watching premium channels such as HBO and Showtime, an astonishing 85% of the shows contain violence. If that is not bad enough, of those shows that contain violence, two thirds contain four or more violent interactions (Smith et al., 1998; Wilson et al., 1997, 1998). Of course, just because a TV program contains violence does not mean that it is promoting violence. Perhaps the message of the program is actually one of anti-violence. Maybe some of these TV shows include violence to

focus on the harmful effects of the violence for the victim and the victim's family and friends. Although such shows do exist, they are rare. Only 4% of the shows during the three seasons from 1994 to 1997 had anti-violence themes (Smith et al., 1998). This means that TV shows are 15 times more likely to contain either pro-violence messages, or *at best* be neutral toward violence, than to contain anti-violence themes.

Figure 8.1 presents the percentages of programs within different types of TV programming that included violence from 1994 to 1997 (with violence defined as intentional physical violence). Clearly, dramas (75%) and movies (90%) contained a lot of violence. In addition, notice the increase in violence in both comedies and music videos over the 3-year period. However, the most disturbing aspect in the figure is the percentage of children's TV shows that contain violence. The fact that approximately two thirds of all children's shows contain violence, and that most of these shows contain multiple acts of violence (just think of the number of acts of violence in one episode of *Power Rangers*), is distressing. The recent proliferation of video games increases the amount of media violence that children are exposed to on a daily basis. The typical child will witness more than 8,000 murders and 100,000 acts of violence on network TV alone before reaching 18 years of age (Bushman & Anderson, 2001). Imagine how high these numbers would be if movies, video games, and comic books were included in that count.

The Consequences of Viewing Media Violence

When you were growing up, your parents may have forbidden you from watching some TV show because it was too violent. Particularly violent or gory movies are rated PG-13 or R so that younger children will not be exposed to this kind of media violence. Why all the fuss about it? One common belief you might have heard is that only violent people, or people with certain characteristics, watch violent TV programs. However, a longitudinal survey in which children were studied when they were just beginning elementary school and then when they were in their early 20s found that violent people are no more likely to watch violent TV programs than are nonviolent people (Huesmann, Moise-Titus, Podolski, & Eron, 2003). Another common belief about violent TV programs and movies is that they may help people to relieve their stress and aggressive impulses, so that violent TV shows and movies may actually *decrease* violence (Feshbach, 1961). This is commonly called the **cathartic effect** of watching violent media. Unfortunately, the vast majority of research studies do not support the idea that TV violence has a cathartic effect (Huesmann et al., 2003; Potter, 2003). Another common belief you may have heard is that people who watch a lot of TV violence are more likely to be violent. Unfortunately, this belief is true (Potter, 2003).

The social scientific literature on media violence is overwhelming. Hundreds of studies, including quasi-experiments, longitudinal studies, and experiments, have examined the effect of TV violence on violent behavior (Potter, 2003). Across all of these studies, the results consistently demonstrate that TV violence increases violent behavior. In fact, Potter (2003) identified more than 30 different effects of watching TV

violence, including increased imitation of violence, short- and long-term increases in aggressive behaviors, increased fear, desensitization to violence, and greater acceptance of violence.

One type of research on TV violence is *quasi-experiments*. Quasi-experiments on TV violence use naturally occurring manipulations of exposure to TV to explore the impact of TV on aggression. When considering the results of the quasi-experimental studies, it is important to realize that the studies consider only exposure to TV *in general* and not exposure to TV violence in particular. For example, the Federal Trade Commission (FTC) stopped granting TV broadcasting licenses from 1949 to 1952 to study how best to regulate this then new communication technology. The FTC's actions created a quasi-experiment with two conditions: cities with TV stations prior to 1950 and cities with TV stations starting in 1952 or later. Hennigan and colleagues (1982) took advantage of this natural manipulation to look at violent crime rates in these two city types. If TV increases violence, then violent crime rates should have increased in the cities that had been granted broadcast licenses prior to 1950 before they increased in the cities that did not receive licenses until 1952 or later. Crime rates did increase sooner in those cities where TV was introduced earlier (Hennigan et al., 1982). However, during the early years of TV, it was not violent crimes that increased; instead, the presence of a TV station in a community increased rates of nonviolent theft (excluding auto theft). Apparently, TV, with all of its commercials, may have made salient to people what they did not have, thereby increasing people's motivations to steal. Although this quasi-experiment did not find evidence that general exposure to TV influenced violence, other quasi-experiments have found such evidence.

Another quasi-experiment occurred in Canada when, in 1973, a small town nicknamed "Notel" (i.e., no television) received TV broadcasts for the first time. There were three conditions in this quasi-experiment: a city with no TV stations (Notel), a city with one TV station (nicknamed "Unitel"), and a city with multiple TV stations (nicknamed "Multitel"). Rates of physical violence in Notel were compared with those in Unitel and Multitel both before and 2 years after the introduction of TV to Notel (Joy, Kimball, & Zabrack, 1986). Unitel and Multitel were similar to Notel in terms of violence prior to 1973. The rates of aggression in Unitel and Multitel children did not change during the 2-year period after 1973. However, rates of both physical aggression and verbal aggression increased dramatically in Notel children after the introduction of TV.

Perhaps the most damning quasi-experiment on the effects of TV violence is Centerwall's (1989) analysis of homicide rates after the introduction of TV in the United States, Canada, and South Africa. Whereas TV was introduced in the United States and Canada at approximately the same time during the early 1950s, the South African government banned TV broadcasts until 1975. Interestingly, following the introduction of TV in each of these three countries, the homicide rates remained fairly constant for roughly 10 to 12 years but then *doubled* by the 15th year. The fact that the homicide rate doubled after the introduction of TV in each of these countries led Centerwall to conclude that TV violence is responsible for approximately half of the violent homicides in each of these countries. However, if TV is the culprit, why was there a 15-year lag between the introduction of TV and the increase in homicide rates? The most likely answer is that children are most vulnerable to the effects of violence on TV (Wilson et al., 2002). But how often do you hear about young children committing murder? Rather, the effect of the introduction of TV on violent homicides may have been delayed until children who were 3 or 4 years old when TV was introduced were old enough to begin committing acts of violence—typically in their late adolescent years—approximately 15 years after the introduction of TV. Clearly, Centerwall's estimate that TV violence is responsible for half of the homicides in the United States, Canada, and South Africa is an overestimate (Giles, 2003). As tends to be the case with quasi-experimental designs, there were many factors that Centerwall did not (and could not) control for in his analysis, including violent social upheavals in two of these countries at the same time that violent homicides increased (the civil rights and anti-war movements in the United States and the

anti-apartheid movement in South Africa). However, the data do indict TV.

Longitudinal studies have also found evidence that TV violence increases violent behavior (Huesmann et al., 2003). For example, in 1977, approximately 600 first- and third-grade children from the Chicago area were interviewed concerning their TV viewing habits. Roughly two thirds of the children were reinterviewed between 1992 and 1995 when they were between 21 and 23 years of age. The levels of violent TV that these children watched in 1977 were a stronger predictor of their levels of violence 15 years later than were their levels of aggression when they were children (Huesmann et al., 2003). This relationship held even when other factors that influence adult aggression were controlled, including parents' level of aggression, socioeconomic status, and intelligence.

Of course, *experimental studies* are the best technique for establishing causal relationships between two variables. Numerous experimental studies have demonstrated such a relationship between TV violence and aggressive behavior. A meta-analysis (i.e., a statistical procedure for assessing the overall results of numerous studies) of 230 experimental studies of media violence with more than 100,000 research participants in total found that exposure to media violence consistently resulted in higher levels of a variety of aggressive behaviors (Hearold, 1986; see also Paik & Comstock, 1994). However, it is important to remember that most of the experimental studies were conducted in a laboratory setting, and so the aggressive behaviors were "milder" than the aggression found outside the laboratory (Giles, 2003). For example, many studies involved giving a person an electric shock or a loud blast of an aversive sound to the victim's ear. Although these behaviors obviously are not "nice," they are certainly not as violent as an aggressive assault or a homicide.

The evidence is overwhelming that TV violence influences people's levels of aggressive behavior. But is that the only effect of watching TV violence? No. Think about recent examples of TV violence that you have watched. Chances are that the people engaged in the violence were performing some fairly risky behaviors. Performing any type of criminal activity is risky because it may result in being arrested and serving time in jail. Likewise, running after and trying to apprehend someone who is trying to kill you is also fairly risky. Survey research suggests that adolescents who watch TV violence are more likely to engage in other risky behaviors as well as being more violent. For example, adolescents who watch more TV violence are more likely to practice unsafe sex, thereby increasing their risk of unwanted pregnancies or of contracting AIDS or other sexually transmitted diseases. In addition, these adolescents are more likely to drive at very dangerous speeds, not wear seat belts, and use illegal drugs (Krcmar & Greene, 2000).

One limitation of the research on media violence is that it has focused nearly exclusively on TV and movie violence. However, when you play a typical video game, how many acts of violence do you view? Of course, the issue of video games is much more complex because you not only are watching the violence but, in many ways, are also committing the acts of violence. Research has shown that playing—or even just watching—violent video games can have the same effects as does watching TV violence (Figure 8.2) (Anderson & Dill, 2000; Hoffman, 1994). Likewise, another media outlet that has been ignored is comic books. Many comic books that are aimed at adolescents contain violence. Again, research suggests that reading violent comic books can have some of the same undesirable effects as does watching violent TV programs or movies (Kirsh & Olczak, 2000).

A final point to remember about violence and the causes of aggression is that aggressive behavior is *overdetermined*. A behavior is said to be **overdetermined** when it has multiple causes. Many different factors can cause a person to be aggressive. For example, males tend to be more aggressive than females. Likewise, some people seem to have aggressive personalities, and this increases their likelihood of acting aggressively. Other factors that have been identified as influencing aggression include frustration and anger, stress, general arousal, the temperature, loud noises, and having been abused as a child (Geen, 2001). Likewise, culture obviously plays a major role in aggressive behavior. The incidence of aggression and violence is higher in the United States than in Canada, even though the TV programming is

Figure 8.2   Playing Violent Computer or Video Games, Which Can Have the Same Effects as Watching TV Violence

SOURCE: Photo courtesy of Juliane A. Coutts.

very similar in the two countries. This is because the United States has a more aggressive culture (Geen, 2001; Nisbett & Cohen, 1996).

Imitation of Violence

On March 9, 2001, Lionel Tate was convicted of murdering Tiffany Eunick. She was 6 years old at the time of her death. In causing Tiffany's death, Lionel used wrestling moves he had seen performed by one of his favorite TV wrestling stars. Tiffany's injuries from the wrestling moves were equivalent to a fall from a three-story building. Lionel was 14 years old when he was convicted of murder and sentenced to life in prison.

You may have heard about some of the early studies focusing on imitating TV violence where children watched a short film of a child beating up a bobo doll. A bobo doll is a large inflatable doll that often looks like a clown and is used as a punching bag. Later, when the children were given an opportunity to play, they imitated the child they watched in the film and also beat up the bobo doll (Bandura, Ross, & Ross, 1963). In one experiment exploring imitative violence (Hicks, 1965), children watched an 8-minute film of a person beating up a bobo doll. The person was either an adult male, an adult female, a boy their age, or a girl their age. The person hit the bobo doll with a bat, hit the doll with a mallet, threw balls at the doll, and sat on the doll and punched it. A final control group of children did not watch any film. The children then were placed in a room with toys that included a bobo doll, a bat, a mallet, and balls. The experimenter observed how much the children imitated the violence they had watched in the film. After a period of 6 months, the children returned to the laboratory to play in the same room with the same toys. Again, the experimenter observed how much the children imitated the violence they had watched in the film 6 months earlier. This experiment was a 2 (age: adult or child model) × 2 (sex: male or female model) × 2 (time of imitation: immediately or 6 months later) design with a control group.

As you can see in Figure 8.3, children who watched either children or adults act aggressively toward a bobo doll imitated that violence when given a chance to play immediately after viewing the violence as well as 6 months later when they were brought back into the setting (Hicks, 1965). You will remember that a control group of children did not watch anyone beat up the bobo doll. These children's data are not included in the figure because they did not act aggressively *at all* either the first time they were allowed to play with the toys or 6 months later (Hicks, 1965).

People often criticize these studies, arguing that the children naturally hit the bobo doll because that is what one does with a bobo doll (although, of course, the control children did not hit the bobo doll). The research is much more complex than this simple criticism would suggest. When children see another child perform aggressive behaviors in a movie and the aggressive child is either rewarded or punished, the children are more likely to act aggressively later

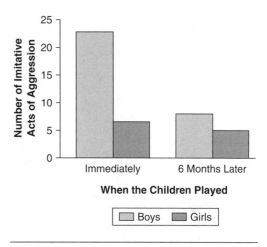

Figure 8.3 Numbers of Imitative Acts of Aggression That Boys and Girls Engaged in Either Immediately After Seeing a Rewarded Actor Perform the Actions or 6 Months Later

SOURCE: Adapted from Hicks (1965).

when the child performing the aggressive behaviors is rewarded than when the child is punished (Bandura, 1965; Bandura et al., 1963; Steuer, Applefield, & Smith, 1971).

Numerous studies have demonstrated that people are more likely to perform behaviors that they are rewarded for performing. However, Bandura (1965; see also Bandura et al., 1963) demonstrated in the bobo doll experiments that even *watching* other people perform a behavior that is rewarded increases the likelihood that the viewer will perform the rewarded behavior. The performing of a behavior because one observes it being rewarded is called **vicarious learning.** Vicarious learning is the foundation of Bandura's (1986, 2001) social cognitive theory of mass communication.

How we learn to imitate violence. Bandura (1986, 2001) argued that much of what you learn is learned vicariously through the media. According to his **social cognitive theory**, there are four processes that must occur for vicarious learning to occur. The first is *attention*. To learn vicariously, people must attend to what is being modeled. Factors influencing whether one attends to the modeled behavior include how salient and attractive the behavior is to the individual. Clearly, media violence is very prevalent, exciting, and salient, and so it attracts attention. The second process is the *representational process,* which entails remembering the modeled behavior. Obviously, people cannot model a behavior that they cannot remember. The representational process also involves mentally rehearsing the behavior, thereby increasing the likelihood that it will be recalled at a later time. How many times have you seen young children play-acting about committing an act of violence they viewed on TV? Through their fantasy, they are rehearsing that behavior. The third process is the *behavioral production process,* which focuses on how people learn to perform the behavior they have observed. Part of this process involves learning how to generalize the observed behavior into other types of related but novel behaviors. For example, a child may observe the bobo doll being hit with a mallet but may generalize this violent behavior to hitting his or her little brother with a mallet or to hitting the bobo doll with a baseball bat. The final element in Bandura's model focuses on the *motivational process.* People do not perform every behavior they observe; rather, they perform those behaviors that they are motivated to perform. This explains why children imitate rewarded behavior but not punished behavior. The reward provides a vicarious motivation for performing the behavior. In sum, according to social cognition theory, viewers are more likely to act aggressively if they watch media violence, remember the violence they watched, figure out how to perform the violent behaviors and practice those behaviors, and are somehow motivated to perform the violent behaviors.

Much of the research on Bandura's social cognitive theory of mass media has focused on the final element of Bandura's model, that is, motivational processes. As already discussed, one factor that increases motivation and the likelihood of performing violent behavior is the rewarding of violent behavior (Bandura, 1965; Bandura et al., 1963). A second motivation-increasing factor is the viewer perceiving the violent behavior as justified (Berkowitz & Powers, 1979; Hoyt, 1970). Examples of justified violence that have been studied include violent behavior that is in self-defense, results in getting even with someone,

and is aimed at a particularly nasty person. A third factor is the viewer perceiving the violence as realistic (Huesmann et al., 2003). A final factor that influences motivation is the viewer identifying with or liking the perpetrator of the violence (Huesmann et al., 2003; Perry & Perry, 1976). If a child identifies with the Power Rangers, then that child will be more likely to imitate the Power Rangers.

Another factor that appears to play an important role in people's motivation to perform violent behavior is *desensitization.* People may learn aggressive behaviors vicariously, but moral concerns and normative pressure will keep most of them from acting violently. However, if people are desensitized to violence, they will be less likely to view violence as morally wrong. Unfortunately, TV violence desensitizes people to violence (Cline, Croft, & Courrier, 1973; Drabman & Thomas, 1974). People who watch a lot of TV violence or have just been exposed to a violent program show less physiological response to media or real violence (Cline et al., 1973). Furthermore, an experiment by Drabman and Thomas (1974) demonstrated that children who are desensitized to violence by viewing TV violence are less likely to help other children who are being hurt. In their study, 22 boys and 22 girls were brought into the laboratory and either watched an excerpt from a violent cowboy film or watched no film. Then the children were asked by the experimenter to help him watch two younger children through a video monitor while he ran a quick errand. The boys and girls in the study were actually watching a film clip of two children who became progressively more aggressive toward each other. This experiment had a 2 (exposure: violent film or no film) × 2 (sex: boys or girls) design. Consistent with the desensitization hypothesis, boys and girls who had watched the violent film took a significantly longer amount of time to tell an adult about the two children's fighting than did boys and girls who watched no film.

In sum, people might want to act violently but do not do so because they know that it is wrong. Desensitization to violence increases people's tolerance of violence and decreases their motivation *not* to act aggressively, thereby increasing the likelihood that they will act violently.

Countering the effects of violence in the media. A concern about children and society demands that some action be taken to counter the effects of watching violent TV. Currently, rating systems are used to indicate whether a TV program or movie contains violence and is suitable for children to watch. But what is the effect of rating systems? Social psychological theory suggests that rating scales may backfire and actually increase children's and adolescents' desire to watch programs rated as violent. Think about it. When someone tries to limit what you can do, how do you react? Often, people react to restrictions on their behavior by wanting to perform the restricted behavior even more. In Chapter 4, this idea was referred to as *psychological reactance* and was identified as a reason why some people resist interventions. "Forbidden fruit" is often the most desirable kind of fruit. Therefore, it is not surprising that research has found that the rating systems used to identify programs that children and adolescents should not watch actually increase the desire of adolescents— particularly boys—to want to watch the programs (Bushman & Stack, 1996; Cantor, Harrison, & Nathanson, 1998).

However, other research based on Bandura's (1986, 2001) social cognitive theory does suggest a way in which to counter the effects of violent TV on children. Recall that watching rewarded violence increases people's tendency to act violently. However, what happens if children see the violence as not rewarding? In that case, children should be vicariously conditioned to not act violently. What can be done so that the violence is not rewarding? What if you thought about the violence from the perspective of the victim? Do you think that the victim of the violence finds the violence rewarding?

To test the idea that decreasing the reward value of violence might decrease its effects, Nathanson and Cantor (2000) conducted an experiment in which they had two groups of boys and two groups of girls watch a *Woody the Woodpecker* cartoon that contained violence. One group of boys and girls simply watched the cartoon. The boys and girls in a second group were instructed to think about the feelings of the person who was the victim of Woody the Woodpecker's assaults. A third group of boys and girls did not watch any TV. This experiment had a 2 (empathy: simply watch or watch and think about victim) × 2 (sex: girls or boys) design with a separate control group (no TV). Nathanson and Cantor found that when children were told to identify with the victim of the aggression by thinking about how the victim felt, they did not enjoy viewing the violence as much as did children who simply watched the cartoon. Furthermore, as can be seen in Figure 8.4, boys who thought about how the victim felt were less aggressive than boys who simply watched the violent cartoon. The empathy manipulation had no effect on the aggression of the girls. However, females are generally less influenced by media violence than are boys (Geen, 2001), as is clearly demonstrated in the figure. This finding indicates that parents and educators should talk with children about the feelings of victims of violence as well as about the feelings of the victims' families. In other words, we need to increase children's sensitization to violence.

Media Violence and Aggressive Thoughts

Imagine that you are sitting at a stoplight and it turns green. The driver of the pickup in front of you is not paying attention and continues to sit there instead of going. Would you be more likely to honk your horn if there were a gun in a gun rack in the back of the pickup than if the gun rack were empty? Regardless of whether you actually honk the horn, according to Berkowitz's (1984) **neoassociationistic model of media priming,** the presence of the gun would increase the likelihood that you would have aggressive thoughts. Of course, the increase in aggressive thoughts heightens the likelihood that you will behave in an aggressive manner and honk your horn—and that might be dangerous given that the person in the pickup has a gun.

The neoassociationistic model of priming is based on research in cognitive psychology and social psychology. **Priming** refers to the effect of some preceding stimulus or event on how we react to some subsequent stimulus. Priming procedures were first used in cognitive psychology to explore the structure and representation of information within network models of memory. **Network models of memory** assume that

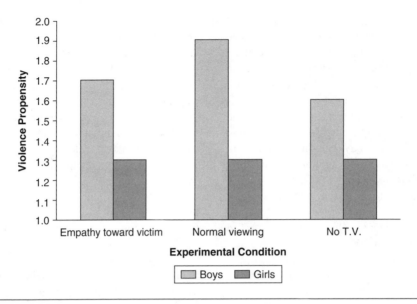

Figure 8.4   Propensities for Children to Act Violently After Watching a Violent Cartoon (normal viewing), Being Instructed to Empathize With the Victim (empathy toward victim), and Not Watching the Cartoon (no TV)

SOURCE: Adapted from Nathanson and Cantor (2000).

information is stored in memory in the form of *nodes* and that each node represents a concept (e.g., there is a "gun" node in memory). Furthermore, these nodes are connected to related nodes in memory by *associative pathways* (e.g., "gun" is linked to "crime" but not to "corn flakes"). An additional assumption of network models of memory is that each node has an *activation* threshold. If the node's level of activation exceeds its threshold, the node fires. When a node fires, it can influence the activation levels of other related nodes. For example, if the gun node fires, activation spreads from the gun node to related nodes such as the crime node. Consequently, the related node now requires less additional activation for it to fire. A typical behavioral outcome of spreading activation is that a judgment (e.g., the judgment that a crime is occurring) is faster when it has been primed by a related concept (gun) than when it has been primed by an unrelated concept (corn flakes). In a slight twist on the earlier example, you would be more likely to interpret an ambiguous behavior (e.g., being bumped) as a hostile act if you had just seen a pickup with a gun in the gun rack than a pickup with an empty gun rack. A final assumption of network models

of memory is that the activation level of a node will go away over time, making it a short-term effect. Priming of aggressive thoughts is a short-term effect of TV violence. You are not going to think about crime for the rest of the day after seeing the gun in the gun rack in the back of the pickup (Roskos-Ewoldsen, Klinger, & Roskos-Ewoldsen, in press). However, it is important to remember that other effects of TV violence, such as increased likelihood of imitation and increased fear, may last for years (Harrison & Cantor, 1999; Hoekstra, Harris, & Helmick, 1999).

Research by both cognitive psychologists and social psychologists has demonstrated that a prime's effect on a target behavior or thought is related to the intensity of the prime (Higgins, Bargh, & Lombardi, 1985). The intensity of a prime refers to either the frequency of the prime (e.g., a single exposure vs. five exposures in quick succession) or the duration of the prime. A TV show with multiple acts of violence— unfortunately, the norm—will prime violent thoughts more strongly than will a show with a single act of violence. Likewise, a show with a particularly graphic act of violence will act as a stronger prime of violence.

FOCUS ON RESEARCH

Many studies have demonstrated that people who are exposed to a violent TV clip are more likely to think aggressive thoughts (Roskos-Ewoldsen et al., in press). However, does priming aggressive thoughts translate into aggressive behavior? Certainly, we do not want people running around thinking aggressive thoughts because of violent TV programs, but the important issue from a societal standpoint is whether violent TV programs prime violent behavior. Josephson (1987) investigated the priming effects of violent media on children's behavior. In that experiment, Josephson gathered measures of young boys' trait aggression by asking the boys' teachers to indicate how aggressive the boys were both in class and on the playground. Later, the boys saw either a violent TV program or a nonviolent one. To test priming, the violent TV segment contained recurring images of violent characters using walkie-talkies, whereas the nonviolent program contained no walkie-talkies. As a result, the walkie-talkies served as a prime for the violent television program but not for the nonviolent program. Josephson was also interested in whether frustration influenced the level of violent priming. When people become frustrated, they are more likely to act violently. Either before or after watching the TV program, half of the boys saw a 30-second nonviolent cartoon segment that had been edited to become increasingly static riddled, eventually worsening to "snow." At that point, the experimenter stopped the cartoon and apologized to the boys for "technical difficulties" with the TV. Stopping the cartoon segment frustrated the young boys because they could not watch a TV cartoon they liked.

After viewing their assigned programs, the boys were mock interviewed and then sent to the school gymnasium to play floor hockey. For the mock interview, either a walkie-talkie or a microphone was used. In this way, half of the boys were exposed to the violence-related cue (the walkie-talkie) and half were not (the microphone). This rather complicated experimental study involved a 2 (TV show: aggressive or nonaggressive) × 2 (trait aggression: high or low) × 2 (frustration: high or low) × 2 (interview method: walkie-talkie or microphone) design.

The boys took turns playing floor hockey and were observed both on and off the floor for signs of aggressive behavior, including pushing down other boys, hitting other players with their hockey sticks, and calling other boys abusive names. After three 3-minute periods of hockey, the boys were returned to their teachers.

The results indicated that the violent TV viewing primed boys who were high in trait aggressiveness to act more violently during initial sports activity (i.e., during the first period of play). This effect on aggressive boys was heightened both when violent programming was coupled with the violence-related cue and when violent programming was followed by frustration. However, as predicted by Berkowitz's (1984) neoassociationistic model, the priming effect lessened with time. The boys were most violent during the first period of play and were about equally violent in the second and third periods. There was no effect of the TV program, presence of the violence-related cue, or frustration on the boys who were low in trait aggressiveness.

Numerous studies have supported Berkowitz's (1984) neoassociationistic model. As noted earlier, the model leads to the prediction that the mere presence of weapons will prime violent thoughts and behavior. This *weapons effect* has been demonstrated in numerous studies (Carlson, Marcus-Newhall, & Miller, 1990). For example, Berkowitz and LePage (1967) conducted an experiment involving research participants evaluating each other's performance on a task by giving mild electric shocks for poor performance. For some of the research participants, a shotgun and a pistol were visible when they entered the room. Other research participants saw a pair of badminton racquets when they entered the room. Control group participants saw no such stimuli when they entered the room. The participants were told that a previous experimenter had left the guns or badminton racquets. Consistent with the weapons effect, participants shocked their partners more when the guns were present than when the badminton racquets were present or when nothing was present. Likewise, recall the earlier example concerning the gun in the gun rack in the back of a pickup that did not move when the light turned green. Turner, Layton, and Simons (1975) actually studied this situation. Despite the fact that the person in the pickup had a gun, people were more likely to honk, and to honk more times, when the gun was present than when it was not present. Think about the number of weapons you see during an average night of TV viewing. What effect do all of these weapons you see on TV or at the movies have on your thoughts, on your interpretations of others' behavior, and on your own behavior?

Media Violence and Fear

How often has a movie made you afraid? Clearly, the Mercury Theatre's broadcast of *The War of the Worlds* terrified many people. However, the fear that resulted from that broadcast was short-lived. Has watching a movie or TV show made you afraid for a long time? During the 1970s, the movie *Jaws* had such an effect on many people. The movie involved a great white shark that attacked swimmers and boaters off a small New England town. Many people (including one of the chapter authors) reported that they would not go swimming in the ocean for years after seeing *Jaws*. In a questionnaire study, Harrison and Cantor (1999) found that more than a quarter of the college students they studied had watched a movie or TV show prior to turning 11 years of age that was still affecting them 8 or more years later (see also Hoekstra et al., 1999). Students reported still having nightmares related to their frightening viewing experiences or still refusing to go to certain places, such as a beach, because of their experiences. Imagine still having fright reactions from a TV program you watched 8 years ago. But think about it this way: If one program can have such a profound effect, what is the effect of watching thousands of hours of TV programs and movies that contain violence

and other frightening events, such as tornadoes, on people's level of fear?

Most research on fright reactions to the media has focused on children. More than 90% of all children are seriously frightened by the media at some point in their young lives (Cantor, 2002). Furthermore, the fright reactions can be very powerful. Children who are frightened by the media may experience nightmares and sleeplessness, high degrees of stress, and even depression (Cantor, 2002). The things that frighten children change as they grow older. Up to 6 years of age, scary-looking things frighten children even if these things are not dangerous (Cantor & Sparks, 1984). For example, children at this age are scared of the Incredible Hulk because he looks scary even though he helps good people. However, after 9 or 10 years of age, things that could realistically happen are scarier than things that just look scary. More abstract threats are scarier to adolescents. The movie *The Day After* depicted the effects of a nuclear war in the United States. A survey study found that younger children were not as scared by the movie as were children over 12 years of age (Cantor, Wilson, & Hoffner, 1986).

The way that children respond to scary media also changes as they grow older. Younger children are more likely to use behavioral coping strategies such as holding onto a favorite toy and covering their eyes. Older children use more cognitive coping strategies such as reminding themselves that the fear-inducing stimuli are not real and minimizing the threat of the threatening stimuli (Cantor, 2002). Do you remember watching a scary movie and repeating to yourself that it was not true?

Cultivation theory focuses on the effects of heavy exposure to TV (i.e., more than 4 hours a day). Cultivation theory maintains that TV operates as the primary socializing agent in today's world; that is, TV is where people learn about their world and their culture (Gerbner, Gross, Morgan, Signorielli, & Shanahan, 2002). In particular, TV cultivates heavy viewers' social reality. Research has consistently found that TV influences heavy viewers' perceptions of the world (Shrum, 1999, 2002). For example, men are characters on TV shows at roughly a 2:1 ratio to women (Gerbner et al., 2002). In addition, women on TV are portrayed in a more stereotypical manner. As a result, questionnaire studies have found that people who are heavy viewers of TV tend to have more sexist views of women (Gerbner et al., 2002; Morgan, 1990). Likewise, commercials for different products promote materialism. Surveys have found that people who watch more TV and more commercials in both the United States and Korea are more materialistic (Kwak, Zinkhan, & Dominick, 2002).

According to cultivation theory, one of the consequences of media violence is that people begin to see the world as more dangerous and "mean" (Gerbner et al., 2002). Considering the amount of violence on TV, what kind of world do people learn about from TV? Cultivation theory suggests that heavy viewers of TV should see the world as a more violent and hostile place than do light viewers. In fact, heavy viewers of TV *do* perceive the world as a more dangerous and hostile place than do light viewers (Signorielli, 1990). Much of the research on cultivation theory has relied on correlations between how much TV a person watches and how hostile he or she perceives the world. However, you now know from reading this book that a correlation between two variables does not tell us which event is causing the other or whether a causal relationship exists between the two events at all. One could argue that people who perceive the world as a dangerous and hostile place may be less likely to engage in activities outside the home and, as a consequence, are more likely to watch TV. But experimental research has demonstrated that watching shows that contain a lot of violence, and where the perpetrators are not brought to justice, causes increases in people's anxiety (Bryant, Carveth, & Brown, 1981). In this research, participants watched 5 hours of prerecorded TV shows once a week for 6 weeks. After the 6-week period was complete, the participants' anxiety levels were measured. For some of the research participants, the TV shows were violent and the perpetrators of the violence were not caught. For the other participants, the shows were violent but the perpetrators of the violence were brought to justice. In this way, Bryant and his colleagues were able to show that watching violent TV programs in which the perpetrators are not brought to justice increases anxiety. Just as TV shows can scare children, viewing a lot of TV can scare adults.

Cultivation theory focuses on overall viewing of TV rather than on watching particular types of shows. However, given the various types of shows on TV, which shows depict the most excessive amounts of realistic violence? The evening news probably has the heaviest concentration of realistic violence of any TV programming. In particular, the local news should be particularly frightening because the violence is occurring where viewers live. In questionnaire studies, parents reported that their children are scared by the local news (Cantor & Nathanson, 1996). Likewise, roughly 25% of children who were in the fourth to sixth grades spontaneously reported during interviews that the local news was scary, and more than half of the children who were interviewed in one study could identify news stories that had scared them (Smith & Wilson, 2002). Interestingly, younger children (first to third grades) reported being scared by news stories covering natural disasters, whereas older children were more likely to be scared by stories dealing with violence and crimes. In fact, children who watch more evening news gave higher estimates of the number of murders that occur in a nearby city (Smith & Wilson, 2002). The local news creates a scary world for these children. Survey research with adults also finds that heavier viewers of the local news are more likely to experience fear and be concerned about crime rates in their community than are lighter viewers (Romer, Jamieson, & Aday, 2003).

In sum, violence is a staple of contemporary TV and movies. Unfortunately, this violence may be literally helping to kill off its audience. As this section of the chapter has demonstrated, the influences of TV violence are subtler than people often realize. TV violence can lead children to model the violence, particularly if the violence is perceived as real and rewarded and if the children identify with the person carrying out the violence. TV violence can also increase people's aggressive thoughts and temporarily increase the likelihood that people will react violently. Finally, TV violence increases viewers' levels of fear.

The next section introduces research on the effects of viewing pornography on people's attitudes, beliefs, and perceptions of the world. Like the research on TV violence, the research on pornography focuses on the negative effects of a specific genre of media programming. Some of the questions concern the effects of pornography on people's attitudes toward women, the family, and rape. As you will see, research on pornography has also focused on ways in which to counter the negative effects of pornography on people's attitudes and beliefs.

WHAT HAPPENS WHEN WE WATCH PORNOGRAPHY?

The first question to ask is what is meant by pornography. There are three kinds of pornography: erotica, nonviolent pornography, and violent pornography (Intons-Peterson & Roskos-Ewoldsen, 1989). All have a sexual theme, but they differ as to their implicit and explicit aggressive components. **Erotica** shows nonaggressive sexual activity between willing, sensitive, and caring partners. In erotica, the partners share in the initiation and choice of activities. In contrast, **nonviolent pornography** is centered on an extreme stereotype of male dominance and female subservience where the more powerful coerce the less powerful. In nonviolent pornography, women are sexual playthings for men to use and discard. Neither men nor women are portrayed as having feelings such as compassion and empathy, let alone self-respect. Women in particular are degraded and demeaned. They are portrayed as having one primary interest—satisfying male sexual desires and fantasies. **Violent pornography,** as the phrase suggests, portrays violence that is juxtaposed with, or an integral part of, sexuality with an underlying theme of coercion and *unequal* status. Violent pornography is limited to X-rated films portraying sadomasochistic behaviors or perhaps the infamous snuff films in which the female victims are tortured sexually and then killed. **Violent sexuality,** on the other hand, is found in any R-rated film that includes an erotic scene followed immediately by, or juxtaposed with, graphic violence. These films are sometimes called slasher films or women-in-danger films.

You can probably recall a few films where scantily clad young women are shown terrified and running from crazed murderers. The distinction between violent pornography and violent sexuality is important because if you or your friends have brothers or sisters who are young teenagers, they can probably view violent sexuality fairly easily. Because of the ease of viewing violent sexuality even by young teenagers, many experiments in this area have focused on violent sexuality. It is hoped that these same teenagers will have a much more difficult time viewing violent pornography.

Research in this area has focused on whether watching these kinds of pornography has any harmful effects. If exposure to any type of pornography or violent sexuality causes a harmful effect, such as greater callousness toward women, then society at large may want to consider ways of limiting these effects, either by restricting access to the films or by educating the public about their effects. It is probably safe to say that most researchers in this area prefer education to restriction.

One way in which to study the harmful effects of pornography is to look at the association between the availability of pornography in various countries and the corresponding levels of sex-related crimes such as rape, exhibitionism, and voyeurism. Of course, studies of this kind can only examine the effect of general exposure to sexually explicit materials; they cannot examine the effect of exposure to different types of sexuality such as erotica, violent sexuality, violent pornography, and nonviolent pornography. Examples of some of this research include examinations of the effect of loosening restrictions on pornography on sex crimes in Denmark and of relations between the number of sex shops, number of adult theaters, and circulation of sexually explicit magazines and sex crime rates in the United States and other countries (for a review, see Gunter, 2002). Unfortunately, the results of this line of research are unclear (Gunter, 2002). Some *correlational* studies find relationships between the amount of sexually explicit materials available and sex crimes, whereas other studies do not. In addition, there are other extraneous variables that may explain any relationships that exist. For example, the availability of sexually explicit materials may correspond with more lenient attitudes toward sexuality, which may also translate into less reporting of sex crimes (Gunter, 2002).

Experimental research designs are much more informative regarding *causality*. Let us consider some common features of experiments on pornography. They involve showing participants, typically males, a film, video, or video clip that depicts sexuality (erotica, nonviolent pornography, or violent sexuality) and then asking them to fill out various questionnaires. For example, Linz, Donnerstein, and Penrod (1988) had male participants watch either two or five films depicting violent sexuality (R-rated slasher films) or nonviolent pornography. Some studies also include a control condition in which the film or video is nonsexual and nonviolent. In Linz and colleagues' experiment, participants in a control condition watched either two or five nonviolent films aimed at teenagers. Most often, watching the films and filling out the questionnaires are portrayed as two separate studies so that participants will not see a link between watching the films and answering the questionnaires. The particular effects that researchers look for vary widely. For example, Linz and colleagues looked at the influence of these films on desensitization to the female victims in the films or victims of rape. Other typical examples of the effects that are studied include (a) acceptance of rape myths such as "In the majority of rapes, the victim is promiscuous or has a bad reputation" and "Any healthy woman can successfully resist a rapist if she really wants to" (Burt, 1980); (b) callousness of attitudes toward women such as "A man should find them, fool them, fuck them, and forget them" and "A woman doesn't mean 'no' until she slaps you" (Zillmann & Bryant, 1982); and (c) judgments about a victim and perpetrator in a rape trial such as innocence or guilt of the alleged perpetrator and, if guilty, how many years the perpetrator should serve in prison (Linz et al., 1988). Sometimes men's aggressive behavior is measured. In one case, men were given the opportunity to shock a female participant electrically (Donnerstein & Berkowitz, 1981). Of course, in reality there was no shock given because the shock situation is a setup. The female participant was actually a confederate who pretended that she was being shocked.

There are two cases in which potentially harmful effects have been noted: long-term exposure to nonviolent pornography and any exposure to violent sexuality, that is, those R-rated films. These effects are discussed in the following subsections. Absent from this discussion are the effects of erotica, short-term exposure to nonviolent pornography, and violent pornography. These effects are not discussed for several reasons. First, there is very little research on the effects of erotica on people's thoughts and beliefs other than that it arouses both men and women (Gunter, 2002). Although some authors have suggested that erotica may be useful for sex therapy, there is scant research on the utility of erotica in sex therapy and the results are inconsistent (Gunter, 2002). Indeed, the one consistent effect found for erotica is that exposure to erotica increases viewers' tendency to masturbate. Second, research on short-term exposure—less than an hour—to nonviolent pornography has produced inconsistent results, sometimes revealing more callousness toward women and sometimes not (Linz, 1989). However, more recent research suggests that the effects may be subtler than this; men who watched nonviolent pornography briefly were more dominant and less anxious when put in a situation where they had to solve a problem with a female partner (Mulac, Jansma, & Linz, 2002). The men might not have been more callous, but they still attempting to dominate the female partner—albeit in a more subtle manner. Finally, although there is little research on the effects of X-rated violent pornography (probably for ethical reasons), what is true of violent sexuality will also likely be true for violent pornography. After all, they are in the same category in that they both portray sexual violence.

Effects of Long-Term Exposure to Nonviolent Pornography

During the 1980s, the U.S. government convened a commission to evaluate the available evidence on the effects of erotica and nonviolent pornography. The Attorney General's Commission on Pornography (1986) produced a final report that concluded that substantial exposure to nonviolent pornography is causally related to increases in sexual violence and sexual coercion.

Long-term or substantial exposure actually involves less exposure than one might think. Typically, long-term means watching approximately 5 hours of material spread over a 6-week period. In comparison with its conclusion regarding nonviolent pornography, the commission was unable to agree on the harmfulness of erotica but concluded that there is not a causal relation between exposure to erotica and acts of sexual violence.

The actual research on long-term exposure to nonviolent pornography provides more of a mixed bag of results than was suggested by the commission's report (Linz, 1989). The experimental research on exposure to nonviolent pornography has focused on its effects on people's attitudes and beliefs rather than on actual physical violence because of ethical concerns and because attitudes and beliefs influence behavior (Roskos-Ewoldsen, 1997). Some studies have found more leniency toward assailants in rape cases, as well as increased sexual callousness, following exposure to nonviolent pornography (Mullin & Linz, 1995; Zillmann & Bryant, 1982, 1984), whereas others have not (Linz et al., 1988; Padgett, Brislin-Slütz, & Neal, 1989).

Linz (1989) reviewed a number of studies that pointed to a variety of reasons for these discrepancies. Recall that research participants often are told that watching the films and completing the questionnaires are two distinct studies. Linz found that if participants in these studies believe that watching the films is in fact related to the questionnaires, a link between viewing the nonviolent pornography and participants' beliefs is less likely to surface. Perhaps participants are "faking good" when they complete the questionnaires under this circumstance so as not to appear to be influenced by the pornography. Likewise, as the realism of a rape trial increases, films are less likely to have an effect (Linz, 1989). In addition, participants with more sexual experience are less influenced by exposure to nonviolent pornography. Also, if the time lag between the films and the questionnaires increases to 2 days, there is little effect of the films. This suggests that the nonviolent pornography might be priming participants' judgments because priming effects disappear with time. Another factor that Linz identified as moderating the influence of nonviolent

pornography is the ratio of sexual scenes to nonsexual scenes in a film. When there are many nonsexual scenes, the film has less effect. The point of all this is to highlight the fact that the relationship between viewing nonviolent pornography and violence toward women is complex. Simply viewing a lot of nonviolent pornography does not mean that an individual will behave like a rapist. However, as we will see, just because the person does not become a rapist does not mean that there is no effect of viewing nonviolent pornography. There are effects on viewers' attitudes and beliefs.

There are other effects of viewing substantial amounts of nonviolent pornography that are not necessarily directly related to callousness toward women. In particular, some researchers have looked at changes in *attitudes* regarding family *values* (for a summary, see Zillmann, 1994). Family values include, at their core, a parental commitment to the family and to the nurturance of children. Of course, nonviolent pornography portrays just the opposite; it shows a world of transitory relationships that provide the greatest sexual pleasures that can be experienced without emotional involvement (Zillmann, 1994). You can probably see the problem here: One set of values conflicts with the other. Does this conflict matter? Definitely, according to research by Zillmann and Bryant (1982, 1988a, 1988b). In one of their experiments, 70 men and 70 women from the local community either watched nonviolent pornography that could be rented at an adult video store or watched nonsexual videotapes. They watched six 1-hour videotapes over 6 weeks. Roughly a week after the final viewing, they were asked to participate in an ostensibly unrelated study on the American family and aspects of personal happiness. The effects that Zillmann and Bryant found were eye-opening and occurred for both sexes. Figure 8.5 shows that participants who viewed the nonviolent pornography, as compared with participants who viewed nonsexual videos, were (a) less sexually satisfied, (b) more accepting of myths related to health risks of sexual repression, (c) more accepting of nonexclusive sexual intimacy, and (d) more accepting of premarital and extramarital sex, and they also (e) judged the importance of being faithful as less important. In addition, the people who

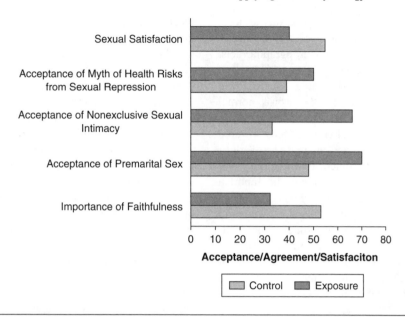

Figure 8.5   The Influence of Long-Term Exposure to Nonviolent Pornography on People's Judgments
SOURCE: Adapted from Zillmann (1994).

watched the nonviolent pornography even wanted fewer children.

Furthermore, Zillmann and Bryant (1986) showed that substantial exposure to nonviolent pornography enhances people's interest in other kinds of pornography. In their experiment, 80 men and 80 women were randomly assigned to one of two conditions. In one condition, participants watched 1 hour of comedies 1 day a week for 6 weeks. In the second condition, participants watched 1 hour of commonly available pornography 1 day a week for 6 weeks. Then, 2 weeks after their final session, participants were brought back to the laboratory. When they arrived, the experimenter apologized for an approximately 15-minute delay in the study and invited the participants to watch any of six videotapes while they waited. They were assured that no one would interrupt them during this delay. The six videotapes were a G-rated movie, an R-rated movie, an X-rated movie, and three XXX-rated movies (the XXX movies consisted of one on bondage, one on sado-masochism, and one on bestiality). Participants who had been exposed to 6 hours of standard X-rated movies were more likely to show an interest in videos depicting less common sexual practices—the bondage, sadomasochism, and

bestiality tapes—than were participants who had seen nonsexual videos. Together, these studies suggest that viewing nonviolent pornography has effects beyond callousness toward women—effects that may change how we view ourselves and our relationships with other people. The findings of this research are consistent with cultivation theory. As discussed earlier, cultivation theory hypothesizes that the social reality of heavy viewers of TV and movies is shaped by what they watch. As this research demonstrates, more exposure to nonviolent pornography changes viewers' social reality, especially their social reality related to sex and sexual relations.

Effects of Exposure to Sexual Violence

The combination of sex and violence has particularly disturbing effects on our thoughts, intentions, and behaviors. A review of research on sexual violence suggests that, in contrast to the effects of nonviolence pornography, even a few minutes' exposure to violent sexuality has many adverse effects (Intons-Peterson & Roskos-Ewoldsen, 1989). Because most of the participants in this body of research are men, the conclusions are mainly about men. The effects on men include (a) increases in sexual arousal, (b) increases in rape fantasies, (c) decreases in sensitivity to the filmed pornographic acts, (d) increases in acceptance of rape myths and of violence toward women, and (e) increases in tolerance toward rapists. In other words, normal males (i.e., showing no propensity for rape) who view portrayals of sexual violence have lowered opinions of women and increased tolerance of violence toward women. Furthermore, after watching violent sexuality, men who report a high likelihood of raping if they could get away with it show more aggression against women in a laboratory setting, are more likely to hold callous attitudes about rape and to believe in rape myths, and show higher levels of sexual arousal to rape depictions than do men who report a lower likelihood of raping (Malamuth, 1981).

As you can see, the effects of exposure to violent pornography in the laboratory have been studied extensively. However, no evidence indicates that viewing violent pornography actually leads to rape or other assaults against women (Intons-Peterson & Roskos-Ewoldsen, 1989). Clearly, there are strong ethical constraints against experimentally studying the causes of rape because this research would require that experimenters show men (perhaps men who are prone to violence against women) sexualized violence and then wait to see whether they actually rape or otherwise harm women. This is not what researchers want to do; in fact, they want to do just the opposite. Researchers want to prevent such occurrences as much as possible, and this is why they have devoted a great deal of effort to figuring out how to lessen the effects of violent sexuality.

Reducing the Harmful Effects of Exposure to Violent Pornography

There are four general ways in which to reduce or eliminate the harmful effects of exposure to violent sexuality. One way is to *legally ban the distribution and sale of these materials.* If you think about this seriously, you can see that this is not feasible except for extreme forms of these materials such as snuff films. However, you have to remember that the films that are used to study violent sexuality are typically R-rated. To ban the sexually violent movies would

mean that many R-rated films—the slasher kind—would be banned. In the United States, any law to ban these materials would likely violate the First Amendment, which includes the right to free exercise of speech. Many other countries have similar rights.

A second way in which to mitigate the harmful effects is to *teach critical viewing skills.* These skills would help people to become more discriminating and discerning consumers of information. Although there are no studies directly related to viewing violent pornography, other studies have shown impressive reductions in violent behaviors in children after critical viewing training (e.g., Huesmann, Eron, Klein, Brice, & Fischer, 1983). Huesmann and colleagues' (1983) study involved children who watched violent TV shows regularly. Half of the children received critical viewing training that focused on violent TV shows (training group), and the other half discussed nonviolent TV shows (control group). The training emphasized that the behaviors seen in violent TV shows do not represent the behaviors of most people (i.e., that these behaviors are not the norm), that the aggressive feats were illusions produced by camera angles and special effects, and that the average person uses other methods to solve problems similar to those encountered in the shows. In other words, the children were taught to perceive the violence as unrealistic. When tested 2 full years after training, these children were less aggressive than children in the control group. The training had affected these children's lives in a positive way, and the effect was long-lasting. It would be of great interest to see if the benefits of developing critical viewing skills generalize to the sexualized violence seen in R-rated slasher films.

A third way in which to mitigate the effects is to *debrief people after viewing violent sexuality.* The debriefing is similar to the training described in Huesmann and colleagues' (1983) study, but it is much shorter in duration. The debriefing typically involves telling the participants about the likely negative effects of exposure to violent sexuality, including information to counter rape myths. All of the studies in the area of sexual violence include a debriefing of some sort. It would be unethical to do otherwise. Researchers strive to undo any potential harm that may have been caused by their experiments. To address the question of whether the debriefings actually work, a meta-analysis was conducted examining all studies that measured the efficacy of debriefings by comparing the post-debriefing rape myth scores of participants exposed to pornography with either pre-debriefing scores or the scores of a control group (Allen, D'Alessio, Emmers, & Gebhardt, 1996). The researchers found that debriefing was effective in undoing the negative effects of exposure. In all of the studies considered, educational debriefings negated the impact of exposure to sexually violent material. One obvious difficulty with debriefings, however, is that it is probably infeasible to append a debriefing to all, or even most, commercially available media. Many producers would probably not add them unless they were legally forced to do so. Even if producers were to add them, would viewers wait around after a movie to watch one? Probably not.

A fourth (and better) way in which to mitigate the harmful effects of exposure is to *inform people about the effects ahead of time.* This would inoculate them against the effect before they were exposed to the material. These prebriefings are basically educational in nature. One variant is to explicitly warn people of the possible effects of exposure to violent sexuality, dealing specifically with the desensitization and callousness that are likely to occur. Another variant includes sex education programs focusing on the similarities and differences of female and male sexual responses, with the differences including what the two sexes consider to be sexual signals, communication skills, and consideration for one's partner. This type of education is intended to make people less susceptible to myths encountered in the media. Yet another variant includes movies aimed at larger audiences that are designed to raise awareness and understanding about rape (e.g., *A Scream of Silence, Behind Closed Doors, Rape Is Not Just a Woman's Problem*) and violent pornography (*Not a Love Story*). As with the debriefings, the question is whether these prebriefings reduce the negative effects of exposure to violent sexuality. The answer is yes. In the meta-analysis by Allen and colleagues (1996), the prebriefings were found to be even more effective than the debriefings.

● FOCUS ON INTERVENTION

A study by Intons-Peterson, Roskos-Ewoldsen, Thomas, Shirley, and Blut (1989) illustrates how prebriefings can serve as effective interventions for the effects of exposure to violent sexuality. In this experiment, 90 adult participants from the local community and university were recruited through local advertisements and were paid for their participation. Only participants who were low to moderate on a set of aggression scales participated in the experiment. Participants high in aggressiveness were precluded from the study for ethical reasons because these people show the strongest long-term effects of exposure to violence. Participants were told that the major purpose of the project was to evaluate the appropriateness of various kinds of information about sex for use with high school audiences and that, because two projects needed to have films evaluated, the participants would take part in two sessions spaced 2 weeks apart. They were also advised that they might be exposed to violent pornography.

This, however, was simply a cover story. The study actually investigated the influence of two types of prebriefing film on participants' acceptance of violent sexuality. The first film, called the *rape prebriefing,* presented participants with current information about rape and general rape myths and also included a discussion of rape's traumatic effects on victims. The second film, called the *sex education prebriefing,* had as its theme the desirability of respecting and being considerate of one's sexual partner. Participants were randomly assigned to view either the rape prebriefing, the sex education prebriefing, or no prebriefing film (the control group). On arriving at the laboratory, participants completed demographic questionnaires and a rape myth acceptance scale, watched one of the prebriefing films (except for control group participants), and then watched a 15-minute segment of one of three types of commercially available videos. One portrayed violent sexuality (*Toolbox Murders,* R-rated), another portrayed nonviolent sexuality (*Pretty Girls,* X-rated), and a third was nonviolent and nonsexual (*The Great American Wilderness,* G-rated).

Afterward, participants responded to a number of questionnaires. Included in this questionnaire package was a rape myth acceptance scale. At the end of the first testing day, all participants watched a *debriefing* video (as opposed to a *prebriefing* video) that explained the effects commonly associated with the viewing of pornographic films and the likely consequences. It also discussed and debunked rape myths (recall from Chapter 3 that debriefing participants is an important component of ethical research). All participants returned 2 weeks later to complete the second session, ostensibly to evaluate more materials. In fact, the session consisted simply of completing the rape myth acceptance scale and many other questions about the films.

Note that participants were tested about their acceptance of rape myths three times: once before the prebriefing, a second time after watching the commercial films, and a third time 2 weeks later. Thus, the experiment involved a 3 (prebriefing type) × 3 (commercial video type) × 3 (time of testing) design with 10 participants in each condition. The dependent variable was the measure of rape myth acceptance.

The results for the rape myth acceptance scale are shown in Figure 8.6. Higher scores indicate more rape myth acceptance, whereas lower scores indicate less rape myth acceptance. As you can see, the two prebriefing films were equally effective at mitigating the negative effects of exposure to violent sexuality or to nonviolent sexuality. There are three findings of note. First, at the first test, rape myth acceptance was similar for all groups. Second, rape myth acceptance increased among control participants immediately after watching the sexual violence commercial film, which is the typical research finding in the literature. In contrast, for both of the prebriefing groups, rape myth acceptance declined immediately after watching sexual violence. This decline indicates that prebriefings lessened the negative effects of exposure to violent sexuality. Finally, at the third testing that occurred 2 weeks after the debriefing, everyone's rape myth acceptance was either back at its normal level (control condition) or at a decreased level (prebriefing conditions), suggesting that both the prebriefings and the debriefings were effective. The only exception was the group that saw no prebriefing and saw the nonviolent, nonsexual commercial film. (There was reason to believe that some members of this group were angered that they did not see any pornography!) These results show clearly that prebriefings emphasizing concern for one's sexual partner or about rape education lessen the effects of exposure to violent sexuality. In addition, both kinds of prebriefing appear to be equally effective in mitigating the negative effects of exposure to violent sexuality. These results are encouraging because the kinds of information incorporated into the prebriefings can easily be presented to groups within an educational setting.

In sum, there are three kinds of pornography: erotica, nonviolent pornography, and violent pornography/sexuality. There is little research on erotica other than that it arouses both men and women. Substantial exposure to nonviolent pornography has its effects mostly on attitudes about family values and happiness. On the other hand, even minimal exposure to violent sexuality, including R-rated slasher films, leads to greater callousness and acceptance of violence toward women. Fortunately, educational programs that emphasize respect for other people, and especially toward one's partner, lessen these negative effects.

The final section of this chapter explores the interaction between the media and political systems. The previous two sections focused on the social psychological study of the influences of two specific types of media content: TV violence and pornography. The research on the media and politics focuses much more on the influence of political news coverage and political advertising on beliefs and behavior. For example, what effect does the media's coverage of an issue have on people's beliefs about that issue? Like the research on TV violence and pornography, the research on the media and politics again suggests that the media do influence our beliefs, thoughts, and attitudes.

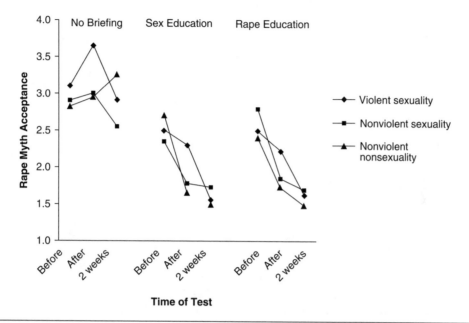

Figure 8.6 Effects of Educational Prebriefing and Content of Video on Rape Myth Acceptance

SOURCE: Adapted from Intons-Peterson, Roskos-Ewoldsen, Thomas, Shirley, and Blut (1989). Reprinted with permission from Guilford Press.

Does Political News Coverage Affect Us?

During the early part of the last century, people thought that the media could have profound effects on how people perceived the world. The *War of the Worlds* radio broadcast suggested that the media could shape people's thoughts. A classic example of "powerful" media comes from Walter Lippmann's book, *Public Opinion* (Lippmann, 1922). In 1914, there was a small island where people from France, England, and Germany lived together. A steamer that stopped every 60 days was the only connection this small island had with the outside world. On a particular day in September, the steamer arrived and delivered newspapers announcing the outbreak of hostilities in Europe that turned out to be the beginning of World War I. All of a sudden, the French and British citizens on the island were also at war with the German citizens on the island. Nothing had changed on the island, yet people who had been friends were now enemies simply because they had learned of the start of World War I. The residents' reality changed because of the delivery of a newspaper.

How the Media Influence Our Thoughts

The view that the media could have such powerful effects on what people think began to change as more research was conducted using newspapers, radio, and TV. During the 1950s and 1960s, social scientists began to argue that the media have little or no influence on how people perceive the world (Rogers, 1994). Recall Senator Knowland's telethon, where the telethon had minimal impact on whether people voted for him. Studies such as this one led to the conclusion that the media do not determine what we think. But does that mean that the media have no influence?

Influencing people's thoughts. During the late 1980s, the U.S. public's concern about the problem of illegal drug use steadily increased. In November 1985, no respondents to a national political survey listed drugs as the number one problem facing the United States. However, by November 1989—just 4 years later—more than 50% of the respondents listed drugs as the number one problem in the country (Dearing & Rogers, 1996). This occurred even though objective measures of the drug problem suggested that, if anything, the drug problem was

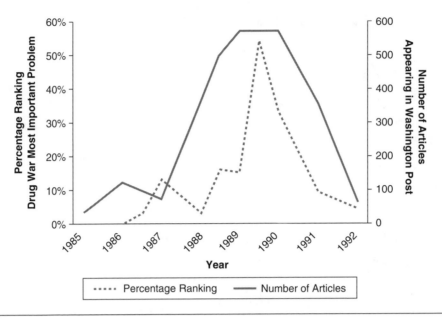

Figure 8.7   The Relationship Between Newspaper Coverage of the War on Drugs and the Public's Judgment That Drugs Were the Number One Problem in the United States

SOURCE: Adapted from Dearing and Rogers (1996).

decreasing. For example, drug-related deaths decreasing during this time period. What was going on? Why were people becoming more concerned about the "drug problem" when the drug problem appeared to be under control? Obviously, no single factor can explain why the U.S. public became more concerned about the problem. One factor that certainly played a role was the media's focus on drugs. Several studies have documented that the news media's extensive coverage of drugs during the mid- to late 1980s certainly raised public concerns about the drug issue (Dearing & Rogers, 1996; Gozenbach, 1996). Figure 8.7 shows how media coverage of the drug issue—in this case the *Washington Post*—predated the country's concern about the drug issue. As you can see, shortly after the number of articles on the drug problem increased, the number of people rating drugs as the most important problem facing the United States increased. Also of interest, the figure shows that later, as people began to judge the problem as less important, the press decreased the number of articles devoted to the drug problem.

The idea that the media can shape what issues we think about or what issues we think are important is referred to as **agenda setting**

(Iyengar & Kinder, 1987; McCombs & Reynolds, 2002). When the media set the agenda, the media are not influencing what people think; rather, the media coverage is influencing what people think about. The media did not influence whether people thought that the use of drugs was wrong or whether the real problem was unfair sentencing of drug offenders. Media coverage of the drug issue resulted in people thinking that the drug issue was an important one. Several hundred studies in the United States and in Europe have demonstrated that the media do set the public's agenda (Dearing & Rogers, 1996; McCombs & Reynolds, 2002). Furthermore, media coverage of an issue can result in the public becoming more concerned about the issue even when real-world indicators of the problem may suggest that the problem is declining (Gozenbach, 1996).

When discussing agenda setting, it is important to keep in mind that there are really three kinds of agenda that are important. The **public agenda** involves the issues that the public thinks are important. The **policy agenda** involves the issues that government officials and policymakers think are important. The **media agenda** involves the issues that the media are covering extensively. Research suggests that the media often set the public's agenda and that the public sets the policy agenda (Dearing & Rogers, 1996). For example, a famine in Ethiopia had been going on for 2 years before the U.S. media picked up on the issue based on an October 1984 BBC report with startling footage of children starving in Ethiopia. The 3½-minute segment that aired on NBC on October 23 caught the public's attention, and calls for aid increased. The media's coverage of the famine continued (media agenda), and this heightened the public's concern about the issue (public agenda). Consequently, policymakers began to see the famine in Ethiopia as an important issue (policy agenda) because it was attracting so much public attention and because polls indicated that the American people thought that this was an important issue. Interestingly, a drought that was going on in Brazil at the same time did not catch the media's attention. Unlike the situation in Ethiopia, the people in Brazil who were affected by the drought were spread out over a vast territory. This situation made gathering information about the drought much more difficult. The Brazilian drought never became an important issue for the American people or the U.S. government, probably because it was not on the media's agenda. The media decided that the drought in Brazil was too difficult to cover (Dearing & Rogers, 1996).

The reason why the media can influence the public's agenda is that extensive media coverage of an issue makes that issue *salient* (Iyengar & Ottati, 1994). The **availability heuristic** suggests that people make judgments based on how easy it is to recall instances of something from memory (Tversky & Kahneman, 1974). For example, if someone calls you as part of a survey and asks what is the major problem facing the country, the availability heuristic predicts that you would answer with the issue that came to mind first. Consequently, anything that makes an issue more salient to you increases the likelihood that you will recall it and report it as an important issue. When you read the newspaper and the front-page headlines report a drought in a distant country, they will make the issue more salient. If the media include graphic pictures of starving children, they will also increase the salience of the issue.

Likewise, if all of the media are covering the issue, that will increase the likelihood that you will see multiple stories about the issue and will increase its salience. Also, if the media continue to cover the issue over weeks or even months, that will further increase the salience of the issue. So, there are a lot of different ways in which the media can increase the salience of an issue. All of these different elements of how the media cover the issue work to make you think that the issue is important.

Although there are many impressive examples of how the media set the public's agenda, it is important to understand that the media do not always set the agenda. For example, survey research has demonstrated that the media are not likely to set the agenda for local issues (Behr & Iyengar, 1985). Of course, if you think about it, this makes sense. If the issue is a local issue or it affects your life directly, do you need the media to tell you that this is an important issue? For example, think about a person who has been laid off during a recession. Do you think that media coverage of the economy is necessary for that person to think that the economy is a major issue? An additional factor that influences the media's role in setting the public agenda involves the need for orientation (McCombs & Reynolds, 2002). People have a high need for orientation when an issue is personally important to them but they do not know a lot about the issue. In this situation, the media are more likely to influence the public's agenda. Finally, people who are less educated or who are not politically involved are more likely to be influenced by the media's agenda (Iyengar & Kinder, 1987).

What information do we use to judge the president? One area that has been studied extensively is political priming. **Political priming** is the idea that the issues that the media are covering influence the information that people use to judge the president and other politicians (Iyengar & Kinder, 1987; Roskos-Ewoldsen et al., in press; Roskos-Ewoldsen, Roskos-Ewoldsen, & Carpentier, 2002). In 1991, President George Bush enjoyed very high approval ratings. Indeed, many political pundits did not think the Democratic party would be able to field a candidate that could beat Bush in the 1992 presidential election given how popular he was in early 1991. However, if you are familiar with recent U.S. history, you know that Bush did not win reelection in 1992. Instead, he was defeated by a young Democrat from Arkansas named Bill Clinton. How did Bush go from such a high level of public approval to losing the election to Clinton?

There are a number of factors that influenced the outcome of the 1992 election. Research on media coverage of events suggests that the media's preoccupation with domestic issues during late 1991 and 1992 certainly played a role in the declining popularity of President Bush. When you judge how well the president is doing his or her job, you have a lot of different pieces of information that you could use to make the judgment. You could use the president's performance on the economy, civil rights, or international affairs, or you could use how well the president dresses. Political priming is concerned with the role that the media play in what information you use to judge the president. Thus, the idea behind political priming is that the media do not influence what you think specifically; rather, they influence *what information you use* to make your judgment of the president. Calling this political priming is unfortunate because it is easy to think that political priming is like Berkowitz's (1984) model of media priming of violence that was discussed earlier. However, the two are very different. For example, when the media prime violence, the effect goes away relatively quickly, but political priming effects from the media can last for weeks (Roskos-Ewoldsen et al., in press).

Arguments about calling this phenomenon priming aside, according to the research on political priming, if the media are focusing primarily on international affairs, then people will use their impressions of how well the president is doing in international affairs to judge how well the president is doing overall. However, if the media are focusing primarily on domestic affairs, then people will use their impressions of how well the president is doing on domestic issues to judge how well the president is doing overall. People tended to have very positive impressions of how well President Bush handled international affairs but tended to have negative impressions of how well he handled domestic affairs. A combination of survey research and content analysis of the major stories on the evening news and in major newspapers demonstrated that when the media were covering the first war in Iraq, people who had positive evaluations of Bush's handling of international affairs formed a positive impression of his overall performance despite the fact that people generally did not think he was doing a good job of handling the U.S. economy. In late 1991 and 1992, when the media turned their attention away from the Middle East and focused on domestic issues, people used their negative evaluations of Bush's handling of domestic affairs to judge his overall performance. Consequently, the ratings of Bush's job performance plummeted despite the fact that the people thought that he did a good job of handling international affairs (Iyengar & Simon, 1993, Krosnick & Brannon, 1993). In other words, the media agenda seemed to be implicated in the outcome of the 1992 election because the media primed the criteria that people used to judge Bush's job performance.

Effects of Negative Media Coverage of the Government

People's confidence in political institutions has dropped precipitously in the United States over the past 40 years. In 1964, roughly 75% of the U.S. population trusted the nation's government. By the mid-1990s, the number of people in the United States who trusted the government had fallen to approximately 25% (Moy & Pfau, 2000). The declining trust of the government has gone hand in hand with declining rates of voter turnout at national and local elections. The declining confidence in the government may undermine the effectiveness of the president, Congress, the courts, and law enforcement agencies. Furthermore, if people do not trust the president and Congress, the mistrust can undermine efforts at reforming the political system. For example, recent attempts at campaign finance reform in the United States have been met with growing cynicism as to whether the reforms will have any real influence. Others have gone so far as to argue that if confidence sinks too low, the country might not be able to respond to a crisis as effectively (Moy & Pfau, 2000).

Many people argue that there is good reason for the declining trust in the U.S. government (Cappella & Jamieson, 1997; Moy & Pfau, 2000). During the 1960s, the civil rights movement and the war in Vietnam both undermined confidence in the government. During the 1970s, President Richard Nixon resigned because of the Watergate scandal. During the late 1970s, the Iran hostage crisis, where a handful of students in Iran held U.S. embassy personnel hostage for more than a year, further undermined people's confidence in the presidency. During the 1980s, the U.S. elected an *actor* as president, and the Iran–Contra scandal and numerous other scandals rocked Ronald Reagan's presidency. And of course, President Clinton was nearly impeached because of his sexual involvement with White House intern Monica Lewinsky. However, there are good reasons to believe that the various scandals that have occurred are not the only reason why people's confidence in the U.S. government is so low. Many people charge that the media have played a key role in the declining image of the government (Moy & Pfau, 2000).

Do the media undermine confidence in the government? You have probably heard people complain that the news media focus only on the negative. People often lament the fact that the news media cannot seem to show anything positive or uplifting about the country or the government. In particular, the media are often accused of presenting overly negative portrayals of politicians. Surprisingly, a recent content analysis of the media found that although most media (e.g., newspapers, newsmagazines, the local news) are somewhat negative in their treatment of the government, they are not the worst. Radio talk shows (e.g., *Rush Limbaugh*) and TV entertainment talk shows (e.g., *David Letterman, The Tonight Show*) are particularly negative in their portrayals of the government (Moy & Pfau, 2000).

But does this negative coverage of the government and politicians influence the public's knowledge of, and confidence in, the government? Numerous surveys and studies have found that people who are exposed to negative coverage of the government trust the government less. The most extensive study, involving a survey of more than 1,200 adults on this issue, revealed some interesting things about the media and perceptions of political institutions in the United States (Moy & Pfau, 2000). Consistent with most people's folk wisdom, this research suggested that reading newspapers and watching TV news programs (e.g., *60 Minutes*) increased people's understanding of the political system. However, other types of TV programming, such as entertainment talk shows, actually decreased people's understanding of the government. People who read newspapers and newsmagazines or watched their local TV news had higher confidence in the government. Conversely, people who watched the national news on TV or listened to politically oriented radio talk shows were more cynical of the government—especially of the president. Of course, it is important to remember that although Moy and Pfau's (2000) study is by far the most extensive one on this issue, only surveys were used. As a consequence, it is difficult to know the direction of causation. Listening to radio talk shows may increase people's cynicism of the government. However, it also may be the case that those people who are particularly cynical of the government are more likely to listen to radio talk shows. Probably both occur; radio talk shows probably attract people who are already cynical of the government, but radio talk shows certainly reinforce cynical views of the government.

How is the story told? The framing of stories. There are many different slants or angles that a reporter can take for a story. **Framing** refers to how the story is presented or its angle (Iyengar, 1991). Assume that a reporter is going to write a story about the latest war in Iraq. The reporter could focus on the issues that led up to the war such as the United Nations' inspectors and disagreements between the United States and Britain, on the one hand, and France, Germany, and Russia, on the other, over the war itself and the charges that Iraq had weapons of mass destruction. The reporter might instead focus on President George W. Bush's motivations for wanting to go to war with Iraq, including Iraq's oil reserves and the attempt by Iraqis to assassinate the president's father. The reporter might choose to use a human interest angle and focus on one of the U.S. soldiers who fought in Iraq or on an Iraqi family's experiences during the war. These are just a few of the different ways in which the reporter could frame the story.

How a story is framed is important because the story's frame will make certain aspects of the story salient while other elements are deemphasized or ignored (Iyengar, 1991). For example, if the story focused on the experiences of a U.S. soldier fighting in Iraq, then the story might highlight the dangers of the war in Iraq and the fanatical zeal of certain paramilitary groups within Iraq. This kind of frame would likely fuel negative Western stereotypes of people from the Middle East.

How a story is framed can have important influences on the judgments people make related to the story (Iyengar, 1991; Kahneman & Tversky, 1982). For example, Iyangar (1991) found that when stories about poverty took a human interest angle and focused on a particular poor person, people were more likely to blame the individual as responsible for being poor. However, when the stories provided thematic coverage of poverty and focused on the history of poverty in this country and government programs to aid the poor, people were less likely to blame individuals for being poor and focused more on poverty as a problem that society is responsible for causing.

How political stories are framed contributes to the growing mistrust of the government (Cappella & Jamieson, 1997). In covering a political campaign, a reporter could use what is called an **issue frame** and focus on the issues that are important, the background of the issues, and the pros and cons involved with the issues. For example, an issue in the 2000 U.S. presidential campaign concerned the role of the United States as a peacekeeper in various countries. A story that took an issue frame might focus on the history of the United States acting as a peacekeeper in Somalia and Eastern Europe during President Clinton's administration and the impact of these activities on how other countries perceived the United States. On the other hand, a story could use what is termed a **strategy frame.** A strategy frame focuses on the motivations behind the different positions that politicians are taking. For example, a story with a strategy frame might argue that Bush was opposed to the U.S. acting as international

peacekeepers because polls have shown that most Republican voters are opposed to it. Because of a strategy frame's focus on the motivations for why a politician supports a policy, the strategy frame tends to make the politician look self-interested and not particularly concerned about the greater good for the country.

In a series of experiments, Cappella and Jamieson (1997) demonstrated that reading articles with a strategy frame increased participants' cynicism toward politics to a greater extent than did reading articles with an issue frame. This increase in cynicism occurred whether the strategy frame focused on a politician's motivations for a stance on an issue (health care reform) or on the motivations of a candidate while running for office (mayor's race in Philadelphia). The public generally wants politicians who are concerned about their well-being. However, by focusing on the motivations behind a politician's stance on an issue, the strategy frame tends to make the politician look as though his or her primary concerns are with how he or she looks to the general public and with getting elected or reelected. Because most strategy frames focus on the negative motivations of politicians, these frames reinforce the public's perceptions that politicians are only out for their own good. In our everyday lives, we tend not to trust people who look out only for themselves, and the same holds true for politicians who we perceive as looking out only for themselves. Clearly, journalists can play an important role in the political process because what they choose to focus on—the frame for the story—can influence the readers' interpretation of the story.

Political advertising gone bad. The elements of a political campaign that make it "negative" involve an emphasis on the undesirable characteristics of the opponent. Unfortunately, in the United States, most negative campaigns do not focus on the disadvantages of the opponents' positions on the issues. Rather, the typical negative campaign focuses on what a despicable individual the opponent is. Negative political campaigning has been around for a long time. For example, in the presidential election of 1800, the Republicans attacked the Federalist candidate, John Adams, by arguing that he was a hypocrite and a fool, had no virtues, and was a wretch (Johnson-Cartee & Copeland, 1991). However, as many commentators have noted, political campaigns began getting much more negative during the last 30 years of the 20th century (Johnson-Cartee & Copeland, 1991). At the same time that negative political campaigning has been increasing in the United States, voter turnout has been dropping (Ansolabehere & Iyengar, 1996). The question is whether negative campaigning turns off the electorate.

Several experimental studies demonstrate very clearly that negative campaigns decrease voter turnout. In an experiment using actual advertisements from a California senate campaign and the Los Angeles mayoral campaign, it was found that negative advertisements decreased people's intentions to vote (Ansolabehere & Iyengar, 1996). In addition, several experimental studies have demonstrated that when *both* candidates run negative advertisements, as opposed to just one or neither candidate running negative advertisements, this seems to create a synergy that results in *both* candidates being evaluated as less desirable. Furthermore, research participants reported that they would be much less likely to vote when they witnessed campaigns where both candidates were negative (Houston & Doan, 1999; Houston, Doan, & Roskos-Ewoldsen, 1999; Houston & Roskos-Ewoldsen, 1998). Specifically, it appears that negative campaigns create the perception that voting is a lose–lose situation. Lose–lose situations are those that people try to avoid. How do you feel when you are placed in a situation where you have to choose between two undesirable options, for example, continuing to have a painful tooth or going to the dentist? These are situations that people find to be aversive. It is no wonder that negative campaigns have turned off the voting public and increased people's cynicism.

In sum, the research on agenda setting and political priming clearly show that the media can and do effect what political issues people think about and what information people use to make political judgments. However, the influence of the media is more subtle than people tend to think. The media clearly do not *dictate* what people think. If the media influenced what people thought, there would not be so much disagreement about various issues. The media

do not influence whether people think a particular proposal for welfare reform is a good idea or a bad idea. However, the media can influence whether people think that welfare reform is an important issue. Likewise, the media can influence whether people's judgment of how well the president handles welfare reform influences their evaluation of the president. These effects of the media are subtle, but they can be important. The media also play a role in people's increased cynicism of the government. The media's focus on negative events, how they frame stories, and the negative campaigns that politicians run in the media all create a deepening distrust of government.

SUMMARY

As the topics covered in this chapter have demonstrated, the psychological effects of the media are varied. When a particular type of content, such as violence, is prevalent in the media, the effects can be quite pronounced. Media violence can lead to long-term imitation of violent behavior. Quasi-experiments suggest that the media can play a large role in the number of homicides in a country. Conversely, TV violence can temporarily increase one's aggressive thoughts. Likewise, TV and movies can result in fright reactions that can be short term or last for years, or they can increase heavy viewers' perceptions of the world as a dangerous and hostile place in which to live.

Pornography, another popular genre of media, can also have serious consequences. Although little research has been done on erotica, research on nonviolent pornography demonstrates that both men and women have more negative views of family life after watching a substantial amount (six videos) of nonviolent pornography. Violent pornography—in the form of XXX-rated movies, snuff films, or R-rated slasher films—has the most serious psychological effects. Even short-term exposure to violent sexuality can increase men's acceptance of rape myths and result in more negative views of women.

The research on political news coverage suggests that the media can have very subtle psychological effects. The media can influence what people think are the important issues facing the country. How a story is framed can influence people's interpretation of an issue. Heavy coverage of an issue will influence how people judge the job that the president is doing. In addition, the media can create cynicism toward political leaders and institutions.

It is hoped that this chapter has demonstrated why social psychologists and other social scientists are interested in studying the media. There are many more areas where media psychology

has been studied, including prosocial benefits of the media, the effects of the media on racism, the factors that influence how enjoyable a movie is, and why people watch the shows they watch. In other words, a lot of research has been conducted. However, there are still many issues that need to be addressed. Given the rapid changes that are taking place in the media, there will always be a need for social psychologists to study the psychological consequences of the media.

 ## CULTURE CAPSULE: MEDIA INFLUENCE ACROSS CULTURES

One area where much more research is needed concerns the influence of the media in different cultures. As was noted in the beginning of this chapter, the majority of research on the psychology of the media has been conducted in the United States. However, there has also been research conducted on the media in other countries. For example, most of the interesting research on agenda setting has been conducted in Europe. Likewise, research on cultivation theory has been conducted in Europe, Asia, South America, and the Middle East. Heavy viewers of TV in all of these areas show cultivation effects in that TV influences their perceptions of their social reality.

However, there is research suggesting that culture can play an important role in the psychological influences of the media. St. Helena is a remote island in the South Atlantic Ocean. Indeed, Napoleon's second exile was to St. Helena, and he died on the island. St. Helena is so remote that the first TV broadcast occurred there on March 31, 1995. Obviously, this event provided researchers with another opportunity to conduct a quasi-experiment on the influence of TV, and that is what researchers did (Charlton, Gunter, & Hannan, 2002). In particular, research focused on the effects of the introduction of TV on children's aggression, much like the research that was conducted in the town of "Notel" in Canada during the 1970s (Joy et al., 1986). However, unlike Notel, there have been no increases in violence since the introduction of TV on St. Helena (Charlton et al., 2002). Why? Of course, one possibility is that there has not been enough time for TV to influence the aggressiveness of the children. Recall that Centerwall (1989) argued that it took 15 years for the effects of TV to influence homicide rates. However, the research on Notel found increases in both verbal aggression and physical aggression just 2 years after the introduction of TV to that town. TV has been on St. Helena for more than 5 years with no increase in children's physical or verbal aggression. Why the difference? The best explanation is that St. Helena is a unique culture. In particular, people on St. Helena are much more prone to watch out for each other than are people in other Western cultures (Charlton et al., 2002). The greater sense of responsibility for others that characterizes this culture may serve as a buffer that protects children from the negative consequences of exposure to TV.

9

APPLYING SOCIAL PSYCHOLOGY TO HEALTH

KATHRYN D. LAFRENIERE

KENNETH M. CRAMER

CHAPTER OUTLINE

During the summer of 2002, the story of a New York man's lawsuit against the fast-food industry for contributing to his obesity made newspaper headlines and was widely discussed on television news. The man, who was 5 feet 10 inches tall and weighed roughly 270 pounds, had filed a lawsuit claiming that many of the major fast-food chains were guilty of false advertising because they were misleading about the nutritional value of their food. The man had been eating fast food several times a week for most of his life, and at 56 years of age he had a number of health problems that tend to be linked to obesity, including diabetes, high blood pressure, and a series of heart attacks. During the same summer, a similar lawsuit was filed in New York by the parents of two teenage girls who were also obese and suffered from high cholesterol, high blood pressure, heart disease, and diabetes. This lawsuit was directed at McDonald's and two of its branches, claiming that they had failed to clearly disclose the ingredients and effects of their food, which tends to be high in fat, sodium, and cholesterol. The parents claimed that, in the absence of information to the contrary, they believed that fast food was healthy for their children. Samuel Hirsch, the lawyer who filed both of these cases, suggested that McDonald's food was "addictive" and that the corporation's billion-dollar advertising campaigns tend to unduly target and influence children to make unhealthy choices.

These lawsuits came on the heels of several well-publicized lawsuits against the tobacco industry in which extremely high punitive damages awards were made to plaintiffs who argued that the tobacco companies failed to adequately warn consumers about the risks of smoking. In one tobacco lawsuit case, the original amount awarded was as high as $28 billion but was later reduced to $28 million. To date, the fast-food lawsuits have not met with the same success as the tobacco industry lawsuits have.

When you read about these kinds of lawsuits, what is your initial reaction? Are these just frivolous lawsuits in which opportunistic lawyers are trying to profit from multi-billion-dollar industries by using current knowledge about the health risks associated with obesity and smoking? Are decisions about what kind of food to eat and whether or not to smoke simply individual choices whereby people need to take personal responsibility and not shift the blame onto others (Figure 9.1)? Or, do industries that spend billions of dollars on advertising campaigns also bear some responsibility to guide individuals toward making positive health choices?

Most of you will probably come out on the side of individual responsibility and dismiss these lawsuits as frivolous. The majority of people who responded to a WNBC online poll said that restaurants are not responsible for the health of their customers. Most adults in our society clearly understand that smoking is a dangerous habit and that a steady diet of fast food does not constitute a nutritious balanced diet. However, a group called the Physicians Committee for Responsible Medicine, which promotes preventive medicine, recently published a commentary that discussed why fast-food lawsuits are good (Barnard & Kursban, 2002). In the article, they pointed out that the fast-food industry manipulates American perceptions about food and influences people's choices through billion-dollar advertising campaigns as well as through more direct means such as contracts with school food service departments and sponsorship of educational events. In other words, the power and political clout of a multi-billion-dollar industry means that we are not necessarily on a level playing field when it comes to nutritional choices.

In fact, although it is easy to suggest that an obese person should simply make better nutritional choices and lose weight, or that a smoker should safeguard his or her health by quitting smoking, the reality of the situation is much more complicated. One thing that we know about health is that the better off people are financially and educationally, the healthier they tend to be. As we go down the socioeconomic ladder, health outcomes become poorer as well (Adler et al., 1994). Again, this suggests that we are dealing with an uneven playing field where adopting healthier behaviors is harder for some people (those who are financially disadvantaged) than it is for others. Smoking habits lead to smoking addiction, and many current smokers have made very strenuous attempts to quit that have failed repeatedly. So, although we might want people to assume greater personal responsibility for their health choices, we also need to recognize that there are substantial barriers to doing so. If there were no such barriers, we all would be fit, trim, and healthy nonsmokers.

An area of applied social psychology that addresses such concerns is *health psychology*. Although health psychologists can also be trained in clinical psychology, many of the principles of health promotion, health behavior change, and adjustment to illness are based on social psychology theories and concepts, and these are the focus of this chapter.

As you read through the chapter, keep the following questions in mind:

Figure 9.1   Eating Habits: A Major Contributor to Physical Ailments

- Who is responsible for my health? Is it entirely up to me, or are there social and societal influences that operate as well?
- How can psychology be used to promote healthy choices?
- How do we go about changing our unhealthy behaviors and adopting healthier ones?
- Can psychological factors contribute to our likelihood of getting particular illnesses?
- Does psychology have anything to offer to people who already suffer from physical illnesses or symptoms?

HEALTH PSYCHOLOGY DEFINED

Health psychology is the branch of applied psychology that is concerned with examining psychological influences on physical health. There are a number of aspects to this relationship between psychological considerations and physical health. The classic definition of **health psychology** that is most often cited includes all of these aspects:

> Health psychology is the aggregate of the specific educational, scientific, and professional contributions of the discipline of psychology to the promotion and maintenance of health, the prevention and treatment of illness, the identification of etiologic and diagnostic correlates of health, illness, and related dysfunction, and the analysis and improvement of the health care system and health policy formation. (Matarazzo, 1980, p. 815)

In other words, health psychology is concerned about how we can promote better health habits and help to prevent illness, how psychological factors might influence our likelihood of becoming ill, and how knowledge from psychology can be used to help those who already suffer from particular illnesses. In addition, it also enables us to examine how health care can be provided to patients in the best possible way.

Health psychology is a relatively new area of concentration within psychology. It first appeared during the 1970s and really took hold during the early 1980s, when a select group of universities began to offer undergraduate and graduate health psychology courses and the journal *Health Psychology* was first published. Now health psychology courses are widely available at many universities, and there are a number of journals devoted to psychological and social influences on health.

A number of factors contributed to the rise in popularity of health psychology through the end of the 20th century (Brannon & Feist, 2000). For one thing, medical and technological advancements have meant that people are living longer, yet few elderly people are completely free of disease or dysfunction. Many people live with chronic illnesses such as hypertension (high blood pressure), diabetes, and heart disease. Although medical science is concerned with developing medications and technologies to help control these diseases, psychology can help to manage psychological aspects of living with chronic illnesses so that patients can enjoy a better quality of life throughout their life spans. In addition, the chronic illnesses that are most predominant today (e.g., heart disease, diabetes, cancer) are different from the acute infectious diseases that people tended to die of a century ago (e.g., tuberculosis, influenza, pneumonia). Chronic illnesses are influenced by lifestyle factors such as whether or not people smoke, their diets and levels of physical activity, and even their stress levels. Thus, psychological factors can play a much stronger role in helping to prevent and manage chronic illness than is the case for infectious diseases. Another factor that helped to set the stage for health psychology's rise in popularity is the high cost of health care. Although an extraordinary number of high-tech diagnostic and treatment options exist today (e.g., CT [computed tomography] scans, MRIs [magnetic resonance images], radiation treatments), they are extremely costly and the idea of allocating resources toward promoting healthy habits to prevent illness seems to be a cost-effective choice. Again, psychology makes an important contribution in helping people to alter their bad habits and make healthier lifestyle choices.

In addition to these other factors, toward the end of the 20th century there was growing dissatisfaction with the traditional **biomedical model** of health and illness (Brannon & Feist, 2000). The biomedical model is the theoretical framework that guided medical advances leading to the ability to conquer a number of life-threatening diseases. The biomedical model is based on the idea that illness can be completely explained by examining problems in an organism's biological functioning. This approach leads us to focus on lower level biological processes (e.g., cell functioning, biochemical imbalances) rather than to examine health in a broader context that also includes psychological functioning and social influences (Taylor, 2003). The biomedical model also tends to focus on disease more than on health, and it conceptualizes health quite simply as the absence of disease. The biomedical model was important in leading to the discovery of a number of specific disease-causing agents, such as bacteria and viruses, and these discoveries in turn led to advances in medical technology to cure a number of life-threatening infectious diseases. Despite the importance of the biomedical model, it was limited in that it failed to account completely for the fact that not everyone who is exposed to the same virus will acquire a particular disease; furthermore, even when people do get sick, there are large differences among individuals in terms of the severity of symptoms they experience and how they respond to treatment. It seemed clear that a broader model was needed to conceptualize health and illness, and this led to the emergence of the biopsychosocial model, which is the primary model of health and illness underlying health psychology.

The Biopsychosocial Model

In contrast to the biomedical model, the **biopsychosocial model** (as its name implies) sees health as being determined by biological, psychological, and social factors (Engel, 1977). Use of the biopsychosocial model does not mean that we completely reject the biomedical model; instead, it suggests that we recognize that the biomedical model does not lead to a complete understanding of health and illness. Although it is clear that the role of biology will always be important in explaining illness, the biopsychosocial model demands that we also pay attention to psychological and social influences. Consequently, issues such as the particular meanings that patients attach to their illnesses, patients' motivation to recover (or not), patients' response styles (whether they stoically minimize symptoms rather than tending to exaggerate symptom reporting), and to what extent patients benefit from support from other people when they are ill are seen as important determinants of how people experience illness (DiMatteo & Martin, 2002).

Social Variables and Health

The focus of this book is on applications of social psychology, so the emphasis in the remainder of this chapter is on social variables within the biopsychosocial model. Although at first glance it might be easier to understand the relevance of biological variables (e.g., genetic factors, exposure to viruses) and psychological variables (e.g., individual differences in experience of pain or other symptoms, personal coping styles), there are a number of ways in which social factors can have an impact on health. As we have already seen, socioeconomic factors, such as income and educational level, influence our probability of becoming ill. In addition, sometimes we try to adopt good health habits (e.g., exercising) because we are influenced by friends or family members who also engage in these behaviors, or we try to give up bad habits (e.g., smoking) because we know that important people in our lives are concerned about or disapprove of these behaviors. Although it might not always seem to be the case, our interactions with our physicians and other health care providers constitute social relationships, and the nature of these social interactions can affect our health outcomes. Social factors also have a lot to do with how we cope with illness or stress. In general, the presence of others has beneficial effects on our health in that the support we receive from our loved ones can help us to feel better, adopt healthier behaviors, and generally decrease our experience of stress. However, it is sometimes the case that the social influence of other people can have negative effects rather than positive ones. For example, if you work or attend school in a very competitive cutthroat environment, the social presence of others is more likely to add to your stress than to relieve it. Recently, there has been a great deal of research interest in the issue of "caregiver stress," that is, the idea that looking after elderly or disabled family members can place stressful demands on an individual, often leading to negative health consequences (e.g., Schulz & Beach, 1999).

Health psychology is a very broad area, encompassing virtually all of the ways in which we can consider psychological and social factors in relation to health. It would be easy to teach a full-year university course in health psychology and never run out of relevant and exciting material to discuss. Consequently, any brief treatment of health psychology will involve a very limited selection of specific topics within this area of study and is meant to whet the appetite for further study rather than to cover the entire field exhaustively. Following from the definition of health psychology, this chapter focuses on three major areas in which social psychology has been applied to health: (a) promoting health and preventing illness, (b) changing health behavior, and (c) stress, coping, and social support.

PROMOTING HEALTH AND PREVENTING ILLNESS

One of the major areas in which psychology has a great deal to contribute to people's health concerns health promotion and prevention of illness. **Health promotion** refers simply to efforts that are made to encourage people to engage in healthy behaviors such as eating a healthy and balanced diet, exercising regularly, getting enough rest, and refraining from smoking and abusing alcohol. Health promotion is a philosophy that guides action to achieve good health. The actions undertaken to achieve optimal health and well-being occur at multiple levels, including the efforts of individuals, medical practitioners, psychologists, community and government health policymakers, and the mass media (Taylor, 2003).

Prevention typically refers to more targeted efforts to reduce the probability of getting an illness in the first place or to reduce the severity of an illness or disorder once it does occur. Prevention can also take place at multiple levels in terms of who is responsible for undertaking the preventive efforts (e.g., the individual, medical practitioners, the government) and also in terms of the timing of the preventive actions in relation to the illness outcomes. Prevention efforts that are aimed toward healthy individuals so as to keep them healthy and avoid their risk of contracting diseases are called **primary prevention.** For example, a school-based program that educates elementary school students about the health risks of smoking would be considered primary prevention. If this sounds a lot like health promotion, that is because primary prevention and health promotion do overlap to a large extent in that they share the goal of keeping a well population disease free. **Secondary prevention** occurs at a later point, when people are already affected by a medical condition or disorder, and the goal is to prevent the condition from leading to more severe health consequences. For example, getting a mammogram is a secondary prevention strategy for women. If a woman has a malignant tumor in her breast, conducting the breast screening will not prevent the occurrence of cancer altogether, but it might mean that the malignancy was detected early enough for her to be successfully treated before the disease has spread, greatly improving her chances of complete recovery. Finally, **tertiary prevention** refers to situations in which the disease or disorder has not been prevented, but efforts are made to reduce the extent of the disorder's impact on patients (Bishop, 1994). An example of tertiary prevention would be a patient undergoing rehabilitation to attempt to recover some of the skills and abilities that he or she lost as a result of a stroke.

Let us return to a question that was posed near the beginning of this chapter. Who is ultimately responsible for our health? Most of us would probably say that we have to assume responsibility for our own health, and yet many people consistently make unhealthy choices, leading to prevalence rates of illnesses that are strongly influenced by lifestyles. Recent statistics show that the leading causes of death in the United States are heart disease, cancer, and stroke (Taylor, 2003), and some current estimates suggest that roughly half of the current death rate stems from preventable causes such as smoking, poor diet, and physical inactivity (Brannon & Feist, 2000). Clearly, individual efforts at adopting healthier behaviors are not entirely successful. Other initiatives aimed at promoting good health and preventing illness are necessary. These health promotion and primary prevention activities can come from a number of sources, but this section focuses on just a few of these. First, it considers health messages that are delivered through the mass media. Second, it looks at the influence of family members and peers.

Persuasion and Social Influence in Media Health Coverage

Social psychologists have studied the issue of social influence since the 1950s, when Carl Hovland and his colleagues (e.g., Hovland, Janis, & Kelley, 1953) studied attitude change in a series of experiments at Yale University. **Social influence** refers to the idea that interactions with other people can lead to changes in our attitudes, beliefs, values, and behavior. Interventions of any type can be considered a form of social influence. **Persuasion** refers to a specific kind of social influence in which a particular message or appeal is used to try to change someone's attitudes or beliefs (DiMatteo & Martin, 2002). In Chapter 8, you learned about how media messages influence us in a variety of ways. Of particular interest in health psychology is the use of messages to persuade people to adopt healthy lifestyle habits. For example, how do we convince others to exercise more, quit smoking, or refrain from drinking and driving?

Many social psychologists have examined features of persuasive communications to see which factors make a difference in whether the messages will be noticed, remembered, and acted on. In general, these researchers have studied two different kinds of persuasive messages: informational appeals and fear appeals. **Informational appeals** provide people with facts and arguments about why it is important to engage in particular health behaviors. Although this sounds like a simple enough task, it is critical that the informational message be constructed in a way that makes it likely that the target audience actually "gets it." *To be effective an informational appeal must* first grab people's attention, and it must be clear and easily understood. It must also be able to truly persuade the audience, and it must be memorable enough for people to retain it. Finally, and most important, it should stimulate the audience to take appropriate action. For an informational message to persuade people to take action, it generally needs to come from a source that is seen as credible (e.g., a physician, a nutritionist), attractive to the target audience, and perceived as similar to the audience members (Bishop, 1994). A message to an African American community about the importance of nutrition and exercise in preventing diabetes will probably be more convincing if it comes from an African American physician than if it comes from a Caucasian physician.

For a message to be effective, it has to be noticed in the first place. On a daily basis, we are exposed to all kinds of health messages—in newspapers and magazines, in television public service announcements, on billboards and posters in subways and buses—yet we probably retain information from few of these sources and act on fewer still. It is easy to turn the page in a magazine or flip to another channel on the television when we encounter a health message, particularly if its content strikes a nerve about bad habits that already bother us. Media health campaigns that are sponsored by governments or charitable organizations pay advertising companies a great deal of money to develop health campaigns that are noticeable, memorable, and persuasive. One way of grabbing people's attention is through the use of fear. **Fear appeals** are based on the idea that people will be more likely to pay attention to a message, and to subsequently act to change their health behavior, if their related fears are activated. Because diseases, accidents, and death all are intrinsically fear inducing, it is not all that difficult to appeal to people's fears about these consequences of making poor health choices (Bishop, 1994). Most of us are probably familiar with fear appeals in the media such as depictions of the aftermath of fatal car accidents as a result of drinking and driving and pictures of how smoking can damage a person's lungs.

Do these kinds of scare tactics work? Evidence from research studies has shown mixed results. Early studies by Hovland and others suggested that the greater the fear produced by the appeal, the more effective it was in persuading a person to change his or her behavior. Other persuasion researchers, such as Irving Janis and his colleagues (e.g., Janis & Feshbach, 1953), hypothesized that very high levels of fear were probably counterproductive in that people might be so upset that they would simply tune out very threatening messages and that inducing moderate levels of fear would be more likely to

persuade people to follow health recommendations. More recent meta-analyses, in which a number of research studies of fear appeals were examined simultaneously, tended to support the first position, that is, that increases in fear seem to lead to greater persuasion. However, they also found that fear appeals seem to have their greatest impact on people's *intentions* to change their behavior rather than necessarily leading to actual changes in behavior (cited in Devos-Comby & Salovey, 2002). Another concern is that messages that aim to arouse fear might actually elicit other negative emotions such as sadness. Devos-Comby and Salovey (2002) discussed this possibility in relation to fear appeals about HIV prevention. Although fear is seen to be persuasive in motivating people to take action, sadness and thoughts of death and suffering might have an opposite effect, leading to a sense of hopelessness and lack of confidence in one's ability to adopt healthier behaviors.

Other approaches have focused on specifying the *conditions that seem to increase the effectiveness of fear appeals.* For a fear message to have its greatest impact, it should clearly convey that engaging in unhealthy behaviors or not engaging in healthy ones will lead to negative health consequences. The message should also emphasize to people that these negative consequences are real and can happen to them. A fear message should also contain a very specific behavioral recommendation, making it totally clear what actions people should take to avoid the negative health outcomes (e.g., use a condom, wear sunscreen). The message should also emphasize that people can do it, that is, that they will be able to make this change in behavior to safeguard their health (Bishop, 1994; DiMatteo & Martin, 2002). Another issue concerns the timing of the message: When the negative health outcomes are due to happen very soon and immediate action can be taken to prevent them, fear messages are likely to be more effective. Fear appeals that depict middle-aged people having heart attacks, with recommendations to reduce dietary cholesterol and increase exercise, are unlikely to be perceived as requiring immediate action on the part of college students in their early 20s. On the other hand, fear appeals depicting the terrible consequences of drinking and driving accidents that are televised just prior to New Year's Eve are likely

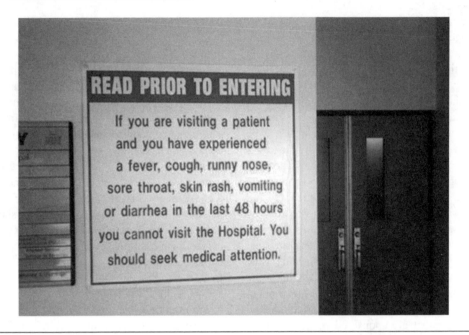

READ PRIOR TO ENTERING

If you are visiting a patient
and you have experienced
a fever, cough, runny nose,
sore throat, skin rash, vomiting
or diarrhea in the last 48 hours
you cannot visit the Hospital. You
should seek medical attention.

Figure 9.2   The Dramatic Effect of SARS on Hospital Procedures in Toronto and Elsewhere

SOURCE: Photo courtesy of Frank Schneider.

to be perceived as more relevant by young people. Even if they are attended to only long enough to persuade young people to take cabs home from New Year's Eve parties, they will have had a very beneficial effect.

Another way in which the mass media exert social influence about health concerns is through reporting dramatic incidents in the news that relate to health issues. During the spring of 2003, media headlines were dominated by stories of the outbreak of SARS (sudden acute respiratory syndrome) in China and in Toronto. In addition, stories about "mad cow disease" (also known by the technical name of bovine spongiform encephalopathy) grabbed the attention of the North American public after a single cow in Alberta was found to test positive for this disease. Although the probability of North Americans getting either SARS or the human form of mad cow disease remained incredibly low, and certainly far lower than the probability of getting injured or killed in the course of everyday activities such as driving a car, there were massive reactions of fear and panic to these perceived health threats. The U.S. government banned imports of Canadian beef, and

polls by Canadian newspapers suggested that a number of Canadians intended to stop eating beef. Toronto and China were the subjects of World Health Organization travel advisories in which people were officially warned not to visit these locations (Figure 9.2). Consequently, the economic impact of behavioral reactions to these health scares was substantial, with severe effects on the Canadian beef industry and on tourism in Toronto and China.

Why do people panic in the face of health risks that are so statistically improbable? If we were truly concerned about all kinds of things that might lead to our premature deaths, wouldn't we also consistently avoid activities that are even riskier such as smoking, engaging in unsafe sex, and even driving a car? Clearly, people's perceptions of risk are often at odds with reality. Many people who fear traveling by airplane, for example, are completely unconcerned about highway driving, where their risk of a fatal accident is actually much greater. Concerning fear of crime, psychologists have sometimes referred to a phenomenon called the **fear–victimization paradox,** that is, the finding that sometimes the people who are most fearful are actually the least likely to be victimized. Elderly women tend to fear crime the most, and yet they are least likely to be victimized. Young men, on the other hand, are the least likely group to fear violent crime, and yet they are the most likely to fall victim to it (Duffy & Wong, 2000). One possible explanation for this paradox concerns media influences (recall media cultivation effects covered in Chapter 8). Whereas the experiences of young men being assaulted in bar fights, for example, rarely attract much media attention, an elderly lady who is the victim of a violent home invasion robbery is likely to be front-page news. That is, the media are selective in their coverage of events, and more unusual (i.e., statistically improbable) occurrences tend to garner a lot of attention. In the minds of media consumers, however, these events appear to be more prevalent than is actually the case.

Experts in risk perception have also identified a number of other factors that explain overblown reactions to rare health risks such as SARS and mad cow disease (Gatehouse, 2003). One factor is *novelty*; new diseases (e.g., SARS) are perceived to be scarier than those with which we are already familiar (e.g., influenza). The degree to which we believe we can *control* something is also a factor that affects our risk perceptions. Thus, we may still be smoking and not exercising but believe that we are in control and can change these habits any time we choose. At the same time, it seems like a mere accident of fate that we could contract a deadly disease by being in the wrong place at the wrong time or by eating a contaminated hamburger. Another factor that elevates our risk perception relates to the *severity of the outcome*. A disease such as the human form of mad cow disease, which attacks the brain and leads to dementia, paralysis, and death, is seen as particularly dreadful and, therefore, of greater risk. Our overall perception of risk can also be altered by well-publicized *dramatic world events*. Halpern-Felsher and Millstein (2002) found that after the terrorist attacks of September 11, 2001, adolescents perceived their risk of dying as being significantly higher than did adolescents surveyed about risk during the years preceding the terrorist attacks. Interestingly, this heightened perception of risk extended well beyond the risk of a terrorist attack, generalizing to unrelated risks, including dying in an earthquake or a tornado. Dramatic media coverage of tragic events appears to increase our sense of vulnerability to all sorts of risks to our health.

Family, Peer, and School Influences

Clearly, the media are not solely responsible for shaping our attitudes and intentions about our health. There are a number of other sources of social influence for health promotion and prevention, including schools, family, and friends. This subsection considers some of these other sources of influence. Although these sources can affect people of all ages, the primary focus here is on social influences that affect young people, from the teen years through young adulthood. During these years, critical choices are made about the kinds of behaviors one will adopt, and habits are formed that may be very resistant to change later in life.

Who has the greatest influence on young people's health behavior—parents or peers? A large number of investigations have examined family influences, peer influences, or both on the health beliefs and behaviors of young people, and different results have emerged for different populations studied. For example, one study of urban minority middle school students found that more than 50% of the sixth to eighth graders in the sample had used alcohol, 20% had smoked tobacco, 13% were sexually active, and 12% had used marijuana. Parent influences were greatest when it came to alcohol use, but overall, peer influences were found to be most consistently associated with engaging in risky health behaviors (Beal, Ausiello, & Perrin, 2001).

One study of students at an elite university showed a different pattern of results, with a much stronger role of parental influence on young adults' health beliefs and behaviors (Lau, Jacobs Quadrel, & Hartman, 1990). Although health behaviors, such as alcohol consumption and eating habits, became worse when the students left home to attend the university, overall, parental influence did not disappear when the students were no longer living at home. The authors suggested a **model of windows of vulnerability**, where the influence of parents on health beliefs and behaviors will be important throughout life but where, during certain critical periods, young people will be vulnerable to the effects of other important social influences that may expose them to different health beliefs and behaviors. Lau and colleagues (1990) speculated that these critical periods occur during adolescence (when the normal developmental process of seeking independence from parents occurs), on leaving home to live on their own, and again later when they set up more permanent homes of their own with significant others. In addition, parental influence was found to be strongest for behaviors in which the parents themselves showed a great deal of consistency among their health beliefs, their behaviors, and how they trained their children. For example, parents who believed in the importance of seat belt use, trained their children to always wear seat belts, and also routinely used seat belts themselves, had stronger "training effects" of this behavior. If parents want their children to adopt healthy habits, it is very important that parents practice what they preach.

A study by Nathanson and Becker (1986) examined the influence of parents, peers, and partners on teenage women's contraceptive-seeking behavior. They found that the majority of nearly 3,000 young women at a family planning clinic reported that their parents or peers had been involved in their actions to obtain contraception. Although the majority of young women who brought others with them to the clinic were accompanied by their girlfriends (54.1%), more young women came with their mothers (16.1%) than with their boyfriends (13.5%). More than half of the young women reported that their mothers knew about their visits to the clinic, and more than two thirds of this group stated that their mothers approved of their decisions to obtain contraception. Approximately one quarter said that their fathers knew, and 42.1% of this group reported having their fathers' approval as well. Having their mothers' approval was rated as very important by a majority of these young women and was seen as more important than having their peers' approval (apart from their boyfriends).

Interestingly, black teens reported significantly higher approval from their mothers than did white teens. The authors speculated that a combination of more powerful extended family networks and greater concern for the consequences of unprotected sex among blacks might account for this difference. Overall, the results of this investigation demonstrate that parents are probably a much more powerful source of social influence over teens' decisions to obtain contraception than one would expect, and so they have great potential to encourage their children to safeguard their sexual health.

Substance abuse in adolescents seems to be influenced by both family and peers. Because adolescents are especially vulnerable to peer pressure, many adolescents begin smoking by experimenting with their friends and then gradually become addicted. When teens try their first cigarette, it is usually in the presence of their peers, but parental smoking is also a source of influence (Sarafino, 2002). Adolescence is a critical period of intervention for substance abuse behaviors. If young people reach 21 years of age without developing a smoking habit, it is extremely unlikely that they will be smokers as adults (Friedman, 2002). Early alcohol use is predictive of higher rates of alcohol dependence during adulthood. Some surveys have shown that those who started using alcohol at 14 years of age had rates of alcohol dependence that were four times greater than those who started drinking at 20 years of age. Those who started drinking by 14 years of age also showed significantly higher rates of injuries while under the influence of alcohol (Spoth, Redmond, Trudeau, & Shin, 2002).

The best way in which to prevent teens from having later substance abuse problems is to try to prevent their initiation into these behaviors in the first place. In other words, primary prevention efforts that target as many young people as possible, before the children develop problems with alcohol, smoking, and/or drugs, are critical. What makes a substance abuse prevention program effective? Various intervention efforts have been attempted, with some being based in schools and others having a focus on families.

● FOCUS ON INTERVENTION

Spoth and colleagues (2002) compared a school classroom-based program alone, the same classroom-based program combined with another program that involved family influences, and a control group whose members did not receive either program to see which type of intervention would be most effective in preventing initiation into substance abuse.

Spoth and colleagues used a very large sample made up of 1,664 seventh graders from 36 different schools that were randomly selected from 22 counties in a midwestern state. This intervention study had three conditions. The first condition involved a group that received two programs. One program was a classroom-based Life Skills Training Program, which aimed at providing knowledge about substance abuse and how to avoid it as well as skills to help teens manage their lives and resist substances in a social situation. The second program was the Strengthening Families Program (for parents and children 10–14 years of age), which had the goal of reducing substance abuse through strengthening parenting skills, parent–child communication skills, and youth skills in resisting peer pressure. In the second condition, a different group of students received the Life Skills Training Program only. A third group, serving as a control condition, received no interventions. The 36 schools were randomly assigned to one of these three conditions so that children within the same school all received the same program (or were in the control condition). The Life Skills Training Program took place over 15 sessions during regular classroom periods and involved interactive teaching techniques plus out-of-class homework assignments. There were also five Life Skills Training Program "booster sessions" for the students the following year, when they were in the eighth grade. These booster sessions emphasized the same skills in self-management and social resistance. The Strengthening Families Program involved weekly evening sessions for 7 consecutive weeks. In each session, there were separate parent and youth curriculum sessions for the first hour, and then the parents and children were together for a family session for the second hour. Similar to the Life Skills Training Program, families in the Strengthening Families Program were invited back to participate in booster sessions 1 year after the initial program.

Spoth and colleagues predicted that children who were in the combined program (Life Skills Training Program + Strengthening Families Program) would show the lowest levels of initiation of substance use, followed by those in the Life Skills Training Program alone, and that the children in the control group would be most likely to initiate substance use. This was the pattern of findings that they observed, with scores on an overall measure of initiating substance use (rates of starting to use alcohol, cigarettes, and marijuana) lowest for those in the combined program and highest for those in the control condition. However, scores for children in the combined program did not differ significantly from those for children who received only the Life Skills Training Program. When the rates for the different substances were examined separately, only alcohol showed the predicted pattern, with rates of initiation for the Life Skills Training Program alone group being significantly higher than those for the combined group and the control group showing initiation rates significantly higher than those for both of the intervention groups.

What do Spoth and colleagues' (2002) results tell us about the effectiveness of these interventions? First, they strongly support the need for some kind of intervention in that the children in the control group showed significantly higher rates of starting to use substances than did those in the groups that received the intervention programs. Second, they suggest that although the Life Skills Training Program was effective in reducing the rate of new use of marijuana, cigarettes, and alcohol, the addition of the Strengthening Families Program produced even stronger results when it came to alcohol use. Given that alcohol is widely available and associated with a number of problem behaviors, such as impaired driving, fighting, and sexual assaults, programs that prevent early alcohol use would seem to be especially valuable. Involvement of parents, in addition to programs that can be delivered through regular school classrooms, would seem to be particularly important in trying to prevent later alcohol-related problems in children.

CHANGING HEALTH BEHAVIOR

The previous section dealt with sources of social influence for promoting healthy behavior and attempting to prevent problems or illnesses from occurring in the first place. In this section, the focus is more specifically on how we can get people to change unhealthy behaviors in favor of healthier ones. A number of theories have been developed to help explain the dynamics of health behavior change and to guide intervention efforts in this area. This section deals with three of the most influential theories: the health belief model, the theory of planned behavior, and the transtheoretical model (or "stages of change" model).

Health Belief Model

A number of factors influence whether people will practice healthy behaviors, including demographic factors (i.e., socioeconomic status), early socialization of health habits, emotional factors, access to the health care system, and cognitive factors (Taylor, 1991). Cognitive factors include our beliefs about how likely it is that we may become ill and our perceptions of how likely it is that particular health practices will prevent illness. The **health belief model** (Janz & Becker, 1984; Rosenstock, 1974) concerns these cognitions and how they predict people's health-protective behaviors.

The health belief model suggests that the actions we take to safeguard our health are influenced by a number of factors, including general health values, perceived susceptibility to illness, perceptions of illness severity, expectation of treatment success, self-efficacy, perceived barriers and benefits, and cues to action. Each of these components is examined briefly in the following subsections.

General health values. The health belief model assumes that we have some interest in our health and concern about maintaining good health in the first place.

Perceived susceptibility to illness. Here we ask ourselves the question, "How likely is it that we will develop this particular problem?" Our perception of a health threat depends on our general knowledge about a particular disease or disorder and the specific knowledge that this condition might be connected with us personally. If you know that smoking, hypertension, and high cholesterol are risk factors for coronary heart disease, and you also know that you are a smoker with high blood pressure and high cholesterol, it should make you feel more personally vulnerable to the threat of heart disease. Media health campaigns attempt to influence our sense of personal vulnerability to health threats by directly stating that a negative health outcome, such as a fatality related to drinking and driving, *can happen to us.*

Perceived severity of illness. Knowing that we may be vulnerable to a particular disease or disorder might not be enough to make us change our behavior. We might also ask ourselves, "How serious are the consequences of this problem?" The way in which we answer this question indicates whether we think the health threat is serious enough to warrant our taking action. If we have seen a family member suffer from breast cancer, for example, we are probably very aware of the toll that this disease can take, will appraise it as being very serious, and be convinced of the need to engage in regular breast screening. On the other hand, we might not bother to get a flu shot because we do not see getting the flu as a severe health threat.

Expectation of treatment success. Here we ask ourselves, "If we change this particular behavior, how likely is it that doing so will reduce this particular health threat?" Sometimes we underestimate the degree to which our health habits might be related to our chances of becoming ill. If we think that our probability of getting a disease is going to be related mainly to family history and genetic predisposition, we might be unconvinced about, for example, developing healthier patterns of eating and physical activity. If we do not think that our actions will make a difference, we probably will not be motivated to change our health behavior.

Self-efficacy. This concept, originated by Bandura (1977a), is one with which you are already familiar. **Self-efficacy** refers to our perception of whether or not we actually have what it takes (e.g., skills, confidence) to carry out a behavior. Most people who smoke know that doing so is a major risk factor for lung cancer and other serious diseases. They also know that quitting smoking is an extremely effective way in which to substantially lower their risk of contracting these diseases. The problem is that knowing these things is not enough if people are convinced that they cannot quit smoking. Unless we have some confidence that we can change our health habits, the health belief model is unlikely to predict our taking healthy actions.

Perceived barriers and benefits. Another component of the health belief model suggests that we do a kind of cost–benefit analysis, weighing the costs of changing health behaviors against any perceived benefits that making such changes might bring. For example, a person who undertakes an exercise program might have to overcome perceived barriers such as not having enough time, not having a good place to exercise, and finding exercise boring but may decide that the health benefits of physical activity outweigh these costs. In some versions of the health belief model, self-efficacy (or, rather, the lack of it) is considered as a perceived barrier to making health changes rather than as a separate part of the model. The idea of a cost–benefit analysis represents another point of intervention: Media health campaigns often focus on the low cost of making a behavior change relative to the high cost of suffering illness consequences.

Cues to action. Some versions of the health belief model have also incorporated the idea of cues to action. **Cues to action** are events or messages that act as triggers to get people to adopt healthy behaviors. Hearing that someone we know was in a serious traffic accident might serve as a cue to action in that we might be more careful about speeding, using seat belts, and not drinking and driving as a result. Some health interventions have deliberately incorporated such cues to action, for example, mailing people reminder postcards when they are due for a dental checkup and giving women waterproof cards (for their showers) instructing them how to perform a breast self-examination.

Research on the health belief model has generally found support for the model or at least for some of its component parts (Bishop, 1994). For example, Out and Lafreniere (2001) conducted a study that employed "Baby Think It Over," a lifelike doll that simulates the functions of a real infant, to see whether exposure to the infant simulator would modify adolescents' attitudes toward teen pregnancy and the consequences of teen pregnancy. After 2 to 3 days of constant exposure to the infant simulator (i.e., caring for the doll 24 hours a day) teens in the intervention group were more likely to accurately assess their personal risk for an unplanned pregnancy, and more likely to produce concrete examples of consequences related to child rearing, than were teens in the comparison group (who were not exposed to the simulated infants). In other words, role-playing parenting tended to increase the teens' *perceived susceptibility* and their awareness of the *severity* of consequences of a teen pregnancy. Other studies have found at least partial support for the health belief model with respect to diverse health behaviors, including the use of sunscreen (Jackson & Aiken, 2000), preventive dental care, breast self-examination, dieting for weight loss, AIDS risk-related behaviors, and participation in health screening programs (Taylor, 2003).

Although the health belief model makes intuitive sense and has been supported by a number of research investigations, it is not without limitations. Not all studies that have tested the model have found supportive results, and most investigations have found only partial support rather than evidence for all components of the model. Some critics have argued that although the health belief model provides a list of relevant variables that influence health behavior, it does not explain precisely the expected relationships among these variables. Furthermore, each study that tests the health belief model tends to use different ways in which to operationalize and measure the variables, and this makes it difficult to compare results across different investigations meaningfully (Bishop, 1994).

Theory of Planned Behavior

Clearly, the goal of any health promotion effort is to get people to change their actual

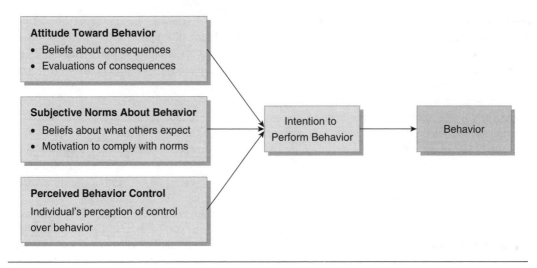

Figure 9.3   Theory of Planned Behavior

SOURCE: Adapted from Azjen (1991).

behavior, for example to get them to exercise more, quit smoking, or use sunscreen. According to the **theory of planned behavior** (Ajzen, 1991), the way to change people's behavior is to alter their **behavioral intentions.** Behavioral intentions are decided on in advance of most behaviors and are the best predictors of what people will do. For people to adopt healthier behaviors, they have to change their behavioral intentions.

According to the theory of planned behavior, behavioral intentions in turn are influenced by three things: attitudes toward the behavior, subjective norms regarding the behavior, and perceived behavioral control (Figure 9.3). To illustrate these components with an example, suppose that Maya, a 21-year-old university student, is a smoker. Obviously, quitting smoking is a target behavior that could result in more positive health outcomes for Maya. Her behavioral intention to attempt to quit smoking will be influenced by the components of the theory of planned behavior. Maya's *attitudes* toward quitting smoking are basically positive. She knows about the health risks of smoking and believes that quitting will ultimately be important for her health. Maya's decision to quit smoking will also be influenced by *subjective norms,* which are her perceptions of what other important people in her life think about smoking and her motivation to comply with what others think.

Maya knows that her parents disapprove of her smoking, as do a lot of her close friends as well. On the other hand, most of her coworkers at the bar where she waitresses are also smokers, and they do not think that quitting smoking is all that important. So, when it comes to this part of the model, it is a bit less clear-cut in that Maya has people in her life who support her smoking behavior and others who really want her to quit. Because the people closest to her are the ones who disapprove of her smoking, Maya's motivation to comply with their wishes is likely to be greater, and so they will act as a positive influence on her behavioral intention to quit.

The last predictor of behavioral intentions is *perceived behavioral control,* that is, the degree to which people believe that they have control over a specific behavior. Perceived behavioral control is influenced largely by a person's sense of self-efficacy (Ajzen, 1998). In Maya's case, she is fairly confident about her ability to quit smoking. Although she has made quit attempts that did not take previously, she believes that she is under less stress now and in a better position to quit smoking at this point. Maya is also determined not to let her previous relapses into smoking discourage her from trying to quit again. In the theory of planned behavior, this component of perceived behavioral control is particularly important. Even if a person has a positive attitude about making the targeted behavior change and subjective norms that favor the change, if perceived behavioral control is low, it is unlikely that the behavioral change will be made. With respect to smoking cessation, for example, a number of previous studies have found perceived behavioral control to emerge as the strongest predictor of both intention to quit and actual smoking cessation (Norman, Conner, & Bell, 1999). Does the same hold true for other health-related behaviors?

The theory of planned behavior has been applied to a number of different health behaviors, including using condoms, using sunscreen while sunbathing, engaging in breast screening practices, performing testicular self-examinations, and participating in exercise (Taylor, 2003). In the majority of studies that have tested the components of the theory of planned behavior, perceived behavioral control has tended to emerge as a strong predictor of both behavioral intentions and actual behavior change (Stroebe & Stroebe, 1995). Thus, enhancing people's self-efficacy—the idea that they have control over health-related behaviors—is extremely important in getting them to make healthy lifestyle changes.

Transtheoretical Model

You are probably pretty familiar with the kinds of healthy habits that are currently recommended such as engaging in regular vigorous exercise, quitting smoking, limiting alcohol intake, eating healthy foods (e.g., fruits, vegetables, whole grains), and getting enough sleep. Even though you are aware of what you *should* be doing to safeguard your health, you likely have some health habits that could stand to be improved. Perhaps you are having trouble fitting exercise into a busy schedule of studies and part-time work or are finding that you are frequently studying late into the night and not getting enough sleep. Stop for a moment and try to think of a health habit for which there is some room for improvement on your part. Once you have identified the health habit that could use some improvement, ask yourself whether you are thinking about changing this situation. Perhaps you are not even thinking about trying to make a change; you've got so much else "on the go" right now that trying to change one of

your health habits is the least of your concerns. Or, perhaps you are thinking about changing this habit not right now but rather way down the road when you have more time to devote to it. Maybe you have plans to change this habit fairly soon but have not actively started yet. Or, maybe you have already started to change this health habit, and so you are actively working on it.

Health psychologists now recognize that people tend to be in different stages of readiness to make a particular health behavior change. Prochaska and DiClemente (1983, 1986) developed the **transtheoretical model** (also known as the *stages of change model*) to account for these individual differences in the course of changing health behaviors. According to this model, people can be classified as being in one of five stages with respect to making a particular health behavior change: precontemplation, contemplation, preparation, action, or maintenance. Each of these stages of change is listed in Figure 9.4 and is discussed in the following subsections.

Precontemplation. During the precontemplation stage, people express no intention to change their health behavior. People may be in the precontemplation stage with respect to a specific health behavior because they do not see that behavior as problematic or because they have considered changing and decided against it.

Contemplation. During the contemplation stage, people are aware that they should undertake a change in a health behavior and are seriously considering doing so. People are classified into this stage if they indicate that they are thinking of making a change within the next 6 months, but in reality people often stay in this stage for years when they do not follow through on more specific actions toward changing their health behavior.

Preparation. People in the preparation stage are ready to make a health change and intend to do so within the next month. Sometimes people who have made an unsuccessful change (e.g., quitting smoking and then relapsing to take up the habit again) are in this stage, preparing for their next quit attempt. During the preparation stage, people usually start to take some action

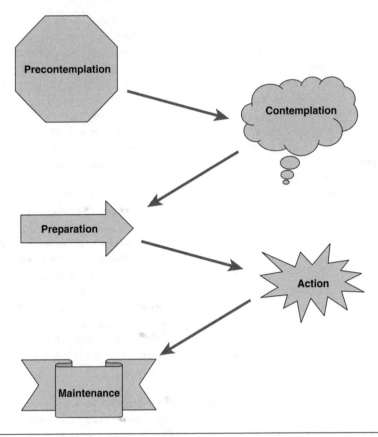

Figure 9.4   The Five Stages of Change in Prochaska and DiClemente's (1983) Transtheoretical Model of
Health Behavior Change

that will lead to their ultimate behavior change. For example, they might sign up for an exercise class that has not begun yet, or they might cut down on the number of cigarettes they smoke per day in advance of quitting altogether.

Action. During the action stage, people are successfully modifying their health behavior. For example, smokers will have quit and be completely abstaining from smoking during this stage.

Maintenance. After 6 months of successful behavior change during the action stage, people are considered to enter the maintenance stage. At this point, they continue to work to maintain the health behavior change they have made. During this stage, for example, ex-smokers try to stay quit, or exercisers try to stick with their regular programs of physical activity. There are some differences of opinion with respect to how

long the maintenance stage lasts. Some formulations of the transtheoretical model include a sixth stage, *termination,* that occurs after people have spent a sufficiently long time in the maintenance stage and have no temptation at all to return to the problem behavior. But with many problematic behaviors such as addictions, relapse—returning to the negative behavior, even if only temporarily—occurs more often than not. For this reason, the realistic goal for most people is to remain in the maintenance stage (Prochaska, DiClemente, & Norcross, 1992).

What are the advantages of conceptualizing health behavior change according to these stages? For one thing, this conceptualization captures the actual processes that people go through in leading up to a health behavior change, actually making the change, and then struggling to maintain it. It also helps to explain why so many health interventions are unsuccessful. If the goal of a health program is to try to get all youth smokers to quit smoking, for example, the program is doomed to fail. Most smoking cessation programs are aimed at individuals who are at least in the preparation stage in that they are ready to change their behavior. Yet many smokers are not at all prepared to make such a change. Prochaska and colleagues (1992) reported that only some 10% to 15% of smokers are in the preparation stage at any given time, whereas some 30% to 40% are in the contemplation stage and 50% to 60% are still in the precontemplation stage. Given that smoking programs are geared toward people in the preparation stage, is it any wonder why their success rates tend to be so low? Thus, another advantage of the model is that it prompts us to consider individual differences in the design and execution of interventions.

Another advantage of the transtheoretical model is that it offers a more optimistic picture of the outcome of relapse situations, where people revert to the negative health behavior they tried to change. Rather than conceiving of relapse as an "all or nothing" situation, the transtheoretical model sees relapse as simply spiraling back to a previous stage and allows for the fact that this happens quite often. People who attempt to quit smoking and then slip up after 3 weeks and smoke a few cigarettes have clearly left the action stage in that they are no longer abstinent from smoking. But what stage describes them now? An "all or nothing" approach to relapse would say that they have to start over at the very beginning. In fact, it is quite unlikely that they really have reverted back to the beginning, according to the transtheoretical model. This would mean a return to precontemplation for most smokers, and yet those who were successfully abstinent from smoking for a few weeks are probably at least at the contemplation stage (i.e., aware of the need to quit again and planning to do so in the future) and perhaps even at the preparation stage (i.e., ready to make another quit attempt fairly soon). Interventions that are guided by this model will help those who are struggling to make difficult health changes to see that all is not lost and that quitting for good might mean that they go through the preparation stage several times.

Perhaps the biggest benefit of the transtheoretical model is that it provides a framework for tailoring health interventions to suit the current stage of each individual who needs to make a health behavior change rather than assuming that a single intervention will work for everyone (Prochaska et al., 1992). Measures have been developed to classify people into the five stages; once a person's stage of readiness to change is known, the approach used to help that person facilitate change can be applied. Although it might seem that people in the precontemplation stage are completely unlikely to respond to intervention efforts, this is not always the case. Costs of their health behavior and benefits of altering it can be pointed out, for example, with the goal of moving them to the contemplation stage, where they will be more responsive to appropriate intervention efforts. For each stage, there are different strategies that can be effective in guiding people to the next stage for ultimately making the behavioral change.

Interventions that are based on the transtheoretical model enable health programs to tailor the messages and materials to a person's current stage of readiness to change. Prochaska, DiClemente, Velicer, and Rossi (1993) conducted research to determine whether programs matched to stage of change were more effective than other smoking cessation programs. They randomly assigned 756 smokers to four different conditions: (a) a *standard condition* in which participants received smoking cessation manuals and booklets; (b) an *individualized condition* in which participants received a series of manuals that were matched to their current stage of change and all of the stages that followed (e.g., someone in the contemplation stage would receive manuals for contemplation, preparation, action, and maintenance); (c) an *interactive computer report condition* in which participants received the manuals appropriate for their stage plus computer reports that fully described their stage of change, individualized feedback on how they were doing on the processes of change, and information on how to cope with tempting situations they might encounter during that stage; and (d) a *personalized counselor condition* in which participants received the interactive computer reports plus manuals appropriate to their stage along with a series of short telephone calls from counselors to provide personalized feedback.

Prochaska and colleagues (1993) found that the interactive computer report intervention showed the best success rates. Individuals in this condition showed more than double the rates of quitting (when quitting was measured in the short term) than did individuals in the standard condition. When they examined long-term abstinence from smoking, they found that participants in the computer condition showed substantially higher rates (nearly three times as high) than those of people in the standard condition. The personalized counselor condition was also found to be more effective in leading people to quit and to maintain their abstinence than was the standard condition, but the counselor condition was less effective than the interactive computer condition. The individualized condition, in which participants were given stage-matched manuals, was also found to be significantly more effective than the standard condition when the participants were contacted for a follow-up assessment 18 months after the intervention.

The overall pattern of results, then, supports the transtheoretical model in that interventions that were tailored to the characteristics of individuals during each stage of change were found to be more effective than a standard "one size fits all" approach. Interestingly, the interactive computer version of the stage-matched intervention worked best of all—even better than the personalized counselor condition. It appears that people do well with individualized feedback, but this feedback might be better received when it comes from an impersonal source such as a computer-generated report rather than an actual counselor. This finding suggests that individualized feedback can be delivered through computer reports in a fairly cost-effective and widespread manner compared with the resources required to deliver feedback through individual counselors.

The transtheoretical model was initially developed to address addictive behaviors, and the majority of research using this model has been on smoking. However, predictions made by the transtheoretical model have been supported in relation to a number of other health behavior changes, including reducing dietary fat, controlling one's weight, getting mammograms, adopting exercise programs, and using safer sex practices (Salovey, Rothman, & Rodin, 1998). Some studies have failed to find support for the predictions made by the transtheoretical model, however, and there have been criticisms of the measures used to classify people into stages and questions regarding whether the stages themselves are identified accurately. Nevertheless, the transtheoretical model is extremely useful in describing the complexity of the processes that people go through to change their health behaviors, and it is likely to remain influential in guiding further research and intervention efforts.

STRESS, COPING, AND SOCIAL SUPPORT

Until this point, the focus of this chapter has been primarily on applying knowledge from psychology to guide health promotion and primary prevention efforts and to determine how people can change their health behaviors. Although it is clear that psychology has a great deal to offer that might enhance the effectiveness of programs to get people to adopt healthier lifestyles, the role of social psychology with respect to people who are already in distress is somewhat less clear. As you saw in Chapter 6, social psychology certainly has much to offer with respect to helping people to deal with psychological disorders. We now address whether social psychology has anything to offer people who suffer from physical illnesses or symptoms of stress.

A great deal of current research, guided by the biopsychosocial model, addresses the psychosocial aspects of various illnesses and disorders. There is growing recognition that treating the body is only one aspect of treating the patient's condition. The course of a number of serious illnesses that people live with today (e.g., heart disease, diabetes, cancer) is affected by psychological and social factors. This section considers two areas in which health psychology has made contributions to the ways in which people experience illness and distress: the study of stress and coping and the influence of social support on health.

Stress and Coping

What sorts of things have stressed you out over the past couple of days? Maybe you are worried about upcoming exams and assignments that are due and you do not know when

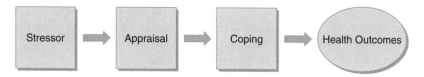

Figure 9.5   Components of Lazarus and Folkman's (1984) Transactional Model of Stress

you will have time to prepare for them. You might be concerned about ongoing issues such as how you are going to afford next semester's tuition and whether the status of your long-distance relationship has changed. Or, perhaps you are just experiencing some little annoyances that drive you crazy such as discovering that your car's gas gauge is right on empty when you are already running late for class and finding out that your work schedule has been changed so that you cannot go out with your friends on Friday night. How would these events make you feel, and what would you do to reduce the stress they cause?

It is easy to identify the feeling of being stressed, but it is not always clear why certain events bother us so much or what we should do to manage our stress. Stress experts have examined the processes of stress and coping so as to help people understand the sources of stress in their lives and learn how to manage stress effectively. Lazarus and Folkman (1984) defined **stress** as "a particular relationship between the person and the environment that is appraised by the person as taxing or exceeding his or her resources and endangering his or her well-being" (p. 19). Lazarus and Folkman's definition reflects their approach, which is referred to as a **transactional model of stress.** The basic idea of their model is that the experience of stress results from ongoing transactions between people and the environment. During the course of these transactions, people will encounter particular situations, events, or other people that may or may not induce the feeling of stress. These are referred to as **stressors** in Lazarus and Folkman's transactional model (illustrated in Figure 9.5). Based on their encounters with these potentially stressful events, people make an **appraisal,** that is, a judgment as to how to respond to the stressors. Do they perceive the stressors as threats (e.g., something potentially

harmful) or as challenges (e.g., an obstacle to be overcome)? Do they feel stress as a result of their encounter with the stressors? The model suggests that if people make a stressful appraisal—seeing the stressors as threatening or harmful—then they will feel stress as a result. According to this model, the experience of stress is an individual phenomenon, and no two people will experience it in exactly the same way. What may be stressful to one person (e.g., driving on a very busy highway) might be quite relaxing to someone else. What is critical here is not the stressor itself but rather how people appraise it.

Once people have appraised a situation as being stressful, they go on to the third stage of the model, where they evaluate their coping options or resources to deal with the problem. **Coping** refers to thoughts, feelings, and behaviors that people engage in when trying to reduce stress. Consistent with the idea that the experience of stress is an individual phenomenon, so too is the way in which people cope with particular stressors. People differ in the coping strategies that they use, and even the same individual will often use different coping strategies in different situations. Coping strategies can be classified into two general types: problem-focused coping and emotion-focused coping (Lazarus & Folkman, 1984; Lazarus & Launier, 1978). With **problem-focused coping,** people deal directly with the problem that has caused them to be stressed. This might involve standing up to others who have wronged them or taking a problem and breaking it down into smaller component parts that people can manage. **Emotion-focused coping** involves people trying to regulate their emotions so that they can minimize the distress caused by the situation. Emotion-focused coping is sometimes the only recourse in situations where people are dealing with an outcome that cannot be altered. For example, if a loved one dies, people cannot change that fact, but they can try to manage their emotions, perhaps by reappraising the situation to try to see something positive in it (e.g., thinking about how grandmother lived a full and happy life and touched so many people's lives before she died). Some emotion-focused coping strategies can be maladaptive, however, in that they involve things such as people trying to pretend that the problem does not exist and trying to comfort themselves by using drugs, alcohol, or other medications. Effective coping tends to reduce the negative effects of stress, whereas ineffective coping does not reduce the stress and might even make things worse.

Negative effects of stress can affect people's health, so the final stage of the transactional model is the predicted *health outcomes*. People who experience a great deal of stress, and particularly those who show poor coping responses, tend to show higher rates of illness. For example, research has shown that people who report higher levels of stress show a higher incidence of respiratory illnesses and other infectious diseases, suggesting that stress has a suppressive effect on the immune system (Sarafino, 2002). In addition, associations between stress and other illnesses, including headaches, hypertension, diabetes, asthma, and rheumatoid arthritis, have been noted (Brannon & Feist, 2000).

Many researchers have focused on the stressor component of this model to determine what kinds of situations or events are potentially stressful. Although the transactional model of stress suggests that we appraise events in unique and individual ways, there are still some general approaches to identifying stressors. One approach to measuring stress suggests that *major life events* that happen in our lives cause us to undergo significant readjustment in our lives. Holmes and Rahe (1967) drew up a list of major life events called the *Social Readjustment Rating Scale*. The events on the list were the ones most commonly suggested by clinical experts as requiring people to make a lot of changes in their lives. Included on the list are events that are both negative (e.g., death of a spouse, divorce, being fired) and positive (e.g., getting married, outstanding personal achievement, vacation), but in all cases they require people to adjust and make changes. According

to this approach, people who have experienced a high number of major life events over the course of a year will be more likely to develop health problems.

Although debate exists about the merits of the life event stress perspective, including criticism of its assumption that even events that are usually experienced as positive can still be experienced as stressful, research studies continue to find that even positive life events can create a considerable amount of stress in people's lives. For example, Cramer and Lafreniere (2003) conducted a study of the stress involved in wedding preparation. In the study, 69 grooms-to-be and 188 brides-to-be were surveyed at a wedding exposition about their wedding plans as well as their wedding-related difficulties, degree of perceived stress, and sources of support available to them. Brides identified family problems, financial constraints, and having an older groom as sources of stress, whereas grooms were stressed by financial constraints, larger weddings, a fast approaching wedding date, and having a young bride. Interestingly, religious or cultural differences between brides and grooms were not related to increased stress, and neither was geographical separation.

Other approaches to stress suggest that it is not necessarily the big events that cause us to feel stressed; instead, it can be the *minor annoyances* that we are subjected to on a daily basis. Lazarus and his colleagues proposed that relatively minor stressors that characterize everyday life can lead to negative health outcomes. They devised a measure of the cumulative impact of these, called the *Hassles Scale* (Kanner, Coyne, Schaeffer, & Lazarus, 1981), which included items about minor annoyances such as misplacing things, having concerns about money, and experiencing problems with neighbors. Kanner and colleagues (1981) found that Hassles Scale scores proved to be a better predictor of symptoms than did major life events. Some researchers (e.g., Pillow, Zautra, & Sandler, 1996) have suggested that major life events tend to result in an increase in the number of daily hassles, thereby increasing our overall amount of distress.

Although appraising events as stressful is an individual process, and not everyone will agree on what is stressful and what is not, there are certain *characteristics of events that make them* more likely to be perceived as stressors (Taylor, 2003). First, negative events are more likely to elicit stress than are positive ones. Even though positive events (e.g., planning a wedding) involve change and require considerable energy, there is clear evidence of rewards for our efforts. This is not the case with negative events, which involve problems, difficulties, or losses but are not associated with any apparent immediate payoffs. Second, events that are unpredictable or uncontrollable are more likely to be seen as stressful than are predictable and controllable events. Third, being overloaded with tasks and having too much to do at the same time increases the likelihood that we will report being stressed out. So, it is not just the characteristics of the individual events, but also the overall quantity of tasks that we have to manage, that contributes to the feeling of being stressed. Finally, events that are vague and undefined tend to be perceived as more stressful than do straightforward clear-cut events. With ambiguous events, we must initially devote time and energy to figuring out what the problems are before we can begin to deal with them effectively.

The transition from high school to university—a major life event—can be a stressful time for many students. Whether students leave home to attend school or live with their parents and commute, embarking on a university career presents significant challenges that can lead to stress and adjustment problems. Although entering university is usually seen as a positive event, it represents a transition that is likely to involve several of the characteristics of stressful events discussed previously. Students have little control over which university accepts them, and many students are forced to leave home to attend university because they are not accepted into a nearby university or because there is no university within close proximity. Compared with the more structured environment of high school, attending university is likely to involve more ambiguous expectations and demands on students. The total picture that emerges is one in which students have to make a great number of changes in their lives that collectively may appear to be overwhelming. Leaving home to live away for the first time is likely to intensify this perception of overload.

FOCUS ON RESEARCH

In a study that examined factors thought to influence the transition to university, Lafreniere, Ledgerwood, and Docherty (1997) compared 50 students (25 males and 25 females) who moved away from their parents' homes to attend university with 50 students (25 males and 25 females) who continued to live at home on measures of family support, perceived stress, and adjustment to university. The researchers hypothesized that students who left home for the first time to attend university would experience more stress and poorer adjustment than would students who continued to live at home with their parents. Students who perceived high levels of family support were also expected to fare better, in terms of showing lower stress and better adjustment, than students who perceived their families to be less supportive.

The findings of this study did not support the hypotheses that students who left home, and those who perceived lower parental support, would experience more stress and poorer adjustment to university. When participant gender was examined in relation to these variables, however, a much more interesting pattern of results emerged. Male students who continued to live at home with their parents while making the transition to university reported the least amount of stress. For female students, the opposite pattern was shown, with continuing to live at home while beginning university being associated with an elevated risk of stress. This finding is illustrated in Figure 9.6. In addition, both male and female students who perceived a high level of support from their families tended to report similarly high levels of adjustment to university, irrespective of whether or not they left home for the first time to go away to school. For students who reported low levels of family support, however, the pattern of results mirrored those seen for perceived stress. That is, females reported significantly better adjustment to university when they lived away from home, whereas males appeared to be better adjusted when they continued to live at home. Lack of support from family, then, appeared to exert differential influences on young women and young men in facilitating adjustment to university.

Lafreniere and colleagues (1997) speculated as to a number of reasons for the differential results by gender. One possibility is that families who are insensitive to the needs of their children might not appreciate the difficulty of the new academic challenges that these children face as they begin university. For example, parents might expect their adolescent children who still live at home to contribute very heavily to housework, cooking, and the care of younger siblings and fail to realize that these responsibilities might be in conflict with the intense demands of attending university. Given that the majority of household responsibilities tend to be shouldered by women in our society (e.g., Hochschild, 1989), it may be that female students who live at home might experience more stress that comes from overload and role conflict than do their male counterparts. In addition, male and female students are likely to differ in terms of how they seek and use social support to ease the stress of the transition to university life. Previous studies have shown that adolescent women are more likely than adolescent men to discuss their problems with peers and that adolescent male students are less likely than adolescent female students to express anxiety about academic demands or to ask their teachers or counselors for help. Consequently, young men who are having difficulty in adjusting to the life changes associated with going away to university might keep their feelings to themselves and not benefit from the support they might be able to receive through building new social networks.

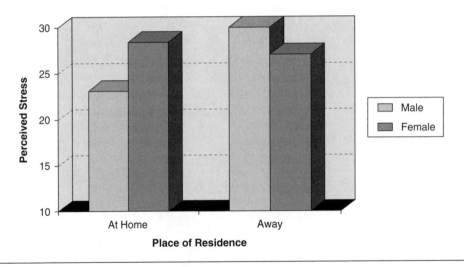

Figure 9.6   Perceived Stress as a Function of Place of Residence and Gender

Social Support

As Lafreniere and colleagues' (1997) study illustrates, the effects of social support are important in helping to alleviate the negative effects of stressful circumstances. **Social support** refers to the resources that we get from other people. One way of conceptualizing social support examines the size of our social network

and the number of links that we have to other people—family members, friends, acquaintances, and others. Social network measures help us to identify who might be socially isolated, for example, with few friends and family members nearby (Brannon & Feist, 2000). Simply having a lot of social contacts does not necessarily mean that we are benefiting from social support. The other aspect of social support refers to the quality of our relationships and to whom we can turn when we have problems or are under stress. The use of social support, or whether we feel comfortable asking others for help when we need it, is also a critical element.

Social support can fulfill many different functions in our lives. We get **emotional support** from others, who provide us with love, empathy, and security. When others let us know that we are valued for our personal qualities and ideas and are accepted despite our faults, we receive **esteem support.** Practical help that we receive from others, such as having them lend us money, give us rides, and help out with our chores, is referred to as **tangible** or **instrumental support. Informational support** refers to getting advice, suggestions, or feedback from others and is especially helpful when we are in a situation, or are encountering a problem, that is new to us. Finally, we get **network support** when we feel a sense of membership in a group that shares our interests or provides us with social companionship (Sarafino, 1998).

There are a number of ways in which social support has been found to contribute to health. One way is through influencing people to practice healthy behaviors. Individuals who are socially isolated have fewer people to encourage them to stick with their diet or exercise program, to distract them from a temptation to relapse to smoking, or to insist that they see a doctor about a health concern (Brannon & Feist, 2000). One study found that even coworkers in a factory setting can be a significant source of encouragement for women over 50 years of age to practice breast self-examination and other breast screening practices (Stamler, Thomas, & Lafreniere, 2000).

Social support can also influence the components of the transactional model of stress and coping (Lazarus & Folkman, 1984). If people are socially integrated and able to use effective social support from others, it is likely that they will encounter fewer stressors in the first place given that loneliness and lack of social contact are stressors in and of themselves. Even if a person encounters a number of potentially stressful events, the presence of others who provide effective support can reduce the probability that the person will make stressful appraisals about these events. For example, if you suddenly find out that you have to move to a new apartment but you know that you have a number of friends who will help you to move and allow you to stay with them during the transition, you will be less likely to perceive the forced move as a particularly stressful occurrence. In addition, knowing that you have support from others can enhance your coping abilities in stressful situations. Friends and loved ones can provide emotional support and esteem support and can remind you that you have the strength to get through some tough times (Brannon & Feist, 2000).

A number of researchers have examined the role of social support in relation to particular chronic and life-threatening illnesses. For example, studies have shown that emotional, informational, and tangible support all are important in reducing depression in AIDS patients (Taylor, 2003). Hegelson and Cohen (1996) reviewed literature that identified helpful and unhelpful aspects of social support for cancer patients. Across a large number of studies, emotional support emerged as being most important to cancer patients, particularly when it came from spouses, family members, and friends. The absence of emotional support from these sources was experienced as harmful to patients' adjustment. Informational support was seen as helpful, but only when it came from health care professionals. Hegelson and Cohen's review also revealed some interesting misconceptions that many people have about providing support to cancer patients. For example, people without cancer believed that they should try to "cheer up" cancer patients, whereas cancer patients themselves said that this kind of unrelenting optimism was more disturbing than helpful. People without cancer also believed that cancer patients would be better off not discussing their illness, whereas cancer patients reported wanting to discuss worries and concerns about their illness. Healthy people perceived cosmetic effects of cancer (e.g., losing a breast) as being a more central concern of cancer patients than it actually was. From the perspective of cancer patients, minimization of the problem, empty reassurances, and forced cheerfulness were unhelpful behaviors, as was misplaced empathy, that is, having people without cancer tell them, "I know how you feel." Probably the most hurtful behavior reported by cancer patients was having friends avoid seeing them because the friends were uncomfortable with their illness. To provide effective support to someone with a life-threatening disease, it is important not to make assumptions about what will be helpful but rather to find out what will be most beneficial from the patient's own perspective.

 ## CULTURE CAPSULE: PATIENT–PRACTITIONER INTERACTIONS

The way in which doctors and nurses interact with their patients undoubtedly affects patient care. Research has shown that there are a number of factors that negatively influence patient–practitioner communication and that poor patient–practitioner communication can lead to negative consequences for the patient, including not following treatment recommendations (Taylor, 2003). When the doctor and patient come from very different cultures, these problems in communication pose an even greater challenge. Many cultures have conceptions of the causes of illness and the appropriate treatments and ways of supporting patients that differ greatly from the typical Western medical approach. For example, in some cultures, illnesses and medical conditions might be believed to result from witchcraft, evil spirits, or the "evil eye" (Turner, 1996). Although no single practitioner can be expected to know all cultural beliefs that relate to illness and healing, awareness of different cultural practices leads to more sensitive patient care (Yox, 2003), which in turn can increase patient compliance with medical treatments.

This issue was brought home by one of the chapter authors' students, who related the following anecdote after hearing a lecture on patient–practitioner interactions and culture. The student's grandmother had recently immigrated to the United States from Africa. Shortly after her arrival, she developed joint pain in her knees and was prescribed anti-arthritic medication. She refused to take the medication, insisting that the pain was a result of a *tokoloshi,* a small mischievous creature that is believed by members of a number of cultures in Southern Africa to be responsible for all kinds of ailments and difficulties. The grandmother believed that the tokoloshi had sneaked into her suitcase and followed her to North America and that, on its release, it had caused the pain in her knees. Her family members were unable to convince her that her pain was the result of a medical condition that could be treated by her medicine, and they eventually took her to see a South African doctor. The doctor understood the grandmother's concern and mentioned that once tokoloshis are released, they detest crossing water. He suggested that by crossing a bridge over the river that ran through their city and taking her medicine, the tokoloshi and the pain it caused would disappear. Sure enough, this proved to be the case!

This anecdote may lead you to believe that the South African doctor was merely humoring his patient as a means of cajoling her into taking the medication that would cure her medical condition. This interpretation misses the point. As we have seen throughout this chapter, psychological factors influence the prevalence and course of physical ailments. The doctor in this story understood that biology, psychology, and social factors interact to produce health. Knowing this, he was able to successfully manage a situation that might have left a patient feeling ill.

SUMMARY

Social psychology has a great deal to contribute to the study of health and interventions to improve people's well-being and quality of life. The field of health psychology is concerned with promoting health and preventing illness, identifying psychological factors that might influence illness, and improving the ways in which health care is delivered. The biopsychosocial model, or the idea that health is determined by biological, psychological, and social factors, underlies health psychology and guides research and interventions that arise from it.

The best way in which to improve the health of the population is to promote healthy choices and prevent people from becoming ill in the first place. Psychologists have applied their knowledge of persuasion to improve the ways in which health promotion efforts can influence their target audiences. Fear appeals, for example, must be carefully designed so that they can arouse fear about negative health consequences in a way that encourages people to pay attention to messages and subsequently to act to change their health behaviors. Family, peer, and school influences have also been shown to affect the health-related behaviors of young people. School-based programs can help to prevent young adolescents from initiating substance abuse, and including parents in these programs seems to help prevent early initiation into alcohol use. Parents are also a powerful source of influence over teens' decisions to obtain contraception and have great potential to encourage children to safeguard their sexual health.

Three influential theoretical models of health behavior change were described. The health belief model suggests that our decisions to engage in healthy behaviors are influenced by a number of factors, including our perceived susceptibility to illness, perceived severity of illness, expectations for treatment success, costs and benefits of health behaviors, and cues to action. According to the theory of planned behavior, the way in which to change people's behavior is to alter their behavioral intentions. Behavioral intentions are influenced by people's attitudes toward the behavior, by subjective norms (i.e., perceptions about what important others think about the behavior), and especially by perceived behavioral control, that is, the degree to which people believe that they have control over the behavior. The transtheoretical model describes the stages of readiness to change a particular health behavior: precontemplation, contemplation, preparation, action, and maintenance. Tailoring health programs to make messages and materials appropriate to each individual's stage of readiness to change seems to hold particular promise.

A major focus in health psychology concerns stress and coping. The transactional model of stress, appraisal, and coping is based on the idea that we experience stress from ongoing transactions with the environment and that the way in which we appraise or evaluate events can trigger stressful reactions. Coping strategies to reduce stress include problem-focused efforts, where we try to change the stressor itself, and emotion-focused efforts, where we try to regulate our emotions to minimize the distress. Social support can help to mitigate the effects of stress and can also provide emotional comfort to people who are ill. Not all social input from others is necessarily helpful, however, and social support is most effective when it is tailored to meet the needs of the patient.

Although this chapter presented theory and research in several of the major areas of health psychology, it actually represents a very limited selection of topics in this subdiscipline of psychology. Health psychology also considers issues such as the use of health services and the experience of hospitalization, adherence to medical treatments, pain and its management, psychological aspects of each of the major chronic and life-threatening illnesses, and experiences associated with dying and bereavement. If you enjoyed reading this chapter, we encourage you to pursue your interests further by reading a book or taking a course in health psychology.

10

APPLYING SOCIAL PSYCHOLOGY TO EDUCATION

LOUISE R. ALEXITCH

In 1996, after 6 weeks of being taught by a group of health care professionals, 11 high school students of Native Canadian and black backgrounds reported on the results of their research projects. Their work was impressive, and so were their experiences; they had the opportunity to observe surgery, work alongside university researchers, and watch health care professionals going about their duties (Galt, 1996). Begun in 1994, the University of Toronto Summer Mentorship Program was established to address a concern over the lack of black and Native Canadians pursuing professions in the health field. The program is designed to expose high school students from minority groups to the university environment and, by having them job shadow professionals, to encourage them to consider careers in science and medicine. The program is aimed specifically at minority students who previously had not considered university as an educational option because they believed that either they were not smart enough or they did not have the skills and means to be successful at the university level. The mentorship program has been so successful that over the years it has been expanded to include other faculties at the University of Toronto such as law, engineering, and social work. The program now admits more than 100 students each year. As an indicator of effectiveness, participants' high school marks have improved by an average of 10%. According to

Miriam Rossi, associate dean of student affairs in the Faculty of Medicine, "Once they see that university is a possibility, they redouble their efforts in high school" (quoted in Sibbald, 1998). As one student put it, "Now I know I can do it" (quoted in Galt, 1996).

- What factors may have affected the students' motivational levels and aspirations?
- Why did these students, who previously viewed themselves as marginal students, come to view their academic abilities more positively?
- How do interactions with mentors, teachers, and role models affect students' academic achievement and aspirations?

We can all remember instances from our school pasts that we cherish—good friends made, inspirational teachers, moments of accomplishment, and the like. We also can recall instances that we would much rather forget—schoolyard bullies, a teacher who made us feel foolish, feelings of isolation, and the like. Social psychology has helped to uncover the intrapersonal and interpersonal processes that operate in the educational environment. For example, there are social psychological theories to explain how students' learning experiences may have led the minority students in the opening vignette to view their academic abilities in a more positive light. In the first section of the chapter, *intrapersonal processes,* such as attitudes, attributions about success and failure, and beliefs about academic achievement, are discussed.

Also, we must not forget that acquiring an education is very much a social process in that teachers interact with students and students interact with each other. In the vignette, it seems that the minority students' interactions with health care professionals led the students to alter their academic aspirations. The second section of the chapter, which discusses *interpersonal processes,* considers how teachers and students interacting together can affect students' beliefs about their abilities and their levels of academic achievement.

Of course, many educators and researchers also have applied social psychology in schools to address more general social issues such as violence, prejudice and discrimination, and health-related behaviors. Interventions based on social psychological concepts are aimed not only at improving the academic achievement of students but also at creating learning environments that foster the development of broad-based emotional,

social, and cognitive skills in students. The final section of the chapter focuses on the problem of school violence. It shows how the school environment reflects broader societal norms regarding violence and how schools can be used as vehicles for addressing this pressing social issue.

INTRAPERSONAL PROCESSES: INCREASING SUCCESS, REDUCING FAILURE

Susan, a psychology major, is worried about her performance in a statistics course. She worries that she "can't do math." To deal with her feelings, she engages in activities that help to distract her from the requirements of the course; for example, she goes out with friends the night before two statistics exams. Susan fails the course. How does she feel about statistics now? How would you feel if you were Susan? Because she failed, Susan believes that her original conception of her ability is correct; that is, she is lousy at math. Can students' beliefs about academic ability be changed? Can these changes result in better academic achievement? Social psychology and decades of research have shown that these changes can occur.

What Factors Affect Student Performance?

What was it about Susan that may have led to her poor performance in statistics? Was it her negative attitude toward math or her previous negative experiences with math courses? Susan attributed her performance to an internal stable characteristic (i.e., low ability). Will this attribution lead her to engage in the same nonadaptive behavior in another similar course? This subsection reviews some of the factors (and related social psychological theories) that may positively or negatively affect academic performance.

Attitudes and academic behavior. In a review of research examining the link between attitudes and behavior, Wicker (1969) indicated that attitudes and behavior might not always be consistent. Susan may value statistics as part of her training in psychology, but her behavior (i.e., going out with friends instead of studying) seems inconsistent with her positive attitude. In an effort to address such inconsistencies, Fishbein and Ajzen (1975) formulated the **theory of reasoned action.** The theory takes into account multiple determinants of behavior (i.e., attitudes and perceived norms) that predict a person's intention to behave in a particular fashion. It is such intentions to behave that predict eventual behavior. Behavioral beliefs (i.e., beliefs that an action will lead to a certain outcome) and the evaluation of the outcome both lead to formation of an *attitude toward the behavior.* For example, you may believe that working hard in college will lead to academic success and that academic success is important; these two beliefs would form your positive attitude toward doing course work. But many behaviors are performed in a social context; we are aware of what others expect of us, and we may (or may not) be motivated to comply with these expectations. Therefore, in addition to our attitudes, *subjective norms* may also affect behavioral intention and behavior. You may be aware that your parents expect you to work hard in college and to be a serious student. Because you do not want to disappoint them, you are motivated to meet their expectations.

But we do not always have control over whether we can, in fact, carry out our intended behavior that will lead to our desired outcome. For example, you would like to get good grades in college. You know that to accomplish this, you must work hard by engaging in behaviors such as keeping up with your readings, studying on a regular basis, and getting all assignments done. You may evaluate college and getting good grades positively (attitudes), and you know that good grades are looked on favorably by your family, friends, and professors (subjective norms). However, you may still end up with a C average simply because you do not have good study skills, lack the ability to comprehend the material, live in a noisy "party" dorm, or have "tough" professors. Any one of these factors may interfere with your intention and ability to work hard in college and, therefore, with the possibility of achieving good grades.

What happens to you when you know that you cannot achieve your desired outcomes due to factors beyond your control? Ajzen (1991) expanded the theory of reasoned action to include an additional component—*perceived behavioral control.* This new theory (see Figure 9.3 in Chapter 9) is called the **theory of planned behavior.** It recognizes that behavioral intentions, and consequently behaviors, may be affected by the extent to which the person believes that he or she has control over the situation. For example, you may have positive attitudes about studying and know that important others encourage studying. However, if you lack the study skills needed to get good grades in college, you might not work very hard. That is, your intention to work hard and the degree to which you work hard will be diminished by your perceived lack of control.

Using the theory of planned behavior as a framework, Sideridis and Padeliadu (2001) compared the importance of achieving good grades in elementary school children who were high-performing readers with that in elementary school children who were low-performing readers. Specifically, the researchers wanted to examine how the children's motivation to achieve good grades was related to the key components of the theory of planned behavior: (a) attitudes toward high academic achievement (beliefs about the consequences of studying and evaluation of the importance of doing well in school), (b) subjective norms about high academic performance (beliefs about the importance that others place on the children's academic performance and how motivated the children are to comply with others' expectations), (c) perceived behavioral control (how easy or difficult the children view studying to be), (d) behavioral intention (how determined the children are to study hard to achieve high grades), and (e) actual academic performance in language and mathematics.

Sideridis and Padeliadu (2001) found that high- and low-performing readers had very different profiles based on the theory of planned behavior. Compared with high-performing readers, low-performing readers undervalued the importance of being a good student, expressed weaker intentions to work hard to achieve, perceived weaker subjective norms about the importance of academic achievement, and demonstrated poorer academic performance. It seemed that the perceived importance of doing well in school predicted attitudes about studying and beliefs about the consequences of working hard, was linked to perceived control over the ability to achieve good grades, and could also be related to the perception of subjective norms. What does this mean for teachers, students, and their parents? It means that if one can increase the importance of learning in students and also increase students' beliefs about their abilities and the amount of control they have over their academic outcomes, students will want to work harder (behavioral intention) to achieve better grades.

Attributions about success and failure. The concept of attributions (i.e., the perceived causes of behavior) has been used extensively to explain students' performance in educational settings, from the types of attributions that students make about their successes and failures to how these attributions influence students' expectations about their subsequent academic achievement. Researchers also have looked at how attributions may be affected by others in students' environment such as peers, teachers, and parents. Of particular interest has been how students' attributions about their academic performance may influence important things such as their choices of areas of study, their decisions to stay in school or drop out, and their feelings of self-worth.

Bernard Weiner developed a three-dimensional framework of attributions that individuals may use when considering their academic outcomes (Weiner, 1986, 2001). Table 10.1 shows Weiner's framework and provides examples for a situation where a student has failed. The first dimension is that of *locus* (internal vs. external). Does the individual believe that the event was caused by something within him or her (internal) or by something outside him or her (external)? For example, if you do poorly on a test, is it due to your lack of study skills or to the fact that the test was difficult? The second dimension is that of *stability* or duration of

the cause (stable vs. unstable). Is the perceived cause of an event something that is constant and not expected to change (stable) or is it temporary and likely to change (unstable)? If Susan attributes her performance in statistics to a lack of ability, this would be a stable cause because ability at math usually is not something that can be changed readily. On the other hand, if Susan explains her poor performance in terms of bad luck, this would be an unstable cause because a person's luck can change from moment to moment. The third dimension, *controllability,* refers to the degree of control that the individual believes he or she has over the cause of the outcome. Effort is something that a person can control (e.g., Susan could study harder and get a math tutor to help her), but some aspects of the task might not be under a person's control (e.g., Susan's professor might be tough on students).

What does it matter whether a student perceives that performance on an assignment is uncontrollable and due to external factors or is controllable and due to internal factors? According to Weiner (1986, 2001), it can matter a great deal to the student's expectations for future performance and can influence the student's emotional reactions to success or failure. Susan believes that she just "can't do math." Susan attributes her poor performance to a lack of mathematical aptitude, a cause that (according to Weiner's framework) is internal, stable, and uncontrollable. As a result, her performance expectations are affected: She fully expects to fail the upcoming test in statistics and will feel embarrassed by her performance (especially if other students do well). Will Susan be motivated to study harder? Probably not; she sees little point to it. She might even be tempted to drop the course or change her area of study altogether.

Table 10.1 Weiner's Three Dimensions of Achievement Attributions

Students' Perceived Causes of Academic Failure							
Internal				*External*			
Stable		*Unstable*		*Stable*		*Unstable*	
Controllable	Uncontrollable	Controllable	Uncontrollable	Controllable	Uncontrollable	Controllable	Uncontrollable
Does not work hard	Low aptitude	Did not complete all assignments	Illness	Teacher has negative impression of student	College has very high standards	Peers were a distraction	Bad luck

SOURCE: Adapted from Weiner (1986, p. 51).

CULTURE CAPSULE: THE ROLE OF CULTURE IN ATTRIBUTING ACADEMIC ACHIEVEMENT

As noted in this chapter, Weiner (2001) observed that students may attribute successful and poor academic performance to different causes depending on the students' perceptions of their own abilities and their expectations about their future performance. Attributions of academic achievement also seem to differ on the basis of culture (Yan & Gaier, 1994). In one study, Yan and Gaier (1994) examined attributions regarding academic performance in 358 students from the United States and Asia (i.e., Chinese, Japanese, Korean, and Southeast Asian) who were enrolled at a large American university. The students rated the extent to which they attributed their successes and failures in the achievement domain to each of the following: ability, effort, task difficulty, and luck. For example, a success item that focused on ability was "I feel my good grades reflect directly on my academic ability," whereas a failure item that focused on luck was "Some of my lower grades have seemed to be partially due to bad breaks."

Based on mean attribution scores, Yan and Gaier (1994) found that students from all groups attributed academic success and failure first to effort and then to ability, task difficulty, and luck. When culture was considered, American students rated ability as a more important factor in academic achievement than did Asian students. In addition, American students believed that effort played a more important role in success and a less important role in failure, whereas Asian students believed that effort was somewhat more important for failure than for success. Also, it is noteworthy that very few differences among the four groups of Asian students were found.

What might be the explanation for the differences in attributions found between American and Asian students? The attribution patterns may reflect cultural and societal beliefs about success and failure in school. One explanation may stem from the degree of individualism and collectivism present in Eastern and Western cultures, with the former being more collectivistic and the latter being more individualistic. The stronger emphasis that is placed on individualism in American culture may lead American students to attribute success more often to internal stable factors (e.g., ability), whereas in collectivistic cultures there is greater emphasis on contributing to one's group and not "losing face" in front of others. Therefore, for the Asian students, both success and failure are reflections of internal but unstable and controllable factors (i.e., effort) (Yan & Gaier, 1994).

Basically, what happens is that Susan's attributions about her past and current academic failures influence her expectations about future academic performance, which in turn affect her level of motivation, which in turn may then affect subsequent academic achievement (Weiner, 2001; Yan & Gaier, 1994). Recall that some (perhaps many) of the minority high school students in the opening vignette initially believed that they lacked the ability to successfully pursue a university education and professional training (i.e., an internal, stable, and uncontrollable attribution). Without any intervention (e.g., the mentoring program), these students very likely would not have bothered to apply to university. If the students had continued to believe that they lacked the ability to achieve successful academic performance, then putting

more effort into their schoolwork would have seemed pointless and of little value to them. Their academic motivation would very likely have decreased. However, once their attributions changed so that it became clear to them that they *could* be successful in a university setting, their academic goals changed and their high school performance improved. In a sense, these students now viewed their academic outcomes as controllable, and past academic difficulties that they may have experienced were not necessarily seen as indicators of their academic abilities.

So, what can be done if students engage in attributions about their academic performance that have adverse effects on motivation? Yasutake, Bryan, and Dohrn (1996) wanted to see whether students who had these maladaptive attribution patterns could be introduced to an intervention in the school environment that would change their beliefs about their academic performance from uncontrollable factors (e.g., ability) to controllable factors (e.g., effort). This kind of intervention procedure is often called *attribution training* and has been shown to have positive effects on academic outcomes. Yasutake and colleagues were especially interested in helping learning-disabled children because it is commonly found that such students develop maladaptive patterns of causal attributions; they attribute their academic successes to external causes, such as "easy tasks," and their academic failures to internal factors, such as a "lack of ability." Consistent with Weiner's (1986, 2001) view about how attributions can affect students' expectations about their academic performance, students with learning disabilities who engage in maladaptive causal attributions can often develop poor self-concepts and show less persistence on academic tasks.

The particular attribution training used by Yasutake and colleagues (1996) involved having grade school children, identified as either learning disabled or at risk for special education, serve as tutors for younger children. The use of this procedure was based on the evidence that peer tutoring involving learning-disabled students leads to academic improvement for both tutors and tutees. The pairs of children (tutors and tutees) were randomly assigned to one of two instructional methods, and the tutors were trained to give feedback on math and reading tasks using the method to which they were assigned. The instructional methods were (a) *problem-solving only,* in which tutors made general positive statements, such as "good job," when tutees made correct responses and suggested problem-solving strategies when incorrect responses were made, and (b) *attribution training plus problem solving,* in which tutors made internal attribution statements, such as "you are smart" and "you are really trying hard," to correct responses and suggested problem-solving strategies when incorrect responses were made. The results showed that the addition of attribution training had significant effects on students' self-concepts. At the end of the intervention, both tutors and tutees in the attribution training condition had more favorable self-perceptions of scholastic ability than did

their counterparts in the problem-solving only condition. It is notable that the positive effects also pertained to self-perceptions of behavior, athletic ability, and physical appearance.

Self-serving biases in the classroom. **Self-serving strategies** (see also Chapter 5) are cognitive and behavioral strategies that can help to protect our self-esteem or enhance our self-image. Often, self-serving strategies are biased in favor of the self and, thus, become **self-serving biases.** When people regard themselves as better than average (e.g., in tolerance and honesty), place particular value on positive qualities they possess and less value on positive qualities they lack, and believe they are less likely than most others to get divorced, we are likely seeing the operation of self-serving biases (Weinstein, 1980). These biases may seem to be harmless, positive, and even adaptive in some cases. For example, if we had more realistic views of our futures instead of expecting "rosy" futures, would we still be as motivated to achieve our goals? However, some social psychologists believe that, in the long run, these self-serving biases and their accompanying behavioral strategies may be self-defeating (Baumeister & Scher, 1988). One example of an ultimately self-defeating strategy, commonly used by students, is self-handicapping, a variable that was considered in Chapter 5 in the context of personal uses of social psychology.

According to Berglas and Jones (1978), **self-handicapping** refers to strategies that people use to handicap their own performance on a task so that they have a ready excuse for failure. Furthermore, self-handicapping not only reduces the cost of failure by shifting blame away from individuals but also enhances the value of success because success occurred despite the handicap. Let us revisit Susan and her statistics course. Suppose that Susan has a statistics test coming up and is afraid that no matter how hard she studies, she will do poorly on the test. She decides, therefore, to go out with friends the night before the test and to study for only a few hours. Handicapping her own performance has two advantages for Susan. If she fails the test, she can attribute her poor performance to not studying enough and being out with friends the night before. If she happens to do well on the test, she can feel especially good about her good performance because she attained it under handicapped conditions. Either way, Susan protects her self-esteem from yet another confirmation of her inability to do math.

This might sound like a good strategy. A number of researchers (e.g., Thompson, 1994), however, have noted that self-handicapping can be habit forming, resulting in negative effects on academic performance and measures of achievement over the long term. For example, Murray and Warden (1992) warned that reliance on self-handicapping as a self-protective strategy in academic settings may lead to the inability to make internal stable attributions about one's performance even when one does well (e.g., "I did well because I am smart"). To examine the performance attributions used by self-handicapping students, Murray and Warden administered measures of self-handicapping, attributions, affect, study habits, and expectations for success on a midterm examination to approximately 200 undergraduate students. The self-handicapping measure was a self-report questionnaire that assessed individuals' tendencies to engage in self-handicapping behaviors in a variety of situations. The students completed all of the measures both before and after receiving their grades on the midterm examination. The researchers found that students who had higher self-handicapping scores were also less likely to make internal and stable performance attributions (e.g., to low or high ability) and also were more likely to believe that their performance was controlled by others (e.g., the professor) and the situation (e.g., the difficulty of the test) and to feel worse about their performance. These results occurred regardless of whether the students had performed well or poorly.

Murray and Warden (1992) suggested that the nonadaptive pattern of attributions that self-handicappers use might lead to lower effort on academic tasks and to performance decrements over time. If students believe that their performance is controlled by external factors, this may protect their self-esteem when failure occurs, but they also might not be able to take full responsibility when success occurs. It is students' perceptions of what affects academic performance, rather than their actual performance, that will determine their efforts in future academic endeavors.

Given that self-handicapping may have detrimental long-term effects, what can educators do to encourage students to put effort into their academic work even if the students may fail at some tasks? How can teachers help students to avoid attributing poor performance to a lack of ability and, instead, to view it as normal part of the learning process? Surprisingly, some classroom environments actually may promote the use of self-handicapping (Turner et al., 2002; Urdan, Midgley, & Anderman, 1998). Urdan and colleagues (1998) found that students in classrooms where ability and competition were emphasized were more likely to report using self-handicapping strategies than were students in classrooms where individual mastery, effort, and learning were emphasized. When the classroom structure is designed to emphasize the idea that performance is linked to ability, students who believe that they are not very good will be more likely to engage in strategies (e.g., self-handicapping) that protect their self-concepts.

To create a classroom environment that emphasizes individual mastery and effort rather than ability and performance, teachers use instructional strategies such as providing students with choices among learning tasks, creating multiple ways in which students can demonstrate their knowledge about a topic, and helping students to set short-term achievable (but still challenging) learning goals. For example, Turner and colleagues (2002) found that sixth-grade students in mathematics classes were less likely to engage in self-handicapping and other avoidant behaviors when they were in classrooms where teachers emphasized learning, motivated students to demonstrate new skills, and emphasized enjoyment of the material. Teachers in these classrooms told students not to feel ashamed when they could not understand some of the math and that it was okay to make mistakes (Figure 10.1).

How Can Student Performance Be Improved?

The research on self-handicapping and achievement attributions suggests that improving students' performance may be accomplished by changing the reward contingencies and teaching strategies in the classroom. In other

Figure 10.1   A Teacher Helping to Make Learning Fun

SOURCE: Photo courtesy of Cassandra Lee Davis

words, if a teacher wants to change a student's behavior, it might be constructive to focus on the situation, or on the interaction of the individual and the situation, rather than solely on the individual. This, of course, reflects the social psychological perspective. The following subsections continue this idea by describing how the emphasis on grades and competition in a classroom can adversely affect students' motivation to learn and by considering what educators can do to prevent this from happening.

Intrinsic motivation and external rewards. It is generally believed that in an *intrinsically oriented* system, people will be motivated to engage in an activity, whether it is a hobby, an exercise, or something new that is being learned. That is, individuals will engage in this behavior not for external rewards (e.g., grades, recognition, fame) but rather because they simply enjoy engaging in the activity. It is also known that providing large rewards for an activity may backfire and undermine people's intrinsic motivation for the activity (Deci, 1978).

Why does such undermining occur? Why would people draw less intrinsic enjoyment from an activity when they receive external rewards for engaging in it? The answer may be found in Daryl Bem's **self-perception theory.** According to Bem's (1972) theory, we infer our own attitudes and beliefs by observing our actions in a detached and logical way. Just as we draw conclusions about other people's attitudes from the ways in which they behave, we also infer our attitudes from observing our own behavior. For instance, you are currently reading this chapter and, thus, might infer that you like what you are doing. According to self-perception theory, when we begin to receive a reward (especially a large reward) for doing something we enjoy even without any recompense, we start to attribute our behavior—engaging in the activity—to the reward (extrinsic factor) rather than to enjoyment (intrinsic factor). Bem proposed that a reward (especially a large reward) is a salient cue to us and that our focus for explaining our behavior shifts from an internal factor to an external factor. As a result, internal factors, such as enjoyment and interest, no longer appear to provide sufficient justification for engaging in the activity. This is called the **overjustification effect** (also discussed in Chapter 5), which refers to the loss of motivation and interest as a result of receiving an excessive external reward (Bem, 1972; Lepper, Greene, & Nisbett, 1973).

What does the overjustification effect have to do with school and with the way in which we educate children? Deci (1978) and others (e.g., Lepper et al., 1973; Tang & Hall, 1995) have argued that schools are very extrinsically oriented. You may remember a teacher giving you a "gold star" when you did well on a school project, or you may recall being embarrassed in front of others when you did poorly. Gold stars, grades, ranks in class, and competition all serve to focus children on the extrinsic aspects of learning. The unintended message conveyed to students is that working on academic tasks is not interesting and of value and that rewards are needed to get people to learn (Deci, 1978). The consequence of the overjustification effect is that intrinsic motivation to learn is undermined.

FOCUS ON RESEARCH

In an experiment to examine the overjustification effect in an educational setting, Lepper and colleagues (1973) relied on the observation that nursery school children enjoyed playing with "magic markers." The children were randomly assigned to one of three experimental conditions: (a) expected award, (b) no award, and (c) unexpected award. Each participant was brought into a playroom by one of the researchers, presented with magic markers and paper, and told that there was a person who was visiting the school to see what kinds of pictures boys and girls like to draw with magic markers. In the unexpected award and no award conditions, the researcher asked the child if he or she would like to draw some pictures for the visitor. In the expected award condition, however, the researcher showed the child a "Good Player Award" (a certificate with a gold seal and ribbon) and informed the child that the visitor would be giving these awards to children who were willing to draw pictures with the magic markers. In all three conditions, the researcher left the room, and the "visitor" (actually a second researcher) was brought into the room to sit with the child. The second researcher asked the child what kind of picture he or she would like to draw. The child was then allowed to draw for approximately 6 minutes with minimal input from the second researcher. At the completion of this session, children in the unexpected award and expected award conditions were given the awards.

For approximately 2 weeks following the experimental session, the participants in all three conditions were observed unobtrusively in their classrooms by the researchers from behind one-way mirrors. The researchers noted the amount of time that the children engaged (without prompting) in the target activity (i.e., playing with the magic markers) from among a choice of other activities and materials (e.g., building blocks, easels). Consistent with the overjustification hypothesis, Lepper and colleagues (1973) found that for children in the expected award condition, interest in the target activity decreased significantly after being rewarded for drawing with magic markers, whereas for children in the unexpected and no award conditions, interest in the magic markers did not decline. The researchers also noted that the *quality* of the drawings produced by the children in the expected award condition was poorer than that produced by the other children in both the experimental session and postsession observations. These findings clearly suggest that the expectation of a reward may affect intrinsic motivation and performance on school tasks. The overjustification effect has been found to occur not only with elementary school children but also with high school and college students (Deci, Koestner, & Ryan, 1999; Tang & Hall, 1995).

Does this mean that teachers should not give students extrinsic rewards for engaging in learning activities? No. Extrinsic rewards can still be used in educational settings in such a way that maintains interest and motivation in students, but there are some conditions that educators need to consider before employing them. Tang and Hall (1995), in their review of the literature on the overjustification effect, noted that other variables, such as the level of initial interest in a task, the expectation of receiving a reward on task completion, and even the characteristics of a reward, are also important in predicting whether the overjustification effect occurs in an educational setting. For example, if students find the learning task to be interesting even without a reward (e.g., building a model of the solar system), then being rewarded will decrease motivation and will decrease subsequent performance on the particular task for the reasons stated earlier. However, if the task is uninteresting to students, then intrinsic motivation will remain unaffected or might even increase when a reward is incorporated (McGraw, 1978).

Remember that in Lepper and colleagues' (1973) study, the children who received an *unexpected* award did not show a decrease in their interest in playing with the magic markers, nor did they show a decrease in the quality of their drawings, as was seen with the children who expected an award. Expecting to receive an award for completing a task connects the task with the reward; in other words, students assume that they are engaging in the activity because they will receive a reward, not because the activity is intrinsically interesting. But teachers should be careful. Unexpected rewards, if given frequently for completing or doing well

on a task, may come to be *expected* by students, and then there may be an accompanying drop in intrinsic motivation due to the overjustification effect.

Finally, the characteristics of a reward may also play a role in the emergence of the overjustification effect. Deci and colleagues (1999) noted that tangible rewards (e.g., money, prizes, good grades), in particular, are likely to have undermining effects on intrinsic motivation, especially if these rewards are large. Furthermore, children tend to be more susceptible than college students to the negative effects of large tangible rewards. In contrast, verbal rewards (e.g., praise) are apparently perceived differently by students than are tangible rewards and can have an enhancing effect on motivation. Deci and colleagues (1999) suggested that this occurs because verbal rewards are often unexpected and provide clear affirmation of competence.

● FOCUS ON INTERVENTION

Amabile, Hennessey, and Grossman (1987) examined whether training students to be more intrinsically motivated would help them to maintain their interest in schoolwork, even when given a reward. In other words, they wanted to develop an intervention that would "immunize" students against the overjustification effect. Using 68 elementary school children (third through fifth grades), the researchers randomly assigned each student to either an intrinsic motivation training group or a control group for the first part of the study. Then, in the second part of the study, half of the students in the intrinsic motivation training group and in the control group were promised a reward for engaging in a creativity task. Therefore, there were four groups of children: (a) intrinsic motivation training/reward, (b) intrinsic motivation training/no reward, (c) control/reward, and (d) control/no reward.

The intrinsic motivation training involved showing children videotapes of two 11-year-olds talking with an adult about various aspects of their schoolwork. The dialogue in the videotapes was designed to get the participants to focus on (a) the intrinsic reasons for doing schoolwork (e.g., "I like social studies the best. I like learning about how other people live in different parts of the world.") and (b) the enjoyment of doing schoolwork and not on the extrinsic, socially imposed rewards for doing schoolwork (e.g., "Sometimes when I know my teacher is going to give me a grade on something I am doing, I think about that. But then I remember that it's more important that I like what I'm doing, that I really enjoy it. . . . "). Children in the intrinsic motivation training met in small groups with the experimenter for two 20-minute training sessions in which they saw and discussed the videotapes. A number of activities were also included in the training sessions to help the children focus on their feelings about doing schoolwork. For example, the participants were asked to indicate their preferences for a variety of school activities. Children in the control condition also met with the experimenter in small groups; however, the focus was on the children's favorite nonschool activities.

After the sessions were over, half of the students in the intrinsic motivation training group and control group were introduced to the reward manipulation. The researcher told them that if they promised to tell a story for the experimenter, they could take two pictures with an instant camera (the reward). The reward was made especially salient to these children by having them sign an agreement that if they told a story, the experimenter would let them use the camera. This agreement was kept in sight of the children for the remainder of the session. For the other half of the participants who were not promised a reward, the picture taking and storytelling were simply presented among a list of things to do during the session, so that one activity was not viewed as a reward for engaging in another activity. For all groups, the storytelling involved making up a brief story to accompany a set of pictures in a book.

In examining the creativity of the children's stories, Amabile and colleagues (1987) obtained some interesting results. First, consistent with the overjustification effect, the control group participants who were rewarded produced stories that were less creative than those produced by their nonrewarded counterparts. Second, and the key part of the research, the children receiving the intrinsic motivation training plus reward produced stories that were more complex and higher in creativity than those produced by children in the control plus reward condition. This finding indicated that the intrinsic motivation manipulation had been effective in preventing the overjustification effect from occurring. Opposite to expectations, however, the children who received the intrinsic motivation training and were rewarded scored *higher* in their creativity than did the children who received the training but were not rewarded. Amabile and colleagues believed that, for the intrinsically motivated children, the reward might have led them to alter their perceptions of the situation such that they actively counteracted the detrimental effects of the reward. Whatever the reason, the results of this study imply that it is indeed possible to develop interventions to alter students' motivation and perceptions of a reward situation so that the usual overjustification effect may be minimized or even reversed.

Students comparing each other. In assessing our performance and abilities, according to Festinger's (1954) **social comparison theory,** we may use two types of standards: objective and social. According to this theory, in the absence of an objective standard (e.g., the proportion of correct responses on a test), we are likely to judge our performance and abilities (as well as our personality characteristics) in comparison with those of other people in our environment (e.g., "Am I smart?" "Do I have many friends?"). Usually, comparisons are made with others who are similar or close to us in terms of the characteristics in question. Furthermore, these comparisons may be made with people who are slightly better than we are on particular abilities and traits (called *upward social comparisons*) or with people who are worse off than we are (called *downward social comparisons*). Both types of comparison serve a useful purpose in that they make us feel better about our current abilities, achievements, and personalities (as in the case of downward social comparisons) or enhance our self-images by giving us attainable goals to strive for (as in the case of upward social comparisons).

The classroom is an environment that readily lends itself to the process of social comparison.

Children and young adults are often grouped in terms of their abilities and academic performance and are regularly evaluated not only on the basis of absolute criteria but also on the basis of how they do relative to their peers (Renick & Harter, 1989). Let us say that you received a B+ on a math test, whereas a classmate of yours received an A on the test. Comparing your performance with that of your classmate, you may end up feeling bad even though the grade you received was a good one. On the other hand, you may react in a more constructive way. You may discuss the test results with your classmate and get useful information on how to improve your grade on the next test. The difference in your grades also may motivate you to try harder the next time, or it may give you a sense of what you are capable of achieving. Because you are making an upward social comparison, comparing your performance with that of your classmate can even raise your self-confidence and feelings of self-efficacy (Blanton, Buunk, Gibbons, & Kuyper, 1999).

Therefore, it seems as though it might be a good idea to encourage children to make upward comparisons with classmates so that their academic performance, motivation, and self-efficacy can improve. But not all classrooms are homogeneous entities with all children close in abilities and with similar chances to achieve. Classrooms are often made up of children of very different backgrounds, abilities to learn, and opportunities to succeed. What happens, for example, when a classroom is made up of children from different ethnic and socioeconomic backgrounds? Consistent with the upward social comparison effect, there is evidence that in classrooms where the majority of children are high-achieving Caucasians, minority children tend to have higher levels of academic achievement than do minority children in classrooms composed predominantly of their own racial groups (Pepitone, 1990). Despite the gains in achievement, however, minority children's academic self-concepts are poorer in integrated classrooms than in racially/ethnically homogeneous classrooms.

So why does upward social comparison not work in all cases? If one observes the interpersonal dynamics in a classroom or even in a schoolyard, those children with similar backgrounds and interests tend to interact with each other. One of the postulates of Festinger's (1954) social comparison theory is that we tend to compare ourselves with others who we perceive as *similar to ourselves*. Making social comparisons to people from outside our group depends on the availability contact with dissimilar others in our environment and the degree to which we come to perceive these others as similar to us in some relevant domain. For comparisons to occur, children from minority ethnic backgrounds must see majority children as relevant comparison figures (Pepitone, 1990). Their mere presence in the same classroom, using the same resources and learning materials, does not guarantee that the higher achieving children will be seen by lower achieving children as similar and, therefore, as appropriate comparisons. That is, minority children must view the areas of competency displayed by the majority children as relevant and important parts of their own self-concepts.

Another factor to consider when examining the effects of social comparison on academic achievement is the notion of perceived control over one's performance and ability. It is critical that students perceive that it is not only important to improve but also that it is *possible* to

improve (Huguet, Dumas, Monteil, & Genestoux, 2001). Keil, McClintock, Kramer, and Platow (1990) argued that the emphasis on social comparison standards and procedures in educational settings may be detrimental to children who consistently perform more poorly than their peers. After repeated lack of improvement in their academic performance, these students may experience less confidence in their abilities, may lose their motivation on academic tasks, and may experience lowered feelings of self-worth, consequently leading to lower academic achievement. In this case, making upward social comparisons can have a negative effect on students if the gap between the students and the targets of comparison never closes.

One group of students who are faced with constant challenges in school is learning-disabled children. Renick and Harter (1989) found that social comparison processes played an important role in how learning-disabled elementary school students perceived their academic competence when they compared themselves with their normal-achieving peers in a regular classroom and when they compared themselves with their learning-disabled peers in their special needs classroom. The researchers also were interested in which group (the normal-achieving peers or the learning-disabled peers) the learning-disabled students spontaneously used as a comparison group. Learning-disabled students reported that they perceived themselves to be more academically competent in the special needs classroom than in the regular classroom and that they spontaneously compared themselves with their regular classroom peers. A disturbing finding was that the learning-disabled students' perceptions of their academic competence decreased across the grades tested in the study (third through eighth grades), suggesting that as these students progress through school they become increasingly aware that there is a discrepancy between their own academic performance and that of their normal-achieving peers, a discrepancy that they may never be able to reduce. According to Renick and Harter, it is this knowledge that may have a detrimental effect on the self-perceptions and feelings of self-worth of learning-disabled children.

In view of the fact that social comparison processes can have both positive and negative effects in the classroom, what can educators do to capitalize on the ego-boosting aspects of making comparisons and, thereby, increase student achievement? The next section may offer some answers by exploring the interpersonal dynamics of the classroom.

INTERPERSONAL PROCESSES: TEACHERS AND STUDENTS INTERACTING

People spend many of their formative years in a school environment. Prior to college or university, they are in school approximately 6 hours a day, 5 days a week, 10 months a year, for approximately 12 consecutive years. Although many school administrators, educators, and researchers focus their attention on how the school environment influences the development of basic academic skills, the capacity to acquire knowledge, and overall scholastic achievement, school also provides a medium for social and emotional development. Asp and Garbarino (1988) called school "the most pervasive socializing institution (outside of the family) in the lives of children" (p. 170). It should come as no surprise that social psychologists have long been interested in how teachers and students interact in the school environment and how these interactions affect the development of individuals.

Teacher Expectations and Student Achievement

One study in social psychology that generated a lot of research, excitement, and criticism is Robert Rosenthal and Lenore Jacobson's Pygmalion in the Classroom. Rosenthal and Jacobson (1968) noticed that teachers had higher expectations for the achievement of good students in their classrooms and wondered whether these expectations could influence students' academic performance. In their classic experiment, Rosenthal and Jacobson told teachers early in the school year that, based on the results of an intelligence quotient (IQ) test, some of their students had above average academic potential (a group labeled "bloomers"). In actuality, the students who they named as bloomers had been randomly selected, meaning

that these students were, on average, no smarter than the other students in their classes. The teachers were unaware that the feedback to them had been falsified, and the students were not told about the label given to them. The results indicated that students who had been labeled as bloomers showed significant increases in their IQ scores by the end of the school year compared with students in the control condition. Remarkably, the teachers' expectations had come true. How did the improvement come about? Rosenthal and Jacobson suggested that because the teachers believed the bloomers to be above average students, they began to treat these students differently. In-class observations revealed that teachers provided the bloomers with the following:

- A warmer climate by giving them more attention, support, and encouragement
- More challenging material to learn
- More feedback on their schoolwork
- More opportunity to respond in class and a longer time to respond

It is important to note, however, that the teachers did not deliberately treat these students differently from others in their classrooms. Indeed, when the results of the study were released, they evoked a great deal of alarm and criticism. According to Babad (1993), the Pygmalion study drew concerns from teachers and other educators that the results could be used to blame teachers for the poor academic performance of some students—expect poor performance, get poor performance. Recall that when the study was published, the United States was in the midst of school desegregation and related busing issues, and many aspects of social institutions were being questioned.

Criticisms aside, it seemed clear from Rosenthal and Jacobson's (1968) research that the expectations of teachers can affect students' IQ scores and possibly academic performance as well. But what mechanism was operating behind the relationship between teachers' expectations and students' subsequent performance? Rosenthal and Jacobson's study was actually an illustration of Robert Merton's concept of self-fulfilling prophecy. A **self-fulfilling prophecy** refers to having expectations about another person that influence how the holder of the expectations behaves toward that other person and that in turn cause the other person to behave in a way that confirms the expectations. In addition, because the target person behaves in accordance with the expectations, he or she may believe that the expectations are justified. Merton (1948) proposed that the self-fulfilling prophecy notion could explain a variety of problems, from bank failures to discrimination against ethnic minorities.

A student may respond to a teacher's high expectations by becoming more interested in schoolwork and working harder, all of which lead to better academic performance. Be aware that the teacher also observes the student's behavior and is likely to conclude that his or her expectations regarding the student are correct and accurate. Thus, the cycle is complete and reinforced. Essentially, what the teacher is doing is changing the student's academic self-concept to conform to the teacher's own expectations and beliefs about the student. This, of course, has serious implications not only for the student's academic self-concept and achievement but also for choices and decisions the student might make later in life (e.g., choice of occupation). It also may help to explain the changes in self-perceptions, performance, and future goals observed in the minority students described in the opening vignette. The mentors held positive expectations for the students and provided them with a variety of learning opportunities and feedback that reflected these expectations. The result was the successful completion of research projects, a change in the way in which the students viewed their academic abilities, improved performance in high school courses, and higher academic aspirations.

Since Rosenthal and Jacobson's (1968) initial study, there have been hundreds of investigations of teacher expectancy effects in educational settings. Rosenthal and Jacobson's study had raised more questions than it had answered. For instance, do teachers' expectations have long-term effects on students' self-concepts? Do positive and negative expectations affect students through similar processes? Also, studies reviewing expectancy effects have consistently found only a small effect of teachers' expectations on the academic achievement of students, accounting for roughly 5% to 10% of students' performance (Brophy, 1983). Kuklinski and Weinstein (2001) suggested that there may be other factors, such as the classroom environment, that interact with the influence of teacher expectancies on students' performance and self-concepts.

Madon, Jussim, and Eccles (1997) also argued that certain conditions may augment the effect of teacher expectancies on students. In their study of 98 teachers and about 1,500 students enrolled in sixth-grade math classes in Michigan, Madon and colleagues examined the relationship between teachers' expectations (whether positive or negative) and the development of self-fulfilling prophecies in certain types of students. For instance, are students who have negative self-concepts or who perform poorly in school (low achievers) more susceptible to the expectations of teachers than are students who have positive self-concepts or who perform well in school (high achievers)? To address this question, teachers' perceptions of their students' self-concepts and their ability, effort, and performance concerning math were surveyed and examined in relation to their students' math achievement.

The results indicated that teachers' perceptions and expectations (whether positive or negative) predicted achievement more strongly for low achievers than for high achievers. That is, low achievers were more susceptible to the development of both positive *and* negative self-fulfilling prophecies than were high achievers. Why might this happen? Madon and colleagues (1997) suggested that the history of past school experiences (mostly negative) may make low-achieving students more sensitive to the expectations of teachers, thereby affecting their motivation and self-concepts more keenly. Therefore, low-achieving students who for years have been deprived of rewarding school experiences in particular may be inspired by teachers' positive expectations. The researchers suggested, on the other hand, that students who are academically more successful may have many more psychological resources to draw on even when faced with teachers' negative expectations and, therefore, are not as greatly affected by teachers' perceptions.

So, does this mean that all that needs to be done is to make sure that teachers hold positive expectations and beliefs about students who are not doing well and then those students' academic performance will improve? The answer is not exactly that simple. Low-achieving students must perceive that teachers' positive expectations are genuine and that any positive feedback they receive from the teachers is based on merit. If a student perceives that positive teacher expectations are based on a feeling of sympathy, for example, the student is likely to discount and mistrust the teacher's positive feedback and support (Crocker & Major, 1989). The result may very well be that the student will disengage from the situation and experience a decrease in self-esteem.

We have seen that teachers' expectations can affect students' academic performance, but what happens when these expectancies fall along racial or gender lines? Many studies (e.g., Steele, 1997) have noted that teachers frequently hold negative expectations related to the academic achievement of African American students. Also, female students are not expected to perform as well as male students in areas of study requiring advanced mathematical and spatial skills (Steele, 1997). Therefore, negative expectations held by teachers and the self-fulfilling prophecy may partially explain why students who belong to marginalized groups (e.g., African Americans, those with low socioeconomic status) tend to

perform more poorly in school than do students who belong to nonmarginalized groups (e.g., whites, middle-class students).

Applying these findings to children from three elementary school grades, McKown and Weinstein (2002) wanted to determine how different types of teacher expectancies (under- or overestimates of students' academic abilities) were related to achievement in mathematics and reading for students in academically stigmatized groups (e.g., girls in math, African Americans in all subjects) and nonstigmatized groups. Specifically, they examined how teachers' expectations for children at the beginning of the school year were related to children's academic performance at the end of the school year. They found that the academic performance of children in the stigmatized groups was affected negatively by teachers' underestimates of their abilities but was not affected positively by teachers' overestimates of their abilities. For children in the nonstigmatized groups, the students benefited from teachers' overestimates of their abilities but were not affected by teachers' underestimates of their abilities. An even more interesting (and disturbing) finding was that the expectancy effects on students' achievement either were constant over time or increased with age.

● FOCUS ON INTERVENTION

Given what we know about the effects of teachers' expectations on students' academic achievement, what do we do about it? Is there a way in which we can counteract the negative effects that teacher expectations can have on academic performance, especially for students in marginalized groups? There has been some attempt to make use of the concepts and empirical evidence on teachers' expectations to design interventions that can be used in educational settings (Babad, 1993).

One approach is to provide teachers with training to help them recognize the differential expectations that they may hold for high- and low-achieving students and to instruct them on how to engage in behaviors that reduce the disparity in students' achievement. The goal of the training is to improve the academic achievement of *all* students (Gottfredson, Marciniak, Birdseye, & Gottfredson, 1991). The Teacher Expectations and Student Achievement (TESA) Program provides teachers with such training (Kerman, Kimball, & Martin, 1980). Recall that Rosenthal and Jacobson (1968) identified a number of teacher behaviors that reflected their expectations of students' abilities (e.g., giving "bloomers" more opportunity to respond in class). The TESA Program focuses on 15 classroom behaviors that teachers commonly display when interacting with students of different achievement levels. The behaviors are similar to those observed by Rosenthal and Jacobson as being indicative of teachers' expectations of students. The behaviors are divided into three categories: (a) response opportunities (e.g., amount of time waiting for students to answer, complexity of questions directed at students), (b) feedback to students (e.g., amount of praise given for success, feedback given on tests and assignments), and (c) personal regard (e.g., number of positive interactions, amount of eye contact with students). Teacher training is provided in five 3-hour sessions, with each session focusing on one behavior from each category. Between sessions, each teacher observes and gives feedback on the classroom behavior of at least three other teachers, and that teacher himself or herself is also observed teaching and given feedback. The main goal of this training is to make teachers more aware of their expectations concerning students and to make them more sensitive to the way in which they respond to students.

Evaluations of the TESA Program reveal that teachers and school personnel find the training to be very helpful, and teachers report making use of the strategies outlined in the program. In addition, the program has been shown to increase teachers' positive interactions with low-achieving students (Gottfredson et al., 1991). Finally, although the effects of this training do not always lead to increases in the achievement of minority students or poorly performing students (as theory and research would suggest), teachers report that students still demonstrate more positive attitudes toward learning (Fenton & O'Leary, 1990).

Students Interacting With Other Students

Forming and maintaining friendships, acquiring leadership skills, learning how to resolve conflicts and cooperate with others, and developing a sense of self all are by-products of attending school. In the classroom, a child learns how to be a student and a member or leader of a group and also is exposed to the norms, language, and values of the community (Asp & Garbarino, 1988). From the standpoint of researchers and educators, these social, cognitive, and emotional skills not only prepare an individual for life outside of school but also can enhance academic achievement.

Academic effects of peer interaction. Children who experience social, behavioral, and emotional difficulties in school are at a disadvantage for reaching their academic potentials. In particular, children who have poor peer relationships, where they are either actively rejected or ignored by their peers, fail to develop competency in many areas of their lives, including academic competency (Bullock, 1992; Coolihan, Fantuzzo, Mendez, & McDermott, 2000). Simply playing with others helps a child to become socially competent, be more self-confident, and do better in school. Indeed, positive peer interactions as early as preschool can have significant effects on later overall adjustment, including academic success (Ladd, Price, & Hart, 1988). Furthermore, some researchers

(e.g., Welsh, Parke, Widaman, & O'Neil, 2001) have also found that the opposite may occur; that is, academic success during the early school years can lead to social competence later.

All in all, then, it seems that doing well academically is very much related to being good at interacting with one's peers and that the relationship between academic success and social competence may be reciprocal. But what happens when no one wants to be a child's friend? Adolescents who continually experience rejection by their peers are at greater risk for dropping out of school, even though many are at least average in intelligence and have the ability to graduate (Bullock, 1992). Although the effects seem to be stronger for boys than for girls, the pattern is the same for both genders: Early poor social adjustment leads to future academic difficulties, a perception that the school environment is aversive, and eventual failure in school (Bullock, 1992; Ladd et al., 1988).

Children and adolescents in disadvantaged groups, such as ethnic minorities, the poor, and the mentally or physically disabled, are especially at risk for "not fitting in" and, consequently, for experiencing difficulties in school. Coolihan and colleagues (2000) investigated how peer interactions may be connected to learning readiness in children who are from poor families. Using more than 500 children enrolled in a Head Start program, they looked at multiple dimensions of peer play and how they related to achievement-orientated variables (e.g., interest in learning, persistence on tasks, cooperative attitude) and problem behaviors (e.g., aggressive outbursts and disruptive play). Three general relationships emerged, namely, that (a) children who demonstrated positive play behaviors also were actively engaged in classroom learning activities, (b) children who hovered around play activities but did not interact with others very much also were inattentive in class and less motivated to learn, and (c) children who were disruptive in their peer play also displayed conduct problems during classroom activities.

Researchers have noted the importance of establishing positive peer relationships in developing academic competence for children and adolescents with disabilities and behavioral difficulties. Children with attention deficit hyperactivity disorder (ADHD) are often at risk for academic underachievement because their behavior disrupts their abilities to attend to teachers and take part in group discussions (DuPaul, Ervin, Hook, & McGoey, 1998). In an effort to increase ADHD students' attention to their school tasks (and thereby improve their academic performance), DuPaul and colleagues (1998) had a small group of elementary school children diagnosed with ADHD tutored by their non-ADHD peers on a variety of school subjects (e.g., math, spelling). The results showed that the ADHD children's disruptive off-task behavior decreased and that their attention to academic material increased. The peer tutoring also contributed to an increase in the academic test scores of the ADHD children, suggesting that peer tutoring might be effective in raising the academic achievement of students with behavioral disorders.

So, what are the implications of the research on peer interactions and academic behaviors? One thing suggested by the research is that if we can improve children's academic performance early on in school (e.g., by providing math and reading tutoring), it can have a positive impact on their later academic and social development. The beneficial effects would be even better if social skills training also were incorporated given that having successful interactions with others can lead to stronger academic motivation and performance in later grades (Coolihan et al., 2000). As was seen in DuPaul and colleagues' (1998) study, encouraging students to help one another learn may be effective in boosting academic achievement, promoting social and personal development, and improving interpersonal skills. The classroom intervention strategies outlined in the next subsection structure peer interactions to achieve not only learning goals but also other social and developmental goals.

Cooperative learning methods. In general, **cooperative learning** (Slavin, 1990) refers to a learning method in which students work together in groups to master academic material presented by the teacher. There are many types of cooperative learning methods, two of which are the *Student Teams–Achievement Divisions* (STAD) and the *jigsaw classroom technique.* Most of the cooperative learning methods have been shown to have positive effects on academic achievement and on the development of students' higher cognitive skills (e.g., critical thinking, problem solving) (Figure 10.2).

The beneficial outcomes are enhanced if the cooperative learning method incorporates both individual accountability and group goals as in STAD (Slavin, 1990). The four-member learning teams used in the STAD technique are heterogeneous, composed of male and female students from different performance levels and ethnic backgrounds (Slavin, 1990). The teacher presents a lesson to the class (e.g., learn about the solar system), and then all members of each team are responsible for making sure that their team members master the content. In essence, students in the group become the "teachers" to their fellow students. Although students work on the lesson in their groups, they are quizzed individually on the material and points are awarded based on the extent to which each student has exceeded his or her own earlier performance. Then each student's points are added to those of the other team members, and the entire team receives a composite score. Teams that meet certain criteria may receive rewards or certificates of achievement.

Another effective cooperative learning method is the jigsaw classroom technique (Aronson, Stephan, Sikes, Blaney, & Snapp, 1978; Slavin, 1990). With this procedure, the students in the class are divided into small groups of five or six members. Each group is

Figure 10.2   Cooperative Learning: Students Helping Each Other to Learn

SOURCE: Photo courtesy of Cassandra Lee Davis

assigned the task of learning about a particular topic, and each student within the group is responsible for learning a small portion of the topic. Each student from the group meets with the members of other classroom groups who have been assigned the same subtopic; these children work together to learn the subtopic. Then the students take the information that they have learned back to their groups and teach the material to other members of their groups. Because each student is evaluated individually, it is important that all group members pay attention to what their fellow group members present. As in STAD, members of the group rely on one another to learn all parts of the assigned material, and no student is considered to be more or less important than another student. What the jigsaw classroom technique does in the long term is improve the overall atmosphere of the classroom to one in which students interact with each other in a positive and constructive

manner that helps them to achieve a goal (Aronson, 2002). In addition, students are given opportunities to interact with classmates with whom they usually might not interact (e.g., peers of different ethnic backgrounds, socially ostracized peers).

But how is it that an individual personal process such as learning can be improved by a group activity? What can social psychology tell us about why cooperative learning is effective in promoting learning? Cooperative learning works in several ways. First, competition among individual students, which can be detrimental to an individual's self-esteem and performance, is reduced. Second, a sense of belonging in the classroom is increased, and this especially can have a positive effect on students who, for whatever reason, may be initially excluded. In addition, even though students work in a group and the group is assigned a score, there is still individual accountability, thereby reducing the potential for *social loafing,* that is, the reduction in individual effort when engaged in collective tasks. Because students are assigned points based on their improvement over their own past performance rather than on an absolute standard of success, any student can be a "star" at any given time. This not only makes learning more rewarding for students but also increases their motivation toward completing schoolwork. Teamwork also adds an element of fun and helps to emphasize that learning is important and valuable, creating an overall positive climate (Ellis & Feldman, 1994; Slavin, 1990). In particular, peers can provide feedback and encouragement to each other, model different levels of thinking, and bring different perspectives to the group. All of this creates an appreciation and positive expectation for the diversity of skills and thinking present in the classroom (Ellis & Feldman, 1994).

So far, we have discussed how student–teacher and student–peer interactions can affect students' academic performance and overall development both positively and negatively. For example, cooperative learning methods can lead to better academic performance and better social interactions among students. Because individuals spend so much time in the social environment of school, some of the negative social behaviors that plague our society, such as

Figure 10.3 The Need for Anti-Bullying Programs to Be Implemented in Schools

SOURCE: Photo courtesy of University of Windsor.

prejudice and violence, also may get their start and receive reinforcement in school settings. As a result, social psychologists view the school system as providing a handy medium to study and address broader social issues such as aggression.

When Interactions Turn Deadly: School Violence

In March 1998, two boys, 11 and 13 years of age, shot to death four students and a teacher at their middle school in Jonesboro, Arkansas. In April 1999, two heavily armed male adolescents, wearing masks and black trench coats, walked into their Colorado high school and opened fire on students, teachers, and staff members. By the time the shooting was over, dozens of people were dead or injured, and the two young gunmen were also dead from self-inflicted gunshot wounds. Just a week later, a 14-year-old high school student in Taber, Alberta, opened fire with a rifle in his high school, killing one student and

seriously injuring another student. Unfortunately, as Table 10.2 shows, these are only three terrible incidents of school violence out of many other similar ones during the past two decades.

Understandably, we are shocked when we learn of such occurrences. We may wonder what is going on in our schools. Are students, particularly adolescents, more violent than ever before? Typically, their classmates describe many of the young perpetrators of school violence as outcasts or outsiders. Some of the shooters report incidents of rejection or bullying by others. Although extreme incidents of school violence are not as widespread as the media would have us believe, there is no denying their tragic results. Furthermore, although there is legitimate concern over the increasing use of weapons by children and adolescents to settle disputes, other types of aggression and violence (e.g., bullying, fighting) are much more common. Can social psychology help to explain what causes some young people to take such harmful actions against others? If we can identify the factors that lead to school violence, perhaps we can develop policies and interventions to prevent such incidents from occurring in the first place (Figure 10.3).

Causes of youth aggression. What makes young people behave violently? Are they suffering from some neurochemical imbalances? Can mental illness or a personality disorder be the culprit? These are, of course, possible answers. Social psychologists, however, have focused on the social environmental factors that can precipitate violent behavior.

Fatum and Hoyle (1996) noted that the way in which today's adolescents react to the harmful or offensive behavior of other individuals may provide some explanation for the incidence of youth aggression. In the past, antisocial interactions, such as those involving rejection, insults, and bullying, were regarded as experiences to be endured as a normal part of adolescence and as opportunities for developing inner strength and maturity. Today, too often such events seem not to be tolerated at any cost. Of course, these interactions have always had detrimental effects on self-esteem and self-image, but it is the way in which children and adolescents deal with them that

Table 10.2   Sample of School Shootings in North America

Date	Location	Perpetrators and Victims
February 10, 2000	Toronto, Ontario	Three teens are seriously wounded in the parking lot of a suburban high school.
April 29, 1999	Taber, Alberta	A 14-year-old boy walks into his secondary school and opens fire with a .22-caliber rifle, killing one teen and wounding another.
April 20, 1999	Littleton, Colorado	Two heavily armed 17-year-olds walk into their high school and start shooting, targeting minorities and athletes. After the rampage, 12 students (including the perpetrators) and 1 teacher are dead, and 23 others are wounded.
March 24, 1998	Jonesboro, Arkansas	Two boys, 11 and 13 years of age, open fire on students, teachers, and staff members from the woods near their middle school after luring people out with a false fire alarm. After the shootings, 4 students and 1 teacher are dead, and 10 others are wounded.
December 1, 1997	West Paducah, Kentucky	A 14-year-old boy opens fire at a high school prayer meeting, killing 3 students and wounding 5 others.
October 27, 1975	Ottawa, Ontario	A 13-year-old boy kills a student and a teacher and injures five others before shooting himself.
May 28, 1975	Brampton, Ontario	A 16-year-old boy kills one student and a teacher and wounds 13 other students at his high school. He also kills himself.

SOURCE: Adapted from news reports in *The Globe and Mail, The National Post,* and *Newsweek.*

has changed significantly. It now seems that any sign of disrespect or intolerance is regarded as justification for immediate retaliation and as a way of maintaining one's status and dignity. As Fatum and Hoyle put it, "The credo becomes 'disrespect deserves disrespect,' and aggression is seen as a tool for defending that credo" (p. 29). Many students see violence and other forms of aggression as the only effective ways of dealing with conflict. The bottom line is that they believe that their aggressive actions are appropriate. This points to a set of values and attitudes that supports the use of aggression. It also indicates that these students see no alternative means of coping effectively with harmful antisocial behavior that is directed at them or others.

Where do these aggressive attitudes and values originate? Why is it that young people come to believe that violence is an effective (sometimes the *only*) response to negative encounters with other individuals? Social psychologists typically view aggression as a learned response that can be precipitated by social and psychological factors. According to the tenets of **social learning theory** (Bandura, 1983; see also Chapter 8), through observation of the aggressive behavior of others (e.g., peers, parents, movie characters), children learn that aggression may be an effective means of obtaining desired goals. Children also observe that aggressive behavior is not always punished and, in fact, is sometimes rewarded. Moreover, they learn how to be aggressive (e.g., what strategies and weapons to use) and learn who are acceptable targets for aggression.

Kashani, Jones, Bumby, and Thomas (2001) identified multiple psychosocial risk factors associated with youth violence; no one causal factor or combination of factors accounts for every instance of youth violence. Risk factors occur at the individual, family, peer group, school, and community/cultural levels. For example, cognitive deficits at an individual level, such as lower levels of moral reasoning and poorer verbal skills, have been associated with aggressive behavior in children and adolescents. In addition, family dysfunction, such as a family history of substance abuse, domestic violence, and little modeling of prosocial behaviors by parents, is also a contributor. One may argue, then, that what we are dealing with is a larger societal issue revolving around the access and use of weapons, the media's glorification of violence as a means of solving problems, and the modeling of aggressive behavior both inside and outside the home.

Violence in the schools. School violence is a heavily researched topic. In a review of the literature on school violence, Furlong and Morrison (2001) identified some general findings:

- Males are more likely than females to be involved in instances of school violence, either as perpetrators or as victims.
- Bullying is more common among elementary school children than among high school students.
- The use of weapons is more common among high school students than among elementary school children.
- There is very little difference among urban, suburban, and rural schools in levels of violence.
- Guns are brought to schools by a relatively small proportion of students (estimates are usually less than 15% and vary widely).
- Students who bring guns to school tend to be male, report frequent use of alcohol and drugs, designate themselves as gang members, and are more likely to be involved in aggressive behavior (e.g., assaults at school, juvenile crimes).

Because children and adolescents spend a great deal of time within the school environment, incidents of aggression resulting in physical and psychological harm have repercussions not only for the students involved in the incidents but also for all students, teachers, and staff members. The overall school climate can be deeply affected. School is no longer seen as a safe environment in which the emphasis is on academic achievement and on building interpersonal skills and relationships. Students can no

longer focus solely on their learning because they also must be very vigilant about who they interact with, where they walk, and so forth. If students notice that teachers, staff members, and others in positions of authority ignore violent behavior, the students are likely to feel that they are alone and that violence is an accepted (or at least tolerated) means of dealing with conflict. Thus, school may be viewed as simply an extension of the community and home environment where violence and aggression may be prevalent and the norm (Furlong & Morrison, 2001).

Based on the thinking of Furlong and Morrison (2001) and Fatum and Hoyle (1996), it seems that a child's behavior in school may influenced by what he or she perceives to be typical, expected, and normal. The child perceives the consequences of certain actions by observing others and then behaves accordingly. A number of researchers (e.g., Cialdini, Kallgren, & Reno, 1991; Deutsch & Gerard, 1955) have identified three normative social processes that may operate within a social setting: (a) **descriptive norms** (i.e., what an individual perceives to be *typical* behavior in a setting), (b) **injunctive norms** (i.e., what people are *expected* to do or *ought* to do in a setting), and (c) **norm salience** (i.e., to what extent the norms are clearly *conveyed* in the setting). Descriptive norms help the individual to define a situation and process the information from the situation efficiently; it may be easier just to follow what others are doing in a setting, especially if the individual is unfamiliar with it. Injunctive norms dictate what ought to be done in a situation and inform the individual of the rewards or punishments associated with following (or not following) the norms. Lastly, descriptive and injunctive norms are said to affect the individual's behavior if the individual is made aware of them; if the norms in a situation are made salient, the individual knows how to behave in norm-consistent ways. We also can relate these processes back to Bandura's social learning theory; the observation of others' behavior and the consequences attached to that behavior are important influences on the individual.

How can social norms, then, operate in the classroom environment in relation to aggression? Aggressive behavior in the classroom may be an everyday occurrence (descriptive norm).

A teacher may discourage aggressive behavior in a student by a look, a gesture, or words indicating that the behavior is not appropriate in the classroom (injunctive norm). The teacher also may make these norms clear to others by excluding the student who has aggressed from the setting (high norm salience). Other students in the class may also convey norms of behavior by actively including or excluding peers who are aggressive (highly salient injunctive norms).

Based on the theoretical concepts developed by Cialdini and colleagues (1991) and others, Henry (2001) studied the normative social processes in the classroom environment that may influence aggressive behavior in children. Using a large sample of elementary school children, he had children report on their perceptions of classmates (i.e., aggressive behavior of peers, popularity and rejection of aggressive peers) and on their beliefs about the appropriateness of physical aggression and verbal aggression. In addition to the children's self-reports, Henry used observational methods to assess teacher and student behaviors in the classroom. He employed these measures to examine the descriptive norms in the classroom (perception of average aggression level of the child's classmates), injunctive norms (the child's expectations concerning aggression in the classroom), and norm salience (the child's views about the popularity of aggressive classmates and the teacher's reactions to aggressive behavior).

Henry (2001) found that children's perceptions of the level of aggression in the classroom (descriptive norms) had no relation to individual child's actual aggressive behavior but that the child's expectations about how he or she ought to behave in the classroom regarding aggressive behavior (injunctive norms) were significantly associated with the child's aggressive behavior. That is, students' beliefs about what was appropriate in the classroom influenced their aggressive behavior more than did their observations of actual levels of aggressive behavior in the classroom. Furthermore, just as theory regarding normative social processes would suggest, children believed that aggressive behavior was unacceptable if they saw that classmates who engaged in it were reprimanded or unpopular among their peers. However, if children believed that aggression was approved of and tolerated in the classroom, they regarded it as acceptable and, thus, aggressive behavior was more prevalent. Henry argued that what really influences the level of school aggression is the "moral climate of the classroom regarding aggressive behavior" (p. 210) rather than the observed behavior of classmates. **Moral climate** refers to children's beliefs about the appropriateness of aggression that are derived from the beliefs of others in the classroom. Therefore, these results imply that both teachers and pupils play important roles in the development of norms related to aggressive behavior in a classroom setting.

Creating a violence-free school environment. What can be done to undermine those aspects of school environments that promote violence? Many schools have implemented policies and programs to help reduce and discourage youth violence and, thus, create a safer environment for students, teachers, and staff members (Schwartz, 1996).

The jigsaw classroom technique discussed earlier is an example of an effective approach to improving interpersonal and intergroup relationships in a classroom, thereby reducing conflict and other antisocial behaviors among students (Aronson et al., 1978; Slavin, 1990). As you may recall, the jigsaw classroom technique is a cooperative learning strategy. Having students representing different backgrounds, social strata, and abilities working together on a common assignment not only enhances learning (as discussed earlier) but also results in the classroom norm becoming one of cooperation and interdependence rather than competition and conflict. Indeed, among students, the jigsaw classroom technique has been shown to promote greater tolerance for diversity, greater empathy and compassion for others, and increased self-esteem (Aronson, 2002; Aronson et al., 1978). Aronson (2002) suggested that the use of the jigsaw approach might have prevented the tragedies that occurred at Littleton, Jonesboro, and Taber. It is difficult to aggress against another person when your feelings and interactions with that individual have been positive.

● FOCUS ON INTERVENTION

The jigsaw classroom technique represents an intervention that occurs in the school itself and is directed toward developing a school climate that does not condone and support violence. Other intervention strategies aim at early childhood prevention. There are a number of prevention programs that have been developed, and many of them incorporate elements of social learning theory (Bandura, 1977b). Eddy, Reid, and Fetrow (2001) described an elementary school program aimed at children who are at risk for developing delinquent and violent behaviors during adolescence. The goal of the program, called Linking the Interests of Families and Teachers (LIFT), is to teach children and their parents prosocial and nonaggressive methods of dealing with anger, frustration, and conflict. Parents are included because they operate as significant role models in the children's lives. Children are encouraged and rewarded to model their behavior on that of their parents. The LIFT program contains three components: (a) a classroom-based social and problem skills training component for the children, (b) a playground-based behavior modification component for the children, and (c) a group-delivered training component for the parents.

For the classroom component, LIFT classroom instructors meet with all students in a classroom for 1 hour twice a week for 10 weeks. Each session includes listening to lectures and role-playing on social and problem-solving skills, practicing skills for interacting with peers, and engaging in unstructured free play on the playground. Students are taught relationship skills such as identifying feelings, dealing with anger, responding appropriately to others, and cooperating and problem solving within peer groups.

For the playground component, students are divided into small groups. The groups engage in various activities together, allowing them to demonstrate (and receive social approval for) prosocial behaviors and the inhibition of negative interactions with peers while playing.

For the third component, sessions are held with parents during the same 3-month period that their children are undergoing their program components. Each parent session involves information and role-playing activities aimed at fundamentals of discipline (e.g., using small positive and negative consequences, paying attention to early signs of problem behaviors) and family management skills (e.g., giving encouragement, controlling negative emotions, making behavior change contracts with children). These activities are based on social learning and behavior modification principles that state that modeling and rewarding prosocial behavior will lead to an increase in the desired behavior.

The LIFT program was implemented in an urban area in Oregon using schools from three school districts (Eddy et al., 2001). During the 3 years the program was in effect, schools randomly chosen for the program were compared with control schools in the same district.

Evaluation research of the effectiveness of the program was conducted using a variety of questionnaires and observations both at school and at home. What did the researchers find? First, there were significant immediate changes (between the fall and spring of the first year) in child and parent behaviors attributed to the LIFT program. For example, children in the LIFT program were less aggressive on the playground and were perceived as more positive by their teachers than were children in the control group. In addition, parents of LIFT children behaved less negatively with their children in parent–child problem-solving sessions. What about the long-term impact of the program? These results were also positive. Three years following the program, LIFT students were less likely to associate with delinquent peers and were less likely to engage in alcohol and drug use than were students in the control group.

Interventions aimed at prevention and reduction of school violence indicate that although violence in our schools is a serious problem, it is not an insurmountable one. It is clear from the preceding discussion that principals, teachers, and school administrators have to provide an atmosphere for students that promotes cooperative (rather than competitive) learning, that rewards prosocial behavior such as sharing and compassion, and that teaches students how to engage in effective (and nonaggressive) problem solving and communication. In short, we need to "change the process of the typical classroom so that our schools can transform themselves into more humane social environments for all students" (Aronson, 2002, p. 214).

SUMMARY

Intrapersonal (or individual) factors associated with academic achievement can affect students' perceptions of their abilities and can affect their academic performance. Attitudes (i.e., beliefs about one's ability to achieve a desired outcome or perceived importance of that outcome), subjective norms (i.e., others' expectations and how motivated one is to comply with those expectations), and perceived behavioral control (i.e., perceived control over the behavior and its outcome) may contribute to students' academic performance. The types of causes that students attach to their academic outcomes (i.e., attributions) may also affect students' motivation and expectations about subsequent academic achievement. Students who attribute their success to ability (an internal, stable, and uncontrollable factor) but who attribute their failure to controllable or unstable factors (e.g., effort) will be motivated to work harder than students who attribute their failure to ability. Belief in their academic abilities, perceived control over their outcomes, and attributing success in the mentoring program to their own abilities all were factors that helped the minority students in the opening vignette to see themselves in a more positive academic light.

Attribution patterns are also linked to self-serving strategies such as self-handicapping (i.e., handicapping one's own performance so that there is an excuse for failure). Students who rely on self-handicapping as a coping strategy for academic failure so as to protect their self-esteem may end up viewing their academic performance as uncontrollable and unstable. As a result, students might not be able to take credit for their academic performance even when success occurs, thereby undermining motivation and confidence.

The emphasis on external rewards (e.g., grades, praise, awards) may reduce the motivation to learn (overjustification effect). Focusing students' attention on the intrinsic aspects of academic tasks and giving them verbal feedback rather than tangible rewards may prevent the decline in intrinsic motivation. Motivation can be affected by how students perceive their academic performance in relation to others (social comparison). Upward social comparisons (i.e., comparisons with those who perform slightly better) may provide students with attainable goals, whereas downward social comparisons (i.e., comparisons with those who perform more poorly) may make students feel better about their own performance.

Because the school setting is a social environment, social psychologists also have looked extensively at the interpersonal processes that occur in the classroom. Teachers' expectations can become self-fulfilling prophecies (i.e., students perform in accordance with teachers' beliefs and expectations about their academic abilities and teachers' views of students are reinforced). Expectations also can be detrimental to academic performance and students' self-concepts when they differ on the basis of students' race, gender, or other preexisting group. Operating as mentors and teachers, the university researchers who interacted with the minority students in the opening vignette held positive expectations for these students and offered them a variety of learning experiences. As a result, the students became more confident in their academic abilities, completed their research projects successfully, showed improved performance in their subsequent high school courses, and expressed higher academic aspirations.

In addition to teachers, interactions with peers can affect students' academic achievement and the development of a variety of social and cognitive skills. Cooperative learning methods (i.e., students working in groups to master academic material) have been used extensively to enhance both academic competence and social competence in students. These methods reduce competition and conflict, increase a sense of belonging for the students, increase students' motivation toward schoolwork, and emphasize the importance of learning. One cooperative learning method, the jigsaw classroom technique, has been applied effectively to address the problem of aggression in schools. Although there is a multitude of causes, school violence may be reinforced through social learning (e.g., observation of others' behavior) and normative (e.g., what one is expected to do in a setting) processes present in the school environment.

11

APPLYING SOCIAL PSYCHOLOGY TO ORGANIZATIONS

LARRY M. COUTTS

JAMIE A. GRUMAN

CHAPTER OUTLINE

The Individual in an Organizational Context
  Making Sense of Others in the Work
    Environment
Job Satisfaction: Antecedents and
  Consequences

Interpersonal Processes in Organizations
  Communication
  Group Decision Making
Summary

"That's it!" Tim said into his videoconference microphone. "I can't talk to you. And I'm tired of you constantly criticizing my ideas. I'm going to lunch. Don't ask me when I'll be back!"

For the past 2 years, employees at Computen Inc. had been experiencing high levels of job dissatisfaction at many of their international subsidiaries, and many of Computen's brightest employees had left the organization to work for competitors. In response, senior managers at Computen had assembled a five-person international task force to examine the job satisfaction issue and to develop recommendations to increase employees' enjoyment of their work and reduce turnover. The task force was instructed to produce a report outlining its recommendations to the regional managers within 6 months. Tim, an American production supervisor, was one of the members of that task force and was frustrated with the behavior of some of his fellow team members.

"I can't talk to these people," he was overheard complaining to a coworker. "They don't seem to understand any of the important issues causing our problems."

229

The rest of the team members were Subir, a marketing manager from India; Chris, a production supervisor from Britain; and Audrey and Veneeta, who together ran the Computen operation in Singapore.

During the first few videoconferences following the formation of the task force, it had become increasingly clear that there were significant differences of opinion among some of the team members regarding how best to examine and address the problem, but in the interest of being collegial, no major conflicts had emerged. Since then, however, nearly every meeting had resulted in disagreements and open confrontations among the team members. Audrey and Veneeta, the only two members who seemed to be getting along, joked that members of the task force were probably experiencing less job satisfaction than were any other employees in the company.

The task force was scheduled to submit its recommendations in less than a month. However, it had made little progress during the 5 months it had been meeting and had virtually nothing to report to the regional managers.

- How might the task force members' perceptions of each other influence their behavior toward each other?
- Why did the task force members seem to have trouble communicating?
- Might a better decision regarding how to deal with the job satisfaction problem have been made if only one person had been assigned to make recommendations to the regional managers?

Attempts to understand the dynamics inherent in organizations by drawing on social psychological concepts are not new. The first major treatise on the topic was titled *The Social Psychology of Organizations* and was published in 1966 by Katz and Kahn. In 1979, Karl Weick published the second edition of *The Social Psychology of Organizing*. These two volumes represent the classic works in this area (Katz & Kahn, 1966; Weick, 1979).

It is difficult to imagine how one could navigate successfully through the whitewater of organizational life without appreciating how and why people interact as they do. Similarly, how would it be possible to effectively manage a group of people if one were ignorant of the interpersonal dynamics that can either lead to fruitless conflicts or produce remarkable achievements?

This chapter discusses some of the social psychological phenomena that influence behavior in organizations. Unfortunately, because of space limitations, it explores in some depth only four of the many topics in the social psychology of organizations: social perception, job

satisfaction, communication, and group decision making. The goal is that, after reading this chapter, you will have developed an appreciation of how social psychology can be applied in organizations and how understanding social psychology can make you a more effective member of an organization.

Before beginning the first major section, however, the next few paragraphs briefly describe three other interesting organizational topics that have captivated the research efforts of social and organizational psychologists: leadership, work motivation, and social influence and power.

Leadership. Researchers have made vast strides toward understanding the essential nature of leadership as a real and powerful influence in organizations. Simply defined, **leadership** "occurs when particular individuals exert influence on the goal achievement of others in an organizational context" (Johns & Saks, 2001, p. 272). The approach to understanding the elusive concept of leadership has taken many roads, including trying to identify leadership traits, explore how leaders emerge in groups, and understand the consequences of various leadership behaviors. In addition, several theories of leadership have been proposed. In *path–goal theory,* for example, House (1971) proposed that the leader's responsibility is to show subordinates the path to valued goals. Moreover, the particular style of the leader (e.g., supportive, directive, participative, achievement oriented) will positively or negatively affect subordinates' satisfaction, motivation, and (ultimately) performance depending on both the subordinates' personal characteristics (e.g., needs, skills) and the work environment (e.g., nature of the task, nature of the work group). (For a concise overview of past perspectives and future directions in leadership research, see House & Podsakoff [1994].)

Work motivation. Employee performance is often described as a joint function of ability and motivation, and one of the primary tasks facing managers is to motivate employees to perform to the best of their abilities (Moorhead & Griffin, 1998). There are several theories of work motivation, all of which are concerned with the reasons, other than ability, that some people perform their jobs better than do others. For example, **need theories,** such as Maslow's (1943) *need hierarchy theory,* are concerned with *what* motivates people, that is, the categories of needs that people are motivated to satisfy (e.g., safety needs, esteem needs). **Process theories** of work motivation focus on *how* motivation occurs. One such process theory is *equity theory* (Adams, 1965), which postulates that employees are motivated to achieve a condition of equity or fairness in their dealings with other people and with their organizations. Specifically, employees compare the inputs they invest in their jobs (e.g., work accomplishments, talents, experience) and the outcomes that they receive (e.g., pay, good treatment, enjoyment, status) against the inputs and outcomes of some other relevant person or group. When these ratios or comparisons are equal, employees should feel that fair and equitable exchanges exist with their organizations. However, inequitable comparisons result in a state of dissonance or tension that motivates employees to engage in behavior designed to relieve the tension. Such behavior may involve raising or lowering work efforts to reestablish equity or withdrawing from the situation that is causing inequity. (For an excellent review of recent motivation research, see Ambrose & Kulik [1999].)

Social influence and power. People advance in organizations partly due to their abilities and efforts but also because they have the capacity to gain influence and power over others. **Social influence** refers to *attempts* to affect another person or group in a desired fashion by means of rational persuasion, inspirational appeal, consultation, ingratiation, exchange, personal appeal, and/or pressure. In contrast, **power** is somewhat narrower in scope and involves using "some aspect of a work relationship to force or compel another person to perform a certain action despite resistance" (Riggio, 2000, p. 374). Power may come from a person's position in the organization (legitimate, reward, and coercive power) or from the person himself or herself (expert and referent power). (For an in-depth review of the concepts of power and influence in organizations, see Kramer & Neale [1998].)

As you undoubtedly have begun to appreciate after reading much of this textbook, understanding social behavior necessarily involves understanding both the person and the situation. Behavior in organizations is no different. For example, knowing why a manager acted toward a subordinate in a particular manner requires that you understand something about the manager and something about the particular situation (e.g., pressure the manager was under, history between the manager and the subordinate). Accordingly, this chapter is divided into two main sections. The first section focuses largely on what individuals bring to the organization, that is, aspects of themselves that affect their perceptions, attitudes, and behavior in the work environment. The second section focuses on how social factors influence individual and group work behaviors. Clearly, however, the two areas are not completely distinct; there is much overlap. As you will see, for example, the amount of satisfaction that an individual derives from a job is a function of his or her personal characteristics and both the nature of the work itself and the work environment.

THE INDIVIDUAL IN AN ORGANIZATIONAL CONTEXT

Making Sense of Others in the Work Environment

In the workplace, as in any other social setting, employees may encounter a wide range of people, from friendly to unfriendly coworkers, pleasant to unpleasant customers, and supportive to unsupportive supervisors. How do people make sense out of all this information about the ways in which others act? Social psychologists have devoted a considerable amount of research effort to addressing this question. Social perception (also called social cognition) is the process of understanding or making sense of people. More formally, **social perception** is the process of selecting and interpreting information about how we view others and ourselves. Because information about people is often subjective and open to interpretation (Fiske, 1993), our behavior is based on our perceptions of what reality is rather than on reality itself. People often have very different views about the environment around them. For example, different employees are likely to have more or less positive perceptions of their company's employee recognition and reward program depending on whether or not they like their jobs, their coworkers, and their boss. Thus, the social perception process serves as a screen or filter through which information passes before it has an effect on people. The quality or accuracy of people's perceptions, therefore, has a major impact on their responses to a given situation.

This section of the chapter considers two key components of social perception and how they relate to the work environment: (a) the perceptual biases that occur in people's attempts to build an overall impression of others based on what they know (or think they know) about them as individuals and as members of groups and (b) how people make attributions about why others behave as they do. Although perceptual biases have been discussed in previous chapters, they are considered here as well to underscore their importance in the social work environment.

Perceptual Biases

Considerable effort is required to perceive and interpret what others do. As a result, we develop cognitive shortcuts to make this task less burdensome. These shortcuts are valuable. Not infrequently, they allow us to reduce ambiguity in social situations and to make accurate perceptions rapidly. In this way, our cognitive shortcuts provide us with valid information for making predictions. For example, if a stranger approaches you on a dark street and demands to see your wallet, you are unlikely to interpret this

event as a harmless request to view pictures of your family. However, our cognitive shortcuts are not infallible. The shortcuts we use to be efficient in interpreting and making sense out of our social world can cause **perceptual biases**—errors that distort the perception process—that in turn lead to faulty judgments. When these biases operate, we short-circuit our search for information and instead rely on our assumptions to fill in the missing information. The following two subsections explore two perceptual biases that affect organizational behavior: selective perception and the halo effect. Later, in discussing the ways in which we attempt to determine *why* others behave as they do (causal attribution), two other types of perceptual distortion—the fundamental attribution error and the actor-observer effect—are considered.

Selective perception. Because it is impossible for us to assimilate everything we see, any characteristic that makes a person, an object, or an event stand out will increase the probability that it will be perceived. This tendency toward **selective perception** explains why a manager may reprimand or reward one employee for doing something that goes unnoticed when other employees do it. Because the manager cannot observe everything going on around him or her, the manager engages in selective perception. Several studies have shown that people's experiences and interests can significantly influence what they notice. For example, Waller, Huber, and Glick (1995) asked the question, "Do executives' functional backgrounds influence what they perceive?" Through the use of questionnaires and interviews, the researchers asked 63 top executives from manufacturing, health care, and other service organizations to identify what important changes had occurred in their organizations during an 18-month period. Waller and colleagues predicted that the changes executives perceived to be important (e.g., productivity, acquisition of resources, development of human resources) would be directly related to the proportions of time they had spent in various business functions such as finance, marketing, personnel, production, and sales. This is indeed what they found.

But how does selectivity work as a shortcut in judging other people? Because we cannot assimilate all that we observe, it is important to reduce the amount of information we have to process. So, we take in bits and pieces selectively chosen and organized around our **schemas,** that is, the mental structures that people use to organize their knowledge about the social world around themes or subjects (Kunda, 1999). For example, if you are led to believe that a new coworker is highly capable and industrious, you will tend to notice each of his or her accomplishments. However, if you expect that the new employee is somewhat lacking in ability and motivation, you will more likely take note of his or her failures. Thus, although selective perception may allow us to get a "quick fix" on others, there is the attendant risk of seeing only what we want or expect to see, thereby drawing unwarranted conclusions from an ambiguous situation (DePaulo, Kenny, Hoover, Webb, & Oliver, 1987).

Halo effect. A **halo effect** operates when we draw a general impression of an individual on the basis of a single characteristic such as intelligence, sociability, or appearance (Nisbett & Wilson, 1977). Solomon Asch conducted an early demonstration of the halo effect. Asch (1946) gave participants a list of traits and asked them to evaluate the person to whom those traits applied. When a list of traits such as "intelligent," "skillful," "practical," "industrious," "determined," and "warm" was used, the person was judged to be wise, humorous, popular, and imaginative. When "cold" was substituted for "warm," a completely different set of perceptions was obtained. Clearly, the participants allowed a single trait to influence their overall impressions of the person being judged.

In the work setting, the halo effect is most likely to show up in a supervisor's appraisal of a subordinate's job performance. In fact, the halo effect is probably the most common bias in performance appraisal (Lowenberg & Conrad, 1998). Think about what happens when a supervisor evaluates the performance of a subordinate. The supervisor may give prominence to a single characteristic of the employee, such as enthusiasm, and allow the entire evaluation to be colored by how he or she judges the employee on that one characteristic. Even though the employee may lack the requisite knowledge or ability to perform the job successfully, if the employee's work shows enthusiasm, the supervisor may very well give him or her a higher performance rating than is justified by knowledge and ability. Murphy and Anhalt (1992) suggested that the halo bias is not necessarily a general characteristic of supervisor ratings. Instead, they showed that the halo effect is dependent on specific features of the rating situation such as the amount of contact the supervisor has had with the employee and the occurrence of some significant performance problem.

A powerful factor that can create a halo is the **similar-to-me** effect. This effect occurs when people perceive others who are like themselves more favorably than they do others who are dissimilar. This potential source of bias was demonstrated by Pulakos and Wexley (1983), who found that when supervisors evaluate employees, the more similar the parties are, the higher the ratings the supervisors give. However, Turban and Jones (1988) provided evidence of an alternative explanation for this effect in the work environment. They suggested that perceived similarity may result in more confidence and trust between the supervisor and the employee. This could lead to a more positive and informed working relationship, which in turn would lead to deeper insights (rather than bias). Such insights could contribute to more accurate, and sometimes more favorable, performance appraisals. Nevertheless, it should be obvious that the similar-to-me effect could potentially have significant negative implications in an increasingly culturally diverse workplace where other employees are bound to be different.

The Attribution Process

In our interactions with others, we often want to know *why* they behave or perform the ways in which they do. For example, you might notice that a new employee has been putting in extra hours at work. You wonder whether the new employee is simply behaving in a way that most people would in starting a new job or whether he or she is a particularly conscientious and hard-working person. In other words, you want to know what *causes* the

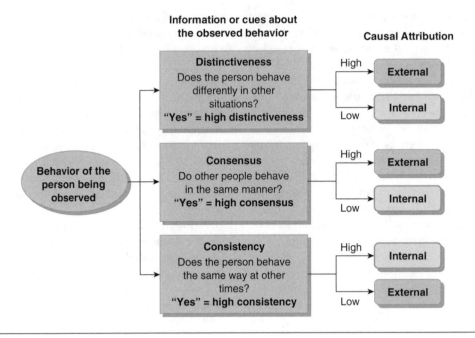

Figure 11.1   Model of the Attribution Process

SOURCE: Adapted from Robbins and Langton (2001). Reprinted with permission by Pearson Education Canada, Inc.

new employee's behavior. The process of assigning a cause to a behavior is called the **attribution process.**

Harold Kelley, a social psychologist, developed a theory of attribution that focused on how people decide whether the cause of a behavior is external or internal. According to Kelley's (1973) **covariation model,** when we observe the behavior or performance of another person, we consider whether the individual is responsible for the behavior (internal cause) or whether something outside the individual caused the behavior (external cause). When we believe that behavior is *internally* caused, we view it as under the personal control of the individual—the result of his or her personality, values, and ability. *Externally* caused behavior is viewed as resulting from factors beyond the control of the person—situational factors such as the physical setting, task difficulty, and the presence and behavior of other people. As depicted in Figure 11.1, the covariation model suggests that, in trying to explain the reason(s) why a person engages in a particular behavior or performs at a certain level, people rely on three types of information:

- *Distinctiveness.* Does the person engage in the behavior in many types of situations, or is it distinctive to one type of situation? If the person behaves the same way in other situations, distinctiveness is low; if he or she behaves differently, distinctiveness is high.
- *Consensus.* Do most people engage in this behavior, or is it unique to this person? If others behave similarly, consensus is high; if they do not, consensus is low.
- *Consistency.* Does the person engage in the behavior regularly and consistently? If the person acts the same way at other times, consistency is high; if he or she does not, consistency is low.

Notice in Figure 11.1 that, depending on how we perceive these three types of information, we are likely to make either an external attribution or an internal attribution. We are likely to conclude that this person's behavior stemmed from *external* causes if we know that (a) this person does not act in the same manner in different types of situations (high distinctiveness), (b) other people also act like this person in this situation (high consensus), and (c) this person does not behave in the same manner at other times (low consistency). In contrast, we will probably conclude that this person's behavior stemmed from *internal* causes if we know that (a) this person acts in the same manner in other situations (low distinctiveness), (b) other people do not act like this person (low consensus), and (c) this person behaves in the same manner in similar situations at other times (high consistency).

To illustrate, suppose that you are the supervisor of an employee who performs well across a variety of tasks (i.e., different situations); in other words, the employee's success on a particular task is not unusual (low distinctiveness). Furthermore, you notice that he or she is the only employee who performs this task well; other employees do not succeed on this task (low consensus). Finally, you observe that the employee performs this task well at different times (high consistency). Given these observations, you are likely to attribute the employee's successful performance to internal factors such as ability and effort. Now imagine another employee who is successful on one particular task but not on others (high distinctiveness), where other employees also succeed on this task (high consensus) and the employee is not always successful on this type of task (low consistency). Under these circumstances, you are likely to attribute the employee's success on the task to external factors such as the (easy) nature of the task and luck.

Biases in Attribution

One of the more interesting findings from attribution theory is that there are perceptual biases that distort our attributions. Although the covariation model suggests that determining causal attribution is a completely rational process, you probably suspect that people do not always appear to draw conclusions about internal or external causality through a careful and systematic analysis of distinctiveness, consensus, and consistency cues. And you would be correct! In fact, there is substantial evidence that when we judge the behavior of other people, we tend to underestimate the influence of external or situational factors and to overestimate the influence of internal or personal factors (Miller & Lawson, 1989; Ross, 1977). You will recall from

some earlier chapters that this is called the **fundamental attribution error.** This phenomenon stems from the fact that it is usually far easier to explain others' actions in terms of their personal dispositions than to be aware of and recognize the complex pattern of situational factors that may have affected their actions (Gilbert & Malone, 1995).

As you might imagine, this tendency can have a significant impact in organizations to the extent that supervisors assign employees too much blame for their failures and too much credit for their successes. For example, Mitchell and colleagues (e.g., Mitchell & Kalb, 1981; Mitchell & Wood, 1980) investigated factors that influence a supervisor's causal attribution of poor work performance on the part of an employee. Consistent with the fundamental attribution error, they found that supervisors were more likely to attribute an employee's poor performance (e.g., high rate of errors) to internal factors than to external ones regardless of the extent to which other employees performed as poorly. (Note that this finding is inconsistent with the high consensus prediction of the covariation model.) Moreover, the supervisors' reactions to the poor performance were directly related, in a predictable manner, to their attributions such that the more internal the attribution, the more likely they were to recommend disciplinary action. Interestingly, Struthers, Weiner, and Allred (1998) reported that supervisors are likely to put more weight on effort than on ability in appraising employee performance. That is, if a supervisor believes that a particularly high level of performance is the result of great effort on the part of a worker, that worker will receive a more positive performance appraisal than if his or her high level of performance is perceived as resulting from ability or talent. Similarly, a performance failure attributed to a lack of sufficient effort will be judged more harshly than will a failure attributed to lack of ability.

Finally, an interesting twist on the fundamental attribution error is that we judge the causes of our own behavior differently than we judge the causes of others' behavior. This bias in causal attribution is called the **actor–observer difference** (Jones & Nisbett, 1972). It refers to the fact that whereas we tend to see others' behavior as being caused by (internal) dispositional factors, we are more likely to see our own behavior as resulting from (external) situational factors. Thus, the same behavior can trigger internal attributions in the observer of the action and external attributions in the actor, that is, the person performing the action. For example, in the case of a supervisor (observer) evaluating the performance of an employee (actor), the supervisor has a tendency to attribute the level of performance to personal characteristics of the employee such as ability, effort, and personality. That is, the supervisor tends to believe that the employee's performance is due primarily to his or her personal qualities and tends to deemphasize the role that situational factors might have played in the performance outcome. Thus, in some situations, the supervisor may blame the employee for poor performance when the failure was actually due to circumstances beyond the employee's control. On the other hand, the employee (actor) is likely to overemphasize situational factors and, in cases of failure, will try to lay the blame elsewhere, for example, by faulting the working conditions, coworkers, or even the supervisor. The actor–observer bias not only leads to inaccurate perceptions of work performance but also is likely one of the main reasons why supervisors and employees frequently disagree when it comes to performance appraisals. There is some evidence to indicate that this situation may be more frustrating for employees than for supervisors. Krueger, Ham, and Linford (1996) found that employees (actors), but not supervisors (observers), were aware of the actor–observer bias in specific rating situations, suggesting that employees may realize that supervisors are being biased but might not be able to make their supervisors aware of it.

FOCUS ON RESEARCH

In a laboratory experiment, Pfeffer, Cialdini, Hanna, and Knopoff (1998) investigated the extent to which the amount of supervision provided by a manager would influence his or her subsequent evaluation of both the quality of a subordinate's work and the subordinate's ability. M.B.A. students were invited to participate in a study of "how differing management styles and levels of information affect the quality of a finished work product." Participants arrived at the laboratory in pairs and were separated into individual rooms, where they were told that they would be chosen randomly to assume the role of either a manager or a worker in an advertising agency. Supposedly, the agency had been asked by a wristwatch manufacturing company to design a print ad for a new watch that the company was marketing. Through a bogus draw, each participant was assigned the role of manager and informed that the participant in the other room would take the role of a worker who had been assigned by the agency to design the ad. Participants were told that their role was to supervise the worker's creation of the advertisement and to subsequently evaluate its quality and the ability of the worker. However, "because of other demands on their time," the opportunity to interact with the worker would be limited. This allowed the researchers to set the stage for the manipulation of the amount of supervision provided.

In the *low-supervision* condition, participants were told that they would have no opportunity to interact with or provide feedback to the worker until the ad was completed. In this condition, after the worker supposedly had completed the ad, participants evaluated both the quality of the ad and the ability of the worker. In the *high-supervision* condition, participants were told that they could review the first draft of the ad and give written feedback (delivered by the experimenter) to the worker prior to completion of the final product using a standardized checklist of suggestions (e.g., provide pricing information). Similar to the low-supervision condition, after the worker completed the ad, the participants evaluated both the ad and the worker. The ad was exactly the same for all participants in both supervision conditions. Participants' evaluations of the final ad were based on four 7-point scales ranging from 1 (*poor*) to 7 (*outstanding*) on which they rated its (a) creativity and originality, (b) interest level, (c) demonstrated "business sense," and (d) overall quality. The ratings on these four items were combined to form an overall evaluation index. The worker's ability to develop marketing concepts was rated by participants on a 7-point scale ranging from 1 (*very low*) to 7 (*very high*).

Did the amount of supervision provided affect participants' evaluations of the ad and the worker? Yes. In fact, the results were quite dramatic. On average, participants gave the ad a rating of 5.0 in the high-supervision condition and only 3.5 in the low-supervision condition. (Remember, it was the same ad in both conditions.) In addition, participants rated the worker's ability higher in the high-supervision condition (mean approximately 5.5) than in the low-supervision condition (mean approximately 4.2). Thus, when participants played a more active role in supervising the work, they evaluated the quality of the exact same product *and* the ability of the worker substantially higher than when they played a more passive role—a striking instance of perceptual bias.

Pfeffer and colleagues (1998) concluded that as managers become more involved in the supervision of a subordinate's work, their evaluation of that work is likely to become much more favorable. As the researchers noted, "Self-aggrandizing perceptions of this sort are perhaps not surprising given extensive evidence of self-enhancement tendencies in much of human functioning" (p. 319). They suggested that the tendency for supervisors to evaluate the quality of work they were involved in overseeing more positively helps to explain why they may be reluctant to empower employees with greater autonomy and decision-making authority. On the positive side (at least for employees), managers who supervise in a more controlling fashion might not assume all of the credit for themselves. It appears that managers also assign greater credit to subordinates' abilities as their estimates of work product quality rise.

Job Satisfaction: Antecedents and Consequences

People in organizations form attitudes about many different things, including their amounts of pay, their opportunities for promotion, their coworkers, their bosses, and (of course) *their jobs*. These feelings about one's job are known as job satisfaction. **Job satisfaction** can be defined as a person's attitude toward his or her overall job as well as toward various aspects of the job; it is a predisposition to respond to one's work environment in a favorable or unfavorable manner (Steers & Porter, 1991).

Whether or not you are aware of it now, job satisfaction will be important to you. In fact, it may very well underlie the reason you are in college, that is, to maximize the likelihood that you will have the knowledge, skills, and abilities to obtain the kind of job you want when you graduate. If it seems that you have been in school forever, think about how long you are likely to work over the course of your life—8 hours a day, 5 days a week until approximately 65 years of age. Needless to say, you will be much happier if you are satisfied with the job(s) you have during that time.

The two most widely used approaches in measuring job satisfaction are the global approach and the facet approach. The **global** approach considers overall job satisfaction and simply asks an employee to respond to one general question such as the following: "All things considered, how satisfied are you with your job?" Answers usually are provided on a 5-point rating scale ranging from *highly satisfied* to *highly dissatisfied*. The **facet approach** is more sophisticated. In this approach, job satisfaction is considered to be composed of feelings and attitudes about a number of different key aspects, or facets, of the job. Typical facets that would be included are the nature of the work itself, quality of supervision, pay, fringe benefits, promotion opportunities, job conditions, and relations with other people such as supervisors and coworkers. These facets are rated on a standardized scale and then summed to create an overall job satisfaction score (e.g., Price & Mueller, 1986). Much of the research on job satisfaction uses the facet approach in its measurement.

This section discusses two areas of job satisfaction that have captured the attention of researchers during the past several decades: (a) the factors that determine job satisfaction and (b) the effects of job satisfaction on both individual and organizational outcomes. Unfortunately, it is only able to scratch the surface of this fascinating and important topic because research studies on job satisfaction number in the thousands (Hulin & Judge, 2003) and, given

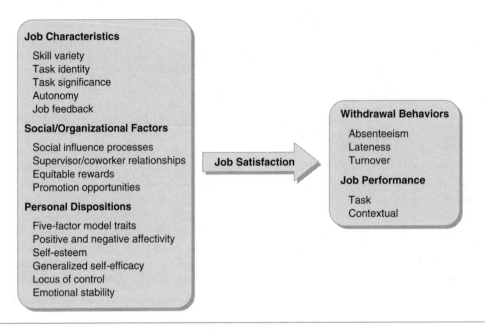

Figure 11.2   Antecedents and Consequences of Job Satisfaction

SOURCE: Adapted from Levy (2003) with permission from Houghton Mifflin Company.

recent theoretical and empirical developments in the area, are likely to continue for some time to come.

Determinants of Job Satisfaction

Now that we know a little about what job satisfaction is and how it is measured, let us consider the determinants of job satisfaction. In other words, what "causes" people to like their jobs and, perhaps more interesting, why do some people have different attitudes toward the same job in the same organization? These questions have been addressed in hundreds of empirical studies and several theoretical models such as Thibaut and Kelley's (1959) *comparison level model of satisfaction,* Hackman and Oldham's (1976) *job characteristics model,* and Salancik and Pfeffer's (1978) *social information processing model.*

With regard to empirical work, one early review of the literature indicated that the most important factors contributing to job satisfaction reflect characteristics of the job and work environment—mentally challenging work, equitable rewards, supportive working conditions, and

supportive colleagues (Locke, 1976). More recent research has revealed that personal dispositions also play a major role in determining how satisfied people are likely to be with their jobs (Ilies & Judge, 2003). A summary of some of these factors is shown in Figure 11.2. The left side of the figure shows those factors considered to be related to the extent to which a person will be satisfied with his or her job: the perceived characteristics of the job, the social work environment, and the person's personal characteristics. The right side of the figure shows the consequences or outcomes of job satisfaction (discussed later). Because of space limitations, only a few of the antecedents of job satisfaction are considered: (a) the core characteristics of a job as proposed by Hackman and Oldham's (1976) job characteristics model, (b) the role of the social context as proposed by Salancik and Pfeffer's (1978) social information processing model, and (c) personal dispositions.

Job characteristics. **Job characteristics** refer to the content and nature of job tasks themselves. Five such core characteristics, listed in Figure 11.2, are central to Hackman and

Oldham's (1976) influential job characteristics model, which is based on the premise that workers can be motivated by the intrinsic nature of job tasks. Considerable empirical support exists for the relationship between the five job characteristics and job satisfaction. Based on a meta-analysis, Fried and Ferris (1987) estimated that the mean correlations between the five job characteristics and global job satisfaction are as follows:

- *Skill variety* (degree to which job allows employees to perform different tasks): +.29
- *Task identity* (degree to which one can see one's work from beginning to end): +.20
- *Task significance* (degree to which one's work is seen as important and significant): +.26
- *Autonomy* (degree to which one has control over how to conduct one's job): +.34
- *Job feedback* (degree to which the work itself provides feedback concerning one's effectiveness): +.29

The preceding relationships between job characteristics and job satisfaction are consistent with the more general finding that, among the major job satisfaction facets (pay, promotion opportunities, coworkers, supervision, and the work itself), satisfaction with the work itself typically emerges as the most important facet for overall job satisfaction (e.g., Rentsch & Steel, 1992). Not surprisingly, most of us want our work to be personally interesting and meaningful for it to be satisfying. Moreover, according to Hackman and Oldham (1976), the relationship between challenging job characteristics and job satisfaction should be even stronger for those employees with high **growth need strength** (GNS), defined as employees' receptiveness to challenging job characteristics, that is, the extent to which they want their jobs to contribute to their personal growth and development. This appears to be the case. Frye (1996) reported average correlations between job characteristics and job satisfaction of .68 for high-GNS employees and .38 for low-GNS employees.

Before leaving our discussion of job characteristics as potential determinants of job satisfaction, a few cautionary notes are appropriate. One limitation of most studies that have investigated the role of job characteristics in job satisfaction is that job characteristics were assessed by means of self-report questionnaires. That is, the employees complete a job satisfaction measure as well as a measure describing the characteristics of their job, rating it on skill variety, autonomy, and so forth. As discussed in Chapter 3, merely demonstrating that variables are correlated does not mean that one variable necessarily causes the other variable. Although it might be intuitively appealing to conclude that more interesting and meaningful jobs are likely to result in higher job satisfaction, it could also be the case that people who like their jobs are inclined to describe them more favorably than are people who are dissatisfied with their jobs. Thus, job satisfaction might be the cause, rather than the consequence, of job characteristics as rated by workers on questionnaires. Or, the relationship between perceptions of job characteristics and job satisfaction might be bidirectional in that each influences the other (James & Tetrick, 1986).

Social/Organizational factors. As shown in Figure 11.2, a variety of social and organizational factors play an important role in determining the extent to which employees are satisfied with their jobs. For example, the nature of an employee's relationships with supervisors and coworkers and the extent to which one perceives his or her work rewards (e.g., pay, promotions, working hours) to be equitable in comparison with the rewards obtained by other employees have a significant impact on the employee's feelings of job satisfaction.

Social influence processes also affect one's level of job satisfaction. For example, the **social information processing** model of job satisfaction (Salancik & Pfeffer, 1978) is based on the premise that people "adapt attitudes, behavior, and beliefs to their social context and to the reality of their own past and present behavior and situation" (p. 226). In other words, employees develop their levels of job satisfaction based on the information available to them, including the immediate social environment. According to Salancik and Pfeffer, the social environment provides cues that individuals use to construct and interpret the nature of their jobs. One such process involves employees observing the levels of motivation and satisfaction of other employees and then modeling those levels. This modeling occurs because jobs are often complex and ambiguous stimuli and employees might be uncertain about how to react to the multidimensional components of their jobs (e.g., job characteristics, supervisors, pay). Knowledge of how an employee's coworkers evaluate their jobs gives the employee some idea as to how to react. For example, if you are continually exposed to negative statements from your coworkers about their lack of decision-making authority, you too may come to perceive your job as lacking in such autonomy and, therefore, as less satisfying. Conversely, if your coworkers talk positively, you are likely to be influenced by these positive evaluations and, thus, to be more satisfied with your job.

In sum, the job characteristics model holds that job satisfaction is determined largely by objective features of the job such as the variety of skills required to perform the work and the importance of the work performed. On the other hand, the social information processing model posits that job satisfaction is based on the effects of social influence in the work environment. As noted previously, there is considerable empirical (albeit correlational) support for the job characteristics model. In general, research also has supported the social information processing model. For example, in a laboratory experiment, Mirolli, Henderson, and Hills (1998) found that participants rated a task as more enjoyable when they were exposed to a confederate's positive comments about the task than when they were exposed to a confederate's negative comments about the task. In a field study of 66 civilian employees at a U.S. military base, Pollock, Whitbred, and Contractor (2000) reported that information from the social environment had a significant effect on individuals' job satisfaction. Thus, both the social environment and job characteristics seem to be important factors in the extent to which people are satisfied with their jobs. So too are personal dispositions, which are discussed next.

Personal dispositions. Few studies prior to the mid-1980s focused on individual differences, much less personality, as sources of job satisfaction (Hulin & Judge, 2003). Since that time,

however, two seminal studies by Staw, Bell, and Clausen (1986) and Arvey, Bouchard, Segal, and Abraham (1989) have provided considerable impetus to investigations of the role of dispositional factors as determinants of job satisfaction. Staw and colleagues (1986) made use of data from the Intergenerational Studies initiated at the University of California, Berkeley, during the 1920s. Beginning in adolescence, participants were assessed on a number of characteristics using interviews and questionnaires several times during their lives. Scores on 17 of the characteristics were combined into a measure of affective disposition (e.g., "cheerful," "warm," "negative"). Staw and colleagues reported striking results showing that positive affective disposition assessed as young as early adolescence was significantly correlated (.34) with overall job satisfaction assessed at 54 to 62 years of age.

In an even more provocative study, Arvey and colleagues (1989) found significant similarity in job satisfaction levels of 34 pairs of identical twins reared apart from early childhood (i.e., each pair was identical in genetic makeup but lived in different environments). The intraclass correlation between the twins' ratings of job satisfaction was .31, meaning that if one person tended to be satisfied with his or her job, so did the person's identical twin. It appears that individuals are born with characteristics that predispose them to be more or less satisfied with their work. In the words of Hulin and Judge (2003), "Heritability of job satisfaction is very likely indirect, operating through heritability in personality or other dispositions" (p. 263). However, as noted by Ilies and Judge (2003), neither Staw and colleagues' (1986) study nor Arvey and colleagues' (1989) study documented any direct evidence for the relationship between specific personality traits and job satisfaction.

Subsequent research has attempted to address this issue, focusing on a variety of personality traits, including those that are central to the *five-factor model* of personality (e.g., neuroticism), *core self-evaluation traits* (e.g., self-esteem), *positive affectivity* (the tendency to experience enthusiasm, confidence, cheerfulness, etc.), and *negative affectivity* (the tendency to experience anxiety, hostility, anger, etc.). Various meta-analyses of the findings of these

Table 11.1   Mean Estimates of the Relationship Between Personality and Job Satisfaction

Personality Trait (and meta-analysis source)	Mean Corrected Correlation
Five-factor model traits (Judge, Heller, & Mount, 2002)	
Neuroticism	−.29
Extraversion	.25
Openness to experience	.02
Agreeableness	.17
Conscientiousness	.26
Core self-evaluation traits (Judge & Bono, 2001)	
Self-esteem	.26
Generalized self-efficacy	.45
Locus of control	.32
Emotional stability	.24
Positive and negative affectivity (Connolly & Viswesvaran, 2000)	
Positive affectivity	.49
Negative affectivity	−.33

SOURCE: Adapted from Hulin and Judge (2003). This material is used by permission of John Wiley & Sons Inc.

studies have been conducted, and the results (summarized in Hulin and Judge, 2003) are shown in Table 11.1. Generalized self-efficacy and positive and negative affectivity appear to be the most highly correlated with job satisfaction. Thus, the more people believe in their own competence and effectiveness, and the more they are disposed toward positive emotions rather than negative emotions, the more likely they are to be satisfied with their jobs.

Although research investigating the extent to which individual differences in personality influence job satisfaction is likely to continue with fervor, it is important not to minimize the impact of environmental and social factors (e.g., job characteristics, social influence processes) on job satisfaction.

In this regard, **person–job fit** models posit that job satisfaction results from complex interactions between personal dispositions and environmental (job) characteristics (Hulin & Judge, 2003). Researchers pursuing this approach argue that a person's job satisfaction will be higher to the extent that there is a good match between his or her personal characteristics and the nature of the job (Kristoff, 1996). For example, the empirical evidence is fairly consistent in showing that the closer the correspondence between what people say they *want* in their jobs (e.g., autonomy) and what they say

they *have* in their jobs, the greater their job satisfaction (Edwards, 1991).

Consequences of Job Satisfaction

What consequences may be expected from workers who are satisfied or dissatisfied with their jobs? This question has generated a vast amount of research during the past several decades, with particular attention being given to how job satisfaction affects job performance. In addition, the effects of job satisfaction on many other important organizational and personal outcomes have been well documented. Such outcomes include employee withdrawal behaviors (e.g., absenteeism, turnover), counterproductive behaviors (e.g., theft, sabotage, interpersonal violence), and employee well-being (e.g., physical and mental health, general life satisfaction). This subsection briefly reviews the research on employee withdrawal behaviors and then turns its attention to the relationship between job satisfaction and job performance. It concludes with a discussion of the causal nature of this relationship.

Employee withdrawal behaviors. As you might expect, people who dislike their jobs are more likely to avoid or *withdraw* from them, either in the form of absenteeism (i.e., missing work) or in the form of voluntary turnover (i.e., quitting).

Absenteeism is an expensive behavior in North America. According to one estimate (Lu, 1999), sick pay, lost productivity, and overstaffing to compensate for absentee workers annually cost American and Canadian organizations up to $46 billion and $10 billion, respectively. Obviously, not all absenteeism can be attributed to job dissatisfaction. People miss work for many unavoidable reasons, including illness, family problems, and weather conditions. Nevertheless, several researchers have investigated the relationship between absenteeism and job satisfaction. In an early review of the literature, Porter and Steers (1973) concluded that both voluntary turnover and absenteeism increase as job satisfaction decreases. But these relationships are not especially strong. For example, in a meta-analytic review of research findings pertaining to absenteeism, Hackett and Guion (1985) reported an average correlation of only –.09 between absenteeism and job satisfaction. They also found that absenteeism was more closely related to some facets of job satisfaction than to others, particularly satisfaction with the nature of the work itself.

Voluntary turnover is also costly to organizations. By the time an employee is recruited, hired, trained, and evaluated, an organization has invested a considerable amount of time and money in that individual. As noted by Levy (2003), when an employee quits, not only is the initial investment in the person lost, but the organization also must spend additional money in a new cycle of recruitment, selection, and training. There are many factors that contribute to turnover such as age, level of education, marital status, and number of dependent children (Cotton & Tuttle, 1986). Employees who are young, are well educated, and do not have families to support are more mobile and, therefore, more likely to seek out alternative employment opportunities. In addition to perceived ease of movement, researchers also have looked at the role that job satisfaction plays in decisions to leave an organization. In general, research indicates a moderately strong relationship between job satisfaction and turnover, with less satisfied workers being more likely to quit (e.g., Steel & Ovalle, 1984).

In sum, the empirical evidence suggests that although job satisfaction is related to various types of employee withdrawal behavior, it is more predictive of turnover propensity than of absence propensity. Needless to say, not all employees who dislike their jobs quit, so this begs the question: Do those employees who are dissatisfied and stay on the job perform more poorly? The next subsection tries to answer this question.

Performance. As noted by Judge, Thoresen, Bono, and Patton (2001), the investigation of the relationship between job performance and job satisfaction is one of the most venerable research traditions in applied psychology. Since the Hawthorne studies of the 1920s and 1930s, researchers and managers alike have been captivated by the intuitively appealing notion that "a happy worker is a productive worker." Until recently, however, this notion received little empirical support. For example, in an influential meta-analytic review of the research literature, Iaffaldano and Muchinsky (1985) concluded that job performance is, at best, only weakly related to job satisfaction. Their estimated correlation of .17 between satisfaction and performance was based on the average of the correlations between specific job satisfaction facets (e.g., pay, coworkers, promotion opportunities) and job performance.

Recently, the Iaffaldano and Muchinsky (1985) meta-analysis has been criticized on both statistical and conceptual grounds (Judge et al., 2001). The statistical flaws are beyond the scope of our current purpose, so only the latter is addressed here. Judge and colleagues (2001) argued that averaging the correlations between job performance and specific *facets of job satisfaction* is conceptually different from the relationship between performance and *overall job satisfaction.* Accordingly, they suggested that one must create a composite of the job satisfaction facets as opposed to averaging the individual correlations between each facet and job performance. Using this approach in their own meta-analysis, Judge and colleagues estimated the corrected correlation between job satisfaction and job performance to be .30, nearly twice as high as the earlier estimate reported by Iaffaldano and Muchinsky (1985).

Another aspect of performance is organizational citizenship behavior. As initially defined

Table 11.2   Models of the Relationship Between Job Satisfaction and Job Performance

Model	Description
1	Job satisfaction causes performance (i.e., attitudes lead to behavior)
2	Job performance causes job satisfaction (i.e., attitudes follow behavior)
3	Job satisfaction and job performance are reciprocally related (i.e., attitudes lead to behavior and, in turn, are changed by behavior)
4	Job satisfaction and job performance are only spuriously related (i.e., the satisfaction–performance relationship is due to the relationship of each of these variables to one or more unmeasured variables)
5	The job satisfaction–job performance relationship is moderated by other variables (i.e., the relationship exists only to the extent that other factors are present, e.g., job performance affects job satisfaction if it leads to important job rewards such as pay)

by Organ (1988), **organizational citizenship behavior** refers to employee behavior that is "discretionary, not directly or explicitly recognized by the formal reward system, and that in the aggregate promotes the effective functioning of the organization" (p. 4). Organizational citizenship behavior can be distinguished from specified job requirements, that is, what an employee must do according to his or her job description. For example, organizational citizenship behavior involves performance behaviors such as voluntarily assisting coworkers, alerting others to work-related problems, conscientiously performing one's own work (e.g., not wasting organizational resources, involving oneself in the life of the organization such as going to meetings and keeping abreast of the larger issues affecting the organization), and tolerating the inevitable inconveniences and impositions of work without complaint. It may have occurred to you that job satisfaction must surely have some impact on the extent to which an employee will "go above and beyond the call of duty" to get the job done. If so, you are right.

In fact, research has shown that the more people are satisfied with their jobs, the more good citizenship contributions they tend to make (Konovsky & Organ, 1996). However, the relationship appears to be moderated by perceptions of fairness. When fairness is controlled, job satisfaction is unrelated to organizational citizenship behavior (e.g., Moorman, 1991). In other words, when employees perceive organizational processes and outcomes to be fair, they are more likely to trust their employers. And when employees trust their employers, they are more willing to engage in behaviors that go beyond their formal job requirements (Organ, 1990).

The question of whether satisfaction "causes" performance. Although you know by now that correlation does not imply a causal relationship between two related variables, some people might assume that job satisfaction "causes" job performance. After all, as mentioned previously, for many years both managers and social scientists assumed that a happy worker was a productive worker, reflecting the belief that satisfaction causes performance. On the surface, the notion that people who are satisfied with their jobs are subsequently likely to expend greater effort on their jobs seems logical. But a simple "satisfaction produces performance" relationship might not necessarily be the case. There are other possibilities. Judge and colleagues (2001) reviewed seven different theoretical models that have been used to describe the satisfaction–performance relationship. A simplified description of five of the models is shown in Table 11.2. Because of space limitations, only the first two models are considered here. This will give you at least a taste of the theoretical complexity surrounding this area of inquiry.

Model 1, often attributed to the human relations movement, represents the traditional perspective that people who like their jobs work harder and, therefore, perform better. As noted by Judge and colleagues (2001), this model is grounded in the broader stream of social psychology attitude research in which researchers have assumed that attitudes (e.g., job satisfaction) have direct implications for behavior. For example, Eagly and Chaiken (1993) stated that, depending on whether we evaluate an object favorably or unfavorably, we will tend to engage in behaviors that foster/support it or hinder/oppose it, respectively. Within this attitude–behavior perspective, it follows that if a person evaluates his or her job favorably (i.e., has high job satisfaction), the person will put in greater effort to perform well. Obviously, the converse also is true. Few studies have actually hypothesized a unidirectional "satisfaction causes performance" relationship, and of those that have the results are inconclusive (Judge et al., 2001).

In Model 2, the implied causal relationship between satisfaction and performance is reversed. Performance is deemed to cause satisfaction in the sense that people who perform well are likely to benefit from that performance, and those benefits could enhance satisfaction. In this regard, Lawler and Porter (1967) suggested that performance leads to job satisfaction through the provision of intrinsic and extrinsic rewards. For example, if effective job performance leads to extrinsic rewards (e.g., an increase in pay, a promotion) or intrinsic rewards (e.g., a sense of accomplishment), and these rewards are perceived as fair, receiving these rewards leads to job satisfaction. Although several studies have tested this model, the results are mixed, with some claiming a significant "performance causes satisfaction" relationship (e.g., Brown, Cron, & Leigh, 1993) and others showing no causal relationship (e.g., Brown & Peterson, 1994).

In concluding this section, we should note that Judge and colleagues (2001), following their extensive review of the literature, proposed an integrative model of the relationship between job satisfaction and job performance because they believed that several of the models are best considered in a unified framework. In their integrative model, Judge and colleagues suggested that there likely is a bidirectional causal relationship between satisfaction and performance (i.e., Models 1, 2, and 3 in Table 11.2). However, the relationship could be moderated by other variables such as personality (i.e., Model 5). For example, Mount, Harter, Barrick, and Colbert (2000) found that job satisfaction was more strongly related to job performance for less conscientious employees than for conscientious employees. Presumably, conscientious employees who are dissatisfied are less willing to reduce their levels of performance (i.e., because they are still conscientious even though they are not happy with their jobs). In addition, Judge and colleagues (2001) suggested that the causal effects between satisfaction and performance may be mediated by other variables such as positive affect. Thus, job satisfaction might lead to better job performance because employees who like their jobs are more likely to be in good moods at work, and this in turn facilitates job performance through higher levels of motivation (Isen & Baron, 1991).

CULTURE CAPSULE: JOB SATISFACTION ACROSS CULTURES

Many studies conducted in North America have shown that job characteristics are related to job satisfaction. As with research in all areas of psychology, we cannot be certain that the results of studies done with workers in Western societies will generalize to countries with very different cultures. Pearson and Chong (1997) investigated the differential effects of various predictors of job satisfaction in a sample of 286 nurses working in a Malaysian public health organization. Because of the Chinese values and collectivistic culture of Malaysia, the researchers hypothesized that Malaysians would be more sensitive to collectivist-related *interpersonal aspects* of work, such as feedback from others and dealing with others, than to individualist-related *job characteristics,* such as skill variety, task identity, task significance, autonomy, and job feedback. In turn, Pearson and Chong predicted that the collectivist-related aspects of work would be more highly correlated with job satisfaction than would the individualist-related factors.

As expected, there were no significant correlations between any of the five job characteristics and job satisfaction (the correlations ranged from –.09 to +.07). Thus, job content had a negligible impact on the extent to which the Malaysian nurses were satisfied with their jobs, a finding that is considerably different from findings typically reported in North American studies. However, the informational attributes of feedback from others (measured by the appropriate section of Hackman & Oldham's [1980] Job Diagnostic Survey) had a substantial influence on the nurses' job satisfaction; the correlation was .40. Pearson and Chong (1997) explained these results as reflecting the collectivistic culture of the Malaysians, whereby individuals place great value on the relationship-oriented components of their work environment, enabling the development of harmonious relations with supervisors and coworkers. This study clearly indicates that we must be cautious in assuming that research findings in Western organizations can be replicated in the organizations of other cultures.

INTERPERSONAL PROCESSES IN ORGANIZATIONS

Communication

Organizations can range in size from small, two-person "mom and pop" corner stores to large transnational companies with tens of thousands of employees. Regardless of their size, to carry out work within and across these organizations, employees, managers, and executives need to communicate with each other regularly. In fact, managers spend approximately 80% of their time communicating (Trevino, Daft, & Lengel, 1990). By definition, **communication** involves social behavior, that is, two or more people interacting with each other and transmitting information. However, the precise nature of this behavior is not as simple as it may appear. There are a number of subtle activities involved in the act of communicating. Some of them might not be immediately apparent but are nonetheless essential for conveying information effectively. To better understand the significance of each of these activities, let us consider a simple model of the communication process.

A Model of Communication

As depicted in Figure 11.3, when communication occurs, a **message** is conveyed. A message refers to the verbal and nonverbal information that is imparted from one party to another. This message must be conveyed by way of a **channel,** which refers to the medium through which the message is transmitted (e.g., computer cables, telephone wires, air molecules in the case of face-to-face communication). During this process, the **sender** refers to the individual who conveys the message. Note that before the sender can transmit a message, that message must be **encoded,** constructed from the sender's thoughts, and transformed into a communicable form. After being transmitted, the message is then **decoded** (perceived and interpreted) by a **receiver.** Communication is, of course, not a one-way process. The receiver may decide to offer feedback to the sender. When this occurs, the receiver becomes the sender and the entire process is reversed.

You probably can imagine ways in which the communication process can break down at any point along this chain. In fact, you may remember the delight you experienced noticing these breakdowns occurring when playing the "broken telephone" game as a child. As you may recall, this game involves seating children in a line and having the first child whisper a short made-up story into his or her neighbor's ear. Each successive child whispers the "same" story to his or her neighbor farther down the line until the end of the line is reached. The last child then tells his or her version of the story, and the child who first made it up notes whether it remained intact by repeating the original story to the group. Invariably, it is found that the story

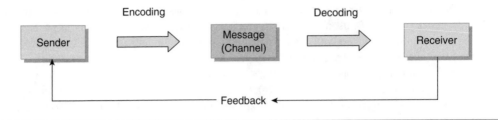

Figure 11.3   Communication Process

mutates as it progresses down the line. How should we account for this phenomenon, and what might be some of the implications for communication in small and large organizations?

Perspectives on Communication

With our model of communication in mind, let us consider a few different ways in which organizational communication can be viewed. Krone, Jablin, and Putnam (1987) distinguished among the mechanistic, psychological, and interpretive–symbolic perspectives of communication. (They also discussed a systems interaction perspective that is not elaborated here.) Each of these perspectives involves a different **locus of communication,** that is, the point in the communication process that is the focus of the particular perspective (Fisher, 1978). For example, in the **mechanistic perspective,** the locus of communication is the channel (Figure 11.3) and communication is viewed primarily as a transmission process with a primary focus on the mechanics of sending a message. Because effective transmission is considered central in this perspective, research in this tradition might focus on factors such as the communication skills of managers, including their choice of medium, and on the overall effectiveness of their transmission of information. These skills should be important given the multiple departments and layers of hierarchy that are characteristic of most large organizations.

Research within the mechanistic perspective has provided evidence that communication skills can, in fact, have a number of practical consequences in organizations. For example, Sypher and Zorn (1986) measured the communication skills of employees at a large U.S. insurance company and found that those possessing stronger communication skills tended to occupy higher levels in the corporate hierarchy and tended to be promoted more often. Similarly, Penley, Alexander, Jernigan, and Henwood (1991) found that managers with better developed communication skills outperformed those with less developed skills. Finally, it has been shown that managers who choose to use communication media that match the complexity and ambiguity of the messages they send are rated as higher performers (Trevino et al., 1990). Given the need to clarify objectives, coordinate activities efficiently and effectively, and provide feedback to people in organizations, the results of the preceding studies should not be surprising.

In the **psychological perspective,** the locus of communication is people's conceptual filters (Krone et al., 1987). **Conceptual filters** consist of attitudes, cognitions, and perceptions (Fisher, 1978) that may distort information exchange. The basic idea within this tradition is that, as discussed earlier in the chapter, there is too much information in the environment for people to attend to all of it. As a result, people learn to automatically filter out what they consider to be unnecessary information. This is a form of *selective perception.* A potential problem with filtering information is that what is considered unimportant by one person may be considered important, or even vital, by another person. As a consequence of incongruent conceptual filters among communication partners, breakdowns in communication may occur. The psychological perspective focuses on the way in which conceptual filters affect encoding by the sender and decoding by the receiver.

It is important to recognize not only that conceptual filters limit the information to which people attend but also that psychological processes will tend to make people confident that the particular pieces of information they focus on are important and that the ignored pieces are less important. Consider the breakdowns in communication that could occur between a marketing manager, whose primary focus is sales, and an operations manager, whose primary focus is efficient production. Because these managers focus on different objectives, the conceptual filters they use in thinking about their work will likely be different, and this may produce communication problems that lead to conflict.

An example of research within the psychological perspective is a study conducted by Dunkerley and Robinson (2002). These investigators explored the communication styles of American and British managers working in the United Kingdom. Dunkerley and Robinson found that the style of communication of American managers tends to be direct and task focused, whereas the British managers' style tends to be more circuitous, cautious, and focused on maintaining the work relationship. This may appear to be a simple example of cultural differences, and in fact it is. However, more fundamental than the overt differences in behavior are the underlying differences in conceptual filters that lead these groups to focus on different aspects of their shared interactions. Of particular relevance to our discussion is that managers from each country believed that their own communication style was superior and that the managers from each country tended to denigrate the communication style of the managers from the other country. For example, one American manager commented that "the British approach is inefficient" (p. 399), whereas one British manager thought that "the American approach is simplistic" (p. 402). Both parties' conceptual filters influenced the information they attended to and deemed important.

Given these findings, we might expect that an American manager would be susceptible to filtering out a British colleague's comments about their relationship because the comments are deemed irrelevant. Similarly, we might expect that a British manager might get offended when an American manager curtly makes direct requests. Note that in Dunkerley and Robinson's (2002) study, managers were explicitly asked about their thoughts regarding the communication style of their "foreign" colleagues. However, when people are at work, they typically are not asked to think about these types of issues. Evaluations of other people and other people's ideas occur automatically, and we generally do not notice the effects that our filters may have on our judgments.

The third approach to understanding organizational communication is called the **interpretive symbolic perspective** (Krone et al., 1987). In this perspective, the locus of communication is the shared meaning that develops between or among the parties involved in the act of communicating. Referring back to Figure 11.3, we would say that just like the psychological perspective, the focus of this perspective is on encoding and decoding. However, this time we are not concerned about the biasing effect of filters; instead, we are concerned about the development of categories of thought (i.e., the filters themselves) that allow communication to occur. Consider the following example. If a friend speaks to you about one of your professors, you and your friend need to have a shared understanding of the word "professor" before any effective communication can take place. In fact, you need to have a shared understanding of every word in every sentence. The interpretive symbolic perspective suggests that categories of thought (e.g., "professor") are not objective features of our environment but rather are created by people through a process that is sometimes called **consensual validation,** defined by Weick (1979) as the development of a "common sense" that people agree on because their collective experiences make it seem correct. Consensual validation reduces the level of uncertainty we experience by allowing us to share meaning and by imposing order on a potentially confusing and chaotic environment.

The interpretive symbolic perspective has its roots in the theory of **social constructionism** (Gergen, 1985), which posits that reality is constructed by means of the consensual validation achieved through social interaction. As Edley (2001) noted, we should not make the mistake of believing that there is no reality apart from that which we create socially. We should, nonetheless, recognize that our interpretations of much of that which we experience are influenced by our socially constructed categories. The terms we use to label people (e.g., secretaries vs. executive assistants), situations, and events influence the ways in which we think about them, how we react to them, what we expect from them, and what we consider to be normal and appropriate.

The example of research within the interpretive symbolic tradition considered here involves an observational field study. Bennington, Shetler, and Shaw (2003) analyzed the communication of representatives from three organizations— a waste disposal company, a state regulatory agency, and a community activist organization— who were participating in a public meeting to discuss changes in the waste disposal company's operations. Bennington and colleagues noted that some of the words that the company representatives and community activists used were identical but had different connotations; that is, the representatives did not create shared meaning among the three groups. As a result, the representatives of the three organizations found it difficult to effectively explain their respective points of view to each other, and the meeting ended with no resolution to the main issue under consideration. In this case, the parties did not agree on the categories of thought that shaped their understanding of reality, and this precluded their negotiating an agreement.

Do you think that the broken telephone effect and the problems encountered by the task force in the opening vignette might best be explained by the mechanistic, psychological, or interpretive symbolic perspective? You should be able to imagine how each perspective could play a role.

Nonverbal Aspects of Communication

No discussion of communication would be complete without addressing its nonverbal aspects. **Nonverbal communication** refers to all information conveyed by a sender, apart from the words themselves, that plays a role in the transmission of meaning. The tone of your voice, the way in which you are dressed, the mannerisms you use, the features of your smile, and whether you make eye contact when speaking all are examples of nonverbal aspects of communication. It is important to know that in certain situations, people's nonverbal signals can

sometimes convey more accurate information than do the actual words they use (Burgoon, 1994; Mehrabian & Ferris, 1967).

In a survey of applications of nonverbal behavior in marketing and management, DePaulo (1992) noted that researchers and consultants have addressed issues of nonverbal behavior in areas such as advertising, sales, public relations, service delivery, leadership, supervision, and security. DePaulo concluded that nonverbal behaviors play a significant role in many areas of organizational functioning. Following are examples of a few studies that attest to this. In an experiment where a variety of nonverbal behaviors were manipulated, Leigh and Summers (2002) found that salespeople who made more eye contact were perceived by buyers to be more believable and that those who were less hesitant in their speech were perceived as more interesting and persuasive. The importance of nonverbal behavior also has been demonstrated in studies of the employment interview, which happens to be the work-related topic area in which the most amount of nonverbal communication research has been conducted (DePaulo, 1992). For instance, in an experiment using videotaped interviews, Howard and Ferris (1996) found that interviewers rated job candidates as more suitable for employment when the candidates displayed high levels of certain nonverbal behaviors—direct eye contact, smiling, and head nodding—than when they displayed low levels of these behaviors.

It may surprise you to learn that it also has been shown that the *nonverbal behavior of interviewers* can influence the behavior and perceived suitability of job applicants. Liden, Martin, and Parsons (1993) conducted an experiment in which job applicants were interviewed by an interviewer who displayed either warm or cold nonverbal behaviors. In the warm condition, the interviewer maintained eye contact most of the time, leaned forward in his chair, smiled occasionally, and faced the applicant. In the cold condition, the interviewer made no eye contact, leaned back in his chair, did not smile, and sat sideways relative to the applicant. The results revealed that the verbal and nonverbal behaviors of applicants interviewed by the cold interviewer were rated more negatively by independent judges than were the verbal and nonverbal behaviors of those interviewed by the warm interviewer. It seems not only that an applicant's nonverbal behavior matters in job interviews but also that the interviewer might actually be able to influence the verbal and nonverbal behaviors that the applicant exhibits.

As just noted, interviewers may use nonverbal behaviors to infer the personalities of job applicants and determine their suitability for a position. If accurately decoding an applicant's nonverbal behavior is necessary to determine his or her suitability for a position, might the effectiveness of a job interview be compromised if it were conducted in such a way that some nonverbal behavior was missing? This was precisely the question posed by Blackman (2002). Blackman had pairs of university students conduct mock job interviews. In each pair, one student was randomly selected to play the role of interviewer and the other to play the role of job applicant. The interviews were conducted either face-to-face or over the telephone. Subsequent to each interview, both participants completed personality questionnaires assessing the personality of the job applicant. The purpose of the study was to determine whether there would be a difference in the degree of agreement between the interviewer's and applicant's assessments of the applicant's personality as a result of the interview method. As it turned out, there was. Blackman found that the difference was greater in the telephone interview condition than in the face-to-face interview condition. She concluded that the lack of nonverbal information available to the interviewer in the telephone condition might have reduced the accuracy of the interviewer's assessment of the job applicant's personality.

Nonverbal communication is also lacking among employees who work together despite being physically distant from each other, as occurs in virtual organizations. DeSanctis and Monge (1999) reviewed research on electronic communication and found that within virtual organizations the volume of information tends to increase and, as a result, efficiency tends to decrease. They also concluded that message comprehension is lower relative to face-to-face communication. Those who communicate exclusively using electronic media such as e-mail may have a more difficult time in achieving consensual validation (Weick, 1979) because decoding social cues that are helpful in establishing meaning is more difficult. Technology and social psychology do not always mix well.

Group Decision Making

Small groups have always been a major focus of social psychological inquiry (Levine & Moreland, 1998). As Levine and Moreland (1998) indicated, an understanding of groups is necessary for the analysis of social behavior because groups provide the social context in which much social behavior occurs. Because of this, researchers have long been interested in better understanding the effects of group-level phenomena such as cohesion (e.g., Brawley, 1990), culture (e.g., Rentsch, 1990), composition (e.g., Pfeffer, 1983), and conflict (e.g., Levine & Thompson, 1996). Although these topics are interesting in and of themselves, they also are important because of their practical implications for group decision making.

Traditionally, how groups make decisions and what factors promote high-quality versus low-quality decisions have been important concerns for organizations because most important decisions in organizations are made by groups (Donaldson & Lorsch, 1983). Today, however, these concerns are even more significant due to the growing prevalence of semiautonomous and self-managed work teams. In the United States, 80% of Fortune 500 companies have at least half of their employees working in teams (Joinson, 1999). In contemporary organizations, teams are often responsible for making group decisions that previously had been under the purview of individual managers. As organizations move to being more team based, group decision making becomes much more prevalent and the consequences of group decision making become more extensive. Under these conditions, understanding the social psychology of group decision making becomes more important than ever before.

You might think that the trend toward group decision making is a good idea and that it is obvious that groups should make better decisions than individuals. However, our intuitions about the results of group decision making often are inaccurate (Davis, 1992). Groups do not always make better decisions than individuals. This is because groups can, for example, exert pressure on people to conform to bad ideas and exacerbate individual decision-making biases.

Groupthink

As discussed in Chapter 2, Janis (1982) proposed that a number of tragic decisions in history (e.g., the Kennedy administration's Bay of Pigs invasion) could be explained by his theory of groupthink. **Groupthink** essentially refers to a process of flawed decision making that occurs as a result of strong pressures among group members to reach agreement. That is, one or more of several antecedent conditions induce concurrence-seeking tendencies that override effective decision making by preventing a group from engaging in careful and thorough consideration of all relevant information.

Among the antecedent conditions that Janis proposed were high group cohesiveness, directive leadership, high stress, and insulation of the group from outsiders (Janis, 1983; Janis & Mann, 1977). In addition, Whyte (1998) suggested that groupthink might arise from an exaggerated sense of collective efficacy, for example, when overconfidence among group members leads them to falsely assume that it is unnecessary to fully examine possible advantages of alternative decisions. The evidence concerning which antecedent conditions in fact do promote the development of groupthink is somewhat equivocal, with virtually all proposed antecedents supported by at least some research. Whether or not some of the proposed antecedent conditions lead to groupthink seems to be moderated by the presence or absence of other conditions (Brehm, Kassin, & Fein, 1999). For instance, there is some experimental evidence that high stress (e.g., necessity of reaching a fast decision) promotes groupthink especially under conditions of high cohesiveness (Turner, Pratkanis, Probasco, & Leve, 1992).

Notwithstanding the importance of understanding the determinants of groupthink, of particular relevance to the focus of this chapter is that problems connected to groupthink can victimize groups in a wide variety of organizational contexts. For example, groupthink tendencies have been identified by Hensley and Griffin (1986) in a university board of trustees and by Manz and Sims (1982) in battery assembly work teams.

Because strong concurrence-seeking tendencies can adversely affect the quality of decisions made in organizations, it is important to understand how organizations can take steps to ensure that groups engage in effective decision-making processes. Recall from Chapter 2 that Janis (1983) proposed a set of prescriptions for preventing groupthink (see Figure 2.4 in Chapter 2). The prescriptions generally focus on helping a group to carefully examine all relevant information and courses of action to ensure that it does not rush into making a poorly informed and reasoned decision. Clearly, the leader has a critical part in initiating steps to prevent groupthink. For example, the leader should ensure that each member of the group assumes the role of "critical evaluator." In addition, the leader should, as much as possible, remain impartial and not voice his or her preferences and expectations until all other group members' views have been heard. Research supports the importance of intervention strategies to reduce the possibility of the flawed decision-making processes connected with groupthink (Brehm et al., 1999).

If, in the case of groupthink, concurrence-seeking tendencies can propel groups into making bad decisions, another group phenomenon may serve to enhance the group's tendency to reach agreement on those (bad) decisions—group polarization.

Group Polarization

More than 40 years ago, Stoner (1961) demonstrated that when people made decisions after engaging in a group discussion, the decision made by the group as a whole tended to be riskier than the average of the decisions the people had made individually prior to the discussion. Initially, this effect was called the **risky shift.** However, the label changed when researchers later noted that sometimes group decisions were actually more conservative than decisions initially made by the group's individual members. This phenomenon eventually was relabeled **group polarization** because it was determined that the group tended to polarize (make more extreme) the initial position of the majority of its members. That is, if group members' views on average are mildly supportive of a position, then as a result of group discussion the group's final decision tends to be more strongly supportive. Conversely, if before entering the group discussion individual members moderately oppose an issue, the group's decision tends to be more strongly opposed.

Group discussions polarize other kinds of decisions as well as those involving risk. In fact, group polarization can influence the deliberations of any kind of group, including most certainly those in the world of organizations. One example comes from a study by Whyte (1993). Business students were asked to imagine having to decide whether they would sink additional money into various business projects that were doing badly. Evidence of polarization occurred when the students were more likely to invest more money when deciding as a group than when deciding as individuals. The results have serious practical implications because group polarization exacerbated the notion of "too much money to quit," a phenomenon that has been financially damaging to many companies.

We should return to the likely connection between groupthink and group polarization. For one thing, the polarization process may underlie a group's tendency to rush into a premature decision in the case of groupthink. Also, perhaps the overconfidence hypothesized to be an antecedent of groupthink may result from the polarization of confidence among individual group members. Let us consider what social psychological mechanisms help to account for group polarization.

The most likely explanation for group polarization involves the concepts of normative influence and informational influence (Deutsch & Gerard, 1955), both of which are present to varying degrees in every social situation. **Normative influence** refers to pressure to conform to the expectations of others so as to gain social approval or avoid negative social consequences such as being ostracized. For example, in a group meeting, if an employee has reservations about the majority view but goes along with it because he or she does not want to annoy the other members of the group, the employee is experiencing normative influence. **Informational**

influence refers to changes in behavior or attitudes as a result of information obtained from other people that provides evidence about the nature of the social situation. In ambiguous situations that are not readily amenable to objective verification, we often turn to others to provide us with information about what is correct and to guide our behavior. For example, if an employee in a group meeting changes his or her position on an issue based on the convincing nature of the arguments presented by the other group members, the employee is experiencing informational influence. Essentially, the distinction between normative influence and informational influence involves the difference between conforming in order to be accepted and conforming in order to be right, respectively.

So, which is it? If you were taking part in a group discussion, do you think your views might become more extreme because you felt pressure to conform so as to be accepted by the group (normative influence) or because your definition of the situation was guided by information provided by other members of the group (informational influence)? It turns out that there is evidence to support both forms of influence in producing polarization. Support for normative influence has centered on demonstrations that mere knowledge of the positions or opinions of other people (without exposure to discussion) can produce polarization and that whether or not polarization occurs depends on whether or not individuals believe that the positions or opinions derive from members of their in-group (Eagly & Chaiken, 1993). These demonstrations suggest that pressure to conform to the expectations of important reference groups serves as one ingredient in producing group shifts toward more polarized positions.

Evidence of informational influence rests on studies that support what is termed **persuasive arguments theory** (Burnstein & Vinokur, 1977). According to this theory, polarization occurs when most of the arguments that group members hear favor one position over another. In a group where most or all members favor a particular position, most of the arguments raised during the group deliberation will reflect that position. Because the preponderance of information supports the position, the members become even more persuaded and, thus, polarization occurs. Eagly and Chaiken (1993) pointed out that the degree of polarization toward a position correlates directly with (a) the number of pro-position arguments available to group members and (b) the extent to which the arguments are valid. So, it seems that polarization can occur as a result of the desire to be accepted by the members of one's group and also as a consequence of being exposed to many strong arguments favoring a particular position. As organizations implement more team-based structures, group members and managers should learn about these types of social processes and be vigilant about the effects that these processes may have on group decisions.

Normative influence and informational influence serve as useful constructs in helping us to understand the decisions made by groups and how they may differ from those made by individuals. In addition to shedding light on why decisions become polarized, these constructs may help us to understand why groups fail to reduce, and sometimes actually intensify, certain decision-making biases that we observe in individuals.

Decision-Making Biases in Groups

Human beings have a limited capacity to hold information in memory and have great difficulty in evaluating numerous pieces of information simultaneously or in quick succession. As discussed earlier in the chapter, to help in the processing of information, people regularly and automatically use cognitive shortcuts, or **heuristics**, when making judgments. These heuristics allow people to make efficient decisions without taxing their mental resources. We saw earlier that cognitive shortcuts can result in perceptual biases. Another consequence of using heuristics is that they sometimes lead people to make decisions that are inferior in quality to objective standards. For example, in Chapter 18, you will read about the *availability heuristic* (Tversky & Kahneman, 1973). The availability heuristic can have the effect of making people think that issues are more common and/or more likely than they actually are.

There are a number of decision-making biases to which people fall victim, and it has

been demonstrated that groups do not always diminish—and sometimes even exacerbate—these biases. This might sound surprising. Would it not always be the case that individual group members would serve as *error checkers* and that groups would produce more accurate solutions to problems? Not always. Group members do tend to serve an error-checking function when the demonstrability of a solution is high, for example, when someone in the group has access to data that clearly indicate the correct information. This is sometimes referred to as a *truth wins* process of decision making. However, when the demonstrability of a solution is low (i.e., the solution is very hard to discover), a *majority wins* process, in which the group accentuates the dominant tendencies of its members, seems to characterize group decision making (Tindale, 1993). When the demonstrability of a solution is low, the group may fall victim to the same biases that affect individuals.

One well-known bias to which people regularly succumb is called the *hindsight bias* (Fischoff, 1975). The **hindsight bias** refers to people's tendency to believe, in retrospect, that an event was more predictable than it actually was. For example, before the launch of a new product, employees in a company may have conflicting views as to whether the product will succeed in the marketplace. However, if the product eventually does succeed, people retrospectively considering their prior confidence levels will often claim that they knew all along that the product would be well received. Simply put, people believe that they are better at predicting outcomes than they actually are, and once an outcome is known they tend to believe that they would have predicted it. Despite the reasonable conjecture that error-checking group members could serve to eliminate or at least reduce the hindsight bias, research has demonstrated that groups have no appreciable effect on its magnitude. Studies by Stahlberg, Eller, Maass, and Frey (1995) and Bukszar and Connolly (1988) indicate that the hindsight bias is present to the same extent in group judgments as it is in individual judgments.

A second bias to which individuals regularly fall victim is the **confirmation bias** (Wason, 1960) that was discussed in Chapter 6. This bias refers to people's tendency to seek out and pay attention to information that supports their favored positions and to ignore disconfirming information. In a recent experiment, Schulz-Hardt, Frey, Lüthgens, and Moscovici (2000) explored the magnitude of the confirmation bias in groups and individuals. They had 200 participants read a case study involving a chemical company that had to make the decision of whether or not to invest in a developing country. Some participants were placed in groups and informed that, after a 10-minute discussion, they would be asked to make a preliminary group decision and then, after more group discussion, a final group decision. The remaining participants were simply asked to make an initial individual decision and, later, a final individual decision. After they had made their initial decisions, and before they were asked to make their final decisions, the groups and individuals were provided with the opportunity to receive additional separate pieces of information that either favored or opposed investment in the developing country. Schulz-Hardt and colleagues' results revealed that confirmation bias occurred in each condition in that both groups and individuals demonstrated a clear preference for additional information that supported the initial decisions they had made. Interestingly, the researchers also found that groups chose significantly more supporting information than did individuals. Thus, confirmation bias was significantly stronger in groups, a convincing illustration of groups failing to serve the error-checking function. Based on the preceding discussion of normative influence and informational influence, what do you think might have caused the intensification of this bias in groups? What consequences do you think group confirmation bias might have on the effectiveness of organizations?

A third bias we consider is based on the **representativeness heuristic** (Kahneman & Tversky, 1972), which leads people to make categorical judgments based on the extent to which an object, event, or individual is perceived to fit or represent a particular category. This heuristic can produce a bias in which base rate information (i.e., statistical probability) is insufficiently weighted. For example, imagine being at a party where you know that 30 doctors and one jockey are in attendance. Imagine next that you are introduced to a very short man. How likely would you be to guess that this man is the jockey? According to Kahneman and Tversky (1972), you are likely to allow the fact that the short man is representative of jockeys bias your judgment and conclude that the person races horses for a living. Notice that in this case you are ignoring base rate information that would suggest that the person is most likely a short doctor. This bias has been demonstrated repeatedly in individuals, but only a few studies have explored the extent to which the representativeness heuristic is present in groups.

One such study was conducted by Argote, Seabright, and Dyer (1986), who presented participants working alone or in five-person groups with base rate information that there were 9 engineers and 21 physicians in a group of 30 people. Participants were then provided with descriptions of 3 members of the group and were informed that each description had been randomly drawn from a set of file cards containing descriptions of all the group members. One description, Ben's, was made to sound like an engineer. Another description, Jonathan's, was made to sound neutral. The final description, Roger's, was intended to sound like a physician. Participants were simply asked to indicate the probability that the individual in each description was one of the engineers in the group. Note that the statistical probability of randomly drawing an engineer from the group is .30. The results of the study revealed a clear bias based on the representativeness heuristic. Individuals' probability estimates that Ben, Jonathan, and Roger were engineers were .63, .36, and .21, respectively. The corresponding group estimates were .74, .36, and .20. Both individuals and groups were greatly influenced by the description of Ben and allowed it to substantially bias their estimates. However, groups tended to amplify this bias; when judging the likelihood that Ben was an engineer, groups were significantly more influenced by the description than were individuals and produced an estimate further from the base rate. Argote and colleagues explained these results in terms of persuasive arguments theory, suggesting that group discussion tended to expose members to additional arguments in favor of relying on the individuating information.

These results are only a sample of the research on biases in group decision making. However, the conclusion is clear: Groups do not always produce higher quality decisions than individuals. As discussed, social psychological processes help to explain why this is the case. Today, as more and more employees work in teams, it is important that they and others pay attention to how social dynamics may influence their group decisions.

Decision Making and Information Technology

Earlier, this chapter discussed the virtual organization and how communication is affected when employees who are physically separated work together through the use of information technology. As you might expect, collaborating by way of computers can also affect group decision making. For example, McGuire, Kiesler, and Siegel (1987) demonstrated that groups interacting face-to-face (FTF) displayed greater bias in their decision making than did groups engaging in computer-mediated communication (CMC). McGuire and colleagues' results suggest that there may be less social influence exerted on group members when they interact by way of computers. But which form of influence is reduced—informational or normative? The prevailing view is that with the use of information technology, normative influence decreases relative to informational influence (Reid, Ball, Morley, & Evans, 1997). In his review of the literature, Bordia (1997) concluded that there is greater equality of participation in CMC groups and that CMC groups perform better than FTF groups on idea generation tasks. Bordia's conclusions imply that there is less normative pressure in CMC groups and suggest that McGuire and colleagues' (1987) results—less biased decision making in CMC groups—also can be attributed to a reduction in normative influence.

In a direct test of the relative impact of normative influence and informational influence in computer-mediated decision making, Reid and colleagues (1997) examined the discussion patterns of FTF and CMC groups as they tried to reach a decision about how to handle an alleged case of child abuse. In examining the comments made by participants in both conditions, the researchers found that CMC members made fewer comments that demonstrated informational influence and made more comments that demonstrated normative influence. These results counter the prevailing view that CMC reduces normative influence relative to informational influence. This certainly is an interesting and somewhat counterintuitive finding that raises many questions about how normative and informational social influence processes may operate during CMC. Further research is required to sort out these questions.

Group decision making is affected not only by social influence processes but also by the communication processes discussed earlier. Effective decision making may be negatively affected during CMC because social cues necessary for accurately decoding messages are reduced. Baltes, Marcus, Sherman, Bauer, and LaGanke (2002) concluded that nonanonymous CMC groups are less effective in their decision making, particularly when they are under time pressure, and take longer to reach decisions than do FTF groups. Why does this occur? Strauss and McGrath (1994) suggested that CMC is most likely to adversely affect group decision making when there is a need to perceive the emotions of others, when persuasion is required, or when value-based consensus building is needed (i.e., when social cues greatly facilitate interaction). In this regard, Baltes and colleagues (2002) suggested that the more lifelike the medium (e.g., real-time exchange of information and presence of nonverbal information), the better computer-mediated decision making will be.

So, it appears that computer-mediated decision making is affected not only by changes in social influence processes that occur when people interact through computers but also by difficulties inherent in communicating using information technology. Organizations are well advised to take these issues into account and to carefully consider task requirements when considering whether to promote decision making by groups interacting by way of computers.

● FOCUS ON INTERVENTION

Recall that Schulz-Hardt and colleagues (2000) found that one of the biases that affects groups (more than individuals) is that they engage in biased information seeking and tend to gather data that confirm their original positions. This is clearly not a recipe for effective organizational decision making based on a thorough consideration of available data. In a follow-up investigation designed to test the effectiveness of interventions aimed at reducing this bias, Schulz-Hardt, Jochims, and Frey (2002) examined the effect of intentionally producing conflict during a group decision-making task. In a manner slightly different from that in the study conducted by Schulz-Hardt and colleagues (2000), an experiment was conducted in which 201 employees and managers read an economics case involving a company that had to make a decision regarding whether to transfer some of its operations to "Country A" or "Country B." After evaluating the case individually, participants were asked to choose which country represented the best alternative and then were provided with the opportunity to receive new information (i.e., brief articles) regarding the choices they had made. Participants were told that each article was written on a separate sheet of paper and was either in favor of or opposed to an investment in Country A or Country B. Participants made their choices but were informed that the articles would not be distributed prior to a subsequent group discussion. Based on participants' choices regarding the countries in which they chose to invest, homogeneous and heterogeneous three-person groups were then formed and instructed to make group decisions about which country should receive the investment. Homogeneous groups consisted of participants who had chosen the same country, whereas heterogeneous groups consisted of a two-person majority and a one-person minority. At the same time, one member in half of the groups in both conditions was assigned a "devil's advocacy" role in which he or she was required to identify all disadvantages, mistakes, and false assumptions underlying the investment choice that his or her particular group was considering. Both of these manipulations—group composition and devil's advocacy role—were designed to stimulate conflict in the groups. After discussing the case, groups made their final decisions and were again provided with the opportunity to receive new information regarding the countries in question (the same articles provided to individuals previously). The articles that the groups chose served as an indication of the extent of confirmation bias.

The results revealed that, as expected, homogeneous groups displayed the confirmation bias; however, heterogeneous groups showed no confirmation bias. Also, groups with a member playing the devil's advocacy role facilitated the search for information conflicting with the groups' tendencies and reduced the confirmation bias. It should be noted, however, that genuine dissent (present in heterogeneous groups) was more effective in eliminating the confirmation bias than was contrived dissent (i.e., devil's advocacy).

These results clearly underscore the potential for designing interventions to reduce bias in group decision making. It appears that training group members to consciously explore alternative ideas and carefully choosing members of groups such that a diversity of opinions is available are successful interventions for reducing the bias inherent in some group decisions. In fact, the devil's advocacy procedure in particular is often employed as an intervention to reduce groupthink.

Summary

This chapter has attempted to convey to you the breadth of application of the theories, principles, and research findings of social psychology to understanding social behavior in organizations. The first main section of the chapter focused on individual psychological processes in an organizational context. It began by exploring social perception and noted how certain perceptual biases, such as selective perception and the halo effect, influence the ways in which we view and interpret the behavior of others in the work environment. It then discussed the attribution process and noted how our perceptions of the distinctiveness, consensus, and consistency cues of another person's behavior influence whether we conclude that the person is responsible for the behavior (internal cause) or that something outside the person caused the behavior (external cause). It also discussed how the fundamental attribution error and the actor–observer effect distort the accuracy of our attributions.

Next, the first section focused on job satisfaction, a topic that is likely to be of interest to most of you throughout your working careers. It first touched briefly on how job satisfaction is measured by social scientists and then explored some of the factors thought to be related to job satisfaction, including the characteristics of the job itself, the social and organizational environments in which the job is situated, and the personal dispositions of the job incumbent. It also looked at some of the potential consequences of job satisfaction, including the relationship of job satisfaction to employee withdrawal behaviors and job performance. The section concluded with a discussion of the complex question of the nature of the causal relationship between job satisfaction and job performance.

The second main section of the chapter addressed the role of interpersonal processes in organizations. It examined three ways in which to conceptualize organizational communication by considering the mechanistic, psychological, and interpretive symbolic perspectives. It noted that all three perspectives contribute to a fuller understanding of effective communication in organizations. It also discussed the importance of nonverbal behavior in the communication process, particularly how it can affect judgments made during an employment interview.

Finally, the second section explored decision making in groups. It showed how certain phenomena, such as groupthink and group polarization, can victimize groups in a wide variety of organizational contexts. It also discussed how certain biases, such as hindsight bias, confirmation bias, and the representativeness heuristic, are not necessarily diminished through group input and, in fact, may be exacerbated in group discussions and decision making. The section ended with a brief discussion of the effects of information technology on group decision making. In general, it appears that computer-mediated decision making may be adversely affected not only by changes in social influence processes but also by difficulties inherent in communicating using information technology.

12

APPLYING SOCIAL PSYCHOLOGY TO THE CRIMINAL JUSTICE SYSTEM

DAVID M. DAY

CHAPTER OUTLINE

The Crime and the Criminal
  The Social Psychology of a Crime
  The Origins of Criminal Behavior
The Response of the Criminal Justice
    System

The Police Investigation
The Courtroom
The Prison Setting
Summary

On the evening of November 14, 1999, Dimitri "Matti" Baranovski, a 15-year-old high school student from Toronto, sat with about six friends in the Harryetta Gardens playground in a park near their school and not far from where Matti lived with his mother. They often would come to the park to talk, socialize, and just hang out.

At approximately 8:45 pm, they were approached by a group of 10 to 12 older teens and were asked whether they had any cigarettes and money. The intruders were wearing balaclavas over their faces so that their identities were not readily apparent. When Matti and his friends told them they had no cigarettes or money, the young men persisted in their demands. At this point, Matti stood up against the group and told the older teens to stop bothering him and his friends.

The details of what happened next are not entirely clear. According to newspaper reports, three of the young men began to punch and kick Matti about his face and body. Matti's friends fled, leaving him alone with his assailants. As a result of the attack, Matti fell to the ground as they continued to brutally hit and kick him. One kick caused Matti's head to snap back, tearing an artery in his neck and killing him. The attack lasted a few minutes, after which the assailants fled.

One of Matti's friends had run across the street to a residence to summon help. The first 9-1-1 call came in at 9:02 pm (Wong, 1999). By the time the paramedics arrived on the scene, Matti's body was lifeless. Although he was revived later at the hospital, Matti died during the early morning hours of the next day.

It was later revealed that the young men had apparently come to the park looking for a fight with another group whose members failed to show up. They then turned their attention to Matti and his friends and decided to rob them. It also was revealed that at least two cars had passed by the scene that evening on the busy street that runs by the park. The drivers, on hearing Matti's screams, had slowed down or even stopped. In all cases, no one came to assist Matti or called for help. According to one newspaper report (Wong, 1999), a woman driving by stopped her car when she and her two sons, who were passengers in the car, heard the noises from the attack. They reported hearing a loud cry for help and a lot of Russian words, followed by someone yelling "Get to the ground!" At that point, the woman, fearing that there might be weapons involved, became scared and drove off.

This vicious attack raises many questions about the nature of criminal behavior and about people's responses to criminal acts that may be examined from a social psychological perspective. Moreover, beyond the particular criminal incident, social psychological theory and research can be applied to understand and address other aspects of the criminal justice system, including the police investigation, the criminal trial, and the incarceration and rehabilitation of criminal offenders. Some of the questions that social psychologists could address include the following:

- What situational factors of that evening might have influenced the behavior of Matti's assailants?
- What factors might account for the responses of the bystanders who, on hearing the commotion, slowed down but did not stop to assist?
- Once the police become involved in a crime, what elements make for an effective investigative interview with witnesses, victims, and suspects?
- In a court case, how might the personal characteristics of a defendant or the situational characteristics of the courtroom influence decisions made by the judge or jury members?
- Can we increase the effectiveness of prisons by altering their social climates and creating more "humane" environments behind bars?

With regard to the potential role of social psychology in answering these questions, consider the following statement made by Schuller and Ogloff (2001): "Given that public policies, laws, and court decisions are based on assumptions about human behavior, the very subject matter of psychology, psychologists can play a vital and important role in this area" (p. 6). Consider also that criminal behavior is a social act, involving violations of socially defined laws. Some crimes are committed against people directly, including both violent offenses (e.g., murder, robbery, uttering a death threat) and nonviolent offenses (e.g., fraud, voyeurism, exhibitionism). In many cases, particularly among youths, crimes are committed by groups of individuals acting together. What social psychologists bring to these issues are theories and methodologies that take into account the role of both the person and the situation to account for behavior. This approach provides a more integrative and multilevel framework for addressing the issue of crime than does focusing only on the person or only on the environment.

To illustrate, criminal acts may be viewed from a **social ecological perspective,** that is, as the result of an interaction between the person and the environment. This notion derives from Kurt Lewin's famous theorem, $B = f(P, E)$, which states that *behavior* is a function of the *person* (*P*), the *environment* (*E*), and the *interaction* between the two (Lewin, 1951b). With regard to criminal behavior, an individual may be compelled to offend only in the presence of an environmental stimulus that acts as a sort of "trigger." For example, a person might shoplift only after walking into a large department store; indeed, some offenders can be quite picky regarding the stores from which they will steal. In the absence of the large department store, the crime would not take place. As another example, a drug addict might start "Jonesing" or craving a "hit" on seeing drug paraphernalia sitting on a table.

In practice, social psychology has been of value to the police in developing techniques for interviewing suspects, to defense attorneys in demonstrating how a person can come to be wrongfully accused of a crime, to lawyers in selecting possible jurors for a trial, and to forensic psychologists in conducting risk assessments of offenders to predict the probability of future criminal behavior. Whereas many such topics may be explored, a full discussion of the contributions of social psychology is beyond the scope of this chapter. The topics examined here relate to four aspects of the criminal justice system in which the application of social psychology has been particularly fruitful: (a) explaining criminal behavior, (b) conducting the criminal investigation, (c) conducting the trial, and (d) incarcerating offenders. The chapter first examines criminal incidents from a social psychological perspective, focusing in particular on the attack on Matti.

THE CRIME AND THE CRIMINAL

The Social Psychology of a Crime

In some respects, the tragedy of the beating death of Matti Baranovski, described in the opening vignette, is reminiscent of the story of Catherine "Kitty" Genovese, who in 1964 was also killed by her attacker in Queens, New York. When reporters went around the neighborhood looking for witnesses, they found 38 people who admitted to having seen or heard the attack but having done nothing in response.

Research on bystander intervention (Darley & Latané, 1968; Latané & Nida, 1981) has shown that various factors influence a person's decision to assist in an emergency situation, including the ambiguity of the situation and the perceived similarity of the victim to the potential helper. Another factor is the number of bystanders who witness the emergency. There is considerable research evidence of a phenomenon known as the **bystander effect,** which states that people are less likely to help in an emergency when other bystanders are present (also discussed in Chapter 3). One explanation for the bystander effect is that the presence of others lowers the individual bystander's sense of responsibility. The drivers who passed by the Toronto park and heard Matti's cries that evening might not have intervened because they thought that, given the busy road nearby, others would intervene. Moreover, this **diffusion of responsibility** (i.e., the diminished sense of responsibility a person feels when he or she believes that others would or should intervene) is more likely to occur when a bystander can remain anonymous (the driver may remain in his or her car and continue driving without much notice), when there are relatively few victims (only Matti's voice was heard screaming), and when the victim is perceived to be dissimilar to the potential helper (Russian words were heard). What would you have done if you had been a passerby that evening? Unfortunately, it seems that many of us would not have offered help. On December 7, 2002, the body of 19-year-old Breann Voth was found in the shallow banks of the Coquitlam River in Port Coquitlam, British Columbia. Despite Breann's screams for help, which at least three people were reported to have heard as she tried to fight off her attacker, no one came to her aid, leaving members of the community angry and in search of answers to explain their apparent "apathy" (Armstrong, 2002).

What about the behavior of Matti's assailants? What situational factors might have accounted for their actions? We could begin by asking questions such as the following. Would these young men have attacked Matti if they had not been wearing masks over their faces? Would they have engaged in this violent behavior if they had not been in a group, that is, if they had been on their own with Matti and his friends? To what extent did such factors contribute to Matti's beating? Although we cannot know for sure, we can speculate based on sound principles derived from well-controlled social psychological research.

Wearing balaclavas over their faces provided the young men with a sense of anonymity and loss of personal identity, much like members of the Ku Klux Klan wearing hooded robes. Research on **deindividuation** (i.e., a diminished sense of self-awareness) suggests that people, under the cover of anonymity in which their identities are concealed, may deliberately choose to engage in behavior about which they might otherwise be inhibited, including aggression. For example, Zimbardo (1969) demonstrated in a laboratory experiment that female research participants wearing Ku Klux Klan-type hoods and outfits delivered shocks for twice as long to an experimental confederate as did other research participants whose identities were revealed by large nametags.

The young attackers also were not acting alone. Moreover, they had come to the park prepared to fight. The notion of **social facilitation** (Zajonc, 1965) informs us that a person's performance on a well-learned task will be enhanced by the heightened arousal caused by the presence of others. Perhaps the aggressive behavior of these young men was well learned—something they were accustomed to doing and, indeed, something they were primed to do that evening. Within their antisocial peer group, such behavior might even be considered "normative." As a result, the presence of the group might have heightened the young men's levels of arousal, which in turn enhanced their tendencies to engage in aggression, resulting in the vicious unprovoked attack.

Furthermore, it was alleged that Matti's assailants had come to the park intending to fight with another group whose members failed to show up. This aborted confrontation may have led to a heightened sense of frustration and anger among the young men. According to the **frustration–aggression hypothesis** (Berkowitz, 1989), frustration—defined as anything that blocks a person from attaining a goal—may have been a trigger for their aggressive behavior in the presence of a new set of potential victims.

A fourth factor that may influence antisocial behavior, and aggression in particular, is the presence of *situational cues* that incite the behavior. Recall the laboratory experiment by Berkowitz and LePage (1967), discussed in Chapter 8, in which the presence of a gun, rather than a badminton racquet, was shown to increase the aggressive behavior of research participants. Moreover, according to Anderson and Bushman (2002), some social contexts restrict opportunities to act aggressively, whereas others provide ample opportunities:

> Church services contain many impediments to aggression—witnesses, strong social norms against aggression, and specific nonaggressive behavioral roles for everyone in attendance. Country/Western bars on Saturday nights present better opportunities for aggression. Many aggression facilitators are present: alcohol, aggressive cues, aggression-prone individuals, males competing for the attention of females, and relative anonymity. (p. 43)

Perhaps, under the cool cover of night in a secluded area of a park, the stage was set for violence to erupt as a group of deindividuated, frustrated, and aggressive young men turned their sights on Matti and his friends.

But these factors do not explain all of the events of that evening, nor do they explain the events leading up to or subsequent to the attack. In fact, although deindividuation and social facilitation are good examples of some of the **proximal variables** (i.e., those occurring close in time to the event) that can influence criminal behavior, there is another set of factors that also is important, referred to as **distal variables** (i.e., those occurring in the distant past relative to the event). As we will see, a comprehensive social psychological theory of criminal behavior should include both sets of determinants.

It should be noted that recognition of the situational determinants of criminal behavior is not meant to imply that an individual's *personal responsibility* for engaging in antisocial acts should be reduced or diminished in any way. Rather, it is meant to acknowledge that many factors—both situational and individual differences—are needed to fully explain crime.

The Origins of Criminal Behavior

Existing theories of criminal behavior implicate a wide range of variables that reside within the person, the person's immediate environment, and the broader sociological context. Presented in what follows are some of the major theoretical paradigms from biology, sociology, and social psychology that have been put forth to explain criminal behavior. Although this chapter emphasizes the social psychological perspective, it is important to always remember that the perspectives of other disciplines contribute to a more complete understanding of psychological phenomena, including the etiology of criminal behavior. A general discussion of the biological and sociological theories is presented first, followed by a consideration of several social psychological approaches.

Biological Theories

Biologically based theories view criminal behavior as the result of genetics, psychophysiology, neurological functioning, and biochemistry. Studies of genetic influences, for instance, have noted a greater preponderance of criminals among sons whose biological parents also were criminals (Lytton, 1990). The well-documented finding that males have a greater propensity for physical aggression than do females has been attributed to higher levels of testosterone (Dabbs, Carr, Frady, & Riad, 1995) and the presence of an extra Y chromosome (XYY) (Crowell, 1987), although the latter observation has been disputed (Mednick, Moffitt, Gabrielli, & Hutchings, 1986). In addition to these inherited biological characteristics, acquired biological deficits may influence criminal behavior. Even before birth, factors may conspire against the developing fetus, predisposing it to impulsive, hyperactive, or aggressive behavior. For example, a lack of proper nutrients during critical periods of prenatal development or pre- or postnatal exposure to toxic agents (e.g., alcohol, cigarettes, lead, drugs) may result in mild or severe deficits in cognition (e.g., learning disabilities, social information-processing deficits) and behavior (e.g., poor motor coordination, poor self-control) (Hodgins, Kratzer, & McNeil, 2002)—factors that are known to be markers of aggressive behavior in children.

Sociological Theories

Some of the most enduring theories of crime are those that are based on sociological principles. These traditional theories (e.g., anomie, strain, control, subculture), although widely diverse, attempt to explain crime in relation to various factors in society such as social class, poverty, and social inequity. Thus, a person's socioeconomic status, determined by education, occupation, income, and neighborhood characteristics, explains substantial variability in criminal behavior. Lower socioeconomic status is associated with a higher rate of crime. However, the causal mechanisms purported to connect these variables will differ depending on the particular theory. For example, according to strain theory (Cohen, 1960), criminal behavior is said to be caused by undue strain (frustration) experienced as a result of pathological social structures (e.g., social inequality, poverty) that prevent a person from achieving the middle-class expectations for material success. The strain leads the person to engage in socially deviant behavior, such as crime, to attain goods and social prestige. Subculture theory (Wolfgang & Ferracuti, 1981) states that individuals who engage in criminal activity are merely conforming to the hedonistic, hostile, and destructive values of lower-class culture. Indeed, in the deviant subculture, the nonconformists who do not engage in theft, drug use, and gang affiliation are said to be the true deviants (Andrews & Bonta, 2003).

Social Psychological Theories

Theories of criminal behavior from a social psychological perspective tend to consider the influence of both dispositional and situational factors. For example, as Hoge (2001) noted, social ecological models explain crime as a function of the interaction among multiple "forces operating at the level of the individual, their immediate social environment, and more distal factors within the larger social environment" (p. 58).

According to Bandura's (1977b) **social learning theory,** criminal activity represents learned behaviors that develop through a person's interactions and experiences with the social environment. This learning takes place as a result of various processes, including observing and imitating the criminal behavior of others, receiving positive consequences for engaging in criminal behavior (e.g., peer approval), realizing that such behavior can effectively lead to desired outcomes (i.e., have instrumental value), and developing a high sense of self-efficacy in using antisocial means to achieve one's aims. As we will see, these notions have greatly influenced the development of current social psychological theories of crime.

This subsection focuses on the **general personality and social psychological model of criminal behavior** that has been developed by Andrews and Bonta (2003). According to Andrews and Bonta's model, the likelihood that a person will develop a tendency to engage in criminal behavior is increased by the presence of risk factors in his or her life. Six categories of risk factors—some personal and some environmental—are proposed:

1. An early age of onset for antisocial behavior

2. Negative parenting and family experiences (e.g., harsh and abusive discipline, low family cohesion, parental criminality)

3. Temperamental and personal characteristics that are conducive to criminal activity (e.g., impulsivity, aggressive energy, weak problem-solving abilities)

4. Low levels of school or vocational achievement

5. Association with pro-criminal peers and isolation from noncriminal associates

6. Antisocial attitudes, values, and beliefs

In addition, characteristics of the immediate situation are considered to interact with characteristics of the individual to further increase the likelihood of criminal activity.

The factors in Andrews and Bonta's (2003) model are viewed from a developmental perspective, either appearing early in a person's life (e.g., temperamental factors, family factors) or emerging over time through middle childhood and into adolescence (e.g., antisocial attitudes, negative peer influences). In addition, the amount of influence of each set of factors on the propensity to engage in antisocial acts will vary depending on the stage of a person's life. For instance, the influence of family factors will be greater during childhood, and the influence of peer factors will be greater during adolescence (Moffitt, 1993).

Clearly, Andrews and Bonta's model recognizes that the factors that influence the development of individuals who are predisposed to criminal activity are numerous, and their interrelationships are complex.

Drawing on Andrews and Bonta's (2003) model and a social learning perspective, one can see how the factors that the person brings to the situation, such as antisocial attitudes and perceived self-efficacy, in interaction with factors in the immediate situation, such as peer support for antisocial acts, are related to criminal behavior. For example, a person who values the use of antisocial behavior (e.g., violence, theft) as a means of achieving certain ends (e.g., settling a personal score, obtaining money), who feels competent in so doing (i.e., has high perceived self-efficacy), and who does not feel constrained in any way to behave in an antisocial manner has a high probability of committing an offense, particularly in the presence of an opportunity and antisocial peers. Add the influence of other social psychological factors discussed earlier, such as deindividuation and frustration, and there may be a recipe for disaster. Two elements of Andrews and Bonta's model—antisocial attitudes and antisocial peers—are examined in more detail in the following paragraphs.

The study of attitudes, including *antisocial attitudes,* and their relation to behavior is an important endeavor in social psychology. Attitudes are generally thought of as evaluative judgments that a person makes about an issue, an object, an event, or a person. Thus, a person's attitudes toward crime may be relevant to his or her tendency to commit a crime.

Andrews and Bonta (2003) identified five elements that comprise an antisocial pattern of attitudes (including values and beliefs): (a) high tolerance for deviance in general, (b) rejection of the validity of legal authority and institutions, (c) use of cognitive distortions (e.g., rationalization, denial) to make one's antisocial behavior acceptable, (d) interpretation of a wide range of environmental stimuli as a reason for anger, and (e) a style of thinking that is generally antisocial. Sample items from the Measures of Criminal Attitudes and Associates (Mills & Kroner, 1999), a self-report inventory of antisocial attitudes, are presented in Table 12.1. Taken

Table 12.1 Sample Items From the Measures of Criminal Attitudes and Associates

	Response	*Alternative*
It's understandable to hit someone who insults you.	Agree	Disagree
I have a lot in common with people who break the law.	Agree	Disagree
I could see myself lying to the police.	Agree	Disagree
Rules will not stop me from doing what I want.	Agree	Disagree
I would run a scam if I could get away with it.	Agree	Disagree

NOTE: Individuals who agree with these and similar types of items score high on antisocial attitudes.

SOURCE: Mills and Kroner (1999).

together, antisocial attitudes, values, and beliefs, once stabilized, have been shown to be among the strongest predictors of criminal behavior, more so than social class, personal distress variables (e.g., low self-esteem, anxiety), and family–parenting characteristics (Gendreau, Little, & Goggin, 1996). Correlations between antisocial attitudes and criminal behavior have been found to be in the range of .35 to .40 (Andrews, Leschied, & Hoge, 1992).

Studies have shown that offending behavior, particularly among adolescents, is apt to be deeply embedded within an *antisocial peer group.* The influence of the peer group can come about in one of two general ways: through a relatively casual and time-limited association with delinquent peers or through a clearly indoctrinated, long-term affiliation with other antisocial youths such as membership in a street gang. Adolescents who follow the first path are identified as the adolescence-limited group, and those who follow the second path are identified as the life-course-persistent group (Moffitt, 1993).

For **adolescence-limited individuals,** antisocial behavior is limited, as the name implies, to the teen years. The onset of their problem behaviors is largely explained as resulting from an association with delinquent peers. These individuals experience few developmental risk factors (e.g., harsh and punitive parenting, academic problems) and include as many females as males. Their criminal behavior is typically mild in nature, involving primarily nonviolent offenses (e.g., property, drug, truancy) rather than violent offenses. The criminal activity tends to end within a few years of onset.

Indeed, the adolescence-limited group comprises the vast majority of adolescents given that rule-breaking behavior becomes common during this period. For example, Moffitt, Caspi, Dickson, Silva, and Stanton (1996) found that only 6% of male adolescents in their survey reported *not* engaging in some form of delinquent activity (e.g., drug use, underage drinking or smoking).

The process by which an association with a delinquent peer group and the subsequent criminality of the adolescence-limited group comes about is related to a perceived "maturity gap" experienced by these young people. This is the discrepancy between what they would like to do as they strive for greater autonomy and self-reliance and what they are allowed to do given the social and legal constraints on their behavior. It becomes increasingly apparent to the adolescence-limited group that the small numbers of youths who already display antisocial characteristics, including a flagrant disregard for rules, do not experience the maturity gap to the same extent as they do. Consequently, this antisocial precocity "becomes a coveted social asset" (Moffitt, 1993, p. 687), leading some youths to mimic the antisocial behaviors and attitudes of the antisocial group. During this period of development, participation in delinquent activities becomes normative social behavior. As Moffitt (1993) explained, for those youths who become adolescence-limited delinquents, their antisocial activity "is an effective means of knifing-off childhood apron strings and of proving they can act independently to conquer new challenges" (p. 688). For healthy adolescents, the antisocial behavior is discontinued within a few years of its onset with the impending social and emotional maturity and responsibilities of early adulthood.

For the **life-course-persistent group,** the influence of the delinquent peer group follows a more lengthy and complex developmental pathway (Moffitt, 1993). This precocious antisocial group, comprising less than 10% of adolescents, is more likely to consist of males than females, experience many developmental risk factors, and show an early age of onset for problem behaviors (i.e., before 12 years). These individuals tend to engage in a wide variety of antisocial acts (e.g., violence, drug use, vandalism) referred to as "versatility." They are also at

particular risk for becoming chronic and serious offenders with lengthy criminal careers (Day, 1998). Their trajectory often begins with exposure to harsh and punitive discipline practices during childhood, lack of effective parental monitoring, parental criminality or psychopathology, failure at school, and rejection by nondeviant peers, leading them into the company of similarly fated individuals (Patterson, DeBaryshe, & Ramsey, 1989). The antisocial behavior of life-course-persistent adolescents is further reinforced within their delinquent peer group, where it becomes more serious and diverse in nature, often including violence. The process by which this peer reinforcement takes place is referred to as **deviancy training** (Dishion, 2000).

FOCUS ON RESEARCH

Deviancy training was the focus of an observational study by Dishion, Spracklen, Andrews, and Patterson (1996), who sought to examine how the socialization process in a deviant peer group takes place. Given the considerable evidence of the causal role of the antisocial peer group in the commission of serious delinquent behavior, studying how this influence is exerted is important to the development of effective early intervention and prevention programs.

The major goal of Dishion and colleagues' research was to examine the relationship between the social interactions of pairs of 13- and 14-year-old males and their rates of antisocial behavior 2 years later. The researchers analyzed the conversations of 186 boys, each with one of his friends, as they engaged in a 25-minute problem-solving task in a clinic-based laboratory setting. The sample of 186 boys was part of a longitudinal study of antisocial behavior in high-crime neighborhoods. The problem-solving task for each pair of boys involved five segments: (a) planning an activity together, (b) solving a problem that occurred recently for the target boy (from the sample of 186) about not getting along with his parents, (c) solving a problem that occurred recently for the target boy about not getting along with his peers, (d) solving a problem that occurred recently for the friend about not getting along with his parents, and (e) solving a problem that occurred recently for the friend about not getting along with his peers.

The videotaped interactions were coded to assess normative and rule-breaking talk during the task. The boys' reactions during the interactions and the discussions also were coded as either positive (i.e., characterized by laughter) or negative (i.e., characterized by pauses in the conversation). Long-term data also were gathered. At the end of a 2-year follow-up, based on police records, the pairs were classified as either not arrested, mixed arrested (one boy arrested), or both arrested. In addition, at the end of 2 years, the boys' self-reported delinquent behavior was measured.

The analyses of the boys' interactions revealed that the most common *normative topics* included recreation, school, family, money, social, and peer relations. The most common *deviant topics* included mooning the camera, using drugs, stealing, vandalizing, victimizing women or minorities, making obscene gestures, and getting into trouble at school. As shown in Table 12.2, boys in all three groups discussed both topic types. However, there was an important difference. The *no delinquent group* (neither boy arrested at the end of the 2-year follow-up) and *mixed group* (one boy arrested) spent much more time discussing normative topics than rule-breaking topics. On the other hand, and importantly, the *delinquent group* (both boys arrested) spent more time discussing rule-breaking (deviant) topics than normative topics. In addition, the conversations of the no delinquent and mixed groups were characterized by approval through laughter for talk about prosocial topics. The delinquent group showed approval through laughter for talk about antisocial activities. Thus, only the delinquent group demonstrated a pattern of social interaction that encouraged the display of deviant behavior. It was further revealed, at the end of the 2-year follow-up, that the tendency to discuss rule-breaking topics (but not normative topics) at 13 and 14 years of age was associated with increases in self-reported delinquency at 15 and 16 years of age, even after controlling for prior levels of delinquency. Dishion and colleagues (1996) concluded that the types of social interaction that reinforce rule-breaking discussions that they observed in their study (i.e., providing approval and acceptance for antisocial values and attitudes) are indications of the deviancy training that takes place within delinquent peer groups on the streets. They further suggested that such interactions contribute to an escalation in criminal behavior over time. At the same time, caution must be exercised in generalizing the findings of this study given the questionable *ecological validity* (see Chapter 3) of the investigation's problem-solving task. Interactions between boys who are observed in a contrived setting of a clinic might not be reflective of the interactions that take place away from the prying eyes of social scientists.

Table 12.2   Mean Number of Topics Discussed per Minute by Arrest Status of the Dyads

	Neither Boy Arrested	*One Boy Arrested*	*Both Boys Arrested*
Rule breaking	1.90	3.01	8.59
Normative	14.61	12.49	6.27

SOURCE: Dishion, Spracklen, Andrews, and Patterson (1996).

Treatment Implications

In keeping with the general personality and social psychological approach, the effective treatment of antisocial behavior involves targeting the factors that support or maintain the criminal behavior. As outlined in the model, this includes targeting factors such as antisocial attitudes, beliefs, and peer associations as well as family factors. For example, treatment programs that target antisocial thinking as one component of a rehabilitation strategy have been shown to yield positive effects in reducing the risk of reoffending or recidivism (Coates, Miller, & Ohlin, 1978).

One successful intervention strategy, the Multisystemic Treatment Program for seriously violent youths (Henggeler, 1999), attempts to influence the multiple social systems in which young people are embedded (e.g., family, school, peer, neighborhood, justice system) to bring about a decrease in criminal behavior. Thus, program staff members intervene in several ways

and areas, including working with the families to modify parenting practices and dysfunctional dynamics within the youths' homes, linking the families to community supports, diverting the youths from negative peer associations, providing individual counseling, and providing supports at school.

Outcome evaluations of the Multisystemic Treatment Program, using experimental and quasi-experimental designs, have found the intervention to be promising. Pointing to its clinical utility, the program has been shown to be superior to usual services for offenders such as psychiatric hospitalizations and individual counseling. Positive gains in reducing the rates of recidivism have been observed for up to 5 years after treatment (Edwards, Schoenwald, Henggeler, & Strother, 2001; Henggeler, 1999). For example, Borduin and colleagues (1995) reported that the rate of recidivism 4 years after discharge from a treatment program was only 22% for program youths, compared with 72% for youths who received individual counseling and 87% for youths who refused either type of treatment. This is a sizable difference in program effectiveness and speaks clearly to the value of an approach that addresses both the personal and social factors that influence criminal behavior.

The general personality and social psychological approach also suggests that efforts to *prevent* the onset of antisocial and delinquent behavior may begin during early childhood. Appropriate targets for prevention and early intervention strategies include (a) young children who show signs of aggression, impulsivity, and poor social skills; (b) the home environment to provide parent training in the use of inductive discipline techniques (e.g., instructing, explaining) rather than punitive discipline techniques (e.g., hitting, yelling); and (c) the school environment to support children who display academic or behavior problems (Day & Golench, 1997). One can only wonder whether Matti would be alive today if his assailants had been involved in an early intervention program or a program such as the Multisystemic Treatment Program.

THE RESPONSE OF THE CRIMINAL JUSTICE SYSTEM

The previous section suggested that myriad factors, both proximal and distal, likely led the young men to pick on Matti and his friends and then brutally beat Matti to death. Once a crime has been committed, various areas of the criminal justice system become involved. For instance, in an effort to bring a case to its proper resolution, the police have to identify and interview witnesses and possible suspects and have to gather evidence to build a strong case for the prosecution to be presented in a court of law. This section examines several ways in which social psychology has been applied in three areas of the criminal justice system: (a) the criminal investigation, (b) the events in the courtroom, and (c) the prison setting (which is where defendants are likely to end up if they are convicted).

The Police Investigation

Once the police determine that a crime has occurred, they begin their investigation. This means that evidence about the crime should be carefully and systematically gathered in an effort to substantiate an allegation against one or more suspects who, in the face of sufficient evidence, may be tried in court. The process of conducting an investigation can be extremely complex. Eyewitnesses, victims, and suspects must be properly interviewed, and evidence must be gathered in ways that are in keeping with the law (e.g., no entrapment, no beating a confession out of a suspect, no improper searches, no contaminating "trace evidence" such as hair, fingerprints, and bodily fluids).

The inordinate attention to detail required in following proper police procedure places considerable demands on the investigating officers. In this regard, social psychological theory and social psychological research have played significant roles in identifying possible sources of bias and error in carrying out an investigation and in developing procedures for increasing the accuracy and integrity of police officers' work. The practical utility of this work has been to assist police in guarding against systematic biases that may invalidate their investigations and in applying empirically valid procedures, for example, in conducting investigative interviews and constructing police lineups (Wells et al., 2000). Some of this literature has contributed considerably to the development of a document called *Eyewitness Evidence: A Guide for Law Enforcement* (Technical Working Group for Eyewitness Evidence, 1999), which was put together by a panel of experts convened by the U.S. attorney general. The panel included social scientists, prosecutors, defense lawyers, and law enforcement officers. The guide provides a set of national guidelines for "the collection and preservation of eyewitness evidence for criminal cases" (Wells et al., 2000, p. 581) and has been distributed to more than 17,000 police services across the United States and Canada.

Let us consider some social psychological contributions to improving the effectiveness of police interview procedures.

The Investigative Interview

Interviewing witnesses, victims, and suspects constitutes a significant part of a criminal investigation. Sometimes a distinction is made between *interviewing* a witness or victim and *interrogating* a suspect (Bennett & Hess, 2001). However, this distinction is problematic and leads to the misconception that different methods and styles are used for each purpose (e.g., "hard" and "soft" approaches). In fact, the objective of both interview types is identical— to elicit the most information, and the most accurate information, from the interviewee. Good interviewing skills must be used in both cases. The broader term, the *investigative interview,* suits both purposes. At the same time, as Leo (1992) observed, a unique objective of the interview with a suspect "is to create a psychological atmosphere that will facilitate the act of confessing" (p. 43).

How should the investigative interview be conducted to elicit the most accurate, complete, and detailed information? How might the social dynamics of the interview context influence the effectiveness of the interview? It is clear that the way in which an interviewer behaves can alter the behavior of the interviewee. For instance, Akehurst and Virj (1999) demonstrated that fidgety behavior (e.g., continuous fiddling with a pen) by an investigating officer can elicit fidgety body movements in an interviewee. Such parallel behavior is in keeping with the notion of **interactional synchrony,** that is, the tendency of people to coordinate their body movements during conversations. Of course, in this instance the danger is that the fidgetiness of an interviewee might be interpreted by the investigating officer as suspicious and possibly as a sign of lying and deception. This is in spite of the evidence, reported by Akehurst and Virj, that suggests that people who are lying (i.e., engaged

in a cognitively complex task) usually make fewer body movements than do people who are being truthful.

Applied social psychological research has led to the identification of some of the key variables that distinguish a productive interview from an unproductive one. In numerous studies conducted over the past three decades, Elizabeth Loftus, Gary Wells, and their colleagues (e.g., Loftus & Palmer, 1974; Wells et al., 2000) have identified some of the more *common errors* that police make in conducting interviews. For example, a content analysis of 11 police interviews selected at random from the Miami–Dade Police Service in Florida (Fisher, Geiselman, & Raymond, 1987) revealed that police make mistakes such as asking too many close-ended questions (e.g., "Was the offender tall or short?"), asking too few open-ended questions (e.g., "Tell me everything you saw"), interrupting witnesses in the middle of their narratives, asking leading questions (e.g., "Did you see the knife?"), and asking questions in a fixed and inflexible order. Such questioning techniques may have the effect of drawing out brief concise answers that contain few details and leading an interviewee to selectively attend to certain aspects of the incident to the exclusion of other—perhaps more important—elements.

When interviewing a possible suspect, false and possibly incriminating information may be elicited in an improperly conducted interview, particularly if the suspect is vulnerable (e.g., due to young age, low intelligence, or anxious mental state) or if the interviewing officer already has made up his or her mind about the guilt or innocence of the person.

FOCUS ON RESEARCH

A fascinating laboratory experiment by Kassin and Kiechel (1996) demonstrated how easily people can be led to confess to crimes they did not commit and to not only confess but also internalize the false confessions and confabulate details of the events to make them consistent with their false confessions. A total of 75 university students participated, one at a time, in the experiment. They were led to believe that they were participating in a study on reaction time in which they had to type letters on a computer keyboard as quickly as possible as the letters were read to them by another person. The other person was actually an experimental confederate. The participants also were warned by the experimenter against pressing the "ALT" key because doing so would cause the computer to crash and all of their data would be lost. Shortly after the task began, the computer ceased functioning, and a very distressed experimenter accused the participant of pressing the forbidden ALT key. Initially, each participant denied hitting the key. The experimenter then tinkered with the computer, confirmed that the data had been lost, and asked whether the participant had hit the ALT key. The experimenter also asked the confederate what had happened and wrote out a handwritten confession for the participant to sign. The experimenter explained that the consequence for signing was a telephone call from the principal investigator.

How the participants responded to the accusation of hitting the ALT key depended on the experimental condition to which they had been randomly assigned. Two independent variables were manipulated: low versus high vulnerability and absence versus presence of a false incriminating witness. In the low-vulnerability condition, the pace of the task was slow, so a participant might be reasonably certain that the ALT key had not been pressed. In the high-vulnerability condition, the pace of the task was very fast, decreasing a participant's certainty about not having pressed the key. In the absence of a false incriminating witness condition, the confederate told the experimenter that she had not seen what happened. In the presence of a false incriminating witness condition, the confederate said that she had seen the participant press the ALT key. Thus, there were four conditions: low vulnerability/no incriminating witness, low vulnerability/incriminating witness, high vulnerability/no incriminating witness, and high vulnerability/ incriminating witness.

A full 69% of the participants signed the confession admitting that they had hit the ALT key when, of course, they had not. In the condition that was most biased toward yielding a confession—high vulnerability/ incriminating witness—100% of the participants signed the confession. Moreover, 65% of these participants internalized the belief that they were guilty (i.e., were overheard admitting to a waiting research participant that they had ruined the experiment), and 35% confabulated information about how and when they hit the ALT key when asked by the experimenter to reconstruct the event (e.g., "I hit it with my right hand when I typed the letter "G").

Kassin and Kiechel's (1996) study represents another example of the power of the situation. It highlights the powerful effect of the social context on eliciting false confessions, particularly the use of providing false incriminating evidence, a ploy often used by police. In California, 19-year-old Bradley Page confessed to the murder of his girlfriend after detectives told him, during a 16-hour interrogation, that he had flunked a lie detector test, he was seen near the scene of the crime, and officers had found his fingerprints nearby. None of those details was true. The suspect confessed to the crime after being befriended by the detective, who "put his arms around him and called him 'son'" (Kassin, 1997, p. 226) and whose trust the suspect desperately wanted. His confession came in spite of the fact that there was no evidence whatsoever against him. He seemed to have solid alibis and no motive. Nonetheless, he was sentenced to 9 years in prison as a result of his statement.

In contrast, research has determined a number of *techniques of a good interview* (Turtle & Watkins, 1999). Among them are asking simple and nonleading questions, using strategic silence, and continuing to reevaluate working hypotheses in light of new information. Furthermore, employing follow-up questions (e.g., "You said before that the person who stabbed the student looked angry. Can you tell me more about what that means for you?") and the interviewees' own words to phrase questions conveys good listening skills, and this in turn facilitates rapport, gains trust, and provides opportunities to elicit additional and more accurate information. Allowing interviewees to tell their stories with minimal interruption or redirection elicits better information than does asking a barrage of questions. The use of mnemonic instructions or situational cues may facilitate recall of events. Bringing interviewees back to the scenes of the crimes, either physically or psychologically, is a valuable technique that may trigger important memories.

Overall, laboratory and field studies have shown that, compared with the typical police interview, addressing the social dynamics and patterns of communication between the interviewer and the interviewee by applying the preceding interviewing principles can increase the amount of information recalled by a witness by between 35% and 75% without sacrificing accuracy (Wells et al., 2000). In one study, Fisher, Geiselman, and Amador (1989) compared the amount of information that was gathered from victims and witnesses of a crime by two groups of detectives from the robbery division of the Miami–Dade Police Department. One group ($n = 7$) was trained in the proper interviewing techniques, and the other group ($n = 9$) was not so trained. The content of 47 tape-recorded interviews conducted by the 16 detectives was analyzed for the amount of relevant information that was elicited. The results indicated that the two groups were equivalent prior to the training. However, after one group received the training, the trained detectives elicited 63% more information than did the untrained detectives without losing accuracy.

Special steps must be taken when interviewing witnesses or victims who are children, particularly young children (e.g., preschoolers), because they may be especially susceptible to the demand characteristics of the interview context, that is, responding in ways they believe are expected of them. For example, repeating a question to a child may signal to the child that his or her first answer was not acceptable. The child might then change his or her response even though the first answer was correct (Köhnken, 1996). As a result, the reliability of children's testimony can easily become contaminated through the use of improper procedures, leading to a miscarriage of justice. At the same time, there is widespread agreement in the literature (e.g., Lamb, Sternberg, Orbach, Hershkowitz, & Esplin, 1999) that children are capable of providing accurate and reliable testimony "provided they are questioned in a neutral, non-suggestive manner" (Köhnken, 1996, p. 269).

Witness Identification of Suspects

Imagine that you are sitting in class. Your professor is writing notes on the board about the upcoming exam. Suddenly you detect, out of the corner of your eye to your left, several students getting into what appears to be a heated, although muffled, argument. Although you try to ignore the ruckus and pay attention to your instructor, you notice, again to your left, the flash of something shiny and metallic. In an instant, you realize that one of the students has just been stabbed with a knife. In the moments that follow, through all the commotion that has transpired, as your professor and classmates become aware of the situation, you glance back to see three students running out of the room through the rear exit, with one of these students appearing to be leaving behind a trail of blood.

You have just witnessed a crime. As an eyewitness, you are asked to be interviewed by the police. How much information are you able to provide about what you saw? How accurate is your perception of the events that transpired? Can you recall what the person who stabbed the student was wearing? Was the victim a male or a female? Will you be able to identify the perpetrator in a police lineup?

As an eyewitness, you may be asked to identify a perpetrator from a variety of formats, including a set of photographs (i.e., "mug shots") or a "live" police lineup. The identification of a suspect by an eyewitness represents one of the most important pieces of evidence in building a case for the prosecution. Given the importance of this kind of information, there is an essential need to develop lineup identification procedures that reduce eyewitness errors, including the very serious problem of *false identifications.*

The consequences of wrongly accusing an innocent person of a criminal offense can be dire. Scheck, Neufeld, and Dwyer (2000) reported that of 62 criminal cases in which a convicted person was subsequently exonerated through DNA testing, 52 had been convicted as a result of mistaken eyewitness identifications. One such individual is Ronald Cotton, who in 1984 was convicted of raping a 22-year-old woman. He was positively identified from a police lineup by the victim as the man who attacked her. As a result, he was sentenced to prison for life. In 1987, the case was retried because another man who was in prison at the time for another crime, Bobby Poole, had bragged that he was the actual perpetrator. In court, however, Poole denied committing the offense, and again Cotton was found guilty. This time he received two life sentences. In 1995, the victim was asked to provide a blood sample so that DNA tests could be done on evidence from the case. She gladly complied because she was certain this evidence would confirm what she had known all along. However, the DNA results indicated that Poole was, in fact, the man who had attacked her. As a result, Poole was sentenced for the crime and Cotton was released from prison after serving 11 years for a crime he had not committed (Dowling, 2000).

Based on a prodigious body of social psychological research, it is now well established that witnesses are prone to making errors in judgment under certain circumstances (Wells et al., 2000). Experimental studies on eyewitness identification typically involve staging a mock crime (e.g., robbery) in front of a group of research participants and then having the participants identify the perpetrator from an array of suspects. The conditions of a crime scene that are thought to affect a witness's ability to accurately identify the culprit are manipulated by the researcher to identify factors that may facilitate or undermine eyewitness accuracy. For example, studies have shown that witnesses tend to make fewer errors when the perpetrators have distinctive faces (e.g., highly attractive) than when they have ordinary-looking faces, when the perpetrators are the same gender or race as the witnesses, and when witnesses can attend to perpetrators' entire faces rather than to select features (Shapiro & Penrod, 1986).

The conditions under which participants are asked to identify the culprit from a police lineup also have been manipulated in studies to identify the optimal procedures for reducing errors. Lineups can vary in terms of composition, using either all suspects or a suspect and several **foils** (i.e., people who are known to be innocent). In a review of the literature, Wells and Turtle (1986) reported that when a lineup consists entirely of suspects rather than a suspect and foils, witnesses are more likely to identify an innocent person as the perpetrator, resulting in charges being brought against the innocent person. Wells and Turtle explained that the use of foils allows for the possibility of the eyewitness making a *known error*. Without foils, there can be no known errors.

To further reduce errors, the foils must be carefully selected to ensure that they share certain physical characteristics with the suspect. Wells and colleagues (2000) reported that, in the absence of clear guidelines, a common procedure is for lineups to be constructed so that only

the suspect fits the eyewitness description. This would bias the witness toward selecting the person who the police believe committed the offense (Figure 12.1).

Furthermore, research has shown that the foils must not be *too* similar to the perpetrator because that would make it difficult for the witness to discriminate among the lineup members. As a middle ground, the foils should generally fit the description of the suspect given by the witness prior to the lineup, for example, a tall man with a medium build, dark hair, and a mustache. Witnesses also should be told prior to the procedure that the suspect *might or might not* be in the lineup. This serves to guard against a witness feeling pressured to identify one of the individuals as the perpetrator, for example, the one who matches the description most closely. Presenting the **lineup** individuals one at a time (**sequential lineup**) rather than all at once (**simultaneous lineup**), and asking the witness to state whether that person is the perpetrator, further serves to reduce the rate of misidentifications. Finally, the lineup should be conducted by an officer who is unaware of the identity of the suspect so as not to consciously or unconsciously guide the witness.

Recommended procedures for composing an effective mug book or lineup are presented in the aforementioned document, *Eyewitness Evidence: A Guide for Law Enforcement* (Technical Working Group for Eyewitness Evidence, 1999). Sample recommendations for a photo lineup are presented in Table 12.3.

The Courtroom

A lengthy police investigation led three men to be charged with beating Matti Baranovski to death. Their criminal trial was conducted according to the adversarial model of the legal system that is adopted in North American, Britain, and a few other countries. Under the **adversarial model,** two sets of lawyers, one for the defense and one for the prosecution, present their arguments, question witnesses, and make their case before a judge and, perhaps, a jury, who will determine the guilt or innocence of the defendant(s).

Since the publication in 1908 of Hugo Münsterberg's book, *On the Witness Stand:*

Figure 12.1   Example of a Biased Lineup After the Witness Described the Perpetrator as a Short, White, Balding Male in His 30s

SOURCE: Photo courtesy of the University of Windsor.

Table 12.3   Some Recommended Procedures for Preparing a Photo Lineup

The officer should ensure that:

1. Photos are grouped by type of format (e.g., color or black & white, Polaroid, 35 mm, digital) so that none unduly stands out.

2. Photos are of individuals who have similar characteristics (e.g., age, sex, race).

3. Photos are grouped by specific types of crime (e.g., sexual assault, gang activity).

4. Positive identifying information, such as names and addresses, exists for all individuals portrayed.

5. Photos are reasonably contemporary.

6. Only one photo of an individual appears in the mug book.

SOURCE: Technical Working Group for Eyewitness Evidence (1999, p. 17).

Essays on Psychology and Crime, applied psychologists have been actively involved in conducting research on the courtroom, including the behavior of jurors (Münsterberg, 1908). Social psychologists have been particularly interested in understanding the social processes (e.g., attributions, social influence, group decision making) that take place within the courtroom among the lawyers, judges, witnesses, defendants, and jurors (Figure 12.2).

This subsection examines three issues that are relevant to understanding how jurors think and behave as individuals and as members of a group: jury size, juror impartiality, and inadmissible evidence.

Jury Size

A jury of "one's peers" is composed of individuals from the community-at-large who are selected at random from voter registration and enumeration lists and are summoned to appear for jury duty. In the United States, a jury may be composed of either 6 or 12 members. The smaller number is meant to be a time- and cost-saving measure. In keeping with the British tradition, Canadian law only allows for a 12-person jury. The jury that rendered the verdict in Matti's case was highly unusual in that it was

Figure 12.2 The Courtroom: A Legal and Social Arena in Which People's Lives Can Be Dramatically Affected

SOURCE: Photo courtesy of the University of Windsor.

made up of 11 jurors (6 men and 5 women) after 1 juror was dismissed from the jury because she failed to disclose that she worked in a bank that had been robbed and was subpoenaed midway through the trial to testify as a witness.

Is there a functional difference between 6- and 12-member juries? An abundance of social science research concerning social perception, minority opinion, and normative and informational social influence (see Chapter 11) has had a bearing on answering this question. However, problems applying knowledge gleaned from research have sometimes occurred because the courts have not always interpreted the findings correctly. For example, in *Williams v. Florida* (1970), the U.S. Supreme Court ruled that no adverse effects would result from reducing the size of the jury from 12 members to 6 members, in other words, that the 6- and 12-person juries are "functionally" equivalent. Drawing on social science research at the time, including Asch's (1951) classic studies of conformity in groups, the Supreme Court erroneously concluded that a juror in a 5-to-1 split faces the same pressure to conform as does a juror in a 10-to-2 split. However, Asch actually had demonstrated the

opposite—that having at least one ally in a group increases an individual's ability to resist pressure to conform (see also Saks & Marti, 1997).

What else does the research show about the effect of jury size? The results of a meta-analysis conducted by Saks and Marti (1997) indicated that jury size tends to have a greater impact on the deliberation process than on the jury's verdict. Although the overall distribution of verdicts (i.e., guilty, not guilty) from small and large juries tends not to differ, smaller juries tend to spend less time deliberating, and this leads to quicker decisions. Moreover, consistent with what Asch (1951) found, studies confirm that it is easier to be a minority member in a 10-to-2 split than to be a minority member in a 5-to-1 split. Indeed, a 12-person jury is twice as likely to arrive at a hung verdict than is a 6-person jury (Ellsworth & Mauro, 1998). Finally, statistically, larger juries are thought to be more representative of the diverse community from which they are drawn (Zeisel, 1971).

Much of the social psychological jury research has used mock (simulated) juries for hypothesis testing. Like staging a crime in eyewitness research, mock jury simulations allow social psychologists to systematically manipulate independent variables (e.g., jury size) to study their effects on various dependent variables (e.g., length of deliberations, memory for evidence, verdicts). As an example, Davis, Kerr, Atkin, Holt, and Meek (1975) recruited 647 university students who were randomly assigned to one of four experimental conditions in a 2 (6- vs. 12-person jury) by 2 (requirement of a unanimous decision vs. a two-thirds majority decision) experimental design. Within their groups, the participants listened to a 45-minute tape-recording of an abbreviated version of an actual rape trial. They were then asked to deliberate the case based on the evidence to a maximum of 30 minutes and to reach a verdict of guilty or not guilty. The time spent deliberating and the vote of each juror (guilty, not guilty, or no response) were recorded.

The results indicated that neither jury size nor decision rule affected the distribution of verdicts. However, within the 12-person juries, the unanimity condition was significantly more likely to result in a hung jury than was the two-thirds majority rule condition. No difference was found for the 6-person juries. Finally, a significant interaction effect revealed that unanimous juries of 12 took significantly longer to deliberate than did two-thirds majority juries of 12. The 6-person juries showed only a negligible difference. These findings suggest that with 12-person juries, when all jurors have to agree on the verdict, dissenting viewpoints will be less likely to be suppressed and the evidence will be discussed at greater length and more thoroughly.

That Davis and colleagues' (1975) study found only partial support for the effect of jury size on the decision process contradicts other studies that have yielded clearer evidence for an effect (see, e.g., Saks & Marti, 1997). However, contradictory findings reflect the often equivocal and inconclusive nature of social science research. Such apparent inconsistencies can lead to misrepresentations of data (e.g., obscuring subtle effects) when members of a lay audience, such as representatives of the legal system, attempt to glean unequivocal answers from the extant literature (Zeisel & Diamond, 1974). This kind of flawed integration of social science research into legal decisions, as reflected in *Williams v. Florida* (1970) and subsequent court

rulings, can be a source of great frustration for researchers (Grofman, 1980), although it can also spur social psychologists to conduct more and better research, as we have seen.

Juror Impartiality

The strength of the jury, rather than a single judge, is that consideration of the facts of the trial evidence are based on the combined perspectives of 12 ordinary individuals who are brought together to function as a group to reach a unanimous decision. As Vidmar and Schuller (2001) explained,

> Because jury verdicts are rendered by members of the community, their legal decisions about guilt or innocence are assumed to have greater legitimacy and public acceptance than decisions by a single judge. The jury also serves as the conscience of the community because it is drawn precisely from the community in which the crime was committed. (p. 130)

Therefore, for a jury to function as intended, the members not only must be representative of the community but also must be free of any preconceived biases that might prevent them from rendering a fair decision. In other words, jury members must be impartial. But what does this mean, and how is it achieved? In *R. v. Parks* (1993), the Court of Appeals of Ontario defined **partiality** as a social psychologist would, having an attitudinal (i.e., prejudicial) and a behavioral (i.e., discriminatory) component that could potentially affect an individual juror's verdict on a case. What has the research found about the relationship between juror attitudes and verdict decisions?

Considerable research on the attitude–behavior link has shown that attitudes and behavior are strongly correlated, but only under certain conditions. For example, Ajzen and Fishbein (1977) reported that attitudes correlate with behavior when the attitudes are *specific* to the behavior, for example, when predicting whether a person will start jogging based on his or her attitude toward jogging rather than on his or her attitude toward exercising in general. Schuller and Yarmey (2001) report that, within the courtroom, attitudes that are specifically relevant to a particular case will predict a juror's verdict (e.g., a juror's attitude toward sexual abuse will predict his or her verdict in a sexual assault case). Similarly, Ellsworth (1991) found that favorable attitudes toward the death penalty are predictive of guilty verdicts in capital murder trials (in which the defendants can be sentenced to death).

What are the possible sources of bias in a juror? Vidmar and Schuller (2001) identified four types of juror prejudice: interest, specific, generic, and normative prejudice. First, **interest prejudice** refers to a juror having a particular interest or stake in the outcome of a trial. For example, a juror might be related to someone who is called to testify or might know someone who has been charged with the same offense. Second, **specific prejudice** occurs when the juror holds attitudes or beliefs that might interfere with his or her ability to be impartial in a particular case. Specific prejudice might arise from exposure to pretrial publicity presented in the media that biases the juror's judgment of the case. Third, **generic prejudice** refers to possessing general attitudes (e.g., racist views) that would interfere with an unbiased evaluation of the evidence. Finally, **normative prejudice** refers to a juror believing that there is such strong community sentiment supporting a particular outcome of the case that his or her ability to decide the case impartially based on the evidence becomes compromised in favor of the perceived normative attitude.

There are several remedies that could be invoked to deal with biased jurors. First, as stated, if a potential juror is deemed to be biased, he or she may be removed during the voir dire, that is, the preliminary examination to determine the competency of a juror. Second, with a high-profile crime, extensive pretrial publicity sometimes can make it difficult to select impartial jurors from the community in which the crime took place. In such an instance, the location or venue of the trial could be moved, for example, to another city. Third, if during a trial one or more members of a jury become aware of information that might bias their judgment (e.g., hearing a rumor, seeing information in the media), the trial might need to be adjourned until such time passes that the prejudicial information becomes less salient. Vidmar and Schuller (2001) noted that the latter is the most rarely used solution.

Inadmissible Evidence

The function of the jury is to reach a decision about the guilt or innocence of the defendant beyond a reasonable doubt based solely on the admissible trial evidence. The jury sometimes may be exposed to evidence that is determined to be unreliable or deemed by the judge to be legally inadmissible, in which case the jury members may be instructed to "disregard" what they had just seen or heard. In the Matti Baranovski case, for example, the jury heard that the prosecution's star witness, a 16-year-old boy, had told the police that he saw the whole thing and reported in considerable detail what had happened, describing how each of the three suspects had "soccer kicked" Matti "like a lifeless bag . . . like a rag doll" (Gadd, 2003, p. A11). Under cross-examination, however, the witness admitted that he had fabricated the whole story 3 days after the killing to protect himself from prosecution. He was repeatedly caught in lies under oath, and it also was revealed that he had his own criminal history for robbery, theft, and drug offenses, leading the judge to refer to him as an "unsavory witness." Moreover, the defense attorney claimed that the police, acting under intense pressure from the public to make an arrest, adopted his version of the crime and failed to consider disconfirming evidence. All of this negative information about the witness and the actions of the police led the judge to instruct the jury to disregard the witness's testimony in arriving at the verdict. How does a jury deal with evidence that they have been exposed to but that turns out to be inadmissible, fabricated, or otherwise false?

Research suggests that it is difficult for jurors to simply erase such information from their minds. In a laboratory experiment by Kassin, Williams, and Saunders (1990), university students, acting as mock jurors, read a transcript of a court case. Half of the participants were given information that implied that an expert witness had a tarnished reputation. The other half of the participants received no such information. Participants were then asked to disregard the information about the witness. When later asked to estimate how credible the witness was, the group that received the unflattering information rated the witness as less credible—even though it had been instructed to ignore this information—than did the group that did not receive the information. Although the findings in the literature are by no means unequivocal (e.g., London & Nunez, 2000), Lieberman and Arndt (2000) noted that various social psychological theories, including belief perseverance, the hindsight bias, and reactance, may account for this effect.

On July 23, 2003, after a 4½-month trial and 7 days of deliberation, the jury found two of the three young men accused in Matti's case guilty of manslaughter. The third was acquitted due to a lack of evidence. In the end, did the three defendants receive a fair trial given the complexities of the case? Based on the admissible evidence, did the jurors construct a valid narrative or "story" of what happened that November evening (Pennington & Hastie, 1986), or—as the defense claimed—was justice denied? Although the case has ended, at the time of this writing, it was about to be appealed, leaving that determination up to an appeals court judge.

CULTURE CAPSULE: SENTENCING CIRCLES—AN ABORIGINAL APPROACH TO SANCTIONING

Sentencing circles represent a unique, community-based approach to criminal sanctioning that draws on traditional healing practices of North American Aboriginal cultures. The underlying philosophy of the sentencing circle is *restorative justice* or repairing harm. There is a focus on healing (the victim, the offender, and the community), engaging in respectful dialogue, taking responsibility, achieving consensus, condemning the behavior and not the person, and rebuilding community relations. The sentencing circle involves a process in which people sit together in a circle and face each other. The people typically include victims, offenders, friends, family members, and various members of the community, including elders and representatives of the traditional criminal justice system (e.g., judges, lawyers, police). Indeed, a fundamental principle of the sentencing circle is that the process is seen as more important than the sentence (Griffiths & Cunningham, 2000). In deciding to use a sentencing circle, all relevant stakeholders, including the victim and the offender, must agree to the process. Ensuring that the sentencing circle is seen as a safe place for open dialogue is of paramount importance. Sentencing circles are coordinated by community members in collaboration with representatives from the criminal justice system. They may be used for a variety of offenses for both adult and juvenile offenders.

Within the sentencing circle, each member has a chance to speak while holding a *talking piece,* which can be anything that has a connection to, and meaning for, the community (e.g., feather, stone, stick, piece of sculpture). At the end of the process, the participants as a group formulate a sanction that addresses the needs of all stakeholders. The agreement that is reached is signed by the offender, the victim, and the police with the understanding that the agreement will be implemented by the community. As a result, the community, rather than the justice system alone, has control over the disposition of the case and ensuring that the sanction is carried out. The agreement may include conditions such as an apology to the victim and the community, compensation payment to the victim, community work, house arrest, banishment to a wilderness location, surrendering weapons or ownership of a vehicle, and entering a counseling program for substance abuse, anger management, or domestic violence (Griffiths & Cunningham, 2000). Although there is very little formal evaluation of sentencing circles (Wilson, Huculak, & McWhinnie, 2002), the available evidence suggests that they are a promising alternative to the traditional criminal justice system's response to crime that far too often excludes the community and the victim from the justice process (Braithwaite, 2000). Indeed, there has been a slow but steady movement across North America toward restorative community justice practices as a response to crime.

The Prison Setting

The guilty men were sentenced to 10 years in prison. Unless the sentence is overturned on appeal, they will join the many thousands of other people, both in Canada and in the United States, who are already confined to prison. In the United States, as of June 30, 2000, there were 1,305,253 inmates serving time in state, federal, or private prisons (U.S. Department of Justice, 2001) at a cost of roughly $3.6 billion (for correctional activities only), just a fraction of the $26.7 billion in the total federal criminal justice budget (Office of Management and Budget, 2001). In addition, these individuals represented only a small percentage of people serving time in the two countries given that the vast majority of convicted criminals—71% in the United States—serve their sentences in the community such as through probation or parole (U.S. Department of Justice, 2003).

If asked to reflect on what it is like inside a prison, you might draw on images you have seen in the media, for instance, on television shows such as *Oz* or in movies such as *The Shawshank Redemption, The Green Mile,* and *Dead Man Walking.* Your sense might be that prisons are hard, cold, and brutal places; where inmates keep their mouths shut and mind their own business; where the sound of slamming heavy steel doors pervades the place as access from one corridor to the next is carefully monitored and controlled; where there is a clear hierarchy among the prison population that is controlled by the toughest "solid" inmates and the sex offenders are on the bottom rung; and where the correctional officers, also known as guards or "screws," look askew from this coercive environment or even contribute to it.

On the other hand, your impression might be that prisons are quite the opposite, that is, that they are places where inmates enjoy many rights and privileges; where they receive a bed and "three squares" a day and can engage in recreational activities; and where they can upgrade their educations, acquire valuable trade skills, and participate in treatment programs (and all at no financial cost to them). To an extent, these depictions might characterize some maximum (the former) or minimum (the latter) security facilities. However, the reality is more complex than this given that there is a wide range of social environments—from very repressive to more humane—found within prison walls across North America. This subsection examines the social climate of correctional facilities, including the impact of a "therapeutic" prison environment on offenders' chances for rehabilitation and subsequent reintegration into society.

Goals of Prison

What purpose is served by a prison sentence? Prisons serve different (sometimes conflicting) functions, one of which is to protect society by removing a criminal from the streets, and this also serves as a form of punishment for the criminal's antisocial behavior. This function represents the goal of incapacitation. Other goals include general deterrence (for society), specific deterrence (for the individual), rehabilitation (i.e., to correct or modify the criminal behavior and prepare the offender for reintegration into society), denunciation (i.e., to send a message that this type of behavior will not be tolerated), and retribution (i.e., to serve a sentence as "repayment" for the crime). Each goal reflects a different conceptualization of justice, equity, and fairness dating back to the ancient philosopher Aristotle. Since the 1970s, we have seen a shift away from a philosophy that endorses the goal of rehabilitation to one that places greater emphasis on punishment and a "get tough on crime" perspective (Benson, 2003).

How effective is the practice of incarceration in preventing future crime? Research suggests that it is of limited value and may, in fact, contribute to an increase in the risk of recidivism. Furthermore, longer sentences have been found to be unrelated to the risk of recidivism (Griffiths & Cunningham, 2000). Although there are many possible reasons to explain the limited effectiveness, one possible explanation is that the prison environment is not conducive to the offender making the kinds of personal changes that lead to a reduced risk of reoffending. In other words, there is a poor *fit* between the environment and the needs of the inmate. If we change the prison environment to match the needs of the offender, would the result be a better outcome? The answer is a resounding yes, although matching the individual to the appropriate environment is by no means an exact science.

Social Climate of Prisons

One way in which to think about the social dynamics of a prison environment, or its social climate, is in terms of the notion of the keeper and the kept. At the most basic level, the role of the prison staff members is to enforce the rules, and the role of the inmates is to toe the line. Moving beyond this simplistic paradigm, as you extend the concepts of roles and relationships, there exists a vast array of social climates.

The notion of social climate derives from various streams of psychology, including the work of Barker (1968) on the impact of environments (i.e., "behavior settings") on human behavior and Murray's (1938) theory of personality. Murray proposed that behavior is determined by the degree of fit between the needs of the individual (e.g., need to affiliate, need to achieve) and environmental *press* (demands), which entail aspects of the environment that either facilitate or impede the likelihood of the individual's meeting these needs. For example, a designated study area in a student residence building that is furnished with sofas, a television, and a bar refrigerator might impede satisfaction of achievement needs but promote satisfaction of affiliation needs.

Measuring the social climates of prisons. Moos (1973) seized on the notion of the person–environment relationship and suggested that environments, like individuals, have "personalities" similar to the needs put forth by Murray (1938) (e.g., achievement-oriented environments, interpersonally supportive environments, controlling environments). Moos believed, furthermore, that these environmental personalities could be assessed, at least as they are perceived by the setting members. As a result, he developed a number of scales to assess the environments of various settings, including psychiatric wards, university residence halls, and sheltered care settings for the elderly. One scale, the Correctional Institutions Environment Scale (CIES), measures correctional environments (Moos, 1987).

According to Moos (1987), the social climate of a correctional setting, such as a prison, jail,

detention center, or group home for offenders, is composed of three broad dimensions, each of which can be assessed by three subscales. The dimensions and subscales are as follows: Relationship-Oriented (involvement, support, and expressiveness), Personal Development (autonomy, practical orientation, and personal problem orientation), and System Maintenance and System Change (order and organization, program clarity, and staff control). To measure a correctional environment, the 90-item CIES may be completed by both residents and staff members. The result is a profile of their shared or combined perceptions across the nine subscales. In addition, each informant group (staff members and residents) may complete the scale twice—once in terms of the "real" environment and once in terms of the "ideal" environment. The difference between the residents' and staff members' averaged profiles and between the averaged real and ideal profiles reflects the different perceptions of the social climate and may identify areas for program development. For example, if staff members rate their ideal version of a group home for adolescent sex offenders as being high on the three Personal Development dimension subscales but rate the home in which they work as low on the subscales, the discrepancy might suggest areas for improvement to bring the facility in line with the staff members' vision of an effective group home that will meet the needs of the client population.

Moos (1987) further suggested that the profile of scores across the nine subscales of the three primary dimensions reflects a setting's particular orientation. Some facilities may place particular emphasis on supporting residents and fostering their involvement in helping each other (Relationship-Oriented). Other settings may encourage residents to take responsibility for their personal growth and development and to develop practical life skills (Personal Development). Moreover, some residences may emphasize the value of maintaining order and structure and ensuring that residents follow the rules (System Maintenance and System Change). Although no study has directly tested the notion of a person–environment fit with criminals, in theory offenders should be matched with the type of facility that best suits their needs. For instance, offenders who have

Figure 12.3   Stanford Prison Simulation

strong needs to work toward self-improvement may be better served by the second type of setting, whereas residents who require a great deal of structure and staff control may be best suited to the latter type of facility.

The Stanford Prison simulation. As stated previously, the social climate of a prison is composed of various dimensions that define the "personality" of the setting. These dimensions reflect the nature of the roles and relationships between staff members and inmates, including the ways in which the inherent power imbalance is negotiated, the role of static (e.g., electronic surveillance) versus dynamic (e.g., relationships among staff members and residents) security barriers between staff members and inmates, and the ways in which rules are enforced and order is maintained.

If the social climate of a prison were placed on a single continuum of the staff–inmate relationships, we might place the Stanford Prison simulation (Haney, Banks, & Zimbardo, 1973) and its demonstrated potential for the cruel treatment of prisoners near one end and a "therapeutic community" (see next subsection) and its humane approach to the treatment of prison inmates (Lipton, 1998) near the other end.

The Stanford Prison simulation was a powerful demonstration of how social roles influence behavior. In this investigation, 21 healthy male volunteers, screened on various personality measures, were randomly assigned to one of two roles: a mock prisoner or a mock guard. After being "arrested" at their homes, the prisoners were taken to a mock prison constructed in the basement of the psychology department building at Stanford University and placed in cells, to be watched over by the prison guards. The results, as they unfolded over the next few days, were startling and unexpected. While playing out their assigned roles, some of the guards became increasingly abusive and cruel, using degrading forms of punishment, including locking prisoners in a closet and withholding food. The prisoners experienced various negative psychological effects, including disorganized thinking, fits of rage, and acute depression. As a result of these deleterious outcomes, the simulation was halted after only 6 days, although the original plan called for it to last for 14 days (Figure 12.3).

Although only a simulation, the Stanford Prison simulation reminds us of the inherent power imbalance that exists within a correctional setting and its potential for abuse. The oppressive conditions in prisons for women have been particularly well documented, although reforms over the past decade have brought about some improvements (Hannah-Moffat, 2002). The harsh and degrading conditions of prisons come in many forms and degrees of severity, including poor sanitary or health conditions, overcrowding, limited opportunities to exercise, assaults on staff members and inmates, hunger strikes, and prison riots. There is also some evidence that staff members are complicit in peer-on-peer violence. In a survey of 100 incarcerated young offenders, 47% stated that they were aware of prison staff members who had either said or done something to put an inmate at risk for harm, for example, starting a rumor or letting an inmate into another inmate's cell (Peterson-Badali & Koegl, 2002).

A riot on February 29, 1996, at Bluewater Youth Centre, a 90-bed secure custody facility for young offenders in Goderich, Ontario, stands as a stark reminder of the potential for abuse of prison inmates. Correctional officers were on strike at the time, and substantial changes were made to inmates' routines and schedules, including a reduction in supervision, activities, and treatment programming. During the angry rampage, inmates set fires, broke windows, and plundered bathrooms, causing $250,000 in damage. Staff members may have "planted" matches and barbecue fluid and may have encouraged the dissent that triggered the riot. As a result of the incident, 52 male youths were transferred to other facilities, including a detention center designed primarily for adult offenders. During the course of being either transported to a facility or held at the detention center, some youths were punched, kicked, hit with batons, and/or yelled at by managers acting in the place of correctional officers. Several youths had hair yanked out of their heads as they were escorted into the building, and some were kicked so hard that they had boot marks across their faces. Staff members said that they needed to intimidate the youths to maintain order. At a second detention center, a 16-year-old boy with serious behavior problems who had become identified as a "rat" was placed in a "segregation" cell with another youth, contrary to institutional policy. Two days later, the cellmate

beat the 16-year-old to death in spite of the victim's repeated calls for assistance. In the end, 30 charges were laid against seven managers and two bailiffs, and 12 youths received $1 million in total compensation from the province of Ontario. A public inquest into the death of the 1 youth resulted in 119 recommendations, many of which dealt with the transportation and treatment of young people in custody.

Prison Approaches to Rehabilitation

Therapeutic communities. Near the other end of the social climate continuum, we find a more humane prison environment known as a therapeutic community. Maxwell Jones is the person most closely associated with therapeutic communities. Jones (1953) developed a number of principles on which the traditional therapeutic communities were based, including democratization, communalism, reality confrontation, and peer group influence.

Drawing on various perspectives within social psychology and clinical psychology, including social ecological, social learning, and humanistic theories, a **therapeutic community** is a holistic residential environment that is designed to promote the personal growth and development of the residents. The primary aim is to bring about changes in attitudes, beliefs, and behaviors that lead to a healthier and more adaptive lifestyle on return to the community than the lifestyle that led the person to be admitted into the facility in the first place (e.g., substance abuse, criminality). The core concept is *living learning* as the therapeutic community adheres to the principles of honesty, openness, self-governance, and learning from individuals' efforts to live together (Grant, 1980). The distinguishing feature of the therapeutic community, in contrast to other therapeutic approaches, is the role of the community, which is the primary vehicle for promoting social and psychological change.

Extending the therapeutic community concept to correctional settings, additional principles include building relationships with one another, authority figures, and women and children; attending to antisocial attitudes, values, and beliefs as well as victim awareness, contrition, and consequences for the victim; and developing strategies for avoiding reoffending (Lipton, 1998). A prison-based therapeutic community builds on the notion that prisons are microcosms of the larger coercive and maladaptive environments that inmates often inhabit on the streets. As such, therapeutic communities provide opportunities for offenders to experience a highly structured setting that models a cooperative prosocial environment. However, residents must be carefully screened before being admitted to a therapeutic community because the approach is only for those prisoners who are motivated to participate in the unique environment. Furthermore, as Wexler (1995) noted, a prison-based therapeutic community must recognize that it "is a 'guest' of corrections and that while treatment is highly important, it is secondary to security" (p. 62). At the same time, for the therapeutic community to succeed, it must be seen as separate, and in other ways reasonably autonomous, from the custodial prison environment. Prison-based therapeutic communities have been implemented in many states, including New York, California, Oregon, and Texas, as well as in Canada and elsewhere in the world.

● FOCUS ON INTERVENTION

The Stay'n Out program is an example of a well-defined prison-based therapeutic community. Developed in 1977 in New York State, Stay'n Out is a 12-month program for male and female prisoners with substance abuse problems (Lipton, 1998). Program participants are phased into the program over three stages: (a) induction, (b) treatment, and (c) consolidation of treatment gains and reentry into the community.

The *first stage* (*induction*) involves orientation, assessment, and assimilation into the therapeutic community model. The *second stage* (*treatment*) is aimed at personal growth. The treatment program is highly structured with daily schedules for group, work, and community activities. This orderly and regimented schedule is meant to counter the disorder that many offenders experience on the streets and that may be suffused with boredom, negative thinking, and drug use. On a day-to-day basis, residents involve themselves in group seminars, often led by other residents, in which they discuss a wide range of issues focusing on positive and prosocial behaviors, such as self-reliance and personal responsibility, rather than dwelling on negative issues, such as criminality and addictions. Residents are expected to participate in group counseling that focuses on self-discipline, self-worth, respect for authority, and acceptance of guidance for problem areas. Although there is little formal written curriculum, the programming is communicated orally and derived from the day-to-day experiences of the residents.

During this phase, residents are able to earn positions of increased responsibility through hard emotional work (e.g., engage in appropriate sharing and expressing of feelings within a therapeutic context). The *final stage* (*reentry*) involves strengthening and reinforcing the treatment gains that have been made and developing a discharge plan. At each stage, there are clearly defined goals, activities, and expectations with both positive and negative consequences when deserved.

Conceptually, in terms of the Moos (1987) dimensions described earlier, Stay'n Out would be characterized as high on both the Relationship-Oriented and Personal Development scales and as moderate to high on the System Maintenance and System Change scale. From a theoretical standpoint, drawing on self-help traditions (Levy, 2000), social learning theory (Bandura, 1977b), and theories of intergroup relations (Yalom, 1995), the focus of each Stay'n Out program component is on learning to respect oneself and others through positive interpersonal relations within the shared environment. The more seasoned residents model appropriate behavior, share their insights with new members, and directly and immediately confront and neutralize any negative or "jailhouse" attitudes and behaviors that are displayed by the residents. Moreover, some of the staff members are "ex-addicts/felons who serve as credible role models" (Wexler, 1995, p. 63).

Is the Stay'n Out program effective? Over the past 25 years, evaluation research has consistently demonstrated its effectiveness with drug-using offenders. For instance, using a quasi-experimental design, Wexler, Falkin, and Lipton (1990) followed up several hundred men who had participated in either Stay'n Out, a nontherapeutic community milieu drug treatment program, or a drug counseling treatment program as well as a "no treatment" comparison group (i.e., offenders who volunteered for Stay'n Out but never entered). The results indicated that 3 years after release from prison, 26.9% of the Stay'n Out group had recidivated, compared with 34.6%, 39.8%, and 40.9% of the milieu, counseling, and no treatment groups, respectively. The Stay'n Out group also had fewer parole violations than the other groups. Moreover, the longer the individuals participated in the Stay'n Out program (up to 12 months), the more positive were the postrelease outcomes. The annual cost per treatment bed for the Stay'n Out program was found to be relatively inexpensive at less than $3,000 over the cost of incarceration in a state facility (Lipton, 1998). Compare that figure with the lifetime cost to society of a heavy drug user, estimated to be between $483,000 and $1.26 million (Cohen, 1998). Similar positive treatment gains have been observed with male and female offenders in other prison-based therapeutic communities implemented around the world (Lipton, 1998; Wexler, 1995). Today, in contrast to a political climate that increasingly favors punitive measures for criminal offenders, prison-based therapeutic communities such as Stay'n Out stand out in embracing the philosophy of rehabilitation over punishment and favoring the humane treatment of prisoners. As a result, the practice of therapeutic communities remains controversial and is not widespread, although their effectiveness with certain populations of offenders, particularly those with substance abuse problems, has clearly been demonstrated.

Boot camps. Over the past decade, the boot camp (also known as shock incarceration) has become an increasingly popular alternative to imprisonment for young offenders. By the year 2000, there were at least 70 boot camps for juveniles in the United States (MacKenzie, Wilson, & Kidder, 2001). Although the specific elements of boot camps vary considerably from one boot camp to another, they are generally designed as highly structured residential programs that last between 6 and 30 weeks. Boot camps use military-type components, including uniforms, drills, physical training, chain of command, manual labor, and a focus on strict discipline. There is an emphasis on immediate punishment for misconduct, usually involving a form of physical activity (e.g., push-ups). These programs are rigorous and highly regimented with activities that keep the youths occupied from dawn to dusk. Additional components may include life skills training, academic education, and drug and alcohol treatment. Aftercare community-based programming, which lasts from 6 to 9 months, also may be included. The aim of boot camps is to teach life skills and instill a sense of self-discipline and personal responsibility, factors that are believed to be causally related to a reduction in criminal behavior.

Evaluations of boot camp programs suggest that, despite their many advocates, they are of limited value in reducing the risk of recidivating after discharge. A 5-year quasi-experimental evaluation conducted by the California Youth Authority (1997) indicated that youths who participated in a boot camp program did not differ from youths in a control group on a variety of important indicators—rates of criminal activity and rearrest, severity of subsequent offenses, school attendance, number of days worked, and number of positive drug tests. These negative findings were corroborated by a meta-analysis of 29 experimental or quasi-experimental evaluation studies by MacKenzie and colleagues (2001). These researchers found no differences in the rate of recidivism between the youths who participated in a boot camp and youths who participated in comparison programs.

As you may have noticed, the social climate of boot camps differs greatly from that of therapeutic communities. In terms of Moos's (1987) framework, boot camps are especially high on the dimension of System Maintenance and System Change. The apparent ineffectiveness of this kind of programmatic intervention contrasts sharply with the promise shown by the more relationship-oriented Stay'n Out intervention. As MacKenzie and colleagues (2001) stated, "Critics argue that many of the components of the camps are in direct opposition to the type of relationships and supportive conditions that are needed for quality therapeutic programming" (p. 128). Certainly, one lesson that has been learned from the boot camp experience is that positive treatment gains will be limited when programs place a greater emphasis on surveillance and control, which support the principles of incapacitation and punishment, than when programs address the youths' psychological and social needs by providing treatment and aftercare services, which are in keeping with the principles of rehabilitation.

SUMMARY

Social psychologists have pursued many avenues in the application of theories and well-controlled research methodologies to explain and investigate matters concerning crime and the justice system. With regard to the criminal event, this chapter described how, rather than focusing exclusively on the personal characteristics of the individual offender, factors in the environment, such as the presence of others and situational cues that incite aggressive behavior, also may be implicated as determinants of criminal activity. The notion of a person–environment interaction has been incorporated into the general personality and social psychological model of the etiology of criminal behavior. Moreover, given the influential role of the peer group in the criminal activity of youths, the chapter described a study that identified a pattern of social interaction displayed by pairs of 13- and 14-year-olds that facilitates antisocial thinking and behavior.

Social psychological research has contributed to the development of more effective police interviewing techniques that have led to appreciable increases in the amount of information recalled by witnesses without sacrificing accuracy. Research-based procedures for conducting police lineups and constructing mug books have been developed to reduce the incidence of eyewitness error in the identification of witnesses. The chapter reviewed evidence regarding three factors—jury size, juror impartiality, and inadmissible evidence—that influence interpersonal dynamics and decision making involving the key players in a court case (e.g., lawyers, judge, witnesses, defendants, jurors).

The work of Moos in assessing the social climates of social settings (e.g., prison settings) was discussed. Therapeutic communities, representing prison environments that have relationship/personal growth orientations, have been shown to be effective in reducing the risk of recidivism among certain offender types (e.g., those with substance abuse problems). On the other hand, there is little evidence that the more control and discipline-oriented boot camps have rehabilitative value.

13

APPLYING SOCIAL PSYCHOLOGY TO THE COMMUNITY

STEWART PAGE

KATHRYN D. LAFRENIERE

April 8, 1974, surely began as a normal enough day in North America's cities. Undoubtedly, the usual quota of crimes was committed, both major and minor. Statistical chances are that rapes, assaults, and burglaries were committed, probably in a city environment and perhaps in the midst of observers, witnesses, or others who did little or nothing to intervene. In New York City, pedestrians crossed the street (green light or not) after checking to see whether others were about to cross. In Los Angeles, still others were affected by pollution and smog. Some citizens wondered about the formation of community groups with which to protest industrial pollution, toxic wastes, and numerous assaults on the environment.

But that evening in Atlanta, Georgia, a major and historic event occurred in Major League Baseball. The event and its aftermath are relevant to the interface of social psychology and community psychology today. Henry Aaron, a member of the Atlanta Braves, hit career home run number 715, thereby eclipsing the former record of 714 career home runs held for many years by Babe Ruth. Home run number 715 was a historic and fitting reward for a renowned athlete. But in 1973, throughout the previous baseball season as Aaron was approaching the home run record, his life was made difficult by many people and groups. They issued death threats against him and threatened the safety of his children both at home and at school. He was forced to hire security guards for himself and his family. Although many were happy and excited about what was happening, some baseball fans accepted Aaron's accomplishments rather passively and without much enthusiasm or admiration. Still others verbally abused him, hurled gross and insulting racial comments, and even threw objects at him during games while (perhaps surprisingly) the other fans nearby typically did nothing to object or intervene. Many citizens could not tolerate the fact that a black player was threatening to break a white player's home run record—untouched for 39 years.

- How can we understand the responses to Aaron's accomplishment?
- As Aaron was threatening to break Ruth's record, what factors account for the positive reactions of some, the passive reactions of others, and the negative reactions of still others? Although some fans were apparently less than thrilled, why did others run onto the field and try to run the bases with Aaron after the historic home run number 715?
- Which of these groups of people basically followed the crowd, so to speak, and followed the path of least resistance in responding, and which ones held racial attitudes at a deeply meaningful psychological level, that is, a "gut" level?

This book concerns theoretical applications, that is, instances where the discipline of social psychology might be used to help us understand events in the real world—social psychology taken out of the laboratory, as it were.

Students now have an enormous reference literature as a source of information, and indeed there is an entire universe of possible chapters that might be written about social psychology in the community. This chapter presents a selective but representative survey of events and theoretical ideas that should be of value to readers encountering this kind of material perhaps for the first time, for example, in the context of an undergraduate university course. In fact, our main "guideline" has been the belief that an introduction to this sample of ideas will enable these readers to become significantly more familiar with, and better informed about, the kinds of activities in which community-oriented social psychologists have engaged.

The chapter begins with some historical information about how community psychology came into being and about its connection with social psychology. In fact, most of the descriptions proceed as if social psychology and community psychology were closely related and intertwined; effective research and intervention, if performed in a community setting, presupposes knowledge of ideas drawn from social psychology. Also, social and practical problems, referred to in the title of this book, often occur *in the community.* As such, this chapter is necessarily a collage, that is, a mixture of ideas and findings that have significance in their own right but that are also relevant to, and part of, many of the topics covered elsewhere in the book. As such, perhaps the chapter could serve to help connect and bring together these other topics.

WHAT IS COMMUNITY PSYCHOLOGY?

The Origins of Community Psychology

There is no single definition of community psychology on which all community psychologists would agree. Dalton, Elias, and Wandersman (2001) offered one definition that is consistent with the treatment of community psychology in this chapter: "**Community psychology** concerns the relationships of the individual to communities and society. Through collaborative research and action, community psychologists seek to understand and to enhance the quality of life for individuals, communities, and society" (p. 5, emphasis added). In other words, community psychology is the study of social forces, and of collectives of humans, on behavior, including the study of social rules and norms as these are encountered in the real world, that is, in settings outside the confines of the laboratory so often relied on to generate knowledge in psychology.

Much of community psychology in North America developed during the 1960s out of the general area of mental health. Several problems with institutional (i.e., hospital-based) mental health services came to light during these years. One problem was the high cost associated with in-hospital treatment of persons with mental disorders. Many institutionalized patients, often persons of modest or low financial means, were experiencing long hospital admissions, and

there were few other means available for their care. But the social environments of mental health institutions themselves became a source of concern among mental health professionals and observers of mental health practices (e.g., Goffman, 1961; Rosenhan, 1973). Institutions were criticized as being dehumanizing and ineffective in terms of helping patients to develop skills needed to function adequately in the community after hospitalization. Little was done about prevention of mental disorders or exploring means of assistance other than through hospitalization. Another problem was that the labeling of persons as "mental patients" bore negative effects; that is, having received mental health treatment in an institution too often became a stigmatizing and negative characteristic. Personal and employment difficulties often resulted—and still do—when authorities, such as potential employers, discovered that individuals had received such treatment.

From these roots, there developed a desire for "something better" in mental health practices, including the wish to develop means of providing help as close as possible to the individual's own place of residence and community contacts. There also developed the wish to study communities themselves as sources of psychiatric difficulty—sources "outside" rather than "inside" the person—and to study how these factors contribute to personal hardships and a variety of health problems. Thus, this new approach became focused less on personality or life history factors and more on the study of what external stresses are affecting an individual in his or her life at the current time. Thus, communities, like people, can be relatively healthy or sick, relatively stressful or nonstressful, and so forth. There also has developed an interest in the question of what kinds of community resources are needed to assist formerly hospitalized (or **deinstitutionalized**) persons to reenter and live successfully in the community and, thus, to avoid rehospitalization—or to avoid hospitalization in the first place.

In May 1965, a group of 39 psychologists met in Swampscott, Massachusetts, to discuss new directions for the field of clinical psychology. These psychologists shared a view that many mental health problems were influenced by social conditions outside the individual, and they believed that efforts at treatment needed to target change at the community level. The Swampscott Conference is often regarded as the official "birthplace" of the field of community psychology (Dalton et al., 2001).

Although early community psychology issues were mostly related to mental health concerns, psychologists in social psychology and environmental psychology also became involved in the community movement. This was because they generally have interests in **action research,** which involves applying knowledge actively, promptly, and directly to social problems in the community as well as increasing the empowerment and well-being of citizens (for a fuller discussion of action research, refer to Chapter 16). Increasingly, many psychologists also wanted to test theories and findings from laboratory research to see how well these would hold up when applied to real-life settings. Moreover, many topics studied by psychologists in laboratory settings also have a community aspect or application, for example, the study of social conformity or racial prejudice. Dalton and colleagues (2000) provide a comprehensive summary of how community psychology developed.

The Relevance of Social Psychology to Community Psychology

As described in Chapter 1, **social psychology** is the branch of psychology that seeks to understand how people influence each other based on how they think about, feel about, and relate to one another. **Applied social psychology** attempts to apply social psychological knowledge toward a better understanding of real-life situations (Rudkin, 2003). That is, it draws on social psychological theories, principles, methods, and research evidence to help us understand and develop effective interventions for social and practical problems and to lead to enhanced functioning of individuals, groups, organizations, and communities. Community psychology has a great deal in common with applied social psychology in its emphasis on studying people in their real-world context and in its attempts to find effective solutions for social and practical problems. However, the roots of community psychology lie in its concern with the treatment and general situation of people with mental health problems, and this distinguishes it somewhat from the broader field of applied social psychology. Consistent with this book's emphasis on applied social psychology, the topics covered in this chapter focus on the more "social" aspects of community psychology rather than dealing primarily with mental health concerns.

Community Psychology Approaches and Goals

Community psychology is characterized by a number of underlying philosophical approaches and goals. Duffy and Wong (2003) identified several of these. Community psychology places importance on prevention rather than treatment, and it emphasizes the enhancement of individuals' strengths and competencies rather than focusing on their weaknesses and problems. It employs an **ecological perspective,** that is, the idea that we should examine the fit between people and their environments in understanding their circumstances and that we should strive to achieve an ideal person–environment fit to create a healthy situation in which each individual can function optimally and experience a positive sense of community. Community psychology respects *diversity,* valuing differences among people rather than assigning negative and stigmatizing labels to those who are not members of the dominant group or culture. Other goals of community psychology are to analyze social change and guide social action toward resolving social problems. Community psychology takes an approach to addressing social problems and promoting well-being through **empowerment** of individuals and communities, that is, helping people to gain control over their own lives and to take an active role in participating in issues that affect their communities.

Although this chapter does not provide in-depth coverage of all these concepts and goals, they should be kept in mind as important themes that underlie a community psychology approach. This chapter introduces a particular research method that is used in some research relevant to community psychology and then focuses on selected issues related to the goals and approaches discussed heretofore. Environmental influences on individuals and communities are subsequently discussed in relation to some classic social psychological studies. The issue of stigmatization and labeling of those who are *different* in some respect is then considered, and relevant research investigations are described. Finally, the chapter examines perspectives on achieving social change through prevention approaches and addressing social problems such as community violence and the challenge of meeting the global needs of diverse populations in a rapidly changing world.

PERSPECTIVES ON COMMUNITY-BASED RESEARCH: UNOBTRUSIVE METHODS

Although the topic of research methods was dealt with formally in Chapter 3, it must be mentioned here briefly because it has been an area of special identity and special significance for those interested in the interface of social psychology and community psychology. For example, social psychologists have learned much from **unobtrusive research,** that is, community-based research studies in which research participants are not aware that they are being studied or observed. These methods are significant as well because we can use them to compare what people say with what they actually do in different types of community settings. This approach was stimulated by the publication of Webb, Campbell, Schwartz, and Sechrest's (1966/1981) book titled *Unobtrusive Measures.* "Unobtrusive" means subtle or hidden, that is, "in the background." Although community psychology was not well established when *Unobtrusive Measures* was first published, several important studies using these measures exist in the relevant literature. For example, a classic study by LaPierre (1934) showed that restaurant managers who described on the telephone their policy of not serving Chinese couples seldom refused to serve such couples when they actually visited these managers' restaurants. Dutton (1981) also found that restaurant managers who advertised formal dress requirements for customers rarely enforced this requirement when visited by customers who deliberately violated it. Interestingly, this was especially the case for black couples.

Some types of community settings have been used to test a provocative idea called the *repressed affect* hypothesis (Weitz, 1972). This is the Freudian idea that anxieties or negative dispositions toward certain persons or groups can be repressed or "bottled up" inside us (Freud would say that they have been rendered unconscious) but may show "leakage" under certain everyday situations in which we interact with these persons or groups. Frequently, the interaction in which leakage may occur is quite subtle and may involve quite "normal," routine, and unremarkable behavior. Weitz found, for example, that although samples of white research participants indicated high acceptance of blacks on questionnaire measures, these participants still showed subtle nonverbal and gestural signs of rejection toward blacks when they were observed unobtrusively in cooperative, racially mixed work situations. Taylor (1979) found that white teachers, who indicated high acceptance of blacks on questionnaire measures, showed negative nonverbal behaviors toward black students when these teaching interactions were observed unobtrusively through hidden one-way mirrors. Also, Page (1997) found that students at a Canadian university, who were studied unobtrusively over time in a large cafeteria and who had shown strong acceptance of minority groups in questionnaire data, selected black cashiers less often than they did white cashiers on exiting the cafeteria. These unobtrusive research methods allow psychologists to effectively study aversive racism, that is, racist behavior among people who might think they are not racist. Racism is discussed in greater detail in Chapter 15.

The public's affection for the classic *Candid Camera* television series (and its currently popular updated version), as well as its recognition by social scientists, is testimony to its significance as a method for the unobtrusive study of human behavior. Similarly, a more recent episode of ABC's *Prime Time Live* program used hidden videotaping procedures to show that blacks tended to receive poorer service in stores and to be quoted higher prices for used cars by dealers relative to prices given and quoted to white shoppers.

Milgram (1970) is also responsible for developing another type of unobtrusive research measure, particularly suited for the study of beliefs and social attitudes within a community environment, called the "lost letter" technique.

In this technique, letters addressed to persons who appear to belong to certain organizations (e.g., political parties) are left ("lost") in public places such as subways and buses. The rate of return for such materials can be a useful measure of the level of positive regard toward the organizations indicated on the letters. Milgram has used this method, for example, to predict results of political elections. Others also have used the procedure in contexts involving measurement of attitudes. Page (1981), for example, found that letters appearing to be written to (or by) psychiatric patients were far less likely to be mailed than were letters with neutral or no information about apparent social status of the sender or receiver. The unobtrusive measures approach is revisited later in the chapter in connection with the issue of stigmatization.

ENVIRONMENTAL INFLUENCE: CLASSIC STUDIES RELEVANT TO COMMUNITY PSYCHOLOGY

The goal of understanding communities by way of applying social psychology has not always been oriented toward immediate solution of community problems, nor has the "applying" always been a successful endeavor. Not all social psychologists have a community interest or background. However, many have been interested in trying to apply social psychological ideas and research to community-based problems and in trying to understand how communities function with respect to topics such as stigmatization, prejudice, and conformity. This section summarizes some classic studies relevant to such topics.

Behavior as Autonomous Versus Social Conformist

Have you ever looked at other drivers to see whether their windshield wipers were on or looked at others to see whether they were going to laugh at a joke or agree with a controversial statement? A telling demonstration of the effects of groups (as a "mini-community" or organization) on an individual's behavior is taken from the research of Solomon Asch on **conformity,** defined as changing one's behavior to act in a way that is consistent with the behavior or expectations of others. Asch's (1956) work has become important as a paradigm, that is, as a general technique for research on social conformity and its connection with events in many community settings.

If you were a participant in Asch's research, you would take your seat at a long rectangular table with others believed by you to be other participants in the research. By prearrangement, you would always find yourself seated at the end of the table. Using a series of charts, Asch would ask which of several vertical lines was the same height as another comparison line. On several trials, your fellow participants (whose behavior was actually prearranged by Asch) would make incorrect—sometimes obviously incorrect— choices. In turn, each person at the table would give an answer, one by one, before you would give yours. (From time to time, you probably find yourself in this same dilemma. Do you go along with the group's consensus even when the group seems to be offering clearly wrong answers?) Asch found that approximately 75% of his participants made errors of judgment; that is, they went along at least once with what appeared to be the group's opinion even when this opinion could clearly be seen as inaccurate by an objective observer. Some participants were strong in terms of resisting the group consensus, but many others went along with it consistently throughout these experiments.

The "moral" of Asch's (1956) work is important, and in various forms it reappears in much social psychological research. Other people often cause us to believe (or publicly state) that something is true even when objective independent observers can see that it is not so—and even when we, if giving our honest opinion in private, would also see it as untrue. This general social psychological situation—having to deal with the social influence pressures of our social environment—is one that is found frequently in community settings.

Prejudice as Conformity to Social Rules and Community Norms

Conformity pressures are also apparent in the community research of Thomas Pettigrew on the matter of racial desegregation. With particular reference to community norms about racial separation, Pettigrew (1961, 1988) studied communities in both the northern and southern United States. He found that much discriminatory behavior by whites against blacks was related less to the internal personality characteristics of whites (e.g., their scores on measures of authoritarianism or rigidity) than to their need to *conform* to what they believed were the racial preferences of *others around them,* hence the reference to Pettigrew's notion of following the path of least resistance in the opening vignette. The community norms in these instances tended to be anti-black and supportive of racial segregation. However, Pettigrew found no evidence that authoritarianism, a personality trait associated with racism, was greater in the southern areas where racial problems have tended to be more intense. Similarly, he also found that many northern communities, in comparison with southern areas, showed less racial discrimination and less intense norms favoring segregation but were no less authoritarian or dogmatic in terms of the basic personality orientation of their residents.

Pettigrew also pointed out that most (seemingly) prejudiced individuals were also quite capable of changing their practices and behaviors once they found themselves in job situations, certain geographical areas, or communities whose norms did not support segregation. Pettigrew referred to these individuals as "latent liberals." Their liberalism and potential for change were hidden, but they were capable of immediate change once the norms of the surrounding situation called for different behavior. You may be a latent liberal yourself in terms of considering your response to controversial issues where there are conformity pressures, for example, if you find yourself not speaking up in groups about something even though you privately disagree with the group's views or if you find yourself pondering some action but then wondering, "What would the neighbors think?"

Thus, many discriminatory practices appear to have a strong foundation in individuals' needs for conformity to community or group norms and do not usually represent authoritarian or other types of negative personality characteristics. From Pettigrew's framework, we realize the relative ineffectiveness of "therapy" or other procedures aimed at "repairing" individual personalities one by one given that the origin and functioning of many social problems can be seen as social and community based rather than individual in origin or causation. Again following Pettigrew, the most effective interventions for problems concerning racial prejudice would be those in which role models, such as well-known athletes and community leaders, could be seen presenting views opposing discrimination and conveying that these views represent the norms and preferred moral positions of the community. You may recall that Chapter 4 presented an intervention designed to change drinking behavior by altering people's perceived norms. How might you use norms as the basis of an intervention to change racist behavior?

Thus, we see that our **attitudes** (i.e., our beliefs, opinions, and feelings about particular issues, objects, or situations) often follow our need to conform to what we see around us, both in our immediate social groupings and in the community generally. Some of our attitudes are not deeply "internalized"; that is, they do not matter to us so much psychologically that they cannot change when the norms of our social surroundings are changed. On this point, one should refer to Kelman's (1958) important observations about attitudes. An attitude can be held at three different levels of psychological depth or importance. Kelman called the first (shallowest) level **compliance,** where you go along with something (e.g., obeying a police officer's instructions, generally supporting the idea of free speech) but do not care about it that much internally; it is not that important to you psychologically. Kelman called the second (next deepest) level **identification,** where an attitude is a bit more stable and more meaningful and important to the person psychologically (e.g., giving money to an organization, allowing your name to be on a petition). Kelman called the third (deepest) level **internalization,** where an attitude held is one that *really matters* to you deeply. At this level, you might not only give money to an organization but also openly support it, march in a parade about it, or try hard to convert others to it. At this level, you do not hesitate to take action to back up your belief. Attitudes held at this level do not easily change as the surrounding social norms change because they are internalized and part of the individual's self-definition. Some subgroups in the community may manifest internalized attitudes, for example, racial extremists, distributors of hate literature, and those who shout racial insults at high-achieving black athletes such as Henry Aaron.

Bystander Effects

We often believe that human behavior is caused by certain internal traits or personal characteristics. We are always classifying people as healthy or sick, normal or abnormal, criminal or law abiding, and so forth. That is, we tend to believe that good people will do good things and that bad people will do bad things. We make this assumption based on what people's *personality characteristics* seem to be like, possibly as a result of how they scored on a personality test or similar measure. Yet we are taught, and retaught, by research that our social behavior depends largely on how we assess and are affected by the surrounding social situation.

One powerful example of the influence of the social situation involves a phenomenon known as **bystander nonintervention** (e.g., Darley & Latané, 1970), which occurs when multiple people who witness an emergency situation fail to intervene. It is believed that this occurs partly as a result of what is called **diffusion of responsibility,** where observers do not help because they believe that *other* observers will help. In a series of studies in which they arranged for fake but realistic emergency situations to occur in public places, Darley and Latané (1970) found results that seemingly contradicted common sense. If a crime or accident victim (e.g., someone experiencing a fall, someone apparently being robbed) was victimized in the midst of several people or in a crowd, the person was less likely to receive assistance than in instances where the incident occurred in the presence of one person alone. Darley and Latané, for example, staged a robbery in a real store. Bystanders witnessed the robbery either alone or in a group. Bystanders reported the robbery and took action much more frequently when they were alone. One explanation offered by Darley and Latané was that a diffusion, or spreading out, of responsibility occurs when there are others around, that is, a much reduced

likelihood that any individual person will feel personally and individually responsible for taking action. Each such person can easily "hide" psychologically by attributing responsibility to others without feeling undue guilt or bringing attention to oneself. The individual in a group perceives that he or she will not be individually blamed for failing to act. Indeed, there are many real-life examples in community settings where such events have occurred. These examples all follow the same basic pattern in which helpful action, rescue, or other assistance to a victim is less likely when the emergency occurs in the presence of a group as opposed to one person alone. A notorious example was the 1964 case of Kitty Genovese, a young nurse who was murdered as she walked toward her apartment in Queens, New York. A total of 38 neighbors witnessed or became aware of the attack, which lasted approximately 30 minutes, yet nearly an hour passed before anyone took action to help or call police. Similarly, Milgram (1970) studied reactions of passersby to a child who appeared to be lost and confused. The child (supervised carefully throughout) was taken to a busy corner in New York, where he proceeded to ask pedestrians for change so that he could make a phone call. In general, the child was helped infrequently, with most people pausing or hesitating but then continuing on their way. Why would they do this? What would your own reaction to the child be? We see then that the phrase "safety in numbers," which we may hear in connection with many community situations, can be misleading.

These findings, like many others in community settings, are actually not unlike those from Asch's (1956) laboratory-based studies of conformity. The lesson for us is that what people say or do when they are alone does not always predict what they will do in a social or community setting. Suppose that tonight, as you are walking home, you find a crowd forming an "audience" around someone who is being assaulted or ridiculed. What would you do? What factors are involved? How long do you need to think about it to know? Are you sure?

Life in the City

Cities, which are urban environments that tend to have multiple sources of stress, contain many things of interest to psychologists based on the knowledge that behavior reflects the characteristics of the surrounding social context and physical environment. Some of the earliest research on the character of city environments was conducted by Phillip Zimbardo and his colleagues at Stanford University during the late 1960s and early 1970s. For example, Zimbardo's researchers deliberately abandoned vehicles on city streets and then observed how, over time, the cars were stripped down and then finally deserted. These events were, and still are, seen by many social psychologists in terms of certain explanatory themes—apathy, overstimulation, depersonalization, a loss or reduction in one's sense of individual responsibility within a city environment, and so forth. We know that community stressors, of virtually any type, can and do enhance our chances of becoming ill, either physically or psychiatrically. Cities are a known source of many disadvantages that we know have negative effects on behavior and health (e.g., pollution, crime, noise, crowding, poor housing, less likelihood of receiving help from strangers). They also serve as constant sources of fear and stress. Devlin (2000), for example, found that most persons, particularly women, tend to become more fearful and take more precautionary measures when visiting a large city than when visiting a smaller location. A useful way in which to compare city environments involves the use of **cognitive maps** (Bell, Fisher, & Loomis, 1978). The idea is that different cities are kept in mind and stored in memory in different ways and with different imagery, according to variations in their buildings, general layouts, atmospheres, and general features. Las Vegas is this way, New York is another way, and Montreal is still another way. It is widely believed that differences in cognitive maps are factors in our stereotyped beliefs about cities and, furthermore, that such maps are factors in how we feel about and behave in them. Because our behavior can be influenced by the structural elements of cities and other built spaces, we return to the issue of effective design of cities and spaces in Chapter 14.

Milgram's (1970) theory on cities states that the stress of cities traces to something called **stimulus overload,** a condition in which our nervous systems are frazzled and we cannot keep track of everything—traffic, honking horns, distractions, and so forth—and so we psychologically retreat; that is, we cut down (perhaps unconsciously) on what we pay attention to.

Milgram (1970) indicated six ways in which this retreat occurs. First, we try to rush through social situations and get them over with quickly. Saul Alinsky, whose work is mentioned later in this chapter, described in his book, *Rules for Radicals,* how he roamed the streets of Chicago attempting to give away $20 bills and was usually met with suspicion, or even hostility, from passersby (Alinsky, 1971). Second, we prioritize what we pay attention to so that some things will be avoided, for example, a man begging for money on the street. Third, we depersonalize others and see them only as enacting roles. For example, we see a store clerk or bus driver as just someone hiding behind the role and tend not to see or interact with that someone as a unique person. Fourth, we erect barriers to social interaction such as having locked doors or guards outside apartment buildings. For example, we encounter restaurant servers who pretend that they do not see us, we have answering machines to handle our phone calls and explain that we definitely cannot come to the phone at the time when someone calls, or we walk around listening to music through earphones or finding reasons to use our cell phones—even in social situations and even while driving. Fifth, we use *filters;* that is, communications or complaints (e.g., in a large store or government office) often are made to go through several people or layers of people before they reach their intended targets. Sixth, we create special agencies to deal with particular problems, and so people with problems are quickly referred elsewhere, for example, when we are shuffled around in a department store, thereby relieving someone's responsibility to help or interact. This process is reminiscent of Darley and Latané's (1970) idea about diffusion of responsibility mentioned earlier.

Complete reviews of existing research on urban environments are beyond the scope of this chapter but may be found in Marsella (1998), Black and Krishnakumar (1998), and Wandersman and Nation (1998). The majority of studies show that many types of interventions have been effective in helping urban residents with issues such as neighborhood relations, gang activity, disease prevention, health promotion, stress reduction, and child-rearing issues. Black and Krishakumar (1998), for example, described programs based in schools and shopping malls where videotaped or computerized presentations have assisted low-income and urban adolescent mothers in dealing with parenting and health issues. The effectiveness of many such programs may be credited to the community application of social learning theory (Bandura, 1986), in which participants are exposed to live or taped role models appropriate to the participants' situations and cultures. Another type of community intervention is the effort to maintain in a community setting people who would otherwise be institutionalized or clearly limited in their daily living arrangements. Page, Lafreniere, and Out (1999) found, for example, that **psychiatric "consumer-survivors"** (i.e., former recipients of treatment within the mental health system) profited financially, personally, and socially from the experience of running their own business in a community (city) environment, in this case a restaurant, and that many participants felt that this type of involvement was critical in avoiding rehospitalization. By whatever means, many successful stress reduction programs in cities involve helping participants to increase their levels of empathy for others, that is, others who also have to deal with the stressful impacts of city life. *Empathy* is the ability to see things as others do and to realize that most people, despite many differences, are capable of cooperation and that they share common values and life goals.

As mentioned previously, other successful interventions by psychologists and other professionals have been based on **social learning theory** principles. These principles are generally based on the idea (advanced by theorists such as B. F. Skinner and Albert Bandura) that behavior will repeat itself (or not) based on its consequences and that if someone is reinforced or sees another person being reinforced for the behavior (i.e., being given something that rewards the behavior), then its occurrence will become more likely. Many years ago, Robert Schwitzgebel performed the first major demonstration of these principles in a community setting. In a large American city, Schwitzgebel's (1967) research

team informally contacted 48 male youths who had been standing around on street corners and eventually arranged for them to meet on a regular basis with the researchers and talk about their problems, gripes, and so forth into a tape recorder. For some of the participants, the research team applied positive reinforcers (e.g., verbal agreement, a small gift, money, food bought in a restaurant) when the participants said something positive in terms of its social meaning (e.g., wanting to support or help someone in some way). They applied negative consequences (e.g., disagreement) when negative statements were given (e.g., reporting a hostile action or antisocial act). Following the application of the positive reinforcers, Schwitzgebel found significant increases in the participants' frequency of positive (e.g., helping) behaviors and verbalizations and positive changes in their behavior generally. The evidence basically supports his conclusion that the application of social reinforcement has the potential to be effective in dealing with and reshaping behavior in young offenders, even when carried out in tough and stressful city environments.

STIGMATIZATION AND RELATED ISSUES IN THE COMMUNITY

Self-Fulfilling Effects in a Community Context

People will often do what they believe others expect of them and, in turn, will treat others in line with their beliefs about them. Many have heard the phrase **blaming the victim** (Ryan, 1976). This is another commonly found error in interpreting behavior, similar to the fundamental attribution error mentioned earlier in the book. (In fact, blaming the victim might well be a special case of the fundamental attribution error.) Ryan's (1976) phrase refers to our interpreting a person's behavior (e.g., depression) as resulting from an individual's weakness or foibles rather than understanding it as a product of factors in the person's environment such as a depressing, often unfair, or contradictory environment.

One such factor that is extremely important for understanding community-based events concerns the phenomenon known as the **self-fulfilling prophecy** (Merton, 1948; Rosenthal, 1976). If you believe that something will happen, you often behave in such a way as to inadvertently cause it to happen. The sociologist Robert Merton described the situation where a rumor began that a town's bank (the "Last National Bank") was in poor financial shape and would have to close. The town's citizens fearfully withdrew their money at once, thereby taking away the bank's ability to do its daily business and, indeed, causing it to close. The belief was initially unfounded, yet the towns-people's actions made it come true. Many health situations may also be seen as reflecting self-fulfilling effects, for example, the person who worries continually about having a heart attack and becomes so continually anxious that a heart attack becomes the actual result.

Clearly, schools are a critical type of community setting, and although they were also covered in detail in Chapter 10, this chapter makes reference to them here briefly in the context of social psychological research concerning self-fulfilling effects. Kenneth Clark, a former president of the American Psychological Association, spoke many years ago about racial differences in intelligence quotient (IQ) test scores as reflecting an educational self-fulfilling prophecy. Clark meant that black children, relative to other children, tended to be deprived of educational reinforcements and opportunities—and many believe that this is still true today. Thus, these children's IQ scores, which tend to depend heavily on academic knowledge, were bound to be unreliable and biased. Racial IQ "differences" were, in Clark's view, a result of differential educational opportunities and lower expectations rather than of "real" IQ differences. Clark's comments alerted people to the possibility that many other events in the community could be interpreted similarly (Keppel, 2002).

Self-Fulfilling Effects in the Classroom

Let us look briefly at a classic study illustrating the self-fulfilling prophecy to which Clark was referring. In 1968, Robert Rosenthal and Lenore Jacobson tested Clark's view that IQ measurement could reflect a self-fulfilling mechanism such that children believed to be bright might profit by being given advantages that would serve to increase their IQ scores (Rosenthal & Jacobson, 1968).

The particular mechanism examined by Rosenthal and Jacobson (1968) was *teacher expectations.* They informed the teachers at an elementary school that they, as visiting researchers (from Harvard University), were trying out a new instrument called the "Harvard Test of Inflected Acquisition." They informed the teachers that this instrument would be able to identify pupils most likely to show rapid IQ gains over the year or so following testing. (In fact, the test was a standard intelligence test and did not really have any special ability to predict rapid IQ gains.) After administering the test to the children, Rosenthal and Jacobson gave the teachers the names of approximately 20% of the students whose performance supposedly indicated that they were going to be "academic spurters." Rosenthal and Jacobson returned to the school several months after the initial testing and found that pupils who were members of the special 20% group had made significantly greater IQ gains than did control pupils not in the special group. But in reality, the names of children in the special group had been selected *entirely at random,* and in the beginning there were no particular differences at all between their characteristics or abilities and those of the control children. The "difference" was only in the minds of the teachers, who believed that the special students—although only randomly selected in the first place—were brighter.

We do not know for sure, even today, how the children believed to be brighter were treated differently by their teachers. There is fairly strong evidence, however, that teachers unintentionally tend to teach and behave generally in a warmer fashion toward children who are believed to be brighter. They also tend to give such students other advantages such as trying to teach them more material, giving them better feedback about their performance, and having greater patience with them. These factors concerning the communication of self-fulfilling mechanisms—more and better feedback, warmer interactions, increased amount of material taught, and increased patience with children believed to be brighter—have together been termed the "four-factor theory" (Rosenthal, 1976). This theory and general perspective have continued to be of much concern to researchers and educators during recent years. Children, whether in schools or as members of society generally, are affected by what others believe they can or cannot do and by *what they believe others believe about them.* In fact, a recent and important series of studies showed that being a member of a negatively stereotyped minority group can adversely affect a person's academic performance when the person believes that his or her intellectual ability is being directly assessed (Steele & Aronson, 1998, cited in Kaplan & Saccuzzo, 2001). We would hypothesize here that the four factors of expectancy transmission may be relevant to the results of Steele and Aronson (1998) concerning how racial differences may be created but also to how persons of lower social class are treated generally in the community. The issue of class will be elaborated in Chapter 15.

Studies of Stigmatization

Because it can be used to illustrate frequently occurring issues in the study of communities, one important area of community research involves **stigmatization,** that is, the labeling of someone as being deviant, different, or flawed in some way. On publication of sociologist Erving Goffman's books *Asylums* and *Stigma,* the issue of stigmatization led to several community-based studies in the United States (Goffman, 1961, 1963). It was Goffman's view that a stigmatizing characteristic would often function as a **master status,** that is, a dominant prism through which other people judge the individual, discarding or ignoring other statuses or roles the individual might have. Many of the pioneering studies of stigma, during the late 1960s and the 1970s, were undertaken by Amerigo Farina and his colleagues at the University of Connecticut.

Regarding stigmatization of the mentally ill, more recent studies in several cities (described in Page, 2000; Page & Day, 1990) have assessed the level of community acceptance of persons believed to be, or to have formerly been, psychiatric patients. The level of verbal acceptance (i.e., what people *say*) of these individuals is typically found to be high, for example, when interviews, surveys, or questionnaires are used to assess acceptance. Many studies (e.g., using unobtrusive research methods) have found, however, that the actual level of behavioral acceptance (what people *do*) is usually much lower. At the University of Windsor, for example, we have examined a critical problem faced by many stigmatized persons, namely, that of finding accommodations in the community. In these studies, we frequently have used a research method used in the U.S. civil rights movement. Although many variations are possible, the basic method uses telephone inquiries that are placed to landlords who are publicly advertising rooms or apartments for rent in the community. After we have confirmed that a room or an apartment is actually unrented, calls inquiring about the room or apartment are then made later by, or on behalf of, a person described as a current or former psychiatric patient portraying himself or herself as in need of accommodations. In approximately 90% of such situations, we have found that inquiries made by callers supposedly bearing some stigmatizing characteristic will elicit deliberately falsified information concerning the rental status of the advertised room. Again, the basic results have followed a single theme: *public acceptance but private rejection*— in other words, data showing acceptance when responses are obtained with "I don't want to look bad" measures (e.g., surveys, interviews) combined with other data showing rejection when responses are obtained with measures in which participants' responses are believed by them to be private and unobserved by others.

But the series of room-for-rent studies also found something intriguing and paradoxical about stigma and how we react to others. Specifically, although landlords in the community often gave false information when confronted by someone (usually a male in our research) with a stigmatizing characteristic, they also frequently did the same thing when the characteristic was *neutral or even positive,* for example, when the person inquiring was a stutterer, spoke with a strange voice, was elderly, or said he was very active in politics, was a police officer, or was a professor. Apparently, individuals will seek to avoid situations in which they must somehow face or deal with a person bearing a negative characteristic, especially where they believe that their means of avoidance is undetectable. But if individuals also do this when the characteristic is not negative, it appears that they are rejecting not only the person who is "negatively different" but also those who are just *different*. Simply put, having to deal with *difference* involves the expectation of having to put out extra effort or to undergo some kind of hassle—experiences that most people would prefer to avoid. Of note here is the early, although still highly relevant, theory of Thibaut and Kelley (1959) called **social exchange theory.** Thibaut and Kelley pointed out that in real or anticipated social situations such as the potential rental situations in our examples, persons will usually (instantly and internally) calculate the anticipated psychological "rewards" and "costs" of various actions (e.g., renting vs. "getting out of" renting a room) and then behave according to these personal calculations. That is, they will ultimately carry out the action perceived as likely to bring lower psychological costs and/or higher rewards—in effect, the least hassle.

But Thibaut and Kelley's (1959) view is interesting on still another count. Because we are used to interpreting problematic behavior in terms of personality characteristics "inside" us, we often wonder about finding the criminal or terrorist personality, the "typical" shoplifter profile, and so forth. Thus, we might try to persuade someone to stop doing something wrong by using persuasion, therapy, discussion, or counseling. But we generally find, perhaps surprisingly, that many problem or criminal behaviors are not limited to supposedly abnormal groups or "special" personalities at all and, in fact, are carried out by nearly everyone—at least everyone who calculates (i.e., perceives) that the likely rewards will be greater than the likely costs. Most of us do not commit criminal acts because, for starters, we figure that the stakes for getting caught are too high and also because we are not so sure we can get away with the acts and remain unidentified anyway. (Would your behavior be greatly different if you knew for certain that you would get away with something and that the act would never be discovered or punished?) We know that we can now reduce harassing or obscene phone calls by being able to identify the phone numbers or locations of callers. We can greatly reduce shoplifting and other crimes by using video cameras. In so

doing, we are not concentrating on, or even concerned with, shoplifters' personalities or motivations. We are focusing on their calculations about the likelihood of potential rewards and costs, for example, the probability and perceived consequences of getting caught. In fact, some effective shoplifting strategies involve posting signs as well as cameras in stores, explicitly reminding potential thieves about specific costs and consequences following apprehension—embarrassment, legal problems, and so forth.

Weiner (1995) put forward a complicated but commonsense theory about stigmatization. Weiner's view is that we tend to be more negative and rejecting toward someone if we judge that the person was "blameworthy," for example, that he or she was personally able to control an action or stigmatizing condition (e.g., getting lung cancer from smoking, getting AIDS from unprotected sexual contact) but failed to do so, and also that we tend to be more rejecting if we believe that the person truly had the moral responsibility to avoid the action or condition but did not exercise it. No attempt will be made to fully evaluate Weiner's view. However, it would seem that, if Thibaut and Kelley (1959) are right, it might not matter so much whether the person's behavior was controllable and so forth; it might only matter whether the person is *different* in some way and, thus, is likely (or so we perceive) to cause us some type of cost or extra hassle in our interaction with him or her. If we are the manager of a restaurant with formal dress requirements, for example, we might well decide to serve persons violating the requirements given that we do not want an embarrassing or ugly scene and possibly legal hassles and expenses as well.

Acceptance of research data from certain types of research methods frequently leads to interpretations about community issues that are seriously in error. For example, Crocetti, Spiro, and Siassi (1973), on the basis of *questionnaire and interview research,* concluded that the stigma of mental illness had disappeared and that the mentally ill need not fear community rejection. Other studies that have drawn similar conclusions, mainly in a Canadian context, are described in Page and Day (1990) and Page (2000). These studies have found that many individuals within the general public have learned, as a result of educational efforts and programs initiated by mental health authorities, to become more accepting in terms of their verbal and written reactions toward the concept of "mental patient." We have found, however, that when the community's *actual behavior* toward stigmatized groups is studied in situations where rejection is believed to be hidden and undetectable, such rejection can and does occur. Such actions contravene the Canadian Human Rights Code, the Canadian Charter of Rights and Freedoms as well as the U.S. Fair Housing Act, the U.S. Human Rights Act, the U.S. Federal Housing Act, and the U.S. Civil Rights Act.

Readers interested in knowing the current status of how former psychiatric patients and members of other stigmatized groups are treated in the community, together with suggestions for future research, are referred to the review by Corrigan and Penn (1999). Drawing on social psychological research about stereotyping and attitude change, Corrigan and Penn pointed to the value of programs and interventions that involve personal contact with stigmatized individuals in real community situations, especially where the contact is cooperative and egalitarian in tone. This kind of positive contact can enhance and make more positive the community norms concerning our interactions with these groups and can also enable us to become more positive role models for others.

The Media and Stigmatization

A major concern regarding the problem of stigmatization in the community concerns the media's role, particularly with regard to newspaper, television, and movie portrayals. Here is another area that is badly in need of future research and perhaps social action toward change. As discussed in Chapter 8, many social psychologists believe that the mass media greatly influence their consumer-customers through social learning mechanisms such as imitation and modeling. This view is clearly associated with the research and theory of Bandura (1986) discussed earlier. For example, with regard to mental illness, we find that television portrayals frequently tend to be negative and unflattering toward persons connected with this label. This is particularly so in portrayals where aggression or violence have been committed and where reference is made at the same time, as it almost always is, to mental illness in the perpetrator's past (Diefenbach, 1997). Unfortunately, these portrayals are generally inaccurate in their assumption that the mentally ill are generally violent or aggressive toward others. Moreover, news broadcasts seldom report positive or outstanding accomplishments by those bearing the mental illness label.

FOCUS ON RESEARCH

Thornton and Wahl (1996) conducted an experiment to explore the effect that newspaper articles promoting negative stereotypes of the mentally ill could have on people's attitudes and whether these effects could be modified through an intervention. The researchers had 120 university students participate in what was described as a study of newspaper articles. The study had four conditions. In the three experimental conditions, participants read an article representing the kind of media portrayal that stigmatizes mental illness. The article graphically described a murder committed by a mentally ill person who was characterized as different, without social identity, unpredictable, and dangerous. However, before reading the stigmatizing article, participants in the three experimental conditions read either (a) a factual article on mental illness (stigma condition), (b) an article that addressed misconceptions and the truth about mental illness (prophylactic information condition), or (c) an article that described media distortion of mental illness (prophylactic media condition). The first articles that participants read in the two prophylactic conditions were designed to inoculate, or protect, participants from the biasing effects that the stigmatizing article was anticipated to have on their attitudes toward the mentally ill. The factual article in the stigma condition was expected to have no effect. Participants in a fourth condition did not read the stigmatizing article (control condition). Instead, they read two health-related articles that were not related to violence or mental illness. The control condition served as a baseline against which the three experimental conditions could be compared.

Subsequent to reading their second articles, participants completed two questionnaires: The first had four subscales that assessed participants' attitudes toward mental illness. Each subscale tapped a different dimension of this attitude. The second questionnaire measured two variables: (a) participants' expected reactions of fear and anxiety and (b) participants' perceived danger of mentally ill people.

The results revealed that, as might be expected, participants in the stigma condition were less accepting of the mentally ill after reading the stigmatizing article. They also displayed greater fear, anxiety, and perceived danger with respect to mentally ill people. Thus, exposure to a stigmatizing newspaper article clearly made the participants' attitudes toward the mentally ill more negative.

The results also revealed that both prophylactic manipulations succeeded in inoculating participants against the biasing effect of the stigmatizing article. Participants in both prophylactic conditions demonstrated a pattern of results that were similar to those in the control condition, revealing that the attitudes toward the mentally ill of those exposed to a prophylactic were virtually identical to those of participants who were not exposed to the stigmatizing article. In fact, participants in the prophylactic information condition had attitudes that demonstrated even *less* desired avoidance of the mentally ill than did participants in the control condition. The intervention was clearly effective. However, more research is still needed to address questions regarding how frequently the inoculation effect might be observed outside of laboratory conditions, how temporary or permanent it might be, and what would happen if the counterinformation were presented after, instead of before, being exposed to a media depiction.

Wahl and Lefkowits (1989), in an earlier study, found that presenting counterinformation (reminding viewers that the mentally ill are seldom perpetrators of violence) did not positively affect attitudes toward mental illness as expressed by viewers who saw a film portraying violent acts committed by a supposedly mentally ill individual. One cannot conclude for certain, therefore, that giving counterinformation will always help in affecting attitudes elicited by media portrayals. An idea for future research, however would be to examine whether the negativeness of attitudes toward persons bearing a stigmatizing characteristic is directly related to the number of repeated pairings or connections made in media portrayals between that characteristic and instances of undesirable or violent behavior.

Osofsky (1995), in her review of studies concerning the effects of exposure to violence on young children, had a very important conclusion for current purposes. That is, exposure to violence appears to be harmful in many ways and threatens to adversely affect the development and future abilities of children. Although much more research is needed, her review also found that family- and community-based programs would likely be effective in moderating these effects. Osofsky stated, "The media contribute to the problem of children and youth violence by glamorizing violence, thereby encouraging

involvement in violent activities" (p. 786). Moreover, our social responsibilities toward children seem to be made even clearer by Osofsky's comment that "the cooperation of television and the media is needed to change the image of violence in American society from an acceptable and even admirable quality to one that is disdained without tolerance" (p. 786). Another observation, taken from the review of media violence effects carried out by Bushman and Anderson (2001), is relevant here. These authors pointed out that, over the past couple of decades, news reports and figures in the media have apparently tended to downplay, question, or negate the negative effects of media violence, yet during the same period, psychologists and other researchers have actually become increasingly confident that such effects are real. This interesting and important issue regarding the psychological effects of violent media was further elaborated in Chapter 8.

SOME ISSUES RELATED TO SOCIAL CHANGE AND PREVENTION

Prevention is a term that appears frequently in community psychology literature. It refers to the view that illnesses, social problems, and disorders of various kinds can be attacked at their source before they become problematic or even begin at all. This section discusses some selected issues relevant to this view.

Social Action

As background, the influence of Saul Alinsky in the social psychological study of communities must be acknowledged here. Alinsky (1971) was an "organizer," that is, a community-based strategist who helped to organize and mobilize poor neighborhoods and communities when they needed help with regard to more responsible behavior by landlords and improvements in living conditions. His goal was basically that of empowerment, which involved finding and implementing community strategies that would redistribute power—real power and not just bureaucratic jargon saying "thank you for your views" and so forth—away from the "haves" and toward the "have-nots." Alinsky pointed out that powerful and wealthy community groups or city governments, like people in general, have psychological needs. They all have "selves." They need to be liked and to "look good." They can easily refuse, delay, or turn down polite and reasonable requests (or complaints) from citizens' organizations or spokespersons so long as their need to look good is not threatened by the potential for unflattering publicity and so long as they are sure to remain in charge. Thus, Alinsky knew that bringing about community change depended on protesters being able to use tactics that went "outside the experience" of those in charge. As mentioned earlier, Alinsky roamed the streets of Chicago, handing out money at random. Passersby were suspicious and seldom receptive or overly friendly toward him. Alinsky described his own behavior as being "outside their experience." He organized communities by helping them to adopt protest tactics that carried the potential to embarrass the powerful and that were not the kinds of tactics with which the haves were already prepared to deal.

In one scenario, Alinsky and fellow protesters threatened to use teams of jobless individuals to simultaneously occupy all of the restrooms at Chicago's O'Hare airport, just when these facilities would be needed by passengers exiting from incoming flights, as a means of protesting unfair municipal employment practices. Fearing the reactions of business travelers and other passengers who might be inconvenienced by this tactic, the municipal politicians swiftly agreed to meet to discuss concessions regarding the employment conditions. In another scenario, Alinsky and his associates threatened to organize a "shop in" of a department store that engaged in discriminatory hiring practices. In this tactic, large numbers of black shoppers would tie up the Chicago department store for long periods, examining merchandise over and over again with mock seriousness and without buying anything. When threatened by Alinsky's tactics, the store owners arranged a meeting with the protesters to discuss making changes to their hiring practices. Like the municipal politicians, the store owners realized that these tactics could not be opposed gracefully or effectively. They saw that further publicity would only bring more attention to Chicago's community problems and the poverty that created them.

In the context of calls for social action and change, community psychologists are also interested in examining factors in the physical environment that affect behavior and general well-being. Social action and political action are often needed to address the risks related to living in threatening environments. Sometimes, for example, entire communities or cities are particularly vulnerable to the effects of low air or water quality or of pollution generally. Research evidence generally shows that high levels of environmental pollutants, as a major source of community stress, are related to increased frequency of adjustment and health problems, both medical and psychiatric. If you were a citizen or parent living in this type of geographical area or another similarly affected location, *what would you do*? Are you in favor of one type of environmental strategy, adopted by certain cities, whereby citizens are reinforced (e.g., with social approval or financial reward) for responsible environmental behavior or are charged a fee for garbage collection in excess of a specified weekly amount?

A General Perspective on Community Prevention

Perhaps the most influential advocate of community prevention programs was Emory

Cowen. Cowen believed in promoting health and well-being from birth onward, particularly through programs promoting development of life skills in young children rather than concentrating resources on treatment procedures for mental health and other personal problems after they had developed and become serious. As described in his obituary (Cicchetti, Rappaport, Sandler, & Weissberg, 2001), Cowen and his colleagues founded the Primary Mental Health Project (PMHP) based at the University of Rochester. The PMHP focused on school-based prevention and treatment/intervention strategies for identifying early signs of maladjustment in primary-grade children.

There is a sizable literature on prevention of illness or other problems through interventions (e.g., counseling or informational programs, home or school visits, distress or hotline services) in community settings. Many of these are attempts at what is called primary prevention, which was also considered in Chapter 9. **Primary prevention** (Caplan, 1964; Dalton et al., 2001) refers to attempts to increase the ability of community residents to cope with problems and early warning signs before illness or other serious problems occur. Some primary prevention measures require medication (e.g., taking an aspirin every day to prevent heart disease), and others require the person to change his or her behavior, for example, regarding the use of tobacco or an increase in exercise (Kaplan, 2000). Some prevention programs are referred to as involving **secondary prevention.** These are attempts to reduce problems associated with illnesses or problems that have already occurred. According to Kaplan's (2000) review of U.S. studies, programs generally have been less successful when they are not implemented until the disease or disorder has occurred. Conversely, the results from programs based on primary prevention seem much more promising. But Kaplan also pointed out that, unfortunately, due to the difficulty in conducting primary prevention research, most resources seem to have gone toward secondary prevention programs.

In terms of scope, prevention strategies can be directed toward the individual or family or toward communities and societies themselves (Nelson, Laurendeau, & Chamberland, 2001). Again, the key idea here is the belief that many

illnesses have social and community origins and that if community settings could be used to prevent or anticipate problems, or if persons could receive early treatment for problems in the community, many hospitalizations could be prevented. But it is vitally necessary, before interventions are initiated, to know the target community well. Sometimes interventions intended to be helpful turn out to be negative or indecisive (Dishion, McCord, & Poulin, 1999). For that matter, sometimes the professional disciplines involved (e.g., psychology, medicine) have not always cooperated well or agreed on the wisdom of community prevention in the first place.

Sometimes community interventions can be very positive in terms of providing information and relevant role-playing experiences for participants. For example, based on earlier findings (e.g., Saltz, Perry, & Cabral, 1994), Out and Lafreniere (2001) asked 114 female high school students to carry a lifelike vinyl doll (capable of simulating human functions) with them continuously for 3 days to simulate the experience of caring for a baby and to help them confront the common illusion that pregnancy "can't happen to me." Compared with a control group whose members did not carry the doll, students in the intervention group subsequently showed greater ability to assess their risk for pregnancy and more realistic knowledge about the demands of parenthood and child rearing.

Different Perspectives on Prevention

Clearly, we need to know much more about community prevention of illness as well as about community programs and prevention efforts directed toward young offenders and youths in general. But we also must be aware of our own values and perspectives. What kinds of violence, for example, concern us the most? Can we agree on these? Given that many precursors of violence seem to be found in poorer neighborhoods, how do we attack the problems of poverty, hopelessness, and social disengagement? Again, the need arises for effective political action to address community-based problems, many of which are so familiar that we seldom even think of them. Because their symptoms and warning signs are not always dramatic or clear-cut, they seldom receive daily coverage or huge headlines to compete with the latest rape, whale rescue, murder, or kidnapping of a child from a wealthy family. In a column in the *Detroit Free Press* titled "Child Abuse: Let's Combat This Form of Terrorism Too," Susan Silverman observed that although many recent world events have been horrendous, we are nevertheless faced with other tragedies of equal magnitude—the realities of child abuse, domestic violence, and numerous forms of family disruption and disintegration (Silverman, 2002). According to Silverman, a child is sexually abused in America every 10 seconds, and one of every four girls is sexually assaulted by 18 years of age. She added that Child Help U.S.A. reports that approximately 1,100 children die annually from parental abuse or neglect and that 4 million American women are seriously assaulted by their husbands or partners.

There are still more value issues about prevention measures such as how to draw the line between individual rights and the imposition of mandatory health or safety measures. Individuals retain the right to indulge in practices that may be harmful such as neglecting exercise, eating junk food, and smoking. Some recent media reports have referred to a strong connection between infant breast-feeding and lowered cancer risk, yet clearly infant care also remains under the personal discretion of parents. We have much to learn about prevention and about how to predict (and protect) the future development of children. But we also have to think critically about the issue. There are some areas where our predictions or assumptions might go amiss or where we seem to blame someone for being poor as though the person was responsible for his or her hardships or problems. Or, sometimes we need to be careful in evaluating the experts themselves. We might see some practices as dangerous to children when, in fact, they might not always be. In a recent case in Michigan, criminal charges were brought against parents who apparently taught their young children to fight each other and who also made videotapes of this activity. The couple said that they wanted to teach their children the horrors of violence so that they would avoid it in later life. Several experts said that the children would be "emotionally scarred" for life. But how do

these experts know this? In fact, who is wise enough to know whether the children will be scarred or not? How would the scarring be later measured and at what point? How could it be clearly linked to being taught to fight one's sibling? How could it be reliably assessed and measured, and how do we rule out other causes? Also, many children and families are able to pull through tough times and are able to rise above early traumatic events in their lives (Garmezy, 1987). Therefore, we need more research to better understand why these events affect some children much more than they do others— even others within the same family. These are issues affecting all types of community-based research.

In our zeal to establish community programs, we also must be careful not to unintentionally change the community situation so that it is no better than it was before. Shadish (1984), for example, described difficulties with the approach of treating the mentally ill within the community. Many former patients have experienced a lack of acceptance, financial difficulties, and lonely and isolated experiences while living in community residences—indeed, sometimes in poor urban areas and unsatisfying, or even unhealthy, living arrangements. By an act of the U.S. Congress in 1963, the movement toward establishing community mental health centers was started based on the goal of "treatment in the community." But many community centers, although based on the goal of short-term help for the mentally ill and other citizens, seem to have had only mixed success. Funding is always an issue (and a problem). The ability of persons housed in the community to support themselves, financially and otherwise, is another. Friction between mental health professions (e.g., between those who favor the "community approach" and those who do not) is another. The failure of some communities to allow these centers to be located in their midst is another (would you object to having such a center in your neighborhood?). Also, the failure of many mental health staff members to get meaningfully involved in community life, and their tendency to instead concentrate on giving individualized treatment such as psychotherapy (often in noncommunity settings such as offices), is still another. Faced with difficulties in community living, the question arises as to whether some persons without means of community support (or family) should be allowed (or even encouraged) to remain in a hospital or an institution. This view stands in contrast to, and questions, the idea that a place of residence within the community must necessarily be found for every single person (Rosenblatt, 1984). Also, it is possible that the goal of preventing future problems has been overemphasized given that it tends to make us forget the importance of what is happening in the present, for example, the importance of enriching a child's life *right now.*

The Internet as a Community and Source of Help

The Internet as a community. Here we depart from the typical view that communities mean the physical presence of others and that ideas from psychology apply only to "real life." With the development of the Internet during the past several years, we now have a new type of real community, that is, an electronic or virtual one (Rheingold, 1993; Turkle, 1984; Wallace, 1999).

The Internet has provided social psychologists with a new source of research data, for example, studies of chat rooms, discussion groups, and communications as well as characteristics of advertisements and "home pages" (Lee, 2000). Following a theme mentioned earlier, we now can examine and study the things that people do and say within a virtual community, where their actions and real identities are usually kept anonymous.

Most people do not question or consider the possible negative consequences of virtual life because the advantages of computers are assumed to be unquestionable. Yet with increased development of the Internet, to which approximately 63% of North American households had access at the end of 2003 (Madden, 2003), some warning signs about virtual life can be noticed. A study by Putnam (1995, cited in Kraut et al., 1998) found that in the United States, there has been an increasingly steep decline in what Putnam described as "civic engagement and social participation" (Kraut et al., 1998, p. 1017). That is, people seem to belong to organizations less, are generally less "social," and are seemingly less able to form significant connections with others.

Putnam noted that if this is true, there are consequences for the community; schools do not run as well, politicians care less, and the streets may be less safe as the amount of time devoted to virtual living increases.

But there is evidence that virtual living and social disengagement also have personal consequences, that is, if we assume that live social contact generally means better health and a greater sense of well-being (Cohen & Wills, 1985; Gove & Geerken, 1977). Thus, we will likely see much more social psychological research in the future exploring the social and personal effects of the Internet on its citizen-users. In one study, Kraut and colleagues (1998) gathered data on 169 Internet users in 73 households over a 2-year period. They found that although the Internet was used frequently for communication purposes, there were declines in communication among family members and in the size of family members' social subgroups. There were also increases in loneliness and depression. Kraut and colleagues referred to the Internet's effects as causing a "disengagement from real life." Moreover, we now have fairly solid, and perhaps alarming, evidence that exposure to pornography, which is instantly reachable on the Internet (Wallace, 1999), increases various forms of men's sexual aggression and acceptance of numerous myths about rape and also decreases the favorability of attitudes toward women (Malamuth & Donnerstein, 1984; Page, 1990). Therefore, we encounter this issue no less than we do in the case of "real" community settings, where pornography has long been a concern of citizens' groups and, more recently, of social scientists. A major social psychological theory relevant to these issues as they appear in the community is that of social learning (Bandura, 1986). This concerns the view (discussed more fully in Chapter 8) that exposure to violent pornography in magazines, videos, or other forms of media expression can and often does increase the likelihood of violent acts and other forms of aggression against women. There is also related evidence that the mere presence and repeated depictions of violent materials, such as guns and other symbols of violence, in the community can increase the likelihood of aggressive acts being committed, especially in situations where people have already become irritated or angry for some reason (Berkowitz & Alioto, 1973). If we support controls on pornographic material such as the material likely to be found at the local convenience store, do we also support them with regard to the Internet? Do we want to contemplate and live in a (virtual) community full of pornographic images and negative messages to children about the nature of sexuality and the "place" of women therein?

We are in dire need of more research on these and other personal and social consequences of Internet use and of living virtual lives—and accepting them as "real"—within virtual communities. An excellent discussion of the social and psychological side effects of new technology and Internet use may be found in Kipnis (1997). In fact, we must add the Internet, with its positive and negative effects, to the growing list of global issues of relevance for social and community psychologists (Marsella, 1998). In this context, we are reminded that psychologists are becoming increasingly obligated to become involved in social or political advocacy and in efforts to address community problems and inequities. These kinds of obligations are now becoming more prominent in psychologists' professional ethical codes (American Psychological Association, 2002; Canadian Psychological Association, 2000).

The Internet as a source of help. The general movement toward receiving counseling help or treatment in nonvirtual communities (rather than through hospitalization) is mirrored in the increasing use of online help for both medical and psychiatric problems, often in the form of online community self-help groups. These can provide both factual information and social/emotional support for people dealing with a common problem. In many ways, this development reflects the virtual equivalent of well-known nonvirtual "face-to-face" community groups such as Alcoholics Anonymous and those associated with community crisis centers. The thinking among developers of online groups is that traditional sources of help, although still valuable, cannot deal with all of the complexities involved in personal, social, and medical problems. Of course, the development of online help groups creates many questions, for example, issues about anonymity and confidentiality of users and help givers and about how the effectiveness and integrity of these groups might be evaluated. Other questions arise as to which individuals are best qualified and most skilled to be involved as virtual community helpers or counselors. These same questions may, of course, also be asked about face-to-face groups.

● FOCUS ON INTERVENTION

Being a young single mother who lacks a social support network can be very challenging. Young mothers face tremendous stressors that can result in increased physical and mental health problems, isolation, and alienation. In their efforts to help such mothers deal with the stresses associated with their difficult circumstances, Dunham and colleagues (1998) evaluated a trial intervention designed to provide social support and a sense of community to young single mothers. The researchers recruited 42 mothers from community agencies that specialize in providing social and medical services. All of the mothers were between 15 and 20 years of age, and their children averaged 5.2 months of age. None of the mothers was employed full-time outside of the home, and all but 3 were receiving some form of government assistance. Dunham and colleagues provided all participants with computers and 6 months of access to an electronic bulletin board system on which they could discuss their lives, discuss the situations they faced, and share information with other young single mothers. The bulletin board was accessible 24 hours a day, 7 days a week, and served as a computer-mediated social support network by allowing for multiuser, text-based teleconferencing, public exchanges of messages, and private e-mail interactions for up to 8 online participants at a time.

To determine whether the social support provided by accessing the bulletin board affected participants' stress levels, a measure of parenting stress was administered to all mothers before the intervention began and again 6 months later during a postintervention interview. On completion of the intervention, participants also completed a scale assessing the sense of community they felt toward the computer-mediated social support group.

The high frequency of system use revealed how valuable some of the mothers found the electronic support group to be. Over the 6-month period, the system was accessed 16,670 times, that is, an average of 397 times per participant, although there was great disparity in the amount of use among participants. Some accessed the bulletin board regularly (high participation rate), others were more sporadic (moderate participation rate), and some stopped using the board altogether (low participation rate). The analysis of the pre- and postintervention measures revealed the value of accessing the bulletin board. For example, Dunham and colleagues (1998) found a significant relationship between consistency of participation in the bulletin board and decreases in parenting stress. They also found that the young mothers who accessed the bulletin board more frequently developed a stronger sense of belonging to a community. Given that young mothers often report high levels of stress and a sense of isolation, these results are encouraging. They suggest that access to online peer support networks can serve as an effective intervention in helping to mitigate the stressors associated with being a young single mother.

It should be noted, however, that because there was no control group, this study was a quasi-experiment. This research design does not allow us to conclude that the positive outcomes were necessarily due to the online social support intervention. It is possible that an uncontrolled extraneous variable accounted for the relationship between accessing the online support group and the outcome measures employed in this intervention (see Chapter 3). However, as noted in what follows, there is other evidence suggesting the benefits of online social support.

Winzelberg (1997) summarized the results of several studies showing that online support groups can be helpful as supportive communities in terms of providing information as well as social and emotional support for women (and some men) suffering from various types of eating disorders. Winzelberg also noted another positive factor unique to online community groups, namely, that users are able to participate during late night or early morning hours. Obviously, this is an advantage over conventional support services in nonvirtual communities.

Some recent research by Davison, Pennebaker, and Dickerson (2000) reminds us that virtual community support groups form a strong and usually low-cost alternative to traditional or professional forms of medical assistance. These authors studied live support groups in Dallas, New York, Chicago, and Los Angeles as well as two online domains, namely, America Online and Internet newsgroups. The nonvirtual groups met in all kinds of places—churches, empty offices, shopping malls, and so forth. Support group activity generally was highest for medical conditions usually seen or experienced as stigmatizing or embarrassing, such as AIDS, alcoholism, breast cancer, and prostate cancer, and was lowest for serious but less embarrassing conditions such

as heart disease. Online support group activity was greatest for people with conditions limiting their mobility such as multiple sclerosis and chronic fatigue syndrome. Davison and colleagues concluded that virtual support groups appear to be well suited for "those whose disability impairs mobility, and more striking, the online community allows for anonymity. Potent social factors like physical attractiveness, vocal characteristics, ethnicity, and social skills are neutralized" (p. 211). Davison and colleagues noted that both virtual and nonvirtual support groups are attractive to people attempting to cope with embarrassing, stigmatizing, or disfiguring conditions. These results are actually at odds with an earlier perspective called *social comparison theory* (e.g., Sarnoff & Zimbardo, 1961), which held that people suffering from embarrassing situations or problems are less likely to affiliate with each other. However, Davison and colleagues (2000) offered the explanation that sufferers can, through the use of both virtual and nonvirtual community support groups, escape their usual social networks (e.g., friends, relatives, fellow workers) and that this lessens the anxiety they normally experience in having to deal with the social consequences (e.g., looks, glances, perceived evaluations of others) of their illnesses. More needs to be known about the characteristics of both virtual and nonvirtual support group users. It appears, however, that their numbers have increased rapidly. Surely, then, the effectiveness of traditional health services could be enriched by including health professionals, as well as other helpers or facilitators, as participants in both virtual and nonvirtual support group activities.

REFLECTIONS ON COMMUNITY VIOLENCE AND FUTURE RESEARCH

This section, based on material discussed in this chapter, presents a few selected questions for your own consideration but also as a basis for future research:

As one such question, do you believe that exposure to violence in a community, of whatever sort, contributes to future problems and increased likelihood of aggression in some form? This question is posed in the context of a community-based study (Berkowitz, 1981) concerning the effects—especially on younger people—of violent stimuli and scenarios that seem to be always around us. Admittedly, we are using this example arbitrarily, but it is germane to the many issues involved in our discussion and it helps us to focus on what the issues are in the interface of social psychology and community psychology. Berkowitz and associates took an old truck out to a busy city intersection and then intentionally stalled it when the light turned green. If you were the driver behind the truck when this happened, what would you do? How patient with the truck driver would you be? How would your reaction differ if you saw a rifle in a gun rack on the back of the truck? What if you saw a rifle plus a bumper sticker that read "VENGEANCE"? Berkowitz found, perhaps surprisingly, that drivers behind the old truck were more—not less—likely to show aggression (e.g., honking, becoming hostile) toward the driver when his truck carried the rifle. They were even more hostile when they also saw the VENGEANCE bumper sticker. Berkowitz and many other professionals have concluded that the more violent stimuli a person encounters, the more likely he or she is to think of, and possibly carry out, some aggressive or violent act. Therefore, we seem to be affected by stimuli that we easily associate with aggression such as guns, knives, and other violent images we usually encounter in a normal day. This repeated exposure, including events such as continued media coverage of kidnappings and crimes involving coercion, likely tends to "desensitize" us, that is, to make violence seem "normal" and routine. Violence is then, in a sense, more tolerable—and more likely to cause someone to imitate it (Malamuth & Donnerstein, 1984; Page, 1990).

A radio station in Detroit, Michigan, recently started to post its monthly crime statistics on a flashing sign. Detroit also features a huge statue of the boxer Joe Louis in its downtown core. The statue shows Louis with a menacing look and raised fist, again contributing yet one more "normal" ingredient to the collection of violent stimuli with which communities are bombarded. As a citizen, would you oppose developments in your city that would increase the presence of violent stimuli? Would you be willing to join an organization to promote this view? Can you tolerate a community or society full of violent stimuli given the message they send to young children about the type of society in which we live?

- Do you believe that the large number of aggressive stimuli and symbols of violence in society contributes to instances of "road rage" and other forms of aggressive behavior?
- Are you in favor of community regulations that would prohibit the sale or availability of pornographic material? Should this material be regulated somehow yet made available at least to adults? Should sexually explicit material be available if it is nonviolent in its content? Do you believe that pornography, especially violent pornography, leads to increased aggression or more negative attitudes toward women or to more lenient attitudes toward the issue of sexual assault?

CULTURE CAPSULE: RELATIVITY
OF NEEDS AND PROBLEM SOLVING

Fish, someone once said, do not realize that they live in a wet environment. That is, we must remember that our findings are most understandable within a given culture but often less so within another culture. Particular community mental health programs, for example, are based on prevailing assumptions about what is healthy, desirable, and scientifically informed. Yet these might not fit well in other societies where goals such as simply staying alive, avoiding military conflicts, avoiding abuse, avoiding disease and hunger, and hoping for live births are major priorities. We might believe, for example, that arranging and taking an airline flight alone, or checking into a hotel alone, would enhance a person's self-confidence. Yet in some societies, these very activities might be inconceivable, impossible, or even illegal—at least for women. In Kashmir, persons with anxiety problems have only recently been able to seek help from mental health counselors rather than automatically being given electroshock treatment. Thus, in the context of the surrounding culture, we have to examine our own values, our view of what is healthy adjustment, and what are acceptable means of solving problems. Also, we must keep in mind the issue of *cultural relativity of needs.* Our means of solving problems—and what we consider to be problems in the first place—will differ according to the surrounding culture. We think here of many people starving in poor countries or areas because they do not have the simplest of foods. With little or no food (or financial income), they have to figure out how to survive the day. We contrast this with the situation of citizens interviewed during the North American power blackout of August 14, 2003, where many people expressed serious concern, even helplessness, when they could not *shop* for food—or could not do so at familiar stores.

Beneath the apparent differences, it is a common belief that most people in different cultures still support pretty much the same values and needs—a need for love and basic security, meaningful links with others, justice, freedom, health, and a general sense of well-being. Thus, the community concerns of psychologists extend well beyond our own culture and geographical boundaries. Readers interested in how learning theory principles might be applied in a global sense are referred to Walsh's (1985) suggestions in his book *Staying Alive.* Politicians at all levels might be reinforced with praise, attention, and approval (or reelection) when their statements favor preservation of the environment and community resources. They might also be reinforced when they state globally friendly messages that acknowledge the universality of human needs and values such as getting together face-to-face and attacking problems through means other than war. Walsh and others are saying that we, as environmentally concerned citizens, must *immediately* do everything possible to keep politicians and authorities on their toes. We must make clear our reactions to their statements, and we must selectively praise and encourage them depending on the content of what they say. In psychological jargon, this could be referred to as giving or withholding reinforcement. (Kenneth Clark, mentioned earlier, once said that elected politicians should be forced to take tranquilizing medication so as to avoid what he called the "pathos of power," that is, the tendency for persons in power to seek attention and headlines, to compete with each other, to increase conflict, and sometimes to wage war.) Moreover, our efforts to prevent, comment on, and study social/community problems will be different depending on the stage or theoretical aspect of a problem on which we are focusing. That is, when we find a problem or disease being suffered by a particular person, we can usually trace the problem back to much broader factors—siblings, family, society, and the state of the world itself.

Readers are referred to Marsella (1998), who provided an extensive list of problem areas of immediate concern, but also of global concern, to community psychologists and all concerned citizens.

306 • **APPLIED SOCIAL PSYCHOLOGY**

SUMMARY

This chapter has described the relevance of social psychological theory and knowledge to various problems existing in community settings, briefly outlined the origins of community psychology, and outlined several classic studies based on various aspects of social and community psychology. It reported some recent findings and theories about problems existing in today's cities and outlined some community problems that exist not only locally but also globally. It indicated ways in which the Internet now exists as a virtual community from which many users derive benefit in terms of self-help and support groups but which also has shown negative effects in terms of psychological disengagement and social disengagement from the nonvirtual community. Throughout, the chapter has tried to raise additional issues by asking further questions, many of which can well serve as ideas for future research.

14

APPLYING SOCIAL PSYCHOLOGY TO THE ENVIRONMENT

ROBERT GIFFORD

CHAPTER OUTLINE

"A California student linked to a radical environmentalist group is being held without bail as he faces charges for allegedly firebombing 125 sport utility vehicles [SUVs] last August [2003]. . . . Human life is risked by the nature of these offences," U.S. Magistrate Carolyn Turchin said during a hearing Wednesday as she decided not to release 23-year-old Billy Cottrell.

The Pasadena, California, man was arrested on March 9, 2004, and accused of damaging or destroying vehicles at car dealerships and homes in the Los Angeles area. The bill for the property damage was an estimated $2.3 million. At the time, Cottrell was a second-year graduate student in physics at the California Institute of Technology, and e-mails from computers at that school had claimed responsibility for the SUV mayhem on behalf of the extremist Earth Liberation Front. On its website, the Earth Liberation Front called Cottrell "an environmental campaigner."

Federal Bureau of Investigation (FBI) officials said in an affidavit that Cottrell was also involved in a plot to plaster SUVs with 5,000 bumper stickers that read "My SUV

Supports Terrorism." Many environmentalists disapprove of SUVs because of their high gas consumption. If convicted, Cottrell could spend 40 years behind bars. One charge that he faces, using a destructive device during a violent crime, carries a minimum sentence of 30 years in federal prison ("Suspected SUV Bomber," 2004).

One might ask the following questions:

- Why is gas consumption such a contentious issue?
- If SUVs consume so much gas, what interventions can be implemented to discourage people from buying them?
- As more people drive SUVs, does that encourage still more people to purchase them?

"Wherever you go, there you are." This old saying is another way of conveying the idea that no matter what you do—whether you are interacting with others or are alone, and no matter what behavior or thought you are engaged in— you do it *somewhere*. This somewhere is the physical environment, and it is often a crucial influence on our actions, thoughts, and well-being. But our actions, both individually and collectively, also have an enormous impact on the physical environment—sometimes beneficial, but sometimes harmful.

The task of psychologists interested in the environment is to examine a great variety of topics besides the issues involved in extreme actions aimed at defending the natural environment. Environmental psychologists study not only how the physical environment (e.g., buildings, weather, nature, noise, pollution, street arrangements) affects our behavior, thinking, and well-being but also how our behavior (e.g., energy conservation, vandalism, activism, automobile use, recycling, water use) affects the environment.

There are social psychological aspects to many topics examined by environmental psychologists such as violence in jails; weather and altruism; the design of the built environment in relation to crime, privacy, crowding, and territoriality; the effects of noise and lighting on interpersonal relations; spatial arrangements in offices and schools; and social aspects of managing natural resources.

It is not possible to describe everything that environmental psychologists do in one chapter. One recent textbook (Gifford, 2002) describes more than 3,000 published studies in environmental psychology, and even that represents only a fraction of the field's research literature. However, to give you a taste of environmental psychology, including the contributions of social psychology, this chapter focuses on three major topics that should give you a good sample of the field as a whole.

The first topic is **resource dilemmas,** which are sometimes called commons dilemmas. These are situations in which individuals must choose between self-interest (taking or using unsustainable amounts of a natural resource such as water or fish) and the interests of the community or environment (taking a sustainable share, or less, of the resource). Which social factors do you think might come into play as individuals make these decisions? Given that no one person is likely to be given control of an entire water supply or fishing grounds, how might you conduct some research to understand what causes greed or cooperation in these situations?

Second, **social design** refers to a process by which any building (e.g., office, school, residence, factory, retail store, prison) may be designed in collaboration with those who will actually use that building so that they are more user-friendly, as opposed to being designed solely by an architect who will never use the building. Outdoor spaces, such as streets and plazas, can also be designed either to support human interaction or to ignore it. What social factors might be important in a process like this? Have you ever worked, gone to school, or visited a building that did not facilitate your work, your purpose for using the building, or your social life? Social design could have helped.

Third, **defensible space** represents a way of fighting crime through careful arrangement of the physical aspects of communities, retail buildings, and residences. The way in which a building or community is designed can encourage or discourage burglars, robbers, and vandals. What could those design factors be? How could social psychology be a part of this kind of research?

Just like the efforts of other psychologists, the work of those who study environmental issues may be grouped into two complementary branches: experimental and applied. Nearly all of environmental psychology is applied in the broad sense that its efforts are stimulated by the recognition of problems in interactions between individuals and their built and natural settings. Virtually all environmental psychologists hope to help solve these problems eventually. Even the most experimental of environmental psychologists hope that the results from their studies will be considered in the design of offices, factories, homes, streetscapes, and/or parks (even parks have some buildings and trails) or in programs designed to improve environment-related behaviors such as recycling, energy conservation, and reductions in car use.

Environmental psychologists have learned an enormous amount about person–environment relations during the 35 years the field has formally existed. They know much about social environmental dynamics such as how typical interpersonal distances change with different situations, which social factors are likely to improve or inhibit pro-environmental attitudes, how interpersonal relations lead to water conservation, how crowding affects social interaction, how noise influences helping behavior, and how temperature is related to interpersonal violence. Many have designed behavioral interventions to change and improve behavior toward more sustainable practices.

As discussed in Chapter 1, however, good social scientists also want to understand *why* people act the way they do. Therefore, psychologists who focus on the physical environment have developed interesting theories to help explain things such as who will cooperate and who will not when resources are scarce, how cultures vary in seeking privacy, the cultural meanings conveyed by building facades, the strategies residents use for dealing with spatial conflicts within their homes, how children learn to find their way around their neighborhoods,

and which furniture arrangements encourage social interaction (Gifford, 2002).

However, as mentioned earlier, this chapter considers only a small sample of these efforts: resource dilemmas, social design, and defensible space.

RESOURCE DILEMMAS

As environmental problems and concerns grow, social scientists must learn more about individual and small-group contributions to ecological degradation. As humans who dwell in societies, we extract, refine, use, and dispose of many natural resources. However, societies are composed of individuals, and ultimately people make these choices *as individuals and small groups* in their homes, at work, and during their leisure hours.

The crucial aspect of resource management decisions by each of us is that they sum, from person to person, across billions of individuals' actions to large-scale effects on the environment in ways that are partly rational, partly irrational, and yet all-important. Mundane everyday choices to turn on the air-conditioning, drive the car a short way instead of walking or riding a bike, or take a 15-minute shower instead of a 5-minute shower add up to resource depletion on a larger scale.

Once the macroenvironment is affected (e.g., less forest cover, depleted aquifers, more landfills, more pavement), it affects us in return. Most of us realize that we should waste less, but we are tempted to lead lives that use many natural resources (e.g., water, oil, wood). Our divided goals lead us to experience this as a dilemma, one or another of a family called *social dilemmas*.

A Family of Dilemmas

The focus of this section is on resource dilemmas, which represent one of several kinds of dilemma situations that fall under the general category (family) of social dilemmas. **Social dilemmas** are a group of situations in which individuals face important choices. Sometimes individuals do not realize how important their choices are—or even that they are making choices—but that is a separate problem. In social dilemmas, the rewards to the individual for noncooperation are greater than the rewards for cooperation no matter what others do; however, if most individuals involved fail to cooperate, then everyone receives lower rewards (Dawes, 1980). A simple example would be a person washing a car during a dry spell. This person gains a clean car by using scarce water—the reward (a clean car) seems greater than having no reward (an unclean car)—and this clean car reward occurs, in the short term, regardless of what other community residents do. If this person is one of very few people washing their cars, a clean car reward is gained with little loss to the community water supply. However, if many persons wash their cars, serious damage might be done to the water supply and everyone receives a lower reward—having no water, or perhaps muddy water, from the community supply—and this consequence is worse than merely having a dirty car.

Three main forms of social dilemma are recognized: public goods problems, social traps, and resource (or commons) dilemmas. **Public goods problems** involve dilemmas about whether to contribute (e.g., time, effort, money) to a project that would benefit everyone when such a contribution is voluntary. For example, one may decide to help (or not help) build a neighborhood children's playground. The dilemma is that contributing costs something (in this case, one's money or time devoted), but if not enough others contribute, the playground project will not be successful.

A person is tempted to *avoid* contributing to the public good (to not cooperate) for two reasons. First, if enough others contribute their time and/or money so that the public good succeeds, the person benefits (gets a neighborhood playground) without having to contribute anything. Second, contributing is risky in that a person might donate money or time, only to find that not enough others do so; if this happens, the project fails and the person's contribution is wasted.

Of course, the ideal outcome is that everyone helps and the project succeeds. Unfortunately, there are usually some who do not help, leaving the outcome uncertain, and then each person begins to wonder whether participation is a good idea (and this is precisely the public goods

dilemma). Public goods dilemmas are surprisingly common in our lives (just look around with the concept in mind). Unfortunately, many worthwhile projects fail.

Social traps are a second form of social dilemma. They involve short-term pleasure or gain that, over time, leads to pain or loss (Platt, 1973). Some classic social traps include smoking, overeating, and using pesticides. They are dilemmas because individuals must choose between an immediate reward (e.g., the pleasure of smoking, the pleasure of eating an extra dish of ice cream) and the long-term negative outcome to which the reward can lead (e.g., lung cancer, obesity) versus short-term deprivation (e.g., quitting smoking, refusing to eat the extra dish of ice cream) and the long-term positive outcome to which the deprivation can lead (e.g., a longer life, a slimmer build).

Two problems create the dilemma in a social trap. First, the long-term outcome usually is not certain (e.g., not every smoker dies of smoking-related disease, nor does every person who abstains from smoking live a long time). In the case of the environment, the long-term uncertainty makes it easier to rationalize choosing the environmentally damaging option (e.g., using excessive water in the spring when the state of the community reservoir later in the summer is not yet known). Second, individuals tend to *discount* (i.e., downplay) the negative outcomes; for example, pesticide users usually do not think about how their pesticide use can lead to ecological problems in the future, or they believe that their own small contribution does not matter all that much.

Public goods problems and social traps are important social dilemmas that clearly are pertinent to the well-being of the physical environment. All of us must deal with these two forms of dilemma in our lives. However, as noted previously, the focus in this chapter is on a third form of social dilemma, the resource dilemma, which is sometimes called the commons dilemma, a term first used by Dawes (1973).

What Is a Resource Dilemma?

Early perspectives on resource dilemmas. The car-washing example given earlier is a specific form of resource dilemma. For a more general understanding, let us start with a little background based on an allegory told long ago by William Lloyd. In some older societies, "the commons" referred to a central open space in the heart of a village. By mutual understanding, this commons was jointly owned by all citizens in good standing without any borders or fences inside it. All citizens were allowed to use its grass and open space to graze their animals. The unwritten rule was that each family could have one cow. There was enough grass for all of the citizens' animals, and the commons worked well for many years (Lloyd, 1837/1968).

However, the day eventually came when one citizen decided to make a little extra money by having a second cow, from which more milk could be produced and sold. There is nothing wrong with "getting ahead," is there? (Another possibility is that more families moved to the village, and each family wanted to add one more cow. Everyone is entitled to one cow, right?) The problem is that the amount of available grass remained the same; the alternative is to cut down more of the forest surrounding the village, but that is just another form of resource dilemma. Whether someone wanted to get ahead or the number of shareholders in the commons grew, there was more use of the same amount of grass. As demand for a limited resource increases, the issue becomes one of *freedom in the commons,* according to Garrett Hardin. Do citizens have the right to take what they want (individual freedom to get ahead) or to increase the number of families, all of whom want equal grazing rights, or should there be restrictions so that the commons is protected (Hardin, 1968)?

When the supply of a resource seems large or nearly limitless, individuals seem to feel free to exploit the resource as much as possible. One reason for this was advanced by the famous 18th-century economist Adam Smith. Smith (1776/1976) argued that in exploiting resource for one's own benefit, an individual allegedly is guided by an "invisible hand" to benefit the whole community. For example, a whaler who becomes rich would employ people, buy equipment, and donate to social, educational, and charitable causes—and would generally aid the economy. At one time, the supply of whales seemed nearly endless.

Lloyd (1837/1968), a 19th-century economist, appears to have been the first (in relating the preceding village allegory) to see a fundamental problem with Smith's logic. Lloyd recognized that many resources are, in fact, finite and limited. When that is the case, a big problem arises. In a limited commons consisting of some desirable resource, individuals acting in self-interest might lead to a process called the **tragedy of the commons,** which occurs when "each [person] is locked into a system that compels him to increase his [harvesting] without limit—in a world that is limited. Ruin is the destination toward which all [persons] rush, each pursuing his own best interest" (Hardin, 1968, p. 1244).

The classic example of a commons dilemma is grazing land (as in the commons example), but the extreme importance of resource dilemmas is that many other resources are limited and essentially held in common—fresh water, forests, habitat, and even our one and only atmosphere. Resource dilemmas are a matter of life and death for all life on the planet.

The conclusion to Lloyd's allegory was that once the commons was overused, the grass ran out and so the cows perished, and then the villagers did not have enough to eat and so they too died. Lloyd's story was an amazingly prescient vision of our modern notion of the limited "spaceship earth" given that he first presented the story more than 165 years ago.

The nature of the dilemma itself. What is a resource dilemma? One occurs each time you want to do something that uses a limited natural resource (e.g., fresh water, oil or gas, wild fish) that would make your life easier, more fun, or more comfortable. Some resources regenerate relatively quickly (e.g., grass for grazing, water in reservoirs), others regenerate not so quickly (e.g., fish, trees), and some regenerate very slowly or not at all (e.g., oil, endangered species). When resources regenerate more slowly than people can harvest them, the danger of resource exhaustion arises. Users of such resources face a choice: either get ahead quickly at the expense of the commons (the resource and/or the environment) and other harvesters or restrain harvesting to preserve the commons and increase one's contentment or wealth more slowly. The radical environmentalist Billy

Cottrell apparently believed that oil, from which gas is produced, is a natural resource that is being harvested too quickly.

Not all natural resources are in short supply, even those that are created very slowly (e.g., sand). But when people are able to harvest a desirable resource faster than it can regenerate through improved technology or sheer person power, the potential dilemma becomes an actual dilemma. Harvesters must choose between rapid, resource-destructive, short-term, self-interested harvesting ("get it while you can") and restrained, long-term, community-, and resource-oriented harvesting.

The consequences of resource dilemmas. Hardin's (1968) article in the journal *Science* on the ultimate consequences of resource dilemmas has been very influential. He concluded that commons dilemmas probably would be fatal to the entire planet eventually. However, environmental psychologists have not accepted without question Hardin's tragedy of the commons argument that most (too many) individuals will act in their short-term self-interest. They believe that the issue of how individuals will behave in a limited commons is an open question that will be resolved through empirical research. Hardin was a biologist and had a fairly pessimistic outlook on the future, based on some clear examples of nonhuman animal populations that followed a tragedy of the commons path to destruction. There is no doubt that the growth of the earth's human population, over the long term, resembles the same pattern observed in some instances of animal populations that collapsed after extremely rapid growth. The explosive growth of the population of humans is depicted in Figure 14.1.

However, humans have greater cognitive capacity than do animals, and they can anticipate difficulties and solve problems—usually. Can our species do better, or are we just another animal in the sense that we will not be able to escape the tendency to greed that will eventually destroy us? Social scientists have pursued this question and created sizable bodies of work in their attempts to try to answer it (e.g., Gardner, Ostrom, & Walker, 1990; Gifford, 2002, chap. 14; Komorita & Parks, 1994).

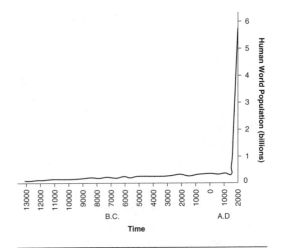

Figure 14.1 The Growth of the Human Population on Earth

The case of water: A dose of reality. One of the most important resources in the world is fresh water, and it is bound to become more important in the future. You will recall that Lloyd pointed out a flaw in Smith's 18th-century influential economic theory that was based on the assumption that natural resources are essentially unlimited. It was acceptable—even admirable—for entrepreneurs to use them at will to create wealth because others in society also would benefit. This rationale still is used today to justify the "necessary" growth of business and the economy.

We now know well that at least some natural resources are not unlimited and that people have been fighting over limited natural resources for centuries. In his book *Resource Wars,* Michael Klare recalled the biblical accounts of the Israelites' drive from the desert into the "Promised Land," that is, the fertile valleys of the Jordan River basin that contained good supplies of water (Klare, 2001). This drive involved a successful invasion (led by Moses) of these lands that were held by several groups that the Israelites expelled from the fertile region (e.g., Canaanites, Amorites, Hittites).

Klare (2001) argued that the 1967 Arab–Israeli war essentially was a modern repetition of the same struggle. He quoted former Israeli Prime Minister Yitzhak Rabin, who once said, "If we solve every other problem in the Middle

East but do not satisfactorily solve the water problem, our region will explode." Ancient and modern Egyptian rulers likewise have struggled to control the waters of the Nile, which during modern times flows through nine countries. Boutros Boutros-Ghali, the former Egyptian minister of state for foreign affairs, said, "The next war in our region will be over the waters of the Nile, not politics."

Today's natural resource struggles are over oil, fish, and trees as well as water. The ancient legacy of war and armed conflict in the Jordan and Nile regions could well be repeated as sources of water, fish, oil, and trees recede. Indeed, there have already been many oil wars and fish wars during recent times. Thus, cooperation in the use and management of natural resources is not some kind of academic parlor game; it is of vital importance in the real world of politics and war. Lives depend on finding ways of sharing natural resources in equitable ways.

To summarize, we all play a part in the management of a steady stream of natural resources (e.g., fresh water, oil, wood, fish) that have been converted into products that we use every day. Some of these resources come from limited sources. Commons dilemmas occur when improved technology or increased person power enables the harvesting of resources faster than the resource can regenerate.

All of us who use natural resources or products derived from them (i.e., everybody) must decide whether to maximize our own gain in the short term or, instead, to help maximize the gain over the long term for everyone, including ourselves (and, in the course of so doing, to preserve the resources themselves rather than wiping them out). The crucial aspect of all these individual decisions is that they add up to society's success or failure in managing natural resources.

Studying Resource Dilemmas

For environmental psychologists, two important questions are as follows. First, under which conditions will individuals act in self-interest to the detriment of others and the resource? Second, under what conditions will individuals

not act in self-interest and, thus, act to the benefit of others and the resource? The first question concerns understanding the problem, whereas the second question relates to addressing the problem. Often it is easier or more rewarding, at least in the short run, to engage in self-serving behavior than to behave in the public interest. In a limited commons, the cooperative or public-spirited act often is more expensive, difficult, and/or time-consuming and less immediately rewarding than is the self-serving act. As we will see, social factors are among the most important in answering these questions.

More than 100 recent scientific studies have examined many influences on the choices that individuals and groups make in these resource dilemmas. Altogether, perhaps 35 different factors have been found to influence whether harvesters tend to be greedy or cooperative in resource dilemmas (Gifford, 2002, chap. 14; Komorita & Parks, 1994). These studies have, in general, focused on three kinds of influence on cooperation in the commons. The first is the nature of the resource itself (e.g., how much of it is available, how much of it is certain to exist). This is of less importance to social psychologists than are the other two factors. One of these factors involves the social conditions or rules surrounding the harvesting (e.g., how well the harvesters know and trust each other; whether a leader exists, is elected, or acts in a certain way). The other factor is characteristic of the harvesters (e.g., the size of the harvester group, how the harvesters think about or interact with each other).

Each study typically examines two or three specific variables at a time. As an example, our own recent research has focused on the thinking processes of participants as the dilemma evolves over time (Hine & Gifford, 1997) and on the attributions made about the actions of the self and other harvesters (Gifford & Hine, 1997; Hine & Gifford, 1996). Decision making and behavior in resource dilemmas depend, in part, on what we think about the other harvesters and *their* choices.

A microworld. When you think about it, no government or corporation is likely to give anyone,

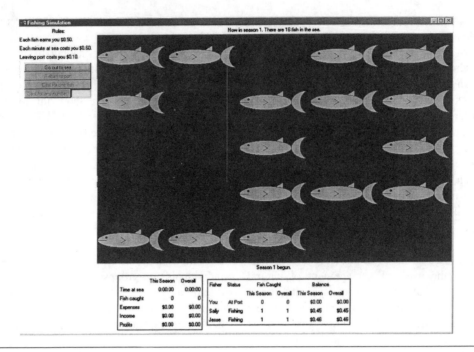

Figure 14.2   Screen Shot from FISH 3

including a social scientist, complete control over any large real resource merely to conduct an experimental study. Thus, we scientists sometimes use **microworlds,** that is, dynamic, computer-based, virtual environments that exist in laboratories but reasonably simulate real-world conditions (DiFonzo, Hantula, & Bordia, 1998). It is tempting to think that participants in these simulated environments do not respond in the same way as they do in everyday life, but there is good evidence that a well-constructed microworld will elicit strong emotions that seem to indicate that the participants are taking the microworld as seriously as they would a full-scale resource.

One such microworld is FISH 3 (Gifford & Gifford, 2000), which recreates in the laboratory the situation faced by real fishers as they choose how much of a fish stock to harvest. The program creates a context that includes many of the essential elements of a real resource dilemma. If you were a participant fisher, you would be able to choose, if you wish, to catch fish more quickly than they can spawn. In fact, you could catch all the fish at any time. But if you (or another fisher) do that, the fish will not exist to reproduce in the future, so the quick gain comes at the expense of any future harvests. So, you may also choose to restrain your harvests in the interest of conserving the stock of fish. Each fisher in a fleet (group) has equal and full access to the resource. Thus, one big concern is what the other fishers will do; can they be trusted to restrain their harvests? Figure 14.2 shows a screen shot from FISH 3.

FOCUS ON RESEARCH

Experimental research on resource dilemmas has been very productive and has generated a number of important findings (Komorita & Parks, 1994). Most such studies set up various conditions for their participants and then observe the resulting behaviors. However, more might be learned by examining the "inner" process by which harvesters make their decisions. An approach that seeks to "get into the heads" of participants, **grounded theory analysis** (Glaser & Strauss, 1967), is useful for this purpose. (Grounded theory analysis was discussed in Chapter 3 as an example of qualitative methods.)

Grounded theory analysis is a sophisticated way of learning how people think about particular issues by asking them what they are doing, and why, *as* they are considering something such as making a decision about using some resource. It uses the **think-aloud procedure,** in which individuals explain their decisions moment by moment as they make them. This procedure enables the researcher to track online cognitive processing as it naturally occurs. As noted earlier, in most resource dilemma studies, researchers simply impose a set of conditions on the harvesters and then observe their resultant decisions. This tells us little about exactly how the decision makers arrived at their decisions because it ignores what goes on in the "black boxes" of the people's minds.

One resource dilemma study used this grounded theory approach to find out what goes on in harvesters' heads (Hine & Gifford, 1997). In this microworld study of fishing, one real participant (at a time) was seated in front of a personal computer and a tape recorder to collect his or her thoughts. Two computer-simulated fishers also harvested fish, and their harvesting behavior was programmed to range from quite cooperative to quite greedy. The real fishers were faced with a harvest choice: to take fish for which they receive payment or to leave the fish in the water to reproduce.

Before the fishers fished, and as they fished, the think-aloud technique was used to gather the fishers' action strategies, heuristics, and cues that triggered their decisions of whether to take fish or not. The results showed that several main *action strategies* were employed by harvesters, including the following:

- Close monitoring of others' harvest practices
- Imagining the future harvests of others
- Trying to avoid overuse of the resource
- Attempting to influence the harvests of others through one's own harvest practices (strategic harvesting)

Notice that three of these goals were social; they related to what other fishers were doing. This shows that social interaction, whether direct or indirect, is an important part of decisions about whether to use natural resources. Interestingly, two of these social strategies—imagining the future harvests of others and strategic harvesting—had received little or no attention previously in the general experimental research literature. By uncovering them, the study helped to point the way toward a fuller understanding of harvesters' decision making, which in turn leads toward improved policymaking in real resource dilemmas. The results suggest that when policymakers consider strategies to encourage conservation of natural resources, they should be aware that people do try to imagine or guess what other harvesters might choose to do (a very social factor) and that people use their own harvests to send messages to others (another very social act). How would you turn this knowledge into concrete policy?

Field studies of strategies for inducing pro-environment behavior. Psychologists who are interested in environmental issues also study other uses and abuses of resources such as pollution, the rate of energy use in households and work organizations, recycling, and transportation. Usually they consider the potential power of a few factors that they think might influence people to engage in a more pro-environment behavior such as to reduce their use of some resource, to pollute less, or to recycle more.

Some of the main factors include the following: appeals from authorities, improvements in educational campaigns, goal setting and public commitment by individuals to change their behavior, feedback, modeling, and norm activation (Gifford, 2002; Schultz, 1998). The first two of these have not been found to be particularly effective in changing behavior. This might be surprising in the case of educational campaigns given that they represent a widely used strategy and cost considerable sums to implement. The value of educational campaigns lies in their *priming ability;* that is, they get people *ready* to make a change rather than actually *get* them to change.

The goal-setting and public commitment strategies work better. If a person decides, for example, to reduce household energy use by a specified and reasonable amount (say, 10%) and also announces this goal to family and friends, actual behavior change is more likely. The change has become a personal "item" that the individual "wears around" like a new coat, whereas a plea from the mayor or president, or a television ad, are easy to listen to or look at without becoming incorporated in the person's identity.

The use of role models has proven to be effective in facilitating the increase in pro-environment behavior. We learn from watching others. This basic principle of **social learning theory** (Bandura, 1977b) has been shown to increase energy conservation behaviors in studies of university students' showering practices and to improve home energy conservation (Aronson & O'Leary, 1977). In the shower study, despite signs imploring them to do so, only 6% of students soaped up while the water was off and took short showers. A larger sign increased compliance to 19%, but the sign became a target for hostile remarks and minor vandalism. But when a confederate model displayed the desirable behaviors, roughly half of the students followed suit, and when two confederates did so, roughly two thirds of the students followed suit. The confederates changed an environmentally important behavior without saying a word about it; that is an excellent example of social influence. Also, recall that Chapter 3 reported that cognitive dissonance theory has been applied successfully in reducing shower water use (Dickerson, Thibodeau, Aronson, & Miller, 1992).

Modeling can be used to encourage other environmentally conscious behaviors as well. Kahle and Beatty (1987) demonstrated that recycling will increase when significant others are depicted as recycling. A similar strategy combining role models and persuasion is to identify individuals in a neighborhood (e.g., block leaders) who can encourage their neighbors to recycle (Hopper & Nielsen, 1991).

● FOCUS ON INTERVENTION

In 1998, Wesley Schultz examined the effectiveness of several interventions designed to promote recycling among the residents of a California community of 32,000. Schultz's (1998) idea was to capitalize on using norms to produce changes in people's recycling behavior. As you may recall from Chapter 4, norms are shared beliefs about what behaviors are and are not acceptable for group members. Schultz attempted to increase residents' recycling behavior by making norms about their own and others' recycling behavior salient to them, thereby highlighting existing discrepancies between the norm (i.e., "I should be recycling every week") and a resident's actual level of recycling.

During the first stage of this field experiment, Schultz and his colleagues spent 8 weeks observing the levels of recycling among a large number of households. These data served as a baseline measure of recycling behavior. The households (actually small groups of houses that bordered each other) were randomly assigned to the experimental conditions (see below), with approximately 120 houses per condition.

During the second stage (9 weeks after the baseline period), a green door hanger was placed on the front doorknob of every household in the study. The door hangers indicated to the residents that their households had been chosen to be part of a study of recycling and that they should recycle as much as possible. Some households were not contacted any further. These households constituted the *plea to recycle condition*. The households in the other three conditions were contacted on one occasion during each of the next 4 weeks.

On one morning each week, participants' recycling materials were collected by truck. For each of the remaining treatment conditions, door hangers were placed on household doorknobs within 24 hours after recycling materials were collected. In the *information condition,* the hangers had printed information about recycling (e.g., what materials were recyclable, the recycling process). The information on the hangers changed each week. Households in the *individual feedback condition* received door hangers that provided feedback about the level of recycling (i.e., recycle or not, amount of material) at their houses for the previous week, for the current week, and for the course of the study. Participants in the *group feedback condition* received feedback about the level of recycling in their entire residential area for the previous week, for the current week, and for the course of the study.

Schultz's research team systematically observed and recorded levels of household recycling for all of the households during the 4-week intervention period and also during the 4 weeks following the intervention period. Based on theory and evidence regarding the effects of activating norms by providing feedback, Schultz predicted that feedback of either kind (individual or group) would be more effective in promoting recycling than would either merely providing information or simply making a plea.

Schultz's predictions were supported. During the intervention period, the households receiving individual feedback increased their frequencies of recycling relative to the baseline period. Attesting further to the power of the norm manipulations, those receiving either individual or group feedback continued to show higher frequencies of recycling relative to the baseline during the postintervention period. Neither the plea condition nor the information condition showed significant increases. Also, households in the individual feedback and group feedback conditions increased the *amount* of material they recycled relative to the baseline during both the intervention and postintervention periods. Again, there were no significant effects for either the information condition or the plea condition.

Schultz's experimental intervention was by no means a simple field study. Imagine the amount of time and money required to carry out the project. The two norm-based interventions worked, but were they too costly? Schultz took his research a step further by conducting a cost–benefit analysis. He calculated the costs involved in implementing the interventions (e.g., cost of door hangers, labor to record recycling materials and to distribute feedback, preparation of intervention materials) and the short-term financial benefits (e.g., monies received for recycling materials, reduction in funds needed to pay for trash disposal). Schultz determined that if the interventions were implemented on a citywide basis, the savings to the city for either feedback intervention would be $23,000 or more. He further noted that the implementation procedures could be streamlined (reducing costs substantially and further increasing savings) and that the very important environmental benefits (e.g., conservation of resources, reduced pollution) had not been factored into the benefits of the interventions but clearly add to their value.

Schultz's (1998) results demonstrate that interventions designed to promote recycling can be productive in changing people's behavior. They also highlight the usefulness of using theory in the development of effective interventions. It is interesting to consider how Billy Cottrell might have used norm-based interventions to try to change the purchasing behavior of SUV buyers.

Let us consider one other approach to ameliorating resource dilemmas—*environmental audits.* Energy utility companies and governments have tried to provoke conservation through programs in which a company representative visits a household and examines its energy-wasting capacity. Typically, the auditor points out problems, suggests repairs, offers an attractive grant or loan for major refits, and suggests reputable contractors for doing the needed work. The success of such programs has been variable. For instance, Gonzales, Aronson, and Costanzo (1988) reported that the U.S. national average was approximately 15% of household residents going on to make at least some of the necessary changes to their residences.

The environmental audit program, which on the surface might not seem to have anything to do with social psychology, actually does. Gonzales and colleagues (1988) improved the 15% success rate by training auditors how to communicate more effectively with household residents. Drawing on several established social psychological techniques of persuasion, they instructed auditors to use *vivid examples,* for example, "If you were to add up all the cracks under these doors, it's the same as if you had a hole the size of a basketball in your wall." Also, they told the auditors to *focus on loss rather than gain,* for example, "If you don't fix cracks, it's your hard-earned cash going right out the window." The auditors also were trained to induce residents to invest in the audit process by getting them to follow the auditors around the house, help take measurements, and actually look at the cracks. The researchers reasoned that household residents who personally took part in locating cracks in their homes and realized that they were playing a role in wasting energy would experience *cognitive dissonance*. They predicted that the residents would be motivated to increase their energy conservation behavior (e.g., fill the cracks) so as to reduce dissonance. Together, the changes to the auditors' social influence strategy produced a cooperation rate of approximately 60%, roughly four times the usual rate and a truly impressive outcome. Imagine the overall impact that the improved communication and persuasion processes could have if that fourfold improvement were applied to residences on a large-scale basis.

In conclusion, Hardin (1968), whose famous article in *Science* stimulated monumental modern debate and study on resource dilemmas, was not optimistic that humans can avoid the tragedy of the commons, that is, the complete collapse of our resources and, therefore, life as we know it. However, environmental and social psychologists have not accepted without question Hardin's argument that individuals will always act in their short-term self-interest. They consider the issue of how individuals behave in a limited commons to be an open question that will be resolved through empirical research, including implementing and evaluating interventions designed to induce people to put aside self-interest so as to preserve scarce and essential resources before they are destroyed. The material covered in this section has suggested that interventions that draw on social psychological theory and evidence show promise with respect to helping to counter Hardin's very pessimistic position.

SOCIAL DESIGN

Many aspects of the physical environment have been shown to influence behavior, including lighting, noise, and temperature. This section considers the behavioral effects of the physical design and layout of buildings. Have you ever had to study, live, or work in a school, home, or workplace that just did not work well and foster the types of behavior the situation called for? Certainly, some parts of the built environment need much improvement. One well-known example is a large apartment complex in St. Louis, Missouri, that was completed in 1954. The Pruitt–Igoe project was designed with the admirable intention of replacing deteriorating inner-city housing. The design for this complex, which contained 43 eleven-story buildings to house 12,000 people, was praised in an architectural journal for having vandal-resistant features, individualistic design, and no wasted space ("Slum Surgery in St. Louis," 1951).

The Pruitt–Igoe design saved space in part by having elevators stop only at every third floor, so that most residents would walk up or down one flight of stairs to their apartments. Pruitt–Igoe cost much less per unit than did comparable buildings. The design changes were considered so admirable that the architect even applied for a patent on the design.

But problems appeared soon after Pruitt–Igoe opened. The failure to carefully examine its design in relation to human social behavior contributed to high rates of fear, vandalism, serious crime, and vacancy. A particular problem was crime in the stairwells that residents were forced to use due to the "innovative" elevator savings plan. The situation was so bad that, after only 18 years, the city began to demolish the entire complex. In this example, insufficient consideration of how the physical structure would influence social behavior led to the ultimate failure of the project. Whether the architect ever received his patent is unknown.

Pruitt–Igoe is the most dramatic example of building design failure, but many other buildings also pose problems for their users. Take a look at Figure 14.3 for a different example of architecture that fails to suit human needs. *Hard architecture* is aimed at preventing vandalism but goes so far toward that goal that it is uncomfortable and, therefore, rarely used.

There is a way to design more humane buildings. This process, developed over the past three decades, may be called social design (Sommer, 1972, 1983) or social design research. In general, it involves studying how settings can best serve human desires and requirements. It must be distinguished from **technical design,** that is,

Figure 14.3   Hard Benches

the engineering aspects of the building such as the performance of building materials. Robert Sommer, a social design pioneer, characterized social design as follows:

> Social design is working with people rather than for them; involving people in the planning and management of the spaces around them; educating them to use the environment wisely and creatively to achieve a harmonious balance between the social, physical, and natural environment; to develop an awareness of beauty, a sense of responsibility, to the earth's environment and to other living creatures; to generate, compile, and make available information about the effects of human activities on the biotic and physical environment, including the effects of the built environment on human beings. Social designers cannot achieve these objectives working by themselves. The goals can be realized only within the structures of larger organizations, which include the people for whom a project is planned. (Sommer, 1983, p. 7)

Social design also may be distinguished from formal design, which is the traditional approach (Sommer, 1983). **Formal design** favors an approach that may be described as large scale, corporate, high cost, exclusive, authoritarian, tending to high-tech solutions, and concerned with style, ornament, the paying client, and a national or international focus. In contrast, social design favors an approach that may be described as small scale, human oriented, low cost, inclusive, democratic, tending to appropriate technology, and concerned with meaning and context, the occupant or paying client, and a local focus. These two approaches to design lead to the construction of buildings that differ dramatically, with important implications for human behavior and welfare inside them.

A Growing Collaboration

Design education and design competitions often encourage designers to emphasize the aesthetic dimension of architecture at the expense of the setting's functional value. Environments should, of course, be both beautiful and functional for their occupants. Unfortunately, attempts to create fashionable works of art dominated architecture for a long time—and still do. Architectural magazines still use expensive photography and glossy paper to show off buildings, but often no people are even visible in the scenes.

It is tempting to conclude that these "unpeopled buildingscapes" accurately reflect many designers' interests. One of the most influential architects in the world, Philip Johnson, said, "The job of the architect is to create beautiful buildings. That's all" (quoted in Sommer, 1983, p. 4). Where in this view is consideration of the residents' social lives and interpersonal relations? Who will live, work, and learn in the building—the architect or people like you?

But times are changing. Many architects and designers now recognize the importance of designing for the human use of buildings (without sacrificing technological or aesthetic considerations). For example, decades ago the American Institute of Architects sponsored a conference that served as an early summit meeting between social scientists and designers (Conway, 1973). This conference outlined several key roles that social scientist consultants might play, including evaluating building habitability, defining the psychological needs of occupants, and training occupants in the optimal use of buildings.

Actually, an early form of social design had been practiced long before, at least in one project, although perhaps it had been forgotten by many. Back in 1914, one office design team "spent several months in consultation, asking advice, and studying the needs of every department and of every individual" (Dempsey, 1914), although these consultations primarily concerned one elemental aspect of social design, that is, the physical distance between employees.

Nevertheless, even now, many architects are still mesmerized by the aesthetic properties of geometric space, and mainstream psychology largely neglects the physical context of behavior. However, when architects and social designers do collaborate, they begin to think of architecture as **placemaking,** that is, real people imagined in real spaces (Sime, 1986; Schneekloth & Shibley, 1993). To "make a place," architects and social designers work together to create an "envelope for behavior," meaning that they think mainly about what people actually do in a building rather than think of the building mainly as a sculptural object without much regard for the people who will be using it.

The social versus formal design dispute need not be adversarial. If formal designers try to make beautiful buildings for the multisensory pleasure of the building's *users,* aesthetic pursuits serve at least part of the social designer's goals (Stamps, 1989). Beautiful buildings may improve our perceptions of each other, facilitate social interaction, and assist occupants in some less direct ways such as enhancing tourism or a city's reputation.

When and How Social Design Helps

Social design is not *always* needed in the design process. It is not required, for example, in times, places, and cultures where buildings are constructed by small communities in which everyone works together in accordance with a time-tested architectural tradition. These traditions, called **preindustrial vernacular** (Rapoport, 1969), evolved an architecture that already fits community and cultural norms, individual interests, local climate, geography, and building materials quite well. When community members are both builders and occupants, the design process does not need separate financiers, architects, boards of directors, and construction firms (for an example of vernacular architecture, see Figure 14.4).

In the developed nations of the world, division of labor has produced material benefits for all of us. However, in the design professions (as in other occupations), it has produced considerable role specialization. Because the work of designing and constructing buildings is split more narrowly and each person's entire career is reduced to just one phase of it, there is a tendency for communication among the *principal players* in the process to diminish. The principal players in building design include the client (who puts up the money), the designer (architect and/or planner), the engineer (on larger projects), and (most important) the everyday building resident, customer, worker, or visitor.

Therefore, social design research has become necessary in industrial and postindustrial societies. Two of its major roles are to both reestablish and facilitate communication among the principal players in the design process. A third role is to remind everyone involved that the everyday building user *is* one of the principal players.

After the rise of industrialism and before the advent of environmental psychology, the

Figure 14.4   Vernacular Architecture

building user was nearly forgotten in architecture. The dazzling technology produced by the industrial revolution provided a vast array of design possibilities—in building materials, construction principles, and international communication among designers. Today, the design of some buildings requires so much attention to technical factors that the future occupants are completely forgotten.

Six Goals of Social Design

Social design researchers and practitioners have six main goals, with some being broader than others and some overlapping with others:

1. Create physical settings that match the needs and activities of their occupants. This goal is probably the most important one of all.

2. Satisfy building users. Occupant satisfaction is important because occupants must spend significant parts of their lives working, residing, or relaxing in the setting.

3. Change behavior. Such changes might include increasing office worker productivity, enhancing social ties among institutionalized elderly people, reducing aggression in a prison, or increasing communication among managers in an administrative office. As we will see, the behavior change goal can be both difficult to attain and controversial.

4. Enhance the building users' personal control (Holahan, 1983). The more building users are able to alter the setting to make it suit their needs, the less stressful that setting will be.

5. Facilitate social support (Holahan, 1983). Designs that encourage cooperation, assistance, and support are desirable primarily for building occupants who are disadvantaged in one way or another but also for active and successful individuals.

6. Employ "imageability." This refers to the ability of the building to help occupants, and (especially) visitors and newcomers, to find their way around without getting lost or confused.

Let us examine each of these goals more closely by considering the design of buildings.

Matching. How well the occupants' activities and needs are met by the setting is called **matching.** An example of poor matching might be a gymnasium when it is used for final examinations. It is done, but gyms are not very well suited to that task. Ideally, of course, buildings should match their occupants' needs and behaviors perfectly. However, whether the degree of match is high or low sometimes depends in part on whose viewpoint is considered (Michelson, 1976). For university administrators' purposes, the gym might seem to be a fine way in which to manage a space problem during final examinations; for students taking exams in the gym, the noise and distractions might seem to be quite inappropriate for an exam atmosphere.

The personality theorist Henry Murray and his collaborators distinguished between two forms of **press,** which refers to properties or characteristics of environmental features that shape behavior (Murray, 1938). **Alpha press** refers to actual reality that can be assessed through objective inquiry. **Beta press** refers to people's interpretation of external reality. For example, a person may act toward a conversation partner in an objectively neutral fashion (alpha press) but be perceived by the partner as aggressive (beta press). Similarly, there are alpha and beta forms of matching.

Alpha matching, or **congruence,** refers to how well the setting fits the person from an objective point of view. For example, there is a good (objective) height for kitchen counters for persons of different heights. Beta matching, or **habitability,** is "environmental quality as perceived by occupants of buildings or facilities" (Preiser & Taylor, 1983, p. 6). Some kitchen workers might not think that a certain counter height is good for them, even if experts claim that the existing counter height *is* correct.

All of the principal players in the design process hope, of course, that both perceived and actual matches are good. The possibility remains, however, that a team of design experts could *declare* that matching has been achieved when the occupants believe that it has not. Unfortunately, significant disagreements between experts and users have indeed been demonstrated in several studies of residential environments. For example, one study found that professional planners believed that a high-quality neighborhood was related to how open, interesting, and pleasant it was, whereas neighborhood residents believed that high quality was related solely to how pleasant it was (Lansing & Marans, 1969). Such clashes mean that efforts must be made not only toward improving the fit between users and their environments but also toward reducing differences between designer and occupant definitions of good design.

When alpha and beta matching are the same, such as when a building user has an objective need on which everyone agrees, the design implications are clear but the design still does not always meet this need. For example, persons with physical disabilities often have obvious clear-cut needs such as smooth ramps for those in wheelchairs. Yet there are still many buildings that lack ramps even though they are used by people in wheelchairs. Similarly, aged people whose perceptual and cognitive abilities have declined markedly have specific design needs that are often not provided for (Christenson, 1990; Cohen & Weisman, 1990; Rule, Milke, & Dobbs, 1992).

Nevertheless, building design guidelines for individuals with specific characteristics are a good idea, and many lists of guidelines have been prepared. For example, some have considered the proper design for relatively able-bodied older people (Hunt, 1991). Recommended design features for mental patients were among the first to receive attention from social designers (Osmond, 1957), and new ones continue to be issued (e.g., Gulak, 1991; Remen, 1991). Another setting that has been the focus of many recommendations is the children's day care center (Kennedy, 1991; Striniste & Moore, 1989). A set of design guidelines has been created to reduce a drastic behavior—suicide—among jail inmates (Atlas, 1989).

Satisfaction. Habitability (beta matching) corresponds to occupant satisfaction; congruence (alpha matching) is the expert's opinion that the occupants are satisfied. But principal players *other* than the occupants may or may not be satisfied with the project. Some architects, for example, hope that their buildings will work as statements of certain aesthetic design principles. The paying client (the building's developer) might be primarily satisfied if the project is completed within its budget. Most social designers would be happy if their work contributed to a habitable structure.

Change behavior. Many projects implicitly or explicitly embody people's hope that occupant behavior will change for the better. When all principal players, including occupants, agree that a certain pattern of behavior needs encouragement or discouragement from the design, the design process may steam merrily ahead. In a New York psychiatric hospital, the violent behavior of some severely regressed psychotic patients was one target when renovation designs were considered (Christenfeld, Wagner, Pastva, & Acrish, 1989). The new design significantly reduced the incidence of violence. In another study, museum visitors paid more attention to exhibits after careful design changes (Harvey, Loomis, Bell, & Marino, 1998).

Sometimes rather simple design modifications can change behavior. For instance, by merely adding tabletop partitions between pairs of students with profound retardation, researchers increased the amount of on-task behavior of the students (Hooper & Reid, 1985).

Unfortunately, principal players sometimes disagree about who should change which behaviors. Clients who pay for new or renovated workplaces, for example, often expect that the new designs will increase employee productivity. When faced with this expectation, the social researcher is in the uncomfortable position of being asked to use the environment to squeeze productivity out of employees. The very thought of attempting to manipulate employees for the benefit of an organization is unpleasant for many social design practitioners. (Recall the discussion in Chapter 1 of the role of personal values in applied psychology.)

Occupant satisfaction, on the other hand, is usually the goal of social design practitioners and other principal players who are particularly sympathetic to the needs of the building users. Some social designers see the process as part of a worldwide concern for human rights; social design began with attempts to provide the benefits of design to the unfortunate (e.g., mental patients) and to the poor (Sommer, 1983). This activist tradition still fuels the efforts of many social designers.

Let us consider a couple of examples of how social design can influence performance and behavior in the college classroom. Wollin and Montagne (1981) changed a typical plain introductory psychology classroom into one with softer lighting, plants, posters, cushions, and rugs. Student exam scores after 5 weeks in the room were higher than exam scores of students who spent 5 weeks in a similar room that had not been modified. The renovations cost only a few hundred dollars and appear to have produced improved learning for many.

Around the same time, Robert Sommer and Helge Olsen redesigned a plain, 30-seat college classroom (Sommer & Olsen, 1980). With a very small budget, they changed it into a *soft classroom* with semicircular, cushion-covered bench seating, adjustable lighting, a small carpet, and some mobiles. Compared with traditional classrooms of similar size, student participation increased markedly in the classroom. The number of statements per student tripled, and the percentage of students who spoke in class doubled. Besides the dramatic increase in participation, students using the soft room wrote many glowing comments about it in a logbook placed in the classroom. The room was still producing more student participation 17 years later (Wong, Sommer, & Cook, 1992). That represented a lot of added discussion considering the hundreds of students who had used the room over those years. The research of Sommer and his associates, together with Wollin and Montagne's (1981) work, suggests a tentative conclusion: College classrooms need not be plain and hard; inexpensive changes to make them more pleasant can have very tangible benefits, including better grades, better discussions, and occupant satisfaction (habitability).

Personal control. Good social design will provide building occupants with real options to control their proximate environment. What does this mean in specific terms? Consider, for example, children in hospitals. It is unpleasant enough being in a hospital, but if all of the furniture and equipment are adult-sized, the place is that much more intimidating. To increase children's independence and sense of control, one researcher published body measurement data for people from 0 to 19 years of age in the hope that hospital designers would use it for things such as beds, furniture, and bathrooms (Mirrer, 1987).

A second example is publicly funded residential space for students (dormitories) and poor people (housing projects). Some buildings, high-rises in particular, seem designed to overload residents with social stimulation. Too few elevators and long, narrow hallways, for example, result in the sense that people are everywhere and inescapable. Residents may develop the feeling that they cannot control the number of social contacts—especially unwanted social contacts—they must face daily. This loss of control can negatively affect feelings of security and self-esteem.

Two other common examples of low-control settings are crowded retail stores and traffic jams. **Crowding** refers to the feeling that there are too many people around; it may be distinguished from **population density,** which is an objective measure of persons per unit area. High density does not always lead to crowding, and crowding is not always the result of high density. Crowding is caused, in part, by social overload and informational overload, which in turn lead to the sense that one has lost control. Designing *against* crowding is, in part, designing *for* personal control. Again, simple design changes can be effective. By merely adding a few entrances to a mental health center, clients' sense of freedom (and thus control) was increased. Furthermore, the various treatment units within the center experienced a greater sense of identity because therapists felt as though they had their "own" entrances (Gutkowski, Ginath, & Guttman, 1992).

Stress is often related to lack of personal control over physical and social input. Noise, unwanted social contact, congestion, and a lack of places of refuge are examples of primary sources of stress (Evans & McCoy, 1998). Good social design can anticipate and attempt to overcome such sources or at least buffer the user from them.

Social support. Personal control is an individual phenomenon, whereas social support is a group phenomenon. **Social support** is a process in which a person receives caring, kind words, and helpfulness from those around him or her. Many social problems would be eased if more and better social support were available (Holahan, 1983). Common psychological problems, such as depression and anxiety, have been shown to increase when social support is absent or inadequate. Social support may be seen as an anti-stress process (Moos, 1981).

What can social design do to facilitate social support? On a small scale, furniture can be arranged in a sociopetal fashion instead of a sociofugal fashion. **Sociopetal arrangements** are those that encourage social interaction (e.g., when people sit facing each other), whereas **sociofugal arrangements** discourage social interaction (e.g., when people sit in rows or even facing away from one another) (Mehrabian & Diamond, 1971). At the building level, open-space areas may be arranged to facilitate social interaction (Holahan, 1972). Of course, if the personal control goal, as well as the social support goal, is to be met, the increased social interaction must be controllable; occupants should be able to find social interaction when and if they want it but should not be faced with unwanted social encounters.

In office buildings, social support may be fostered through the provision of high-quality lounge space for employees. The mere existence of such space does not guarantee that valuable social support will be available, but with inadequate space for employees to share coffee and conversation, the likelihood of supportive social networks declines.

Finally, in some cases social support may result from a design that provides optimal privacy (being able to filter one's interactions). Consider shelters for victims of domestic violence. A study of alternative designs for such shelters showed that designs characterized by anonymity and safety were most preferred (Refuerzo & Verderber, 1990). Sometimes social support is maximized when a person simultaneously can be near a helper and far from an abuser. The difference in helpfulness and caring is especially large when the contrast is between a residence that is full of hostility and violence and one that is dominated by caring and understanding.

Imageability. Buildings should be **imageable** (i.e., clearly understandable or legible) to the people who use them (Hunt, 1985). When you walk into a building, you should immediately be able to find your way around or, in more technical terms, be capable of **purposeful mobility.** In simple terms, you should not get lost.

It is astounding how often a person enters a building that is unfamiliar and is unable to figure out where to go next. Unless we realize that buildings *should* be imageable, there is a tendency to blame ourselves (e.g., "I never did have a good sense of direction"). Sometimes observation reveals that you are not the first to have problems. Perhaps you have seen hand-made signs that occupants have made to be helpful and/or to save themselves from answering the same question about where such-and-such is "for the hundredth time." Such signs represent a failure to make the building image-able, either through good signage or good and legible design of the building itself.

To conclude this section on building design, social design is architectural design that begins with the principle that the needs and preferences of those who will be working, living, or otherwise using a building are important or even para-mount. If a building can also be beautiful, that is a wonderful bonus because people do also need beauty in their lives. By virtue of its effects on the way in which people feel and interact, social design is intimately related to applied social psychology. Slowly, for the past 35 years, social design has increasingly become the goal of most architects. However, goals and reality are not always compatible, and not all new buildings are models of successful social design.

Outdoor Spaces

Many of the same social design ideas apply to outdoor public areas such as plazas, parks, and streets. In one of the most widely used changes wrought by environmental psychology principles, the very fabric of many cities has been changed by a concept called *density bemusing,* which can be traced to the pioneering work of William Whyte. Recognizing the need for some open space in the city core in 1961, the City of New York offered developers a deal: For every square foot of plaza they included in a new project, their new building could exceed normal zoning restrictions by 10 square feet. Developers liked the idea, and this deal certainly increased New York City's supply of open space downtown.

Unfortunately, the new plazas tended to be vast empty spaces, with the developers doing the least possible work to obtain their bonuses. Consequently, New York City revised its offers to developers. It would allow extra floors in new buildings only if developers offered plazas that included many of the amenities identified by Whyte (1980) that are associated with greater use and enjoyment of plazas such as "sittable space," water (fountains and pools), trees, and accessible food outlets. New plazas based on Whyte's ideas represent marked improvements over the alternatives, that is, cities with "canyons" but no open space, or empty concrete spaces. The new plazas have increased the pleasantness not only of New York City but also of many cities around the world.

A worthwhile exercise is to return to the six goals of social design and consider the extent to which they (some more than others) are served by the implementation of Whyte's thinking. Do likewise with respect to the contributions of Brower (1988) reviewed in the following paragraphs.

Sidney Brower has spent years developing and testing ideas for enlivening urban neighborhoods in Baltimore. Two of his key guidelines that have been used to improve the quality of life on the residential streets of that city are (a) keeping the street front alive by encouraging residents to walk, stroll, and play on the sidewalks and (b) finding a legitimate use for every public space so that people routinely visit all areas of the neighborhood and there are no "dead" or unowned spaces. Once some residents are outside and using the public space, others will feel safe in doing so; security and socializing go hand in hand.

Brower has encouraged more use of the street front by giving residents things to do and places to be. For some, this might mean benches; for others, it might mean horseshoes, hopscotch, bocce, street vendors, and/or library vans. Recreation on public streets can be encouraged by blocking off streets, alleys, and parking lots to cars. Some areas, such as side-walks themselves, must be free of fast and rough play by young people so that older people can enjoy walking or watching. At the same time, young people need open space that *can* be used for fast and rough play.

Brower also has reduced the speed and number of cars with speed bumps or temporary barricades. This reduced accidents by up to 30%

and accidents with injuries by roughly 25%. Residents tend to accept the barriers because they feel safer and the neighborhood is quieter and more suitable for walking (Vis, Dijkstra, & Slop, 1992; Zaidel, Hakkert, & Pistiner, 1992).

DEFENSIBLE SPACE

As noted previously, in Baltimore the use of speed bumps and barriers has helped to promote feelings of safety among residents of neighborhoods. How might the physical setting influence the actual likelihood of crime? Most evidence bearing on this question has emerged from the observations and ideas of Jane Jacobs and Oscar Newman that led to **defensible space theory,** a theory that deals with both crime and the fear of crime (Jacobs, 1961; Newman, 1972). This theory proposes that certain design features will increase residents' sense of security and decrease crime in the territory. Some of the features include the use of real or symbolic barriers to separate public territory from private territory and the provision of opportunities for territory owners to observe suspicious activity in their spaces (surveillance).

Quite a number of field studies have tested defensible space theory, and most of them provide support for it (Brown & Altman, 1983; Schneekloth & Shibley, 1993). For example, one would expect more crime in areas that offer fewer opportunities for surveillance and do not appear to be controlled by anyone. A study of crime in university residence halls showed that halls with defensible space features (e.g., more areas over which residents could feel some control and exercise more "surveillability") suffered less crime than did halls on the same campus without such features (Sommer, 1987). A survey of 16 well-conducted studies in which multiple design changes were made in accordance with defensible space theory found reductions in robberies of 30% to 84% (Casteel & Peek-Asa, 2000). In what follows, we consider the notion of defensible space in several settings.

Convenience Stores and Banks

Convenience stores have been frequent robbery targets. Those with smaller parking lots and those that do not sell gas, both of which decrease the surveillability of the stores' interiors, are held up more often (D'Alessio & Stolzenberg, 1990). A fascinating study of bank robberies found that several design features are related to increased chances of a holdup (Wise & Wise, 1985). Among these, more robberies occur when the bank has a smaller lobby, a compact square lobby (as opposed to a wide rectangular lobby), and larger distances between its teller stations. These features may be influential because they affect surveillability in the bank lobby.

Residences

In a study involving convicted burglars, convicts examined photos of 50 single-family dwellings and rated each one's likelihood of being burglarized (MacDonald & Gifford, 1989). The defensible space features of the houses were then assessed. As the theory predicts, easily surveillable houses were judged to be unlikely burglary targets. However, actual barriers (e.g., fences, visible locks) had no effect on the perceived vulnerability of the houses, although defensible space theory predicts that they should. According to defensible space theory, symbolic barriers, such as extra decorations and fancy gardens, are supposed to communicate to criminals that the residents are especially concerned about their property and, therefore, are more likely to defend it; symbolic barriers should make burglars shy away. However, the burglars saw houses with symbolic barriers as *more* vulnerable to burglary (Figure 14.5).

Why? Interviews after the study revealed that burglars viewed actual barriers as challenges that they could overcome; most fences and locks were not seen as serious barriers to them. The symbolic barriers were interpreted not as signs that the residents were especially vigilant but rather as signs that the houses probably contained more than the usual amount of valuables; if the residents have the time and money to decorate their houses and gardens, the burglars reasoned, the houses are probably full of "goodies." A study of apartment building burglaries confirmed that accessibility (actual barriers) made little difference but that surveillability reduced burglary (Robinson & Robinson, 1997).

Burglars cannot accurately pick out houses that have been burglarized from those that have not, but they do use social and physical cues in

Figure 14.5   An Undefensible House.

their guesses (Brown & Bentley, 1993). As discussed in the previous study, they do not see locks and bars as serious impediments, but they do worry about neighbors seeing them and about the residents' territorial concerns.

Interestingly, research has revealed that residents and police do not use the same house features as do burglars to infer that houses are vulnerable to burglary (Ham-Rowbottom, Gifford, & Shaw, 1999; Shaw & Gifford, 1994). These studies imply that residents and police need to understand burglars' perspective before they can stop burglary through residential design.

As for other features of residences, more crime occurs in taller apartment buildings and in buildings with more than 5 units per floor or 50 total units (Rand, 1984). This probably occurs because residents of larger buildings are less likely to know one another, tend to treat each other as strangers, and lose the ability to recognize who lives in the building and who does not. This makes entry by criminals easier.

Communities

Crime and vandalism are linked to, or facilitated by, certain aspects of the physical nature of a community. Many gated communities have sprung up, partly out of fears about crime.

Residents do feel safer in gated communities, according to one study, but actual crime rates were no lower, and sense of community was lower, than in nongated communities (Wilson-Doenges, 2000). But perhaps residents do not need to completely cut themselves off from the rest of the world.

Defensible space theory asserts that the actions of both the resident and the criminal are affected by defensible space features. Certain streets in St. Louis have defensible space features, including gateway-like entrances, alterations that restrict traffic flow (through narrowing roads or using speed bumps), and signs that discourage traffic (Newman, 1980). Residents who live on such streets are more often seen outside their homes, walking and working in their yards. Such behaviors might not be overtly territorial; residents might not think of themselves as guarding the neighborhood, yet they seem to have the effect of discouraging antisocial activity. Presumably, intruders are discouraged by this naturally occurring surveillance.

Another neighborhood with a high crime rate—in Dayton, Ohio—incorporated some defensible space changes (Cose, 1994). Many entrances to the neighborhood were closed, speed bumps were installed to slow down traffic, gates with the neighborhood logo were installed, and the community was divided into five mini-neighborhoods with physical barriers. Two years later, traffic was down 67%, violent crime was down 50%, and total crime was down 26%.

When an area seems more residential, with few through-streets and little public parking, it usually will experience less crime than will houses on the edges of such areas (Brantingham & Brantingham, 1977; Krupat & Kubzansky, 1987). The general principle is to reduce passage by strangers through the area, which increases bonds among residents and helps everyone to spot suspicious activity.

Blocks with houses that have been burglarized tend to have more street signs (Brown, 1980). It is possible that streets with more signs indicate a more public area with less control by residents and so may be attractive to criminals. Apartments nearer parking lots and recreation areas are burglarized more, as are stores and residences near corners. Somewhat contrary to this overall picture, streets with heavier traffic may experience less crime; perhaps more cars means more chance of being observed (Rand, 1984). This notion that areas that are more public are more vulnerable is confirmed by reports that more crimes are committed at the edges of central downtown districts (Rand, 1984). People go downtown, are not familiar with the darker areas near the main corners, and may be attacked as they leave or arrive for an evening's entertainment.

However, some areas that *have* defensible space characteristics still have serious crime problems. That is partly because *defensible* space (the physical layout) does not necessarily translate into **defended space** (i.e., residents actually acting against crime by keeping an eye out or reporting suspicious activity). This can happen, for example, if the neighborhood is not sufficiently cohesive for residents to act together against criminal elements (Merry, 1981). Defensible space *sets the stage* for crime reduction by making it easier—nearly automatic—for residents to fight crime through visual surveillance of outdoor areas, but if residents are unable or unwilling to act on what they see, crime will not be deterred.

A second reason that defensible space does not guarantee a crime-free neighborhood is that not all criminals pay attention to the environment. Less experienced criminals who are motivated by thrill seeking or social approval use less rational criteria for choosing a target and may simply not pay attention to defensible space features of the setting (Rand, 1984). Also, some criminals are impaired by drugs or alcohol as they work and pay less attention to the environment.

When the crime scene is a particular place (e.g., a convenience store) rather than an entire neighborhood, defensible space design principles may be more successful. One chain of stores incorporated a series of changes such as putting cash registers right in front of windows and removing window ads to make the interior more surveillable. Robberies declined by 30% relative to other stores that were not redesigned (Krupat & Kubzansky, 1987).

Researchers in The Netherlands have developed a checklist for assessing the crime vulnerability of neighborhoods (van der Voordt & van Wegen, 1990). This checklist consists of six main elements that discourage criminal behavior:

- The potential visibility of public areas (lines of sight)
- The actual presence of residents (to take advantage of these sight lines)
- Social involvement (residents caring enough to maintain buildings and act against criminals)
- Poor access and escape routes for criminals but good ones for potential victims
- Attractive surroundings that evoke care in residents (with decay informing criminals that residents are not vigilant)
- Structural safeguards or not (e.g., locks, presence of easily vandalized walls, phone booths)

The checklist's primary aim is to identify areas that are susceptible to vandalism, but it may be further developed as a tool against other crimes such as burglary and violent crime.

Vandalism is a widespread destructive behavior. Not every alteration of public territory is vandalism, of course. We can distinguish between vandalism and *people's art* (Sommer, 1972). Part of the distinction involves motive; the artist's goal is to beautify an ugly environment. Vandals are destructive or egocentric; instead of painting a mural that reflects a social concern, they break off a branch of a young tree or scrawl their own names on a subway wall. In contrast, public artists usually seek anonymity yet creatively enhance a bleak place.

Vandals' motive often may be revenge. **Equity theory,** emphasizes the idea that social and other behaviors are influenced by each person's perception that social (or other) rewards and costs should be fair. The theory suggests that vandals often are persons who feel they are dealt with unfairly (Baron & Fisher, 1984). Vandalism may be particularly likely when perceived unfairness is combined with a perceived lack of control, a feeling that the injustice cannot be rectified through normal channels. Whether or not potential vandals have role models who engage in vandalism may also be important (Baron, 1984).

CULTURE CAPSULE: CULTURAL DIFFERENCES IN PERSONAL SPACE

Environmental psychologists are acutely aware that human behavior varies considerably around the world. The ways in which people celebrate birth, teach their children, dress, get married, work, and are treated at death are like a colorful tapestry of swirling colors. Yet in another way, and at another level, people are the same everywhere. They celebrate births, teach their children, dress, get married, work, and recognize death in some kind of ceremony. Personal space is like that; the distance across which individuals interact with one another varies from culture to culture. Yet in every culture, there are rules that govern the choice of those interactional distances.

Personal space has been described as hidden, silent, and invisible, yet everyone possesses and uses personal space every day. Personal space stretches and shrinks with circumstances. It is interpersonal, so it depends on with whom people are interacting. It refers to the distance people choose to stay from others, but social interaction, such as angle of orientation and eye contact, is also part of personal space. Finally, personal space can be invaded, although such invasions are a matter of degree (Patterson, 1975). In sum, **personal space** is the geographic component of interpersonal relations, that is, the distance and angle of orientation (e.g., side by side, face to face) between individuals as they interact (Gifford, 2002).

Beyond these within-culture variations, personal space is used differently around the world. In one study, for example, groups of four male students came to the laboratory and were told that they would be observed but were given no other instructions (Watson & Graves, 1966). Half of the groups were composed of Arabs, and half were composed of Americans. The average interpersonal distance chosen by Arabs was about the length of an extended arm, whereas the average interpersonal distance chosen by Americans was noticeably farther. The Arabs touched one another much more often, and their orientation was much more direct. In general, the Arabs were much more "immediate" (close) with one another than were the Americans.

Such findings might lead to overly simplistic generalizations or stereotypes about cultural differences, for example, that some cultures are "close" and others are "distant." However, two studies (Forston & Larson, 1968; Mazur, 1977) revealed that students from supposedly close cultures (Latin America, Spain, and Morocco) chose seating positions that were farther apart from one another than did students from a supposedly distant culture (United States). Furthermore, not all Latin Americans use the same amount of space (Shuter, 1976). Costa Ricans, for example, choose smaller interpersonal distances on average than do Panamanians and Colombians.

Despite some oversimplifications, personal space does vary with culture. In one study, for example, Japanese people used more distance in conversations than did Americans, who in turn used more than did Venezuelans. But when the same Japanese and Venezuelans spoke English instead of their first languages, their conversational distance moved toward that of the Americans (Sussman & Rosenfeld, 1982). Language, an important part of culture, can modify one's cultural tendencies to use more or less interpersonal distance.

The study of personal space is not merely academic; it also has important implications for cultural understanding and conflict. For example, a researcher taught some English students how to act more like Arabs in their nonverbal behavior (Collett, 1971). Arabs who interacted with the trained students liked them more than they did students who had not received such training. Consider the implications for diplomats or even ordinary tourists.

EPILOGUE

Psychologists have the most difficult scientific job in the world. Natural scientists, even those who study tiny particles or immense galaxies, have the advantage of investigating phenomena that are inherently less complex than they are. Therefore, they can—at least theoretically and at some future time—fully understand the phenomena they study. Psychologists have a more difficult task—to understand entities (people) at their own level of complexity. This is as difficult as frogs trying to understand how and why frogs operate. But beyond that, much of psychology ignores or underplays the important dynamic interaction between people and their physical settings. Thus, environmental psychologists are like frogs trying to understand not only their fellow frogs but also the manner in which frogs fit into the pond's ecology. No other scientists are faced with a more daunting task.

Nevertheless, for a field of inquiry and action that is only roughly 35 years old, environmental psychology has made some very significant improvements in the world. One wonders whether other branches of psychology, or even other disciplines, have so positively affected the quality of life of so many people within their first 35 years. From ubiquitous transit maps to international diplomacy, from more humane city plazas to the widespread acceptance of social design principles, from encouraging more environmentally responsible behavior to fighting crime, and from saving lost hikers to facilitating better learning in classrooms, environmental psychology has much to be proud of and can truly say that it has made a difference in the quality of life for millions of people.

SUMMARY

This chapter began by discussing social dilemmas with a particular focus on resource dilemmas that occur in situations where a natural resource may be consumed at a nonrenewable rate, potentially leading to severe environmental and human consequences. The dilemma is that individuals must choose between self-interest (overconsuming the resource) and the interests of the community (cooperating by not overconsuming). Consideration was given to the factors that affect the decisions of people faced with resource dilemmas, with particular emphasis placed on factors, including intervention strategies, that lead people to avoid acting on the basis of self-interest.

Next, the chapter explored issues related to social design, which involves the physical design of buildings and outdoor settings and places an emphasis on the needs and requirements of people as opposed to more technical and stylistic considerations. Social design has six goals: (a) matching the needs of occupants, (b) satisfying building users, (c) changing behavior, (d) enhancing control, (e) facilitating social support, and (f) employing imageability. Of particular importance is the significant role that architecture plays in shaping human behavior, performance, and feelings of well-being.

Finally, the chapter discussed defensible space theory, which posits that certain physical design features influence the likely occurrence of crime and feelings of security. We considered the application of the theory to commercial enterprises, residences, and communities.

15

APPLYING SOCIAL PSYCHOLOGY TO DIVERSITY

CATHERINE T. KWANTES

SHERRY BERGERON

RITU KAUSHAL

CHAPTER OUTLINE

When the United States created treaties with indigenous nations during the 1800s, many treaties included the right of the native peoples to continue to hunt and fish on land that they had ceded to the U.S. government. Since that time, many changes have occurred in how these treaties have been interpreted and the degree to which they have been respected. For example, in some cases, land that was ceded to and owned by the government is now owned privately. In other cases, the boundaries of the land allocated for reservations has changed, leading to conflict among native peoples, individual landowners, and the government. The issue of fishing and hunting rights has also become a source of conflict between members of indigenous nations and nonmembers.

The conflicts have generally related to limits for members of indigenous nations in terms of allowed locations, times of the year, and methods of fishing and hunting.

During the late 1980s and early 1990s, intense conflict erupted in Minnesota over fishing and hunting rights claimed by the Ojibwe nation. Native Americans contested their right to use spearfishing while members of the non-Indian community reacted negatively, arguing that this means of fishing constituted harvesting more than fishing and threatened their ability to engage in sport fishing on lakes where spearfishing took place. In 1988, violence—including rock throwing and attempts to capsize Ojibwe boats—escalated the conflict to the point where Minnesota's attorney general called on the federal government to help deal with the situation. In 1999, the U.S. Supreme Court upheld the rights of the Ojibwe to hunt and fish without state regulation on 13 million acres of public land.

Similarly, in Burnt Church, New Brunswick, clashes occurred over the rights of Mi'kmaq, Maliseet, and Passmaquoddy natives of the Burnt Church area to set lobster traps in accordance with treaty provisions allowing lobster fishing to the extent of earning a moderate living. Non-native fishers resented these actions, contending that their livelihoods were being threatened. Clashes erupted involving property damage to the lobster traps, boats ramming into each other, and fishers threatening each other with firearms. In 2002, an agreement was reached between the government of Canada and members of the Burnt Church First Nation.

- To what extent do cultural factors play a role in these disputes?
- What aspects of cultural diversity do you think are most important in understanding these issues?
- To what extent do demographic diversity factors play a role in these disputes?
- What aspects of demographic diversity do you think are most important to understanding these issues?

The world is diverse; people have diverse values, diverse behaviors, and diverse customs, and they wear diverse clothing. So, what does it mean to have diversity around us? In this chapter, the approach to understanding diversity and its implications is derived from the discipline of applied social psychology. Applied social psychology is, first and foremost, *psychology.* Therefore, this chapter focuses on the level of the individual and individual experiences, examining the effects of diversity in our lives. Because this is *social psychology,* attention is also paid to the effect that social groups have on individuals and what some of the implications are of being an individual who differs in some way from most others with whom he or she interacts. Finally, being *applied social psychology* means that the focus of this chapter is on research that can be used by both individuals and groups not only to understand diversity but also to deal effectively with issues that result from diversity.

But what is diversity exactly? The obvious answer is that diversity refers to differences in how people look, how they think, and how they behave. The meaning of the term **diversity** within psychology extends beyond simply acknowledging that differences exist to understanding that diversity can arise from many different sources. Some of the more common ones include ethnicity, nationality, religion, sex, sexual orientation, physical ability, and social class. Differences across these categories reflect the layers that make us who we are, and it is these differences that coexist in each of us. Some aspects of diversity are the result of learned ways of doing things. For example, in some cultures individuals learn that the best way in which to eat is with a knife and fork, in other cultures chopsticks are favored, and in still other countries fingers are the utensils of choice. Other aspects of diversity are the result of birth, for example, sex and ethnicity. This chapter takes a look at culture as one source of learned diversity and then focuses on three major domains of demographic diversity: ethnicity, sex, and social class.

Diversity has consequences. Some of these consequences are positive. For example, diversity brings a sense of excitement as we discover new perspectives and ideas. In a sense, creativity itself stems from diversity in viewpoints. Problem solving is enhanced as a diversity of perspectives allows groups to be more flexible. Some consequences of diversity, however, are negative. News stories of individuals and groups who have suffered because they are different in some way are all too commonplace. The final portion of this chapter is devoted to the consequences of diversity—creativity and innovation, then conflict, and then its management and resolution.

CULTURAL DIVERSITY

Cultural diversity is increasingly a part of all of our lives. Urban, suburban, and even rural areas are becoming more culturally diverse, and with increased globalization this diversification will continue both in the interactions in our daily lives (e.g., schools, workplaces) and in the broader social structure (e.g., social functions, media). Most urban and suburban schools no longer teach only Christmas songs in December; songs related to Hanukkah and Kwanzaa are also brought into the classroom. Decades ago, a white male entering the workforce could be relatively sure that he would be working with white males in his career; this assumption no longer holds true. Culture has a pervasive influence on the lives of individuals within it. Its reach extends from the more obvious factors, such as values and beliefs, to the less obvious ones, such as nonverbal behavior and communication styles. Broadly speaking, the term **culture** refers to factors, such as race and ethnicity, that exert differential influence over the lives of individuals in different groups. More specifically, culture may be defined as

> a dynamic system of rules, explicit and implicit, established by groups in order to ensure their survival, involving attitudes, values, beliefs, norms,

and behaviors, shared by a group but harbored differently by each specific unit within the group, communicated across generations, relatively stable with the potential to change across time. (Matsumoto & Juang, 2004, p. 10)

As you can see by this definition, there are many aspects to culture, and these aspects can result in many differences across groups of people. For example, people from different countries may sometimes be identified by the type of clothing they wear. The photograph in Figure 15.1 was taken by one of the chapter authors in a rural village in India. You can immediately see that the women come from a culture with specific and unique ideas regarding dress and jewelry. Similarly, an individual's religion can sometimes be identified by how the person dresses such as with some members of the Amish and Islamic communities. Behavioral differences can also result from culture. Although shaking hands when meeting someone is the norm now in many parts of the world, the traditional greeting in Japan is a bow while placing one's hands together in front of the face, whereas nodding is the appropriate greeting in India. However, not all of culture's effects on behavior are as immediately visible as greetings. Think back to the opening vignette. Methods for fishing and gathering food may be culturally based, and so may other traditions. In some cultures it is a given that a young person will live with his or her parents until marriage, and maybe even after marriage, whereas in North America the norm is for newlyweds to establish a home apart from their parents.

Given the fact that culture is such a multifaceted construct and affects the diversity of values and behaviors in so many ways, it can be difficult to grasp without creating subdivisions within the construct. Developing taxonomies, or classification systems, provides a way in which to examine the influence of culture more effectively. Within the field of social psychology, two taxonomies are currently dominant.

Hofstede's Cultural Taxonomy

The first large-scale study of cultural diversity began roughly 40 years ago. During the 1960s, Geert Hofstede was asked to survey the

Figure 15.1   Women in Rural India

employees of a large multinational organization. He collected data from individuals in more than 50 countries and realized that there were distinct patterns in the data that reflected national cultures. Hofstede (2002) referred to these differences as the "software of the mind" and defined culture as "the collective programming of the mind that distinguishes the members of one group or category of people from another" (p. 9). In other words, humans are born with the same biological brain (the "hardware"), but they learn to value different things and to view the world differently based on the cultures in which they are raised (the "software"). More specifically, Hofstede used a statistical technique called factor analysis to derive four dimensions of culture from his survey data: individualism/collectivism, power distance, masculinity/femininity, and uncertainty avoidance. He later added one more dimension based on work by Bond (1988): long- or short-term orientation. Each of these dimensions is related to diversity among humans. Cultures differ along these dimensions, and each of these differences results in different learned values and preferences.

Individualism and collectivism. When you have a major decision to make, do you discuss it with anyone? Do you turn to family or friends? And if their advice does not match what you want to do, would that affect your decision? Would you opt for what you want to do, or would you conform to what your family or friends think is best? The way in which an individual answers these questions is at the heart of **individualism and collectivism.** Someone with an individualistic orientation, an **idiocentric,** will tend to follow his or her own goals regardless of the opinions of family or friends. On the other hand, someone with a collectivistic orientation, an **allocentric,** will tend to do what is seen as best for the group, even if it means giving up personal goals (Triandis, 1995).

Every person grows up in a society that reflects certain values and preferences. Individualism and collectivism refer to the values that society places on the group as opposed to the individual, and these values are taught to most individuals within the society. Harry Triandis pointed out that in individualistic societies, social experiences are structured around individuals, whereas in collectivistic countries, social experiences are structured around social groups (Triandis, 1994). For example, in societies with individualistic tendencies, such as the United States and Canada, marriage has traditionally been viewed as the choice of the couple; two people fall in love and then get married. However, in collectivistic societies, such as Japan and India, marriages were traditionally arranged by the parents or other elders in the family, and in some cases they still are. The purpose of marriage is not viewed as providing happiness to the two individuals involved; rather, it is viewed as developing alliances between families. Differences on this dimension not only are found between nations but also may be found between regions within countries. Vandello and Cohen (1999), for example, found that within the United States there were striking regional differences in individualism and collectivism, with individualism being more predominant in the North and East and collectivism being more predominant in the South and West. Individualism/collectivism and power distance are the cultural dimensions that have been most widely examined in research. The degree to which a person is from a culture that emphasizes individualism or collectivism has been shown to make a difference in many of that person's attitudes and behaviors. For example, differences have been found in work behaviors such as looking for another job and doing little "extras" to help out the organization in which one works—even without added pay. In the United States, an individualistic country, the intensity with which an employee looks for a new job, or how much extra the employee does for his or her company, depends on how much the person likes the company. However, in India, a collectivistic country, these behaviors depend not only on how much an employee likes his or her company but also on the extent to which the employee feels obligated to the company (Kwantes, 2003).

In the intergroup and interpersonal arena, Gelfand and colleagues (2001) suggested that in collectivistic countries such as Japan, conflict is viewed and experienced more as a situation that calls for compromise, whereas in more individualistic countries such as the United States, conflict is experienced more as a win–lose

situation. Even children show noticeable differences on this dimension. Barbopoulos, Fisharah, Clark, and El-Khatib (2002), for example, found that children in Canada, an individualistic culture, exhibited more independent attitudes than did children from Egypt, a more collectivistic culture. Other more global attitudes may also be related to these cultural dimensions. For example, people in collectivistic societies are more likely to view the thoughts and business of others in their group as their own business, whereas people in individualistic societies are more likely to desire privacy (Triandis, 1995).

Power distance. **Power distance** refers to the extent to which people in a society accept inequalities based on social status, wealth, power, laws, and/or physical characteristics (Robert, Probst, Martocchio, Drasgow, & Lawler, 2000). In countries with high power distance, such as Malaysia, Guatemala, The Philippines, and many Arab countries, it is normal to find conformity among the people and to find that most power is held by a small group of individuals with authoritarian values. It is not uncommon for individuals with this value orientation to view those who have a high status in society as fundamentally different from other humans. Because of this, the inequality is accepted. In contrast, those in countries with low power distance, such as New Zealand, Germany, Great Britain, and the Scandinavian countries, view individuals as essentially equal. In such countries, the exercise of power is accepted only if there is agreement with the rationale behind it (e.g., as with elected officials), and independence of thought is valued over conformity. You can sometimes see the effects of power distance in how people address each other. In low-power distance societies, people tend to use first names very quickly regardless of whether the other person is senior in position. In high-power distance societies, titles are used for those who are senior in position by virtue of either employment (e.g., one's boss) or age (e.g., an elderly neighbor). There tends to be a strong relationship across cultures between power distance and individualism/collectivism, with high power distance correlating with collectivism and lower power distance correlating with individualism (Triandis, 1994).

Masculinity and femininity. The name for this dimension comes from different values placed on work goals. Hofstede (2002) noted that surveys on work goals nearly universally indicate that women place higher values on social goals such as relationships and helping others, whereas men place higher values on what Hofstede called "ego goals" (p. 279) that relate to money and careers. Hofstede applied this masculinity/femininity distinction to differences in values among countries. Individuals in cultures high on femininity are taught to value relationships and harmony, whereas those in cultures high on masculinity are encouraged to emphasize competition, advancement, and recognition in jobs. Societies that emphasize masculinity, such as Japan, Venezuela, Italy, and Mexico, often exhibit great differences between men and women in the values they endorse. Men, for example, place much stronger emphasis on ambition and career goals than do women (Hofstede, 1997). Societies that emphasize femininity, such as Sweden, Norway, The Netherlands, and Costa Rica, generally do not demonstrate large differences in values between men and women. Hofstede further pointed out that in feminine countries, both males and females are expected to be modest and nonassertive.

Uncertainty avoidance. High levels of uncertainty can lead to anxiety and stress. Common ways of dealing with uncertainty can characterize cultures because each society teaches that some ways of coping are more acceptable than others. Technology, religion, social customs, and even family customs are used to help cope with uncertainty. For example, individuals from societies with low uncertainty avoidance, such as Singapore and Jamaica, generally accept the fact that some uncertainty is unavoidable. These individuals believe that it is important to "go with the flow" and are often willing to take a certain amount of risk. On the other hand, individuals from cultures characterized by high uncertainty avoidance, such as Portugal and Greece, learn to feel threatened by uncertainty; thus, these individuals tend to take fewer risks, behave more carefully regarding laws, and avoid things (and people) that are different from that to which they are accustomed.

Long- or short-term orientation. After Hofstede's original research, other psychologists also began to investigate how culture affects diverse values, attitudes, and behaviors. Because Hofstede's survey research was carried out in one organization, namely IBM, most of his survey questions were developed from a Western cultural perspective and, therefore, did not capture some cultural values that might be more immediately obvious to someone from an Eastern cultural perspective. A fifth classification, long- or short-term orientation, was added to the original four based on values in a Chinese context (Bond, 1988). In cultures with a long-term orientation, such as Taiwan, Japan, and South Korea, individuals learn to value future rewards, thereby placing an emphasis on persistence, thrift, patience, and harmony. On the other end of the spectrum, cultures that emphasize a more short-term orientation, such as Canada and the United States, place value on short-term rewards and emphasize immediate gratification over long-term considerations (Hofstede, 2002).

Hofstede's taxonomy has made possible comparisons of cultures along specific dimensions. Using his original data (Hofstede, 2002), an example comparing the three North American countries on Hofstede's original four dimensions is illustrated in Figure 15.2. You can see how each country has a different profile on the graph, indicating different value emphases. For example, people in Mexico place a much stronger emphasis on uncertainty avoidance and power distance than do people in Canada and the United States. In contrast, people in Canada and the United States emphasize individualism more than do people in Mexico. There is very little difference among these three countries, however, in terms of the emphasis that people place on the masculinity/femininity dimension of culture. Using these dimensions, it is possible to get a quick "snapshot" of some of the values in a culture and to be able to compare and contrast different cultures in terms of these values.

Although this taxonomy has stimulated a lot of research and has provided a useful perspective for understanding the effects of culture on values, attitudes, and behaviors, not everyone agrees with Hofstede that this taxonomy is universal and that it can be used to describe all

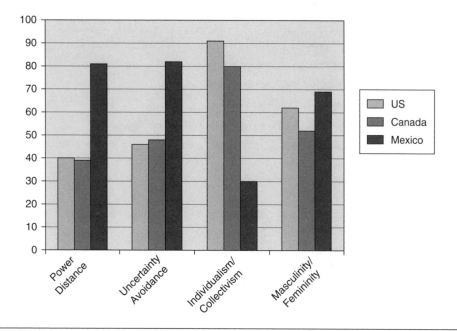

Figure 15.2   Hofstede's Cultural Dimensions

cultures. The sample that was used in the original research constituted individuals who were all working for the same company, and so it was not necessarily representative of all individuals in a given culture. Also, the kinds of people that worked in those types of jobs (e.g., educated men) limited the range of characteristics represented in the group. However, psychologists do agree that this work is extremely important because it represents the first attempt to examine global cultural differences and to look for dimensions across which it is possible to contrast and compare cultures.

Schwartz's Values Framework

Rather than looking for ways in which to find differences between cultures, it is possible to look for ways that culturally learned values and, therefore, cultures may be similar. Shalom Schwartz developed a theoretical framework that may be used to understand the content and structure of value systems in cultures and how these values affect the ways in which individuals in different groups organize their understanding of the world around them (Schwartz, 1992;

Schwartz, Lehmann, & Roccas, 1999). In research spanning 20 countries, Schwartz has established that a set of 10 value types is comprehensive enough to be useful in a global context. In other words, the value types are universal and different groups agree on their meanings. Core values have been grouped into value types that encompass an overarching or defining feature. For example, the value type termed *tradition* is based on the core values of respect and commitment (Table 15.1).

A great deal of research has shown that this framework holds across numerous cultures and can be used to predict attitudes and behaviors. For example, values have been found to be important predictors in determining the degree to which Israeli Jews, Israeli Arab Muslims, and Israeli Christians would be willing to engage in contact with individuals outside their own cultural groups (Sagiv & Schwartz, 1995). Similarly, in their sample of more than 150 teachers, Sagiv and Schwartz (1995) found that values predicted willingness to engage in contact with dissimilar others. Specifically, those who scored higher on universalism demonstrated more of a willingness to engage in

Table 15.1   Definitions of Motivational Types of Values and How They Affect Behavior

Power	Social status and prestige, control or dominance over people and resources
Achievement	Personal success through demonstrating competence according to social standards
Hedonism	Pleasure and sensuous gratification for oneself
Stimulation	Excitement, novelty, and challenge in life
Self-direction	Independent thought and action, choosing, creating, and exploring
Universalism	Understanding, appreciation, tolerance, and protection for the welfare of all people and for nature
Benevolence	Preservation and enhancement of the welfare of people with whom one is in frequent personal contact
Tradition	Respect for, commitment to, and acceptance of the customs and ideas that traditional culture or religion provides
Conformity	Restraint of actions, inclinations, and impulses likely to upset or harm others and to violate social expectations or norms
Security	Safety, harmony, and stability of society, relationships, and self

SOURCE: Adapted from Schwartz, Lehmann, and Roccas (1999, p. 109).

contact with others than did those who scored higher on tradition or conformity. As another example, in research focusing on values and worries, Schwartz, Sagiv, and Boehnke (2000) found that there were few differences between respondents in Israel and Germany in the relationships between specific values and the types of worries they had. An emphasis on power, for example, correlated with "micro-worries"; that is, worries related to the self or the group to which a person belongs (Boehnke, Schwartz, Stromberg, & Sagiv, 1998). Fear of war has been found to be greater in individuals from both Germany and Israel who attach a high priority to values related to concern for others, such as benevolence, and who attach importance to issues of equality and social justice (Boehnke & Schwartz, 1997).

As you can see, by developing dimensions of culture, researchers have tried to reduce the complex notion of the effect of culture on values and behaviors, allowing us to look at some aspects of diversity that are learned by individuals within groups and societies. Do you see either of these ways of viewing cultural differences as being able to explain the tensions and conflicts related to the hunting and fishing rights of native and non-native peoples? Are there fundamental learned value differences between the two groups that might explain some of the differences in perspective?

There is always a bit of a danger, however, in looking to large groups for explanations of differences in individual behavior. One reason for this is that groups, and especially large groups, are never completely homogeneous, and individual differences, such as ethnic background, sex, and social class, can also contribute to individual experiences related to diversity.

DEMOGRAPHICS: PERSONAL DIVERSITY

Just as cultural diversity reflects complex phenomena, demographic diversity is also complex. People differ on core characteristics that are key determinants of life experiences. These characteristics and experiences affect how we see ourselves and create different pieces of identity that are like links on a chain; one never exists without the others. A man from an upper-class background cannot necessarily differentiate the parts of his experience that are related to being upper class from the parts that are related to being male. Similarly, our own experiences are intertwined with our own characteristics. People respond to us because of a combination of these factors and rarely to any one factor alone. When examining the sources of diversity and how these affect individual experience, it is important to remember that these sources typically do not operate in isolation from each other, nor do they necessarily affect everybody in the same way. Rather, these different aspects of identity become important to us at different times depending on the context or circumstances (Kawakami & Dion, 1995).

Is differential treatment based on one's race, sex, or class (e.g., racism, sexism, classism) still a problem in our society? Do you think that your own race, sex, or social class affects how you would answer this question? Some people believe that North American societies provide equal opportunities for all of their citizens, skin color does not create advantages or disadvantages, gender makes no difference, and equal opportunity exists for all regardless of social class. Admittedly, blatant "in-your-face" discrimination rarely occurs today, but discrimination and bias continue to exist in more sophisticated, convoluted, and subversive ways. Racial segregation of schools is no longer an official policy, although in many areas it continues to be a practical reality. Women have penetrated the borders of many traditionally male workplaces yet are still drastically underrepresented in the upper echelon of the corporate world. Social class still has an effect on the availability of educational and occupational opportunities. This section takes a closer look at race, gender, and social class, each of which continues to influence one's experiences and opportunities.

Gender

Although many people use the terms *sex* and *gender* to mean the same thing, there is actually a difference between them. The term **sex** refers to the biological distinction of being male or female, whereas the term **gender** refers to the social or learned characteristics that are associated with being male or female. Gender, unlike sex, is the result of sociocultural influences throughout an individual's development. Boys are molded to become what society considers to be masculine (e.g., extraverted, independent, assertive), whereas girls are molded to become what society considers to be feminine (e.g., obedient, dependable). Behaviors that match these expectations are rewarded (Robinson & Howard-Hamilton, 2000).

An individual's sex is often used as a primary source of social categorization or, more simply, as a way in which to place people into groups. From the beginning, babies are wrapped in the color of blanket that is matched with their sex—blue for boys and pink for girls. Descriptors of behaviors are also often gender typed from birth. For example, early research by Condry and Condry (1976) found that when a male child cries, people will often explain the behavior by saying that he is angry, whereas when a female child cries, they will often describe her as frightened. This process continues as an individual grows into adulthood, where descriptors are often still distributed differentially based on sex. In fact, a well-known study by Williams and Best (1982) not only demonstrated that adjectives were viewed as being differentially associated with men and women but also revealed that this happened with a surprising amount of consistency across participants from the 30 countries represented in their sample. Men, for example, were more frequently associated with descriptors such as *aggressive, capable,* and *rational,* whereas women were more frequently associated with descriptors such as *affectionate, dependent,* and *emotional.*

Are women and men actually more similar than they are different, or are they more different than they are similar? Do any differences across the sexes justify social inequalities? Early research on sex differences held men as the standard to which women were compared. Differences between the sexes were put up as evidence of the innate superiority of men and, thus, were used to justify differences in social power. For example, the sizes of male and female brains were compared, and when male brains were found to be larger, this was used to explain the superior intellect of men (instead of the equally plausible, but politically incorrect, proposition that women's brains were more efficient). The greater social power held by men was merely a natural derivative of this superior intellect (Shields, 1975).

Although things have changed from the time when women were thought to be too intellectually inferior or too weak and frail to participate in many aspects of society, a belief in the fundamental difference between the sexes is still evident in modern cultures (Benokraitis & Feagin, 1995).

Even in presumably advanced societies, books that suggest that women and men are seen not only as different but as (figuratively) coming from different planets (Mars and Venus) can become best-sellers.

The focus on differences and the ignoring of similarities have been the basis of much of the feminist critiques of research on gender (Hyde, 1991). If differences do exist, what do they really mean and are they substantial enough to be weighted more heavily than the similarities? One of the responses to differences between the sexes (whether real or perceived), or to gender diversity, is **sexism,** that is, differential and often detrimental treatment of a person based on that person's sex. The term *sexism* likely brings to mind thoughts of negative or demeaning attitudes toward women. Negative comments, such as "a woman's place is in the home" and "women are bad drivers," are frequently assumed to be the only way in which sexism can be expressed. However, this is not the case.

An article by Peter Glick and Susan Fiske explored the concept of sexism and revealed some of its more complex and subtle nature. In its purest sense, **sexism** refers to any bias against an individual or group of individuals based on the individual's or group members' sex. That bias does not necessarily have to be expressed in the form of negative attitudes or behaviors. Glick and Fiske (1996) proposed a tripartite, or three-part, understanding of the different forms of sexism.

Negative expressions, or behaviors that reflect negative attitudes toward women, are referred to specifically as **hostile sexism**. Some forms of sexism, however, involve the attribution of typically positive traits or qualities. This is referred to as **benevolent sexism**. Although this might seem to be a contradiction in terms, the problem (according to Glick and Fiske) is that the attributions associated with benevolent sexism, even though they sound they are positive, are derived from stereotypes that see women in limited ways and often stem from a male-centered perspective. Imagine for a moment that a female executive is about to sit down at a negotiation table when a male coworker comments, "You look very good in that suit." Glick and Fiske suggested that, although the comment might not be intended as negative or hostile, it is nonetheless sexist. The remark sounds pleasant but in effect emphasizes traditional stereotypic notions of women and trivializes the fact that competence rather than beauty was behind the executive's promotions to her current position. According to Glick and Fiske, not only can people hold both hostile and benevolent sexist attitudes, but also these attitudes and beliefs can be held simultaneously. They named this **ambivalent sexism**. An illustration of ambivalent sexism, they suggested, is when an individual believes both that women need to be protected by men (benevolent— helping those who are perceived to need help) and that women are incompetent (hostile).

FOCUS ON RESEARCH

These different forms of sexism can play out in many different ways. Imagine, for example, a woman standing with a group of men at a social gathering. One of the men in the group makes a comment that is clearly sexist and derogatory toward women. What does she have to gain or lose by responding? What does she have to gain or to lose by choosing not to respond? Do you think that she would be more or less likely to respond if there were other women present?

A recent series of experiments by Janet Swim and Lauri Hyers examined how women would respond both publicly (what they said or did) and privately (what they thought) in such a situation. When women encounter sexism, Swim and Hyers (1999) suggested, they must decide not only how to respond but also, more fundamentally, whether to respond at all. Although there are things to be gained by responding, there are also potential costs associated with speaking up against sexism. In their first experiment, Swim and Hyers recruited from a pool of female students in an introductory psychology class. Participants were told that the study was on group decision making and were placed into groups of four, where the other three people were actually experimental confederates. In the "solo" condition, the participant was placed with three male confederates. In the "nonsolo" condition, two of the confederates were female and one was male. The apparent group task was to choose from a list of 15 women and 15 men with different occupations the 12 people whom group members felt would be most able to survive on a deserted island. The four group members were seated in a predetermined order, and each member was asked to give reasons for inclusion or exclusion of each of the 30 people listed. Each group member made comments in a clockwise direction. A male confederate who was seated to the participant's right made scripted responses to each of the hypothetical candidates. In the sexist condition, three of the comments directed at female candidates were sexist. In the nonsexist condition, three similar comments were made but the sexism was removed. For example, when discussing whether to include a man whose occupation was a chef, in the sexist condition, the confederate said, "No, one of the women can cook" (p. 73), whereas in the nonsexist condition, the confederate said, "No, one of the others can cook." The participants' actual responses to the sexist remarks formed the basis of the public response measure. After the group had made all of the choices, the experimenter directed each of the group members to a private room; at this point, the participant was asked to complete a questionnaire. After completing the questionnaire, the participant was taken to another room where she was told that the group decision-making task had been videotaped. The participant was then asked to watch the tape to improve her recall of her thoughts and feelings during the task. She was instructed to stop the tape whenever she remembered something that she was thinking or feeling at that particular time and to write down what she remembered. This formed the basis of the private response measure. Finally, the participant rated her feelings toward each of the experimental confederates.

After analyzing the women's public responses to the sexist remarks, Swim and Hyers reported that 45% of the women confronted the men who made the sexist remarks in some way (e.g., using humor or sarcasm, questioning the person who made the comment, displaying exclamations of surprise) but that only 16% directly confronted the men with verbal responses that challenged the stated reasons for the candidate choice (e.g., "You can't pick someone for that reason. Pick another person" [p. 76]). Interestingly, when the participant was the only woman among three male confederates, she was more likely to respond to the initial sexist remark than when other women were present.

Using social psychological theory, Swim and Hyers offered an explanation for this seemingly curious finding. If more than one woman is present when the sexist remark is made, each woman may look to the other women to respond and might feel that the responsibility for addressing the comment does not fall on her shoulders alone. This concept is termed the **diffusion of responsibility** and is useful for providing insight into the response patterns of the women in this study.

Examination of the participants' private responses (what they reported thinking or feeling during the group discussion) revealed that the absence of public responses did not mean that the participants did not notice or did not disagree with the sexist comments. Of the 55% of women who did not publicly respond, 75% rated the confederates who made the comments as prejudiced, and nearly all of them (91%) viewed the confederates negatively.

In a follow-up study performed by Swim and Hyers, an identical situation was described to female participants, and they were asked to indicate how they thought that they would respond in that situation. Not surprisingly, far more women indicated that they would respond publicly and directly than those that actually did in the first study. In fact, only 1% of the respondents indicated that they would ignore the comments, whereas 55% actually did ignore the comments in the first study. Swim and Hyers proposed that these two studies suggest that most women might not be responding to the sexist comments they encounter in their everyday lives in the way they would like. The social situation, they suggested, controlled not only *whether* the women would respond but also *how* the women would respond. For example, even when women did choose to respond, they typically did so in a polite, and more socially acceptable, manner. Awareness of the powerful impact of the situation on our behavior can help us to understand reactions to sexism but also provides us with clues on how to effect change.

Ethnic Background

Another domain of diversity is ethnic diversity. Like gender, ethnicity is often used as a way in which to group people together. A common response to ethnic diversity is, unfortunately, racism. **Racism** can be defined as bias against an individual or group of individuals based on the individual's or group members' race/ethnicity. It may seem likely that racism no longer exists given that official policies that condone overt discrimination rarely exist. However, reality tends to show otherwise. For example, Jones (1997) pointed out that the United States ranks sixth in the world on the Human Development Index, a UN index based on measures of life expectancy at birth, literacy, years of schooling, and economic data. He further noted that if this index were computed based on data from African Americans alone, the United States would rank 31st; if data from Hispanic Americans alone were used, the ranking would be 34th globally. Unfortunately, the negative effects of racism are still prevalent in American society today.

In North America, modern forms of racism are often difficult to measure because most displays of bias or negative attitudes have become very subtle and might not match our common understanding of the term. Typically, people's beliefs about minorities appear to be positive or at least do not appear to be overtly negative. In most (but not all) situations, it is no longer considered acceptable to make directly racist comments, and so racism tends to reveal itself in indirect ways. Direct and blatant attacks on minority group members have become less frequent in North America, and negative attitudes are expressed only if situations are ambiguous or if the attitude can be attributed to something other than a response to the target group (Nelson, 2002). It is obvious that the persecution of Jews in Nazi Germany and the lynching of blacks by the Ku Klux Klan, among many other historic examples, constitute prejudice, racism, and discrimination. The fact that nearly all of the professors in a given psychology department are white, or that nearly all of the chief executive officers of the major corporations across North America are white, might not strike you as indicative of prejudice or discrimination, yet such situations also may be the result of some form of racism.

What most people commonly understand to be racism is actually more similar to the **blatant racism** that was more common in the past than to modern forms of racism. Racism in the past was often blatant in that it took obvious forms such as segregation and clear differential treatment based on skin color. Blatant racism is easier to measure than more contemporary forms of racism because blatant racists will usually admit to holding negative attitudes and beliefs. Accessing this information may be as simple as asking.

During more recent years, other forms of racism have been identified. In many cases, people do not believe that they are racist or that they hold prejudiced attitudes toward specific racial/ethnic groups. In other cases, perceived social norms against racism inhibit the likelihood that someone will admit to racist attitudes or beliefs. As such, these forms of prejudice may be more subtle and indirect. An example of a form of modern racism is **aversive racism** (Gaertner & Dovidio, 1986). Despite holding racist beliefs, aversive racists believe that they are not prejudiced against people from races other than their own. They do not acknowledge their racial biases because this perspective is inconsistent with their view of themselves as egalitarian. Therefore, although racism is present, the racist attitudes are not conscious (Nelson, 2002).

Similarly, **symbolic racism** (Sears, 1988) also does not manifest itself in obvious ways. In instances of this type of racism, a negative attitude is associated with something other than the target. For example, an individual may insist that he or she is not racist and has "nothing against blacks." However, the individual may also say that there is a problem with affirmative action, something that he or she believes gives an unfair advantage to blacks over whites in hiring practices. Aversive racism and symbolic racism are similar concepts in that people who manifest either type do not acknowledge racism explicitly. That is, the actual negative attitudes are associated with some other proxy-type factor (e.g., affirmative action) and not with the target. So, the attitudes appear as though they are tied to politics rather than to groups of people (Hilton & von Hipple, 1996).

Ambivalent racism (Hass, Katz, Rizzo, Bailey, & Eisenstadt, 1991), like ambivalent sexism, contends that people can simultaneously hold two attitudes that are inconsistent with each other. With this type of racism, people are not overtly prejudiced and do recognize the unfair treatment of minorities and racial disparities, but at the same time they believe that the system is based on meritocracy, that is, the principle that hard work will pay off—the "American Dream" (Hilton & von Hipple, 1996). As a result of holding this attitude, these individuals are more willing to accept different outcomes for people of different races/ethnicities in the belief that everyone has had the same opportunities but that individuals from some groups have not taken full advantage of the opportunities available to them.

Despite the many obvious visible changes since the time when it was acceptable to have "whites only" drinking fountains and bus seats, racism does still exist. Its expression has changed to more subtle forms, but racism has not yet been eradicated. The good news is that this may be slowly changing. In 2000, researchers examined how the expression of aversive racism had shifted over the 10-year period between 1989 and 1999 (Dovidio & Gaertner, 2000). Coinciding with their expectations, self-ratings of prejudice were much lower in 1999 than in 1989. In addition to self-reports of racial prejudice, participants were asked to engage in a simulated employment situation and make selection decisions. The researchers found that in situations where candidates presented with strong credentials, no prejudice or discrimination was shown to black candidates. Black candidates whose credentials were not as strong, however, were still selected for employment at a lower rate than were white candidates with the same credentials. This study is optimistic in that some things do appear to be changing, but it is also pessimistic in the sense that in many ways real change is making only very slow progress.

Social Class

Issues relating to social class constitute another example of how the ideal of equal opportunity, and the belief that individual effort always pays off, pervades many Western societies, allowing people to avoid acknowledging structural and systemic inequalities.

Those who are economically disadvantaged have historically been described as belonging to a "culture of poverty" (Mincy, 2000). This culture has been assumed to be the result of values and attitudes held by impoverished individuals and is viewed as part of what separates those in the lower socioeconomic strata from those in other strata. Research suggests that social class is indeed a determinant of how we "size people up." For example, Kirby (1999) found that class bias was involved in people's impressions of new neighbors. She found that people were more likely to object to their new neighbors if they believed that the neighbors were receiving public assistance and that this bias was one that participants expressed candidly.

Issues related to poverty and social class have been likened to an elephant in the room that everyone knows is there but that nobody wants to talk about (Younge, 2003). The huge economic disparities in the lives of people across North America are undeniable, and the United States has been described as the most stratified industrial society in current times (Mantsios, 2000). Because this inequity is undeniable, it is often justified or excused.

Younge (2003) suggested that the notion of equal opportunity is often used to excuse the huge disparity in economic realities. The concepts of the deserving poor and the undeserving poor are rooted in people's perceptions of those who comprise the lowest socioeconomic classes (Mincy, 2000). The **undeserving poor** are those whose economic conditions are assumed to be through no fault of their own. For example, individuals who are handicapped, are mentally ill, or have some other life circumstances that have clearly affected their ability to earn a living are often given sympathy, and we are less likely to hold their economic circumstances against them. However, most individuals are assumed to have equal opportunity and equal access to earning a living. Those who fall into the **deserving poor** category are those whom others think should have taken advantage of the supposed opportunities but have not done so due to their own lack of initiative. This artificial and frequently erroneous pattern of assumptions allows others, especially those who are more privileged, to justify the existence of social class inequalities. In fact, a recent study by Fiske and her colleagues, conducted with a sample of university students, indicated that among the 16 groups in their analysis (Asians, African Americans, Latinos, Jews, gay men, feminists, rich people, businesswomen, disabled people, blind people, retarded people, northerners, southerners, migrant workers, house cleaners, and housewives), those who received welfare were the only group of people that were rated as both disliked and disrespected (Fiske, Xu, & Cuddy, 1999).

Gender, ethnicity, and social class constitute three of the many ways in which we are demographically diverse. As mentioned at the beginning of this section, each of these differences does not operate in isolation; we are complex individuals with many different aspects to our identities. Do you think that any of these aspects of demographic diversity might help to explain the conflict described in the opening vignette? Might race and/or social status play a role?

DIVERSITY: OPPORTUNITIES

Although cultural diversity may foster misunderstandings and xenophobia, and demographic diversity may give rise to social problems such as sexism, racism, and classism, diversity has the potential to produce positive results as well. Research on the positive effects of diversity has focused mainly on how diversity enhances group processes. The logical question to ask, then, is what aspects of diversity affect how people behave in groups. To answer this, a distinction needs to be made between functional diversity and the other types of diversity that we have been discussing. **Functional diversity** refers to the fact that each person in a group brings different strengths and talents to the group process. Although a greater number of people working on a problem provides more chances for important information to be brought to light than does an individual working alone on a problem (Triandis, Kurowski, & Gelfand, 1994), functional diversity enhances group effectiveness even further by contributing to a group's ability to be innovative and creative (Amabile, 1983). Functional diversity is related to both cultural and demographic diversity. When groups are composed of members who

belong to different cultures or demographic categories—whether ethnic background, sex, or other categories—they have built-in functional diversity (Schneider & Northcraft, 1999) simply as a result of having members with diverse experiences and being exposed to different perspectives from their own in-groups. For example, a Hispanic individual who grew up in an urban neighborhood will have different experiences, and therefore will bring different insights to an issue, than will an Asian individual who grew up in a suburban neighborhood.

Creativity and Innovation

These different perspectives can lead group members to rely less on past ways of dealing with things and may result in a reduced emphasis on conformity to the group. Some of the positive outcomes related to diversity within groups include creativity, better problem solving, and innovation (Cox, 1991). It has also been suggested that minority points of view can challenge the prevailing way of thinking and, therefore, can stimulate greater creativity (Nemeth, 1986).

In a study of university teachers, those who described their working environment as diverse were the ones who were the most creative (Ryhammer & Smith, 1999). Of course, diversity may take many forms, and some differences may matter more than others. In a laboratory experiment, it was found that more creative solutions to problems emerged when groups were composed of both men and women than when they were composed of just men or just women (Schruijer & Mostert, 1997). McLeod, Lobel, and Cox (1996) found that groups composed of only Anglo-Americans came up with less effective solutions in a brainstorming task than did groups composed of multiple ethnicities. Yet research is not always so clear about the effect of diversity on creativity and innovation. A study conducted with 50 work teams from a Fortune 500 company indicated that diversity in the teams related to age, sex, and race had no effect on the innovative quality of group-generated solutions (Cady & Valentine, 1999). On the other hand, they found that sex diversity had a negative impact on the number of innovative ideas generated in response to a given problem, whereas racial diversity had a positive impact. It seems that there must be a balance between the diversity of the group members and the similarity of their values and goals (Ofori-Dankwa & Julian, 2002). Research is continuing in this area to try to untangle just what aspects of diversity are important to creativity and innovation in groups and how the different aspects of diversity interact.

Problem Solving

Problem solving tends to be better when groups are of diverse backgrounds and abilities (Cox & Blake, 1991). When a group can draw on a rich variety of perspectives and experiences, decision making is often of a higher quality than if the perspectives and experiences shared by the group members are similar. Yet, as was the case with creativity and innovation, the most effective problem solving emerges when a balance of diversity exists. Diversity without any shared values and goals is likely to break a group apart; however, shared values and goals may lead to what Irving Janis has termed *groupthink*. As you may recall from Chapters 2 and 11, groupthink describes what happens when groups converge on a single answer to a problem and, rather than critically evaluate the solution, they convince themselves and each other that the solution they came up with is the best one (Janis, 1983, 1996). As discussed in earlier chapters, this type of decision making can have disastrous consequences. Unfortunately, group homogeneity may exacerbate the likelihood of groupthink occurring. For example, during the Bay of Pigs fiasco, the similarity of the individuals within John F. Kennedy's presidential advisory council fostered a high degree of group cohesion, and shared values and goals helped to intensify this cohesion. In contrast, diverse groups are much less likely to have this sort of cohesion, thereby minimizing the likelihood that groupthink will occur (Cox, 1991) and maximizing the likelihood that many different possible solutions will be examined.

DIVERSITY: CHALLENGES

Although diversity presents many opportunities, there are also a number of challenges present when individuals with diverse backgrounds and experiences interact.

Prejudice and Discrimination

One challenge related to diversity is dealing with prejudice and discrimination against those who are in some way different. **Prejudice** is "an attitude toward others based solely on group membership" (Moghaddam, 1998, p. 330). When prejudiced attitudes get translated into behavior, discrimination results. So, the term **discrimination** is reserved for use when referring to the "actual behavior directed at others on the basis of category membership" (p. 332).

Social psychology has played a prominent role in research on both prejudice and discrimination. For example, early research on racism and discrimination focused on the characteristics of people who are prejudiced or who discriminate against others based on their race or ethnicity (Dovidio, 2001). More recently, many social psychologists have begun to include an examination of the effects that prejudice and discrimination have on the targets of these attitudes or behaviors. For example, how does being a target of discrimination affect the way in which people feel about themselves? The scope of interest has also expanded beyond racism to include other types of diversity, including the sexism and classism mentioned earlier in this chapter.

Where does prejudice originate? Some believe that prejudice stems from our thoughts and belief systems or from cognitive sources (Nelson, 2002). The mistaken belief that two things are related simply because they are seen as occurring together is one cognitive process that contributes to the formation of stereotypes (Jones, 1997). So, for example, you may begin to believe that all people with red hair have terrible tempers because the last several times you saw someone yelling and upset in a restaurant, the person pitching the tantrum had red hair. Another perspective on the origins of prejudice suggests that we are motivated to hold particular beliefs. Examples of this view would be illustrated in some theories of conflict that are discussed later in the chapter (e.g., social identity theory, realistic group conflict theory, theory of relative deprivation).

Stereotypes are "beliefs about the characteristics, attributes, and behaviors of members of certain groups" (Hilton & von Hipple, 1996, p. 4), and many stereotypes are culturally based (Moghaddam, 1998). Within social psychological research, stereotypes have been studied as a process (how people come to believe what they do), as content (what traits comprise a particular stereotype), and as varying in their strength or intensity (how firmly people believe what they do about particular social groups) as well as for their consequences (Madon, 1997). Over the past few decades, process and consequence issues have dominated researchers' attention, and it is only recently that there has been a shift in focus to return to analysis of stereotype content (Madon, 1997). Knowledge of the content of stereotypes is important both because of real-life implications (Fitchen & Amsel, 1986) and because of the potential that this information holds for providing insight into possible avenues of social change for stigmatized groups.

Stereotype content may affect the target in many different ways. One of the more subtle effects is referred to as stereotype threat. **Stereotype threat** is a fear or nervousness that your behavior will exemplify a negative stereotype about your in-group, thereby in essence confirming the accuracy of the stereotype. Unfortunately, this may capture some of the attention of the target and affect the target's performance on the task at hand (Steele & Aronson, 1995). For example, if a woman was due to take a math exam and she knew that women are not expected to perform well in math, she might get nervous about her performance (see Figure 15.3). The nervousness may negatively affect her score by affecting her level of concentration, thereby contributing to the stereotype. Recognition that stereotypes are not always exclusively negative, and that in fact positive traits (e.g., Africans are good dancers, Asians are good at math, gay men are good at decorating) are included in the stereotypes of many social groups, is central to further enhancing our understanding of the complexity of stereotype content and the effects that stereotypes may produce.

Figure 15.3   Women Who May Be Likely to Experience Stereotype Threat

SOURCE: Photo courtesy of the University of Windsor.

● FOCUS ON INTERVENTION

Stereotypes can help us to organize the world around us, but we must be careful about the negative effects that they have for relationships between groups and for our society. They can make it seem as though the differences that exist between certain people, or groups of people, are larger than the similarities or that these differences are larger than they really are. This perception of differences can sometimes lead to problems. This idea is at the crux of a recent intervention designed to reduce stereotyping and increase tolerance of diversity through educating children to decategorize their perceptions of people from diverse ethnic backgrounds (Jones & Foley, 2003). In general, decategorization involves changing how we categorize people so that the new categories emphasize similarities rather than differences.

In this experiment, 65 fourth graders were randomly assigned to either a control condition, in which they were read a story, or an experimental group, in which they were read a presentation with material that focused on various topics related to diversity. Specifically, the presentation covered the topics of anthropology (emphasizing our common human ancestry), biology (emphasizing our common genetic background), and the "melting pot" (emphasizing that most people living in the United States are from immigrant families). All children were asked to complete an adapted version of the Racial Decategorization Scale, a 30-item questionnaire designed to assess their feelings and beliefs about people of diverse ethnic backgrounds and stereotypes, and a questionnaire assessing their knowledge about anthropology, biology, and diversity in the United States. Responses to the questions were recorded on a 5-point Likert scale (1 = *strongly agree*, 5 = *strongly disagree*), with higher scores indicating more racial categorization and negative perceptions of diverse ethnic groups. Study results demonstrated that the experimental group scored lower on the Racial Decategorization Scale than did the control group (*Ms* = 50.4 and 58.9, respectively). These findings support the assertion that children can and do benefit from material that stresses decategorization and that shifting the focus to emphasizing similarities across groups, rather than differences, is potentially useful. This has implications for the reduction of prejudice in children. Often, biases that form the basis of prejudice are developed early in life. To combat them, interventions aimed at reducing or correcting these biases should be put into place as early as they are observed, if not earlier. Perhaps if we spend more time emphasizing the overlap between ethnic groups, we will make it harder for people (especially children) to treat people differentially based on race. At the very least, making use of interventions such as these would be another step toward fostering an increased tolerance for diversity.

CONFLICT

Ideally, society would recognize, appreciate, and even celebrate its diversity by acknowledging the richness and value that diversity brings, but this is not always the case. Attention to diversity and misperceptions involving the people around us often brings the threat of **conflict,** which has been defined as "a perceived incompatibility of interests" (Moghaddam, 1998, p. 513). Often the person or group is competing for limited resources with another person or group that holds incompatible goals.

Examples seem to be in the news on a constant basis—ethnic clashes in the Balkans and Rwanda, religious and political conflicts in Northern Ireland, armed clashes between Pakistan and India over Kashmir, and angry clashes between natives and non-natives over fishing rights. Conflicts inevitably arise out of clashes of values, attitudes, and/or behaviors, and these conflicts must be dealt with effectively.

This definition of conflict is not the only one. In fact, Deutsch (1973) suggested that conflict may occur when persons or groups hold either competitive or cooperative interests. For example, consider school projects in which students are paired up to work together. Both students may have been motivated to do a good job but may have disagreed on how to go about this. Maybe one student wanted to use information collected from interviews about personal experiences, whereas the other student wanted to use more general information collected from magazines, books, and research journals. Despite the fact that both students have compatible goals and an equal desire to succeed, conflict can still result. In this scenario and others like it, the competitive interests produce the conflict ("I want the project to be done my way"), and the cooperative interests serve as motivation to reach an agreement ("I want the teacher to be impressed with our work").

It is often assumed that conflict is always a bad thing. Because of this, conflict is often given a bad name. Granted, most conflict that we hear about is of the negative variety. Negative conflict may waste both time and valuable resources, and it can result in resentment and animosity. However, conflict is not necessarily negative. Conflict can represent honest differences of opinion and may be healthy or functional when people take the opportunity to express themselves assertively yet respectfully and, thus, open the lines of communication. This type of conflict can serve as the basis for the creativity and innovation discussed earlier. Viewed from this perspective, conflict provides a stimulus to foster positive change.

Despite the fact that conflict may be beneficial in the sense that it stimulates needed change, it can also become a very serious problem with enormous implications across organizational, community, and national settings (Fisher, 1990). Within organizational settings, conflict has the potential to decrease the effectiveness of employees through lost work time, lowered morale, wasted energy, and various other negative effects. Within the community, it may lead to increased levels of prejudice and discrimination among groups. At the international level, conflict can be even more dangerous, as demonstrated by numerous armed conflicts throughout human history.

As noted in earlier chapters, we often see others and ourselves as members of groups, that is, in-groups and out-groups. Usually such perceptions are harmless and often work to increase group cohesiveness. At a football game between rival universities, for example, the fact that you attend one of the universities is much more important than what your major is (a sense of cohesion exists across majors, ages, fraternities, and other groups). You quickly identify with your own team and university, and you view people from the other university as the out-group. Focusing on groups rather than individuals, however, also leads to the perception of exaggerated group differences and, thus, creates the potential for conflict. In situations such as those in New Brunswick and Minnesota, reports of the conflicts quickly come to include comments by those involved that refer to "them," meaning members of the other group. These comments are rarely positive and typically apply a characteristic (e.g., stubborn) to everyone in the other group simply on the basis of group membership. Understanding the dynamics of group interaction is important for understanding the development of conflict, its management, and its resolution. Some of the relevant theories of intergroup relations with respect to conflict and conflict management include social identity, relative deprivation, and realistic group conflict.

Social identity theory. **Social identity theory** (SIT) is a popular theory in the study of intergroup behavior (Karasawa, 1991). Although SIT was not developed as a theory of conflict, it does provide insight into how conflict may arise from relations between groups. SIT posits that an individual's self-knowledge is based on two types of identity (Tajfel & Turner, 1986). One type, known as *personal identity,* reflects an individual's sense of his or her own personal qualities and characteristics. Personal identity, for example, may be reflected by characterizations of the self as smart, outgoing, and funny. The other type, *social identity,* reflects a sense of identity based on the social groups to which individuals belong or with which they identify. Being a student, a woman, and an American could reflect a person's social identity. Which identity is expressed at any given time is often determined by the situation or the context within which a given behavior occurs. For example, going to a movie with a friend or out to dinner with a date brings personal characteristics and, hence, personal identity to the fore. On the other hand, marching in a student protest against tuition hikes, playing basketball against a rival university team, or becoming involved in a dispute over native fishing rights could evoke one's sense of social identity. Think about this: Would you fail to notice if you were the only person of color in a room full of white people or you were the only woman in a room full of men? In essence, SIT suggests that it is the context within which individuals find themselves that determines which type of identity—personal or social—will predominate.

A fundamental assumption of SIT is that people want to feel good about who they are and about the groups to which they belong; that is, they strive toward achieving (or maintaining) a positive social identity (Tajfel & Turner, 1986). So, as an American, a person might think great things about people from the United States because these positive comments also apply to him or her as a member of that category. Although this is true in some cases, it is especially so in situations involving intergroup relations. When in a group, being motivated to feel good about oneself and one's group often goes hand in hand with being motivated to evaluate members of the other group negatively. This is where the danger lies.

Awareness and critical evaluation of group membership forms the basis of the social identity process in that there must be an awareness that one belongs to a particular group. Then, through a social comparison process, evaluation of group status occurs. This evaluation results in a negative social identity (i.e., a status differential exists between an individual's group and the comparison group, with one's own group comparing unfavorably) or a positive social identity (i.e., either no status differential exists or one's own group compares favorably with the comparison group). Thus, perception of group differences and status differentials play an important role in the potential for conflict by setting the stage for "us versus them" comparisons. In situations where there is high tension between groups, such as in the opening vignette, the differences between "my" group and the "other" group become even more exaggerated.

It is important to note that the categorization of groups does not have to be based on real or observable between-group differences and that one needs only to perceive oneself as being part of a particular group and different from another group to induce a sense of group membership. Such comparisons, if left unchallenged, may be the building blocks for stereotypes and other forms of prejudice and discrimination.

Relative deprivation. Like SIT, the **theory of relative deprivation** acknowledges the importance of both perceptual comparative processes and social comparative processes between groups in conflict. Originally developed by Stouffer, Suchman, DeVinney, Star, and Williams (1949), the theory of relative deprivation suggests that a person may feel deprived of some desirable thing relative to his or her own past; to another person(s), group, or ideal; or to some other social category. It is important to note that this sense of deprivation is based on a relative comparison with some "other" thing and that the person does not have to be "deprived" in the absolute sense of the word (Runciman, 1972). For example, even if an individual has received what would be considered a "fair share," conflict may still occur as a result of the perception that one has received less than the individual believes he or she is due. Thus, conflict arises only after an individual has compared himself or herself with some standard and judged himself or herself to be deprived.

Although the theory of relative deprivation has its limitations, it can provide a useful framework for understanding some types of conflict. When individuals experience relative deprivation, they are motivated to act in a way that serves to reduce or eliminate the deprivation. This action may sometimes result in conflict. The theory of relative deprivation may be used to explain the origins of many political conflicts because individuals believe that this relative deprivation is the result of social injustice (Auvinen & Nafziger, 1999). This theory also helps to explain conflicts over fishing and hunting rights between native and non-native peoples. When natives and non-native fishers have different restrictions placed on them, it is understandable that the more restricted group feels deprived in comparison with the other group. Similarly, when native people believe that restrictions are being placed on activities where no restrictions existed previously, a sense of relative deprivation may occur.

Realistic group conflict theory. In essence, **realistic group conflict theory** (RGCT) suggests that intergroup hostility is produced by competition in the form of conflicting goals. Basing their theory on the work of Sherif (1966a), LeVine and Campbell (1972) suggested that conflict is reduced by cooperation in the form of common goals that are attainable only through cooperation. The basic premise of this theory is that conflict between groups is a result of real conflicts of interest. Unlike the theories of social identity and relative deprivation (where perception plays a central role), RGCT suggests that perception is not enough and that a real and immediate conflict of interest must exist for actual conflict to occur. Once in-group identity is threatened, awareness of in-group identity is heightened and feelings of in-group solidarity are increased along with negative feelings toward those in the out-group. The presence of all these factors can be clearly seen in the ongoing conflict over fishing rights in the United States and Canada.

The basis for RGCT was the classic field experiment conducted by Muzafer Sherif that was discussed in Chapter 1. You may recall that the study, known as the Robber's Cave Study, involved boys at a summer camp and consisted of three phases: a *group formation* phase during which groups with distinct norms formed, an *intergroup conflict* phase during which conflict between groups and the denigration of out-group members surfaced, and a *reduction of conflict* phase during which the introduction of superordinate goals led to the reduction of conflict between the groups (Fisher, 1990; Sherif, Harvey, White, Hood, & Sherif, 1961).

In Sherif's field study, the boys were ultimately able to reduce (if not eliminate) their out-group biases and eventually get along. This study provided some definite insights into the consequences of conflicts of interest and the development and resolution of intergroup conflict. Furthermore, this study provided clear evidence that superordinate goals play a key role in conflict management and that the resolution of conflict takes more than mere contact with out-group members.

As mentioned in earlier sections of this chapter, it is simply human nature to categorize people into different groups. From an early age, individuals learn to place people into groups based on obvious differences such as gender, ethnic background, and social class. In fact, Sherif and colleagues' (1961) pioneering field studies have demonstrated that, even when the differences are completely arbitrary, people still categorize others into groups and behave in ways that correspond with in- and out-group membership. Thus, Sherif and colleagues' work emphasized the importance of self–other differences, whether concrete or perceived, when establishing group or social identity.

Although the experimental work that has been done in the area of conflict management is important, it must be noted that such experimental work is of limited value if it cannot be applied to real-world situations. In this way, the work of Sherif and colleagues has greatly helped to identify some of the conflict management and resolution strategies that could be applied in settings ranging from home to school to the workplace.

RGCT has also been used successfully to understand the effectiveness of team-based organizations. Hennessy and West (1999) looked at the effects of identification with a work group and perceptions of competition between groups at a community health care hospital in England. The teams used in the research were composed of individuals working at 17 different day centers of the hospital. As part of the survey, participants were given scenarios where they were asked to make decisions on how they would distribute a pool of funds between the day centers. They found that participants who strongly identified with their team and who perceived some competition between groups made decisions that benefited their team at the expense of the other teams, allocating significantly more money to their team than to the others. RGCT provides a useful tool to understand how individuals and groups may, even unintentionally, initiate conflict situations when limited resources are available. The health care workers in this research were more concerned with their own needs and the benefits that the additional funding could provide for patients in their own program than with equitable distribution among the day centers.

In the real world, this type of situation is often the beginning of conflict, even though nobody was behaving maliciously or even intending for conflict to occur. This is especially true in cross-cultural situations where there may be great differences in expectations for how resources ought to be divided (Fischer & Smith, 2003). In collectivistic countries, for example, norms typically dictate that resources be distributed equally; everyone gets the same regardless of how hard they worked or what their rank is. In individualistic countries, however, the norm is for rewards to be equity based; the more one puts into a project in terms of work, materials, and so forth, the more of the reward that person receives. It is extremely difficult to reach a consensus on reward allocation when individuals from both cultural perspectives must arrive at a solution, and this sets the stage for conflict (Leung, 1988). Let us reflect back for a moment on the intervention example used for prejudice reduction. How would you extend these techniques from simple prejudice reduction to conflict management and resolution?

Conflict Management and Resolution

Although understanding the causes of conflict is extremely important, understanding the ways in which we can manage and potentially resolve conflict is perhaps more so. At the group level, two promising theories of conflict management and resolution are the contact hypothesis and coalition building.

The contact hypothesis. In his classic book *The Nature of Prejudice,* Gordon Allport suggested that negative intergroup relations could be improved by increasing positive contact between members of two groups. Known as the **contact hypothesis,** the assumption was that positive contact with members of an out-group could decrease negative stereotyping of the out-group by the in-group and lead to improved intergroup relations. However, Allport (1954) pointed out that contact in and of itself is insufficient to produce positive change without other important criteria being met. For example, improvement

can be anticipated only if both the in-group and the out-group are perceived as relatively equal in status and power. Here, even the perception of status equality between the groups is enough to help resolve a conflict situation. In addition, a perception that the two groups share a common goal should exist along with a perception that their environments support their movement toward that goal. When attempting to reach a desired outcome that is common to both groups, it is necessary for them to work together to achieve this. The interaction that occurs as a result of working together helps to overcome some of the barriers that caused the conflict in the first place. If two groups have a common goal and yet engage in competition rather than cooperation with one another, this will serve to impede the process of conflict resolution. For example, if two groups are competing for the same limited resources, prejudice will increase rather than decrease, as was the case during the early phases of the situations described in the opening vignette. This theory has been the basis for attempts to minimize conflicts between groups in a number of settings. Many attempts to reduce conflict in Israel have begun by bringing together young Israelis and Arabs. However, a high degree of interaction does not always occur when groups are brought together (Maoz, 2002), and more than mere contact seems to be required for meaningful change.

One example of a conflict intervention that uses the preceding principles in a group setting is the "graduated and reciprocated initiatives in tension reduction" (GRIT) strategy, which involves building on successive attempts at conciliation (Osgood, 1962). The initiation of the GRIT strategy involves one "side" or party taking the first step by engaging in a few deescalatory actions to demonstrate an attempt at conciliation. This step is meant to notify the opposing party of the initiating party's intent to deescalate conflict as well as to invite the opposing party to respond by taking their own steps to deescalate the conflict. This first step serves two purposes: (a) to clarify the intent of the initiating group (so as to make clear that this is a step toward peace and not a trick) and (b) to publicly demonstrate the attempt at conciliation in such a way as to allow for external pressure (by the public, the media, or the international community) to be placed on the opposing party to reciprocate. If the opposing party responds in kind, step-by-step the conflict can be reduced. Osgood (1962) suggested that if the opposing party does not respond in kind, the initiating party should try again to make a small concession a second or third time.

The GRIT strategy will be successful only if each of the conflicting parties responds appropriately. However, the potential remains for the initiating party to take a conciliatory step and, if the opposing party chooses not to respond, to leave itself vulnerable to being taken advantage of by the opposing party. In this respect, the GRIT strategy also emphasizes the need for both conflicting parties to protect their own interests by ensuring that they are capable of retaliation if the need arises. The nature of the GRIT strategy is such that it encourages gradual steps in tension reduction, a process that ensures the safety of both parties because it does not leave any one party more vulnerable than another party. Given what you know about the groups described in the opening vignette, do you think that those interested in decreasing conflict would be wise to try to increase contact between the two groups?

Coalition building. Research on **coalition building** has identified a set of pivotal factors required for making positive changes to intergroup relations. These factors include acquaintance potential, social norms, cooperative tasks and reward systems, and the characteristics of individuals (Fisher, 1982, 1990).

A high *acquaintance potential,* meaning a greater opportunity for personal and informal interaction between groups, would serve to help members of different groups to get to know each other. This would increase the potential for positive interaction between groups. Also, *social norms* that encourage positive intergroup interaction would allow for more accepted relations between groups. If such norms were institutionalized, communication between groups would become more commonplace because it would not be looked on so negatively. As mentioned previously, introducing *cooperative tasks* and *reward systems* would also create common cooperative goals that members of different groups could work together to achieve. Having

to work together often starts off feeling like forced interaction, but as people get to know each other on a more personal level, relations between them start to change and become more positive in nature (Fisher, 1982, 1990). Efforts to resolve conflicts such as the fishing disputes described earlier often involve creating coalitions with members from both groups convening to seek solutions to the problem that would aid members of both groups.

Finally, *individual characteristics* also serve to influence intergroup interactions—both the individual who may hold a negative attitude and the target of that attitude. The strength with which people hold prejudicial ideas may determine how open they are to changing their stereotypes of people from other groups. For example, being introduced to a member of a minority group who is highly competent may make a person think about the stereotypes that he or she holds about that particular group and might even motivate the individual to change his or her thinking (Fisher, 1982, 1990).

Desforges and colleagues (1991) investigated the effects of different types of social contact with a former mental patient (two types of structured cooperative contact and a control condition) on attitudes toward former mental patients and found support for the contact hypothesis as a way in which to reduce conflict. Specifically, the study explored the potential for attitude change as a result of contact with a representative from a stigmatized social group. The results demonstrated that attitudes toward former mental patients changed from being negative to being more positive in nature after individuals engaged in a cooperative task with a confederate playing the role of a former mental patient. In addition, contact was linked to more positive attitudes regarding the typical former mental patient and to more positive general attitudes toward former mental patients. Thus, as Desforges and colleagues demonstrated, contact may indeed foster a change in negative attitudes toward mental patients and other stigmatized social groups, a finding that has several implications for the reduction of prejudice through contact.

Another example of a conflict intervention is illustrated by the United Nations' efforts in developing peace-building support offices in postconflict areas where help is needed to restore a sense of balance in the legal, political, economic, and/or social systems of the regions. The UN website is a great source of information regarding the peace-building support offices as well as other interventions aimed at reducing tensions between conflicting groups. The aim of these peace-building offices is to provide support throughout the peace process, essentially helping to prevent further conflict. The mandate of such offices is often part of a "disarmament–demobilization–reconciliation" (DDR) process in which the primary aim of peace building is to encourage conflicting parties to disarm, demobilize, and reconcile their differences. Each peace-building office is headed by a representative of the secretary-general who is responsible for overseeing each peace-building initiative. Often these individuals serve as negotiators between the government and the international community. Although they are responsible for encouraging and monitoring communication between conflicting parties, they must take care not to cross the boundary between helping and interfering with the internal affairs of the region. Peace-building offices have come into existence only during recent years and can be found in regions that have recently dealt with conflict such as Liberia, Tajikistan, Guinea-Bissau, and the Central African Republic. In each of these areas, the nature of the peace-building activities taking place is different, although the function of such activities remains the same. For example, peace-building activities monitored by the offices may range from monitoring elections and ceasefire agreements to temporarily taking over the functions of government.

Headed by Felix Downes-Thomas, the peace-building office in the West African nation of Liberia is one such attempt at rebuilding a region recovering from civil war. In Liberia, some disarmament and demobilization goals have been met, but the goals of reconciliation still remain. To this end, Downes-Thomas has facilitated meetings between government and rebel leaders, advising the two groups on ways in which they could improve economic cooperation between them. In addition, the country's president recently released some political prisoners from jail. Such efforts at peace building help to encourage reciprocal actions that, in turn, help to deescalate the conflict. So far, these peace-building efforts have been maintained successfully. However, as with any peace-building initiative, any progress that has been achieved can be undone just as quickly. In Liberia, less than a year later, clashes reerupted in the North as a result of dissident groups whose members feel that their needs were not being met during the process of conflict resolution. This highlights the need, during the post-conflict phase, for the UN peace-building support offices to do their job and help to reestablish a sense of peace within the region. How might one use this approach to help reduce the conflict discussed in the vignette at the beginning of the chapter?

Throughout this section, much of the focus has centered on conflict at the group level. However, we also experience conflict in our daily interactions with others, that is, at an interpersonal level. Understanding interpersonal conflict can provide insight into group processes and improve conflict management skills. At the interpersonal level, Rahim and Bonoma (1979) provided an understanding of the different styles of managing conflict.

Interpersonal conflict management. The contact hypothesis and coalition building focus on strategies for managing conflict between groups (intergroup conflict). However, conflict also occurs between individuals (interpersonal conflict). According to Rahim and Bonoma (1979), interpersonal conflict is best managed when individuals balance their personal goals and the requirements of the task in such a way as to meet both personal and group goals. The most effective strategy in a given situation depends on specific factors embedded in the situation. Rahim and Bonoma identified distinct styles of conflict management, each of which can be placed on two dimensions: concern for the self and concern for others. The *concern for self* dimension represents the extent to which an individual is motivated to look out for himself or herself. In contrast, the *concern for others* dimension represents the extent to which an individual places the needs of others before those of himself or herself. Figure 15.4 graphically represents each style as a function of the degree of concern for self and the degree of concern for others.

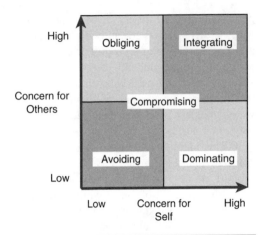

Figure 15.4   Rahim and Bonoma's Interpersonal Conflict Management Styles

SOURCE: Based on Rahim, A., & Bonoma, T.V. (1979). Reprinted with permission.

The *integrating* style of conflict management involves problem solving through the exchange of information. Individuals who handle conflict in this way make use of any and all information provided to them about the context of the conflict and attempt to achieve an agreement on a particular course of action that fully satisfies the interests of both parties. This style of managing conflict reflects an attempt to balance a high concern for one's own needs with a high concern for the perceived needs of others. Rahim and Bonoma (1979) suggested that this strategy is most useful in dealing with issues that are complex in nature.

The *obliging* style of handling conflict involves making adjustments to satisfy others. Individuals who manage conflict with this style try to emphasize any and all common ground while ignoring differences, emphasizing the concern for others more strongly than the concern for self. This strategy is most useful when someone believes that he or she may be incorrect or that he or she cares much less about the outcome than do others.

Forcefully controlling the behavior of others to get what one wants is the focus of the *dominating* style of conflict management. When using this strategy, individuals effectively focus only on their own goals without much concern for others. Individuals who are dominating are often willing to "risk it all" to gain an unfair advantage against others. This conflict management style is most useful in situations where a decision needs to be made under pressure of time.

Rahim and Bonoma (1979) suggested that when an issue is simple and insignificant, *avoidance* is the most effective way of managing conflict. Neither concern for self nor concern for others comes into play because the conflict is basically ignored. Handling conflict through avoidance usually involves some form of denial or distraction. The inherent risk in this strategy is that if the conflict is not minor or insignificant, individuals who select this strategy often end up disappointing themselves as well as others.

The *compromising* style of conflict management involves reaching an agreement that is mutually satisfactory to one's self as well as to others. Individuals who make use of this style of conflict management are willing to give in a little bit to achieve a common goal. There is a moderate focus on their own needs and goals as well as a concern about the needs of others.

SUMMARY

Anywhere humans exist, diversity will exist; people differ in how they look, how they feel, and how they behave. Some of these differences are the result of learning. The social culture in which an individual grows up teaches its members to value certain behaviors or perspectives over others. Other differences are not the result of learning, for example, differences in sex, ethnic background, and socioeconomic status. None of these aspects of diversity operates in isolation from the others, and all of these differences have implications for how the world is experienced.

Some of the implications of diversity are positive, and some are negative. Diversity brings about the opportunity to learn new perspectives and, in so doing, to increase creativity and innovativeness for both individuals and groups. However, it can also lead to negative effects such as prejudice, discrimination, and even conflict. A clear understanding of when diversity leads to conflict is important because conflict itself may be beneficial or harmful. It can move us toward innovation and change, but it can hinder such efforts as well. Research and theories relating to conflict management and resolution offer ways in which to deal with conflict constructively so that negative outcomes are minimized and positive outcomes are maximized.

16

YOU CAN CHANGE THE WORLD

Action, Participatory, and Activist Research

CHARLENE Y. SENN

The newspaper, magazine, and television coverage of psychology often makes it sound as though the only way in which psychology makes a difference in people's lives is through clinical psychology and the process of therapy. Often research is talked about as though it is something very separate from life, from helping, and from making things better. All of the applied social psychological research you have read about in this book proves that this is not the case. Research findings can be used in various ways to improve society. But beyond that, there are many research projects that, by the very act of being conducted, help to change the world one step at a time.

When you read the title of this chapter, you may have asked yourself whether this whole book is not about changing the world one piece at a time. The answer to that question is "yes and no." All of applied social psychology by definition has real-world relevance, and much of it will end up changing the lives of individuals or communities. Findings from these studies may assist other researchers or practitioners in

Figure 16.1   The Difficulty of Distinguishing Types of Social Change Research

SOURCE: Cartoon by Simon Kneebone (Wadsworth, 1998).

seeing fruitful avenues for social interventions. The results of applied social psychology studies may be used by social activists to inform their demands or by government officials to help devise their policy recommendations. But in most of these cases, the goal of the research has not been to deliberately create social change. The research that you will read about in this chapter has explicit social or situational change goals. That is, the research, to a greater or lesser extent, was developed to change something about the specific situation right at that time rather than, or as well as, later.

These distinctions between research that deliberately sets out to change society and research that has other goals are, however, not always clear-cut (Figure 16.1). Who is to say that a health promotion study that compares three different types of smoking cessation programs is not changing the world? If the study helps to reduce a dangerous behavior (smoking) in a small or large group of individuals and to thereby reduce health risk and economic hardship, is that not improving society? Of course it is. The research covered in this chapter, however, has as its purpose an immediate impact on policy and/or the improvement of social conditions for a whole society, group, or community of disadvantaged people.

DEFINITIONS OF DIFFERENT TYPES OF SOCIAL CHANGE RESEARCH

Applied social psychologists are not the only people who do research to effect social change. The labels and definitions for the types of research that do this are somewhat different across disciplines. This section defines what we mean in psychology by each of the terms we commonly use. But it would be very difficult to discuss these terms without also relying on the work of sociologists, anthropologists, and the like because this field tends to be **multidisciplinary** (i.e., people from many disciplines working together) and **interdisciplinary** (i.e., people who use knowledge and skills from across disciplines). By necessity, this chapter can only scratch the surface of the breadth and depth of research that tries to make a real difference in society. It is hoped that this will give you a flavor of the types of research possible and perhaps

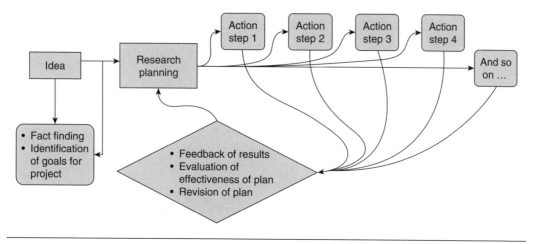

Figure 16.2   The Action Research Process as Described by Lewin (1947)

even a desire to do this kind of research yourself. You should note that there are no new research *methods* for you to learn in this chapter because these types of research use a variety of methods that you already know. These studies are still correlational, descriptive, and/or experimental and use the same tools for gathering data.

The most common terms for research that has the goal of changing situations in society are **action research, participatory research,** and **activist research.** Each of the first two terms (action and participatory) describes both a way of approaching research (e.g., epistemology, values, assumptions about research) and a particular research process. The last term (activist) is used less often and refers to a particular standpoint that the researcher takes toward the research process and the project at hand. It is not unusual to see combinations of these terms (e.g., participatory action research [Wadsworth, 1998]) if a study takes components of each type and uses them in one study. This chapter looks at some of these hybrid approaches later.

Action Research

Action research is the oldest of all the types of research discussed in this chapter, having been developed and advocated for use in psychology by Kurt Lewin in an article published in 1946. Lewin (1946) argued that when psychologists seek to facilitate social change, they must conduct "comparative research on the conditions and effects of various forms of social

action and research leading to social action" (p. 35). He went on to criticize the academic focus of much of psychology at that time, saying, "Research that produces nothing but books will not suffice" (p. 35). In Lewin's view, change can occur only if an iterative process of research is followed (Figure 16.2), that is, planning that includes appropriate "fact finding," execution of the plan, evaluation of the effectiveness of the action taken (usually involving more fact finding), followed by another cycle of planning, action, and evaluation, and so forth.

The process that Lewin suggested is different in emphasis and content from the standard research process that we all learn in research methods (for a review, see Chapter 3 in this book). In that model, the process for a single research project is much more like a straight line. The planning takes place, the study is carried out, and the project is considered to be complete when the original plan has been executed and the data have been analyzed and interpreted. The data from that study may then be used to evaluate the theory driving the research. Future studies to continue the process may be planned by that researcher or other researchers. But the essence of a good research study, according to the principles underlying mainstream psychological research design, is that a study is planned well and then carried out exactly as specified.

Lewin was not discarding all aspects of the standard research process, but he placed more emphasis on the effectiveness of the particular intervention to solve the social problem. He believed that for any research plan to accomplish this, it must be flexible and revised constantly according to new information. This requires multiple cycles of planning, data gathering, and plan revising by the same researcher(s) and within the same project. Lewin also thought that for any social change to be long-lasting, the action plan must be developed based on diagnosis of the problem within the specific social context (e.g., the local community or factory) and must involve the cooperation of the people from that setting (Lewin, 1946).

It is clear that Lewin, as someone who had escaped from fascism, had strong views about many topics that he studied. But he thought that this did not get in the way of "good science," that is, that action research was an objective process well within the appropriate role for social scientists. He argued that carrying out research in this way gave greater insight into how situations worked in comparison with other methods (e.g., surveys) of social research. He also thought that action research, because of its applied context, was a superior process for testing psychological theories and producing knowledge.

Lewin died a few years after he proposed this approach. During his life, he applied his plan for action research to issues ranging from improving intergroup relations (i.e., race relations) to democracy and democratic leadership to modifying the food-buying and preparation habits of wartime housewives to support the war effort (Lewin, 1946, 1947).

If you look at the diagram of Lewin's view of how action research should work (Figure 16.2), you can see that it would be possible to follow Lewin's directions as a *research process* (e.g., by attempting to find the best bottle or aluminum can design to sell more sparkling beverages) without using his underlying assumptions that the method should be used to understand social phenomena and to effect social change. But most action research (Peters & Robinson, 1984) does keep the key elements of Lewin's model even if the research has tended to focus on closed group change (e.g., making change within a specific organization) rather than on general societal change (e.g., reducing prejudice in one community while gaining an understanding of how to reduce conflict between groups in

society more generally). Most of the published studies during recent years have been of workplace or educational applications in which negative work environments (e.g., those that cause injury or stress to workers) or school practices (e.g., how to best teach learning-disabled students) are modified through cycles of action research (e.g., Cunningham, 1993). This is important research that makes meaningful changes in those specific workplaces or schools.

For example, Pasmore and Friedlander (1982) were hired by the management of a factory where an outbreak of sore arms (diagnosed as tenosynovitis) among the workers had resulted in a drop in productivity, high absenteeism, sick leaves, and surgeries across a 5-year period. If the problem could not be solved, the factory would shut down and all workers would lose their jobs. On previous occasions, the company had hired medical researchers to try to ascertain the cause of the injuries. None of these actions had been successful. Pasmore and Friedlander realized very quickly that the workforce, whose members were local, rural, and primarily women (90% female vs. 100% male supervisors transferred in to the plant from elsewhere), had very little control or say over their work environments. They had, in fact, never been asked about what they perceived to be the cause of the injuries. A committee, the Studies and Communication Group, was created by the researchers and was composed of five workers (with or without injuries), two foremen, the employee relations manager, and the researchers. These group members were introduced to **action research principles** (e.g., that an understanding of the problem and decisions about a solution could not be reached before several rounds of data gathering, discussion, reexamination, and revision had been done, that cooperation and trust were crucial to the process) and were encouraged to discuss their beliefs about the "soreness problem." Across months of meetings, members of the committee designed an interview and survey, were trained in a number of research skills (e.g., participant observation), conducted the research, and prepared recommendations for change based on analysis of 50 interviews and a survey of all employees. The results of this research were then fed back to all employees and the management (the latter of

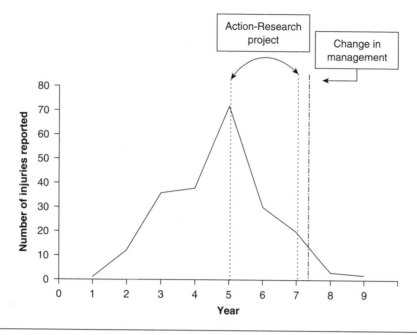

Figure 16.3   Arm Injuries Reported Prior to, During, and Following the Research Project

SOURCE: Adapted from Pasmore and Friedlander (1982, p. 357). Copyright © 1982 Cornell University.

which initially did not take kindly to many of the recommendations that blamed the management style of the organization for increased work stress) and resulted in many small and large changes in the work environment.

You can see, by examining the graph in Figure 16.3, that the research itself caused a reduction in injuries long before a full management change was effected. This should not be mistaken for a simple **Hawthorne effect,** that is, the phenomenon where productivity is increased because researchers single out and pay attention to workers. In fact, some researchers argue that action research capitalizes on the Hawthorne process and goes much further (Gottfredson, 1996). Pasmore and Friedlander (1982) agreed, suggesting that the nature of an action research project makes changes in the environment. They identified a number of features of their project to support this claim. The cooperation and trust built between employees and managers in designing and carrying out the various data collection stages, the massive publicity campaign that informed workers about the project and ensured them that the problem was being taken seriously, and the disruption of power dynamics between the plant manager and the employees all were integral parts of the research process and became key factors in the reduction of the stress that was responsible for the injuries.

This example follows the procedures that Lewin set out for action research; the researchers planned, did research to gather facts, and implemented a series of changes, each time coming back to the group to pass on the information and to reassess the plan before moving to the next action. What you may have noticed as well is that this project involved in-depth collaboration with the people in the particular setting to accomplish the action research cycle. This is not a requirement for action research, but as you may recall from the discussion earlier in the chapter, Lewin believed that collaboration of any kind would make the action research more successful in sustaining changes. When real collaboration is present, as it was in the "sore arms" study, these researchers have much in common with those who describe their work as "participatory."

Participatory Research

Participatory research evolved in Latin America and other parts of the "Two-Thirds World"—Asia, Africa, and Central and South

America (this term is used by activists to illustrate that the so-called First World is only a small proportion of the world's countries and peoples)—from roots quite separate from action research traditions (Park, 1999). Paulo Freire is often given credit for beginning this tradition through his popular education process. Freire (1970) dedicated his book *Pedagogy of the Oppressed* (translated from the original Spanish) "to the oppressed, and to those who suffer with them and fight at their side" (p. 7). It was Freire's view that "authentic education" was truly working *with* an oppressed group rather than providing information *for* or *about* the group. Freire put this into action with peasants in Brazil who learned to read as they also learned about their own culture, heritage, and status within Brazilian society. He facilitated social action based on people's own discovery of their social position and their solutions for change. He suggested that many social and political change efforts had been unsuccessful because they were designed based on the perspectives of the educators and politicians rather than on the perspectives of the people for whom the plans had been developed. Can you see how this point of view could be applied to research in psychology?

Have you ever participated in a psychological study? How much did you contribute to the direction of the research? To what was studied? To how the conclusions were used? If you are like most undergraduate students, you probably have been asked to fill out a survey or be part of an experiment. Although your beliefs, behaviors, attitudes, and perceptions were no doubt of great value to the researchers in completing their study, your role as a participant was quite limited. **Participatory research** involves a very different level of involvement. A study can be said to be participatory when it requires the involvement of people from the group or community of interest in some or all of the stages of research. Maguire (1987) suggested that "participatory research combines three activities: investigation, education, and action" (p. 29). The *investigation* part of the process is a "social" investigation "involving participation of oppressed and ordinary people in problem posing and solving" (p. 29) and is not an academic library exercise (although no one says that

you should not also make yourself aware of any previous research or theory about the problem). Both the participants in the study and the researchers are *educated* in the process about the possible causes of the problem "through collective discussion and interaction" (p. 29). Finally, both the researchers and the participants "join in solidarity to take collective *action,* both short and long term" (p. 29, emphasis added). The reasoning is clear. The people who are going to be affected by change efforts should be involved in directing that change, and mutual education will be necessary for that to occur. Take a minute now to compare Maguire's outline of the process of participatory research (investigation, education, and action) with Lewin's plan for action research in Figure 16.2. Can you see the differences and similarities?[1]

Have you read many studies from researchers who took a participatory approach to their work? If you are like most undergraduates in psychology courses, you have not. Have researchers who care about the lives of those in poverty asked single mothers what they thought were the most important issues in their lives? The answer in most cases is no. Participatory research is fairly rare in psychology, even in applied social psychology. But it is gaining popularity.

So, how would a researcher tackle issues such as those facing poor single mothers? A participatory researcher would, at a minimum, involve this group of women in brainstorming about the problems they face and would like to see solved. The experts in this case would be the women whose life experience this is and, to a lesser extent, the researcher who has expertise in research. Studies using this type of approach range from those involving some participation during the early stages of research to those involving some individuals from the community/group during every phase of the research and action up to and including the desired social change. Sometimes researchers call their work "participatory" even when a social action or change is not part of the study. However, Maguire (1987) and others (Park, Brydon-Miller, Hall, & Jackson, 1993) would not call this participatory research. "Participatory research includes political action, especially actions that cultivate 'critical consciousness' and are oriented towards structural change, not towards adjusting people to oppressive environments" (Cancian, 1993, p. 94). In this way, we could differentiate between research that is "participatory" in nature (involving the affected people more fully in the research process, which looks more like the collaboration described in the Pasmore and Friedlander [1982] example of action research) from "participatory research" (which follows the full process outlined by Maguire [1987]).

In participatory research, researchers often diminish their own expert status by providing training in research skills, such as interviewing and developing questionnaires, so that participants can be actively involved in carrying out the research. Sometimes this training and work would be paid, and this may have the additional benefit of providing an immediate temporary remedy to participants' financial situations. But even if this is not the case, the skills gained from being part of the research may be beneficial for participants' self-esteem and life and career skills in many ways beyond the issue that is the focus of the research.

A good example of participatory research is the study carried out by Davidson, Stayner, Lambert, Smith, and Sledge (1997). This study was undertaken after another more traditional approach they tried had failed dismally. Working in the psychiatry department of an academic medical center, Davidson and his colleagues had previously attempted to design and implement an elaborate relapse prevention program for psychiatric patients who were released from the hospital. This program included education for patients about the nature of their disorders and the symptoms of relapse that were unique to them while they were still in the hospital, preparation of an "action plan" for dealing with symptoms while they were living on the outside, groups held twice a week to reinforce the program, and availability of the groups for patients once they were released. All of this sounds like a good idea, doesn't it? That is what the doctors and other clinicians associated with the program thought. To their dismay, the program was completely and utterly ineffective, with many readmissions to hospital. Even more surprising to the staff members and researchers was that not one patient used the program following his or her release.

Davidson and colleagues (1997), on reflection, realized that they had taken all of the professionals into account in their formulation. Based on the views of these experts, their plan to prevent relapse was based on the assumption that readmission to the hospital was the result of a clinically definable relapse, that is, a person's return to a severely symptomatic state. (Recall that Freire believed that basing programs on the perspective of professionals alone would lead to failure.) They began to wonder whether there were other reasons—even more important ones—why a person might be readmitted. So, the researchers started again, this time with the goal of "learning how patients might view the problem of recidivism differently and how they might be involved in a fuller and more constructive way of addressing the problem" (p. 771). Can you see how this shift in focus begins to move the research into a participatory research framework?

Of the patients who had been readmitted to the hospital two or more times, 12 were invited in open-ended interviews to talk about "their experiences of rehospitalization, the circumstances of this event, and the functions it served in their lives" (Davidson et al., 1997, p. 772). They were also asked to reflect on the relapse prevention program they had gone through and why they had not participated after they left the hospital as well as what things they felt might have been more useful to them. The most important finding that emerged was that the desire to prevent hospital readmission was entirely the clinicians' agenda. For the patients themselves, the hospital provided "safety, respite, food, and privacy" (p. 774) along with caring. To some, it was a "vacation." This was in extreme contrast to their lives outside of the hospital, where most of the patients were "homeless, broke, [and] unemployed" (p. 775), living on the streets or in homeless shelters where the beds were less than 12 inches apart. Moreover, the patients felt powerless to control their illnesses and did not see mental health treatment as effective, with the exception of their medications in some cases. They perceived the programs in the hospital to be more like school exercises where they were expected to perform, but they did not see these as being related to improvements in their well-being. Their views could not have been more different from the clinicians' views. The hospital still wanted to prevent readmissions where possible because hospital stays are expensive. These findings made it clear that any programs based solely on the assumptions of clinicians were doomed to fail; success could be achieved only by "follow[ing] the lead of the patients in assuming that their restoring a decent quality of life for themselves in the community would make the hospital a less appealing alternative" (p. 777). In other words, there had to be a social change.

Further discussions were held with patients and other individuals who had once been patients but were now leading "productive lives in the community" (Davidson et al., 1997, p. 777) (i.e., self-labeled mental health consumers) to guide the direction of new solutions. On the basis of these discussions, groups were moved out of the hospital and into the community to overcome transportation barriers and to provide a new social community in the city. The groups were changed to be more focused on social support than on education and relapse prevention. Support for patients from one another was encouraged in various ways. For example, mental health consumers were hired to arrange social and leisure activities that were desired by the patients, to provide transportation to the groups, and to accompany patients on outings. They were also taught to co-lead the support groups, providing role models of success. A number of other changes were aimed to reduce "feelings of powerlessness." Not only did these changes reduce hospital admissions and the length of hospital stays for people who participated in the new programs by 70% to 90% in comparison with people who did not have the program, but also the new community of mental health consumers acted to sustain the groups beyond the 3-month plan and helped to change the program to accommodate budget cuts and other obstacles. In other words, this participatory project changed the communities into which these patients were released and facilitated the move out of their patient role. It is a great example of how a participatory research study can make a large difference in a community and can even create a sense of community where one did not exist previously.

Activism in Research

Most participatory research is also activist research. That is, the researchers are taking a position and action on a controversial issue or social problem (Merriam–Webster, 2003). Usually, the researcher is working for the benefit of the oppressed group. For example, Cancian (1993), a self-described participatory researcher, described the process as "a radical type of activist social research in which the people being studied, or the intended beneficiaries of the research, have substantial control over and participation in the research" (pp. 93–94). You can see in the example of the treatment of psychiatric patients (Davidson et al., 1997) how the program changed as a result of the research from something designed and controlled by clinicians to a program designed jointly and controlled on an ongoing basis by the mental health consumers themselves. Clearly, this is activism, even if it was not originally intended to be.

Not all activist research is participatory. It is possible to conduct research using a variety of methods and processes where direct participation of the people involved most directly with the issue is not included. Nancy Russo's empirical work debunking "post-abortion trauma syndrome," a condition fabricated by the anti-abortion lobby, is one such example (Russo & Denious, 2001; Russo & Zierk, 1992). Russo worked as part of a task force of the American Psychological Association's Division 35 (Society for the Psychology of Women) to investigate this issue.

Russo and her colleagues conducted a secondary statistical analysis of survey data gathered for the U.S. Bureau of the Census. It was a very well-conducted national probability sample of male and female youths ages 14 to 21 years. This study was originally designed to examine youths' experiences in the labor market but included many questions on health and fertility, including follow-up surveys of 5,295 women 8 years later. This follow-up included measurement of women's self-esteem and adjustment, that is, variables that the anti-abortion lobby had claimed were irreparably harmed by abortion. Russo found that women who had abortions had higher overall levels of well-being on follow-up than did women who had not had abortions, even though the stresses of unwanted pregnancies were experienced. Delaying child-birth and having fewer children spaced further apart were also related to higher levels of self-esteem and well-being. Russo found no evidence that abortion is harmful to women. She did *not* claim that abortion is directly related to a sense of empowerment and well-being but rather argued that it has an indirect relationship through reducing the number of children to which a woman gives birth. The task force then collaborated with a pro-choice group, Pro-Choice Forum, that had a large international online audience to disseminate the information from Russo's and others' studies. Russo stated, "This is our attempt to let people know the facts" (quoted in Crawford, 2003). You should note that there is no participation of a group of women who have had abortions in the design, conduct, or interpretation of the results from this study. The researcher is the sole force driving the research. Therefore, this is an example of activist research, which takes a stand on an issue (pro-choice on abortion) and action (conducting a study and disseminating the results in a politicized forum), but not of participatory research.

You may have noticed that the amount of coverage devoted to activist research in this section was much less than that devoted to the action and participatory research processes. This emphasis represents the amount of research of each kind in the applied social psychology literature more generally. There are relatively few researchers who describe their research as strictly activist in character. This does not mean, however, that components of each of these approaches are not found in other applied social psychologists' work.

DIFFERENCES AND SIMILARITIES BETWEEN ACTION RESEARCH AND PARTICIPATORY RESEARCH

Some authors believe that there are key ideological differences between action research and participatory research that have kept their literatures separate. According to Brown and Tandon (1983), "The two traditions focus on different levels of analysis, use conceptual tools from different disciplines, hold fundamentally different assumptions about the nature of society, and attend to different central problems" (p. 283). Table 16.1 provides a summary of these comparisons. Yet there are many similarities between research that is called action research and studies that are participatory. (These similarities are examined in more detail in the next section on comparisons between these approaches and mainstream research.)

The **level of analysis** (individual/group vs. societal) is probably the most distinct difference between the two approaches. Researchers who hold an action research perspective often focus on *the individual within the group* for their analyses. Consider the example of the research to deal with sore arms in an electronics factory, where Pasmore and Friedlander (1982) were hired to solve the sore arms problem. The researchers were aware of many features of the group, that is, the management's relationship with the workers and the style of management that were affecting the individuals' work lives. They were not, however, focused on the world outside the factory, where the gendered dynamics of the work world reinforce the dominance of male managers over female employees, or on the class dynamics, where men from the cities were transferred in to take over management of the local and primarily rural workers. The authors were aware of all these societal realities, but they chose solutions that made modifications to the existing system rather than trying to overhaul it substantially. They were sensitive to the realities of the workers, but they were hired by the employer. The researchers collaborated with all of the stakeholders within the factory, but they were bound to come up with solutions that met with management's approval or else they would have been completely ineffective. This makes the project an excellent example of action research, but the research is not participatory in the meaning used in this chapter, nor is it activist.

Davidson and colleagues' (1997) example of the psychiatric patients could have been focused within the confines of the hospital and its programs, but instead the researchers' design and process allowed for changes on a societal level. The authors chose to take the perspective of the

Table 16.1   Comparison of Action Research and Participatory Research Approaches

	Action Research	*Participatory Research*
Starting place • Values • Beliefs • Assumptions	• *Critique of mainstream psychological research approaches* • *Change is necessary and positive* for efficient and effective environments • People within setting will have common interest in solving problems; consensus possible	• *Critique of mainstream psychological research approaches* • *Change is necessary and positive* to enable improvement of situation for oppressed groups • There will be conflict between those in power and those without power; empowerment and transformation necessary
Stance in research setting	• *Focus is on knowledge developed in the specific situation that requires change* • Problem solving to facilitate efficiency and effectiveness	• *Focus is on knowledge developed in the specific situation that requires change* • Strategies to increase equitable distribution of resources and enhance self-reliance of oppressed groups
Level of analysis	• Individual within the group (individual, interpersonal, group)	• Societal (community, social structures)
Participation/Collaboration	• Collaboration will improve longevity of change but is not necessary	• Participation of group most affected is critical
Research process	• Spiral process of data gathering, intervention, evaluation of effectiveness, and refocusing research plan	• No specific process recommended beyond real involvement of members of oppressed group

NOTE: Italicized items are those that approaches have in common.

SOURCE: Details and analysis of differences and similarities between the approaches are adapted from Brown and Tandon (1983).

people without power seriously. One might have presumed that the researchers, as clinicians internal to the hospital, would want to "balance" the views of the patients with the perspectives of the clinical staff members. However, they made it clear from the beginning of the project that they were going to take the patients' views as expertise about the problem and possible solutions. In other words, they assumed that the views of the two groups might be in conflict. In this example, the patients were not involved until the data-gathering stage, but that data gathering was done in a very open-ended nondirective way so as to maximize input. The patients were an integral part of the interpretation of the data and of the development and implementation of potential solutions. In fact, participation was expanded by including former patients (mental health consumers) during the latter parts of the process. This is great participatory research, but it is not action research because it does not have the cycles of intervention and evaluation that are necessary features as defined in this chapter.

We could imagine a continuum of action research and a continuum of participatory research where one end of each continuum is the "pure" form of research (if such a thing exists) that has all of the attributes of its method and none of the other method and where the other end is the place where projects that have only some of the features of the process fit. Those projects at the extreme end of the action research continuum (representing purity) would be the most different from projects at the extreme end of the participatory research continuum and would be clearly and easily distinguishable. However, for the majority of studies categorized as action or participatory research, the differences are much less clear and would fall somewhere along the two continua. Many successful studies borrow from both traditions, as you will see later.

In all of our discussions to this point, you have seen that the relationship between researchers and participants is not the kind described in your standard research methods course. But it is the kind of relationship that you could foster within your own communities, your own workplaces, and your own social and political action groups.

DIFFERENCES BETWEEN TRADITIONAL PSYCHOLOGICAL RESEARCH AND SOCIAL CHANGE RESEARCH

Table 16.1 compares the action research and participatory research approaches. The previous section discussed the *differences* between the two approaches. Now we examine the principles that the approaches have *in common*. These are the features that distinguish them both from mainstream psychological research. For example, both approaches begin with criticisms of traditional research approaches and translate into doing research differently (Wadsworth, 1998). What do you think some of the differences are between the various kinds of research covered in this chapter and the kind of research you are most used to reading about? (Think about this for a minute before you read on.)

One difference between mainstream research and social change research is that in most cases, researchers who are trying to effect social change are not relying on one of the underlying principles of **positivism** (the philosophy driving the standard research method, as detailed in Chapter 3), that is, "objectivity." This does not mean that researchers do not take a "scientific" approach; rather, it means that they are clear that their values and assumptions matter and do affect their take on the research. How could you want to change the world or any specific situation or environment and not have an idea of

what is wrong with it as it stands now or how you think it should change? This approach is in direct contrast to mainstream psychological research, where researchers are trained to attempt to be objective.

There are many critiques of the concept of objectivity in research (DuBois, 1983; Prilleltensky & Fox, 1997), but consensus among most social researchers is that objectivity is an impossible goal (Pyke & Agnew, 1991). Many community psychologists, feminist psychologists, and critical psychologists believe that the principle of objectivity hides support for the status quo. Who appears to be objective? Usually it is someone who shares our views or the views of the dominant culture. Biases are very obvious when someone is disagreeing with our point of view. On a social issue such as poverty, what would it mean to be objective? Could we ever be objective? Would we want to be? For this reason, social researchers with social change objectives, including feminist researchers across disciplines and critical psychologists, believe that the best way in which to proceed is to state their values and assumptions up front so that consumers of the research can judge for themselves the quality of the research and how it was influenced by values.

Another difference that comes out of critiques of mainstream research and the idea of objectivity is who we mean when we say "the researcher." Is it the same in research for social change as it is in other areas of social psychology? Not in most cases. In other social psychological research more generally including many applied domains, the researcher has an idea (often from shared activities/collaboration with other colleagues, reading, and/or making observations in daily life) and then plans and carries out the research on his or her own or with the help of research assistants (voluntary or paid) who are usually undergraduate or graduate students in psychology. And you will see examples of social change research that follow this pattern where the trained researcher approaches a group or an organization in the community with his or her idea. But much more commonly, the researcher is approached (or hired) by an employer or members of the community to start a research project that comes from ideas generated within that community or workplace. Sometimes the researcher himself or herself is a member of that social group and so has additional vested interest in the solution. In many cases in participatory research, the trained researcher is only one of many researchers because the research skills are passed on to the group or team.

Another difference from mainstream research is that research for social change is more concerned about **specificity** (i.e., knowing in-depth what the situation is for a group of people, and for people in similar circumstances, and how their position could be made better) rather than being concerned about **generalizability** (i.e., knowing enough to generalize to all people or to all communities). In Table 16.1, this commonality between action research and participatory research is described as a focus on developing knowledge in the particular situation. Brown and Tandon (1983) called it a focus on "useful knowledge." If you think about the two main examples you have read so far, the researchers would have had to take very different approaches to the questions or problems they began with if their intent was to generalize the results to all factory workers or to all psychiatric patients. If they had taken approaches that were more appropriate for generalizability, they would have been hampered in their ability to find solutions for these specific people in these specific locations. Of course, this is not to say that sometimes the results of a participatory or action research project are not helpful to another similar situation, just that the research was not focused on that goal.

Similarly, you may have noticed that this focus on specificity or on the local situation or context means that researchers do not tend to talk a lot about testing or developing social psychological theory. But neither is there a neglect of theory. Lewin, the parent of action research, argued strenuously both for a focus on useful knowledge *and* for the development and use of theory. He stressed that good theories are practical. Theories that can be used in specific social situations are critical to our work. Social change researchers do not get their ideas for how change could be implemented by pulling them "out of the air." They use their social psychological training and knowledge of theories of attitude and belief development, of social

cognition, of social behavior and behavior change, and of group decision making—among many other theories—to assist them. In the process, theories are often refined, discarded, or strengthened.

MOVING AWAY FROM STRICT DEFINITIONS: RESEARCH THAT INFLUENCES SOCIETY

This chapter has spent a fair amount of time describing action research, participatory research, and activist research so that you have a clear idea of what they are and are not. To people who have never been exposed to these kinds of approaches previously and who are taking an introductory course on the topic, being sure that the differences and similarities are understood is important. However, as is often the case in the world outside the university classroom, a focus on the goals of the research process is usually more important than the definitions themselves to the researchers who are doing the work. There are many ways in which to influence the world, and to change things for the better, that do not fit strictly into one definition or the other. Researchers do not worry about this so long as they can meet their goals for their projects. So, this section covers some examples of different types of change efforts organized by the type of change that each is trying to effect. These particular examples were chosen because they highlight the breadth of approaches to social change. There are many other excellent examples, but there is insufficient space to discuss all of them here.

Influencing Policy Directly

Policies are plans and procedures that governments have for specific issues to ensure that certain overall goals can be met (Merriam–Webster, 2003). It is not unusual for researchers to want to influence social policy. Many researchers have press conferences or send reports of their findings to government offices in the hope that decision makers will take them into account. Some government officials peruse the scholarly literature for assistance with policy problems. During times of openness to the social sciences (this fluctuates quite dramatically over time), researchers are even hired by the government to study problems or test possible solutions. But there are many times when social scientists watch in horror as governments and government officials make policy decisions that fly in the face of the empirical literature. For example, Jeremy Travis, former director of the National Institute of Justice within the U.S. Department of Justice, summarized the social science research on crime deterrence. In a speech to the United Nations, he pointed out that decision makers, in attempting to deter crime, have consistently moved to increase the "severity of punishment" when in fact research shows that changing the "certainty of punishment" is more effective (Travis, 1995, p. 1). Another good example of policies that were not based on empirical evidence is found in the Canadian laws surrounding pornography. Until the early 1990s, Canadian law focused on the sexual explicitness of images. Decisions about what materials to prohibit or restrict were made on this basis even though there was no scientific evidence that explicitness was harmful. It was not until a Canadian Supreme Court decision, *R. v. Butler* (1992), that lawmakers took the views of social scientists into account and began to focus on content that had been empirically demonstrated to be harmful (e.g., representations of violence, degradation and/or dehumanization of persons). Representations of adult sexuality without these qualities, no matter how explicit, are now protected under Canadian law.

Although they may want to influence social policy, it is unusual for researchers to directly attempt to do so. A study by Jason and Rose (1984) is an example of this rare approach. First, you need some background. Strict seat belt laws in Canada have resulted in 90% compliance by citizens. Legislators across states in the United States have been much less consistent in their application of regulations, resulting in only 70% compliance (American College of Emergency Physicians, 2001). Child restraint legislation (i.e., mandatory use of car seats) came much later historically, with both countries having abysmal records of correct car seat use. Yet there is incontrovertible evidence that many children's lives would be saved by the correct use of car seats.

Many states did not have child restraint legislation when Jason and Rose began their investigation. Illinois had already defeated a law once, and the issue was coming up again. Jason and Rose planned an experiment to test whether provision of scientific information about the issue would influence the state senators who would be voting on the new Illinois legislation on child restraints. The experimental study used personally addressed letters containing empirical and technical information about child restraints. The information in the letters came from two studies that the authors had conducted: an observational study set up at intersections in several states to examine the use of car seats with children under 5 years of age (very low levels of correct restraints were observed) and a survey of attitudes toward the bill being put forward (nearly 80% of citizens would support the law). Half of the state senators were selected at random to receive the letter. The vote in the Illinois Senate was recorded. Significantly more of the senators who had received the letter voted in favor of the bill (79%) than did senators who had not received it (53%). The bill, which had been narrowly defeated during the previous round, was supported and became law.

Researchers who do their work in the world outside of the university have to be even more careful in their consideration of the ethical implications of their research. Among many other ethical issues, they must push themselves harder to consider the ramifications of doing the research versus not doing it. They must decide between carrying out their studies in the best way possible from a research standpoint (and thereby increasing the validity of the findings but perhaps risking some adverse consequences) versus doing it in a less controlled way (and thereby losing the ability to be sure about the cause of the result). These decisions are always important to researchers, but applied social psychologists' decisions may have more impact on society. The authors of the child restraint study pointed out that they took a risk by carrying out an experiment in this situation because many children's lives were at stake. If the support for car seats had not been so high to begin with, sending the letters to only half of the senators was a risk that probably should not have been taken. The random assignment of senators to conditions was a necessary feature of an experimental design that could test the effect of the letters on subsequent voting behavior. Now that we know that letters of this type can make a difference, would you insist on random assignment on the next issue? Why or why not? You may want to bring up this issue in class to get the views of your classmates and professor. Ethical decisions are always about balancing risks and benefits. There are no easy answers.

When we look at this study, we can see that it was definitely attempting to change social policy, in this case child restraint legislation, but by our definitions was it action research, participatory research, or activist research? Think about this for a minute before you read on.

The researchers used multiple methods to approach their topic: an observational study to examine how children were currently being restrained, a survey of public attitudes toward the legislation, and an experiment. But was there a cycle of planning with fact finding, intervention, and evaluation? If you were going to argue that it was action research, you would need to identify the specific components that match the action research framework. Because there was only a single cycle of intervention, this is *not* an example of action research. You might now ask yourself how you could change this study to make it action research. (Again, take a minute to think about this before you read on.) If the researchers now proceeded to other phases of the project, adding new components beyond the letters to try to influence senators in other states and evaluating those interventions, the project would fit the action research framework. Is the research participatory? No. The parents and/or children were not involved in the research in any substantive way beyond being observed or giving their opinions in a survey developed by the researchers. Neither were the state senators involved in the project except as the targets or recipients of the experimental intervention. Is this activist research? Yes. The researchers had strongly held beliefs from the outset that child restraint legislation would save lives, and they designed a series of studies to help change existing laws for the better.

Another researcher who has attempted to change policy, in this case policy on a community level rather than on a governmental level, is David Riley with his work on "latchkey" children, that is, children who are left at home unsupervised for some part of the day. Riley (1997) described the transition in his career from the standard university researcher to someone who "gives psychology away." Although there is some evidence in the research literature that having more responsibility can provide children with opportunities to grow in positive ways, other research suggests that young children left unsupervised can be plagued by fears or can develop increased dependence on drugs, alcohol, and/or cigarettes during their teenage years. When Riley first began thinking about this, he used public lectures, radio shows, and press releases to raise public awareness about the prevalence of latchkey situations and the risks of this lack of supervision for the children. He described all of these efforts as having had "zero effect" (p. 425). People in the communities where the reports were publicized dismissed Riley's work because they felt that it did not apply to them in their towns or cities. Riley doubted that this was the case, but he took some time to understand that these people from the general public might have a point. He stated, "At the time, I did not realize that they were voicing a cogent methodological critique: They were questioning the external validity of the research I cited" (p. 425). When Riley finally listened, he suggested that they (the researcher along with people from the community) do research in those communities to see whether the issue of latchkey children was or was not a problem. As a result, he embarked on 10 years of mainly successful studies and interventions.

This is an example of research that affects local nongovernmental policy. This type of policy develops when communities and organizations choose a plan of action to help them make future decisions (Merriam–Webster, 2003). In each community, a planning committee made up of teachers, parents, and men and women from the business community was created. With Riley's assistance, the planning committee developed and administered a mail survey of parents of school children up to the sixth grade. The survey asked the parents about situations in which the children were left without adult supervision and about the safety knowledge possessed by their children (e.g., whether they know about fire safety). A report was written describing the results, including direct quotes from these local surveys. This report was then presented to the broader community in a variety of ways, and the community planning committee almost always took action.

An immediate outcome of the pilot survey in the first community studied was the number of parents who called their local schools to ask about the types of safety and self-care information that their children were receiving. From this, the researchers (Riley and the community planning committee) realized that the survey itself was an intervention that produced change. As a result, the research projects in all subsequent communities were changed to survey *all* parents of children of a particular age rather than a selected sample of parents.

Riley agreed to help other communities set up similar projects in the state. His own involvement became less and less as the number of communities involved increased. Riley described this as an accidental (it began due to his being overwhelmed by the workload) but empowering component of the research. The expert status of the researcher was undermined, and the communities themselves "owned" their research and the research process.

Riley evaluated the effectiveness of the actions taken within the project. He found that the local planning committees felt obliged to act on their own reports and that many changes resulted. Long- and short-term changes in the communities over a 7-year period included new jobs (e.g., new businesses related to child care needs) and new school-age children's programs, with thousands of children being served. The project has been replicated in another 12 states, and in many communities within those states, being carried out by other researchers and community planning committee members who obtained the needs assessment materials from Riley. Calculating the impact by multiplying the effects by the number of communities shows us how a simple participatory approach can support major community and social policy change around an issue. Without the community planning groups, whose members tailored the project for their own communities, would people have listened to the results? Riley maintained that they would not listen. Before you go on,

make sure that you can identify whether or not this study has action research or activist components.[2]

Influencing Society by Changing Structural or Social Barriers

Researchers have tried to change society by going into the communities where injustice exists (entering groups of people who are disadvantaged by common identities/experiences) and developing research projects whose aims are to overcome structural or social barriers. Sometimes this is done by empowering the social group or facilitating its members' social action in some way. This is not to imply that the groups "need" research to take action. Many groups are already active before they meet the researchers. In all cases, however, the research projects provide something additional, usually expertise or skills training to gather data required to strengthen community positions or demands. In other situations, researchers must try to influence society at a more basic level by giving voice to people, a point of view, or a perspective that has not been heard. Other times, researchers try to change long-standing attitudes in communities. In many of these situations where researchers try to make long-term changes, they must use a research process that is a hybrid of the types of research discussed up to this point in the chapter. The following subsections discuss three very different examples to show how the research process can work for larger scale social change.

Overcoming physical barriers. Mary Brydon-Miller has been involved in a number of participatory projects on diverse issues. The example focused on here is her work in the community of people with physical disabilities in western Massachusetts (Brydon-Miller, 1993). The members of this community had long been involved in the independent living movement (active all over North America), working for autonomy and control for persons with disabilities. In this instance, the group, which was based in the Independent Living Center, asked for Brydon-Miller's help in identifying the accessibility needs of people with physical disabilities and in assessing the best routes for their advocacy to take. Brydon-Miller had a number of objectives for the project that built on the group's existing strengths. She wanted to ensure that the members of the group had sufficient skill and information to engage in productive self-advocacy, that people in the community understood the specific problems related to accessibility, and that the design and implementation of advocacy actions matched the consensus understanding of the disabled community in that area. Brydon-Miller also had "more process-oriented objectives," including a desire to ensure that members of the disabled community saw themselves as "experts in the field of disability" (p. 127) and that they had ownership of the research and advocacy that resulted. She also wanted to demonstrate that advocacy, and particularly self-advocacy, was an effective tool for social change. That is quite a laundry list of objectives and gives you a sense of the breadth of goals that a study can have.

Brydon-Miller used face-to-face interviews as a first step not only to identify information about "accessibility-related concerns" and "strategies for dealing with inaccessible environments" (p. 128) but also to encourage participants to reflect on their own experiences in more detail. She conducted all of the interviews. She then summarized these interviews and presented the summary at a workshop at the center. Prior to this meeting, Brydon-Miller believed that the most useful action to take would be to organize a large-scale conference with policymakers and politicians. The participants at the workshop had very different views and were not at all interested in her idea. Many new issues and possible solutions were identified, and a different advocacy project was chosen. The participants wanted to work toward greater accessibility of a local shopping mall (a project idea that disturbed the researcher at first because she dislikes malls). A committee was created and named itself the Community Accessibility Committee.

The first research action taken was to investigate (through observation) the current state of accessibility of the mall. Then discussions were held about possible strategies and tactics to overcome the many barriers to accessibility that had been identified. Suggestions ranged from a protest outside the mall during the Christmas shopping season to writing to the mall executives. Letter writing had been attempted in the past by the center staff members and had been unsuccessful. However, it was eventually decided that writing a detailed letter with all of the relevant details from the mall survey would be more appropriate. Not much happened as a result of that first letter, but the group did not give up. The group followed up with a complaint submitted to the Architectural Barriers Board. Five years later, after extensive negotiation and a number of court battles, all requested changes to the mall were made, including an elevator to the second floor, providing full accessibility to those in wheelchairs. The committee has continued its work on other sites of inaccessibility in the community since that achievement.

The researcher initiated the research based on her knowledge of the community, carried out the early phases of the research, and did all report writing. All other aspects of the research process and advocacy were shared between Brydon-Miller and the committee. There is a strong activist focus to the entire project. In this example, action research cycles of planning, implementation, and evaluation were carried out by the researcher and the committee within a fully participatory process that culminated in social action and social change.

Overcoming social barriers: Giving voice and making change. Sometimes the kinds of changes that are needed in a society are more basic; changes are needed to the very fabric of the society. As you can imagine, changes such as these take considerable time, but research can play a role in making them occur. Since 1983, Mary Brinton Lykes has been involved in a number of projects in Guatemala with the Mayan people, particularly (but not exclusively) with women and children (Brinton Lykes, 1997). Guatemala had been at war for 36 years when her 1997 article was written. This war, similar to those in other countries around the world, is based on conflicts between a military-backed government that "defend(s) gross inequities in the distribution of economic resources within the country" (p. 727) and popular revolutionary forces. Violence has been a constant reality for the people of Guatemala, creating a state of "normal abnormality"

(Martin-Baró, 1989) or "terror as usual" (Taussig, 1986–1987). At the same time, the people are prohibited, through fear and social convention, from speaking of their experiences and trauma. A number of the projects in which Brinton Lykes has been involved have focused on giving voice to these children and adults, thereby breaking the silence in the community. One of these projects was developed over a period of years of reflection and trial and error with local workers in child care, education, and health care settings "to accompany child survivors and develop a firmer knowledge base from which to make meaning of children's experiences of war and its effects" (Brinton Lykes, 1997, p. 729). Workshops were held in which theater, art, music, and movement were used as resources to encourage play (which is often suppressed in child victims) and the expression of feelings, thoughts, and anxieties. The artwork and stories produced by the children were used directly to help children understand themselves and their peers and to help the professionals involved with those particular children to base their interventions on relevant information (individual-level changes). When this artwork was displayed in the local community along with other educational media (e.g., pamphlets, dramatization), it also helped other professionals and community members to educate themselves about children's lives in the community more generally and to create new ways of dealing with the trauma of war in the communities (a societal intervention). For example, a health educator who was involved in the project said,

> Based on my observation, I believe that it is necessary that the children know what has happened to their parents, [and] how and why, especially because the children themselves are asking. I realize that it may not be something that we want them to know. However, we, as mature people, should speak the truth. It would be unjust for us to invent a false history in order to provide the explanations. We must tell the truth, for it is the truth the children seek. (quoted on p. 731)

On a very different scale, a project was begun to develop and deliver resources to young people across four countries—Guatemala, Argentina,

Chile, and El Salvador—that had been similarly ravaged by war. This was an extremely challenging task because there were many differences as well as similarities in the experiences of grief and loss within these different cultures. But because of the data gathered from the research, the interventions that were developed were able to take cultural and community specificity into account. For example, rituals and other attempts at providing healing communities in Chile and Argentina had to be focused around mourning of individual family members because that was what was discovered to be crucial in the children's stories. A program in Guatemala would have to take into account the grief over loss of clothing, in addition to loss of family members, houses, animals, and land, because clothing plays a significant part in the conception of self in that community.

The participatory aspects of this project were, in this case, not with the minor children themselves but rather with the many workers in the community who were with the children every day. However, the children themselves were an integral part of the workshop process, which was driven by their actions. The education of all involved—children, adults, and researchers—was also evident. The ongoing nature of the project, with multiple cycles of reflection and trial and error, also suggests that an action research process may have been approximated, although it is not clear whether this was the original intention of the researcher. Given the goals of the study to give voice to the traumatized and to change the way in which a community was dealing with the effects of war, the project is activist.

Overcoming social barriers: Changing prejudicial attitudes and stereotypes. Sometimes it is easy to distance ourselves from the examples from the Two-Thirds World, believing that social change is not so necessary here in North America. A Canadian example of a 40-year project that has addressed this need for change is the work of Wallace E. Lambert at McGill University (Lambert, 1992). Lambert and his colleagues have been attempting to influence attitudes and stereotypes toward French Canadians and bilingualism in an increasingly multicultural Canada. Beginning with experimental studies involving audiotapes of bilingual Canadians speaking in either French or English, the research documented much less favorable impressions of persons speaking French than of persons speaking English. The most surprising finding was that this bias existed in samples of French Canadian participants as well, demonstrating an in-group prejudice. The authors of the study were dismayed when the media and other colleagues interpreted these results in ways that supported the status quo rather than challenging it (e.g., as proof of French inferiority, as proof that English dominance had created "losers"). Three decades later, a replication by Genesee and Holobow (1989) demonstrated no change in the phenomena. Lambert (1992) concluded that focusing research on a social question does not ensure social change.

Lambert continued doing research to dissect the workings of prejudice in this context and to identify possible solutions. Lambert suggested that his work with English Canadian parents in developing and initiating "immersion education" in the schools has had the most impact (on social change) of all his work. English-speaking students were taught in French by French teachers nearly exclusively for the first 3 years of their schooling. Parents were actively involved in pushing for these program developments. The researchers helped to design the program and then evaluated its effects over time. They were able to demonstrate the efficacy of this model of education to facilitate bilingualism without damaging children's skills in other areas. Perhaps more important for Lambert and his colleagues, the students not only became fluently bilingual but also resisted prejudice and became open to the benefits of other languages and cultures.

The idea spread, and many other schools across Canada, as well as in the United States and Europe, have adopted similar educational programs. But as Lambert (1992) pointed out, "The tolerance and appreciation ran the risk of being one way, not mutual" (p. 537). He followed this study with investigations of parenting differences between French Canadian and English Canadian parents. There were no differences on the basis of language. Only social class, sex of the child, and sex of the parent were related to differences in parenting styles. He then moved to thinking about education for the children of minority languages. With his colleagues Cazabon and Hall, Lambert has been continuing his work with experiments in "two-way bilingual immersion," where equal numbers of students with different home languages (e.g., English and Spanish) spend half of the day being taught in one language by English-speaking teachers and the other half of the day being taught by Spanish-speaking teachers. Lambert reported that the results look very promising both for these children and for the possibility of truly democratic, multicultural, and multilingual societies. His research with colleagues over many years continues to examine attitudes of parents (both majority and minority groups) toward bilingualism, the protection of home cultures, and the benefits of multiculturalism.

One part of the research program just outlined had participatory components. The study that launched immersion programs in the schools could not have been successful without the intense involvement of English-speaking Canadian parents who wanted a bilingual future for their children. Most of Lambert's other studies use laboratory or survey methods in which students or other citizens provide data in the more standard way. So, this research project as a whole is not participatory research. The research program does provide an interesting example of something that did not *start out* being action research but that, in retrospect over 40 years of work, *is* action research. After each study, the researcher, his colleagues, and students adjusted their views and perspectives, thought about the problem in a different way, and implemented another phase of the research to address the new concerns. Would you classify the research program (or any individual study within that program) as being activist? Why or why not?[3]

DIFFICULTIES AND LIMITATIONS OF RESEARCH FOR SOCIAL CHANGE

As you may have noticed in these examples of action, participatory, and activist research, the timelines for the research are often very long— from several years to decades. This is not research for the fickle or for those with attention span problems. Any researchers who take on these projects must have an enduring commitment. Because social problems often develop across many years, the attempts to intervene and change things cannot be accomplished overnight. However, although the projects are slow, they are often very effective. But the very features of the research that make it more productive (e.g., participation of the groups involved, multiple cycles of planning, data gathering, interpretation) also make it a slow process. It is possible for an action research design within a factory to be carried out in a shorter time frame, but any study involving in-depth voluntary community participation will necessarily take much longer. If you are considering doing a project like this for your fourth-year undergraduate research, you could consider it only if you were already very involved with a community group or workplace or if your adviser invited you to take part in an ongoing project. However, if you are considering a graduate education and/or a job in a community organization or business, you could consider participatory or action research.

Another potential pitfall of social change research is again created by the decisions you have made to involve others who are experts in their own experiences. When you are doing a research project in an academic setting with undergraduate students, the only limits are your ideas, the ethical guidelines of your profession, and any timelines that may be imposed by your education or career. When you are doing a research project in an applied setting, you add the complications of: changing administration within the organization and other workplace realities such as new contract negotiations, new government policies being implemented, turnover on the board of directors, and staff members or volunteers who were integral to your project being transferred or leaving town. And then there is always the unexpected—plagues, floods, pestilence, and so forth. Well, this might be a slight exaggeration, but even these latter problems are not out of the question in some places around the world where you might have research and humanitarian interests.

In social change research, you are taking a stand not only as a researcher but also as a human. You are standing up for something you believe in. This means that if things go wrong, not only your professional ego but perhaps also your personal emotional well-being will suffer. Doing "passionate scholarship" makes you more effective but also more vulnerable. But these are risks worth taking, as the researchers who you have read about would tell you.

SUMMARY

This chapter has discussed a number of different kinds of research that attempt to make a difference in the world. You may have noticed that there is not one way in which to do this, nor is there one research method or process that is required. Change can be created out of all the research methods and tools you have read about in this book, including experiments, surveys, interviews, focus groups, and workshops. Change efforts are based on a range of social psychological theories. Researchers who work in universities, hospitals, and community groups, as well as consultants, can work toward change. And people who are in the most powerful positions (e.g., state senators, managers) as well as those in the least powerful positions (e.g., physically disabled citizens, mental health consumers) can play a part in transforming their workplaces, services, and communities. In fact, you could take the lessons you have learned from this book and, with some guidance from books and articles on the process and perhaps from a more experienced researcher, take on a project in your community that matters to you now.

Many psychologists, including presidents of the American Psychological Association, have called on psychology to give more of its work away. George Miller stated, "We should have contributed more" than we have contributed (Miller, 1969). During more recent years, people still bemoan the difficulty in translating psychological knowledge into knowledge that can be used by governments, communities, and individuals. All of applied social psychological research tries to do just that. Action, participatory, and activist research aims to make social change directly, and this makes it more likely to be useful.

NOTES

1. First, action research's stages of fact finding, goal identification, and research planning are similar to the problem-posing activities conducted in participatory research at the "investigation" stage. But Lewin's plan does not *require* that this be a social or group process, whereas Maguire's plan does. Second, research planning in the action research model is where decisions are made about possible explanations for the problem (based on fact finding and the results of action steps), and so this again is in some ways similar to what is accomplished at the "education" stage of participatory research. However, it is different in *how* it is accomplished. In participatory research, this is a fully collaborative project accomplished within the group. In action research, it is something that could be accomplished by a researcher or researchers with or without collaboration from people in the setting, although it would be better to have cooperation of the people in the situation. Third, both research processes have action/change goals. Participatory research requires that the action be taken by the people most involved and that the action be aimed at long-term change as well, whereas action research does not require this.

2. A pilot survey of parents was carried out in a single community, and the researchers evaluated the survey and changed their research plan based on the findings. They discovered that the tool they were using to gather data was actually an effective intervention. They expanded the survey to all parents instead of sampling from among the parents, thereby adding an intervention and increasing the impact of their overall project. They also gathered data from each community, fed back that data to the community in multiple ways, and then based their actions on the specific findings. This research fits the action research process framework even though the researcher did not use these words to describe his project. The project is also activist because the researcher was acting in the interests of children who could not speak for themselves and was firmly on one side of the issue.

3. Lambert's research program is activist research because it was carried out on behalf of a language minority.

REFERENCES

Abela, J. R., & D'Alessandro, D. U. (2001). An examination of the symptom component of the hopelessness theory of depression in a sample of schoolchildren. *Journal of Cognitive Psychotherapy, 15,* 33–48.

Abela, J. R. Z., & Payne, A. V. L. (2003). A test of the integration of the hopelessness and self-esteem theories of depression in schoolchildren. *Cognitive Therapy and Research, 27,* 519–535.

Abelson, R. P., Aronson, E., McGuire, W. J., Newcomb, T. M., Rosenberg, M. J., & Tannenbaum, P. H. (Eds.). (1968). *Theories of cognitive consistency: A sourcebook.* Chicago: Rand McNally.

Abramson, L. Y., Seligman, M. E., & Teasdale, J. D. (1978). Learned helplessness in humans: Critique and reformulation. *Journal of Abnormal Psychology, 87,* 102–109.

Adams, J. S. (1965). Inequity in social exchange. In L. Berkowitz (Ed.), *Advances in experimental psychology* (Vol. 2, pp. 267–299). New York: Academic Press.

Adler, N. E., Boyce, T., Chesney, M. A., Cohen, S., Folkman, S., Kahn, R. L., & Syme, S. L. (1994). Socioeconomic status and health: The challenge of the gradient. *American Psychologist, 49,* 15–24.

Ainsworth, M. D., Blehar, S. D., Waters, E., & Wall, S. (1978). *Patterns of attachment.* Hillsdale, NJ: Lawrence Erlbaum.

Ajzen, I. (1991). The theory of planned behavior. *Organizational Behavior and Human Decision Processes, 50,* 179–211.

Ajzen, I. (1998). Models of human social behavior and their application to health psychology. *Psychology and Health, 13,* 735–739.

Ajzen, I., & Fishbein, M. (1977). Attitude–behavior relations: A theoretical analysis and review of the literature. *Psychological Bulletin, 84,* 888–918.

Akehurst, L., & Virj, A. (1999). Creating suspects in police interviews. *Journal of Applied Social Psychology, 29,* 192–210.

Alinsky, S. (1971). *Rules for radicals.* New York: Random House.

Allen, M., D'Alessio, D., Emmers, T. M., & Gebhardt, L. (1996). The role of educational briefings in mitigating effects of experimental exposure to violent sexually explicit material: A meta-analysis. *Journal of Sex Research, 33,* 135–141.

Allen, V. L., & Wilder, D. A. (1975). Categorization, belief similarity, and intergroup discrimination. *Journal of Personality and Social Psychology, 32,* 971–977.

Alloy, L. B., & Clements, C. M. (1998). Hopelessness theory of depression: Tests of the symptom component. *Cognitive Therapy and Research, 22,* 303–335.

Allport, G. W. (1954). *The nature of prejudice.* Reading, MA: Addison–Wesley.

Amabile, T. M. (1983). The social psychology of creativity. *Journal of Personality and Social Psychology, 45,* 357–376.

Amabile, T., Hennessey, B. A., & Grossman, B. (1987, April). *Immunizing children against the negative effects of reward.* Paper presented at the biennial meeting of the Society for Research in Child Development, Baltimore, MD.

Ambrose, M. L., & Kulik, C. T. (1999). Old friends, new faces: Motivation research in the 1990s. *Journal of Management, 25,* 231–292.

American College of Emergency Physicians. (2001). NHTSA update on safety belt effectiveness; crowded emergency departments urged to prepare for mass casualty incidents. *Annals News Releases.* Retrieved October 17, 2004, from www.acep.org/1,2727,0.html

American Psychiatric Association. (1994). *Diagnostic and statistical manual of mental disorders* (4th ed.). Washington, DC: Author.

American Psychological Association. (2002*). The ethical principles of psychologists and code of conduct.* Washington, DC: Author.

American Psychological Association Committee on Accreditation. (2000). *Guidelines and principles for accreditation of programs in professional psychology.* Retrieved April 29, 2004, from www.apa.org/ed/gp2000.html

Anderson, C. A., & Bushman, B. J. (2002). Human aggression. *Annual Review of Psychology, 53,* 27–51.

Anderson, C. A., & Dill, K. E. (2000). Video games and aggressive thoughts, feelings, and behavior in the laboratory and in life. *Journal of Personality and Social Psychology, 78,* 772–790.

Andrews, D. A., & Bonta, J. (2003). *The psychology of criminal conduct* (3rd ed.). Cincinnati, OH: Anderson.

Andrews, D. A., Leschied, A. W., & Hoge, R. D. (1992). *The prediction and assessment of youth at risk: A social psychological approach.* Toronto: Ministry of Community and Social Services.

Ansolabehere, S., & Iyengar, S. (1996). *Going negative: How political advertisements shrink and polarize the electorate.* New York: Free Press.

Apple, K. S. (1993). *The antecedents and consequences of multidimensional cohesion throughout an intercollegiate baseball season.* Unpublished master's thesis, Purdue University.

Argote, L., Seabright, M. A., & Dyer, L. (1986). Individual versus group use of base-rate and individuating information. *Organizational Behavior and Human Decision Processes, 38,* 65–75.

Armstrong, J. (2002, December 14). Teen's dying cries went unanswered. *The Globe and Mail,* p. A6.

Aronson, E. (1968). Dissonance theory: Progress and problems. In R. P. Abelson, E. Aronson, E. (1999b). *The social animal* (8th ed.). New York: Freeman.

Aronson, E. (1992). Stateways can change folkways. In R. Baird & S. Rosenbaum (Eds.), *Bigotry, prejudice, and hatred: Definitions, causes, and solutions* (pp. 185–201). Buffalo, NY: Prometheus Books.

Aronson, E. (1999). Dissonance, hypocrisy, and the self-concept. In E. Harmon-Jones & J. Mills (Eds.), *Cognitive dissonance: Progress on a pivotal theory in social psychology* (pp. 103–126). Washington, DC: American Psychological Association.

Aronson, E. (2002). Building empathy, compassion, and achievement in the jigsaw classroom. In J. Aronson (Ed.), *Improving academic achievement: Impact of psychological factors on education* (pp. 209–225). San Diego: Academic Press.

Aronson, E., Fried, C., & Stone, J. (1991). Overcoming denial and increasing the intention to use condoms through the induction of hypocrisy. *American Journal of Public Health, 81,* 1636–1638.

Aronson, E., & Mills, J. (1959). The effect of severity of initiation on liking for a group. *Journal of Abnormal and Social Psychology, 59,* 177–181.

Aronson, E., & O'Leary, M. (1977). The relative effectiveness of models and prompts on energy conservation: A field experiment in a shower room. *Journal of Environmental Systems, 12,* 219–224.

Aronson, E., Stephan, C., Sikes, J., Blaney, N., & Snapp, M. (1978). *The jigsaw classroom.* Beverly Hills, CA: Sage.

Aronson, W. J. McGuire, T. M. Newcomb, M. J. Rosenberg, & P. H. Tannenbaum (Eds.), *Theories of cognitive consistency: A sourcebook* (pp. 5–27). Chicago: Rand McNally.

Arvey, R. D., Bouchard, T. J., Segal, N. L., & Abraham, L. M. (1989). Job satisfaction: Environmental and genetic components. *Journal of Applied Psychology, 74,* 187–192.

Asch, S. E. (1946). Forming impressions of personality. *Journal of Abnormal and Social Psychology, 41,* 258–290.

Asch, S. E. (1951). Effects of group pressure upon modification and distortion of judgements. In H. Guetzkow (Ed.), *Groups, leadership, and men.* Pittsburgh, PA: Carnegie Press.

Asch, S. E. (1955). Opinions and social pressure. *Scientific American, 193*(5), 31–35.

Asch, S. (1956). Studies of independence and conformity: A minority of one against a unanimous majority. *Psychological Monographs, 70,* 416.

Asp, E., & Garbarino, J. (1988). Integrative processes at school and in the community. In T. D. Yawkey & J. E. Johnson (Eds.), *Integrative processes and socialization: Early to middle childhood* (pp. 167–183). Hillsdale, NJ: Lawrence Erlbaum.

Atlas, R. (1989). Reducing the opportunity for inmate suicide: A design guide. *Psychiatric Quarterly, 60,* 161–171.

Attorney General's Commission on Pornography. (1986). *Attorney General's Commission on Pornography: Final report.* Washington, DC: U.S. Department of Justice.

Auvinen, J., & Nafziger, E. W. (1999). The sources of humanitarian emergencies. *Journal of Conflict Resolution, 43,* 267–290.

Axsom, D. (1989). Cognitive dissonance and behavior change in psychotherapy. *Journal of Experimental Social Psychology, 25,* 234–252.

Axsom, D., & Cooper, J. (1985). Cognitive dissonance and psychotherapy: The role of effort justification in inducing weight loss. *Journal of Experimental Social Psychology, 21,* 149–160.

Azjen, I. (1991). The theory of planned behavior. *Organizational Behavior and Human Decision Processes, 50,* 179–211.

Babad, E. (1993). Pygmalion: 25 years after interpersonal expectations in the classroom. In P. D. Blanck (Ed.), *Interpersonal expectations: Theory, research, and applications* (pp. 125–153). New York: Cambridge University Press.

Babbie, E., & Benaquisto, L. (2002). *Fundamentals of social research.* Toronto: Thomson–Nelson Canada.

Bales, R. F. (1950). *Interaction process analysis.* Reading, MA: Addison–Wesley.

Baltes, B. B., Marcus, W. D., Sherman, M. P., Bauer, C. C., & LaGanke, J. S. (2002). Computer-mediated communication and group decision making: A meta-analysis. *Organizational Behavior and Human Decision Processes, 87,* 156–179.

Bandura, A. (1965). Influence of models' reinforcement contingencies on the acquisition of imitative responses. *Journal of Personality and Social Psychology, 1,* 589–595.

Bandura, A. (1977a). Self-efficacy: Toward a unifying theory of behavioral change. *Psychological Review, 84,* 191–215.

Bandura, A. (1977b). *Social learning theory.* Englewood Cliffs, NJ: Prentice Hall.

Bandura, A. (1983). Psychological mechanisms of aggression. In R. G. Geen & E. I. Donnerstein (Eds.), *Aggression: Theoretical and empirical reviews,* Vol. 1: *Theoretical and methodological issues* (pp. 1–40). New York: Academic Press.

Bandura, A. (1986). *Social foundations of thought and action: A social cognitive theory.* Englewood Cliffs, NJ: Prentice Hall.

Bandura, A. (1997). *Self-efficacy: The exercise of control.* New York: Freeman.

Bandura, A. (2001). Social cognitive theory of mass communication. *Media Psychology, 3,* 265–299.

Bandura, A., Ross, D., & Ross, S. A. (1963). Imitation of film-mediated aggressive models. *Journal of Abnormal and Social Psychology, 66,* 3–11.

Bandura, A., & Walters, R. H. (1963). *Social learning and personality development.* New York: Holt, Rinehart & Winston.

Barak, A., & Fisher, W. A. (1989). Counselor and therapist gender bias? More questions than answers. *Professional Psychology: Research and Practice, 20,* 377–383.

Barbopoulos, A., Fisharah, F., Clark, J., & El-Khatib, A. (2002). Comparison of Egyptian and Canadian children on a picture apperception test. *Cultural Diversity and Ethnic Minority Psychology, 8,* 395–403.

Barker, R. G. (1968). *Ecological psychology: Concepts and methods for studying the environment of human behavior.* Stanford, CA: Stanford University Press.

Barnard, N., & Kursban, M. (2002, August 4). Why fast-food lawsuit is good news. *Physicians Committee for Responsible Medicine Commentary.* Retrieved March 26, 2003, from www.pcrm.org/health/commentary/commentary020804.html

Baron, D. A., & Byrne, D. (2000). *Social psychology* (9th ed.). Boston: Allyn & Bacon.

Baron, R. M. (1984, August). *A social-psychological perspective on environmental issues.* Paper presented at the annual meeting of the American Psychological Association, Toronto.

Baron, R. M., & Fisher, J. D. (1984). The equity-control model of vandalism: A refinement. In C. Levy-Leboyer (Ed.), *Vandalism: Behavior and motivations.* Amsterdam: North Holland.

Bartholomew, K. (1990). Avoidance of intimacy: An attachment perspective. *Journal of Personal and Social Relationships, 7,* 147–178.

Baumeister, R. F., & Scher, S. J. (1988). Self-defeating behavior patterns among normal individuals: Review and analysis of common self-destructive tendencies. *Psychological Bulletin, 104,* 3–22.

Beal, A. C., Ausiello, J., & Perrin, J. M. (2001). Social influences on health-risk behaviors among minority middle school students. *Journal of Adolescent Health, 28,* 474–480.

Beaman, A. L., Barnes, P. J., Klentz, B., & McQuirk, B. (1978). Increasing helping rates through information dissemination: Teaching pays. *Personality and Social Psychology Bulletin, 4,* 406–411.

Beck, A. T. (1976). *Cognitive therapy and the emotional disorders.* New York: International Universities Press.

Beck, A., & Katcher, A. (1996). *Between pets and people.* West Lafayette, IN: Purdue University Press.

Beck, B. L., Koons, S. R., & Milgrim, D. L. (2000). Correlates and consequences of behavioral procrastination: The effects of academic procrastination, self-consciousness, self-esteem, and self-handicapping. *Journal of Social Behavior and Personality, 15*(5), 3–13.

Behr, R. L., & Iyengar, S. (1985). Television news, real-world cues, and changes in the public agenda. *Public Opinion Quarterly, 49,* 38–57.

Bell, J., Fisher, W., & Loomis, B. (1978). *Environmental psychology.* Philadelphia: W. B. Saunders.

Bem, D. J. (1972). Self-perception theory. In L. Berkowitz (Ed.), *Advances in experimental social psychology* (Vol. 6, pp. 1–62). New York: Academic Press.

Benjamin, L. T., Jr., & Crouse, E. M. (2002). The American Psychological Association's response to *Brown v. Board of Education. American Psychologist, 57,* 38–50.

Bennett, W. W., & Hess, K. M. (2001). *Criminal investigation.* Belmont, CA: Wadsworth.

Bennington, A. J., Shetler, J. C., & Shaw, T. (2003). Negotiating order in interorganizational communication: Discourse analysis of a meeting of three diverse organizations. *Journal of Business Communication, 40,* 118–143.

Benokraitis, N. V., & Feagin, J. R. (1995). *Modern sexism: Blatant, subtle, and covert discrimination* (2nd ed.). Upper Saddle River, NJ: Prentice Hall.

Benson, E. (2003). Psychology and the prison system: Rehabilitate or punish? *APA Monitor, 34*(7), 46–47. (American Psychological Association)

Berglas, S., & Jones, E. E. (1978). Drug choice as a self-handicapping strategy in response to noncontingent success. *Journal of Personality and Social Psychology, 36,* 405–417.

Berkowitz, A. (2003, January). *The social norms approach: Theory, research, and annotated bibliography.* Retrieved April 29, 2003, from www.socialnorm.org/bibliography.html

Berkowitz, L. (1981, June). How guns control us. *Psychology Today,* pp. 11–12.

Berkowitz, L. (1984). Some effects of thoughts on anti- and prosocial influences of media events: A cognitive–neoassociationistic analysis. *Psychological Bulletin, 95,* 410–427.

Berkowitz, L. (1989). Frustration–aggression hypothesis: Examination and reformulation. *Psychological Bulletin, 106,* 59–73.

Berkowitz, L., & Alioto, J. (1973). The meaning of an observed event as a determinant of its aggressive consequences. *Journal of Personality and Social Psychology, 28,* 206–207.

Berkowitz, L., & LePage, A. (1967). Weapons as aggression-eliciting stimuli. *Journal of Personality and Social Psychology, 7,* 202–207.

Berkowitz, L., & Powers, P. C. (1979). Effects of timing and justification of witnessed aggression on the observers' punitiveness. *Journal of Research in Personality, 13,* 71–80.

Bernal, G., & Scharron-del-rio, M. R. (2001). Are empirically supported treatments valid for ethnic minorities? Toward an alternative approach for treatment research. *Cultural Diversity and Ethnic Minority Psychology, 7,* 328–342.

Bickman, L. (1981). Some distinctions between basic and applied approaches. In L. Bickman (Ed.), *Applied social psychology annual* (Vol. 2, pp. 23–47). Beverly Hills, CA: Sage.

Biglan, A., Mrazek, P. J., Carnine, D., & Flay, B. R. (2003). The integration of research and practice in the prevention of youth problem behaviors. *American Psychologist, 58,* 433–440.

Bishop, G. D. (1994). *Health psychology: Integrating mind and body.* Boston: Allyn & Bacon.

Bjork, R. (2000). Giving away and selling the behavioral sciences. *Monitor on Psychology, 9*(11), 27. (American Psychological Association)

Black, M., & Krishnakumar, A. (1998). Children in low income, urban settings: Interventions to promote mental health and well-being. *American Psychologist, 53,* 635–647.

Blackman, M. (2002). The employment interview via the telephone: Are we sacrificing accurate personality judgments for cost efficiency? *Journal of Research in Personality, 36,* 208–223.

Blanton, H., Buunk, B. P., Gibbons, F. X., & Kuyper, H. (1999). When better-than-others compare upward: Choice of comparison and comparative evaluation as independent predictors of academic performance. *Journal of Personality and Social Psychology, 76,* 420–430.

Boehnke, K., & Schwartz, S. (1997). Fear of war: Relations to values, gender, and mental health in Germany and Israel. *Peace and Conflict: Journal of Peace Psychology, 3,* 149–165.

Boehnke, K., Schwartz, S., Stromberg, C., & Sagiv, L. (1998). The structure and dynamics of worry: Theory, measurement, and cross-national replication. *Journal of Personality, 66,* 745–782.

Boggiano, A. K., Barrett, M., Weiher, A. W., McClelland, G. H., & Lusk, C. M. (1987). Use of the maximal-operant principle to motivate children's intrinsic interest. *Journal of Personality and Social Psychology, 53,* 866–879.

Bond, M. H. (1988). Finding universal dimensions of individual variation in multicultural studies of values: The Rokeach and Chinese value surveys. *Journal of Personality and Social Psychology, 55,* 1009–1015.

Bordia, P. (1997). Face-to-face versus computer-mediated communication: A synthesis of the experimental literature. *Journal of Business Communication, 34,* 99–120.

Borduin, C. M., Cone, L. T., Mann, B. J., Henggeler, S. W., Fucci, B. R., Blaske, D. M., et al. (1995). Multisystemic treatment of serious juvenile offenders: Long-term prevention of criminality and violence. *Journal of Consulting and Clinical Psychology, 63,* 569–578.

Botwin, M. D., Buss, D., & Schackelford, T. K. (1997). Personality and mate references: Five factors in mate selection and marital satisfaction. *Journal of Personality, 65,* 107–136.

Bowlby, J. (1982). *Attachment and loss,* Vol. 1: *Attachment* (2nd ed.). New York: Basic Books. (Original work published 1969)

Braithwaite, J. (2000). Shame and criminal justice. *Canadian Journal of Criminology, 42,* 281–298.

Brannon, L., & Feist, J. (2000). *Health psychology: An introduction to behavior and health.* Belmont, CA: Wadsworth.

Branswell, H. (2003, March 4). A third of teens ride with drunk drivers. *Windsor Star,* pp. A1, A4. (Windsor, Ontario)

Brantingham, P. S., & Brantingham, P. L. (1977). *A theoretical model of crime site selection.* Paper presented at the meeting of the American Society of Criminology, Atlanta, GA.

Brawley, L. R. (1990). Group cohesion: Status, problems, and future directions. *International Journal of Sports Psychology, 21,* 355–379.

Brawley, L. R., Carron, A. V., & Widmeyer, W. N. (1992). The nature of group goals in sport teams: A phenomenological analysis. *The Sport Psychologist, 6,* 323–333.

Bray, C. D., & Whaley, D. E. (2001). Team cohesion, effort, and objective individual performance of high school basketball players. *The Sport Psychologist, 15,* 260–275.

Brehm, J. W. (1956). Postdecision changes in the desirability of alternatives. *Journal of Abnormal and Social Psychology, 52,* 384–389.

Brehm, J. W., & Cohen, A. R. (1962). *Explorations in cognitive dissonance.* New York: John Wiley.

Brehm, S., & Brehm, J. W. (1981a). *Psychological reactance: A theory of freedom and control.* New York: Academic Press.

Brehm, S. S., & Brehm, J. W. (1981b). *Reactance: A theory of freedom and control.* New York: Academic Press.

Brehm, S. S., Kassin, S. M., & Fein, S. (1999). *Social psychology* (4th ed.). Boston: Houghton Mifflin.

Brehm, S. S., Miller, R. S., Perlman, D., & Campbell, S. M. (2002). *Intimate relationships* (3rd ed.). Boston: McGraw–Hill.

Brewer, M. B., & Brown, R. J. (1998). Intergroup relations. In D. T. Gilbert, S. T. Fiske, & G. Lindzey (Eds.), *The handbook of social psychology* (4th ed., Vol. 2, pp. 554–594). New York: McGraw–Hill.

Brinton Lykes, M. (1997). Activist participatory research among the Maya of Guatemala: Constructing meanings from situated knowledge. *Journal of Social Issues, 53,* 725–746.

Brophy, J. E. (1983). Research on the self-fulfilling prophecy and teacher expectations. *Journal of Educational Psychology, 75,* 631–661.

Broverman, I. K., Broverman, D. M., Clarkson, F. E., Rosenkrantz, P. S., & Vogel, S. R. (1970). Sex role stereotypes and clinical judgments of mental health. *Journal of Consulting and Clinical Psychology, 34,* 1–7.

Brower, S. (1988). *Design in familiar places: What makes home environments look good.* New York: Praeger.

Brown, B. B. (1980). *Territoriality, defensible space, and residential burglary.* Unpublished master's thesis, University of Utah, Salt Lake City.

Brown, B. B., & Altman, I. (1983). Territoriality, defensible space, and residential burglary: An environmental analysis. *Journal of Environmental Psychology, 3,* 203–220.

Brown, B. B., & Bentley, D. L. (1993). Residential burglars judge risk: The role of territoriality. *Journal of Environmental Psychology, 13,* 51–61.

Brown, L. D., & Tandon, R. (1983). Ideology and political economy in inquiry: Action research and participatory research. *Journal of Applied Behavioral Sciences, 19,* 277–294.

Brown, S. P., Cron, W. L., & Leigh, T. W. (1993). Do feelings of success mediate sales performance–work attitude relationships? *Journal of the Academy of Marketing Science, 21,* 91–99.

Brown, S. P., & Peterson, R. A. (1994). Effects of effort on sales performance and job satisfaction. *Journal of Marketing, 58,* 70–80.

Bryant, J., Carveth, R. A., & Brown, D. (1981). Television viewing and anxiety: An experimental examination. *Journal of Communication, 31*(1), 106–119.

Brydon-Miller, M. (1993). Breaking down barriers: Accessibility self-advocacy in the disabled community. In P. Park, M. Brydon-Miller, B. Hall, & T. Jackson (Eds.), *Voices of change: Participatory research in the United States and Canada* (pp. 125–144). Westport, CT: Bergin & Garvey.

Buchanan, G. M., & Seligman, M. E. P. (1995). *Explanatory style.* Hillsdale, NJ: Lawrence Erlbaum.

Bukszar, E., & Connolly, T. (1988). Hindsight bias and strategic choice: Some problems in learning from experience. *Academy of Management Journal, 31,* 628–641.

Bullock, J. R. (1992). Children without friends: Who are they and how can teachers help? *Childhood Education, 69,* 92–96.

Burgoon, J. K. (1994). Nonverbal signals. In M. L. Knapp & G. R. Miller (Eds.), *Handbook of interpersonal communication* (pp. 229–285). Thousand Oaks, CA: Sage.

Burk J. P., & Sher, K. J. (1990). Labeling the child of an alcoholic: Negative stereotyping by mental health professionals and peers. *Journal of Studies on Alcohol, 51,* 156–163.

Burnstein, E., & Vinokur, A. (1977). Persuasive argumentation and social comparison as determinants of attitude polarization. *Journal of Experimental Social Psychology, 9,* 236–245.

Burt, M. R. (1980). Cultural myths and supports for rape. *Journal of Personality and Social Psychology, 38,* 217–230.

Burton, D. (1989). Winning isn't everything: Examining the impact of performance goals on collegiate swimmers' cognitions and performance. *The Sport Psychologist, 3,* 105–132.

Bushman, B. J., & Anderson, C. A. (2001). Media violence and the American public: Scientific facts versus media misinformation. *American Psychologist, 56,* 477–489.

Bushman, B. J., & Stack, A. D. (1996). Forbidden fruit versus tainted fruit: Effects of warning labels on attraction to television violence. *Journal of Experimental Psychology: Applied, 2,* 207–226.

Business as usual. (2002, August 5). *Sports Illustrated.* Retrieved November 15, 2002, from http://sportsillustrated.cnn.com/baseball/news/2002/08/05/dominating_braves_ap

Buss, D. M. (1985). Human mate selection. *American Scientist, 73,* 47–51.

Cabbage, M., & Harwood, W. (2004). *Comm check: The final flight of shuttle Columbia.* New York: Free Press.

Cady, S. H., & Valentine, J. (1999). Team innovation and perceptions of consideration: What difference does diversity make? *Human Relations, 30,* 730–750.

California Youth Authority. (1997). *LEAD: A boot camp and intensive parole program—Final impact evaluation.* Sacramento, CA: Department of the Youth Authority.

Campbell, D. T. (1969). Reforms as experiments. *American Psychologist, 24,* 409–429.

Canadian Psychological Association. (2000). *Canadian code of ethics for psychologists* (3rd ed.). Ottawa: Author.

Cancian, F. M. (1993). Conflicts between activist research and academic success: Participatory research and alternative strategies. *The American Sociologist, 24,* 92–106.

Cantor, J. (2002). Fright reactions to mass media. In J. Bryant & D. Zillmann (Eds.), *Media effects: Advances in theory and research* (2nd ed., pp. 287–306). Mahwah, NJ: Lawrence Erlbaum.

Cantor, J., Harrison, K., & Nathanson, A. I. (1998). Ratings and advisories for television programming. In Center for Communication and Social Policy (Ed.), *National television violence study* (Vol. 2, pp. 269–322). Thousand Oaks, CA: Sage.

Cantor, J., & Nathanson, A. I. (1996). Children's fright reactions to television news. *Journal of Communication, 46*(4), 139–152.

Cantor, J., & Sparks, G. G. (1984). Children's fear responses to mass media: Testing some Piagetian predictions. *Journal of Communication, 34*(2), 90–103.

Cantor, J., Wilson, B. J., & Hoffner, C. (1986). Emotional reactions to a televised nuclear holocaust film. *Communication Research, 13,* 257–277.

Cantril, H., Gaudet, H., & Herzog, H. (1940). *The invasion from Mars: A study in the psychology of panic.* Princeton, NJ: Princeton University Press.

Caplan, G. (1964). *Principles of preventive psychiatry.* New York: Basic Books.

Cappella, J. N., & Jamieson, K. H. (1997). *Spiral of cynicism: The press and the public good.* New York: Oxford University Press.

Carli, L. L., Ganley, R., & Pierce-Otay, A. (1991). Similarity and satisfaction in roommate relationships. *Personality and Social Psychology Bulletin, 17,* 419–426.

Carlson, M., Marcus-Newhall, A., & Miller, N. (1990). Effects of situational aggression cues: A quantitative review. *Journal of Personality and Social Psychology, 58,* 622–633.

Carron, A. V., & Ball, J. R. (1977). Cause–effect characteristics of the cohesiveness and participation motivation in intercollegiate hockey. *International Review of Sport Sociology, 12,* 49–60.

Carron, A. V., Brawley, L. R., & Widmeyer, W. N. (1997). The measurement of cohesiveness in sport groups. In J. L. Duda (Ed.), *Advances in sport and exercise psychology measurement.* Morgantown, WV: Fitness Information Technology.

Carron, A. V., Colman, M., Wheeler, J., & Stevens, D. (2002). Cohesion and performance in sport: A meta-analysis. *Journal of Sport and Exercise Psychology, 24,* 168–188.

Cartwright, E. (Ed.). (1951). *Field theory in social science: Selected theoretical papers by Kurt Lewin.* New York: Harper.

Casteel, C., & Peek-Asa, C. (2000). Effectiveness of crime prevention through environmental design (CPTED) in reducing robberies. *American Journal of Preventive Medicine, 18,* 99–115.

Centerwall, B. S. (1989). Exposure to television as a cause of violence. In G. Comstock (Ed.), *Public communication and behavior* (Vol. 2, pp. 1–58). San Diego: Academic Press.

Chansky, T. E., & Kendall, P. C. (1997). Social expectancies and self-perceptions in anxiety-disordered children. *Journal of Anxiety Disorders, 11,* 347–363.

Charlton, T., Gunter, B., & Hannan, A. (2002). *Broadcast television effects on a remote community.* Mahwah, NJ: Lawrence Erlbaum.

Chase, M. A., Feltz, D. L., & Lirgg, C. D. (2003). Sources of collective and individual efficacy of collegiate athletes. *International Journal of Sport and Exercise Psychology, 1,* 180–191.

Chen, M.-W., Froehle, T., & Morran, K. (1997). Deconstructing dispositional bias in clinical inference: Two interventions. *Journal of Counseling & Development, 76,* 74–81.

Christenfeld, R., Wagner, J., Pastva, G., & Acrish, W. P. (1989). How physical settings affect chronic mental patients. *Psychiatric Quarterly, 60,* 253–264.

Christensen, L. B. (2004). *Experimental methodology* (9th ed.). Boston: Pearson.

Christenson, M. A. (1990). Aging in the designed environment. *Physical and Occupational Therapy in Geriatrics, 8,* 3–133.

Cialdini, R. B., Cacioppo, J. T., Bassett, R., & Miller, J. A. (1978). Low-ball procedure for producing compliance: Commitment then cost. *Journal of Personality and Social Psychology, 36,* 436–476.

Cialdini, R. B., Kallgren, C. A., & Reno, R. R. (1991). A focus theory of normative conduct: A theoretical refinement and reevaluation of the role of norms in human behavior. *Advances in Experimental Social Psychology, 24,* 201–234.

Cialdini, R. B., Trost, M. R., & Newsom, J. T. (1995). Preference for consistency: The development of a valid measure and the discovery of surprising behavioral implications. *Journal of Personality and Social Psychology, 69,* 318–328.

Cicchetti, D., Rappaport, J., Sandler, I., & Weissberg, R. (2001). Emory L. Cowen (1926–2000). *American Psychologist, 56,* 514–515.

Cline, V. B., Croft, R. G., & Courrier, S. (1973). Desensitization of children to television violence. *Journal of Personality and Social Psychology, 27,* 360–365.

Coates, R., Miller, A., & Ohlin, L. (1978). *Diversity in a youth correctional system.* Cambridge, MA: Ballinger.

Cohen, A. K. (1960). *Delinquent boys.* New York: Free Press.

Cohen, M. A. (1998). The monetary value of saving a high risk youth. *Journal of Quantitative Criminology, 14,* 5–33.

Cohen, S., & Wills, T. (1985). Stress, social support, and the buffering hypothesis. *Psychological Bulletin, 98,* 310–357.

Cohen, U., & Weisman, G. D. (1990). Experimental design to maximize autonomy for older adults with cognitive impairments. *Generations, 14*(Suppl.), 75–78.

Collett, D. (1971). Training Englishmen in the nonverbal behavior of Arabs. *International Journal of Psychology, 6,* 209–215.

Condry, J. C., & Condry, S. (1976). Sex differences: A study of the eye of the beholder. *Child Development, 47,* 812–819.

Connolly, J. J., & Viswesvaran, C. (2000). The role of affectivity in job satisfaction: A meta-analysis. *Personality and Individual Differences, 29,* 265–281.

Conway, D. (1973). *Social science and design: A process model for architect and social scientist collaboration.* Washington, DC: American Institute of Architects.

Cook, T. D., & Campbell, D. T. (1979). *Quasi-experimentation: Design and analysis issues for field settings.* Boston: Houghton Mifflin.

Coolihan, K., Fantuzzo, J., Mendez, J., & McDermott, P. (2000). Preschool peer interactions and readiness to learn: Relationships between classroom peer play and learning behaviors and conduct. *Journal of Educational Psychology, 92,* 458–465.

Cooper, J., & Axsom, D. (1982). Effort justification in psychotherapy. In G. Weary & H. Mirels (Eds.), *Integrations of clinical and social psychology* (pp. 214–230). New York: Oxford University Press.

Copeland, B. L., & Straub, W. F. (1995). Assessment of team cohesion: A Russian approach. *Perceptual and Motor Skills, 81,* 443–450.

Coren, S. (1993). When teaching is evaluated on political grounds. *Academic Questions, 6,* 73–79.

Corrigan, P., & Penn, D. (1999). Lessons from social psychology on discrediting psychiatric stigma. *American Psychologist, 54,* 765–778.

Cose, E. (1994, July 11). Drawing up safer cities. *Newsweek,* p. 57.

Cotton, J. L., & Tuttle, J. M. (1986). Employee turnover: A meta-analysis and review with implications for research. *Academy of Management Review, 11,* 55–70.

Cox, T. H. (1991). The multicultural organization. *Academy of Management Executive, 5,* 34–44.

Cox, T. H., & Blake, S. (1991). Managing cultural diversity: Implications for organizational competitiveness. *Academy of Management Executive, 5,* 45–56.

Cozby, P. C. (2004). *Methods in behavioral research* (8th ed.). Boston: McGraw–Hill.

Cramer, K. M., & Lafreniere, K. D. (2003). *Stress in wedding preparation: Results of a pilot study.* Unpublished manuscript, University of Windsor, Windsor, Ontario.

Crano, W. D., & Brewer, M. B. (2002). *Principles and methods of social research* (2nd ed.). Mahwah, NJ: Lawrence Erlbaum.

Crawford, N. (2003). Web site puts out information on reproductive health. *Monitor on Psychology, 34*(2), 17. Retrieved May 20, 2003, from www.apa.org/monitor/feb03/website .html (American Psychological Association)

Crocetti, G., Spiro, H., & Siassi, H. (1973). *Contemporary attitudes toward mental illness.* Pittsburgh, PA: University of Pittsburgh Press.

Crocker, J., & Major, B. (1989). Social stigma and self-esteem: The self-protective properties of stigma. *Psychological Review, 96,* 608–630.

Crowell, D. H. (1987). Childhood aggression and violence: Contemporary issues. In D. H. Crowell, I. M. Evans, & C. R. O'Donnell (Eds.), *Childhood aggression and violence: Sources of influence, prevention, and control* (pp. 17–52). New York: Plenum.

Cunningham, J. B. (1993). *Action research and organizational development.* Westport, CT: Praeger.

Curtis, R. C., & Miller, K. (1986). Believing another likes or dislikes you: Behaviors making the beliefs come true. *Journal of Personality and Social Psychology, 51,* 284–290.

Dabbs, J. M., Carr, T. S., Frady, R. L., & Riad, J. K. (1995). Testosterone, crime, and misbehavior among 692 male prison inmates. *Personality and Individual Differences, 18,* 627–633.

Dale, G. A., & Wrisberg, C. A. (1996). The use of a performance profiling technique in a team setting: Getting athletes and coach on the "same page." *The Sport Psychologist, 10,* 261–277.

D'Alessio, S., & Stolzenberg, L. (1990). A crime of convenience: The environment and convenience store robbery. *Environment and Behavior, 22,* 255–271.

Dalton, J., Elias, M., & Wandersman, A. (2001). *Community psychology.* Belmont, CA: Wadsworth.

Danzinger, P. R., & Welfel, E. R. (2000). Age, gender, and health bias in counselors: An empirical analysis. *Journal of Mental Health Counseling, 22,* 135–149.

Darley, J., & Latané, B. (1968). Bystander intervention in emergencies: Diffusion of responsibility. *Journal of Personality and Social Psychology, 8,* 377–383.

Darley, J., & Latané, B. (1970). *The unresponsive bystander: Why doesn't he help?* New York: Appleton–Century–Crofts.

Davidson, L., Stayner, D. A., Lambert, S., Smith, P., & Sledge, W. H. (1997). Phenomenological and participatory research on schizophrenia: Recovering the person in theory and practice. *Journal of Social Issues, 53,* 767–784.

Davila, J., & Beck, J. G. (2002). Is social anxiety associated with impairment in close relationships? A preliminary investigation. *Behavior Therapy, 33,* 427–446.

Davis, J. H. (1992). Some compelling intuitions about group consensus decisions, theoretical and empirical research, and interpersonal aggregation phenomena: Selected examples, 1950–1990. *Organizational Behavior and Human Decision Processes, 52,* 3–38.

Davis, J. H., Kerr, N. L., Atkin, R. S., Holt, R., & Meek, D. (1975). The decision processes of 6- and 12-person mock juries assigned unanimous and two-thirds majority rules. *Journal of Personality and Social Psychology, 32,* 1–14.

Davison, K., Pennebaker, J., & Dickerson, S. (2000). Who talks? The social psychology of illness support groups. *American Psychologist, 55,* 205–217.

Dawes, R. M. (1973). The commons dilemma game: An n-person mixed motive game with a dominating strategy for defection. *Oregon Research Institute Research Bulletin, 13,* 1–12.

Dawes, R. M. (1980). Social dilemmas. *Annual Review of Psychology, 31,* 169–193.

Day, D. M. (1998). Risk for court contact and predictors of an early age for a first court contact among a sample of high risk youths: A survival analysis approach. *Canadian Journal of Criminology, 40,* 421–446.

Day, D. M., & Golench, C. A. (1997). Promoting safe schools through policy: Results of a survey of Canadian school boards. *Journal of Educational Administration, 35,* 332–347.

DeAngelis, T. (2002). If you do just one thing, make it exercise. *Monitor on Psychology, 33*(7), 49–51. (American Psychological Association)

Darley, J. M., & Latané, B. (1968). Bystander intervention in emergencies: Diffusion of responsibility. *Journal of Personality and Social Psychology, 8,* 377–383.

Dawe, S. W. L., & Carron, A. V. (1990, October). *Interrelationships among role acceptance, role clarity, task cohesion, and social cohesion.* Paper presented at the meeting of the Canadian Society for Psychomotor Learning and Sport Psychology, Windsor, Ontario.

Dearing, J. W., & Rogers, E. M. (1996). *Agenda setting.* Thousand Oaks, CA: Sage.

Deci, E. L. (1971). Effects of externally mediated rewards on intrinsic motivation. *Journal of Personality and Social Psychology, 18,* 105–115.

Deci, E. L. (1978). Applications of research on the effects of rewards. In M. R. Lepper & D. Greene (Eds.), *The hidden costs of reward: New perspectives on the psychology of human motivation* (pp. 193–203). Hillsdale, NJ: Lawrence Erlbaum.

Deci, E. L., Koestner, R., & Ryan, R. M. (1999). A meta-analytic review of experiments examining the effects of extrinsic rewards on intrinsic motivation. *Psychological Bulletin, 125,* 627–668.

DeLeon, P. H. (2002). Presidential reflections: Past and future. *American Psychologist, 57,* 425–430.

Dempsey, F. (1914). Nela Park: A novelty in the architectural grouping of industrial buildings. *Architectural Record, 35,* 469–504.

DePaulo, B. M., Kenny, D. A., Hoover, C. W., Webb, W., & Oliver, P. (1987). Accuracy of person perception: Do people know what kinds of impressions they convey? *Journal of Personality and Social Psychology, 52,* 303–315.

DePaulo, P. (1992). Applications of nonverbal behavior research in marketing and management. In R. Feldman (Ed.), *Applications of nonverbal behavioral theories and research* (pp. 63–87). Hillsdale, NJ: Lawrence Erlbaum.

DeSanctis, G., & Monge, P. (1999). Introduction to the special issue: Communication processes for virtual organizations. *Organization Science, 10,* 693–703.

Desforges, D. M., Lord, C. G., Ramsey, S. L., Mason, J. A., Van Leeuwen, M. D., West, S. C., et al. (1991). Effects of structured cooperative contact on changing negative attitudes toward stigmatized social groups. *Journal of Personality and Social Psychology, 60,* 531–544.

Deutsch, M. (1969). Socially relevant science: Reflections on some studies of interpersonal conflict. *American Psychologist, 24,* 1076–1092.

Deutsch, M. (1973). *The resolution of conflict.* New Haven, CT: Yale University Press.

Deutsch, M., & Gerard, H. B. (1955). A study of normative and social influences upon individual judgment. *Journal of Abnormal and Social Psychology, 51,* 629–636.

Devlin, A. (2000). City behavior and precautionary measures. *Journal of Applied Social Psychology, 30,* 2158–2173.

Devos-Comby, L., & Salovey, P. (2002). Applying persuasion strategies to alter HIV-relevant thoughts and behavior. *Review of General Psychology, 6,* 287–304.

DiBerardinis, J. D., Barwind, J., Flanningam, R. R., & Jenkins, V. (1983). Enhanced interpersonal relation as predictor of athletic performance. *International Journal of Sport Psychology, 14,* 243–251.

Dickerson, C., Thibodeau, R., Aronson, E., & Miller, D. (1992). Using cognitive dissonance to encourage water conservation. *Journal of Applied Social Psychology, 22,* 841–854.

Diefenbach, D. (1997). The portrayal of mental illness on prime time television. *Journal of Community Psychology, 25,* 289–302.

DiFonzo, N., Hantula, D. A., & Bordia, P. (1998). Microworlds for experimental research: Having your (control and collection) cake, and realism too. *Behavior Research Methods, Instruments, & Computers, 30,* 278–286.

Dillman, D. A. (2000). *Mail and Internet surveys: The tailored design method* (2nd ed.). New York: John Wiley.

DiMatteo, M. R., & Martin, L. R. (2002*). Health psychology.* Boston: Allyn & Bacon.

Dinnel, D. L., Kleinknecht, R. A., & Tanaka-Matsumi, J. (2002). A cross-cultural comparison of social phobia symptoms. *Journal of Psychopathology and Behavioral Assessment, 24,* 75–84.

Dion, K. K., Berscheid, E., & Walster, E. (1972). What is beautiful is good. *Journal of Personality and Social Psychology, 24,* 285–290.

Dishion, T. J. (2000). Cross-setting consistency in early adolescent psychopathology: Deviant friendships and problem behavior sequalae. *Journal of Personality, 68,* 1109–1126.

Dishion, T. J., McCord, J., & Poulin, T. (1999). When interventions harm: Peer groups and problem behavior. *American Psychologist, 54,* 755–765.

Dishion, T. J., Spracklen, K. M., Andrews, D. W., & Patterson, G. R. (1996). Deviancy training in male adolescent friendships. *Behavior Therapy, 27,* 373–390.

Donaldson, G., & Lorsch, J. (1983). *Decision making at the top.* New York: Basic Books.

Donnerstein, E., & Berkowitz, L. (1981). Victim reactions in aggressive erotic films as a factor in violence against women. *Journal of Personality and Social Psychology, 41,* 710–724.

Dovidio, J. F. (2001). On the nature of contemporary prejudice: The third wave. *Journal of Social Issues, 57,* 829–849.

Dovidio, J. F., & Gaertner, S. L. (2000). Aversive racism and selection decisions: 1989 and 1999. *Psychological Science, 11,* 315–319.

Dowling, C. G. (2000, August 14). Mistaken identity. *People,* pp. 50–55.

Drabman, R. S., & Thomas, M. H. (1974). Does media violence increase children's toleration of real-life aggression? *Developmental Psychology, 10,* 418–421.

Driscoll, R., Davis, K. E., & Lipetz, M. E. (1972). Parental interference and romantic love. *Journal of Personality and Social Psychology, 24,* 1–10.

DuBois, B. (1983). Passionate scholarship: Notes on values, knowing, and method in feminist social science. In G. Bowles & R. Duelli Klein (Eds.), *Theories of women's studies* (pp. 105–116). London: Routledge & Kegan Paul.

Duffy, K. G., & Wong, F. Y. (2000). *Community psychology* (2nd ed.). Boston: Allyn & Bacon.

Duffy, K. G., & Wong, F. Y. (2003). *Community psychology* (3rd ed.). Boston: Allyn & Bacon.

Dunham, P., Hurshman, A., Litwin, E., Gusella, J., Ellsworth, C., & Dodd, P. (1998). Computer mediated social support: Single young mothers as a model system. *American Journal of Community Psychology, 26,* 281–290.

Dunkerley, K. J., & Robinson, W. P. (2002). Similarities and differences in perceptions and evaluations of the communication styles of American and British managers. *Journal of Language and Social Psychology, 21,* 393–409.

DuPaul, G. J., Ervin, R. A., Hook, C. L., & McGoey, K. E. (1998). Peer tutoring for children with attention deficit hyperactivity disorder: Effects on classroom behavior and academic performance. *Journal of Applied Behavior Analysis, 31,* 579–592.

Dutton, D. (1981). Restaurateurs and reactions to white and black couples violating restaurant dress requirements. *Canadian Journal of Behavioural Science, 14,* 56–66.

Eagly, A. H., & Chaiken, S. (1993). *The psychology of attitudes.* San Diego: Harcourt Brace Jovanovich.

Ebbeson, E. B., Kjos, G. L., & Konecni, V. J. (1976). Spatial ecology: Its effects on the choice of friends and enemies. *Journal of Experimental Social Psychology, 12,* 505–518.

Eddy, J. M., Reid, J. B., & Fetrow, R. A. (2001). An elementary school-based prevention program targeting modifiable antecedents of youth delinquency and violence: Linking the Interests of Families and Teachers (LIFT). In H. M. Walker & M. H. Epstein (Eds.), *Making schools safer and violence free: Critical issues, solutions, and recommended practices* (pp. 128–139). Austin, TX: Pro-Ed.

Edley, N. (2001). Unravelling social constructionism. *Theory and Psychology, 11,* 433–441.

Edwards, D. L., Schoenwald, S. K., Henggeler, S. W., & Strother, K. B. (2001). A multilevel perspective on the implementation of multisystemic therapy (MST): Attempting dissemination with fidelity. In G. A. Bernfeld, D. P. Farrington, & A. W. Leschied (Eds.), *Offender rehabilitation in practice: Implementing and evaluating effective programs* (pp. 97–120). New York: John Wiley.

Edwards, J. R. (1991). Person–job fit: A conceptual integration, literature review, and methodological critique. In C. L. Cooper & I. T. Robertson (Eds.), *International review of industrial and organizational psychology* (pp. 283–357). Chichester, UK: Wiley.

Efran, M. G. (1974). The effect of physical appearance on the judgment of guilt, interpersonal attraction, and severity of recommended punishment in a simulated jury task. *Journal of Research in Personality, 8,* 45–54.

Ellis, A. (1962). *Reason and emotion in psychotherapy.* New York: Lyle Stuart.

Ellis, E. S., & Feldman, R. K. (1994). Creating "thought-full" classrooms: Fostering cognitive literacy via cooperative learning and integrated strategies instruction. In S. Sharan (Ed.), *Handbook of cooperative learning methods* (pp. 157–176). Westport, CT: Greenwood.

Ellsworth, P. C. (1991). To tell what we know or wait for Godot? *Law and Human Behavior, 15,* 205–224.

Ellsworth, P. C., & Mauro, R. (1998). Psychology and law. In D. T. Gilbert, S. T. Fiske, & G. Lindzey (Eds.), *The handbook of social psychology* (pp. 684–732). Boston: McGraw–Hill.

Engel, G. L. (1977). The need for a new medical model: A challenge for biomedicine. *Science, 196,* 129–136.

Esses, V. M., & Webster, C. D. (1988). Physical attractiveness, dangerousness, and the Canadian Criminal Code. *Journal of Applied Social Psychology, 18,* 1017–1031.

Evans, G. W., & McCoy, J. M. (1998). When buildings don't work: The role of architecture in human health. *Journal of Environmental Psychology, 18,* 85–94.

Fatum, W. R., & Hoyle, J. C. (1996). Is it violence? School violence from the student perspective: Trends and interventions. *School Counselor, 44,* 28–34.

Feingold, A. (1990). Gender differences in effects of physical attractiveness in romantic attraction: A comparison across five research paradigms. *Journal of Personality and Social Psychology, 59,* 981–993.

Feldman, R. S. (1998). *Social psychology* (2nd ed.). Upper Saddle River, NJ: Prentice Hall.

Feltz, D. L., & Chase, M. A. (1998). The measurement of self-efficacy and confidence in sport. In J. L. Duda (Ed.), *Advancements in sport and exercise psychology measurement* (pp. 65–80). Morgantown, WV: Fitness Information Technology.

Feltz, D. L., & Lirgg, C. D. (1998). Perceived team and player efficacy in hockey. *Journal of Applied Psychology, 83,* 557–564.

Fenton, R., & O'Leary, N. (1990, February). *Improving student achievement through enhancing the instructional communication competence of teachers.* Paper presented at the annual meeting of the Communication and Instruction Division of the Western States Communication Association, Phoenix, AZ.

Feshbach, S. (1961). The stimulating versus cathartic effects of vicarious aggressive activity. *Journal of Abnormal and Social Psychology, 63,* 381–385.

Festinger, L. (1954). A theory of social comparison processes. *Human Relations, 7,* 117–140.

Festinger, L. (1957). *A theory of cognitive dissonance.* Stanford, CA: Stanford University Press.

Festinger, L. (1999). Reflections on cognitive dissonance 30 years later. In E. Harmon-Jones & J. Mills (Eds.), *Cognitive dissonance: Progress on a pivotal theory in social psychology* (pp. 381–385). Washington, DC: American Psychological Association.

Festinger, L., & Carlsmith, J. M. (1959). Cognitive consequences of forced compliance. *Journal of Abnormal and Social Psychology, 58,* 203–210.

Festinger, L., Schachter, S., & Back, K. W. (1950). *Social pressures in informal groups: A study of human factors in housing.* New York: Harper.

Fetterman, D. M. (1998). Ethnography. In L. Bickman & D. J. Rog (Eds.), *Handbook of applied social research methods* (pp. 473–504). Thousand Oaks, CA: Sage.

Fischer, R., & Smith, P. B. (2003). Reward allocation and culture: A meta-analysis. *Journal of Cross-Cultural Psychology, 34,* 251–268.

Fischoff, B. (1975). Hindsight is not foresight: The effect of outcome knowledge on judgment under uncertainty. *Journal of Experimental Psychology: Human Perception and Performance, 1,* 288–299.

Fishbein, M., & Ajzen, I. (1975). *Belief, attitude, intention, and behavior: An introduction to theory and research.* Reading, MA: Addison–Wesley.

Fisher, B. A. (1978). *Perspectives on human communication.* New York: Macmillan.

Fisher, R. J. (1982). *Social psychology: An applied approach.* New York: St. Martin's.

Fisher, R. J. (1990). *The social psychology of intergroup and international conflict resolution.* New York: Springer-Verlag.

Fisher, R. P., Geiselman, R. E., & Amador, M. (1989). Field test of the cognitive interview: Enhancing the recollection of actual victims and witnesses of crime. *Journal of Applied Psychology, 74,* 722–727.

Fisher, R. P., Geiselman, R. E., & Raymond, D. S. (1987). Critical analysis of police interview techniques. *Journal of Police Science and Administration, 15,* 177–185.

Fiske, S. T. (1993). Social cognition and social perception. In E. W. Porter & M. R. Rosenzweig (Eds.), *Annual review of psychology* (pp. 155–194). Palo Alto, CA: Annual Reviews.

Fiske, S. T., Xu, J., & Cuddy, A. C. (1999). (Dis)Respecting versus (dis)liking: Status and interdependence predict ambivalent stereotypes of competence and warmth. *Journal of Social Issues, 55,* 473–489.

Fitchen, C. S., & Amsel, R. A. (1986). Trait attribution about college students with a physical disability: Circumplex analyses and methodological issues. *Journal of Applied Social Psychology, 16,* 410–427.

Flowers, M. L. (1977). A laboratory test of some implications of Janis' groupthink hypothesis. *Journal of Personality and Social Psychology, 35,* 888–896.

Foa, E. B., Franklin, M. E., Perry, K. J., & Herbert, J. D. (1996). Cognitive biases in generalized social phobia. *Journal of Consulting and Clinical Psychology, 105,* 433–439.

Foa, U. G., & Foa, E. B. (1974). *Societal structures of the mind.* Springfield, IL: Charles C Thomas.

Folkes, V. S. (1982). Forming relationships and the matching hypothesis. *Personality and Social Psychology Bulletin, 8,* 631–636.

Forston, R. F., & Larson, C. U. (1968). The dynamics of space: An experimental study in proxemic behavior among Latin Americans and North Americans. *Journal of Communication, 18,* 109–116.

Forsyth, D. R. (1999). *Group dynamics* (4th ed.). Pacific Grove, CA: Brooks/Cole.

Fowler, F. J. (1998). Design and evaluation of survey questions. In L. Bickman & D. J. Rog (Eds.), *Handbook of applied social research methods* (pp. 343–374). Thousand Oaks, CA: Sage.

Freire, P. (1970). *Pedagogy of the oppressed.* New York: Seabury.

Fried, C., & Aronson, E. (1995). Hypocrisy, misattribution, and dissonance reduction: A demonstration of dissonance in the absence of aversive consequences. *Personality and Social Psychology Bulletin, 21,* 925–933.

Fried, Y., & Ferris, G. R. (1987). The validity of the job characteristics model: A review and meta-analysis. *Personnel Psychology, 40,* 287–322.

Friedlander, M. L., & Stockman, S. J. (1983). Anchoring and publicity effects in clinical judgment. *Journal of Clinical Psychology, 39,* 637–643.

Friedman, H. S. (2002). *Health psychology* (2nd ed.). Upper Saddle River, NJ: Prentice Hall.

Freud, S. (1935). *A general introduction to psychoanalysis.* New York: Liveright.

Frye, C. M. (1996, April). *New evidence for the Job Characteristics Model: A meta-analysis of the job characteristics–job satisfaction relationship using composite correlations.* Paper presented at the annual meeting of the Society for Industrial and Organizational Psychology, San Diego, CA.

Furlong, M., & Morrison, G. (2001). The *school* in school violence: Definitions and facts. In H. M. Walker & M. H. Epstein (Eds.), *Making schools safer and violence free: Critical issues, solutions, and recommended practices* (pp. 5–16). Austin, TX: Pro-Ed.

Gadd, J. (2003, June 3). Matti kicked like a "rag doll," trial told. *The National,* p. A11.

Gaertner, S. L., & Dovidio, J. F. (1986). The aversive form of racism. In J. F. Dovidio & S. L. Gaertner (Eds.), *Prejudice, discrimination, and racism* (pp. 61–81). San Diego: Academic Press.

Gaertner, S. L., Dovidio, J. F., Rust, M. C., Nier, J. A., Banker, B. S., Ward, C. M., Mottola, G. R., & Houlette, M. (1999). Reducing intergroup bias: Elements of intergroup cooperation. *Journal of Personality and Social Psychology, 76,* 388–402.

Gallant, M., & Maticka-Tyndale, E. (2004). School-based HIV prevention programmes for African youth. *Social Science & Medicine, 58,* 1337–1351.

Galt, V. (1996, August 9). Medical mentors a tonic for youths. *The Globe and Mail,* p. A8.

Garb, H. N. (1996). The representativeness and past-behavior heuristics in clinical judgment. *Professional Psychology: Research and Practice, 27,* 272–277.

Gardner, D. E., Light-Shields, D. L., Bredemeier, B. J., & Bostrom, A. (1996). The relationship between perceived coaching behaviors and team cohesion among baseball and softball players. *The Sport Psychologist, 10,* 367–381.

Gardner, R. M., & Dalsing, S. (1986). Misconceptions about psychology among college students. *Teaching of Psychology, 13,* 32–34.

Gardner, R. M., & Hund, R. M. (1983). Misconceptions of psychology among academicians. *Teaching of Psychology, 10,* 20–22.

Gardner, R., Ostrom, E., & Walker, J. (1990). The nature of common-pool resource problems. *Rationality & Society, 2,* 335–358.

Garmezy, N. (1987). Stress, competence, and development: Continuities in the study of schizophrenic adults, children vulnerable to psychopathology, and the search for stress-resistant children. *American Journal of Orthopsychiatry, 57,* 159–274.

Gatehouse, J. (2003, June 9). The good news about the bad news. *Maclean's,* pp. 20–22.

Gaudiano, B. A., & Herbert, J. D. (2003). Preliminary psychometric evaluation of a new self-efficacy scale and its relationship to treatment outcome in social anxiety disorder. *Cognitive Therapy and Research, 27,* 537–555.

Geen, R. G. (2001). *Human aggression.* Buckingham, UK: Open University Press.

Gelfand, M., Nishii, L., Holcombe, K., Dyer, N., Ohbuchi, K., & Fukuno, M. (2001). Cultural influences on cognitive representation of conflict: Interpretations of conflict episodes in the United States and Japan. *Journal of Applied Psychology, 86,* 1059–1074.

Gendreau, P., Little, T., & Goggin, C. (1996). A meta-analysis of the predictors of adult offender recidivism: What works! *Criminology, 34,* 575–607.

Genesee, F., & Holobow, N. (1989). Change and stability in intergroup perceptions. *Journal of Language and Social Psychology, 8,* 17–38.

George, T. R., & Feltz, D. L. (1995). Motivation in sport from a collective efficacy perspective. *International Journal of Sport Psychology, 26,* 98–116.

Gerard, H. B., & Mathewson, G. C. (1966). The effects of severity of initiation on liking for a group: A replication. *Journal of Experimental Social Psychology, 2,* 278–287.

Gerbner, G., Gross, L., Morgan, M., Signorielli, N., & Shanahan, J. (2002). Growing up with television: Cultivation processes. In J. Bryant & D. Zillmann (Eds.), *Media effects: Advances in theory and research* (2nd ed., pp. 43–68). Mahwah, NJ: Lawrence Erlbaum.

Gergen, K. J. (1985). The social constructionist movement in modern psychology. *American Psychologist, 40,* 266–275.

Gifford, R. (2002). *Environmental psychology: Principles and practice* (3rd ed.). Colville, WA: Optimal Books.

Gifford, J., & Gifford, R. (2000). FISH 3: A microworld for studying social dilemmas and resource management. *Behavior Research Methods, Instruments, & Computers, 32,* 417–442.

Gifford, R., & Hine, D. W. (1997). "I'm cooperative, but you're greedy": Some cognitive tendencies in a commons dilemma. *Canadian Journal of Behavioural Science, 29,* 257–265.

Gilbert, D. T., & Malone, P. S. (1995). The correspondence bias. *Psychological Bulletin, 117,* 21–38.

Gilbert, D. T., Pelham, B. W., & Krull, D. S. (1988). On cognitive busyness: When person perceivers meet persons perceived. *Journal of Personality and Social Psychology, 54,* 733–740.

Giles, D. (2003). *Media psychology.* Mahwah, NJ: Lawrence Erlbaum.

Gillham, J. E., Reivich, K. J., & Shatte, A. S. (2001). Building optimism and preventing depressive symptoms in children. In E. C. Chang (Ed.), *Optimism and pessimism: Implications for theory, research, and practice* (pp. 301–320). Washington, DC: American Psychological Association.

Glaser, B. G., & Strauss, A. L. (1967). *The discovery of grounded theory: Strategies for qualitative research.* Chicago: Aldine.

Glick, P., & Fiske, S. T. (1996). The Ambivalent Sexism Inventory: Differentiating hostile and benevolent sexism. *Journal of Personality and Social Psychology, 70,* 491–512.

Goffman, E. (1961). *Asylums.* New York: Anchor Books.

Goffman, E. (1963) *Stigma.* Englewood Cliffs, NJ: Prentice Hall.

Gonzales, M. H., Aronson, E., & Costanzo, M. A. (1988). Using social cognition and persuasion to promote energy conservation: A quasi-experiment. *Journal of Applied Social Psychology, 18,* 1049–1066.

Goodwin, C. J. (2003). *Research in psychology: Methods and design.* New York: John Wiley.

Goodwin, R. (1999). *Personal relationships across cultures.* London: Routledge.

Goodwin, R., & Tang, D. (1991). Preferences for friends and close relationship partners: A cross-cultural comparison. *Journal of Social Psychology, 131,* 579–581.

Gottfredson, D. C., Marciniak, E., Birdseye, A. T., & Gottfredson, G. D. (1991). *Increasing teacher expectations for student achievement: An evaluation.* Baltimore, MD: Center for Research on Effective Schooling for Disadvantaged Students.

Gottfredson, G. D. (1996). The Hawthorne misunderstanding (and how to get the Hawthorne effect in action research). *Journal of Research in Crime and Delinquency, 33,* 28–48.

Gove, M., & Geerken, M. (1977). The effect of children and employment on the mental health of married men and women. *Social Forces, 56,* 66–76.

Gozenbach, W. J. (1996). *The media, the president, and public opinion: A longitudinal analysis of the drug issue, 1984–1991.* Mahwah, NJ: Lawrence Erlbaum.

Graham, J. W., Marks, G., & Hansen, W. B. (1991). Social influence processes affecting adolescent substance use. *Journal of Applied Psychology, 7,* 291–298.

Grant, J. D. (1980). From "living learning" to "learning to live": An extension of social therapy. In H. Toch (Ed.), *Therapeutic communities in corrections* (pp. 41–49). New York: Praeger.

Grau, U., Möller, J., & Gunnarsson, J. I. (1988). A new concept of counselling: A systemic approach for counseling coaches in team sports. *Applied Psychology: An International Review, 37,* 65–83.

Greenlees, I. A., Graydon, J. K., & Maynard, I. W. (2000). The impact of individual efficacy beliefs on group goal selection and group goal commitment. *Journal of Sports Sciences, 18,* 451–459.

Greenlees, I. A., Nunn, R. L., Graydon, J. K., & Maynard, I. W. (1999). The relationship between collective efficacy and pre-competitive affect in rugby players: Testing Bandura's model of collective efficacy. *Perceptual and Motor Skills, 89,* 431–440.

Grieve, F. G., Whelan, J. P., & Meyes, A. W. (2000). An experimental examination of the cohesion–performance relationship in an interactive team sport. *Journal of Applied Sport Psychology, 12,* 219–235.

Griffiths, C. T., & Cunningham, A. C. (2000). *Canadian corrections.* Scarborough, Ontario: Nelson.

Grofman, B. (1980). Jury decision making models and the Supreme Court: The jury cases from *Williams v. Florida* to *Ballew v. Georgia. Policy Studies Journal, 8,* 749–772.

Gross, A. E. (1983). *Date selection: The all-important first meeting.* Unpublished manuscript, University of Maryland.

Gulak, M. B. (1991). Architectural guidelines for state psychiatric hospitals. *Hospital and Community Psychiatry, 42,* 705–707.

Gunter, B. (2002). *Media sex: What are the issues?* Mahwah, NJ: Lawrence Erlbaum.

Gutkowski, S., Ginath, Y., & Guttman, F. (1992). Improving psychiatric environments through minimal architectural change. *Hospital and Community Psychiatry, 43,* 920–923.

Hackett, R. D., & Guion, R. M. (1985). A reevaluation of the absenteeism–job satisfaction relationship. *Organizational Behavior and Human Decision Processes, 35,* 340–381.

Hackman, J. R., & Oldham, G. R. (1976). Motivation through the design of work: Test of a theory. *Organizational Behavior and Human Performance, 16,* 250–279.

Hackman, J. R., & Oldham, G. R. (1980). *Work redesign.* Reading, MA: Addison–Wesley.

Haines, M. P. (1996). *A social norms approach to preventing binge drinking at colleges and universities* (Publication No. ED/OPE/96–18). Newton, MA: Higher Education Center for Alcohol and Other Drug Prevention.

Haines, M. P. (2003). The Northern Illinois University experiment: A longitudinal case study of the social norms approach. In H. W. Perkins (Ed.), *The social norms approach to preventing school and college age substance abuse: A handbook for educators, counselors, and clinicians* (pp. 21–34). San Francisco: Jossey–Bass.

Halpern-Felsher, B. L., & Millstein, S. G. (2002). The effects of terrorism on teens' perceptions of dying: The new world is riskier than ever. *Journal of Adolescent Health, 30,* 308–311.

Hamermesh, D. S., & Biddle, J. E. (1994). Beauty and the labor market. *American Economic Review, 84,* 1174–1195.

Ham-Rowbottom, K. A., Gifford, R., & Shaw, K. T. (1999). Defensible space theory and the police: Assessing the vulnerability of residencies to burglary. *Journal of Environmental Psychology, 19,* 117–129.

Haney, C., Banks, W. C., & Zimbardo, P. (1973). Interpersonal dynamics in a simulated prison. *International Journal of Criminology and Penology, 1,* 69–97.

Hanin, Y. (1992). Social psychology and sport: Communication processes in top performance teams. *Sport Science Review, 1,* 13–28.

Hannah-Moffat, K. (2002). *Punishment in disguise.* Toronto: University of Toronto Press.

Hansen, S., Meissler, K., & Ovens, R. (2000). Kids together: A group play therapy model for children with ADHD symptomalogy. *Journal of Child and Adolescent Group Therapy, 10,* 191–211.

Hardin, G. (1968). The tragedy of the commons. *Science, 162,* 1243–1248.

Harmon-Jones, E., & Mills, J. (Eds.). (1999). *Cognitive dissonance: Progress on a pivotal theory in social psychology.* Washington, DC: American Psychological Association.

Harrison, K., & Cantor, J. (1999). Tales from the screen: Enduring fright reactions to scary media. *Media Psychology, 1,* 97–116.

Harter, S., & Pike, R. (1984). The Pictorial Scale of Perceived Competence and Social Acceptance for Young Children. *Child Development, 55,* 1969–1982.

Harvey, M. L., Loomis, R. J., Bell, P. A., & Marino, M. (1998). The influence of museum exhibit design on immersion and psychological flow. *Environment and Behavior, 30,* 601–627.

Hass, R. G., Katz, I., Rizzo, N., Bailey, J., & Eisenstadt, D. (1991). Cross-racial appraisal as related to attitude ambivalence and cognitive complexity. *Personality and Social Psychology Bulletin, 17,* 83–92.

Hatfield, E., & Sprecher, S. (1986). *Mirror, mirror . . . : The importance of looks in everyday life.* Albany: State University of New York Press.

Haverkamp, B. E. (1993). Confirmatory bias in hypothesis testing for client-identified and counselor self-generated hypotheses. *Journal of Counseling Psychology, 40,* 303–315.

Hayes, M. (2003, February 4). This year, the Gators have the right mix. *The Sporting News.* Retrieved April 2, 2003, from www.sportingnews.com/voices/matt_hayes/20030204.html

Hazan, C., & Shaver, P. R. (1987). Romantic love conceptualized as an attachment process. *Journal of Personality and Social Psychology, 52,* 511–524.

Hearold, S. (1986). A synthesis of 1,043 effects of television on social behavior. In G. Comstock (Ed.), *Public Communication and Behavior* (Vol. 1, pp. 66–135). Beverly Hills, CA: Sage.

Hegelson, V. S., & Cohen, S. (1996). Social support and adjustment to cancer: Reconciling descriptive, correlational, and intervention research. *Health Psychology, 15,* 135–148.

Heiman, G. W. (2002). *Research methods in psychology* (3rd ed.). Boston: Houghton Mifflin.

Heine, S. J., & Lehman, D. R. (1997). Culture, dissonance, and self-affirmation. *Personality and Social Psychology Bulletin, 23,* 389–400.

Hendricks, B., Marvel, M. K., & Barrington, B. L. (1990). The dimensions of psychological research. *Teaching of Psychology, 17,* 76–82.

Henggeler, S. W. (1999). Multisystemic therapy: An overview of clinical procedures, outcomes, and policy implications. *Child Psychology and Psychiatry Review, 4,* 2–10.

Hennessey, B. A., & Zbikowski, S. M. (1993). Immunizing children against the negative effects of reward: A further examination of intrinsic motivation training techniques. *Creativity Research Journal, 6,* 297–307.

Hennessy, J., & West, M. A. (1999). Intergroup behavior in organizations: A field test of social identity. *Small Group Research, 30,* 361–382.

Hennigan, K. M., Del Rosario, M. L., Heath, L., Cook, T., Wharton, J. D., & Calder, B. J. (1982). Impact of the introduction of television on crime in the United States: Empirical findings and theoretical implications. *Journal of Personality and Social Psychology, 42,* 461–477.

Hennigan, K. M., Flay, B. R., & Cook, T. D. (1980). "Give me the facts": Some suggestions for using social science knowledge in national policy-making. In R. F. Kidd & M. J. Saks (Eds.), *Advances in applied social psychology* (Vol. 1, pp. 113–145). Hillsdale, NJ: Lawrence Erlbaum.

Henry, D. B. (2001). Classroom context and the development of aggression: The role of normative processes. In F. Columbus (Ed.), *Advances in psychology research* (Vol. 6, pp. 193–213). Huntington, NY: Nova Science.

Hensley, T. R., & Griffin, G. W. (1986). Victims of groupthink. *Journal of Conflict Resolution, 30,* 497–531.

Herek, G. M., Janis, I. L., & Huth, P. (1987). Decision making during international crises: Is quality of process related to outcome? *Journal of Conflict Resolution, 31,* 203–226.

Heuze, J. P., & Fontayne, P. (2002). A French language instrument for measuring team cohesion. *Journal of Sport and Exercise Psychology, 24,* 42–67.

Hicks, D. J. (1965). Imitation and retention of film-mediated aggressive peer and adult models. *Journal of Personality and Social Psychology, 2,* 97–100.

Higgins, E. T., Bargh, J. A., & Lombardi, W. (1985). Nature of priming effects on categorization. *Journal of Experimental Psychology: Learning, Memory, & Cognition, 11,* 59–69.

Hilton, J. L., & von Hipple, W. (1996). Stereotypes. *Annual Review of Psychology, 47,* 237–271.

Hine, D. W., & Gifford, R. (1996). Attributions about self and others in commons dilemmas. *European Journal of Social Psychology, 26,* 429–445.

Hine, D. W., & Gifford, R. (1997). What harvesters really think about in commons dilemma simulations: A grounded theory analysis. *Canadian Journal of Behavioural Science, 29,* 179–193.

Hirt, E. R., & Markman, K. D. (1995). Multiple explanation: A consider-an-alternative strategy for debiasing judgments. *Journal of Personality and Social Psychology, 69,* 1069–1086.

Hirt, E. R., McCrea, S. M., & Kimble, C. E. (2000). Public self-focus and sex differences in behavioral self-handicapping: Does increasing self-threat still make it "just a man's game?" *Personality and Social Psychology Bulletin, 26,* 1131–1141.

Hobden, K. L., & Olson, J. M. (1994). From jest to antipathy: Disparagement humor as a source of dissonance-motivated attitude change. *Basic and Applied Social Psychology, 15,* 239–249.

Hochschild, A. (1989). *The second shift: Working parents and the revolution at home.* New York: Viking Penguin.

Hodges, L., & Carron, A. V. (1992). Collective efficacy and group performance. *International Journal of Sport Psychology, 23,* 48–59.

Hodges, S. D., Klaaren, K. J., & Wheatley, K. (2000). Talking about safe sex: The role of expectations and experience. *Journal of Applied Social Psychology, 30,* 330–349.

Hodgins, S., Kratzer, L., & McNeil, T. F. (2002). Are pre- and postnatal factors related to the development of criminal offending? In R. R. Corrado, R. Roesch, S. D. Hart, & J. K. Gierowski (Eds.), *Multi-problem violent youth* (pp. 58–80). Amsterdam, IOS Press.

Hodson, G., & Sorrentino, R. M. (1997). Groupthink and uncertainty orientation: Personality differences in reactivity to the group situation. *Group Dynamics, 1,* 144–155.

Hoekstra, S. J., Harris, R. J., & Helmick, A. L. (1999). Autobiographical memories about the experience of seeing frightening movies in childhood. *Media Psychology, 1,* 117–140.

Hoffman, K. D. (1994). *Effects of playing versus witnessing video game violence on attitudes toward aggression and acceptance of violence as a means of conflict resolution.* Unpublished doctoral dissertation, University of Alabama.

Hofstede, G. (1991). *Cultures and organizations: Software of the mind.* London: McGraw–Hill.

Hofstede, G. (1997). *Cultures and organizations: Software of the mind* (Rev. ed.). New York: McGraw–Hill.

Hofstede, G. (2002). *Culture's consequences* (2nd ed.). Thousand Oaks, CA: Sage.

Hoge, R. D. (2001). *The juvenile offender: Theory, research, and application.* Boston: Kluwer.

Holahan, C. J. (1972). Seating patterns and patient behavior in an experimental dayroom. *Journal of Abnormal Psychology, 80,* 115–124.

Holahan, C. J. (1983). Interventions to reduce environmental stress: Enhancing social support and personal control. In E. Siedman (Ed.), *Handbook of social interventions.* Beverly Hills, CA: Sage.

Holman, T. B., Larson, J. H., & Harmer, S. L. (1994). The development and predictive validity of a new premarital assessment instrument: The Preparation for Marriage Questionnaire. *Family Relations, 43,* 46–52.

Holmes, T. H., & Rahe, R. H. (1967). The Social Readjustment Rating Scale. *Journal of Psychosomatic Research, 11,* 213–218.

Hooper, J., & Reid, D. H. (1985). A simple environmental re-design for improving classroom performance of profoundly retarded students. *Education and Treatment of Children, 8,* 25–39.

Hopper, J. R., & Nielsen, J. M. (1991). Recycling as altruistic behavior: Normative and behavioral strategies to expand participation in a community recycling program. *Environment and Behavior, 23,* 195–220.

House, R. J. (1971). A path–goal theory of leader effectiveness. *Administrative Science Quarterly, 16,* 321–338.

House, R. J., & Podsakoff, P. M. (1994). Leadership effectiveness: Past perspectives and future directions for research. In J. Greenberg (Ed.), *Organizational behavior: The state of the science* (pp. 45–82). Hillsdale, NJ: Lawrence Erlbaum.

Houston, D. A., & Doan, K. (1999). Can you back that up? Evidence (or lack thereof) for the effects of negative and positive political communication. *Media Psychology, 1,* 191–206.

Houston, D. A., Doan, K., & Roskos-Ewoldsen, D. R. (1999). Negative political advertising and choice conflict. *Journal of Experimental Psychology: Applied, 5,* 3–16.

Houston, D. A., & Roskos-Ewoldsen, D. R. (1998). The cancellation-and-focus model of choice and preferences for political candidates. *Basic and Applied Social Psychology, 20,* 305–312.

Hovland, C. I., Janis, I. L., & Kelley, H. H. (1953). *Communication and persuasion: Psychological studies of opinion change.* New Haven, CT: Yale University Press.

Howard, D. J., Gengler, C. E., & Jain, A. (1997). The name remembrance effect: A test of alternative explanations. *Journal of Social Behaviour and Personality, 12,* 801–810.

Howard, G. S. (2000). Adapting human lifestyles for the 21st century. *American Psychologist, 55,* 509–515.

Howard, J. L., & Ferris, G. R. (1996). The employment interview context: Social and situational influences on interviewer decisions. *Journal of Applied Social Psychology, 26,* 112–136.

Hoyt, J. L. (1970). Effect of media violence "justification" on aggression. *Journal of Broadcasting, 14,* 455–464.

Huesmann, L. R., Eron, L. D., Klein, R., Brice, P., & Fischer, P. (1983). Mitigating the imitation of aggressive behaviors by changing children's attitudes about media violence. *Journal of Personality and Social Psychology, 44,* 899–910.

Huesmann, L. R., Moise-Titus, J., Podolski, C. L., & Eron, L. D. (2003). Longitudinal relations between children's exposure to TV violence and their aggressive and violent behavior in young adulthood: 1977–1992. *Developmental Psychology, 39,* 201–221.

Huguet, P., Dumas, F., Monteil, J. M., & Genestoux, N. (2001). Social comparison choices in the classroom: Further evidence for students' upward comparison tendency and its beneficial impact on performance. *European Journal of Social Psychology, 31,* 557–578.

Hulin, C. L., & Judge, T. A. (2003). Job attitudes. In W. C. Borman, D. R. Ilgen, & R. J. Klimoski (Eds.), *Handbook of psychology* (Vol. 12, pp. 255–276). Hoboken, NJ: John Wiley.

Hunt, M. E. (1985). Enhancing a building's imageability. *Journal of Architectural and Planning Research, 2,* 151–168.

Hunt, M. E. (1991). The design of supportive environments for older people. *Journal of Housing for the Elderly, 9,* 127–140.

Hyde, J. S. (1991). *Half the human experience: The psychology of women* (4th ed.). Toronto: Heath.

Iaffaldano, M. T., & Muchinsky, P. M. (1985). Job satisfaction and job performance: A meta-analysis. *Psychological Bulletin, 97,* 251–273.

Ilies, R., & Judge, T. A. (2003). On the heritability of job satisfaction: The mediating role of personality. *Journal of Applied Psychology, 88,* 750–759.

Intons-Peterson, M. J., & Roskos-Ewoldsen, B. (1989). Mitigating the effects of violent pornography. In S. Gubar & J. Hoff (Eds.), *For adult users only: The dilemma of violent pornography* (pp. 218, 220–228). Bloomington: Indiana University Press.

Intons-Peterson, M. J., Roskos-Ewoldsen, B., Thomas, L., Shirley, M., & Blut, D. (1989). Will educational materials reduce negative effects of exposure to sexual violence? *Journal of Social and Clinical Psychology, 8,* 256–275.

Isen, A. M., & Baron, R. A. (1991). Positive affect as a factor in organizational behavior. *Research in Organizational Behavior, 13,* 1–53.

Iyengar, S. (1991). *Is anyone responsible? How television frames political issues.* Chicago: University of Chicago Press.

Iyengar, S., & Kinder, D. R. (1987). *News that matters.* Chicago: University of Chicago Press.

Iyengar, S., & Ottati, V. (1994). Cognitive perspectives on political psychology. In R. S. Wyer, Jr., & T. K. Srull (Eds.), *Handbook of social cognition* (2nd ed., Vol. 2, pp. 143–187). Hillsdale, NJ: Lawrence Erlbaum.

Iyengar, S., & Simon, A. (1993). News coverage of the Gulf Crisis and public opinion: A study of agenda-setting, priming, and framing. *Communication Research, 20,* 365–383.

Jackson, K. M., & Aiken, L. S. (2000). A psychosocial model of sun protection and sunbathing in young women: The impact of health beliefs, attitudes, norms, and self-efficacy for sun protection. *Health Psychology, 19,* 469–478.

Jacobs, J. (1961). *The death and life of great American cities.* New York: Random House.

James, J. R., & Tetrick, L. E. (1986). Confirmatory analytic tests of three causal models relating job perceptions to job satisfaction. *Journal of Applied Psychology, 71,* 77–82.

Janis, I. L. (1972). *Victims of groupthink.* Boston: Houghton Mifflin.

Janis, I. (1982). *Groupthink* (2nd ed.). Boston: Houghton Mifflin.

Janis, I. L. (1983). *Groupthink: Psychological studies of policy decisions and fiascoes* (2nd ed.). Boston: Houghton Mifflin.

Janis, I. L. (1996). Groupthink. In J. Billsberry (Ed.), *The effective manager: Perspectives and illustrations* (pp. 166–178). London: Sage.

Janis, I. L., & Feshbach, S. (1953). Effects of fear-arousing communications. *Journal of Abnormal and Social Psychology, 48,* 78–92.

Janis, I. L., & Mann, L. (1977). *Decision making: A psychological analysis of conflict, choice, and commitment.* New York: Free Press.

Janz, N. K., & Becker, M. H. (1984). The health belief model: A decade later. *Health Education Quarterly, 11,* 1–47.

Jason, L. A., & Rose, T. (1984). Influencing the passage of child passenger restraint legislation. *American Journal of Community Psychology, 12,* 485–495.

Jenkins-Hall, K., & Sacco, W. P. (1991). Effect of client race and depression on evaluations by white therapists. *Journal of Social and Clinical Psychology, 10,* 322–333.

Johns, G., & Saks, A. M. (2001). *Organizational behaviour: Understanding and managing life at work* (5th ed.). Toronto: Addison–Wesley Longman.

Johnson, J. G., Han, Y. S., Douglas, C. J. Johannet, C. M., & Russell, T. (1998). Attributions for positive life events predict recovery from depression among psychiatric inpatients: An investigation of the Needles and Abramson model of recovery from depression. *Journal of Consulting and Clinical Psychology, 66,* 369–376.

Johnson-Cartee, K. S., & Copeland, G. A. (1991). *Negative political advertising.* Hillsdale, NJ: Lawrence Erlbaum.

Johnston, L. D., O'Malley, P. M., & Bachman, J. G. (1999). *National survey results on drug use from the Monitoring the Future study, 1975–1998,* Vol. 2: *College students and young adults* (NIH Publication No. 99–4661). Washington, DC: Government Printing Office.

Joiner, T. E., Steer, R. A., Abramson, L. Y., Metalsky, G. I., & Schmidt, N. B. (2001). Hopelessness depression as a distinct dimension of depressive symptoms among clinical and non-clinical samples. *Behaviour Research and Therapy, 39,* 523–526.

Joinson, C. (1999, May). Teams at work. *HR Magazine,* pp. 30–36.

Jones, E. E. (1998). Major developments in five decades of social psychology. In D. T. Gilbert, S. T. Fiske, & G. Lindzey (Eds.), *The handbook of social psychology* (4th ed., Vol. 1, pp. 3–57). New York: McGraw–Hill.

Jones, E. E., & Harris, V. A. (1967). The attribution of attitudes. *Journal of Experimental Social Psychology, 3,* 1–24.

Jones, E. E., & Nisbett, R. E. (1972). The actor and the observer: Divergent perceptions of the causes of behavior. In E. E. Jones, D. E. Kanouse, H. H. Kelley, R. E. Nisbett, S. Valins, & B. Weiner (Eds.), *Attribution: Perceiving the causes of behavior* (pp. 79–94). Morristown, NJ: General Learning.

Jones, J. M. (1997). *Prejudice and racism* (2nd ed.). New York: McGraw–Hill.

Jones, L. M., & Foley, L. A. (2003). Educating children to decategorize racial groups. *Journal of Applied Social Psychology, 33,* 554–564.

Jones, M. (1953). *The therapeutic community: A new treatment method in psychiatry.* New York: Basic Books.

Josephson, W. L. (1987). Television violence and children's aggression: Testing the priming, social script, and disinhibition predictions. *Journal of Personality and Social Psychology, 53,* 882–890.

Joy, L. A., Kimball, M. M., & Zabrack, M. L. (1986). Television and children's aggressive behavior. In T. M. Williams (Ed.), *The impact of television: A natural experiment in three communities* (pp. 303–360). San Diego: Academic Press.

Judge, T. A., & Bono, J. E. (2001). Relationship of core self-evaluation traits—self-esteem, generalized self-efficacy, locus of control, and emotional stability—with job satisfaction and job performance: A meta-analysis. *Journal of Applied Psychology, 86,* 80–92.

Judge, T. A., Heller, D., & Mount, M. K. (2002). Five-factor model of personality and job satisfaction. *Journal of Applied Psychology, 87,* 530–541.

Judge, T. A., Thoresen, C. J., Bono, J. E., & Patton, G. K. (2001). The job satisfaction–job performance relationship: A qualitative and quantitative review. *Psychological Bulletin, 127,* 376–407.

Kahle, L. R., & Beatty, S. E. (1987). Cognitive consequences of legislating postpurchase behavior: Growing up with the bottle bill. *Journal of Applied Social Psychology, 17,* 828–843.

Kahneman, D., & Tversky, A. (1972). Subjective probability: A judgment of representativeness. *Cognitive Psychology, 3,* 430–454.

Kahneman, D., & Tversky, A., (1982). The psychology of preferences. *Scientific American, 39,* 341–350.

Kameda, T., & Sugimori, S. (1993). Psychological entrapment in group decision making: An assigned decision rule and a groupthink phenomenon. *Journal of Personality and Social Psychology, 65,* 282–292.

Kane, T. D., Marks, M. A., Zaccaro, S. J., & Blair, V. (1996). Self-efficacy, personal goals, and wrestlers' self-regulation. *Journal of Sport & Exercise Psychology, 18,* 36–48.

Kanner, A. D., Coyne, J. C., Schaefer, C., & Lazarus, R. S. (1981). Comparison of two modes of stress measurement: Daily hassles and uplifts versus major life events. *Journal of Behavioral Medicine, 4,* 1–39.

Kaplan, R. (2000). Two pathways to prevention. *American Psychologist, 55,* 382–397.

Kaplan, R., & Saccuzzo, D. P. (2001). *Psychological testing.* Belmont, CA: Wadsworth.

Karasawa, M. (1991). Toward an assessment of social identity: The structure of group identification and its effects on in-group evaluations. *British Journal of Social Psychology, 30,* 293–307.

Kashani, J. H., Jones, M. R., Bumby, K. M., & Thomas, L. A. (2001). Youth violence: Psychosocial risk factors, treatment, prevention, and recommendations. In H. M. Walker & M. H. Epstein (Eds.), *Making schools safer and violence free: Critical issues, solutions, and recommended practices* (pp. 39–49). Austin, TX: Pro-Ed.

Kashima, Y., Siegal, M., Tanaka, K., & Kashima, E. S. (1992). Do people believe behaviours are consistent with attitudes? Towards a cultural psychology of attribution processes. *British Journal of Social Psychology, 31,* 111–124.

Kassin, S. M. (1997). The psychology of confession evidence. *American Psychologist, 52,* 221–233.

Kassin, S. M., & Kiechel, K. L. (1996). The social psychology of false confessions: Compliance, internalization, and confabulations. *Psychological Science, 7,* 125–128.

Kassin, S. M., Williams, L. N., & Saunders, C. L. (1990). Dirty tricks of cross-examination: The influence of conjectural evidence on the jury. *Law and Human Behavior, 14,* 373–384.

Katz, D., & Kahn, R. L. (1966). *The social psychology of organizations.* New York: John Wiley.

Kawakami, K., & Dion, K. L. (1995). Social identity and affect as determinants of collective action: Toward an integration of relative deprivation and social identity theories. *Theory and Psychology, 5,* 551–577.

Keil, L. J., McClintock, C. G., Kramer, R., & Platow, M. J. (1990). Children's use of social comparison standards in judging performance and their effects on self-evaluation. *Contemporary Educational Psychology, 15,* 75–91.

Kelley, H. H. (1973). The process of causal attribution. *American Psychologist, 28,* 107–128.

Kelley, H. H., & Thibaut, J. W. (1978). *Interpersonal relations: A theory of interdependence.* New York: John Wiley.

Kelley, G. (1955). *The psychology of personal constructs.* New York: Norton.

Kelman, H. (1958). Compliance, identification, and internalization: Three processes of attitude change. *Journal of Conflict Resolution, 2,* 51–60.

Kennedy, D. (1991). The young child's experience of space and child care center design: A practical meditation. *Children's Environments Quarterly, 8,* 37–48.

Keppel, B. (2002). Kenneth B. Clark in the patterns of American culture. *American Psychologist, 57,* 29–38.

Kerman, S., Kimball, T., & Martin, M. (1980). *Teacher expectations and student achievement: Coordinator manual.* Bloomington, IN: Phi Delta Kappa.

Kimmel, A. J. (2004). Ethical issues in social psychology research. In C. Sansone, C. C. Morf, & A. T. Panter (Eds.), *The Sage handbook of methods in social psychology* (pp. 45–70). Thousand Oaks, CA: Sage.

Kingston, K. M., & Hardy, L. (1997). Effects of different types of goals on processes that support performance. *Sport Psychologist, 11,* 277–293.

Kipnis, D. (1997). Ghosts, taxonomies, and social psychology. *American Psychologist, 52,* 205–212.

Kiragu, K. (2001). *Youth and HIV/AIDS: Can we avoid catastrophe?* (Population Reports, Vol. 29, No. 3). Retrieved April 23, 2004, from www.infohealth.org/pr/112edsum.shtml

Kirby, B. J. (1999). Income source and race effects on new-neighbor evaluations. *Journal of Applied Social Psychology, 29,* 1497–1511.

Kirsh, S. J., & Olczak, P. V. (2000). Violent comic books and perceptions of ambiguous provocation situations. *Media Psychology, 2,* 47–62.

Klare, M. (2001). *Resource wars: The new landscape of global conflict.* New York: Henry Holt.

Klayman, J., & Ha, Y-W. (1987). Confirmation, disconfirmation, and information in hypothesis testing. *Psychological Review, 94,* 211–228.

Kleinknecht, R. A., Dinnel, D. L., Kleinknecht, E. E., Hiruma, N., & Harada, N. (1997). Cultural factors in social anxiety: A comparison of social phobia symptoms and taijin kyofusho. *Journal of Anxiety Disorders, 11,* 157–177.

Kneidinger, L. M., Maple, T. L., & Tross, S. A. (2001). Touching behavior in sport: Functional components, analysis of sex differences, and ethological considerations. *Journal of Nonverbal Behavior, 25,* 43–62.

Knox, R. E., & Inkster, J. A. (1968). Post-decision dissonance at post time. *Journal of Personality and Social Psychology, 8,* 319–323.

Koch, H. (1970). *The panic broadcast.* Boston: Little, Brown.

Köhnken, G. (1996). Social psychology and the law. In G. R. Semin & K. Fiedler (Eds.), *Applied social psychology* (pp. 257–281). Thousand Oaks, CA: Sage.

Komorita, S. S., & Parks, C. D. (1994). *Social dilemmas.* Madison, WI: Brown & Benchmark.

Kondowe, E. B., & Mulera, D. (1999). *A cultural approach to HIV/AIDS prevention and care: Malawi's experience.* Paris: UN Educational, Scientific, and Cultural Organization.

Konovsky, M. A., & Organ, D. W. (1996). Dispositional and contextual determinants of organizational citizenship behavior. *Journal of Organizational Behavior, 17,* 253–266.

Kowalski, R. M., & Leary, M. R. (Eds.). (1999). *The social psychology of emotional and behavioral problems: Interfaces of social and clinical psychology.* Washington, DC: American Psychological Association.

Kozub, S. A., & McDonnell, J. F. (2000). Exploring the relationship between cohesion and collective efficacy in rugby teams. *Journal of Sport Behavior, 23,* 120–129.

Kramer, G. P., Kerr, N. L., & Carroll, J. S. (1990). Pretrial publicity, judicial remedies, and jury bias. *Law and Human Behavior, 14,* 409–438.

Kramer, R. M., & Neale, M. A. (Eds.). (1998). *Power and influence in organizations.* Thousand Oaks, CA: Sage.

Kraut, R., Patterson, M., Lundmark, V., Kiesler, S., Mukopadhyay, T., & Scherlis, W. (1998). Internet paradox: A social technology that reduces social involvement and psychological well-being? *American Psychologist, 53,* 1017–1031.

Krcmar, M., & Greene, K. (2000). Connections between violent television exposure and adolescent risk taking. *Media Psychology, 2,* 195–217.

Kristoff, A. L. (1996). Person–organization fit: An integrative review of its conceptualizations, measurement, and implications. *Personnel Psychology, 49,* 1–49.

Kraus, S. J. (1997). Attitudes and the prediction of behavior: A meta-analysis of the empirical literature. *Personality and Social Psychology Bulletin, 21,* 58–75.

Krone, K. J., Jablin, F. M., & Putnam, L. L. (1987). Communication theory and organizational communication: Multiple perspectives. In F. M. Jablin, L. L. Putnam, K. H. Roberts, & L. W. Porter (Eds.), *Handbook of organizational communication: An interdisciplinary perspective* (pp. 18–40). Newbury Park, CA: Sage.

Kroon, M. B. R., Hart, P., & van Kreveld, D. (1991). Managing group decision making processes: Individual versus collective accountability and groupthink. *International Journal of Conflict Management, 2,* 91–115.

Krosnick, J. A., & Brannon, L. A. (1993). The impact of the Gulf War on the ingredients of presidential evaluations: Multidimensional effects of political involvement. *American Political Science Review, 87,* 963–975.

Krueger, J., Ham, J. J., & Linford, K. M. (1996). Perceptions of behavioral consistency: Are people aware of the actor–observer effect? *Psychological Science, 7,* 259–264.

Krupat, E., & Kubzansky, P. E. (1987, October). Designing to deter crime. *Psychology Today,* pp. 58–61.

Kuklinski, M. R., & Weinstein, R. S. (2001). Classroom and developmental differences in a path model of teacher expectancy effects. *Child Development, 72,* 1554–1578.

Kunda, Z. (1999). *Social cognition: Making sense of people.* Cambridge, MA: MIT Press.

Kwak, H., Zinkhan, G. M., & Dominick, J. R. (2002). The moderating role of gender and compulsive buying tendencies in the cultivation effects of TV shows and TV advertising: A cross-cultural study between the United States and South Korea. *Media Psychology, 4,* 77–111.

Kwantes, C. T. (2003). Organizational citizenship and withdrawal behaviors in the USA and India: Does commitment make a difference? *International Journal of Cross-Cultural Management, 3,* 5–26.

Kyllo, L. B., & Landers, D. M. (1995). Goal setting in sport and exercise: A research synthesis to resolve the controversy. *Journal of Sport and Exercise Psychology, 17,* 117–137.

Ladd, G. W., Price, J. M., & Hart, C. H. (1988). Predicting preschoolers' peer status from their playground behaviors and peer contacts. *Child Development, 59,* 986–992.

Lafreniere, K. D., Ledgerwood, D. M., & Docherty, A. L. (1997). Influences of leaving home, perceived family support, and gender on the transition to university. *Guidance and Counselling, 12,* 14–18.

La Greca, A. M., & Stone, W. L. (1993). Social anxiety scale for children. *Journal of Clinical Child Psychology, 22,* 17–27.

Lamb, M. E., Sternberg, K. J., Orbach, Y., Hershkowitz, I., & Esplin, P. W. (1999). Forensic interviews with children. In A. Memon & R. Bull (Eds.), *Handbook of the psychology of interviewing* (pp. 253–277). New York: John Wiley.

Lambert, W. E. (1992). Challenging established views on social issues: The power and limitations of research. *American Psychologist, 47,* 533–542.

Langlois, J. H., Kalakanis, L., Rubenstein, A. J., Larson, A., Hallam, A., & Smoot, M. (2000). Maxims or myths of beauty? A meta-analytic and theoretical review. *Psychological Bulletin, 126,* 390–423.

Lansing, J. B., & Marans, R. W. (1969). Evaluation of neighborhood quality. *Journal of the American Institute of Planners, 35,* 195–199.

LaPierre, R. (1934). Attitudes versus actions. *Social Forces, 13,* 230–237.

Latané, B., & Darley, J. (1970). *The unresponsive bystander: Why doesn't he help?* New York: Appleton–Century–Crofts.

Latané, B., & Nida, S. (1981). Ten years of research on group size and helping. *Psychological Bulletin, 89,* 308–324.

Lau, R. R., Jacobs Quadrel, M., & Hartman, K. A. (1990). Development and change of young adults' preventive health beliefs and behavior: Influence from parents and peers. *Journal of Health and Social Behavior, 31,* 240–259.

Lawler, E. E., III, & Porter, L. W. (1967). The effect of performance on job satisfaction. *Industrial Relations, 7,* 20–28.

Lazarus, R. S., & Folkman, S. (1984). *Stress, appraisal, and coping.* New York: Springer.

Lazarus, R. S., & Launier, R. (1978). Stress-related transactions between person and environment. In L. A. Pervin & M. Lewis (Eds.), *Perspectives in interactional psychology* (pp. 287–327). New York: Plenum.

Leary, M. R., & Atherton, S. C. (1986). Self-efficacy, social anxiety, and inhibition in interpersonal encounters. *Journal of Social and Clinical Psychology, 4,* 256–267.

Leary, M. R., & Kowalski, R. M. (1995). *Social anxiety: Emotions and social behavior.* New York: Guilford.

Leary, M. R., & Miller, R. S. (1986). *Social psychology and dysfunctional behavior.* New York: Springer-Verlag.

Lee, R. (2000). *Unobtrusive methods in social research.* Buckingham, UK: Open University Press.

Leigh, T. W., & Summers, J. O. (2002). An initial evaluation of industrial buyers' impressions of salespersons' nonverbal cues. *Journal of Personal Selling and Sales Management, 22,* 41–53.

Leippe, M. R., & Eisenstadt, D. (1994). Generalization of dissonance reduction: Decreasing prejudice through induced compliance. *Journal of Personality and Social Psychology, 67,* 395–413.

Leo, R. (1992). From coercion to deception: The changing nature of police interrogations in America. *Crime, Law, and Social Change, 18,* 35–59.

Lepper, M. R., Greene, D., & Nisbett, R. E. (1973). Undermining children's intrinsic interest with extrinsic reward: A test of the "overjustification" hypothesis. *Journal of Personality and Social Psychology, 28,* 129–137.

Leung, K. (1988) Theoretical advances in justice behavior: Some cross-cultural inputs. In M. H. Bond (Ed.), *The cross-cultural challenge to social psychology* (pp. 218–229). Newbury Park, CA: Sage.

Levine. J. M., & Moreland, R. L. (1998). Small groups. In D. Gilbert, S. Fiske, & G. Lindzey (Eds.), *The handbook of social psychology* (4th ed., Vol. 2, pp. 415–469). New York: McGraw–Hill.

Levine, J. M., & Thompson, L. (1996). Intragroup conflict. In E. T. Higgins & A. W. Kruglanski (Eds.), *Social psychology: Handbook of basic principles* (pp. 745–776). New York: Guilford.

LeVine, R. A., & Campbell, D. T. (1972). *Ethnocentrism: Theories of conflict, ethnic attitudes, and group behavior.* New York: John Wiley.

Levy, L. H. (2000). Self-help groups. In J. Rapport & E. Seidman (Eds.), *Handbook of community psychology* (pp. 591–613). New York: Plenum.

Levy, P. E. (2003). *Industrial/Organizational psychology: Understanding the workplace.* Boston: Houghton Mifflin.

Lewin, K. (1936). *A dynamic theory of personality.* New York: McGraw–Hill.

Lewin, K. (1946). Action research and minority problems. *Journal of Social Issues, 2*(4), 34–46.

Lewin, K. (1947). Frontiers in group dynamics: II. Channels of group life—Social planning and action research. *Human Relations, 1,* 143–153.

Lewin, K. (1951a). *Field theory in social science.* New York: Harper. (Original work published in 1944)

Lewin, K. (1951b). Problems of research in social psychology. In D. Cartwright (Ed.), *Field theory in social science* (pp. 155–169). New York: Harper & Row.

Lewin, K., Lippitt, R., & White, R. K. (1939). Patterns of aggressive behavior in experimentally created "social climates." *Journal of Social Psychology, 10,* 271–301.

Lichacz, F. M., & Partington, J. T. (1996). Collective efficacy and true team performance. *International Journal of Sport Psychology, 27,* 146–158.

Lichtenberg, J. W. (1997). Expertise in counseling psychology: A concept in search of support. *Educational Psychology Review, 9,* 221–238.

Liden, R. C., Martin, C. L., & Parsons, C. K. (1993). Interviewer and applicant behaviors in employment interviews. *Academy of Management Journal, 36,* 372–386.

Lieberman, J. D., & Arndt, J. (2000). Understanding the effects of limiting instructions: Social psychological explanations for the failures of instructions to disregard pretrial publicity and other inadmissible evidence. *Psychology, Public Policy, and Law, 6,* 677–711.

Link, B. G., Phelan, J. C., Bresnahan, M., Stueve, A., & Pescosolido, B. A. (1999). Public conceptions of mental illness: Labels, causes, dangerousness, and social distance. *American Journal of Public Health, 89,* 1328–1333.

Linville, P. W., Fischer, G. W., & Salovey, P. (1989). Perceived distributions of the characteristics of in-group and out-group members: Empirical evidence and a computer simulation. *Journal of Personality and Social Psychology, 57,* 165–188.

Linz, D. (1989). Exposure to sexually explicit materials and attitudes toward rape: A comparison of study results. *Journal of Sex Research, 26,* 50–84.

Linz, D. G., Donnerstein, E., & Penrod, S. (1988). Effects of long-term exposure to violent and sexually degrading depictions of women. *Journal of Personality and Social Psychology, 55,* 758–768.

Lippmann, W. (1922). *Public opinion.* New York: Macmillan.

Lipton, D. S. (1998). Therapeutic community treatment programming in corrections. *Psychology, Crime, and Law, 4,* 213–263.

Lloyd, W. F. (1968). *Lectures on population, value, poor laws, and rent.* New York: August M. Kelley. (Original work published in 1837)

Locke, E. A. (1976). The nature and causes of job satisfaction. In M. D. Dunnette (Ed.), *Handbook of industrial and organizational psychology* (pp. 1297–1350). Chicago: Rand McNally.

Locke, E. A., & Latham, G. P. (1985). The application of goal setting to sports. *Journal of Sport Psychology, 7,* 205–222.

Locke. E. A., Tirnauer, D., Roberson, Q., Goldman, B., Latham, M. E., & Weldon, E. (2001). The importance of the individual in an age of groupism. In M. E. Turner (Ed.), *Groups at work: Theory and research* (pp. 501–528). Mahwah, NJ: Lawrence Erlbaum.

Lodzinski, A. (1995). Linking program design and evaluation: Five guiding questions for program designers. In A. J. Love (Ed.), *Evaluation methods sourcebook* (pp. 30–38). Ottawa, Ontario: Canadian Evaluation Society.

Lodzinski, A. (2003). *Effective human service program design and in-house evaluation* (5th ed.). Toronto: Lodzinski Associates.

Loftus, E. F., & Palmer, J. C. (1974). Reconstruction of automobile destruction: An example of the interaction between language and memory. *Journal of Verbal Learning and Verbal Behavior, 13,* 585–589.

London, K., & Nunez, N. (2000). The effect of jury deliberations on jurors' propensity to disregard inadmissible evidence. *Journal of Applied Psychology, 85,* 932–939.

Longman, J. (2000). *The girls of summer: The U.S. women's soccer team and how it changed the world.* New York: HarperCollins.

Loring, M., & Powell, B. (1988). Gender, race, and the DSM-III: A study of the objectivity of psychiatric diagnostic behavior. *Journal of Health and Social Behavior, 29,* 1–22.

Lowenberg, G., & Conrad, K. A. (1998). *Current perspectives in industrial/organizational psychology.* Boston: Allyn & Bacon.

Lu, V. (1999, August 15). Rising sick days cost billions. *Toronto Star,* pp. A1, A10.

Lytton, H. (1990). Child and parent effects in boys' conduct disorder: A reinterpretation. *Developmental Psychopathology, 26,* 683–697.

MacDonald, J. E., & Gifford, R. (1989). Territorial cues and defensible space theory: The burglar's point of view. *Journal of Environmental Psychology, 9,* 193–205.

MacKenzie, D. L., Wilson, D. B., & Kidder, S. B. (2001). Effects of correctional boot camps on offending. *Annals of the American Academy of Political and Social Sciences, 578,* 126–143.

Madden, M. (2003, December). *America's online pursuits: The changing picture of who's online and what they do.* Retrieved June 4, 2004, from www.pewinternet.org/ppf/r/106/report_display.asp

Madon, S. (1997). What do people believe about gay males? A study of stereotype content and strength. *Sex Roles, 37,* 663–685.

Madon, S., Jussim, L., & Eccles, J. (1997). In search of the powerful self-fulfilling prophecy. *Journal of Personality and Social Psychology, 72,* 791–809.

Maguire, P. (1987). *Doing participatory research: A feminist approach.* Amherst: University of Massachusetts Press.

Magyar, T. M., Feltz, D. L., & Simpson, I. P. (2004). Individual and crew level determinants of collective efficacy in rowing. *Journal of Sport and Exercise Psychology, 26,* 136–154.

Main, M., Kaplan, N., & Cassidy, J. (1985). Security in infancy, childhood, and adulthood: A move to the level of representation. *Monographs of the Society for Research in Child Development, 50*(1–2), 66–104.

Malamuth, N. M. (1981). Rape proclivity among males. *Journal of Social Issues, 37,* 138–157.

Malamuth, N., & Donnerstein, E. (1984). *Pornography and sexual aggression.* San Diego: Academic Press.

Mallet, P., & Rodriguez-Tome, G. (1999). Social anxiety with peers in 9- to 14-year-olds: Developmental process and relations with self-consciousness and perceived peer acceptance. *European Journal of Psychology of Education, 14,* 387–402.

Mantsios, G. (2000). Media magic: Making class invisible. In T. Ore (Ed.), *The social construction of difference and inequality: Race, class, gender, and sexuality* (pp. 850–894). Mountain View, CA: Mayfield.

Manz, C. C., & Sims, H. P., Jr. (1982). The potential for "groupthink" in autonomous work groups. *Human Relations, 35,* 773–784.

Manz, C. C., & Sims, H. P., Jr. (1993). *Business without bosses: How self-managing teams are building high performance companies.* New York: John Wiley.

Maoz, I. (2002). Is there contact at all? Intergroup interaction in planned contact interventions between Jews and Arabs in Israel. *International Journal of Intercultural Relations, 26,* 185–197.

Mark, M. M., & Bryant, F. B. (1984). Potential pitfalls of a more applied social psychology: Review and recommendations. *Basic and Applied Social Psychology, 5,* 231–253.

Marks, M. (1999). A test of the impact of collective efficacy in routine and novel performance environments. *Human Performance, 12,* 295–309.

Marsella, A. (1998). Toward a global community psychology: Meeting the needs of a changing world. *American Psychologist, 53,* 1282–1292.

Martens, R., Landers, D. M., & Loy, J. W. (1972). *Sport Cohesiveness Questionnaire.* Washington, DC: AAHPERD Publications.

Martin-Baró, I. (1989, June–July). *La institucionalización de la Guerra* [Institutionalization of war]. Paper presented at the annual meeting of the InterAmerican Psychological Association, Buenos Aires, Argentina.

Maslow, A. H. (1943). A theory of human motivation. *Psychological Review, 50,* 370–396.

Maslow, A. H. (1970). *Motivation and personality.* New York: Harper & Row.

Matarazzo, J. D. (1980). Behavioral health and behavioral medicine: Frontiers for a new health psychology. *American Psychologist, 35,* 807–817.

Matsumoto, D., & Juang, L. (2004). *Culture and psychology* (3rd ed.). Belmont, CA: Wadsworth.

Mayo, C., & La France, M. (1980). Toward an applicable social psychology. In R. F. Kidd & M. J. Saks (Eds.), *Advances in applied social psychology* (Vol. 1, pp. 81–96). Hillsdale, NJ: Lawrence Erlbaum.

Mazur, A. (1977). Interpersonal spacing on public benches in "contact" and "noncontact" cultures. *Journal of Social Psychology, 101,* 53–58.

McAlister, A. L., Perry, C., & Maccoby, N. (1980). Pilot study of smoking, alcohol, and drug abuse prevention. *American Journal of Public Health, 70,* 719–721.

McAllister, H. A. (1996). Self-serving bias in the classroom: Who shows it? Who knows it? *Journal of Educational Psychology, 88,* 123–131.

McChesney, R. W. (1999). *Rich media, poor democracy: Communication politics in dubious times.* New York: New Press.

McCombs, M., & Reynolds, A. (2002). News influence on our pictures of the world. In J. Bryant & D. Zillmann (Eds.), *Media effects: Advances in theory and research* (2nd ed., pp. 1–18). Mahwah, NJ: Lawrence Erlbaum.

McFarland, S. G. (1981). Effects of question order on survey responses. *Public Opinion Quarterly, 45,* 208–215.

McGraw, K. O. (1978). The detrimental effects of reward on performance: A literature review and a prediction model. In M. R. Lepper & D. Greene (Eds.), *The hidden costs of reward: New perspectives on the psychology of human motivation* (pp. 33–60). Hillsdale, NJ: Lawrence Erlbaum.

McGuire, T. W., Kiesler, S., & Siegel, J. (1987). Group and computer-mediated discussion effects in risk decision making. *Journal of Personality and Social Psychology, 52,* 917–930.

McGuire, W. J. (1964). Inducing resistance to persuasion: Some contemporary approaches. In L. Berkowitz (Ed.), *Advances in experimental social psychology* (Vol. 1, pp. 191–229). New York: Academic Press.

McKown, C., & Weinstein, R. (2002). Modeling the role of child ethnicity and gender in children's differential response to teacher expectations. *Journal of Applied Social Psychology, 32,* 159–184.

McLeod, P. L., Lobel. S. A., & Cox, T. H. (1996). Ethnic diversity and creativity in small groups. *Small Group Research, 27,* 248–264.

Mednick, S. A., Moffitt, T. E., Gabrielli, W., & Hutchings, B. (1986). Genetic influences in criminal behavior: A review. In D. Olweus, J. Block, & M. Radke-Yarrow (Eds.), *Development of antisocial and prosocial behavior* (pp. 33–50). San Diego: Academic Press.

Meehl, P. E. (1960). The cognitive activity of the clinician. *American Psychologist, 15,* 19–27.

Meeks, S. (1990). Age bias in the diagnostic decision-making behavior of clinicians. *Professional Psychology: Research and Practice, 21,* 279–284.

Mehrabian, A., & Diamond, S. G. (1971). The effects of furniture arrangement, props, and personality on social interaction. *Journal of Personality and Social Psychology, 20,* 18–30.

Mehrabian, A., & Ferris, S. R. (1967). Inference of attitudes from nonverbal communication in two channels. *Journal of Consulting Psychology, 31,* 248–252.

Mello-Goldner, D., & Jackson, J. (1999). Premenstrual syndrome (PMS) as a self-handicapping strategy among college women. *Journal of Social Behavior and Personality, 14,* 607–616.

Merriam–Webster. (2003). *Online dictionary.* Retrieved May 20, 2003, from www.merriam-webster.com

Merritt, A. C., & Helmreich, R. L. (1996). Human factors on the flightdeck: The influence of national culture. *Journal of Cross-Cultural Psychology, 27,* 5–24.

Merry, S. E. (1981). *Urban danger: Life in a neighborhood of strangers.* Philadelphia: Temple University Press.

Merton, R. (1948). The self-fulfilling prophecy. *Antioch Review, 8,* 193–210.

Michelson, W. (1976). *Man and his urban environment: A sociological approach.* Reading, MA: Addison–Wesley.

Milgram, S. (1963). Behavioral study of obedience. *Journal of Abnormal and Social Psychology, 67,* 371–378.

Milgram, S. (1970). The experience of living in cities. *Science, 167,* 1461–1468.

Milgram, S. (1974). *Obedience to authority: An experimental approach.* New York: Harper & Row.

Miller, A. G., & Lawson, T. (1989). The effect of an informational option on the fundamental attribution error. *Personality and Social Psychology Bulletin, 15,* 194–204.

Miller, G. A. (1969). Psychology as a means of promoting human welfare. *American Psychologist, 24,* 1063–1075.

Mills, J. F., & Kroner, D. G. (1999). *Measures of criminal attitudes and associates: User guide.* Unpublished report available from the Kingston Penitentiary, Department of Psychology, Kingston, Ontario.

Mincy, R. B. (2000). The underclass: Concept, controversy, and evidence. In K. Rosenblum & T. C. Travis (Eds.), *The meaning of difference: American constructions of race, sex and gender, social class, and sexual orientation* (pp. 130–142). Boston: McGraw–Hill.

Miranda, S. M. (1994). Avoidance of groupthink: Meeting management using group support systems. *Small Group Research, 25,* 105–136.

Mirolli, K., Henderson, P., & Hills, D. (1998). *Coworkers' influence on job satisfaction.* Paper presented at the annual Graduate Student Conference in Industrial/Organizational Psychology and Organizational Behavior, San Diego, CA.

Mirrer, S. B. (1987). Using anthropometric data in the design of children's health care environments. *Children's Environments Quarterly, 4,* 6–11.

Mitchell, T., & Kalb, L. (1981). Effects of outcome knowledge and outcome valence on supervisor's evaluations. *Journal of Applied Psychology, 66,* 604–612.

Mitchell, T., & Wood, R. (1980). Supervisor's responses to subordinate poor performance: A test of an attributional model. *Organizational Behavior and Human Decision Processes, 25,* 123–138.

Moffitt, T. E. (1993). Adolescence-limited and life-course-persistent antisocial behavior: A developmental taxonomy. *Psychology Review, 100,* 674–701.

Moffitt, T. E., Caspi, A., Dickson, N., Silva, P., & Stanton, W. (1996). Childhood-onset versus adolescent-onset antisocial conduct problems in males: Natural history from ages 3 to 18 years. *Development and Psychopathology, 8,* 399–424.

Moghaddam, F. M. (1998). *Social psychology: Exploring universals across cultures.* New York: Freeman.

Moghaddam, F. M., Taylor, D. M., & Wright, S. C. (1993). *Social psychology in cross-cultural perspective.* New York: Freeman.

Monto, M. A., Newcomb, M. D., Rabow, J., & Hernandez, A. C. (1992). Social status and drunk-driving intervention. *Journal of Studies on Alcohol, 53,* 63–68.

Moorhead, G., Ference, R., & Neck, C. P. (1991). Group decision fiascoes continue: Space shuttle *Challenger* and a revised groupthink framework. *Human Relations, 44,* 539–550.

Moorhead, G., & Griffin, R. W. (1998). *Organizational behavior: Managing people and organizations* (5th ed.). Boston: Houghton Mifflin.

Moorhead, G., Neck, C. P., & West, M. S. (1998). Tendency toward defective decision-making within self-managing teams: The relevance of groupthink for the 21st century. *Organizational Behavior and Human Decision Processes, 73,* 327–351.

Moorman, R. H. (1991). Relationship between organizational justice and organizational citizenship behaviors: Do fairness perceptions influence employee citizenship? *Journal of Applied Psychology, 76,* 845–855.

Moos, R. H. (1973). Conceptualization of human environments. *American Psychologist, 28,* 652–665.

Moos, R. H. (1981). Social-ecological perspectives on health. In G. Stone, F. Cohen, & N. Adler (Eds.), *Health psychology: A handbook* (pp. 523–547). San Francisco: Jossey–Bass.

Moos, R. H. (1987). *Correctional Institutions Environment Scale manual.* Palo Alto, CA: Consulting Psychologists Press.

Morawski, J. G. (2000). Social psychology a century ago. *American Psychologist, 55,* 427–430.

Moreland, R. L., & Zajonc, R. B. (1982). Exposure effects may not depend on stimulus recognition. *Journal of Personality and Social Psychology, 37,* 1085–1089.

Morgan, M. (1990). International cultivation effects. In N. Signorielli & M. Morgan (Eds.), *Cultivation analysis: New directions in media effects research* (pp. 225–247). Newbury Park, CA: Sage.

Mosher, C. E. (2002). Impact of gender and problem severity upon intervention selection. *Sex Roles, 46,* 113–119.

Moskowitz, J. (1989). The primary prevention of alcohol problems: A critical review of the research literature. *Journal of Studies on Alcohol, 50,* 54–88.

Mount, M. K., Harter, J. K., Barrick, M. R., & Colbert, A. (2000, August). *Does job satisfaction moderate the relationship between conscientiousness and job performance?* Paper presented at the meeting of the Academy of Management, Toronto.

Moy, P., & Pfau, M. (2000). *With malice toward all? The media and public confidence in democratic institutions.* Westport, CT: Praeger.

Muehlenhard, C. L., & Miller, E. N. (1988). Traditional and nontraditional men's responses to women's dating initiation. *Behavior Modification, 12,* 385–403.

Mulac, A., Jansma, L. L., & Linz, D. G. (2002). Men's behavior toward women after viewing sexually-explicit films: Degradation makes a difference. *Communication Monographs, 69,* 311–328.

Mullen, B., Anthony, T., Salas, E., & Driskell, J. E. (1994). Group cohesiveness and quality of decision making: An integration of tests of the groupthink hypothesis. *Small Group Research, 25,* 189–204.

Mullen, B., & Copper, C. (1994). The relation between group cohesiveness and performance: An integration. *Psychological Bulletin, 115,* 210–227.

Mullin, C. R., & Linz, D. (1995). Desensitization and resensitization to violence against women: Effects of exposure to sexually violent films on judgments of domestic violence victims. *Journal of Personality and Social Psychology, 69,* 449–459.

Münsterberg, H. (1908). *On the witness stand: Essays on psychology and crime.* New York: McClure.

Muris, P. (2002). Relationships between self-efficacy and symptoms of anxiety disorders and depression in a normal adolescent sample. *Personality and Individual Differences, 32,* 337–348.

Murphy, J. (1998). Using social psychology. In R. Sapsford, A. Still, D. Miell, R. Stevens, & M. Wetherell (Eds.), *Theory and social psychology* (pp. 161–190). Thousand Oaks, CA: Sage.

Murphy, K. R., & Anhalt, R. L. (1992). Is halo error a property of the rater, ratees, or the specific behaviors observed? *Journal of Applied Psychology, 77,* 494–500.

Murray, C. B., & Warden, M. R. (1992). Implications of self-handicapping strategies for academic achievement: A reconceptualization. *Journal of Social Psychology, 132,* 23–37.

Murray, H. A. (1938). *Explorations in personality.* New York: Oxford University Press.

Myers, D. G. (2002). *Social psychology* (7th ed.). Boston: McGraw–Hill.

Myers, D. G., & Spencer, S. J. (2004). *Social psychology* (2nd Canadian ed.). Toronto: McGraw–Hill Ryerson.

Myers, N. D., Feltz, D. L., & Short, S. E.(2004). Collective efficacy and team performance: A longitudinal study of collegiate football teams. *Group Dynamics: Theory, Research, and Practice, 8,* 126–138.

Nathanson, A. I., & Cantor, J. (2000). Reducing the aggressive-promoting effect of violent cartoons by increasing children's fictional involvement with the victim: A study of active mediation. *Journal of Broadcasting & Electronic Media, 44,* 125–142.

Nathanson, C. A., & Becker, M. H. (1986). Family and peer influence on obtaining a method of contraception. *Journal of Marriage and the Family, 48,* 513–525.

Needles, D. J., & Abramson, L.Y. (1990). Positive life events, attributional style, and hopefulness: Testing a model of recovery from depression. *Journal of Abnormal Psychology, 99,* 156–165.

Nelson, G., Laurendeau, M., & Chamberland, C. (2001). A review of programs to promote family wellness and prevent the maltreatment of children. *Canadian Journal of Behavioural Science, 33,* 1–15.

Nelson, T. D. (2002). *The psychology of prejudice.* Boston: Allyn & Bacon.

Nemeth, C. J. (1986). Differential contributions of majority and minority influence. *Psychological Review, 93,* 23–32.

Newcomb, T. M. (1961). *The acquaintance process.* New York: Holt, Rinehart & Winston.

Newman, O. (1972). *Defensible space.* New York: Macmillan.

Newman, O. (1980). *Community of interest.* New York: Anchor/Doubleday.

Nisbett, R. D., & Wilson, T. D. (1977). The halo effect: Evidence for unconscious alteration of judgments. *Journal of Personality and Social Psychology, 35,* 250–256.

Nisbett, R. E., & Cohen, D. (1996). *Culture of honor.* Boulder, CO: Westview.

Norman, P., Conner, M., & Bell, R. (1999). The theory of planned behavior and smoking cessation. *Health Psychology, 18,* 89–94.

Office of Management and Budget. (2001). *Budget of the United States government, analytical perspectives, fiscal year 2002.* Washington, DC: Government Printing Office.

Ofori-Dankwa, J. C., & Julian, J. D. (2002). Toward diversity and similarity curves: Implication for theory, research, and practice. *Human Relations, 55,* 199–224.

O'Neill, P. (1989). Responsible to whom? Responsible for what? Some ethical issues in community intervention. *American Journal of Community Psychology, 17,* 323–341.

O'Neill, P. (1998). Communities, collectivities, and the ethics of research. *Canadian Journal of Community Mental Health, 17,* 67–78.

Organ, D. W. (1988). *Organizational citizenship behavior.* Lexington, MA: Lexington Books.

Organ, D. W. (1990). The subtle significance of job satisfaction. *Clinical Laboratory Management Review, 4,* 94–98.

Osgood, C. E. (1962). *An alternative to war or surrender.* Urbana: University of Illinois Press.

Oskamp, S. (1991). *Attitudes and opinions.* Englewood Cliffs, NJ: Prentice Hall.

Oskamp, S. (2000). A sustainable future for humanity: How can psychology help? *American Psychologist, 55,* 496–508.

Oskamp, S., & Schultz, P. W. (1997). *Applied social psychology* (2nd ed.). Upper Saddle River, NJ: Prentice Hall.

Osmond, H. (1957). Function as the basis of psychiatric ward design. *Mental Hospitals, 8,* 23–30.

Osofsky, J. (1995). The effects of exposure to violence on young children. *American Psychologist, 50,* 782–789.

Out, J. W., & Lafreniere, K. D. (2001). Baby Think It Over: Using role-play to prevent teen pregnancy. *Adolescence, 36,* 571–582.

Padgett, V. R., Brislin-Slütz, J. A., & Neal, J. A. (1989). Pornography, erotica, and attitudes toward women: The effects of repeated exposure. *Journal of Sex Research, 26,* 479–491.

Page, S. (1981). Social responsiveness toward mental patients: The general public and others. *Canadian Journal of Psychiatry, 15*(2), 34–37.

Page, S. (1990). The turnaround on pornography research: Some implications for psychology and women. *Canadian Psychology, 31,* 359–367.

Page, S. (1997). An unobtrusive measure of racial behavior in a public cafeteria. *Journal of Applied Social Psychology, 27,* 2172–2176.

Page, S. (2000). Community research: The lost art of unobtrusive measures. *Journal of Applied Social Psychology, 30,* 2126–2136.

Page, S., & Day, D. (1990). Acceptance of the mentally ill in Canadian society: Reality and illusion. *Canadian Journal of Community Mental Health, 9,* 51–62.

Page, S., Lafreniere, K., & Out, J. (1999). An evaluation of the Ten Friends Diner: A collaborative community project. *Psychiatric Rehabilitation Journal, 23,* 171–176.

Paik, H., & Comstock, G. (1994). The effects of television violence on antisocial behavior: A meta-analysis. *Communication Research, 21,* 516–546.

Park, P. (1999). People, knowledge, and change in participatory research. *Management Learning, 30,* 141–157.

Park, P., Brydon-Miller, M., Hall, B., & Jackson, T. (1993). *Voices of change: Participatory research in United States and Canada.* Westport, CT: Bergin & Garvey.

Paskevich, D. M., Brawley, L. R., Dorsch, K. D., & Widmeyer, W. N. (1999). Relationship between collective efficacy and team cohesion: Conceptual and measurement issues. *Group Dynamics: Theory, Research, and Practice, 3,* 210–222.

Pasmore, W., & Friedlander, F. (1982). An action-research program for increasing employee involvement in problem-solving. *Administrative Science Quarterly, 27,* 343–362.

Patterson, G. R., DeBaryshe, B. D., & Ramsey, E. (1989). A developmental perspective on anti-social behavior. *American Psychologist, 44,* 329–335.

Patterson, M. L. (1975). Personal space: Time to burst the bubble? *Man–Environment Systems, 5,* 67.

Paulus, P. B. (1998). Developing consensus about groupthink after all these years. *Organizational Behavior and Human Decision Processes, 73,* 362–374.

Pavkov, T. W., Lewis, D. A., & Lyons, J. S. (1989). Psychiatric diagnoses and racial bias: An empirical investigation. *Professional Psychology: Research and Practice, 20,* 364–368.

Pearson, C. A. L., & Chong, J. (1997). Contributions of job content and social information on organizational commitment and job satisfaction: An exploration in a Malaysian nursing context. *Journal of Occupational and Organizational Psychology, 70,* 357–374.

Penley, L. E., Alexander, E. R., Jernigan, I. E., & Henwood, C. I. (1991). Communication abilities of managers: The relationship to performance. *Journal of Management, 17,* 57–76.

Pennebaker, J. W., Dyer, M. A., Caulkins, R. J., Litowitz, D. L., Ackerman, P. L., Anderson, D. B., & McGraw, K. M. (1979). Don't the girls all get prettier at closing time? A country and western application to psychology. *Personality and Social Psychology Bulletin, 5,* 122–125.

Pennington, N., & Hastie, R. (1986). Evidence evaluation in complex decision making. *Journal of Personality and Social Psychology, 51,* 242–258.

Pepitone, E. A. (1990). Social comparison, relative deprivation, and pupil interaction: Homogeneous versus heterogeneous classrooms. In S. A. Wheelan & E. A. Pepitone (Eds.), *Advances in field theory* (pp. 165–176). Thousand Oaks, CA: Sage.

Perkins, H. W. (2003). The emergence and evolution of the social norms approach to substance abuse prevention. In H. W. Perkins (Ed.), *The social norms approach to preventing school and college age substance abuse: A handbook for educators, counselors, and clinicians* (pp. 21–34). San Francisco: Jossey–Bass.

Perkins, H. W., & Berkowitz, A. D. (1986). Perceiving the community norms of alcohol use among students: Some research implications for campus alcohol education programming. *International Journal of the Addictions, 21,* 961–976.

Perry, D. G., & Perry, L. C. (1976). Identification with film characters, covert aggressive verbalization, and reactions to film violence. *Journal of Research in Personality, 10,* 399–409.

Peters, M., & Robinson, V. (1984). The origins and status of action research. *Journal of Applied Behavioral Science, 20,* 113–124.

Peterson, C., Maier, S. F., & Seligman, M. E. P. (1993). *Learned helplessness: A theory for the age of personal control.* New York: Oxford University Press.

Peterson, C., & Vaidya, R. S. (2001). Explanatory style, expectations, and depressive symptoms. *Personality and Individual Differences, 31,* 1217–1223.

Peterson-Badali, M., & Koegl, C. J. (2002). Juveniles' experiences of incarceration: The role of correctional staff in peer violence. *Journal of Criminal Justice, 30,* 41–49.

Pettigrew, T. (1961). Social psychology and desegregation research. In E. Sampson (Ed.), *Approaches, contexts, and problems of social psychology* (pp. 547–557). Englewood Cliffs, NJ: Prentice Hall.

Pettigrew, T. (1988). The ultimate attribution error. In E. Aronson (Ed.), *The social animal* (pp. 325–344). New York: Freeman.

Petty, R. E. & Wegener, D. T. (1998). Attitude change: Multiple roles for persuasion variables. In D. T. Gilbert, S. T. Fishe, & G. Lindzey (Eds.), *Handbook of social psychology* (4th ed., Vol. 1, pp. 323–390). Boston: McGraw–Hill.

Pfeffer, J. (1983). Organizational demography. In L. L. Cummings & B. M. Staw (Eds.), *Research in organizational behavior* (Vol. 5, pp. 299–357). Greenwich CT: JAI.

Pfeffer, J., Cialdini, R. B., Hanna, B., & Knopoff, K. (1998). Faith in supervision and the self-enhancement bias: Two psychological reasons why managers don't empower workers. *Basic and Applied Social Psychology, 20,* 313–321.

Pfeiffer, A. M., Whelan, J. P., & Martin, J. M. (2000). Decision-making bias in psychotherapy: Effects of hypothesis source and accountability. *Journal of Counseling Psychology, 47,* 429–436.

Pillow, D. R., Zautra, A. J., & Sandler, I. (1996). Major life events and minor stressors: Identifying mediational links in the stress process. *Journal of Personality and Social Psychology, 70,* 381–394.

Platt, J. (1973). Social traps. *American Psychologist, 28,* 641–651.

Pollock, T. G., Whitbred, R. C., & Contractor, N. (2000). Social information processing and job characteristics: A simultaneous test of two theories with implications for job satisfaction. *Human Communication Research, 26,* 292–330.

Porter, L. W., & Steers, R. M. (1973). Organization, work, and personal factors in employee turnover and absenteeism. *Psychological Bulletin, 80,* 151–176.

Posavac, E. J., & Carey, R. G. (1997). *Program evaluation: Methods and case studies* (5th ed.). Upper Saddle River, NJ: Prentice Hall.

Potter, W. J. (2003). *The 11 myths of media violence.* Thousand Oaks, CA: Sage.

Prapavessis, H., & Carron, A. V. (1997). Cohesion and work output. *Small Group Research, 28,* 294–301.

Prasad, J. (1950). A comparative study of rumours and reports in earthquakes. *British Journal of Psychology, 46,* 129–144.

Preiser, W. P. E., & Taylor, A. (1983). The habitability framework: Linking human behavior and physical environment in a special education. *EEQ: Exceptional Education Quarterly, 4,* 1–15.

Prentice, D. A., & Miller, D. T. (1993). Pluralistic ignorance and alcohol use on campus: Some consequences of misperceiving the social norm. *Journal of Personality and Social Psychology, 64,* 243–256.

Price, J. L., & Mueller, C. W. (1986). *Handbook of organizational measurement.* Marshfield, MA: Pitman.

Prilleltensky, I., & Fox, D. (1997). Introducing critical psychology. In D. Fox & I. Prilleltensky (Eds.), *Critical psychology: An introduction* (pp. 3–20). London: Sage.

Prochaska, J. O., & DiClemente, C. C. (1983). Stages and processes of self-change of smoking: Toward an integrative model of change. *Journal of Consulting and Clinical Psychology, 51,* 390–395.

Prochaska, J. O., & DiClemente, C. C. (1986). Toward a comprehensive model of change. In W. R. Miller & N. Heather (Eds.), *Treating addictive behaviors: Processes of change* (pp. 3–27). New York: Plenum.

Prochaska, J. O., DiClemente, C. C., & Norcross, J. C. (1992). In search of how people change: Applications to addictive behaviors. *American Psychologist, 47,* 1102–1114.

Prochaska, J. O., DiClemente, C. C., Velicer, W. F., & Rossi, J. S. (1993). Standardized, individualized, interactive, and personalized self-help programs for smoking cessation. *Health Psychology, 12,* 399–405.

Prohaska, V. (1994). "I know I'll get an A": Confident overestimation of final course grades. *Teaching of Psychology, 21,* 141–143.

Pulakos, E. D., & Wexley, K. N. (1983). Relationship among perceptual similarity, sex, performance, and ratings in manager–subordinate dyads. *Academy of Management Journal, 26,* 129–139.

Putnam, R. (1995). Bowling alone: America's declining social capital. *Journal of Democracy, 6,* 65–78.

Pyke, S. W., & Agnew, N. M. (1991). *The science game: An introduction to research in the social sciences* (5th ed.). Englewood Cliffs, NJ: Prentice Hall.

R. v. Butler, 1 S.C.R. 452, File No. 22191 (1992).

R. v. Parks, 24 C.R. (4th) 81, C.C.C. (3d) 353, 15 O.R. (3d) 324, 65 O.A.C. 122 (1993).

Rabbie, J. M., & Horwitz, M. (1969). Arousal of ingroup–outgroup bias by a chance win or loss. *Journal of Personality and Social Psychology, 13,* 269–277.

Rahim, A., & Bonoma, T. V. (1979). Managing organizational conflict: A model for diagnosis and intervention. *Psychological Reports, 44,* 1323–1344.

Rand, G. (1984). Crime and environment: A review of the literature and its implications for urban architecture and planning. *Journal of Architecture and Planning Research, 1,* 3–19.

Rapoport, A. (1969). *House form and culture.* Englewood Cliffs, NJ: Prentice Hall.

Refuerzo, B. J., & Verderber, S. (1990). Dimensions of person–environment relationships in shelters for victims of domestic violence. *Journal of Architectural and Planning Research, 7,* 33–52.

Regan, P. R. (2003). *The mating game: A primer on love, sex, and marriage.* Thousand Oaks, CA: Sage.

Reich, J. W. (1981). An historical analysis of the field. In L. Bickman (Ed.), *Applied social psychology* (pp. 45–70). Beverly Hills, CA: Sage.

Reichardt, C. S., & Mark, M. M. (1998). Quasi-experimentation. In L. Bickman & D. J. Rog (Eds.), *Handbook of applied social research methods* (pp. 193–228). Thousand Oaks, CA: Sage.

Reid, F. J., Ball, L. J., Morley, A. M., & Evans, B. T. (1997). Styles of group discussion in computer-mediated decision making. *British Journal of Social Psychology, 36,* 241–262.

Remen, S. (1991). Signs, symbols, and the psychiatric environment. *Psychiatric Hospital, 22,* 113–118.

Renick, M. J., & Harter, S. (1989). Impact of social comparisons on the developing self-perceptions of learning disabled students. *Journal of Educational Psychology, 81,* 631–638.

Rentsch, J. R. (1990). Climate and culture: Interactions and qualitative differences in organizational meanings. *Journal of Applied Psychology, 75,* 668–681.

Rentsch, J. R., & Steel, R. P. (1992). Construct and concurrent validation of the Andrews and Withey job satisfaction questionnaire. *Educational and Psychological Measurement, 52,* 357–367.

Rheingold, H. (1993). *The virtual community: Homesteading on the electronic frontier.* Reading, MA: Addison–Wesley.

Rhodewalt, F. (1990). Self-handicappers: Individual differences in the preference for anticipatory self-protective acts. In R. Higgins, C. R. Snyder, & S. Berglas (Eds.), *Self-handicapping: The paradox that isn't* (pp. 69–106). New York: Guilford.

Rhodewalt, F., Sanbonmatsu, D. M., Tschanz, B., Feick, D. L., & Waller, A. (1995). Self-handicapping and interpersonal trade-offs: The effects of claimed self-handicaps on observers' performance evaluations and feedback. *Personality and Social Psychology Bulletin, 21,* 1042–1050.

Riess, M., & Schlenker, B. R. (1977). Attitude change and responsibility avoidance as modes of dilemma resolution in forced-compliance situations. *Journal of Personality and Social Psychology, 35,* 21–30.

Riger, S. (1989). The politics of community intervention. *American Journal of Community Psychology, 17,* 379–383.

Riggio, R. E. (2000). *Introduction to industrial/organizational psychology* (3rd ed.). Upper Saddle River, NJ: Prentice Hall.

Riksheim, E. C., & Chermak, S. M. (1993). Causes of police behaviour revisited. *Journal of Criminal Justice, 21,* 353–382.

Riley, D. A. (1997). Using local research to change 100 communities for children and families. *American Psychologist, 52,* 424–433.

Rind, B., & Strohmetz, D. (2001). Effect on restaurant tipping of presenting customers with an interesting task and of reciprocity. *Journal of Applied Social Psychology, 31,* 1379–1384.

Robbins, S. P., & Langton, N. (2001). *Organizational behaviour: Concepts, controversies, applications.* Toronto: Pearson Education Canada.

Robert, C., Probst, T. M., Martocchio, J. J., Drasgow, F., & Lawler, J. J. (2000). Empowerment and continuous improvement in the United States, Mexico, Poland, and India: Predicting fit on the basis of the dimensions of power distance and individualism. *Journal of Applied Psychology, 85,* 643–658.

Robinson, M. B., & Robinson, C. E. (1997). Environmental characteristics associated with residential burglaries of student apartment complexes. *Environment and Behavior, 29,* 657–675.

Robinson, T. L., & Howard-Hamilton, M. F. (2000). *The convergence of race, ethnicity, and gender.* Upper Saddle River, NJ: Prentice Hall.

Rogers, E. M. (1994). *A history of communication study: A biographical approach.* New York: Free Press.

Rogers, P. N., & Schoenig, S. E. (1994). A time series evaluation of California's 1982 driving-under-the-influence legislative reforms. *Accident Analysis & Prevention, 26,* 63–78.

Roloff, M. E. (1981). *Interpersonal communication: The social exchange approach.* Beverly Hills, CA: Sage.

Romer, D., Jamieson, K. H., & Aday, S. (2003). Television news and the cultivation of fear of crime. *Journal of Communication, 53*(1), 88–104.

Rosenblatt, A. (1984). Concepts of the asylum in the care of the mentally ill. *Hospital and Community Psychiatry, 35,* 244–250.

Rosenfield, S. (1997). Labeling mental illness: The effects of received services and perceived stigma on life satisfaction. *American Sociological Review, 62,* 660–672.

Rosenhan, D. L. (1973). On being sane in insane places. *Science, 179,* 250–258.

Rosenstock, I. M. (1974). Historical origins of the health belief model. *Health Education Monographs, 2,* 328–335.

Rosenthal, R. (1976). *Experimenter effects in behavioral research* (enlarged ed.). New York: Irvington Press.

Rosenthal, R., & Jacobson, L. (1968). *Pygmalion in the classroom: Teacher expectation and pupils' intellectual development.* New York: Holt, Rinehart & Winston.

Roskos-Ewoldsen, D. R. (1997). Attitude accessibility and persuasion: Review and a transactive model. In B. Burleson (Ed.), *Communication Yearbook 20* (pp. 185–225). Thousand Oaks, CA: Sage.

Roskos-Ewoldsen, D. R., Klinger, M. R., & Roskos-Ewoldsen, B. (in press). Media priming: A meta-analysis. In R. W. Press, M. Allen, B. M. Gayle, & N. Burrell (Eds.), *Media effects research: Advances through meta-analysis.* Mahwah, NJ: Lawrence Erlbaum.

Roskos-Ewoldsen, D. R., Roskos-Ewoldsen, B., & Carpentier, F. R. D. (2002). Media priming: A synthesis. In J. Bryant & D. Zillmann (Eds.), *Media effects: Advances in theory and research* (2nd ed., pp. 97–120). Mahwah, NJ: Lawrence Erlbaum.

Ross, L. (1977). The intuitive psychologist and his shortcomings: Distortions in the attribution process. In L. Berkowitz (Ed.), *Advances in experimental social psychology* (Vol. 10, pp. 174–221). New York: Academic Press.

Ross, L., Greene, D., & House, P. (1977). The "false consensus effect": An egocentric bias in social perception and attribution processes. *Journal of Experimental Social Psychology, 13,* 279–301.

Ross, L., & Nisbett, R. E. (1991). *The person and the situation: Perspectives of social psychology.* New York: McGraw–Hill.

Rosser, S., Issakidis, C., & Peters, L. (2003). Perfectionism and social phobia: Relationship between the constructs and impact on cognitive behavior therapy. *Cognitive Therapy and Research, 27,* 143–151.

Rothman, A. J., Haddock, G., & Schwarz, N. (2001). How many partners is too many? Shaping perceptions of personal vulnerability. *Journal of Applied Social Psychology, 31,* 2195–2214.

Royse, D., Thyer, B. A., Padgett, D. K., & Logan, T. K. (2001). *Program evaluation: An introduction* (3rd ed.). Belmont, CA: Wadsworth.

Rudkin, J. (2003). *Community psychology.* Upper Saddle River, NJ: Prentice Hall.

Rule, B. G., Milke, D. L., & Dobbs, A. R. (1992). Design of institutions: Cognitive functioning and social interactions of the aged resident. *Journal of Applied Gerontology, 11,* 475–488.

Runciman, W. G. (1972). *Relative deprivation and social justice.* Middlesex, UK: Penguin.

Russo, N. F., & Denious, J. E. (2001). Violence in the lives of women having abortions: Implications for practice and public policy. *Professional Psychology: Research and Practice, 32,* 142–150.

Russo, N. F., & Zierk, K. L. (1992). Abortion, childbearing, and women's well-being. *Professional Psychology: Research and Practice, 33,* 269–280.

Ryan, W. (1976). *Blaming the victim.* New York: Random House.

Ryhammer, L., & Smith, G. J. W. (1999). Creative and other personality functions as defined by percept–genetic techniques and their relation to organizational conditions. *Creativity Research Journal, 12,* 277–286.

Sadava, S. W. (1997). Applied social psychology: An introduction. In S. Sadava & D. McCreary (Eds.), *Applied social psychology* (pp. 1–9). Upper Saddle River, NJ: Prentice Hall.

Sagiv, L., & Schwartz, S. H. (1995). Value priorities and readiness for out-group social contact. *Journal of Personality and Social Psychology, 69,* 437–448.

Saks, M. J., & Marti, M. W. (1997). A meta-analysis of the effects of jury size. *Law and Human Behavior, 21,* 451–467.

Salancik, G. R., & Pfeffer, J. (1978). A social information processing approach to job attitudes and task design. *Administrative Science Quarterly, 23,* 224–253.

Salovey, P., Rothman, A. J., & Rodin, J. (1998). Health behavior. In D. T. Gilbert, S. T. Fiske, & G. Lindzey (Eds.), *The handbook of social psychology* (4th ed., Vol. 2, pp. 633–683). New York: McGraw–Hill.

Saltz, E., Perry, A., & Cabral, R. (1994). Attacking the personal fable: Role-play and its effect on teen attitudes toward sexual abstinence. *Youth & Society, 26,* 223–242.

Sapsford, R., & Dallos, R. (1998). Resisting social psychology. In R. Sapsford, A. Still, D. Miell, R. Stevens, & M. Wetherell (Eds.), *Theory and social psychology* (pp. 191–208). London: Sage.

Sarafino, E. P. (1998). *Health psychology: Biopsychosocial interactions* (3rd ed.). New York: John Wiley.

Sarafino, E. P. (2002). *Health psychology: Biopsychosocial interactions* (4th ed.). New York: John Wiley.

Sarnoff, I., & Zimbardo, P. (1961). Anxiety, fear, and social facilitation. *Journal of Abnormal and Social Psychology, 62,* 597–605.

Schachter, S. (1959). *The psychology of affiliation: Experimental studies of the sources of gregariousness.* Stanford, CA: Stanford University Press.

Scheck, B., Neufeld, P., & Dwyer, J. (2000). *Actual innocence: Five days to execution and other dispatches from the wrongly convicted.* New York: Doubleday.

Schindler-Zimmerman, T. (1993). Systems family therapy with an athlete. *Journal of Family Psychotherapy, 4*(3), 29–37.

Schindler-Zimmerman, T., & Protinsky, H. (1993). Uncommon sports psychology: Consultation using family therapy theory and techniques. *American Journal of Family Therapy, 21,* 161–174.

Schindler-Zimmerman, T., Washle, W., & Protinsky, H. (1990). Strategic intervention in an athletic system. *Journal of Strategic and Systemic Therapies, 9*(2), 1–7.

Schlesinger, A. M., Jr. (1965). *A thousand days.* Boston: Houghton Mifflin.

Schneekloth, L. H., & Shibley, R. G. (1993). The practice of placemaking. *Architecture et Comportement (Architecture and Behavior), 9,* 121–144.

Schneider, F. W., Pilon, P., Horrobin, B., & Sideris, M. (2000). Contributions of evaluation research to the development of community policing in a Canadian city. *Canadian Journal of Program Evaluation, 15,* 101–129.

Schneider, S. K., & Northcraft, G. B. (1999). Three social dilemmas of workforce diversity in organizations: A social identity perspective. *Human Relations, 11,* 1445–1467.

Schramm, W., & Carter, R. F. (1959). Effectiveness of a political telethon. *Public Opinion Quarterly, 23,* 121–127.

Schruijer, S. G. L., & Mostert, I. (1997). Creativity and sex composition: An experimental illustration. *European Journal of Work & Organizational Psychology, 6,* 175–182.

Schuller, R. A., & Ogloff, J. R. P. (2001). An introduction to psychology and law. In R. A. Schuller & J. R. P. Ogloff (Eds.), *Introduction to psychology and law: Canadian perspectives* (pp. 3–28). Toronto: University of Toronto Press.

Schuller, R. A., & Yarmey, M. (2001). The jury: Deciding guilty and innocence. In R. A. Schuller & J. R. P. Ogloff (Eds.), *Introduction to psychology and law: Canadian perspectives* (pp. 3–28). Toronto: University of Toronto Press.

Schultz, P. W. (1998). Changing behavior with normative feedback interventions: A field experiment on curbside recycling. *Basic and Applied Social Psychology, 21,* 25–36.

Schulz, R., & Beach, S. R. (1999). Caregiving as a risk factor for mortality: The caregiver health effects study. *Journal of the American Medical Association, 282,* 2215–2219.

Schulz-Hardt, S., Frey, D., Lüthgens, C., & Moscovici, S. (2000). Biased information search in group decision making. *Journal of Personality and Social Psychology, 78,* 655–669.

Schulz-Hardt, S., Jochims, M., & Frey, D. (2002). Productive conflict in group decision making: Genuine and contrived dissent as strategies to counteract biased information seeking. *Organizational Behavior and Human Decision Processes, 88,* 563–586.

Schwartz, J., & Wald, M. L. (2003, March 9). The nation: NASA's curse? "Groupthink" is 30 years old, and still going strong. *The New York Times.* Retrieved September 15, 2003, from http://query.nytimes.com/search/ restricted/article

Schwartz, S. H. (1992). Universals in the content and structure of values: Theory and empirical tests in 20 countries. In M. Zanna (Ed.), *Advances in experimental social psychology* (Vol. 25, pp. 1–65). San Diego: Academic Press.

Schwartz, S. H., Lehmann, A., & Roccas, S. (1999). Multimethod probes of basic human values. In J. Adamopoulos & Y. Kashima (Eds.), *Social psychology and cultural context* (pp. 107–124). Thousand Oaks, CA: Sage.

Schwartz, S. H., Sagiv, L., & Boehnke, K. (2000). Worries and values. *Journal of Personality, 68,* 309–346.

Schwartz, W. (1996). *An overview of strategies to reduce school violence* (ERIC/CUE Digest No. 115). New York: ERIC Clearinghouse on Urban Education.

Schwitzgebel, R. (1967). Short term operant conditioning of adolescent offenders on socially relevant variables. *Journal of Abnormal Psychology, 72,* 134–142.

Sears, D. O. (1988). Symbolic racism. In P. Katz & D. Taylor (Eds.), *Towards the elimination of racism: Profiles in controversy* (pp. 53–84). New York: Plenum.

Secord, P. S., & Backman, C. W. (1974). *Social psychology* (3rd ed.). New York: McGraw–Hill.

Seligman, M. E. P. (1975). *Helplessness: On depression, development, and death.* San Francisco: Freeman.

Shadish, W. (1984). Policy research: Lessons from the implementation of deinstitutionalization. *American Psychologist, 39,* 725–739.

Shapiro, P. N., & Penrod, S. (1986). Meta-analysis of facial identification studies. *Psychological Bulletin, 100,* 139–146.

Shaver, P. R., & Hazan, C. (1994). Attachment. In A. L. Weber & J. H. Harvey (Eds.), *Perspectives on close relationships* (pp. 110–130). Boston: Allyn & Bacon.

Shaver, P. R., Hazan, C., & Bradshaw, D. (1988). Love as attachment: The integration of three behavioral systems. In R. J. Sternberg & M. L. Barnes (Eds.), *The psychology of love* (pp. 68–99). New Haven, CT: Yale University Press.

Shaw, K. T., & Gifford, R. (1994). Residents' and burglars' assessment of burglary risk form defensible space cues. *Journal of Environmental Psychology, 14,* 177–194.

Shaw, M. E., & Costanzo, P. R. (1982). *Theories of social psychology* (2nd ed.). New York: McGraw–Hill.

Sherif, M. (1966a). *Group conflict and cooperation.* London: Routledge & Kegan Paul.

Sherif, M. (1966b). *In common predicament: Social psychology of intergroup conflict and cooperation.* Boston: Houghton Mifflin.

Sherif, M., Harvey, O. J., White, B. J., Hood, W. E., & Sherif, C. W. (1961). *Intergroup conflict and cooperation: The Robbers Cave Experiment.* Norman: University of Oklahoma, Institute of Group Relations.

Sherif, M., & Sherif, C. W. (1953). *Groups in harmony and tension.* New York: Harper & Row. (Reprinted from *Octagon,* 1966)

Sherif, M., & Sherif, C. W. (1969). *Social psychology.* New York: Harper & Row.

Shields, S. A. (1975). Functionalism, Darwinism, and the psychology of women: A study in social myth. *American Psychologist, 30,* 739–754.

Shoda, Y. (2004). Individual differences in social psychology: Understanding situations to understand people, understanding people to understand situations. In C. Sansone, C. Morf, & A. Panter (Eds.), *The Sage handbook of methods in social psychology* (pp. 117–141). Thousand Oaks, CA: Sage.

Shrum, L. J. (1999). The relationship of television viewing with attitude strength and extremity: Implications for the cultivation effect. *Media Psychology, 1,* 3–25.

Shrum, L. J. (2002). Media consumption and perceptions of social reality: Effects and underlying processes. In J. Bryant & D. Zillmann (Eds.), *Media effects: Advances in theory and research* (2nd ed., pp. 69–96). Mahwah, NJ: Lawrence Erlbaum.

Shultz, T. R., Léveillé, E., & Lepper, M. R. (1999). Free choice and cognitive dissonance revisited: Choosing "lesser evils" versus "greater goods." *Personality and Social Psychology Bulletin, 25,* 40–48.

Shuter, R. (1976). Proxemics and tactility in Latin America. *Journal of Communication, 26,* 46–52.

Sibbald, B. (1998). "The health sciences are for you, too," minority students told. *Canadian Medical Association Journal, 159,* 130.

Sideridis, G. D., & Padeliadu, S. (2001). The motivational determinants of students at risk of having reading difficulties. *Remedial and Special Education, 22,* 268–279.

Signorielli, N. (1990). Television's mean and dangerous world: A continuation of the cultural indicators perspective. In N. Signorielli & M. Morgan (Eds.), *Cultivation analysis: New directions in media effects research* (pp. 85–106). Newbury Park, CA: Sage.

Sikorski, J. F., Rich, K., Saville, B. K., Buskist, W., Drogan, O., & Davis, S. F. (2002). Student use of introductory texts: Comparative survey findings from two universities. *Teaching of Psychology, 29,* 312–313.

Silverman, S. (2002, July 17). Child abuse: Let's combat this form of terrorism too. *Detroit Free Press,* p. A11.

Sime, J. D. (1986). Creating places or designing spaces? *Journal of Environmental Psychology, 6,* 49–63.

Simon, L., Greenberg, J., & Brehm, J. (1995). Trivialization: The forgotten mode of dissonance reduction. *Journal of Personality and Social Psychology, 68,* 247–260.

Slavin, R. E. (1990). *Cooperative learning: Theory, research, and practice.* Englewood Cliffs, NJ: Prentice Hall.

Slum surgery in St. Louis. (1951). *Architectural Forum, 94,* 128–136.

Smith, A. (1976). *The wealth of nations: Book 1.* Chicago: University of Chicago Press. (Original work published 1776)

Smith, S. L., & Wilson, B. J. (2002). Children's comprehension of and fear reactions to television news. *Media Psychology, 4,* 1–26.

Smith, S. L., Wilson, B. J., Kunkel, D., Linz, D., Potter, W. J., Colvin, C. M., & Donnerstein, E. (1998). Violence in television programming overall: University of California, Santa Barbara study. In Center for Communication and Social Policy (Ed.), *National Television Violence Study* (Vol. 3, pp. 5–194). Thousand Oaks, CA: Sage.

Snyder, M., & Ickes, W. (1985). Personality and social behavior. In G. Lindzey & E. Aronson (Eds.), *Handbook of social psychology* (3rd ed., pp. 883–947). New York: Random House.

Snyder, M., & Swann, W. B., Jr. (1978). Hypothesis-testing processes in social interaction. *Journal of Personality and Social Psychology, 35,* 656–666.

Solomon, A. (1992). Clinical diagnosis among diverse populations: A multicultural perspective. *Families in Society, 73,* 371–377.

Sommer, R. (1972). *Design awareness.* New York: Holt, Rinehart & Winston.

Sommer, R. (1983). *Social design.* Englewood Cliffs, NJ: Prentice Hall.

Sommer, R. (1987). Crime and vandalism in university residence halls: A confirmation of defensible space theory. *Journal of Environmental Psychology, 7,* 1–12.

Sommer, R., & Olsen, H. (1980). The soft classroom. *Environment and Behavior, 12,* 3–16.

Spink, K. S. (1990a). Collective efficacy in the sport setting. *International Journal of Sport Psychology, 21,* 380–395.

Spink, K. S. (1990b). Group cohesion and collective efficacy in volleyball teams. *Journal of Sport and Exercise Psychology, 12,* 301–311.

Spoth, R. L., Redmond, C., Trudeau, L., & Shin, C. (2002). Longitudinal substance initiation outcomes for a universal preventive intervention combining family and school programs. *Psychology of Addictive Behaviors, 16,* 129–134.

Sprecher, S. (1986). The relationship between inequity and emotions in close relationships. *Social Psychology Quarterly, 49,* 309–321.

Sprecher, S. (1989). The importance to males and females of physical attractiveness, earning potential, and expressiveness in initial attraction. *Sex Roles, 21,* 591–607.

Sprecher, S., & Chandak, R. (1992). Attitudes about arranged marriages and dating among men and women from India. *Free Inquiry in Creative Sociology, 20,* 59–69.

Stahlberg, D., Eller, F., Maass, A., & Frey, D. (1995). We knew it all along: Hindsight bias in groups. *Organizational Behavior and Human Decision Processes, 63,* 46–58.

Stamler, L. L., Thomas, B., & Lafreniere, K. (2000). Working women identify influences and obstacles to breast health practices. *Oncology Nursing Forum, 27,* 835–842.

Stamps, A. (1989). Are environmental aesthetics worth studying? *Journal of Architectural and Planning Research, 6,* 344–356.

Staw, B. M., Bell, N. E., & Clausen, J. A. (1986). The dispositional approach to job attitudes: A lifetime longitudinal test. *Administrative Science Quarterly, 31,* 437–453.

Steel, R. P., & Ovalle, N. K. (1984). A review and meta-analysis of research on the relationship between behavioral intentions and employee turnover. *Journal of Applied Psychology, 69,* 673–686.

Steele, C. M. (1997). A threat in the air: How stereotypes shape intellectual identity and performance. *American Psychologist, 52,* 613–629.

Steele, C. M., & Aronson, J. (1995). Stereotype threat and the intellectual test performance of African Americans. *Journal of Personality and Social Psychology, 69,* 797–811.

Steele, C., & Aronson, J. (1998). Stereotype threat and the test performance of academically successful African Americans. In E. C. Jencks & E. Phillips (Eds.), *The black–white test score gap* (pp. 401–427). Washington, DC: American Psychological Association.

Steers, R. M., & Porter, L. W. (Eds.). (1991). *Motivation and work.* New York: McGraw–Hill.

Steuer, F. B., Applefield, J. M., & Smith, R. (1971). Televised aggression and the interpersonal aggression of preschool children. *Journal of Experimental Child Psychology, 11,* 442–447.

Stokes, J., Fuerher, A., & Childs, L. (1984). Group members' self-disclosure: Relation to team cohesion. *Small Group Behavior, 14,* 63–76.

Stone, J., Aronson, E., Crain, A. L., Winslow, M. P., & Fried, C. B. (1994). Inducing hypocrisy as a means of encouraging young adults to use condoms. *Personality and Social Psychology Bulletin, 20,* 116–128.

Stoner, J. A. F. (1961). *A comparison of individual and group decisions involving risk.* Unpublished master's thesis, Massachusetts Institute of Technology.

Stouffer, S. A., Suchman, E.A., DeVinney, L. C., Star, S. A., & Williams, R. M., Jr. (1949). *The American soldier: Adjustment during army life.* Princeton, NJ: Princeton University Press.

Strauss, S. G., & McGrath, J. E. (1994). Does the medium matter? The interaction of task type and technology on group performance and member reactions. *Journal of Applied Psychology, 79,* 87–97.

Streufert, S., & Streufert, S. C. (1969). Effects of conceptual structure, failure, and success on attribution of causality and interpersonal attitudes. *Journal of Personality and Social Psychology, 11,* 138–147.

Streufert, S., & Suedfeld, P. (1982). A decade of applied social psychology. *Journal of Applied Social Psychology, 12,* 335–342.

Striniste, N. A., & Moore, R. C. (1989). Early childhood outdoors: A literature review related to the design of childcare environments. *Children's Environments Quarterly, 6,* 25-31.

Stroebe, W., & Stroebe, M. S. (1995). *Social psychology and health.* London: Open University Press.

Struthers, C. W., Weiner, B., & Allred, K. (1998). Effects of causal attributions on personnel decisions: A social motivation perspective. *Basic and Applied Social Psychology, 20,* 155–166.

Sue, S. (2003). In defense of cultural competency in psychotherapy and treatment. *American Psychologist, 58,* 964–970.

Sullivan, P. A. (1993). Communication skills for interactive sports. *The Sport Psychologist, 7,* 79–91.

Sullivan, P. J. (1995). *The relationship between communication and cohesion in inter-collegiate rugby players.* Unpublished master's thesis, University of Windsor, Ontario.

Sullivan, P. J., & Feltz, D. L. (2003). The preliminary development of the Scale for Effective Communication in Sports Teams (SECTS). *Journal of Applied Social Psychology, 33,* 1693–1715.

Suspected SUV bomber held without bail. (2004, March 18). *CBC News Online.* Retrieved October 22, 2004, from www.cbc.ca/stories/print/2004/03/18/world/suv_bombings040318

Sussman, N. M., & Rosenfeld, H. M. (1982). Influence of culture, language, and sex on conversational distance. *Journal of Personality and Social Psychology, 42,* 66–74.

Swim, J. K., & Hyers, L. L. (1999). Excuse me—What did you just say? Women's public and private responses to sexist remarks. *Journal of Experimental Social Psychology, 35,* 68–88.

Sypher, B. D., & Zorn, T. E. (1986). Communication-related abilities and upward mobility: A longitudinal investigation. *Human Communication Research, 12,* 420–431.

Tajfel, H., & Billig, M. (1974). Familiarity and categorization in intergroup behaviour. *Journal of Experimental Social Psychology, 10,* 159–170.

Tajfel, H., & Turner, J. C. (1986). The social identity theory of intergroup behavior. In S. Worchel & W. G. Austin (Eds.), *Psychology of intergroup relations* (2nd ed., pp. 33–47). Chicago: Nelson–Hall.

Tang, S., & Hall, V. C. (1995). The overjustification effect: A meta-analysis. *Applied Cognitive Psychology, 9,* 365–404.

Tangney, J. P., Miller, R. S., Flicker, L., & Barlow, D. H. (1996). Are shame, guilt, and embarrassment distinct emotions? *Journal of Personality and Social Psychology, 70,* 1256–1269.

Taussig, M. (1986-1987). *Shamanism, colonialism, and the wild man: A study in terror and healing.* Chicago: University of Chicago Press.

Taylor, M. (1979). Race, sex, and the expression of self-fulfilling prophecies in a laboratory teaching situation. *Journal of Personality and Social Psychology, 37,* 897–912.

Taylor, S. E. (1989). *Positive illusions: Creative self-deception and the healthy mind.* New York: Basic Books.

Taylor, S. E. (1991). *Health psychology* (2nd ed.). New York: McGraw–Hill.

Taylor, S. E. (2003). *Health psychology* (5th ed.). New York: McGraw-Hill.

Technical Working Group for Eyewitness Evidence. (1999). *Eyewitness evidence: A guide for law enforcement* [booklet]. Washington, DC: U.S. Department of Justice.

Temerlin, M. K. (1968). Suggestion effects in psychiatric diagnosis. *Journal of Nervous and Mental Disease, 147,* 349–353.

Tesser, A., Beach, S. R. H., Mendolia, J., Crepaz, N., Davies, B., & Pennebaker, J. (1998). Similarity and uniqueness focus: A paper tiger and a surprise. *Personality and Social Psychology, 24,* 1190–1204.

Tetlock, P. E. (1979). Identifying victims of groupthink from public statements of decision makers. *Journal of Personality and Social Psychology, 37,* 1314–1324.

Tetlock, P. E., Peterson, R. S., McGuire, C., Chong, S., & Field, P. (1992). Assessing political group dynamics: A test of the groupthink model. *Journal of Personality and Social Psychology, 63,* 403–425.

Thibaut, J. W., & Kelley, H. H. (1959). *The social psychology of groups.* New York: John Wiley.

Thompson, T. (1994). Self-worth protection: Review and implications for the classroom. *Educational Review, 46,* 259–274.

Thornton, J., & Wahl, O. (1996). Impact of a newspaper article on attitudes toward mental illness. *Journal of Community Psychology, 24,* 17–28.

Tindale, R. S. (1993). Decision errors made by individuals and groups. In N. J. Castellan, Jr. (Ed.), *Individual and group decision making: Current issues* (pp. 109–124). Hillsdale, NJ: Lawrence Erlbaum.

Toch, H., & Klofas, J. (1984). Pluralistic ignorance, revisited. In G. M. Stephenson & J. H. Davis (Eds.), *Progress in applied social psychology* (Vol. 2, pp. 129–159). New York: John Wiley.

Tomes, H. (2004). The case—and the research—that forever connected psychology and policy. *Monitor on Psychology, 35*(6), 28. (American Psychological Association)

Topolski, D. (1989). *True blue: The story of the Oxford boat race mutiny.* London: Bantam Books.

Travis, J. (1995, May 2). *Criminal justice research and public policy in the United States.* Speech given at the Ninth UN Congress on the Prevention of Crime and the Treatment of Offenders, Cairo, Egypt. Retrieved May 20, 2003, from www.ojp.usdoj.gov/nij/speeches/ unspeech.htm

Trevino, L. K., Daft, R. L., & Lengel, R. H. (1990). Understanding managers' media choices: A symbolic interactionist perspective. In J. Fulk & C. Steinfeld (Eds.), *Organizations and communication technology* (pp. 71–94). Newbury Park, CA: Sage.

Triandis, H. C. (1994). *Culture and social behavior.* New York: McGraw–Hill.

Triandis, H. C. (1995). *Individualism and collectivism.* Boulder, CO: Westview.

Triandis, H. C., Kurowski, L. L., & Gelfand, M. J. (1994). Workplace diversity. In H. C. Triandis, M. Dunnette, & L. Hough (Eds.), *Handbook of industrial and organizational psychology* (Vol. 4, pp. 769–827). Palo Alto, CA: Consulting Psychologists Press.

Turban, D. B., & Jones, A. P. (1988). Supervisor–subordinate similarity: Type, effects, and mechanisms. *Journal of Applied Psychology, 73,* 228–234.

Turkle, S. (1984). *The second self.* New York: Simon & Schuster.

Turner, C. W., Layton, J. F., & Simons, L. S. (1975). Naturalistic studies of aggressive behavior: Aggressive stimuli, victim visibility, and horn honking. *Journal of Personality and Social Psychology, 31,* 1098–1107.

Turner, D. C. (1996). The role of culture in chronic illness. *American Behavioral Scientist, 39,* 717–728.

Turner, J. C., Midgley, C., Meyer, D. K., Gheen, M., Anderman, E. M., Kang, Y., & Patrick, H. (2002). The classroom environment and students' reports of avoidance strategies in mathematics: A multimethod study. *Journal of Educational Psychology, 94,* 88–106.

Turner, M. E., & Pratkanis, A. R. (1998). Twenty-five years of groupthink theory and research: Lessons from the evaluation of a theory. *Organizational Behavior and Human Decision Processes, 73,* 105–115.

Turner, M. E., Pratkanis, A. R., Probasco, P., & Leve, C. (1992). Threat, cohesion, and group effectiveness: Testing a social identity maintenance perspective in groupthink. *Journal of Personality and Social Psychology, 63,* 781–796.

Turtle, J. W., & Watkins, K. G. (1999). Investigative interviewing: Maximizing information and minimizing errors from witnesses, victims, and suspects of crime. In G. M. Chayko & E. D. Gulliver (Eds.), *Forensic evidence in Canada* (2nd ed., pp. 53–82). Aurora, Ontario: Canada Law Book.

Tutin, J. (1993). The persistence of initial beliefs in clinical judgment. *Journal of Social and Clinical Psychology, 12,* 319–335.

Tversky, A., & Kahneman, D. (1973). Availability: A heuristic for judging frequency and probability. *Cognitive Psychology, 5,* 207–232.

Tversky, A., & Kahneman, D. (1974). Judgment under uncertainty: Heuristics and biases. *Science, 185,* 1124–1131.

UNAIDS/World Health Organization. (2002). *AIDS epidemic update* (Joint United Nations Programme on HIV/AIDS and World Health Organization). Geneva, Switzerland: Author.

Union of Concerned Scientists. (1993). *World scientists warning to humanity* [statement]. Cambridge, MA: Author.

Unrau, Y. A., Gabor, P. A., & Grinnell, R. M., Jr. (2001). *Evaluation in the human services.* Itasca, IL: Peacock.

Urdan, T., Midgley, C., & Anderman, E. M. (1998). The role of classroom goal structure in students' use of self-handicapping strategies. *American Educational Research Journal, 35,* 101–122.

U.S. Department of Justice. (2001). *Census of state and federal correctional facilities, 2000.* Washington, DC: Author.

U.S. Department of Justice. (2003). *Probation and parole in the United States, 2002.* Washington, DC: Author.

Vancouver, J. B., Thompson, C. M., Tischner, E. C., & Putka, D. J. (2002). Two studies examining the negative effect of self-efficacy on performance. *Journal of Applied Psychology, 87,* 506–516.

Vandello, J. A., & Cohen, D. (1999). Patterns of individualism and collectivism across the United States. *Journal of Personality and Social Psychology, 77,* 279–292.

van der Voordt, T. J. M., & van Wegen, H. B. R. (1990). Testing building plans for public safety: Usefulness of the Delft checklist. *Housing and Environmental Research, 5,* 129–154.

Vaughan, E. D. (1977). Misconceptions about psychology among introductory psychology students. *Teaching of Psychology, 4,* 138–141.

Verespej, M. A. (1990). Self-directed work teams yield long-term benefits. *Journal of Business Strategy, 11*(6), 9–12.

Vidmar, N., & Schuller, R. A. (2001). The jury: Selecting twelve impartial peers. In R. A. Schuller & J. R. P. Ogloff (Eds.), *Introduction to psychology and law: Canadian perspectives* (pp. 126–156). Toronto: University of Toronto Press.

Vis, A. A., Dijkstra, A., & Slop, M. (1992). Safety effects of 30 km/h zones in The Netherlands. *Accident Analysis and Prevention, 24,* 75–86.

Voelz, Z. R., Haeffel, G. J., Joiner, T. E., & Wagner, K. D. (2003). Reducing hopelessness: The interaction of enhancing and depressogenic attributional styles for positive and negative life events among youth psychiatric inpatients. *Behaviour Research and Therapy, 41,* 1183–1198.

Vorauer, J. D., & Ratner, R. K. (1996). Who's going to make the first move? Pluralistic ignorance as an impediment to relationship formation. *Journal of Social and Personal Relationships, 13,* 483–506.

Wadsworth, Y. (1998, November). What is participatory action research? *Action Research International,* Paper 2. Retrieved May 20, 2003, from www.scu.edu.au/schools/gcm/ar/ari/p-ywadsworth98.html

Wahl, O., & Lefkowits, J. (1989). Impact of a television film on attitudes toward mental illness. *American Journal of Community Psychology, 17,* 521–528.

Walker, E. L. (1969). Experimental psychology and social responsibility. *American Psychologist, 24,* 862–868.

Wallace, P. (1999). *The psychology of the Internet.* Cambridge, UK: Cambridge University Press.

Waller, M. J., Huber, G. P., & Glick, W. H. (1995). Functional background as a determinant of executives' selective perception. *Academy of Management Journal, 38,* 943–974.

Walsh, R. (1985). *Staying alive.* Boston: New Science Library Books.

Walster, E., Aronson, V., & Abrahams, D. (1966). Importance of physical attractiveness in dating behavior. *Journal of Personality and Social Psychology, 4,* 508–516.

Wandersman, A., & Nation, M. (1998). Urban neighborhoods and mental health: Psychological contributions to understanding toxicity, resilience, and interventions. *American Psychologist, 53,* 647–657.

Wason. P. C. (1960). On the failure to eliminate hypotheses in a conceptual task. *Quarterly Journal of Experimental Psychology, 12,* 129–140.

Watson, J. B. (1913). Psychology as the behaviorist views it. *Psychological Review, 20,* 158–177.

Watson, O. M., & Graves, T. D. (1966). Quantitative research in proxemic behavior. *American Anthropologist, 68,* 971–985.

Webb, E., Campbell, D., Schwartz, R. D., & Sechrest, L. (1981). *Unobtrusive measures.* Chicago: Rand McNally. (Original work published 1966)

Wechsler, H., Davenport, A., Dowdall, G., Moeykens, B., & Castillo, S. (1994). Health and behavioral consequences of binge drinking in college: A national survey of students at 140 campuses. *Journal of the American Medical Association, 272,* 1672–1677.

Wechsler, H., Lee J. E., Kuo, M., Seibring, M., Nelson, T. F., & Lee, H. (2002). Trends in college binge drinking during a period of increased prevention efforts. *Journal of American College Health, 50,* 203–221.

Wegner, D. M., Coulton, G. F., & Wenzlaff, R. (1985). The transparency of denial: Briefing in the debriefing paradigm. *Journal of Personality and Social Psychology, 49,* 338–346.

Weick, K. E. (1969). Social psychology in an era of social change. *American Psychologist, 24,* 990–998.

Weick. K. E. (1979). *The social psychology of organizing* (2nd ed.). New York: McGraw–Hill.

Weinberg, R. S., & Gould, D. (1999). *Foundations of sport and exercise psychology* (2nd ed.). Champaign, IL: Human Kinetics.

Weiner, B. (1986). *An attributional theory of emotion and motivation.* New York: Springer-Verlag.

Weiner, B. (1995). Inferences of responsibility and social motivation. In M. Zanna (Ed.), *Advances in experimental social psychology* (pp. 1–47). San Diego: Academic Press.

Weiner, B. (2001). Intrapersonal and interpersonal theories of motivation from an attribution perspective. In F. Salili & C-Y. Chiu (Eds.), *Student motivation: The culture and context of learning* (pp. 17–30). New York: Kluwer Academic/Plenum.

Weinstein, N. D. (1980). Unrealistic optimism: Present and future. *Journal of Personality and Social Psychology, 39,* 806–820.

Weiss, R. S. (1975). *Marital separation.* New York: Basic Books.

Weitz, S. (1972). Attitude, voice, and behavior: A repressed affect model of interracial interaction. *Journal of Personality and Social Psychology, 24,* 14–21.

Wells, G. L., Malpass, R. S., Lindsay, R. C. L., Fisher, R. P., Turtle, J. W., & Fulero, S. M. (2000). From the lab to the police station: A successful application of eyewitness research. *American Psychologist, 55,* 581–598.

Wells, G. L., & Turtle, J. W. (1986). Eyewitness identification: The importance of linear models. *Psychological Bulletin, 99,* 320–329.

Welsh, M., Parke, R. D., Widaman, K., & O'Neil, R. (2001). Linkages between children's social and academic competence: A longitudinal analysis. *Journal of School Psychology, 39,* 463–481.

Westre, K. R., & Weiss, M. R. (1991). The relationship between perceived coaching behaviors and group cohesion in high school football teams. *Sport Psychologist, 5,* 41–54.

Wexler, H. K. (1995). The success of therapeutic communities for substance abusers in American prisons. *Journal of Psychoactive Drugs, 27,* 57–66.

Wexler, H. K., Falkin, G. P., & Lipton, D. S. (1990). Outcome evaluation of a prison therapeutic community for substance abuse treatment. *Criminal Justice and Behavior, 17,* 71–92.

Wholey, J. S. (1983). *Evaluation and effective public management.* Boston: Little, Brown.

Whyte, G. (1993). Escalating commitment in individual and group decision-making: A prospect theory approach. *Organizational Behavior and Human Decision Processes, 53,* 430–455.

Whyte, G. (1998). Recasting Janis's groupthink model: The key role of collective efficacy in decision fiascoes. *Organizational Behavior and Human Decision Processes, 73,* 185–209.

Whyte, W. H. (1980). *The social life of small urban spaces.* New York: Conservation Foundation.

Wicker, A. W. (1969). Attitudes versus actions: The relationship between verbal and overt behavioral responses to attitude objects. *Journal of Social Issues, 25*(4), 41–78.

Wicklund, R. A., & Brehm, J. W. (1976). *Perspectives on cognitive dissonance.* New York: John Wiley.

Widmeyer, W. N., Brawley, L. R., & Carron, A. V. (1985). *The measurement of cohesion in sport teams: The Group Environment Questionnaire.* London, Ontario: Sport Dynamics.

Widmeyer, W. N., Brawley, L. R., & Carron, A. V. (1990). The effects of group size in sport. *Journal of Sport and Exercise Psychology, 12,* 177–190.

Widmeyer, W. N., & Ducharme, K. (1997). Team building through team goal setting. *Journal of Applied Sport Psychology, 9,* 97–113.

Widmeyer, W. N., Silva, J. M., & Hardy, C. J. (1992). *The nature of group cohesion in sport teams: A phenomenological approach.* Paper presented at the Association for the Advancement of Applied Sport Psychology Conference, Colorado Springs, CO.

Widmeyer, W.N., & Williams, J. (1991). Predicting cohesion in a coacting sport. *Small Group Research, 22,* 548–570.

Williams v. Florida, 399 U.S. 78 (1970).

Williams, J., & Best, D. (1982). *Measuring sex stereotypes: A thirty-nation study.* Beverly Hills, CA: Sage.

Williams, J., & Widmeyer, W. N. (1991). The cohesion–performance outcome relationship in a coacting sport. *Journal of Sport and Exercise Psychology, 13,* 364–371.

Wilson, B. J., Kunkel, D., Linz, D., Potter, W. J., Donnerstein, E., Smith, S. L., Blumenthal, E., & Berry, M. (1998). Violence in television programming overall: University of California, Santa Barbara study. In Center for Communication and Social Policy (Ed.), *National Television Violence Study* (Vol. 2, pp. 3–180). Thousand Oaks, CA: Sage.

Wilson, B. J., Kunkel, D., Linz, D., Potter, W. J., Donnerstein, E., Smith, S. L., Blumenthal, E., & Gray, T. (1997). Violence in television programming overall: University of California, Santa Barbara study. In M. Seawall (Ed.), *National Television Violence Study* (Vol. 1, pp. 3–159). Thousand Oaks, CA: Sage.

Wilson, B. J., Smith, S. L., Potter, W. J., Kunkel, D., Linz, D., Colvin, C. M., & Donnerstein, E. (2002). Violence in children's television programming: Assessing the risks. *Journal of Communication, 52*(4), 5–35.

Wilson, R. J., Huculak, B., & McWhinnie, A. (2002). Restorative justice innovations in Canada. *Behavioral Sciences and the Law, 20,* 363–380.

Wilson-Doenges, G. (2000). An exploration of sense of community and fear of crime in gated communities. *Environment and Behavior, 32,* 597–611.

Winzelberg, A. (1997). Analysis of an electronic support group for individuals with eating disorders. *Computers in Human Behavior, 13,* 393–407.

Wisch, A. F., & Mahalik, J. R. (1999). Male therapists' clinical bias: Influence of client gender roles and therapist gender role conflict. *Journal of Counseling Psychology, 46,* 51–60.

Wise, J. A., & Wise, B. K. (1985). *Bank interiors and bank robberies: A design approach to environmental security.* Rolling Meadows, IL: Bank Administration Institute.

Wolfgang, M. E., & Ferracuti, F. (1981). *The subculture of violence.* Beverly Hills, CA: Sage.

Wollin, D. D., & Montagne, M. (1981). College classroom environment: Effects of sterility versus amiability on student and teacher performance. *Environment and Behavior, 13,* 707–716.

Wong, C. Y., Sommer, R., & Cook, R. (1992). The soft classroom 17 years later. *Journal of Environmental Psychology, 12,* 337–343.

Wong, J. (1999, November 20). Jan Wong's last word: What do we tell our kids if a pal is attacked? Stand by him? Or is it everyone for himself? *The Globe and Mail,* p. A32.

Yalom, I. D. (1995). *The theory and practice of group psychotherapy* (4th ed.). New York: Basic Books.

Yan, W., & Gaier, E. L. (1994). Causal attributions for college success and failure: An Asian-American comparison. *Journal of Cross-Cultural Psychology, 25,* 146–158.

Yasutake, D., Bryan, T., & Dohrn, E. (1996). The effects of combining peer tutoring and attribution training on students' perceived self-competence. *Remedial and Special Education, 17,* 83–91.

Younge, G. (2003, January 27). America is a class act. *The Guardian.* Retrieved January 28, 2003, from www.guardian.co.uk/comment/story/0,3604,882935,00.html

Yox, S. (2003, April 9). Cultural responsiveness improves healing. *Medscape Medical News.* Retrieved April 16, 2003, from www.medscape.com/viewarticle/452137

Zaidel, D., Hakkert, A. S., & Pistiner, A. H. (1992). The use of road humps for moderating speeds on urban streets. *Accident Analysis and Prevention, 24,* 45–56.

Zajonc, R. B. (1965). Social facilitation. *Science, 149,* 269–274.

Zajonc, R. B. (1968). Attitudinal effects of mere exposure. *Journal of Personality and Social Psychology, 9*(2), 1–27.

Zajonc, R. B. (2000). Feeling and thinking: Closing the debate over the independence of affect. In J. P. Forgas (Ed.), *Feeling and thinking: The role of affect in social cognition* (pp. 31–58). Cambridge, UK: Cambridge University Press.

Zeisel, H. (1971). " . . . And then there were none": The diminution of the federal jury. *Chicago Law Review, 38,* 710–724.

Zeisel, H., & Diamond, S. S. (1974). "Convincing empirical evidence" on the six-member jury. *University of Chicago Law Review, 41,* 281–295.

Zillmann, D. (1994). Erotica and family values. In D. Zillman, J. Bryant, & A. C. Huston (Eds.), *Media, children, and the family: Social scientific, psychodynamic, and clinical perspectives* (pp. 199–213). Hillsdale, NJ: Lawrence Erlbaum.

Zillmann, D., & Bryant, J. (1982). Pornography, sexual callousness, and the trivialization of rape. *Journal of Communication, 32*(4), 10–21.

Zillmann, D., & Bryant, J. (1984). Effects of massive exposure to pornography. In N. M. Malamuth & E. Donnerstein (Eds.), *Pornography and sexual aggression* (pp. 115–138). San Diego: Academic Press.

Zillmann, D., & Bryant, J. (1986). Shifting preferences in pornography consumption. *Communication Research, 13,* 560–578.

Zillmann, D., & Bryant, J. (1988a). Effects of prolonged consumption of pornography on family values. *Journal of Family Issues, 9,* 518–544.

Zillmann, D., & Bryant, J. (1988b). Pornography's impact on sexual satisfaction. *Journal of Applied Social Psychology, 18,* 438–453.

Zimbardo, P. G. (1969). The human choice: Individuation, reason, and order versus deindividuation, impulse, and chaos. In W. J. Arnold & D. Levine (Eds.), *Nebraska symposium on motivation* (Vol. 17, pp. 237–307). Lincoln: University of Nebraska Press.

Zimbardo, P. G. (2002a). Going forward with commitment. *Monitor on Psychology, 33*(1), 5. (American Psychological Association)

Zimbardo, P. G. (2002b). Psychology in the public service. *American Psychologist, 57,* 431–433.

Zuckerman, M., Kieffer, S. C., & Knee, C. R. (1998). Consequences of self-handicapping: Effects on coping, academic performance, and adjustment. *Journal of Personality and Social Psychology, 74,* 1619–1628.

AUTHOR INDEX

Subject Index

Aaron, Henry, 284, 290
Actor-observer difference, 235-236
ADHD, 221
AIDS, 9-10, 68, 156, 295
Alcohol use on college campuses
  binge drinking and, 64
  consequences of, 64
  false consensus and, 65
  identifying, 64
  intervention for, 64-68
  mass media campaign for reducing, 65-66
  pluralistic ignorance and, 65
  social norm theory and, 64-65, 67-68
Alinsky, Saul, 298
Allport, Gordon, 351
American Psychiatric Association, 105, 113
American Psychological Association,
  9, 50-51, 53, 69, 126, 362, 373
American Psychologist, 8
Anchoring effect, 124
Applied social psychologists
  ethics of, 72
  everyone as, 19-20
  intervention strategies of, 6, 73.
    See also Interventions
  personal values of, 6-7
  research of, 6
  roles of, 16-18, 73
  See also Applied social psychology
Applied social psychology
  as a science, 6
  behavior and, 9-10, 11-14
  broad approach of, 15-16, 18
  control and, 6, 17-18
  cultural perspective of, 16, 18.
    See also Culture
  defined, 1, 5-9, 16-17, 286
  doctoral programs in, 8-9
  evolutionary perspective of, 16, 18
  historical context of, 7-9

  interdisciplinary approach to, 16, 18
  obedience and, 11-12 (table)
  objectives of, 16
  personal uses of, 10-11, 18
  personality perspective of, 16, 18
  practical problems and, 10, 18
  research. *See* Applied social psychology
    research
  social problems and, 9-11, 18
  social situation and, 11-14, 18
Applied social psychology research
  content analysis and, 41
  context effect in, 38
  control time series design, 46-48, 53
  correlation coefficients of, 47, 53
  correlational studies, 46-48 (figure),
    53, 164
  descriptive studies, 46-49, 53
  designs, 41-42 (table), 43-49, 52
  ecological validity of, 49, 265
  ethics of, 50-51, 53
  examples of, 43 (figure), 44-52.
    See also specific topics
  experimental studies, 155, 165
  field studies, 49-50, 53
  external validity of, 49, 53, 108
  grounded theory and. *See* Theory,
    grounded
  importance of, 355-356
  internal validity of, 44, 53
  interrupted time series design, 46
  laboratory studies, 49-50, 53, 155
  memoing and, 41
  meta-analysis, 136, 137, 155,
    169, 185, 239, 241, 242
  methods of data collection for,
    16, 18, 36-41, 52
  nonequivalent control group designs, 46
  observational methods for, 39-40, 52
  pretest-posttest designs, 45-46, 53, 115

437

ABOUT THE EDITORS

Frank W. Schneider, Ph.D., is Professor of Psychology at the University of Windsor. He received his M.A. in counseling psychology from Ohio University and his Ph.D. in social psychology from the University of Florida. He is a cofounder of the University of Windsor's doctoral program in applied social psychology and is currently coordinator of the program. His current research focuses on community policing and the recruitment and selection of police officers. In addition, he has coauthored a textbook on differential psychology and has published articles related to topics such as group dynamics, organizational effectiveness, evaluation research, social psychology of education, gender roles, domestic violence, helping behavior, race relations, nonverbal communication, attribution theory, and adjustment of the elderly.

Jamie A. Gruman, Ph.D., is Assistant Professor of Organizational Behavior in the Division of Management at the University of Toronto at Scarborough. He earned his Ph.D. in applied social psychology at the University of Windsor. While completing his degree, he taught in both the Department of Psychology and the Odette School of Business at the university. He has published articles in areas such as social psychology, personality, and statistics. His current research interests focus on individual differences and social psychology in the workplace. He has consulted and delivered seminars for corporations and not-for-profit agencies, including Ford Motor Company, Deloitte & Touche, Hiram Walker & Sons, and the Children's Wish Foundation of Canada.

Larry M. Coutts, Ph.D., is Assistant Professor of Psychology at the University of Windsor. He received his Ph.D. in social and personality psychology from the University of Windsor. He currently specializes in research on community policing and organizational psychology. Prior to joining the university in 2000, he held positions with the Royal Canadian Mounted Police as director of the Organizational Design and Job Evaluation Branch and as senior research principal with both the Personnel Research Branch and the Canadian Police College. He also has 20 years of experience as an organizational consultant in both the private and public sectors. He has published several scientific articles in the fields of social psychology and industrial/organizational psychology.

CONTRIBUTORS

Louise R. Alexitch, Ph.D.
University of Saskatchewan
Saskatoon, Saskatchewan

Sherry Bergeron, M.A.
University of Windsor
Windsor, Ontario

Kenneth M. Cramer, Ph.D.
University of Windsor
Windsor, Ontario

David M. Day, Ph.D.
Ryerson University
Toronto, Ontario

Deborah L. Feltz, Ph.D.
Michigan State University
East Lansing, Michigan

Robert Gifford, Ph.D.
University of Victoria
Victoria, British Columbia

Kenneth E. Hart, Ph.D.
University of Windsor
Windsor, Ontario

Ritu Kaushal, M.A.
University of Windsor
Windsor, Ontario

Catherine T. Kwantes, Ph.D.
University of Windsor
Windsor, Ontario

Kathryn D. Lafreniere, Ph.D.
University of Windsor
Windsor, Ontario

David M. Ledgerwood, Ph.D.
University of Connecticut
Farmington, Connecticut

Adam Lodzinski, Ph.D.
Consultant in Private Practice
Toronto, Ontario

Michiko S. Motomura, M.A.
University of Windsor
Windsor, Ontario

Stewart Page, Ph.D.
University of Windsor
Windsor, Ontario

Beverly Roskos-Ewoldsen, Ph.D.
University of Alabama
Tuscaloosa, Alabama

David R. Roskos-Ewoldsen, Ph.D.
University of Alabama
Tuscaloosa, Alabama

Charlene Y. Senn, Ph.D.
University of Windsor
Windsor, Ontario

Randolph A. Smith, Ph.D.
Kennesaw State University
Kennesaw, Georgia

Philip Sullivan, Ph.D.
Brock University
St. Catherines, Ontario

Shelagh M. J. Towson, Ph.D.
University of Windsor
Windsor, Ontario

Ann L. Weber, Ph.D.
University of North Carolina at Asheville
Asheville, North Carolina